BEFORE THE BATTLECRUISER

BEFORE THE BATTLECRUISER

THE BIG CRUISER IN THE WORLD'S NAVIES
1865–1910

Aidan Dodson

Naval Institute Press
ANNAPLOIS, MARYLAND

Title page: The Russian cruiser *Admiral Nakhimov*, one of the very last such ships to carry sail. She is here shown at the Columbian Naval Review, held at New York in April–June 1893. *(Library of Congress LC-D4-21186)*

To the memory of John Leonard Hilton, CEng (1931–2108)

First published in Great Britain in 2018 by
Seaforth Publishing,
A division of Pen & Sword Books Ltd,
47 Church Street,
Barnsley S70 2AS

Published and distributed in the
United States of America and Canada by the
Naval Institute Press,
291 Wood Road, Annapolis,
Maryland 21402-5034

www.nip.org

Library of Congress Control Number: 2018947235

ISBN 978 1 68247 375 7

This edition authorized for sale only in the United States of America, its territories and possessions, and Canada.

Printed and bound in India

CONTENTS

PREFACE

While the battlecruiser, the 'all-big-gun' cruiser developed by the British Royal Navy from 1906 onwards and constructed by or for an number of other navies during subsequent decades, has received considerable attention in print, it was a direct follow-on from earlier generations of ships that in many ways blurred the dividing line between ships for the line of battle and ships for oceanic cruising, and have thus far escaped integrated treatment. With the exception of the British and American vessels of the type, little is available on them in the English language, while nowhere has there been any real attempt at telling their story across the full span of their users – ranging from Europe to the Far East and South America. The present book thus traces the story from the first 2nd class ironclads built for overseas service in the 1860s ('cruising ironclads' in French terminology), through what have been called the first 'true' armoured cruisers, the Russian *General-Admiral* and British *Shannon* of the early 1870s, down to the German *Blücher* and the French *Waldeck-Rousseau*, laid down in 1906 as the last of the breed. By the time that *Waldeck-Rousseau* commissioned in 1911, five all-big-gun, turbine-powered battlecruisers were in service in the British and German navies, making all previous big cruisers obsolescent, relegating such ships to the margins of naval affairs of the coming world war.

Nevertheless, a number played important – and in some cases tragic – roles in that conflict, and although most survivors had gone for scrap by the middle of the 1920s, some continued in service into the Second World War, or even beyond. It was not until the middle of the 1950s that the last seagoing example of the classic big cruiser finished her last deployment, and even today one survives as a museum, to remind posterity of what were once some of the most glamorous of the world's warships.

In producing this book, a major issue has been establishing accurate technical data for vessels, as there are significant contradictions between published sources. The latter range from contemporary year-books[1] (some reflecting propagandistic misinformation and/or over-evaluation of capabilities by compilers or nations' intelligence arms), through more recent 'standard' sources,[2] to articles written in specialist periodicals,[3] derived in whole or part from archival sources, and a handful of monographs similarly sourced. This is particularly the case as far as protection is concerned, with widely differing details given in the various publications.

Likewise, career data given in 'standard' works is often incomplete or in error to a greater or lesser degree, final fates being particularly problematic. Accordingly, priority has been given to data explicitly derived directly from official archival sources (e.g. material in the UK National Archives and US

Naval Historical Branch, and foreign equivalents). There remain, however, areas of uncertainty on technical and career matters, and some ships simply fade from the records, with no certainty of their final ends. All I can say is that the data I have presented is that which seems the most credible in light of the sources available to me. Doubtless there are some areas where correction in still required, and I encourage those with any relevant information to pass it on to me!

Sketches are provided in Part II showing the armour and machinery layouts, and development of the appearance of ships over time. It should be emphasised that the latter are indeed 'sketches', aiming to give an impression of the key changes, and may not be wholly reliable on matters of detail. This is a function of the sources available for drawing them: while some are based on official 'as fitted' plans, many have had to be derived from more schematic drawings and/or estimated from photographs, sometimes of doubtful date. The armour diagrams suffer from all the issues noted above regarding the accuracy of published data, and are thus in some cases 'best estimates', often also simplified for clarity.

Similarly, while every effort has been made to maintain a uniform level of detail and temporal coverage throughout, in practice the issues noted above and lack of accessible documentation has meant that some ships have significantly better coverage than others. Documenting the evolution of the appearance of British vessels has benefitted from the work of Richard Perkins, the relevant volumes of whose invaluable albums of drawings in the National Maritime Museum were published in facsimile while this book was in preparation[4] and should be consulted for deeper details of changes of British ships.

As always, I am indebted to many for their help in producing this book: LaVerle Berry, for help in accessing material in the US Library of Congress; David Chessum, for matters related to naval limitation treaties; Andrew Choong Han Lin, for access to material in the National Maritime Museum's Brass Foundry outstation; Reg Clark for proof-reading; Isabelle Delumeau, for information on the French *Kléber* class; Wilfried Langry, for help with the careers of French ships and the provision of images; Innes McCartney, for material relating to ships sunk at the Battle of Jutland; Stephen McLaughlin on matters Russian; and Richard Osborne for his help with images.

As always, I owe a massive debt to my wife, Dyan Hilton for proof-reading, and for continuing to put up with me! However, all remaining errors, cases of faulty logic, and of incomprehensibility remain wholly my responsibility.

University of Bristol, November 2017

INTRODUCTION

The advent of the 'dreadnought revolution' around 1906 has had a long-term impact on the historiography of naval technology, in that it has become for many a 'Year Zero' in capital ship development. Not only has this led to many writers dismissing 'pre-dreadnought' ships as intrinsically flawed, but also ignoring the way that dreadnought-era vessels were actually lineal heirs of concepts going back to the earliest days of steam, if not before.

This is particularly true when one looks at perhaps the most glamorous manifestation of the 'revolution', the battlecruiser, where dispassionate analysis perceives a line that goes right back to the earliest days of the armoured warship, where a lighter, perhaps faster, kind of ironclad was devised to overmatch any normal cruising vessel and act as a capital unit away from the line of battle itself. Indeed, one can trace such a line back to the razees and American purpose-built big frigates of the late eighteenth and first half of the nineteenth centuries. Into this mix, one can also add the role of commerce raider, suggesting higher speeds and greater radius, neither of which, of course, was inconsistent with the other roles mentioned, and sat well with a role as capital unit in distant waters.

The aim of this book is to explore the story of such vessels, down to the point when they transmogrified into the big-gun battlecruiser – although this final transformation was not the first time that the biggest guns could be found on ships other than fully-fledged battleships. The decision to dub them 'big cruisers', rather than a more 'scientific' description, is based on the extremely wide range of classifications given to the vessels involved by their owning navies (noting in any case that no 'legal' definition of 'battleships' and 'cruisers' existed prior to the 1922 Washington Naval Treaty) – appellations including 'large cruisers', '1st class cruisers', '2nd class battleships',

'cruiser-corvettes' and 'armoured corvettes'. Indeed, there was sometimes a distinct lack of consistency in the terminology applied even within a single navy. For example, there seems no good reason why the British *Imperieuse* class were called 'cruisers', yet the *Centurion* class, designed to meet essentially that same requirement, were 'battleships'. Nevertheless, it is generally possible to identify roles that, jointly or severally, enable one to gather the ships in question into a broadly coherent group: the ability to act as capital ships on distant stations; to act a fast wing of the battlefleet; to act against commerce; and to act against such specialist commerce-raiders. These were underpinned in most cases by a size well in excess of the 'ordinary' cruisers of the era (and in some cases battleships as well), and protection that included side armour, something not found on 'ordinary' cruisers. By the end of the era covered, many of the ships in question were classified (officially or unofficially) as 'armoured cruisers', which might have been considered as a term to use for our whole genre but, as implying the possession of side armour, it could not be so-used, as some ships whose purpose and size certainly placed them in our 'big cruiser' category trusted their protection to just an armour deck.

For the purposes of this book, and as far as possible as a rationalisation of the classificatory issues raised above, the 'big cruiser' has been defined as an armoured vessel, not primarily intended for service in the main battle line, that was begun prior to the completion of HMS *Invincible*, and that possessed side protection and/or exceeded 7500 tons displacement. As well as covering these ships in detail, it will also look at the ancestors of such vessels and collateral developments that met similar requirements and influenced what we are viewing as the main line of evolution, thus effectively viewing international naval history through the lens of the 'big cruiser'.

Sources, Conventions and Abbreviations

References and sources

As far as possible the present work avoids 'standard works' (e.g. *Conway's All the World's Fighting Ships*), with preference given to archival sources and published monographs and articles based on them. Footnoted references are given in particular to articles focussing on specific ships and classes, but key sources also include relevant parts of such works as Burt's *British Battleships 1889–1904*, Feron's *100 ans Marine français: Croiseurs; Gardes-côtes*, Friedman's *U.S. Cruisers: an illustrated design history* and *British Cruisers of the Victorian Era*, Giorgerini and Nani's, *Gli Incrociatori Italiani 1861–1967*, Muscant's *U.S. Armored Cruisers: a Design and Operational History*, and Parkes's *British Battleships* (although this book has problems deriving from its publication before many archival sources were released).

Conventions

For ease of comparison, all measurements have been primarily converted into Imperial units, with conversion tables given at Appendices 1 and 2. Dates in parentheses after a ship's name, unless otherwise indicated, represent their date of launch.

Deck levels are referred to by their British terms. These are shown schematically below, with other contemporary, and modern, designations shown in parentheses. The Upper deck is defined as the highest deck running the whole length of the hull. Only a tiny number of ships had all the features shown, with a Middle deck only normally found in some of the very largest ships.

Abbreviations

AA	anti-aircraft
AMC	Armed Merchant Cruiser
BA	Bundesarchiv (in photographic credits)
BCS	Battle Cruiser Squadron (Royal Navy)
BRT	British Registered Tons
BS	Battle Squadron (Royal Navy)
BuOrd	Bureau of Ordnance (US Navy)
CinC	Commander-in-Chief
CS	Cruiser Squadron (Royal Navy)
cwt	hundredweight (in gun designations)
DF	Destroyer Flotilla (Royal Navy)
FF	Fleet Flagship
FO	Flag Officer
ihp	indicated horsepower
QF	Quick Firing gun
kt	knot(s)
LCS	Light Cruiser Squadron (Royal Navy)
NHHC	US Naval History and Heritage Command (photographic credits)
nm	nautical mile(s)
pdr	pounder (in gun designations)
SG	Scouting Group (*Aufklärungsgruppe* – German Navy)
shp	shaft horse power
Sqn	Squadron
SNO	Senior Naval Officer
SO	Senior Officer
TBF	Torpedo Boat Flotilla
TT	Torpedo tube(s)
WSS	World Ship Society (in photographic credits)

Poop deck
Poop
↓Shelter deck (= Superstructure deck = 02 deck)
↓Forecastle deck (= 02 deck)
↓Upper deck (= 01 deck)
Forecastle
↓Main deck (= Battery deck = First deck = 1 deck)
↓Middle deck (= 'Tween deck = Second deck = 2 deck)
↓Lower deck / Armour deck (= Berth deck = Third deck = 3 deck)
↓Upper Platform deck (= 4 deck)
↓Lower Platform deck (= 5 deck)
Hold (= 6 deck)

Part II data tables

Displacement: Given the lack of any standardised scheme for determining displacement prior to the Washington Naval Treaty of 1922, this is generally the 'Normal' displacement quoted for the ship(s) in contemporary sources. For vessels that remained operational after the signing of the Washington Treaty this became the 'Standard' displacement for treaty purposes, although in actuality wholly unrelated to the legal definition of this under the treaty.

Dimensions: Where available, lengths are given as between perpendiculars (at rudder and forward hawseholes), waterline (wl) and overall (oa); draughts are at normal displacement.

Machinery: Reciprocating engine types are abbreviated as follows:
HC = Horizontal Compound
HAD = Horizontal Direct Acting
HSE = Horizontal Single Expansion
HTE = Horizontal Triple Expansion
HRCR = Horizontal Return Connecting Rod
VTE = Vertical Triple Expansion
In power figures, the suffix FD denotes forced draught
Fuel capacity is quoted as normal/maximum.

Armament: All guns are breech loaders unless otherwise stated (MLR = Muzzle Loading Rifle), and quoted as calibre/bore length; for full details of guns see Appendix 1.

Protection: Thicknesses given from the stern forward, with maximum thicknesses generally quoted; armour deck thicknesses are given flat/slopes.

Complement: Where available, given as officers+other ranks.

Laid down: Definitions varied between navies and unclear as to which is being used in many sources; for French vessels the date of *mis sur cale* is used where available.

Completed: Definitions varied between navies and unclear as to which is being used in many sources; for French vessels the date of *armement definitif* is used where available.

PART I: THE RISE AND

HMS *Suffolk* at the end of her operational career, as British flagship at Vladivostok in 1918 during the UK/US/Japanese intervention in the Russian Civil War. She is shown with typical late-war modifications, with her main-deck secondary guns moved to the upper deck. *Suffolk* was unique among her class in having a stern-walk. In the background is the Japanese battleship *Mikasa* (1900), while behind her on the far left can be seen the bow of USS *Brooklyn* (see p 135). *(WSS)*

FALL OF THE BIG CRUISER

1 | GENESIS

The Sailing Navies

By the late eighteenth century, the Royal Navy had evolved a rating system for warships, inaugurated in 1677, that comprised six bands. During the Napoleonic Wars, the 1st rate had 100+ guns, the 2nd rate 90 to 98, the 3rd rate 64 to 80, the 4th rate 50 to 60, the 5th rate 32 to 44, and the 6th rate 20 to 28. The first three rates were 'ships of the line' – battleships, with multiple gun decks; the last three were 'frigates' – single gun-deck cruising ships, for scouting, trade protection and other ocean service. Other navies used similar concepts, the French with five *rangs*.

When the United States Navy was re-founded under the Naval Act of 1794, it was clear that the fledgling force could not have the luxury of a graduated force of ships of the line and frigates. Instead, the decision was taken to build frigates so powerful that they could defeat any foreign frigate, but capable of outrunning any ship of the line that could outgun them[5] – essentially the concept behind many later big cruisers, and underpinning the concept of the German *Deutschland* class as late as the 1930s. Accordingly, *United States* (44 guns) *Constellation* (38), *Constitution* (44), *Chesapeake* (38), *Congress* (38) and *President* (44) were all launched between 1797 and 1800. All generally carried well above the number of guns for which they were rated, the 44s (normally with over 50 guns)

mounting 24pdrs as their smallest weapons, contrasting with the then-usual 18pdr base armament of a frigate (including the three 38s), emphasising the ships' quasi-capital role.

Another kind of heavy frigate of the period was that created by removing the topmost gun deck of an obsolete two-deck ship of the line to create a razee frigate. Three British 64s became 44-gun frigates in 1794, armed with 24pdrs like the big Americans, and including Sir Edward Pellew's famous *Indefatigable* (originally launched in 1784). The others were *Magnanime* (1780) and *Anson* (1781). More were created between 1813 and 1845 to employ the hulls of 74s, a type increasingly obsolete in the battle line (although not all conversions were completed).[6] The first of the latter conversions were part of crash programme to counter the threat posed by the US 44s during the War of 1812, producing 58-gun vessels that included *Majestic* (1785) which, with the 40-gun frigate *Endymion* (1797), captured *President* on 15 January 1815. The French navy also undertook the conversion of 74s into 54s during the 1790s, and another in 1822. The United States also razeed a 90-gun ship of the line, *Independence* (1814), which became a 54 in 1836.

From Wood to Iron

The ship of the line was never a key part of the United States' order of battle, and the concept of big frigate as principal units of the fleet continued into the nineteenth century, although the realities of artillery of the period meant that the theoretical

Constitution (1797), one of the four big frigates constructed by the United States at the end of the eighteenth century, and in many ways the ancestresses of later big cruisers. She is seen here around 1909, soon after completing her first restoration. (*Author's collection*)

The American-built Russian big frigate *General-Admiral* (i). It would later be proposed that she should be converted to an ironclad, but in the event a new ship, *General-Admiral* (ii – pp 21–2, below) was built instead. (*Author's collection*)

The USN continued to regard the big frigate as a core unit, *Minnesota* (1855) being one of five near-sisters commissioned shortly before the American Civil War. Displacing 3300 tons, she was armed with two 10in, twenty-eight 9in and fourteen 8in guns, with a designed speed of 12.5kt. She spent the post-Civil War years on training duties, being sold for scrap in 1901, and ultimately burned to recover metal fittings. *(NHHC NH 92)*

advantages of ships capable of long-range fire by a smaller number of heavier guns over the those with larger numbers of short-range weapons were not likely to be realised.[7] This culminated in five 40-gunned, nominally 12kt, steam frigates (*Merrimack*, *Wabash*, *Roanoke*, *Minnesota* [all 1855] and *Colorado* [1856]) ordered in 1854 which, with the even bigger frigate *Franklin* (1864) and sloop *Niagara* (1855), were regarded by the British as a threat to their commerce.[8]

Russia had adopted a long-standing dual strategy of coastal defence and commerce raiding in the wake of their defeat in the Crimean War, and also laid down a series of three large frigates in the late 1850s to fulfil the commerce-raiding requirement. The biggest of them, the 5700-ton, 68-gun *General-Admiral* (1858), was built in the USA,[9] with two 4500-ton vessels (*Aleksandr Nevskiy* and *Dmitri Donskoi* [1861]) constructed in Russia.

The construction of the American ships led to the laying

down of British 'replies', which became 'Walker's Big Frigates' (Sir Baldwin Walker [1802–76] being the then-Surveyor of the Navy), the 5500-ton *Mersey* and *Orlando* (1858). Also armed with 40 guns, but much faster than the American-built ships (13.5kt vs. 8.5–9.5kt actual), they proved to be the longest (30ft longer than the slightly bigger *General-Admiral*) and most powerful single-decked wooden fighting ships ever built. However, their tactical value was somewhat nebulous, being too fast for the line of battle and too powerful for normal

Built as an answer to such vessels as *Minnesota*, the two *Mersey*-class frigates (1858, *Orlando* shown here) were the longest wooden warships ever built, and showed that wooden shipbuilding had reached its limits. *(Author's collection)*

Of the six fast commerce raiders authorised by the US Congress in 1863, only three were ever completed; *Wampanoag* (renamed *Florida* in 1869) served a brief commission in early 1868, including as North Atlantic Squadron flagship, but spent the rest of her life in reserve or as a receiving ship until sold in 1885. *(NHHC NH 54159)*

cruising. Indeed, ultimately they were manifestations of the regular tendency to build 'replies' to a given potential enemy vessel, without a real understanding of how the 'opponent' or 'reply' might actually be used – leaving aside the question of whether the two would ever find themselves in the same place at the same time. A similar situation can be seen in the 1890s, with the British construction of the *Powerful* class in reply to the Russian *Ryurik* (i) and *Rossiya* (p 52–3, below).

The 'scare' caused by a further series of American big frigates was also the genesis of the leap in size that produced a series of large iron – but unarmoured – frigates in the Royal

Navy, strength and rigidity problems in the *Mersey*s having shown the limits of wooden construction. In this case, the new Americans' size was driven by a desire for exceptional speed – 15kt – nominally as a counter to Confederate commerce raiders, but seen by the British as a feature allowing the ships in question, *Wampanoag* (1864), *Ammonoosuc* (1864), *Madawaska* (1865), *Neshaminy* (1865), *Pompanoosuc* (never launched) and *Bon Homme Richard* (not laid down), to themselves act as commerce raiders against British trade.

Although, as it turned out, the wooden-built American ships were fast but impractical (and the last three were never completed), they led to the building of HMS *Inconstant* (1868), a thousand tons larger, just as fast and with guns of capital-ship size (9in/12.5-ton and 7in/6.5-ton MLR). She was followed by a half-sister, *Shah* (1873), which also carried capital-ship guns. She, however, marked the end of mounting such guns on seagoing unprotected hulls, a number of similar, but somewhat smaller, vessels (*Raleigh* [1873], *Volage* [1869], *Active* [1869], *Rover* [1874] and the *Bacchante* class [1875–77]), mounting

The British replies to *Wampanoag* and her wooden sisters were a number of large iron unprotected frigates, beginning with *Inconstant* (1868), followed by *Shah* (1870, shown here). Her combat with the rebel Peruvian turret ship *Huascar* in 1877 demonstrated the need for Britain to maintain armoured vessels on distant stations (see p 19). Her lower masts survive in the ship of the line *Victory* (1765), in which they were installed in 1893, when *Shah* was dismantled. *(NHHC NH 71214)*

Tourville (1876) was one of the two French vessels built to similar specifications as the British vessels, but intended for commerce raiding; she was condemned in 1901. *(NHHC NH 66097)*

solely frigate-size (7in and smaller) ordnance. The building of French equivalents was delayed by the Franco-Prussian War of 1870, but under the 1872 Programme (see pp 25–6, below), *Duquesne* and *Tourville* (5905/5698 tons, 1876) were constructed with commerce-raiding as a key function.

Into the Ironclad Age

The appearance of the first armoured battleships, the French *Gloire* (1859) and the British *Warrior* (1860), was an immediate challenge to the conventional system of classification as, while militarily superior to even 1st Rate ships of the line, they were strictly speaking 'frigates' on the basis of their number and placement of guns. However, they were also not intended for the classic frigate roles, rather being capital ships for home waters. Accordingly, the following years saw ships often receiving technically-descriptive classifications (e.g. 'central battery ship'; 'barbette ship'; 'turret ship'),[10] often informally lumped together as 'ironclad', rather than ones that reflected a particular tactical role.

Indeed, that tactical role was often somewhat hazy, ships being often constructed on the basis of required size/cost, rather than the operational requirement that they were to fulfil. Thus, the concept of following a 'full-size' ironclad with diminutives to keep costs down was to be found in the UK in the *Defence* (6150 tons, 1861) and *Hector* (1862–3, 6710 tons) classes that followed the *Warrior*s onto the slips. A third smaller, and 2kt slower, they could not easily tactically combine with the bigger ships (nor *Warrior*'s lineal successors, *Achilles* [1863] and the *Minotaur*s [1863–6]), and thus were of uncertain value as home-waters capital ships. This was reflected by *Defence*'s deployment to the North America station during 1869–70, and *Resistance* becoming the first British ironclad in the Mediterranean in 1864–7, where they both could aspire to full capital rank. The later-completing *Hector* and *Valiant* spent respectively most or all of their careers as guardships in home waters, reflecting their lack of utility as true battleships.

A few even smaller ironclads were also built in Britain during the early 1860s, essentially as experiments to determine whether armour could or should be applied to vessels below capital rank. Two incomplete sloops were converted on the slip into the 1350-ton *Enterprise* (ex-*Circassian*, 1864) and the 1734-ton *Research* (ex-*Trent*, 1863), while an incomplete corvette became the 3230-ton *Favorite* (1864). While the latter was not unsuccessful, spending two commissions on the North American & West Indies station, assessment of these ships resulted in side armour not again being applied to such small vessels in British service (other than coast-defence turret ships) until the twentieth century.

French ironclads, produced as part of the huge fleet expansion programme initiated by Napoleon III in 1857 (and amended in 1863 and 1865), were initially significantly smaller than their British counterparts, only matching them with the *Océan* class (1869–70), and even then with their survivability degraded by wooden hulls. However, as well as such home-service capital ships, from 1863 they also started to build smaller vessels to act in the capital role on foreign stations – to become one of the roles of the 'classic' big cruiser. These ships, *Belliqueuse*, laid down in 1863, and the follow-on *Alma* class, laid down between in 1865, should thus probably be seen as the starting point for the breed to which this book is dedicated.

Gloire, the first armoured frigate, in 1869. *(Author's collection)*

Warrior (1860), the first iron-built ironclad in the 1860s; in her dotage she would be reclassified as an armoured cruiser (p ***). *(NHHC NH 71191)*

The first British 2nd class ironclad, *Defence* (1861). *(NHHC NH 71206)*

2 | THE STEAM AND SAIL ERA

Belliqueuse Challenge

With the 'home' armoured frigate programmes well underway, both the UK and France began to consider the question of how to replace the wooden vessels employed as capital ships of foreign stations. In Britain, issues with the first experimental small ironclads (e.g. *Pallas* [1862]), and the poor habitability of ironclads in the tropics, left wooden vessels on distant stations until the end of the 1860s. But in France a programme of armoured ships intended for overseas service was begun in 1863. The vessels, dubbed 'armoured corvettes', were to be powerful enough to challenge any foreign warship that might be found on an overseas station, and small enough for their maintenance and supply to be within the resources of overseas bases. These roles would be pivotal for many future 'big cruisers', and the line of vessels engendered by this requirement can be seen as starting with these French ships.

The first of them all, to become *Belliqueuse*, was effectively a reduced version of the *Magenta* class (1861), a unique pair of two-deck ironclads. Originally, *Belliqueuse* was to have fourteen guns of the 'heaviest' calibre (and had her battery pierced for such), but completed with four 7.6in and six 6.5in guns, four of the latter in the battery, and the other two on the upper deck as bow and stern chasers. The battery guns were arranged with the 7.6in weapons firing through the aftermost ports, the next-forward with 6.5in, then the other 7.6in, and the remaining pair of 6.5in through foremost ports. Her armour (on a wooden hull) comprised a complete 5.9in belt, covering from the battery deck to 5ft below the waterline. The battery itself had 4.7in armour, but lacked armoured transverse bulkheads fore and aft.

Commissioned in October 1866 as Pacific flagship, she left France in December, returning in 1869, during which time she covered 50,000nm and became the first French ironclad to double Cape Horn. She sailed as flagship for the Levant in November 1869, but went to the Pacific in July 1870, the following month becoming flagship for Western Oceania. Returning to Toulon in 1871, she was flagship for the Far East station from 1872 to 1874. Rearmed in 1876 with new-model main guns, her upper-deck armament was also changed to five of 5.4in calibre, plus some Hotchkiss revolver cannon. During the last half of 1877, she served with the Evolutionary

Atalante (1868), one of the main group of the *Alma* class, showing the barbettes forward of her single funnel. *(Author's collection)*

Belliqueuse, the first of the French armoured corvettes. *(Author's collection)*

Jeanne d'Arc and *Thétis*, the latter shown here in 1865, differed from their sisters in having twin funnels. *(Author's collection)*

16

Squadron, before paying off into reserve. Decommissioned in November 1884, *Belliqueuse* was condemned in May 1886 and became a target ship for testing high-capacity shells (cf. p 41, below).

The design of *Belliqueuse* was judged satisfactory even before she entered service, a whole class of a modified version being laid down in 1865 as the *Alma* class, which were essentially reduced versions of the *Océans*, begun the same year. Compared with the prototype, dimensions were slightly changed, and a 0.6in iron skin was applied over the wood where it was not armoured to lessen fire risk; they also had 5.9in batteries with 4.7in transverse bulkheads. As planned, the ships were to have an upper battery for four 6.5in guns; this was then superseded by four upper-deck 3.9in-armoured barbettes (as also in the *Océans*), the after two then being suppressed owing to weight considerations, but with a decision on 12 March 1868 that the remaining pair be upgunned to 7.5in weapons, thus giving the ships a uniform armament of six guns of this calibre. There were some differences between ships, most noticeably the twin athwartships funnels sported by *Jeanne d'Arc* and *Thétis*.

As with *Belliqueuse*, the *Alma*s gave good service as flagships on distant stations, *Alma* herself spending 1870–2 in the Far East, being relieved by *Belliqueuse*. After a period in the Evolutionary Squadron, she spent 1876 to 1881 in reserve, then deploying to the Levant before once again reducing to reserve in 1883. Condemned in 1886, she was sold for scrap in 1893. *Armide* went to the Baltic during the Franco-Prussian War,[11] and then spent time in the Mediterranean, before going

to the Levant in 1874. After a spell in reserve, the ship became China flagship in 1877; condemned in 1882, she was later expended as a target.

Atalante also served in the Franco-Prussian War, and spent time in reserve before going to the Pacific as flagship from 1872 to 1874. 1876 to 1878 was spent as Pacific flagship, and 1882 to 1885 as Far East flagship, including actions during the Sino-French War of 1884–5. Afterwards decommissioned at Saigon, and condemned in 1887, she subsequently foundered at her berth. *Jeanne d'Arc*, unlike most of her sisters, spent most of her career in home waters, apart from a short period in the Levant in 1879; she was condemned in 1883. *Montcalm* was also in home waters for much of her career, but passed 1874–6 as China flagship and 1882–4 as flagship in the Pacific. On return, she remained laid up until condemned in 1891.

Reine Blanche went to the Levant in 1879, and was Pacific flagship from 1884 to 1886; returning with boilers in a poor state, she was condemned before the end of the year. *Thétis* served in the Levant in 1872 and rammed and nearly sank *Reine Blanche* (which had to be beached). She sailed as flagship for the Pacific in 1885, but had to return under sail after losing her propeller off Madeira. Having finally reached the Pacific, she ended her days as a hulk at Nouméa, New Caledonia.

Audacious Reaction

The building of the *Alma*s prompted the British to consider building something similar to counter the threat to their colonial interests posed by such vessels. While the 1st class turret ships *Monarch* and *Captain* had been ordered in 1866, it was decided that it would be premature to base any overseas diminutives on them prior to trials of the big ships. Full rig was clearly necessary in view of probable difficulties in the

Audacious as completed with a full ship rig.
(WSS John Maber collection)

Triumph at Plymouth in 1873, showing the dummy stern galleries that were painted on their rounded sterns. *(NHHS NH 71217)*

availability of coal on distant stations, for which Edward Reed (1830–1906), Chief Constructor from 1863 to 1870, argued was far more suitable for broadside-armed vessels. Accordingly, the starting point for the design was *Defence*, with a size limitation that led to the first sketches envisaging eight 9in and two 7.5in guns, 6in (5.9in) armour, 12kt speed, and the shallow draught of 21ft. This evolved in 1866 into a somewhat larger ship with ten 9in guns and 8in armour. The guns were arranged on the central-battery principle, first introduced in *Bellerophon* (1866), and now standard for broadside-armed ships. Novel, however, was the fitting of six guns at main-deck

level, with the other four in an upper battery, the latter sponsoned and embrasured to allow fore and aft fire as well as on the beam. These were supplemented by pairs of 6in bow and stern chasers.

Two ships, *Audacious* and *Invincible*, were ordered under the 1867–8 Estimates, out of a total of four ships authorised (albeit with misgivings, particularly since the required shallow draught necessitated twin screws, which could not be made hoisting and thus worked against the requirement for good capability under sail). The remaining pair were the subject of an invitation to private yards to submit proposals; these included broadside, turret and turret-and-broadside designs, but none proved acceptable. Thus *Iron Duke* and *Vanguard* were ordered to the existing design.

The draught requirement was relaxed for a further pair of ships, *Swiftsure* and *Triumph*, built under the 1868–9 Estimates, allowing them to have single lifting screws and thus enhanced sailing qualities, with particular view to service on the Pacific station, where Esquimalt as yet lacked any docking facilities. This was successful, *Swiftsure* being the fastest-sailing of all rigged ironclads. To further refine them for their Pacific role – a station then lacking docking facilities until the late 1880s – the hulls were also sheathed and coppered. In 1878, four 14in torpedo carriages were added fore and aft of the battery, while in the mid-1880s, the 6in MLR guns were replaced by six/eight 4in BL as anti-torpedo-boat weapons, fore and aft and on top of the upper battery.

The class all started their careers as guardships, before *Iron*

Iron Duke while China Station flagship, in dock at Nagasaki during 1872–4. *(WSS John Maber collection)*

Duke proceeded abroad to the China Station from 1871, replacing the wooden-hulled ironclad *Ocean* (1862), and relieving *Rodney* (1833), the last wooden steam ship-of-the-line in full commission, as flagship; en route, *Iron Duke* became the first ironclad to transit the Suez Canal.

She was herself relieved by *Audacious* in 1874 and, while serving as Hull guardship, sank her sister *Vanguard* (Kingstown guardship) in a collision off Dublin Bay in September 1875. *Iron Duke* was then Kingstown guardship until July 1877, when she paid off for refit before going back to China, to relieve *Audacious*. She served there from 1878 to 1883, going aground twice while on station. After returning from China in 1878, *Audacious* went back to guardship duty, and then was extensively refitted, with new boilers and a poop added, before going back to China once again in 1883 for six years. During 1884–6 she was joined by the new battleship *Agamemnon* (1879), sent out as a reinforcement to counter new Chinese battleships (see p 28, below), and also in light of Anglo-Russian tensions over Afghanistan (cf. p 29, below).

As for *Iron Duke*, she was also reboilered during 1883–5 on her return to home waters, serving in the Particular Service Squadron (formed during the aforementioned Russian war scare) during the summer of 1885 before joining the Channel Fleet, and then becoming a guardship. In contrast to her two surviving sisters, *Invincible* only made one brief foray to the Far East, to exchange crews with *Audacious* in 1886 at the juncture of the latter's two commissions. Her career was otherwise concentrated first in the Mediterranean, including acting as flagship during the bombardment of Alexandria on 11 July 1882 owing to her shallow draught. On return from her Far East voyage in 1886, she was dismantled aloft and had 4in secondary guns added, before becoming Southampton guardship until 1893.

Although built for distant service, *Triumph* began her career in the Channel and Mediterranean, until she hurriedly replaced *Shah* as Pacific flagship, serving as such from 1878 to 1882. *Shah* had relieved *Repulse* (1868), the last British wooden-hulled ironclad, in 1877 but the need for an armoured ship in the role had been highlighted by the engagement between *Shah* and the Peruvian turret-ship *Huascar* (1865, then under rebel control) on 29 May 1877, where the much bigger and better-armed, but wholly unarmoured, *Shah* had to attempt to fight at less-effective long ranges to avoid damage.

Swiftsure began a refit in 1878 that reduced her rig to that of a barque, and gave her admiral's quarters, torpedoes and replaced her 6in MLR guns with eight 4in BL battery; in this form she proceeded to the Pacific to relieve *Triumph* from 1882 to 1885. The latter was similarly refitted following her return to the UK, and sailed back west in 1885 to relieve *Swiftsure*, which was reboilered back home, before serving a final commission in the Pacific flagship role from 1888 to 1890. The original intention was that both ships' big refits should have their main batteries replaced by new 8in/26 breech-loaders,[12] as had been done in *Bellerophon* during her 1881–5 reconstruction, but this was not done, as experience

in the latter ship had shown that such longer weapons (6ft longer than her original guns) could not easily be used in space intended for 'short' muzzle loaders.[13] On her return to the UK in 1888, *Triumph* went into reserve, while *Swiftsure* followed her last Pacific deployment with a period of guardship duty before herself going into reserve in 1893.

The Field Widens

In Russia, eight new armoured ships were approved in September 1864, two large seagoing 'corvettes' (to a design tagged 'C'), four smaller broadside vessels for Baltic service ('E' and 'E'), and two small turret ships ('F'), also for Baltic duties.[14] The latter pair were built as the *Charodeika* class (1867), while the other 'Baltic' vessels also actually emerged as turret ships, of the *Admiral Lazarev* and *Admiral Chichagov* classes (1867–8).

In contrast to the limited deployment envisaged for these vessels, the two 'corvettes', which were ordered as *Kniaz Pozharskiy* and *Minin*, were intended to be ocean-going units, with roles that included commerce raiding. This division between vessels intended for coast defence and those intended to prey on the enemy's commerce followed the post-Crimean War strategy noted earlier (p 13). *Pozharskiy*, was ordered on 2 November 1864 as an 'iron-armoured vessel of the large class', and laid down shortly afterwards, with launch scheduled for August 1866 and entry into service for June 1867. Although intended for overseas service, no sheathing and metalling was specified.[15]

Kniaz Pozharskiy as built. (*Author's collection*)

After reboilering in the 1880s, *Kniaz Pozharskiy* had two funnels. (*NHHC NH 101902*)

The original design for *Pozharskiy* and *Minin* was inspired by the British central-battery ship *Bellerophon* and was 265ft at the waterline, with a beam of 45ft, but an extra 4ft was added to the beam to improve stability, while various other modifications increased *Pozharskiy*'s displacement and delayed her launch by a year. However, *Minin*'s design was completely re-cast, ultimately delaying her entry into service by a decade (see below, p 23). The ships' battery was intended to carry eight big guns, originally to be of 9in calibre, but *Pozharskiy* ultimately received 8in weapons (supplemented by 6in chase guns) when these were inordinately delayed. The end guns could either be fired through a broadside port or an adjacent embrasured one. Trials were prolonged, with concerns over her overweight state and consequences for seaworthiness, alterations being carried out to her rig and trim during 1872 leading to significant improvements.

She received a light conning tower in 1871, and after returning from her first deployment to the Pacific during 1873–5, she was extensively refitted over the next two years, receiving wood and zinc sheathing, as well as being reboiled and receiving a second funnel, giving her nearly an extra knot of speed on post-refit trials. A secondary battery of 87mm guns was also added. *Pozharskiy* then had a second period of service in the Mediterranean (following a belated deployment there at the tail-end of the Russo-Turkish War) and Far East during 1880–1. Subsequently, her career was based in the Baltic, new

8in/35 guns replacing her old main battery and another set of boilers being fitted during the 1880s. *Pozharskiy* was reclassified as a 1st class cruiser in February 1892, but was generally employed on training duties, and although plans for a reconstruction were drawn up during the 1890s, her armament was gradually reduced, the ship being formally reclassified as a training ship in 1906, along with other old big rigged cruisers. Reduced to harbour service and losing her name in 1909, she was stricken in 1911.

Meanwhile in France, three improved *Alma*s had been laid down. In the first, *La Galissonnière*, the battery was lengthened to allow the fitting of 9.4in guns, its armour thinned to 4.7in, the thickness that was now applied to the barbettes, which were moved back to abaft the funnel. Two-shaft compound machinery was installed, but not found altogether satisfactory, the remaining pair, the *Victorieuse* class, reverting to a single propeller and also to forward-placed barbettes. They also differed from their half-sister in having a 7.6in gun as a bowchaser and 5.4in, rather than 4.7in, weapons on the upper deck. Although all laid down in 1868–9, they were much delayed in the fallout from France's defeat in the Franco-Prussian War and the fall of the Second Empire, the last ship not completing until 1879.

Nevertheless, for service on distant stations, they still had value, serving like earlier vessels of the type as flagships, *La Galissonnière* going out to the Pacific in October 1874, returning to Brest via Suez in March 1877, having completed a circumnavigation. She was the flagship in the West Indies from 1878 to 1880, and then in the Levant in

Victorieuse, one of the three second-generation French armoured corvettes. *(NHHC NH 66029)*

1883, en route to the Far East, where she served from March 1884, relieving *Victorieuse*, remaining until February 1886, and participating, with *Triomphante*, in the Sino-French War. Laid up after her return, *La Galissonnière* was condemned at the end of 1894.

Victorieuse was flagship in the Pacific from 1878 to 1881, and in the Far East from 1881 to 1884, when relieved by *La Galissonnière*. The remainder of her career was spent in European waters, and she was initially condemned in May 1897. However, she was reprieved and refitted at Brest as a torpedo boat depot ship at Bizerte. Condemned for the second – and last – time in March 1900, she was renamed *Semiramis* as parent ship for vessels laid up at Landévennec, where she remained until broken up in 1904.

Her sister, *Triomphante*, also served extensively in a flagship role, in the Pacific during 1880–2, and from February 1883 in the Levant. However on 28 May, the ship was ordered to Saigon, and subsequently, as part of the Far East Squadron from 1884, participated in a number of actions during the Sino-French War of 1884–5 (see below). She became the flagship of the Far East Squadron on 1 April 1885 and remained as such until reduced to reserve in early 1894. Stricken on 18 July 1896, she then became parent ship for the naval division at Saigon, until sold locally in 1903.

A New Decade

Russia
As follow-ons from *Kniaz Pozharskiy*, Captain 2nd Rank N V Kopytov proposed constructing vessels that would sacrifice armour for speed and range, with just a waterline belt, rather than a fully-protected battery, also omitting *Pozharskiy*'s ram.[16] He also suggested using waterjets rather than screws for propulsion, a system then being trialled in the UK – although it would ultimately prove too inefficient for use with the technology of the time.

Although a suggestion was made by Rear-Admiral Andrei Popov (1821–98) that such a ship might be created by armouring and rearming the wooden frigate *General-Admiral* (pp 12–13, above), a new ship of the same name was built to Kopytov's specification, '. . . to be a cruiser in the full sense of the word, and to inflict damage on the enemy's trade', with 8in guns, protected against 6in ordnance, with a good fuel capacity and full rig. As such, the resulting vessel has often been described as the first true 'armoured cruiser'. Although the design, taking *Pozharskiy* as a starting-point, was completed in 1869, financial constraints meant that two ships were not begun until late the following year.

Their conceptual descent from the 1850s big frigates was implicit in the intent to take their names from two of them, *General-Admiral* and *Aleksandr Nevskiy*,[17] although the latter was later re-named *Gerzog Edinburgskiy*, in honour of the marriage of the British Prince Alfred, Duke of Edinburgh, into the Russian imperial family. Unlike *Pozharskiy*, the new ships

were sheathed and coppered from the outset, while their battery was moved to upper-deck level, leaving an unprotected band above their belt. *General-Admiral* (ii) completed with a main battery of six 8in, mounted in an upper-deck open 6in redoubt, backed up by a pair of 6in chase guns, plus a 6in mortar. Sources differ over her sister's initial fit, but she seems to have had only four 8in, but five 6in.

The ships came out badly overweight, *General-Admiral* having some 500 tons excess on completion, over a third of which was owing to her machinery, which also developed 1000ihp less than designed on trials, its performance deteriorating with time, so that by further trials during 1879–80, power had dropped off to 4470ihp. In normal service, 2800ihp was the best that could be sustained, reducing maximum speed to 12.3kt.

It proved possible to remove 130 tons, but subsequent additions, such as electric lighting, engine-room telegraphs and torpedo equipment, meant that by 1880, 330 tons had been added back, meaning that the belt was almost completely immersed at full load, with stability threatened. As a result, the 6in mortar was removed, as were the forward and aft 6in guns, while the ammunition and coal stowage were both reduced.

A major reconstruction was planned after *General-Admiral*'s first overseas deployment, with new 7000ihp engines and the removal of the belt armour, to bring displacement down to 4830 tons and speed up to 15kt. In the event, the rig was reduced and the upper coal bunkers converted to accommodation, reducing stowage to 630 tons, regarded as sufficient for a 2000nm range, and in 1885 she had six 87mm and eight 37mm guns added.

Both ships had very long careers, although neither was used operationally in war as a cruiser – *General-Admiral* was repairing following grounding and her sister just completing when the Russo-Turkish War was fought in 1877–8, and both were too old for the Russo-Japanese War. They would,

General-Admiral, as completed, in the south of France during the early 1880s. *(NHHC NH 60734)*

however, fight in the First World War in a rather different role. Their armaments were modified on a number of occasions, with a lack of agreement among extant sources, but it seems that *Gerzog Edinburgskiy* received a completely new 6in-only main battery during the 1880s. Early in the twentieth century, armaments were reduced to a few 6in while the vessels were employed for training purposes.

The pair were reclassified as 1st class cruisers in 1892, *General-Admiral* subsequently making some long deployments, both ships spending much of the 1890s and the first years of the twentieth century as training ships. They were reboilered for the first time in 1886 (*General-Admiral*) and *c.*1890 (*Gerzog Edinburgskiy*), receiving cylindrical units, and having their

As with *Kniaz Pozharskiy*, when reboilered *General-Admiral* was fitted with two funnels, as seen here in 1893 at New York. *(Detroit Photographic Co, via Library of Congress)*

single funnels replaced by two. *Gerzog Edinburgskiy* was re-engined in 1897 with an engine removed from the former royal yacht *Livadia* (dismantled as a transport named *Opyt* in 1888), an experimental circular ship whose failure as a seaboat led to her machinery being gradually removed for re-use over the years.[18]

Radical changes occurred in 1909, when the two old cruisers were rebuilt as minelayers, renamed *Narova* (*General-Admiral*) and *Onega* (*Gerzog Edinburgskiy*). As such, the battery and the main deck back to the mainmast was used as primary mine storage, as was most of the lower deck directly below. Rig was reduced to the foremast and a light mainmast and a large bridge erected; *Narova* was reduced to a single funnel when reboilered with Bellevilles in 1913, but *Onega* retained her original two. Both took an active part in the First World War, although *Onega* was reduced to a mine depot hulk in October 1915 and remained on harbour duties until broken up after 1945. *Narova*, however, remained operational, and was taken into Soviet control and employed to lay minefields in November 1918. She was renamed *25 Oktiabrya* in 1924, became a mine training ship in the 1930s and was stricken in 1937, following the commissioning of the newly-converted ex-Imperial yacht, *Marti* (ex-*Shdandart*) in 1936. She then became a floating workshop until discarded in 1944.

A further ship of similar characteristics was commissioned in 1878, after a particularly convoluted building process. As noted above, *Minin* had been planned as a sister of *Kniaz Pozharskiy*, but a review of that design had suggested revisions to the armament, with a number of foreign turret ships exciting the interest of the Russian authorities.[19] Accordingly, *Minin*'s central battery was replaced by a pair of twin turrets, with a pair of light bowchasers in the remaining forecastle. A very similar redesign was carried out a few years later on the German *Großer Kurfürst* (1875).[20] In addition, more powerful machinery was to be installed (4000ihp vs. 2835ihp) and the belt shortened and thickened. Laid down in November 1866, the design was further refined by the decision to fit tripod masts, as in HMS *Captain* (1869).

However, nearly a year after *Minin* had been launched, *Captain* capsized in a gale, calling into question the whole concept of the rigged turret ship. Accordingly, work was suspended while a number of options were considered for *Minin*'s future, including as a turreted coast-defence ship, and with a central battery along the lines of the new *General-Admiral* class. A decision was finally reached in 1874, work re-starting late in the year, with four 8in guns in sponsons at the corners of an unarmoured battery, with eight 6in amidships, plus a pair of the latter in the forecastle and poop, with limited fore and aft arcs. Power was further increased to 6000ihp, and the ship was to be sheathed and zinced.

Minin finally completed in the autumn of 1878, sailing for the Mediterranean in November, transiting the Suez Canal in February 1880 and arriving in the Far East that summer. She headed back to the Baltic in the spring of 1881, arriving home in September. The ship returned east in 1883, arriving

Minin as completed, following a complex building history. (*Author's collection*)

Minin following reboilering in 1887, and reduction in rig in 1891; her funnels were to be heightened in 1895. (*NHHC NH 92224*)

in April 1884 and leaving the following summer, to arrive back at Kronstadt on 20 October 1885.

During 1886–7 she was reboilered with Belleville units, making her the first ship in the Russian navy to have watertube

A number of the early Russian armoured cruisers had second careers as minelayers during the 1910s; here we see *Onega* (ex-*Gerzog Edinburgskiy*) and *Ladoga* (ex-*Minin*) during the first winter of the First World War. (*Author's collection*)

boilers. Her profile was changed to one with two fixed funnels; she was also reduced to a barque rig, with a searchlight fitted half-way up the mizzenmast. *Minin* subsequently served principally as a seagoing training ship, carrying out long voyages during 1889–90 and 1890–1 for cadets and boys. She then became a gunnery training ship in the Baltic, dismantled aloft (with the searchlight moved to the foremast and a fighting top added to the mizzen) and being reclassified as a 1st class cruiser in 1892, along with other ships of the type. Refitted around 1895 with heightened funnels, and in 1901 with a number of more modern guns for training purposes, she continued in her training role until 1908, when an Imperial decree removed all 'sailing ships' from service. The following year, like the *General-Admiral* class, she was rebuilt as a minelayer, capable of carrying 1000 mines, being reboilered and re-engined, the replacement engine being another ex-*Opyt* unit (cf. above). As such, now renamed *Lagoda*, she took part in First World War mining operations, before herself falling victim to submarine-laid mine in August 1915.

The UK

In 1873, the new British First Lord of the Admiralty called for 'ironclads of the second rank . . . which may be good cruizers under sail, draw less water than . . . large ironclads, yet be protected by thicker armour at the waterline and armed with heavier guns than [the *Audacious* class]'. To produce such a vessel, which also should cost half that of the new 1st class

ironclad *Alexandra* (1875), protection of the battery and the forward portion of the belt had to be omitted, albeit with the forepart secured by a submerged armour deck. Additional endurance would be provided by compound engines, estimated to give 10 per cent economy, and a speed a knot greater than the French armoured corvettes.

Named *Shannon*, the ship was ordered under the 1873–4 Estimates, armed principally with seven 9in MLR, supplemented by a pair of 10in. The latter were mounted in the forecastle, embrasured to allow them to fire ahead or on the broadside. Six of the 9in were on the upper deck, firing through the bulwarks, while the seventh was mounted inside the poop, able to fire through embrasures in each quarter. Her guns thus all had a much better command than the main-deck battery of the *Audacious*es, and accordingly more suited to fighting in poor weather. The aforementioned partial waterline belt was topped by a 1.5in armour deck, and closed forward with a 9in transverse bulkhead, which joined the submerged armour deck forward.

Shannon's actual designed speed was 12.25kt, less than the 'second generation' French ships, and also the preceding *Audacious*es, although not dissimilar to that of the earlier French ships, not to mention her Russian equivalents. However, she never made her designed speed, suffering much engine trouble, resulting in much time in dockyard hands. An initial deployment to China was brief, the vessel returning home for modifications after only a few weeks on station in

Shannon in 1877, soon after completion. (*Author's collection*)

Nelson as completed. *(Author's collection)*

While under refit during 1889–92, *Nelson* was dismantled aloft and given fighting tops, as well as a 4.7in secondary battery.
(Author's collection)

July 1878. She made it to the Pacific the following year, but *Shannon*'s tenure was truncated by the fact that no stocks of 10in shells were held at Esquimalt. On her return, she once again went into dock for another long refit, and then spent most of her remaining active years on coastguard duty. Reduced to reserve in 1893, she was sold for scrap in 1899.

The succeeding *Nelson* class, the name ship and *Northampton*, built under the 1874–5 Estimates were intended to remedy the various perceived shortcomings of *Shannon*, with a 40 per cent increase in displacement, gaining a covered-in gun deck, a submerged armour deck replacing the belt aft as well, buoyancy in a riddled condition being entrusted to cofferdams filled with cellulose, which was intended to swell if wet and fill holes. This arrangement was common in the late nineteenth century in a number of navies (e.g. pp 35, 50, 87, below), although experience showed it to be ineffective. The armament was increased by two more 10in, placed aft and one more 9in, the secondary battery now being given a roof. Two-shaft machinery – for the first time in a major British warship installed with vertical cylinders – gave a more respectable 14kt, with bunkerage increased by 50 per cent. As seen by their contemporaries, the pair's status – and that of *Shannon* and the Russian ships – was rather opaque; even the designer, Barnaby, stated that they 'may be looked on from two points of view. They may be regarded as armoured ships, having to meet armoured ships; or as protected cruisers.'

In any case, both *Nelson*s began their careers as overseas flagships, *Nelson* serving on the Australia station from 1881 to 1888.[21] On her return, she underwent a long refit at Chatham, being reduced to military rig and fitted with four 4.7in guns. She then spent three years as Portsmouth before being reduced to reserve, and then housed over and hulked as a stokers' training ship in 1901. *Northampton* relieved the battleship *Bellerophon* as flagship of the North American & West Indies Station in 1881, being relieved herself by *Bellerophon*'s return in 1885. Reaching home the following spring, *Northampton* was reduced to reserve. She recommissioned as a seagoing training and recruiting ship for boys in 1894, retaining her full rig in this role, the only concession to modernity being a military top added in 1886. She served as such for a decade.

France

In the wake of the Franco-Prussian War, a programme of future French construction was set out in 1872, although without any formal approval from the National Assembly, and thus more a statement of aspirations, rather than a formal programme.[22] This gave priority to coastal warfare in home waters and ships for service on distant stations, the latter including further developments of the first generation of armoured corvettes, together with big unarmoured cruisers for commerce raiding (for which see p 15, above).

The former were, as previously, intended to match similar British vessels deployed abroad and to fight the armoured ships that were now beginning to be acquired by regional navies; a further four ships were laid down during 1876–7. The first two, *Bayard* and *Turenne*, were wooden-hulled; the second pair, *Duguesclin* and *Vauban*, had steel. The new ships were 2500 tons bigger than the original *Alma*s and 1200 tons bigger than *La Galissonnière*, with which they shared two shafts. This allowed an extra pair of barbettes to be worked in on the centreline midships and aft, giving the entire main battery of four 9.4in guns the highest command, in an arrangement also found in the contemporary full-size *Amiral Duperré* (1879). The battery, now unarmoured, but mounted on a full-length 1.2in armour deck, was restricted to six 5.4in pieces. 7.6in bow- and stern-chasers were fitted in the first two, replaced by a 6.5in bow-chaser in the second two. The wooden pair were ship-rigged on three masts, and could be distinguished by their funnels, *Bayard* having twin exposed smoke-pipes, while *Turenne*'s funnel was fully cased. The steel ships were two-masted brigs, with the after barbette in the position occupied by the mizzenmast in the wooden pair, thus greatly improving its firing arcs. Sailing gear was later first reduced and then removed, tops being converted to military ones, each with a pair of 47mm guns.

Turenne differed from *Bayard* in having a single cased funnel instead of twin smokepipes. (*NHHC NH 66099*)

Bayard as built, as Far East flagship. (*NHHC NH 32*)

Bayard commissioned in 1882 and following year sailed for Indochina, where she became flagship, taking part in a number of operations during the Sino-French War (see below), but after her return to Toulon in August 1885 she was decommissioned and laid up at Brest until 1894, when she returned to the Far East, serving until May 1899. *Bayard* was then reduced to a hulk at Along Bay (Ha Long, Vietnam); she was broken up five years later. *Turenne* went out to the Far East in 1885, returning to Toulon in 1890. She was then laid up at Cherbourg until stricken in 1900, and sold for scrap the following year.

Duguesclin, which could be distinguished by a unique stern-shape, was the one ship of the type inaugurated by *Belliqueuse* never to serve abroad, going into reserve after only a year's service, during which one man was killed and twenty injured in a capstan accident. Stricken in 1904, she was sold for scrap in 1906. In contrast, *Vauban*, the very last vessel of the line to be completed, left Toulon for the Levant to relieve *Victorieuse* in June 1887, subsequently serving in the Mediterranean from January 1888. She became flagship in the Far East in April 1898, but was then out of commission from May 1899 to July 1900, before returning to service, deploying to Cochin-China (southern Vietnam) during March–November 1901. In January 1903, *Vauban* was placed in special reserve, being stricken the following year and hulked. From 1906 to 1910 she was depot ship for the 2nd Torpedo Boat Flotilla at Along Bay, returning to Saigon as a submarine depot ship from 1911 to 1913; she was sold for scrap in 1914.

A follow-on design was worked out for two vessels to be built under the 1880–1 programme (at Cherbourg and Rochefort),[23] with one 10.6in/30 and two 9.4in/28.5 guns mounted in single barbettes on the centreline, plus ten 5.5in/30 on the broadside. As such, they would have been 6500 tons (fully rigged) diminutives of the contemporary 11,750-ton *Amiral Baudin* class, which arranged their three 14.6in guns in just this way, just as earlier ships of the type had been based on their own 1st class contemporaries. Ordering was, however, deferred owing to delays and cost-growth in ships already under construction. Although two 'station battleships' were included in the 1882, 1883 and 1885 budget requests, with ships now envisaged as being more along the line of the British *Imperieuse* class (pp 30–1, below), the advent of a Navy Minister with a very different set of strategic ideas re-set the French concept of the big cruiser for the second half of the decade.

The final pair of ships descending from *Belliqueuse* differed from their predecessors in being metal-hulled, and also by being brig-, rather that ship-rigged. *Vauban* is seen here after the removal of her sailing rig and the fitting of fighting tops. *(NHHC NH 66028)*

The Sino-French War

In 1875, the Chinese government, reacting to the emerging threat from Japan, established a Sea Defence Fund, and ordering an initial tranche of British-built Rendel gunboats, of small size but armed with guns of up to 15in calibre.[24] In 1880, it was proposed to acquire four modern armoured vessels; plans to buy from Britain (as with the gunboats) having been stymied by Russian objections to the British government, the orders went to AG Vulcan in Germany. First, a contract was placed for a pair of 'armoured corvettes', based on the German *Sachsen* class,[25] together with ten torpedo boats. On 13 September three more armoured corvettes and five (larger) armoured ships were added to the order, but shortages of funds meant that none of the latter were laid down. The other three ships were built, but to designs that were less than half the size of the 7200-ton original pair, completed as the battleships *Ting Yuen* and *Chen Yuen* during 1883–4. One became a 2475-ton protected cruiser ('armoured deck corvette') named *Tsi Yuen*, launched in 1883, armed with two 8.2in/35 and one 5.9in/35, with a 3in deck.[26] The remaining two ships were not begun until 1885 (see p 34).

Both she and the battleships had their delivery held up by the 1884–5 Sino-French War.[27] This had been the culmination of increasing tensions over Chinese support for those opposing the French take-over of Vietnam, full-scale hostilities commencing (without a declaration of war) with an attack on the Chinese naval base of Foochow (Fuzhou) by a French force under Admiral Amédée Courbet (1827–85) on 23/24 August 1885. His usual flagship was *Bayard*, but she, along with *Atalante*, was absent; he therefore flew his flag in the small cruiser *Volta* (1869), although both *Triomphante* and *La Galissonnière* were present, along with the cruisers *Duguay-Trouin* (1879), *Villars* (1881), *d'Estaing* (1881) and *Châteaurenault* (1869), three gunboats and two spar-torpedo boats were in company.

They were faced by a far inferior Chinese force, led by a small wooden corvette, *Yang Wu* (1872), and otherwise comprising scout-transports and four gunboats, exactly the kind of scenario that lay behind the construction of the French armoured corvettes. *Yang Wu* was beached after being successfully hit by a spar torpedo, while most of the remaining ships were disabled by gunfire, *Triomphante* sinking the wooden gunboat *Chen Wei* (1872). The following day, the Foochow dockyard was bombarded, and on 25/26 August, *Triomphante* was involved in the destruction of defences guarding the Min River, although on the 27/28th, *La Galissonnière* was damaged by Chinese gunfire in an attack on a further set of defences.

In February 1885, a force including *Bayard*, *Triomphante* and the cruisers *Nielly*, *Éclaireur* and *Duguay-Trouin* intercepted a Chinese force, comprising the frigate *Yu Yuen* (1873), the cruisers *Nan Chen* (1883), *Nan Rui* (1884) and *Kai Chi* (1882) and the sloop *Teng Ching* (1880), which was tasked with breaking the French blockade of Formosa. A brief action on 13 February off Shipu was followed by the escape of all Chinese vessels except for *Yu Yuen* and *Teng Ching*, which retreated into Shipu harbour, where they were blockaded. Two spar-torpedo boats from *Bayard* entered the harbour on the night of 14/15th, resulting in *Yu Yuen* being torpedoed and sunk, and *Teng Ching* sunk be friendly fire from local shore batteries.

Triomphante later took part in the capture of the Pescadore Islands in March 1885, where Admiral Courbet died of cholera on 11 June. His body was brought back to France on board *Bayard*. The war ended with the Treaty of Paris, signed two days before Courbet's death.

Continuing the Russian Line

In Russia, cruising vessels dominated the programmes of the 1870s, with no ships intended for the line of battle being ordered after *Piotyr Veliky* in 1869, until *Ekaterina II* in 1882 and *Imperator Aleksandr II* in 1883. Most were unarmoured sloops (the *Kreiser* class), but further armoured vessels were planned, *Vladimir Monomakh* and *Dmitri Donskoi*[28] being laid down early in 1881 as a reaction to the Russian navy's inability to deploy worthwhile forces during the Russo-Turkish War of 1877–8 (cf. p 22, above). Much as the *Bayard*s represented an evolution of earlier French armoured cruising vessels, the new

Vladimir Monomakh as completed. (*NHHC NH 88745-A*)

In the early 1890s, *Vladimir Monomakh* was dismantled aloft, and had her machinery replaced. She is shown here in 1902. (*Author's collection*)

Sectioned model of *Dmitri Donskoi* (Central Naval Museum, St Petersburg); note the single-shaft machinery, with two engines in series. *(Author's photograph)*

Russian pair were based on the plans of *Minin*. Like their predecessors, both ships were sheathed and coppered, but there were, however, various changes, including a move to two shafts in the first ship, *Monomakh*, with significantly greater speed; this machinery was based on a set made by Elder in the UK to re-engine the battleship *Piotyr Veliky*, with two three-cylinder compound engines mounted alongside each other. *Donskoi's* construction was slowed for financial reasons, and also to incorporate experience gained in *Monomakh*, which completed before *Donskoi's* launch.

While *Monomakh* followed *Minin's* basic armament arrangement, *Donskoi* had only two 8in, but of a newer type and moved up to sponsons midships at upper deck level, with the battery restricted to a larger number of 6in weapons. This was justified owing to the likelihood that the ships' opponents would be unarmoured cruisers. While *Donskoi* had the same engines as *Monomakh*, in her case they were in series driving a single shaft, to provide an objective comparison of single and twin shafts in ships of the same basic design and machinery.

During the 1890s, both ships were refitted. *Monomakh* had her rig reduced to lower masts and pole topmasts during 1892–3, her boilers being partly rebuilt and new fixed funnels provided. She was further altered during 1896–7, when she was reboilered and completely rearmed, new 6in/45 weapons replacing the 8in (with an additional piece mounted in the bow), while six 4.7in were fitted in lieu of the old 6in guns, leaving two midships and the aft embrasures empty; tops were also fitted to the fore- and mainmasts, with a searchlight high on the former. *Donskoi* received similar alterations during 1893–5, the 8in and endmost 6in guns being replaced by new 6in examples, and 4.7in substituted for all ten remaining old 6in. Her sailing rig was also removed, albeit with the old topmasts kept, and military tops fitted to all three masts. She was also reboilered.[29]

Monomakh deployed to the Mediterranean and Far East during 1884–8, shadowed on her way to the Far East by the British battleship *Agamemnon*: the Admiralty had ordered all Russian ships not in port to be followed by a ship capable of neutralising them at the height of the 1884–5 crisis between the UK and Russia (cf. p 19, above). She was also there during

1889–92 and 1893–1902; a final Baltic refit in 1904 replaced her mainmast with a searchlight platform. Her half-sister also went east on a number of occasions, during 1885–9, 1891–3 and 1895–1902; *Donskoi* sailed for the Pacific once more in October 1903, but was recalled in March 1904, by which time she and accompanying vessels had reached the Red Sea. Back in the Baltic, she joined the 2nd Pacific Squadron, which also contained *Monomakh*, sailing October (see further pp 95–7, below).

Dmitri Donskoi at New York in 1893, in her original form. *(Detroit Publishing Co., via Library of Congress Detroit PC LoC LC-D4-5503)*

As in *Monomakh*, *Dmitri Donskoi* was also extensively refitted in the 1890s, including a reduction to military rig. *(NHHC NH 101967)*

3 | A NEW BEGINNING

The big cruisers built down to the middle of the 1880s had been essentially reduced versions of the 1st class ironclads of the era, and as such stuck to the typical broadside-steam-and-sail concept that most of these adopted, although the fitting of barbettes in the *Alma*s reflected French pioneering efforts to move towards more 'modern' solutions to the location of at least some guns.

Beyond the Broadside

The later 1870s saw the Royal Navy taking more interest in the mounting of heavy guns in barbettes, culminating in the employment of disappearing mountings in the 1st class ironclad *Temeraire* (1876) and then proper barbettes in *Collingwood* (1882). No successors to the *Nelson*s had been planned during this period, and thus when new '2nd class' vessels were next seriously considered for procurement under the 1881–2 Estimates, something more radical than an updated *Shannon/Nelson* or a reduced *Temeraire* – both primarily broadside vessels – was clearly amongst the options, especially as the 'opposing' *Bayard* class, now under construction, had their entire main batteries *en barbette*.

Thus, while initial sketches, with a range of armament arrangements, mixing barbettes and broadside mountings, were based on the earlier British three big cruisers, when the speed requirement was increased from 14kt to 16kt, a radically different approach was investigated, by scaling-up from the 4000-ton *Leander*-class protected cruisers that were now under construction. These were updates of the pioneering fast unprotected steel-built cruisers *Iris* and *Mercury* of 1877–8, which were in many ways the first 'modern' cruisers. The Board preferred, however the side armour of the *Shannon*-derived sketches, but by December 1880 the main armament had changed from the previously envisaged eleven 8in in a mixture of mountings and locations to four of a new breech-loading 9.2in gun mounted at upper-deck level. This was originally envisaged as being of the 26cal Mk I type, but this weapon was abandoned for afloat purposes in 1884, and the cruisers ended up getting an improved 9.2in/31.5, the Mk III in the lead-ship, *Imperieuse*, and Mk V or VI in her sister *Warspite*. This weapon was regarded as more powerful than the 12.5in/16 MLR fitted in the latest *Agamemnon*-class battleships (1879–80).

These guns were mounted in the lozenge arrangement being adopted at that time by the *Hoche* and *Neptune*-class battleships (1886–90) just authorised in France, and which, as in these ships, required a significant tumblehome to enable the beam guns to fire (at least in theory) along the ships' axis. The

mountings were actually based on French practice, drawings of those employed in *Bayard* having been shared in a rare example of Anglo-French amity during the period. A secondary battery for ten 6in/26 BL was to be provided on the main deck, with the end guns capable of axial fire. Six 18in torpedo tubes were fitted on the lower deck, the midships ones fixed but the end pairs trainable. Protection was based on the use of compound armour for the waterline belt, of a uniform 10in thickness over the machinery, topped by a 1.5in deck,

Imperieuse in 1886, with her short-lived barque rig. She and her sister *Warspite* were the last big ships with anachronistic stern quarter-galleries. *(Author's collection)*

Warspite with military rig, at Vancouver while serving as flagship of the Pacific station. She could be distinguished from her sister by having four, rather than six, ventilators around her after funnel. *(Author's collection)*

with a 3in submerged deck fore and aft. Barbettes were 8in thick, extending down to the main deck, with ammunition tubes down to the armour deck.

Two-shaft machinery was provided, with two compound engines on each shaft, to allow the forward pair to be disconnected for economical running at lower speeds. This arrangement would be used in a number of big cruisers down to the 1890s (e.g. pp 38, 50–1), but suffered from the disadvantage that reconnecting the idle engine required engines to be stopped and laboriously realigned, which meant that any sudden need for speed – e.g. an unexpected encounter with an enemy, one of the obvious reasons for requiring full power – could not be accommodated (see p 77 for an actual example).

As with previous cruising vessels, a sailing rig was provided but, owing to the layout of the main battery, this had to be restricted to two masts. Trials showed that this rig was useless, and that its weight simply exacerbated the overweight condition of *Imperieuse*. As a result, she was re-rigged, with her derrick-post extended into a light military mast: her original masts were re-used in refitting *Northampton* as a training ship. The sailing rig prepared for *Warspite* was never fitted, and was later used in a re-rigging of the battleship *Superb* (1875). The ships' overweight condition meant that the endmost four 6in guns were not initially installed, although two were reinstated following re-rigging (with the other two only to be mounted in wartime); in addition, the

torpedo tubes had to be raised by 2ft to keep them sufficiently above the waterline.

Following her rigging trials and refitting in 1886, *Imperieuse* remained in reserve until sailing for China to relieve *Audacious* as flagship in 1889, reflecting the ships' common conceptual heritage. Returning in June 1894, she was then refitted, with her 6in guns converted to quick-firers. She went to the Pacific as flagship in 1896 (carrying all ten 6in guns from February 1897), coming back for a Chatham refit in August 1899. She spent the next few years in reserve, until she replaced *Erebus* (ex-*Invincible* – see pp 37, 111) as destroyer depot ship at Portland at the beginning of 1905, under the name *Sapphire II*, and with her 6in battery unshipped. She remained in this role until the end of 1912, and was sold for scrap the following autumn.

Warspite was also held in reserve following completion in 1888, going to sea only for manoeuvres until sent to the Pacific as flagship to relieve *Swiftsure* in February 1890, staying until 1893. She then was under refit or on guardship duty until she returned to the Pacific to relieve her sister. Coming home in July 1902, she then lay in reserve at Chatham until sold for scrap in 1905.

Although much criticised at home, *Imperieuse* provided the model for the next Russian armoured cruiser, *Admiral Nakhimov*,[30] which was intended as an 'oceanic armourclad', to project power in distant waters. Unlike earlier Russian vessels, she had no overt commerce-raiding role, and was to be protected on a scale to allow her to face foreign equivalents. *Nakhimov* was originally intended as part of a sixteen-ship programme that would, as with previous Russian schemes, comprise a mixture of 'oceanic' vessels, and those intended for coastal defence, the battleships *Imperator Aleksandr II* and

Imperator Nikolai I (1887–9) being *Nakhimov*'s 'Baltic' opposite numbers, and the three *Ekateriana II*-class battleships (1886–92) those in the Black Sea. *Nakhimov* was regarded as having the higher priority of the two types of ship, and would be laid down a year earlier than *Aleksandr II*.

When design work began in 1882, the basic requirement was set as 11in guns, a 10in belt, 15kt speed, a large coal capacity, a maximum draught of 26ft, and a full sailing rig. Models considered included the British-built Brazilian battleship *Riachuelo*, *Nelson*, and *Imperieuse*, with *Nelson* rapidly discarded as of obsolescent layout. The wide firing arcs offered by *Riachuelo*'s en-echelon armament appeared attractive (cf. pp 49–50; she was also regarded as a potential model for *Nikolai I*), but her low coal capacity militated against her. This just left *Imperieuse*, which was agreed to the basis for the new Russian ship on 22 June 1882. Indeed, the formal construction order, issued on 24 October explicitly stated that the new ship should be 'an oceanic armourclad like the *Imperieuse*'.

The final design was approved on 1 December 1882, and included engines that would duplicate those of *Vladimir Monomakh*. As in *Imperieuse*, the intent was to fit single guns in each of the main barbettes, now to be of a new 9in design. However, developmental problems meant that in January 1885 it was decided to substitute twin 8in mountings, which had the incidental benefit of increasing the weight of broadside by some 40 per cent, yet saving mounting weight. A secondary battery of ten 6in was installed, directly imitating the British prototype, with three above-water 15in torpedo tubes, one at the stern and a pair just aft of the forward turret. Protection comprised a 10in belt over the machinery spaces, closed with transverse 9in bulkhead fore and aft, and by a 2in deck; 3in decks extended to the bow and stern. Barbettes were shallow and largely 7in thick.

Again like *Imperieuse*, a brig rig was fitted (this was also planned for *Aleksandr II*), but only with a single funnel, while the hull was sheathed and coppered. During her first high-seas voyage, escorting the Imperial yacht to Copenhagen in the summer of 1887, *Nakhimov* encountered heavy weather, the forecastle being so wet that a suggestion was made that the forward main mounting be removed and an extra deck added. However, as this would have caused trim problems, nothing was done.

In accordance with her intended role, *Nakhimov* spent much of her career abroad, leaving Kronstadt in the autumn of 1888 for the Far East via the Cape of Good Hope, arriving at Vladivostok in May 1889. She joined *Vladimir Monomakh* and *Pamiat Azova* (carrying Crown Prince Nikolai [later Emperor Nikolai II]) on a tour of Eastern ports during the

As refitted in 1899, *Admiral Nakhimov* was partly rearmed and her sailing rig removed. *(Author's collection)*

The Russian *Admiral Nakhimov* (shown at New York in 1893) had a very similar layout to the *Imperieuse* class, albeit with twin main mountings and a single funnel. *(Detroit Publishing Co., via Library of Congress, LC-D4-21138)*

spring of 1891, before returning to the Baltic in September. Following a refit, *Nakhimov* left Kronstadt in May 1893 for the USA, returning to Europe in September, colliding with *Pamiat Azova* off Cadíz and losing her bowsprit. As an indication of the marginal utility of *Nakhimov*'s sailing rig, this component was not replaced at this time, the ship continuing into the Mediterranean, though the Suez Canal, and on to the Far East, where she arrived in the spring of 1894. While there, she led the Russian expedition to Port Arthur in December 1897 that led to Russia taking a 25-year lease on the area in March 1898.

Nakhimov came back to the Baltic in the spring of 1898, paying off for an extensive refit, which involved being dismantled and cut down aloft, the fitting of watertube boilers and triple-expansion engines, and partial re-arming, including new lighter barbette hoods and the 6in battery being replaced by new 4.7in/45 guns. Early in 1900, the ship set out once again for the Far East, via Suez, remaining there until the autumn of 1902, arriving back in the Baltic the following spring for a refit.

The programme promulgated in 1880 was revised in 1885, with a change in the ratio of types, but maintaining the Russian navy's long-term interest in armoured cruisers capable to independent operations. As laid down in 1886, the next such vessel, *Pamiat Azova*, was very different from *Nakhimov*, and in the long-range cruising tradition of *General-Admiral* and her successors down to *Donskoi*.[31] Thus, the new ship was to have the same basic layout as the latter, but lengthened by some 80ft and power increased by 1500ihp with a view to increasing her speed from 16kt to 18kt. She also looked very different from

the earlier vessel, being reminiscent of the French-built *Admiral Kornilov* (p 40, below). In February 1886, it was decided to switch from *Donskoi*'s single-shaft arrangement to one with twin screws, with vertical triple expansion engines, rather than the planned horizontal compound machinery.

Pamiat Azova's main armament comprised two 8in/35 mounted in barbettes abreast the forefunnel, similar to the installations in the French armoured corvettes. This was backed up by thirteen 6in/35 on the main deck, with one gun as a bowchaser (a planned sternchaser was not fitted). 47mm guns were fitted on the forecastle and the quarterdeck, plus 37mm revolver cannon on the upper deck at the very stern and forward, and on the wings of the fore and aft bridges.

Protection was originally intended to cover only the midships 180ft, the ends relying on deck protection. However, while the ship was under construction, it was decided that the belt should be made full-length, but narrowed by 15 per cent amidships and 19 per cent at the ends in part-compensation. 6in thick amidships, it also thinned fore and aft and at its lower edge to 4in. The armour deck was 2.5in amidships, reducing to 1.5in at the ends.

The lengthened belt, additional armour bulkheads, reinforcement of the machinery foundations and the addition of a double bottom contributed to the ship being overweight by some 800 tons as compared to the designed displacement of 6000 tons. To compensate, two 6in, forty mines, torpedo nets and some of the rig were removed, with bunkerage and ammunition stowage also cut. Trials were also a disappointment, only 16.8kt being reached as compared with the hoped-for 18kt.

Pamiat Azova as built. *(Author's collection)*

After a first few months with the Baltic Fleet, *Pamiat Azova* departed for the Far East in the late summer of 1890, picking up the Crown Prince at Trieste in October, and then proceeding east in the company of *Vladimir Monomakh*, making numerous port calls until they formally joined the Pacific Squadron at Singapore in February, Prince Nikolai remaining aboard until they arrived at Vladivostok in May. *Pamiat Azova* acted as Pacific flagship until the middle of 1892, when she sailed for Europe via the Suez Canal, arriving at Kronstadt in October. After a refit, she headed back towards the Far East at the end of the summer of 1893, finding herself in collision with *Nakhimov* en route. She spent a year in the Mediterranean, departing for the final leg of the voyage to the Pacific in November 1894, arriving in February 1895. She was either flag or 2nd flag of the Pacific Squadron for much of her time on station, her rig being reduced at Vladivostok, with yards remaining on the foremast only. *Pamiat Azova*'s Far Eastern service ended in November 1899, when she sailed for home. Arriving in May 1900, the ship paid off for a refit. On completion of this, she became a seagoing gunnery training ship in the Baltic, serving as such until 1904, when she was taken in hand at the Franco-Russian Works for a major refit.

China and Japan

In the wake of her humiliation by the French, China placed orders for a range of new ships.[32] Four vessels were procured abroad, two protected cruisers from the UK (*Chih Yuen* and *Ching Yuen*: 1886; 2300 tons, three 8.2in) and two armoured cruisers (the outstanding 'armoured corvettes' from the pre-war programme [p 28]) from Vulcan in Germany. The latter pair, *Lai Yuen* and *King Yuen*, were essentially enlarged side-

armoured (9.5–5.25in abreast the machinery and forward magazine) versions of *Tsi Yuen*, although with the belts placed such that they were almost submerged at full load. As compared with their prototype, the pair had an extra 5.9in gun, 18in rather than 15in torpedo tubes, triple expansion engines, and two funnels. Both ships were laid down in late 1885, launched in early 1887, and completed that summer. They sailed to China in company with the two British-built vessels, arriving in November, and joining the Peiyang (northern) Fleet the next spring.

In addition to these foreign-built ships, the Foochow dockyard laid down the first Chinese-built armoured vessel, *Lung Wei*, in late 1886. Armed with one 10.2in and two 5.9in Krupp guns, she had an 8in belt, but a speed of only 10.5kt. The ship has often been alleged to have been a cut-down copy of the German-built *King Yuen* class, but these vessels were still on the stocks when the Chinese-built ship was begun, and any inspiration would have come from *Tsi Yuen*, although limited in any case to basic layout. Completed at the end of 1889, she made an initial voyage to Shanghai, for inspection by the CinC, before returning to her builders for the rectification of defects. She was renamed *Ping Yuen* in May 1890, to match the name-pattern of other cruisers, then joining them in the Peiyang Fleet.

In the meantime, Japan was ordering her first armoured cruiser, *Chiyoda*,[33] as a direct (insurance-funded) replacement for the protected cruiser *Unebi* (1886), which had disappeared on her delivery voyage from France after leaving Singapore on 3 December 1886.[34] *Chiyoda* was to be built to a specification laid down by Japanese navy's technical advisor, the French naval architect Emile Bertin (1840–1924), ultimately based

King Yuen as completed. (*Author's collection*)

on the small French unprotected cruiser *Milan* (1884), but some 45 per cent heavier and fitted with side armour. Although to a French model, the order went to a UK yard, as a political move to offset the recent placement of contracts for two of the *Matsushima*-class protected cruisers (1889–91) with a French builder.

As a result, the ship turned out to be something of a Franco-British hybrid, of French conception but built to British standards and with British-pattern fittings. As with the *Matsushima*s, the original intent was that *Chiyoda* should have a single 'battleship-killing' Canet 12.6in/40 gun, but the problems of employing such a huge weapon on such a small platform were already becoming apparent, and she was completed with ten 4.7in/40s of Armstrong origin, fore and aft and in broadside sponsons. These were backed up by 47mm weapons on the main and upper decks. Three above-water torpedo tubes were also fitted. Protection comprised a narrow waterline Harvey steel belt over the machinery spaces, plus a full-length sloped armour deck. The belt was backed by a cellulose-filled cofferdam, typical of ships designed by Bertin, with further reinforcement provided by coal.

Chiyoda's machinery was the first set of vertical engines in the Japanese navy, all earlier vessels having the horizontal type.

Chiyoda, Japan's first armoured cruiser. *(Author's collection)*

Ping Yuen as the Japanese *Hai-yen*. *(NHHC NH 88886)*

Steam was provided by locomotive boilers, again a Japanese first, but, as would be the general case with naval use of this equipment, these proved problematic in service, exacerbated by the use of Japanese coal, which required far more boiler-cleaning than British fuel.

She arrived in Japan in April 1891, but after little over five years' service it was decided in October 1896 to replace *Chiyoda*'s boilers with watertube Bellevilles, the refit being undertaken during 1897–8, fuel economy being greatly improved. As the first Japanese ship with Belleville boilers, she was used to train stokers for later vessels. During the same refit, the ship's fighting tops were removed to reduce topweight.

Towards the Classic British Cruiser

The *Orlando* class

An 1884 study by the Royal Navy's Foreign Intelligence Committee into the navy's materiel needs in the event of war with France highlighted a significant shortfall in a number of categories of ship,[35] including five 2nd class ironclads. Although no link can be proved, it seems likely that the ordering of just this number of side-armoured cruisers under the 1884–5 Estimates was no coincidence.

There had been much debate during the planning process, with the DNC initially favouring a vessel with a heavy torpedo armament, while the Additional Civil Lord, George Rendel (1833–1902), pushed for a gun-oriented ship which could act with the battlefleet; it was this latter conception that would prevail. The ships were based on the *Mersey*-class protected cruisers, four of which had been ordered under the 1883–4 Estimates. As compared with their prototype, which had a pair of 8in and ten 6in guns and a 2–3in deck, what became the *Orlando* class ultimately substituted two 9.2in main guns and added a 10in belt, intended to protect the vitals from heavy shells.[36] Unfortunately, poor control of weights, exacerbated by additions made during construction, meant that the class came out over 15 per cent overweight. This placed the upper edge of the belt 2ft below the waterline – rather than 3.5ft above as designed – even with less than a full load of coal, negating its purpose.[37]

The belt extended the length of the machinery spaces (as compared with the *Mersey*s, now housing triple expansion engines, enhancing endurance), and was topped by a 2in armour deck, which thickened at the ends to 3in. The guns had only splinter protection, with the end most 6in sponsoned-out to give axial fire, 3pdrs being fitted on the main deck as anti-torpedo boat weapons, including in embrasures at the bow and stern. Six torpedo tubes were installed, four above water on the broadside, and a one submerged at the bow and stern, contributing to contemporary descriptions of the class (and the *Mersey*s) as 'torpedo cruisers' (they were also on occasions 'ram cruisers', again reflecting contemporary ideas).

Five vessels (*Orlando*, *Australia*, *Galatea*, *Narcissus* and *Undaunted*) were ordered under the 1885 programme, with two more (*Aurora* and *Immortalité*) following the next year. All were delayed by the late delivery of their main guns, some appearing at the 1889 naval review with wooden dummies. *Orlando* served as flagship of the Australian station for her first decade of service, while the others served in various roles at home and abroad. Refitted during the mid-1890s, they all received heightened funnels, to ensure adequate draught to the boilers,[38] had their 6in guns converted to QF, and in some cases with the original 9.2in Mk V guns replaced by Mk VI weapons.

A question of classification

Prior to 1887, the classification of British armoured ships was descriptive, rather than functional, the *Audacious*es, *Shannon* and the *Nelson*s all being 'iron armour-plated ships' – as were *Warrior* and her other battle-line focussed descendants; the *Imperieuse* class were 'steel armour-plated barbette ships'. That year, ships were formally divided between 'battle ships' and 'cruisers', each category being divided into 1st, 2nd and 3rd classes. Curiously, while *Shannon*, the *Nelson*s and the *Imperieuse*s accordingly became 1st class armoured cruisers, the conceptually all-but-identical *Audacious*es became 2nd class armoured battle ships along with most of the other central-battery ironclads,[39] in spite of also being more lightly armed than any of the newly-minted 'cruisers', and also smaller than any other than *Shannon*.

In May 1892, there was a revision of battleship

Australia, as built with short funnels, at New York in June 1893. *(Detroit Publishing Co, via Library of Congress)*

Orlando, following the heightening of her funnels. *(NHHC NH 57808)*

Achilles was one of a number of old ironclads which were reclassified as cruisers in 1892, but never actually operated as such. After a decade-and-a-half laid up, with her topmasts removed but with light guns added, she is shown here in August 1901, leaving Devonport for Malta to become a depot ship.
(World Ship Society, John Maber Collection)

classifications to reflect the commissioning of the new *Royal Sovereign* class, whose advent relegated many of the former 1st class battleships to the 2nd, and former 2nd class ships to the 3rd (including the *Audacious*es).[40] Furthermore, seven broadside ironclads of the 1860s (the big *Warrior*, *Black Prince*, *Achilles*, *Minotaur*, *Agincourt* and *Northumberland*, plus the smaller *Hector*), all classified as 3rd class battleships in 1887, became 1st class cruisers.[41] Although there had been proposals back in 1883 to convert them into true cruisers, with new machinery, nothing had ever been done, and nothing ever would be, making the reclassification nonsensical.

Except for *Hector*, which was soon afterwards relegated to the non-effective list, all continued to be carried as cruisers until the turn of the century (albeit of no military value and either laid up dismantled, or in use as stationary training ships).

The surviving *Audacious*es and *Swiftsure*s remained active into the 1890s, *Iron Duke* as a guardship until 1900, after which she was cut down for a final five years as a coal hulk at the Kyles of Bute. In 1889–90, *Audacious* was refitted at

The surviving *Audacious*-class vessels served into the 1890s in guardship roles, the name-ship being reduced to a military rig and given a 4in secondary battery during her 1889–90 refit.
(World Ship Society, John Maber Collection)

Chatham, with military rig and a 4in secondary battery, before going to Hull as guardship (for the third time) in 1890. In 1894 she went into reserve, being withdrawn in 1902 to be rebuilt as an unpowered destroyer depot ship, with her machinery removed to make space for extensive workshop and other support functions.[42]

Invincible, in reserve from 1893, and *Triumph*, laid up from 1888, were similarly altered, all then becoming units of artificers' training establishments when the concept of unpowered depot ships was abandoned in 1905. *Invincible*, by now *Fisgard II*, was lost in 1914, but the other two survived in harbour support functions until the 1920s. *Swiftsure* was hulked, under the name of *Orontes*, in 1901, but was not subject to the alterations of her sister and half-sisters, being broken up later the same decade.

At the beginning of the twentieth century, Audacious, Invincible and Triumph were all rebuilt as unpowered destroyer depot ships, Invincible, renamed Erebus, shown here at Portland in 1904. Paid off the following February, on relief by Sapphire II (ex-Imperieuse), she became part of the new Fisgard artificers' training establishment at Portsmouth, commissioning on 1 January 1906 as Fisgard II (her sister Audacious being Fisgard). In September 1914, both ships were withdrawn to provide facilities at the new fleet base of Scapa Flow, but while ex-Audacious would serve in the Orkneys under the name Imperieuse until March 1920, ex-Invincible sank in a storm off Portland en route. (Author's collection)

Triumph, renamed Tenedos, serviced destroyers at Chatham, before becoming name-ship of a new artificers' training establishment at the same port. This closed in 1910, when ex-Triumph became Indus IV, within the mechanicians' training establishment at Devonport. She was withdrawn in October 1914, to become a store hulk at Invergordon under the name Algiers, as shown here. Inboard of her are the likewise-hulked battleships Akbar (ex-Temeraire) and Mars. (Author's collection)

The big protected cruiser

The *Orlando*s would be the last side-armoured cruisers to be built for Britain for over a decade, the Director of Naval Construction from 1885 to 1902, (Sir) William White (1845–1913), being of the opinion that in the current state of ordnance a full-length curved protective deck (introduced in the Armstrong-built Chilean cruiser *Esmeralda* [i – 1883] and to the Royal Navy in the *Mersey*s) was a more effective and efficient means of armouring than one based on a waterline belt.

This system was thus employed in a pair of exceptionally large pair of ships, *Blake* and *Blenheim*, built as a counter to the perceived threat from large liners converted to commerce raiders, whose inherent high speed and endurance would make them difficult for 'ordinary' cruisers to counter, not to mention forthcoming purpose-built French vessels (*Tage* and *Amiral Cécille*; see p 40, below).[43]

Accordingly, the new ships needed to be fast (22kt forced-draught, 20kt continuous), with bunkerage to allow prolonged high-speed steaming, combining to require 20,000ihp on a displacement of 9000 tons. The machinery followed the *Impérieuse* class in that two engines were arranged on each of the two shafts for economic cruising, in this case up to 15–16kt. The armour deck would be 3in on the flat amidships, with 6in slopes (estimated to be equivalent to 12in vertical armour), thinning to 2–2.5in fore and aft, the main guns having 4.5in shields. These were 9.2in/31.5, mounted fore and aft, backed up by ten 6in/26, six in shields on the upper deck, and four in main-deck casemates; the main deck also carried ten 3pdrs, with eight more on the upper deck. There were four 14in torpedo tubes, two above water, two below.

To produce this combination required a massive 60 per cent leap in displacement (and 50 per cent in cost) over the *Orlando* class, most of it attributable to the power requirement. Accordingly, the pair's failure to make 22kt on trial was a great disappointment, while *Blake* suffered considerable boiler problems during her first commission. On the other hand, her French contemporaries also had trials problems, and at more moderate power, the *Blakes*' long range performance was generally very good, although 20kt was regarded as their practical maximum.

Their size and endurance, as well as implicit commerce-protecting role, fitted them well for the role of distant station flagships, *Blake* accordingly going out to relieve the battleship *Bellerophon* on the North American & West Indies Station in 1892, staying there until 1895, when she went to the Channel until 1898. *Blenheim*, on the other hand, went straight into reserve on completion, not being brought forward until 1894, when she joined the Channel Fleet. Both ships went into reserve in 1898, *Blenheim* emerging in June for a brief stint on the China Station, before returning to reserve at Chatham. *Blake* also emerged briefly to take troops to the Mediterranean during 1900–1, while *Blenheim* served a proper commission in China from 1901–4.

In 1902, schemes for modernising the pair were considered, ranging from simply replacing the existing guns with modern ones of the same calibres, to more elaborate changes, including the addition of a 6in belt and increasing the main battery to four or even six guns, the latter cutting the secondary battery to eight guns. In the event, it was clearly considered that the ships were not worth it, *Blenheim* being converted to a destroyer depot ship on her return from China, followed by her sister in 1907. As such, they would serve until after the First World War.

From an early stage, it was recognised that the sheer size of the *Blakes* was not viable for series production, nor were such ships economically viable for peacetime service (cf. the *Blakes*' periods in reserve). A smaller vessel was thus required, the initial proposal from White being to install the armament of *Blake* into a hull based on the cruiser/torpedo boat carrier *Vulcan*, then under construction. The resulting design managed to fit in all guns except six 3pdrs (including the new

The first of the big protected cruisers, *Blake*, shown in 1893. (*Author's collection*)

Although designed as a torpedo-boat carrier (hence the heavy goose-neck cranes), and much more lightly armed than a cruiser of her size, *Vulcan*, launched in 1889, was, like her French opposite number *Foudre* (1895), armoured as a protected cruiser, and formed the basis for the *Edgar*-class design. Her active career was spent in a depot ship role, before she was hulked as part of the *Defiance* training establishment in 1931 (see p 156). *(Author's collection)*

Edgar in the early twentieth century.
(World Ship Society Abrahams Collection)

6in/40 gun in place of the old 26cal version), with the protection having the deck flats thinned to 2.5in and the slopes to 5in, as compared with *Blake*, with a 6in glacis around cylinder heads required by the shallower *Vulcan* hull.[44]

A concern was whether the ongoing development of ordnance might diminish the effectiveness of deck-only protection as compared to that including side armour, especially in light of firing trials against the hulk of the old ironclad *Resistance* from 1885 onwards. As a result both the *Blake*s and the new design, to become the *Edgar* class, were given doubled plating amidships to support any belt that might later need to be fitted – which it never would be. Other adjustments were made as design work continued, including increased boiler power to ensure that the resulting ships could maintain 18kt at sea. Nine ships of the type were built under the Naval Defence Act of May 1889,[45] the culmination of a number years of agitation over the alleged inadequacies of the Royal Navy vis à vis its potential enemies. It thus enshrined the concept of a 'two-power standard' and provided for the laying-down over the following four years of ten battleships and thirty-eight cruisers.

Seven of the vessels were built to the original design, the class name-ship *Edgar*, *Endymion*, *Gibraltar*, *Grafton*, *Hawke* and *St George* all completing during 1893–4, with *Theseus* delayed until 1896. All then began what would be long careers of worldwide service. However, in in early 1890 it was decided that two ships should be completed for service as overseas flagships, with a raised forecastle to provide the requisite additional space, the foremost 9.2in gun being replaced by a pair of single 6in. The ships chosen were *Crescent* and *Centaur* (later renamed *Royal Arthur*), as both in an early stage of

Royal Arthur at Vancouver as Pacific flagship during 1893–6, showing the raised forecastle that distinguished her and *Crescent* from the *Edgar* class. *(Author's collection)*

construction and, as dockyard-built, not subject to the costs that would accrue from amending contracts with private yards. They were both sheathed and coppered, as were also *Gibraltar* and *St George*, which also spent time as overseas flagships.

France: the *Jeune école* and Beyond

The concept of cruisers as commerce raiders continued as a key theme in France during the 1870s, with five unprotected, wooden, fully-rigged vessels of ~3500 tons approved in 1878, four being completed between 1882 and 1886 – a significant step back from the earlier metal-hulled *Duquesne* and *Tourville*. The fifth vessel was, however, eventually cancelled in favour of the first French protected cruiser, *Sfax* (1884), followed by the bigger *Tage* (1886) and *Amiral Cécille* (1888), the latter pair capable of over 19kt. A similar vessel was built

in France at the same time for the Russian navy, *Admiral Kornilov* (1887).

Together with renewed tensions with the UK, a key feature of French naval policy during the 1880s was the emergence of the *Jeune école*, a philosophy based around commerce raiding on the high seas, the defence of the French coast and the bombardment of enemy territory. The subject of discussion for some years, its status crystallized when its prime advocate, Admiral Théophile Aube (1826–90), became French Navy Minister in January 1886. Under this regime, light craft (of 58 tons) were promoted as suitable for all three pillars of the doctrine, even for high-seas commerce raiding, contributing to the suspension of the follow-ons from the 1880 programme's *Neptune*-class battleships, *Charles Martel* and *Brennus*, in favour of the construction of torpedo boats and *bateaux-canons* (torpedo-boat hulls armed with a 5.5in gun), with three coast-defence ships to act as their mother ships. There were also to be six large and ten small protected cruisers.

The light vessels suffered many problems, with the one *bateau-canon* actually built proving unable to handle its gun and subsequently converted to a torpedo boat, while trials showed that the torpedo boats were insufficiently seaworthy for the independent deployment envisaged by the *Jeune école*. Accordingly, the 1888 budget provided for the resumption of battleship building (*Brennus* was completed to a revised design; *Charles Martel* was dismantled on the slip and her name re-used for a wholly-new ship), but Aube's term (which ended with his retirement in May 1887) led to a decade-and-a-half's confusion and dissent within and concerning the French navy.

Tage in the 1890s; she was another French essay into the concept of the dedicated commerce-raider. *(NHHC NH 66092)*

Dupuy de Lôme

A first pair of large cruisers, to be named *Dupuy de Lôme* and
Jean Bart, were ordered in October 1886, originally to be deck-
protected and of 4160 tons. A supplementary grant by the
Chamber in March 1887 provided for two sisters, *Alger* and
Isly, but around the same time a series of firing trials, planned
the previous year, were carried out against the hulk of the old
Belliqueuse, to explore the difference between the effect of
black-powder bursting charges and the new high-explosive
ones now becoming available. The greatly increased damage
seen even with quite modest high-explosive charges led to the
conclusion that side armour was now a requirement for
cruisers. Accordingly, in October 1887, while the other three
ships were built to the original design, it was ordered that
Dupuy de Lôme be re-cast on this basis. Thus was born a ship
that would have an impact on future cruiser construction far
in excess of her own inherent qualities.

Designed by Louis de Bussy (1822–1903), who had built
the world's first all-steel battleship, *Redoutable* (1876), *Dupuy
de Lôme* was protectively a complete departure from the usual
French approach to vertical armour. Rather than a narrow,
thick, waterline belt, she would have an entirely-protected side
(plus a curved armour deck, with a thin splinter deck below it
over the machinery). This was combined with a speed of 20kt
and a relatively heavy armament, two 7.6in weapons being
arranged on each beam, with three 6.5in guns closely bunched
at either end of the ship. When combined with an exaggerated
ram bow and heavy military masts, they gave her a strikingly
martial appearance. The masts were a manifestation of a desire
to increase the number and command of anti-torpedo boat
guns, and would be fitted in all big ships not requiring a full
rig into the 1890s, when their inherent topweight (and the
declining utility of guns light enough to be mounted aloft) led
to their removal (cf. below).

The three-shaft machinery arrangement, the first in a
major warship, was unusual in that the wing shafts were driven
by horizontal triple expansion engines, the middle one by a
vertical unit. During trials, which began in June 1892, the
boilers experienced a number of failures, as a result of which
the ship did not actually commission until May 1895, nearly
three years later.

Nevertheless, her combination of qualities were much
admired, although, the British view was that the deck-protected
approach used in the *Blake*s and *Edgar*s was at least as effective
as the side-and-deck scheme used in *Dupuy de Lôme*. It was
argued at the time that such a vessel as *Dupuy de Lôme* was
equally well fitted for fleet scouting, commerce-raiding and
overseas service, and as such can be seen as the prototype of the
'classic' big armoured cruiser. The French Navy henceforth built
the armoured cruiser almost to the exclusion of all other types
of cruiser (except for a handful of big protected cruisers – see
pp 55–6, below) into the twentieth century,[46] while many other
navies would also build the type extensively.

In service, *Dupuy de Lôme* spent the first part of her career
with the Northern Squadron, including visits to Spain and

Dupuy de Lôme as built. (*Author's collection*)

Dupuy de Lôme in dry dock, showing her unique armament
arrangement; her main guns were mounted in the waist.
(*Author's collection*)

Dupuy de Lôme on trials following reboilering and being fitted with
three funnels. (*Author's collection*)

Portugal in 1899, and representing France at the funeral of
Queen Victoria in 1901. Following that, modifications were
made to her light guns, but the ship continued to suffer from
a number of shortcomings, leading to a reconstruction at Brest
during 1902–6. During this, she was reboilered with watertube
units (requiring three, rather than the existing two) funnels,
and had the mainmast replaced by a pole (early plans had

envisaged replacing the foremast as well, as was done in the refits of the succeeding *Amiral Charner* class – see below).

Recommissioned on 3 October 1906, the ship passed directly into reserve, not undertaking active service until September 1908, when she was assigned to the Morocco Station, based at Tangier. However, her material condition was deteriorating, and *Dupuy de Lôme* went back into reserve, at Lorient, in September 1909. A survey revealed that major hull repairs were necessary, and in spite of having only emerged from a major refit in 1906, she was decommissioned in March 1910 and stricken the following February (see further, p 108, below).

The *Amiral Charner* class

Dupuy de Lôme was rapidly followed by four '2nd class' (2000–4000-ton) diminutives, approved in August in 1888.[47] They were originally to have had a four-masted sailing rig, a battery of two 6.5in and six 5.5in guns and a 3.2in belt, like *Dupuy de Lôme* full-length, but now extending only up to the main deck. In the event, a two-masted military rig was substituted, and the main guns increased in calibre to 7.6in, resulting in ships of 4700 tons. Compared with *Dupuy de Lôme*, the guns were more widely distributed, to avoid a number being disabled by a single hit, and the main guns were placed at the ends, rather than at the waist. Five above-water torpedo tubes were planned, but the stern one was not eventually fitted. Side armour now extended only up to the main deck, 3.6in thick amidships but thinned at the ends. The armour deck was 1.6in thick on the flats and 2in on the slopes. Searchlight platforms were initially placed either side of the stem and just forward of the sternwalk, but the former were removed after trials shown that they were untenable in a seaway.

Six detailed designs were considered, the decision going

Bruix, as built, showing the closed-in upper deck forward that she shared with *Amiral Charner*, and which contrasted with the open area in *Chanzy* and *Latouche-Tréville*; later in their careers the survivors had their military masts replaced by poles.
(Author's collection)

On 20 May 1907, *Chanzy* ran aground in fog on Balard Island in the Chusan (Zhoushan) archipelago, off the Chinese coast, having been serving in the Far East Squadron since the beginning of the year. After ten days' attempts at refloating, she was abandoned in the face of an impending storm, during which the stern sank. The wreck was blown up on 12 June by personnel from *D'Entrecasteaux* (seen laying-off to the right), *Bruix* (left) and *Alger*. The open sides to the forward superstructure can still be seen. *(Author's collection)*

to that by Jules Thibaudier (1839–1918), approved on 1 April 1889. The first ship was laid down that June at Rochefort Dockyard, which was to build two ships; the other pair were contract-built. The first of the latter, *Chanzy*, took the name of what was originally intended as a Societé de Loire-designed companion to the de Bussy-designed protected cruisers *Davout* (1889) and *Suchet* (1893), but cancelled through lack of funds.

The Dockyard-built pair, *Amiral Charner* and *Bruix*, differed from the two built in private yards, *Chanzy* and *Latouche-Tréville*, in that the former had had their forward superstructure extended out to the sides and plated-in, while in the others it was open, making them much wetter than their sisters. *Latouche-Tréville* differed from the other three in having electrically, rather than hydraulically, powered turrets, which were also of oval, balanced form, rather than cylindrical. While the first three ships laid down had horizontal engines (reverting to twin screws, as compared with *Dupuy de Lôme*), *Bruix*, begun a year after her sisters, had vertical engines of slightly higher power.

Although upgraded to 1st class cruisers while still under construction, the purpose of the *Amiral Charner* class seems never to have been made wholly clear, although discussions during the design stage implied that they were to counter contemporary Italian cruisers and carry out coastal-defence activities. Certainly their bunkerage was relatively limited, implying service in home waters, although in the event all but *Latouche-Tréville* also spent time in the Far East. It was while deployed there that *Chanzy* was wrecked off the Chinese coast in May 1907, the second French armoured cruiser to be lost on the station in less than two years (the almost-new *Sully* having been wrecked in October 1905 – see p 71). Torpedo tubes were removed around 1906–7, and *Latouche-Tréville* and *Bruix* had their military masts replaced by poles during 1913–

14. *Charner*'s masts were, however, just cut down to stumps, which were then topped with poles.

Pothuau

In 1890, a new French naval programme, the first since 1872, had been approved by the navy's *Conseil Superieur*, to produce a fleet ten years hence that included twenty-four battleships and thirty-six cruisers for home service, plus thirty-four more cruisers for distant stations. However, as with the 1872 programme, this was not a funded scheme, and would soon be revised.

The 1892 programme contained an enlarged and modified *Charner*, the main difference being an improved arrangement of the secondary guns.[48] Built as *Pothuau*, her design was approved by the *Conseil de Traveaux* on 15 March 1892, and featured four more 5.5in guns, with the *Charners*' turrets replaced by casemates and two open shields. Side armour continued to extend up to the main deck and along the whole waterline, but significantly thinner, while the deck was slightly thicker, the turrets 75 per cent thicker and the conning tower triple the thickness – although the casemates were half the thickness of *Charner*'s secondary turrets. Rig was much lighter, with poles fore and aft; the ship could also be distinguished by three funnels, which were fed by two additional boilers, power being boosted to 10,000ihp.

Commissioned into fleet service in 1897, *Pothuau*

Pothuau as completed. (Richard Osborne Collection)

represented France at Queen Victoria's Diamond Jubilee review in June, and carried the French President to Russia in August. She then served in the Mediterranean until 1905, when she went into reserve. She recommissioned the next year as a seagoing gunnery training and trials ship the following year, and served as such until 1914.

Spain

During the 1880s, a major programme of cruiser construction was undertaken in Spain, ranging from small vessels more akin to sloops, through to the protected cruisers of the *Reina Regente* (i) class (1887–92), and a series of six armoured cruisers. The latter, authorised under the 1887 fleet plan, were begun to a design drawn up by the British firm of Palmers, based upon the British *Orlando* class, sharing their prototypes' protective concept but with a 11.8in belt midships and much heavier main guns, a barbette-mounted 11in, with a domed hood being placed fore and aft; five 5.5in in shields were mounted on each beam. The armour deck was 2in flat on the belt, but beyond it had 3in slopes.

Three were to be built by private yards, and three by state dockyards. The 'private' trio, named *Infanta María Teresa*, *Almirante Oquendo* and *Vizcaya*, were ordered under a royal decree in October 1887, and laid down during the second half of 1889. However, although *María Teresa*, the lead ship was launched the following summer, the other two did not take to the water until 1891, completion being staggered across the summers of 1893, 1894 and 1895. Originally

classified as 1st class protected cruisers, they were reclassified as 2nd class armoured ships shortly before the 1898 Spanish-American War.

Of the three 'state yards' ships, ordered under a royal decree of September 1888, the first ship, *Princesa de Asturias*, was laid down in September 1889 but suffered severe delays, partly owing to modifications to the hull form (most noticeable above water at stern), to provide a longer belt (of the new Harvey armour, which allowed a level of protection to be maintained with a thinner, and thus lighter, plate and more powerful engines.[49] She was not launched until 1896, with final completion not being achieved until the autumn of 1904. The next ship, *Cataluña*, was laid down in January 1890 at Cartagena, the biggest ship yet built there, but remained on the stocks for ten years, taking to the water in the autumn of 1900. *Cardinal Cisneros* was formally laid down in September 1890, but substantive work could not begin until after the launch of the protected cruiser *Alfonso XIII* the following August, owing to shortages of men and materials. Her launch finally took place in the spring of 1897, only after *Alfonso XIII* had left the yard – still not fully complete, and fit only for training duties.[50]

Further modifications had been worked-in while the ships were still on the stocks, it being decided in November 1895 to make a number of changes to the armament. Accordingly, the 1883-pattern Hontoria 11in guns of the earlier ships were to be replaced with more modern 9.4in Canet weapons in a new type of mounting, and the secondary battery reduced to eight

Infanta María Teresa, probably shown at the opening of the Kiel Canal in June 1895. *(NHHC NH 88603)*

The second group of Spanish armoured cruisers were much delayed and completed to a modified design, *Cardenal Cisneros* being shown here at Tangiers. *(NHHC NH 46853)*

guns and protected in casemates. 10in transverse bulkheads were added fore and aft, but the maximum thickness of the armour deck was reduced to 2in. These changes of course delayed work yet further, meaning that the first ship to actually commission, *Cisneros*, did not do so until 1903, closely followed by *Princesa de Asturias*; *Cataluña* did not, however, join the fleet until April 1908.

Also part of the 1887 plan was a considerably larger vessel, ordered in April 1891 and laid down a year later at a private yard in Cadíz. Although over 2000 tons bigger than the other six vessels, she carried the same main battery as the *María Teresa*s, two fewer secondary guns, and was protected primarily by a 2in deck, with 6.5in slopes, supplemented by 2in over the battery; there was no waterline belt. Named *Emperador Carlos V* (shortened before completion to simply *Carlos V*) she was launched in March 1895, and commissioned in June 1897. On account of her size, she was classified as a 1st class

Carlos V, a very different ship from the previous group of Spanish big cruisers, with a unique protective system, comprising a very thick sloped portion of her armour deck, and side armour restricted to the battery. *(LoC LC-H261-4175)*

armoured ship, although her power of offense was no greater than that of the '2nd class' *María Teresa*s.

The Adriatic Powers

Italy
During the late 1870s, the Italian navy had laid down the innovative battleships of the *Italia* class, exceptionally fast (17.5/18.5kt) and deck-protected only, making them in many ways very large cruisers, while succeeding classes were also relatively speedy compared with foreign battleships. Thus the requirement for cruisers suitable for fleet service was less apparent than in navies with slower battle lines. However, the financial crisis that hit Italy at the end of the 1880s meant that there had to be a hiatus in the construction of battleships, and that the building of fleet cruisers had to be considered as a substitute.[51]

During the 1880s, the Italian navy had built a trio of 3500-ton protected cruisers of the *Etna* class (1885–6), armed with two 10in and four 6in, a further, slightly enlarged, ship being projected in 1888. This latter vessel was further enlarged and side armour added, emerging as Italy's first armoured cruiser, *Marco Polo*. The financial situation meant that even this 'cheap' vessel could not be laid down until 1890, being completed in 1894. In 1896, after a long period of trials, *Marco Polo* became flagship of the Flying Division, but from 1898 spent much of her career prior to 1914 in the Far East.

Four larger vessels, to be named *Carlo Alberto*, *Vettor*

Marco Polo as completed. *(NHHC NH 48659)*

Pisani, *Nino Bixio* and *Giuseppe Garibaldi*, and originally also envisaged without side armour, were similarly re-cast as armoured cruisers, some 2000 tons bigger than *Marco Polo*, with double the number of 6in, but four less 4.7in guns, and a belt a third thicker, balanced by a thinner, but sloped, deck. Designed by Edoardo Masdea (1869–1910), the layout of the new design was totally different from previous Italian cruisers, although reminiscent of recent battleships, with the engine room placed between two widely-separated sets of boilers. Installed power was 13,000ihp for a designed speed of 19kt. The main guns were installed in a main-deck battery and on the upper deck abreast the fore and aft bridges; the 4.7in weapons were placed on the upper deck, amidships and as bow- and sternchasers.

Two of the planned vessels were to be built under contract and two in naval dockyards, but the financial crisis meant that only the latter pair, *Carlo Alberto* and *Vettor Pisani* were built to the original design, and even then were delayed, the crisis paralysing ship construction during 1894–6.[52] As a result, although laid down in 1892, the ships were not launched until 1895–6, and finally completed in 1898. *Pisani* served as Italian flagship during the Boxer Rebellion in China during 1900, subsequently making port visits in Russia, Japan and Korea before departing for home in November 1901. Arriving at La Spezia in February 1902, she departed once again for the Far East in April 1903, returning in June 1904; she remained in home waters for the remainder of her career.

Alberto first deployed to South America between June 1898 and February 1899, going to the Far East later that year,

leaving for Italy in January 1900. She served as the royal yacht for King Vittorio Emanuelle III when he attended the coronation of King Edward VII in 1902, diverting to Russia when the ceremony was delayed, and finally attending the Coronation Review on 16 August. Both during this deployment, and for some time afterwards, Guglielmo Marconi (1874–1937) was aboard undertaking experiments in wireless telegraphy. During 1902–3 *Carlo Alberto* was in Venezuelan waters during the crisis there, as part of an international force of British, German, and Italian warships blockading the country in reprisal for her refusal to pay foreign debts. Back in home waters, from 1907 to 1910 *Carlo Alberto* served as a gunnery and torpedo training ship, based at La Spezia, before returning to active service at the beginning of the Italo-Turkish War (see pp 112–13).

Austria-Hungary

Across the Adriatic, the Austro-Hungarian navy had undergone a major strategic and tactical rethink during the 1880s, under the direction of the CinC, Admiral Maximilian Freiherr Daublesky von Sterneck zu Ehrenstein (1829–97), who was very much taken with the ideas of the French *Jeune école*.[53] For his new fleet, the core unit was to be the 'torpedo-ram cruiser', which would be the command ship for squadrons otherwise made up of torpedo boats, undertake gunfire support or ramming attacks to defend its flock, and to provide it with torpedoes, fuel, feedwater and manpower. This would require both heavy and medium guns, to be mounted on a hull of modest dimensions. The 1891 fleet programme envisaged

Vettor Pisani as completed. (*NHHC NH 47790*)

Kaiserin und Königin Maria Theresia in 1895. Her funnels were modified and heightened after a short period of service. *(NHHC NH 88934)*

four squadrons led by such vessels, supported by a smaller torpedo cruiser, a torpedo vessel (large torpedo boat) and six torpedo boats. At that point in time, the first two torpedo-ram cruisers (the 4000-ton protected cruisers *Kaiser Franz Joseph I* and *Kaiserin Elisabeth* [1889–90] armed with two 9.4in and six 5.9in guns) were nearing completion, while three of the torpedo cruisers, of Armstrong design, were already in service. Two further torpedo-ram cruisers were projected, but in the interim the availability of improved armours, providing greater protection for a given thickness, persuaded the authorities that side-protection for medium-sized vessels was now practicable. A lack of consensus among the naval command as to the wisdom of Sterneck's vision also suggested that less specialised ships might be desirable.[54]

Accordingly, *Torpedo-Ram Cruiser C*, whose initial funds were released under the 1890 budget, was re-cast from the intended 4000 tons design. Two options were put forward in 1889, one a 5100 tons side-armoured enlargement of *Kaiser Franz Joseph*, and one a 6220-ton concept, based on *Dupuy de Lôme*.[55] Two versions of the latter were sketched, one following the French prototype in mounting the main guns (two 9.4in/35, as in the *Kaiser Franz Joseph*s) at the waist, the other placing them fore and aft; both were rigged with heavy military masts. The ship was now intended to act as a scout for both the battlefleet and for torpedo forces.

Although the smaller concept was actually adopted, the military masts were incorporated into the new ship, although they would be removed after less than a decade's service, owing to their negative effect on stability. As compared with the big guns of the *Kaiser Franz Joseph*s, which had been manoeuvred hydraulically, those of the new ship were electrically powered; eight 5.9in/35 guns were fitted, with four on the main deck and four (rather than two in the *Kaiser Franz Joseph*s) in upper-deck sponsons. The belt and 9.4in barbettes were all 3.9in thick, with thinner armour protecting the 5.9in guns and the conning tower.

Launched as *Kaiserin und Königin Maria Theresia* in April 1893, and commissioned in March 1895, she formed part of the squadron (also comprising *Kaiser Franz Joseph I* and *Kaiserin Elisabeth*) that represented Austria-Hungary at the opening of the Kiel Canal in the summer of 1895. During 1897–8, along with the battleship *Kronprinzessin Erzherzogin Stephanie* (1887), the three torpedo cruisers and eleven torpedo boats, *Maria Theresia* formed part of the Austro-Hungarian contribution to the international intervention in the Cretan rebellion.

In parallel with the construction of *Maria Theresia*, opposition to Sterneck's theories was hardening, with the view emerging that the torpedo-ram cruisers were too light to engage with battleships and too big to work with torpedo craft. Rather, they should form a cruiser squadron attached to a fleet that would include new armoured ships to replace existing central battery ships. As part of this, *Torpedo-Ram Cruiser D* was postponed in favour of the first of these new vessels, which emerged as the *Monarch*-class coast-defence ships (1895–6).

Battleships or Cruisers?

The issues of classifying powerful vessels not intended primarily for the battle line are neatly illustrated by a pair of ships projected in the UK in the late 1880s as lineal successors to the *Imperieuse* class. Ordered under the 1890 Estimates, they were similarly intended for a capital role on distant stations, capable of overwhelming any foreign adversary likely to be found in foreign waters – especially 8in-gunned Russian cruisers such as the *Imperieuse*-clone *Admiral Nakhimov*. They were intended as improvements on the earlier pair, with shallower draught to allow the navigation of Chinese rivers, and a higher speed – indeed, higher than that of any extant battleship. However, they emerged as reduced versions of the

Royal Sovereign class of battleships (1891–2), rather than iterations of the previous 'armoured cruiser' line. A suggestion that they be deck-protected like *Blake* was rejected, a conventional 'battleship' midships belt (of compound armour for the last time in the Royal Navy) being topped by a conventional full-length flat armour deck. Four 10in guns were provided, in hooded barbettes fore and aft, but the secondary battery was reduced in calibre to 4.7in, from the 6in in *Imperieuse*, although increased in number to ten. Initial plans had them all fitted in shields on the upper deck, but in the event four were placed in main-deck casemates.

While under construction, the two ships, *Centurion* and *Barfleur*, were classified as 2nd class battleships (cf. p 7, above), but by completion they had been reclassified to the 1st class, even though very different ships from the 'true' 1st class *Royal Sovereign*s, and their successors, the *Majestic* class (1894–6). The *Centurion*s remained distant waters 'super-cruisers' or 'cruiser killers', rather than part of in the battle line (with protection only two-thirds that of the *Royal Sovereign*s), something emphasised by their ability to maintain a sea-speed of 17kt (having made 18.5kt on trials). *Centurion* herself spent her entire first-line career on the China Station, relieving *Imperieuse* as flagship in 1894 and remaining as such until 1901. *Barfleur* was also in China from 1898 to 1901, both ships being active during the Boxer Rebellion in 1900, although she had spent time before this in the Mediterranean.

Their secondary guns were condemned from early on as too light, and between 1901–4 both ships were rebuilt with a new 6in secondary battery, a number of items of superstructure being removed as weight compensation, the military foremast also being swapped for a pole. Although *Centurion* served a second tour in the Far East after completion of her refit, British capital ships were withdrawn from the China Station in 1905 as a consequence of the Anglo-Japanese Alliance of 1902, and while the newer *Canopus* class (cf pp 73–4) were redeployed for further fleet service in Home and Mediterranean waters, the days of the 'odd-men-out' *Centurion*s were numbered. In spite of the money recently spent on their rebuilding, both vessels spent the rest of their careers in reserve, and were placed on the sale list in 1909.

A third, very similar, ship was to be laid down three years after the *Centurion*s, but in circumstances that had very little to do with any strategic role to be played by the vessel. It had been intended that the 1892 programme should include the first three of a new 12in-gunned class, the *Majestic*s, but in the event delays in the development of the new gun meant that construction of the first two ships had to be postponed until the 1893 programme. However, this would led to an unacceptable gap in the work programme at Pembroke Dockyard, and accordingly it was decided to build a modified *Centurion* in that yard as the third vessel, incidentally to provide an additional vessel of the type for distant service. In conceptual terms, the 10in main battery had the advantage of coinciding with the views of the current Controller, Rear Admiral John Fisher (1841–1920), who favoured 'the lightest possible big gun and heaviest secondary gun' in battleships.

The new vessel, *Renown*, was some 20 per cent heavier than *Centurion*, with a 6in secondary battery, more power and updated protection. The latter included Harvey armour (allowing a thinner main belt, and a thicker upper belt and

Although built to a battleship-based design, *Barfleur* (shown in 1894) fulfilled a requirement generally met by big cruisers. *(Author's collection)*

Centurion following her 1901–3 reconstruction, including the fitting of prominent two-storey 6in casemates. *(Author's collection)*

Renown spent most of her short seagoing career in prestige roles, here in leaving for the Duke and Duchess of York's 1905–6 tour of India. *(Author's collection)*

barbettes), an armour deck with slopes to the bottom of the belt, oblique armour bulkheads fore and aft, and casemates for the whole secondary battery. This was still below line-of-battle standards (the belt was an inch thinner than that would be fitted in the *Majestics*), and *Renown*'s 'distant stations' design was reflected by her first commission as flagship of the CinC North American & West Indies Station (now Fisher), replacing *Crescent*. She then went on to become Mediterranean flagship at the request of Fisher when he took over there as CinC, whose favourite she had become. In 1902, she was refitted as a temporary royal yacht for a tour to India by the Duke and Duchess of Connaught, losing her main-deck 6in guns in the process. A final year back in the Mediterranean Fleet during 1903–4 was followed by a year in reserve.

Proposals to replace the main battery with newer 10in[56] or single 12in, and/or the secondary battery with new 6in, 7.5in or a mix of the two were not taken forward, the ship undergoing a further refit for royal yacht duties in 1905. This included also taking out her upper deck 6in to provide space for additional accommodation during another Indian tour, this time by the Prince and Princess of Wales (later King George V and Queen Mary). Now a 'subsidiary yacht' in the organisation of the Home Fleet, she carried King Alfonso XIII and Queen Victoria Eugenia of Spain to the UK in the autumn of 1907, but otherwise remained in reserve and was relegated to a stokers' training ship in 1909. Suggestions in 1913 that she might become a depot ship came to naught and *Renown* was sold for scrap in 1914.

The US 'New Navy'

By the middle of the 1880s, the United States, the pioneer of the big cruiser, had shrunk into a power of minimal naval significance, with fleet largely made up of Civil War veterans, mostly only capable of coastal service, with the few major ocean-going vessels of wooden construction, including the 3800-ton *Trenton* (1876). However, in 1883 the first ships of a 'new navy' – the cruisers *Atlanta*, *Boston* and *Chicago*, plus the dispatch vessel *Dolphin* – were authorised,[57] with two 'sea-going armored vessels' of around 6000 tons each and at least 16kt speed authorised on 21 August 1886. These were justified as counters to the threat felt to be posed by the navies of Brazil and Chile, the former having recently commissioned the 5700-ton battleship *Riachuelo* (1883), with the slightly smaller *Aquidaban* (1885) completing in the UK. The two ships were regarded in some quarters as individually superior to the whole US East Coast fleet. The Chileans had an older pair of 3480-ton central-battery ships (*Almirante Cochrane* and *Blanco Encalada* [1874–5]). In the event, the new American ships turned out to be of similar layout to the British-built Brazilian vessels, with their big guns in a pair of en-echelon mountings.

As planned, one of the vessels was to be a 2nd class battleship (to become *Texas* [i – 1892]), but the other was to be an armoured cruiser, with finer lines, lighter main guns and greater endurance, the latter to be bolstered by a 'two-thirds' sailing rig. This vessel, which came to be *Maine*,[58] was designed

by the Bureau of Construction & Repair (C&R; *Texas* was British-designed, although US-built), to carry four 10in (to overmatch *Riachuelo*'s four 9in) and six 6in, with two 2nd class torpedo boats (a feature of other contemporary designs, including the two Chinese battleships) and four 18in torpedo tubes. Protection was of nickel-steel, except for the turrets, which had Harvey armour, the main belt being closed by a bulkhead forward of the foreturret, but by a sloping-down of the armour deck aft.

Although launched in 1890, *Maine* took five years to complete, partly owing to a fire at New York Navy Yard, which was producing drawings, but principally through a three-year wait for her armour. This was the result of late delivery of tooling to the original contractor, Bethlehem, and industrial relations problems at a second contracted source, Carnegie; on the other hand, this allowed her to employ Harvey armour, which became available in the meantime. Before completion, the sailing rig was deleted in favour of two masts with military tops, while funnel plates were originally fitted, but removed when the funnels were heightened during fitting-out. In 1894, while still incomplete, *Maine*'s classification was changed to that of a 2nd class battleship, reflecting the way in which the nature of the big cruiser had changed since she had been laid down (cf. *New York* [see below], laid down two years later than *Maine*, but completed in 1893). Commissioned in September 1895, *Maine* spent her whole career in the North Atlantic Squadron, until destroyed by an internal explosion at Havana, Cuba, in February 1898 (see p 76, below).

On 7 September 1888, Congress authorised a third armoured ship, initially intended as a follow-on from the previous pair. The

The first generation of American capital ships included both the battleship *Texas* and the armoured cruiser *Maine*, the latter's high seas cruising role indicated by the full sailing rig shown in this early sketch. (NHHC NH 76601)

Maine completed, however, without rig and re-classified as a battleship. (Author's collection)

original plans incorporated a twin 12in mounting forward, backed up by six 6in guns. In August 1889, an enlargement was suggested to allow protection for the 6in secondary battery, a speed of 17kt and QF, rather than BL, 6in guns. However, the requisite additional 800–900 tons was not acceptable and 4in weapons were substituted for the 6in, a 10in gun added aft, and the original 12in armour thinned to 11in. An August 1889 proposal changed the main battery to four 11in, but soon afterwards a complete recasting of the design was ordered.

A Naval Advisory Board to determine the future requirements of the navy had been set up back in 1881; now, in July 1889, a new Policy Board was established, to report in January 1890. Its conclusions called for a massively expanded fleet that was far in excess of what Congress was prepared to fund. However, three coastal battleships (to be the *Indiana* class), a cruiser and a torpedo boat were approved in April 1890, while the 1888 armoured ship was to become a proper long-range armoured cruiser, rather than a small battleship akin to *Maine*.

The first attempt at producing this, in the spring of 1890, was deck-protected only, with an 8in mounting fore and aft and ten 5in, although side armour was reinstated in late March, with displacement reduced to 6250 tons but with the same armament, the secondary guns now in turrets. The next iteration switched to two twin 8in mounts, backed up by sixteen 4in, two pairs of which were then given up to allow for a single 8in mount on each beam.

As a result, a design of 8100 tons, with six 8in and twelve 4in guns and 20kt speed, was approved in June 1890, tenders being invited for both a ship to be built to Navy plans, and also one to plans produced by the builder. William Cramp and Son won, the resulting vessel conforming to the C&R design, but with the boilers switched from two to three compartments on the yard's suggestion to improve underwater protection. In contrast to *Maine*, the new ship, to be named *New York*, had nickel-steel armour, the belt also not being closed fore and aft, but had the armour deck lowered and sloped to the bottom edge of the belt, rather than being placed atop it. As with a number of contemporary vessels (including the earlier British *Nelson*s, the American follow-on *Brooklyn*, and many French ships), a cellulose-filled cofferdam extended the full length of the ship along the waterline. As designed, she was to carry heavy military masts, but completed with a lighter rig.

Two engines were arranged on each shaft, to allow one to be disconnected at cruising speeds (as in the contemporary

New York as completed. (*Author's collection*)

New York in 1898, by which time her after superstructure had been built up and the mainmast divested of most of its platforms. (*Author's collection*).

*Blake*s, and in the earlier *Imperieuse* and *Italia* classes – see p 31, above), the use of such an arrangement having been a recommendation of the Policy Board. On trials, *New York* exceeded her contract speed by nearly 2kt, commissioning on 1 August 1893, serving first in the South Atlantic, and then from the summer of 1894 as flagship of the North Atlantic Squadron. She then temporarily joined the European Squadron to represent the US Navy at the opening of the Kiel Canal, before resuming duty in the North Atlantic Squadron. During this period, the mainmast was stripped of its platforms and the aft superstructure built up around it; derricks were also removed from both masts. Her avowed purpose was rather fluid, since although her policy ancestry implied a fleet role, she was also described on occasion as a commerce raider – presumably a relict of long-standing US policy towards this use of cruising vessels (cf. pp 13–14, above).

A further armoured cruiser (to be *Brooklyn*) was authorised by Congress on 19 July 1892,[59] along with the battleship *Iowa*, with which she shared a number of features, including a degree of tumblehome and very tall funnels, for maximum draught. The contract for her went, like that for *New York*, to Cramps, albeit to an unmodified C&R design. This had a distinctly different hull form from the previous vessel, and was very much along contemporary French lines, with a prominent tumblehome and the beam main mountings sponsoned out, an arrangement found in an unbuilt US battleship design of 1893. These were now twins, while the secondary battery was increased in calibre to 5in, albeit reduced in number by two. Electric training was fitted experimentally in the centreline turrets, with the beam mountings powered by steam, the success of the former leading to its adoption in later vessels, beginning with the battleships of the *Kearsage* class. Torpedo tubes were increased in number by two, of the 14.2in Howell (flywheel-powered) pattern, rather than the Whiteheads in *New York*; these were, however, removed before completion,

and later replaced by 18in Whiteheads.

Protection was similar to that of *New York*, albeit with Harvey armour used for the belt, turrets and barbettes. Likewise, machinery largely followed the previous vessel; a proposal by the builder to substitute single four-cylinder quadruple expansion engines, with a disconnecting fourth cylinder for economy running,[60] for the planned tandem sets was rejected by the navy. The height of the engines was such that the armour deck was stepped up over the engine room to allow adequate clearance. All boilers were placed under the armour deck, rather than having two above, as had been the case in *New York*. Commissioned in December 1896, *Brooklyn* represented the USA at Queen Victoria's Diamond Jubilee naval review on 26 June 1897, before joining the North Atlantic Squadron.

The Commerce Raiders: Threat and Reaction

The *Columbia* class

As well the fully battle-worthy type represented by *New York* and *Brooklyn*, the Policy Board had also envisaged large cruisers intended explicitly for commerce-raiding, as well as being able to run down transatlantic liners that might be employed as auxiliary cruisers. Such a type was particularly promoted by Representative Charles A Boutelle (1839–1901), Chairman of the Committee on Naval Affairs, the first (*Columbia*) being authorised in the 1890 programme in the face of considerable opposition. The Secretary of the Navy asserted that six vessels of the type 'would exterminate the commerce of any country under the present conditions of commerce protection', a second vessel (*Minneapolis*) following in 1891. Both orders went to William Cramp & Sons, Philadelphia, the second being the result of the winning tenderer (Bath Iron Works) being unable to meet neither timescale requirements, nor build her engines.

Brooklyn as completed. (*Author's collection*)

Columbia in August 1898, at the post-Spanish-American War celebrations. She could be distinguished from her sister Minneapolis (p 131) by her four, rather than two, funnels. (NHHC NH 55287)

As with most ships intended for commerce raiding, speed and range were the main drivers of the design, resulting in a ship of over 7000 tons, yet a planned main armament of only four 6in, paired fore and aft, backed up by twelve (as completed, only eight) 4in on the beam and a dozen 6pdrs. Before completion, the aft pair of 6in were replaced by a single 8in, presumably to deal with any pursuer. Even then, the ships' armament was considered over-light for their size; in comparison, the contemporary 'conventional' (although on occasion claimed as a commerce-raider) 5865-ton protected cruiser Olympia (1892) had four 8in and ten 5in guns. The Columbias' protection was on the same scale as Baltimore (1888), with a glacis protecting the cylinder heads.

A three-shaft powerplant was adopted, with the intent that the ships could cruise economically at 15kt on the centre shaft only; designed for 22.5kt, they both exceeded this on trial. It was intended that they could stow up to 2130 tons of coal, for a range of 25,500nm, but in practice maximum capacity was 500 tons less. While fast ships, by the time they commissioned in 1894, the fastest transatlantic liners were averaging nearly 22kt across the ocean, while Columbia only managed 18.4kt in 1895.

As part of their role, the two ships were intended to have looks reminiscent of a liner. In Columbia the eight boilers exhausted into four funnels, but in Minneapolis they were trunked into two (original plans had been for both ships to have three), and although reminiscent of certain merchantmen, their overall rig would have left little doubt as to their true nature.

The pair began their careers in the Atlantic Squadron, Minneapolis going to the European Squadron in 1895. Both were reduced to reserve in 1897, illustrative of the limited peacetime use for such specialised vessels, but recommissioned for the Spanish-American War the following year.

Ryurik

Meanwhile in Russia, the long-standing policy of building large cruisers as potential commerce raiders was continued through a requirement for an enlarged, longer-ranged, version of Pamiat Azova, which would emerge as the first of two the Russian armoured cruisers to bear the name Ryurik.[61] An initial design by the Baltic Works was superseded by one produced by the navy itself, resulting in a vessel with four 8in guns in sponsons, backed up by sponsoned 6in and battery-mounted 4.7in weapons. Protection comprised a partial 8–10in belt (Harvey), closed by 10in bulkheads, with a 2in deck above, and a submerged deck at either end beyond the belt. The endurance requirement probably lay behind the inclusion of a full barque sailing rig, reduced in 1899 by the removal of the bowsprit, along with the yards on the mainmast; searchlight platforms were added to the fore and mizzen masts), and finally eliminated in 1904. As she was intended for long detached deployment, the ship was sheathed and coppered. Ryurik's machinery was, like that of New York, composed of four engines on two shafts, although in her case this was owing to difficulties in acquiring engines of sufficient power, rather than the prospect of steaming economy. Laid down in 1890, she went out the Far East soon after completion in 1896, in company with Dmitri Donskoi, and spent her whole career there. Given the poor dockyard facilities in the theatre, few modifications were carried out, apart from the aforementioned rig changes, a proposed reboilering with Bellevilles being beyond Vladivostok Dockyard's capabilities.

The British giants

The advent of Ryurik and her clear commerce-raiding purpose sparked what can only be described as panic in British naval circles, in particular with regard to her coal capacity, which would allegedly be enough to take her from the Baltic to Vladivostok, via the Cape of Good Hope, without refueling. Accordingly, in February 1893 White was ordered to produce a ship for the 1893–4 Estimates that would be clearly individually superior to the Russian vessel and any prospective sisters. On the matter of speed, 22kt sea speed at natural draught, with 23kt with modest forcing, was taken as a baseline, with a maximum coal capacity some 50 per cent above that in Ryurik – giving a massive 3000 tons. The initial

Ryurik (i) with barque rig, intended to increase her range in her commerce-raiding role. (Author's collection)

Terrible running trials, without armament and with her original short funnels. *(WSS, John Maber collection)*

proposal was that the British ship would have twenty 6in guns, with twelve able to fire on each broadside, opposing *Ryurik's* relatively slow-firing 8in with a hail of fire to destroy her largely unprotected sides. In this context, it is important to recognise that at this point in time, the rapid-firing 6in gun was regarded in many ways as a ship's principal weapon, with bigger, slower-firing weapons essentially armour-piercers to finish off an enemy disabled by 6in fire. This was as true for battleships as it was for big cruisers.[62]

To fit as may guns as possible behind protection, two-storey casemates would be introduced. As for protection, White intended to use a protective deck only, arguing that, especially when used in conjunction with coal, it made for more effective protection than the thick narrow belt employed in *Ryurik*, or the extensive, but relatively thin, side-plating found on *Dupuy de Lôme* and the *Amiral Charner* class.

The resulting ship would be big – a minimum of 12,500 tons; in the event 14,000 tons, with a length of 500ft was selected. The power requirements demanded the most economical boilers possible, which implied the use of watertube units; forty-eight Bellevilles were ultimately installed, after a mixed fit has been considered. A two-shaft arrangement with two engines per shaft was adopted, after consideration had been given to a three-shaft installation, but rejected owing to its impact on overall length and pressure on space aft.

The all-6in armament was not looked on favourably, especially in light of the significant 8in batteries in contemporary US ships, not only in *New York* and *Brooklyn*, but also in the smaller *Olympia*. *Brooklyn* was a particular issue, given her eight-gun main battery and a twelve 5in secondary battery, plus an armour belt – all on under 10,000 tons. As a result, a heavier calibre fore and aft was required, either a twin 8in or single 9.2in mounting, the latter being eventually decided upon, the additional weight reducing the 6in battery to twelve mountings (in two double and two single casemates on each side). This was backed up by sixteen 12pdrs, split

between the upper and main decks, as anti-torpedo boat defence, a dozen 3pdrs, and four submerged torpedo tubes.

The main guns were in shallow barbettes with armoured ammunition tubes below and armoured shields. The armour deck was 6in thick over the machinery, thinning to 2.5in at the crown, with 4in over the magazines, 2in forward and 3in aft. Ammunition passages were provided under the deck on each beam to assure supplies to the long line of 6in guns mounted there. This would be a feature of all later British big cruisers but, as experience would show, was a major weakness, allowing flash to pass the entire length of the ship in the event of a propellant fire: at Jutland this would have tragic results (see p 127, below).

Two ships of the design were ordered under the 1893–4 estimates, *Powerful* and *Terrible* both being launched in the summer of 1895, with the lead ship commissioning in June 1897.[63] *Terrible* was also provisionally commissioned that month, to allow both ships to participate in Queen Victoria's Diamond Jubilee naval review, but then paid off for modifications, and commissioned definitively the following spring. Both ships ran trials with short funnels, but these were soon heightened by 10ft. The ships' endurance fell some 25 per cent below that anticipated.

Powerful as rebuilt, showing her new double-decker casemates amidships. While also so-fitted, *Terrible's* lower guns were never actually shipped, leaving her with the same 6in battery as prior to her refit. *(Author's collection)*

Powerful sailed for the China Station in the late summer of 1897, but suffered from a number of machinery problems en route. Heading home in the autumn of 1899, she was diverted to South Africa in view of the deteriorating situation there, which resulted in the outbreak of the Boer War on 11 October, two days before she arrived at Simonstown. There she found *Terrible*, diverted on her way out from the UK to relieve *Powerful* in China, having spent the previous year carrying senior officials, and later relief crews, to the Mediterranean. Both ships and shore-detachments from their crews played important roles in the Boer War, before *Powerful* resumed her voyage back to the UK on 15 March 1900, and *Terrible* hers to Hong Kong on the 27th. *Terrible* arrived as the Boxer Rebellion was getting underway in China, and the ship and her personnel also played a role in this conflict. She returned home in October 1902 and during 1902–4, both ships of the class were extensively refitted.

Their armament was still regarded as inadequate, and the doubling of the midships pair casemates had already been considered on a number of occasions. Although rejected more than once on the grounds that ammunition supply issues would not allow the four additional guns to be proportionately effective, the change was finally carried out during their 1902–4 refits – although *Terrible* never actually mounted guns at the lower midships levels following the refit. This effectively moved her existing midships weapons up to the new higher level, where they were more effective owing to their higher command.

Active service following these refits was discontinuous, punctuated by periods in reserve. *Powerful's* seagoing service ended with a spell as flagship of the Australian Station, from 1907 to 1912. *Terrible* remained predominantly in reserve, but was used to take relief crews out to China from June to December 1904 (and again from November 1906–May 1908), escorted *Renown* to India during April–October 1905, and was 6th CS flagship for the duration of the 1906 summer manoeuvres. *Powerful* was hulked in 1912 and *Terrible* was to have followed suit in 1914 (see pp 120–1).

Although most impressive ships, the *Powerfuls'* sheer size was widely regarded as excessive, especially as their displacement was within a few hundred tons of the contemporary *Majestic*-class battleships. On the other hand, the ship they were intended to counter was much larger than any Russian battleship, with her immediate successors (pp 56–7) maintaining a margin over even the significantly bigger battleships begun by Russia during the 1890s.

The *Diadem* class

Further large cruisers were projected under the 1895–6 and 1896–7 Estimates, with six initially envisaged.[64] The intent was that they should be somewhere between *Powerful* and *Blake* in size, and sheathed and coppered for distant service. As such, they were effectively as follow-ons to the 'overseas' *Edgars*, with commerce protection, including the ability to deal with any existing or planned foreign cruiser, as part of the requirement. The key debates concerned the armament, with

the *Crescent/Royal Arthur* scheme of a 9.2in aft and two 6in on the forecastle (but with the tertiary battery raised from 6pdr to 12pdr), combined with *Powerful's* double-deck casemates and ammunition passages, giving a total of twelve 6in, as a starting point. Single 8in were then proposed potential mountings fore and aft, with the 6in rearranged, one option reducing their number by two.

However, an ongoing rationalisation of gun calibres argued against any 8in-based option, with another version of the 9.2in/6in mix put forward as the provisional way ahead. However, the 9.2in were then dropped in favour all-6in arrangements, the final one giving the ships sixteen 6in, with two on each of the forecastle and quarterdeck, and the same arrangement on the beam as in *Powerful*. Protection remained based around a protective deck, although White was asked to provide an alternate scheme with a 4in belt. However, as built, the ships had a full-length armour deck, 2in on the flat and 4in on slopes, with broadside guns protected by 6in casemates.

The question of machinery was also at issue, with the question of triple shafts again being raised, along with the merits (and otherwise) of the double engine arrangement found in *Blake* and *Powerful*. In the event, a twin shaft installation with a single engine on each shaft was adopted, with steam provided by thirty Belleville boilers. Four vessels, *Diadem*, *Andromeda*, *Europa* and *Niobe* were ordered under the 1895–6 Estimates, and a further four, *Amphitrite*, *Argonaut*, *Ariadne* and *Spartiate*, with slightly more powerful machinery, a built-up aft superstructure and their aft 6in raised on a platform, the following year.

From the very beginning, the *Diadem*s were regarded as too big and too weakly armed and protected for their size, although the former was very much owing to the requirement for high endurance, and they would certainly have been able to deal with most foreign cruisers to be found on distant stations. Nevertheless, during their early years, the ships saw extensive employment both home and abroad. However, by

Essentially reduced *Powerfuls*, the *Diadem* class were generally regarded as underarmed for their size; *Niobe* is shown here in 1911, soon after been transferred to Canada. *(Author's collection)*

1914 a number had already been relegated to secondary duties (see p 111); in addition, *Niobe* had been sold to Canada as that country's first major warship (p108).

France

The big protected cruiser also found a brief popularity in France, for two very different sorts of ship. By the mid-1890s there were three basic strands of French opinion regarding what sorts of cruisers were needed. One, held largely by younger officers, favoured armoured cruisers, supported by smaller vessels, primarily for use with the battlefleet: this had produced *Dupuy de Lôme* and her five immediate successors. A second, rooted among older senior officers, supported ships primarily designed for distant service, while the third perpetuated the commerce-raiding mantra of the *Jeune école*.

In 8 November 1893, influence of the 'distant service' faction led to the ordering of *D'Entrecasteaux*, intended as an overseas station flagship, and thus sheathed and coppered. A requirement for such a vessel had been put together by the *Conseil de Traveaux* in 1891, envisaging a displacement of around 8000 tons, with a main battery of four 9.4in, arranged in a lozenge fashion, although the wing guns were later dropped; an auxiliary rig was also planned. A number of designs were considered, the decision going in favour of one by Amable Lagane, of Forges et Chantiers de la Méditerranée at La Seyne.

The ship carried a single 9.4in gun fore and aft, matching the earlier armoured corvettes and signalling her capital role; the guns were amongst the first to be electrically powered, the ship having a particularly extensive set of electrical installations. The secondary battery comprised eight 5.5in in main deck casemates, plus four more in upper deck shielded mountings, backed up by twelve 47mm and six 37mm, distributed around the superstructure.

Although deck-protected only, *D'Entrecasteaux* was still generally referred to as an 'armoured cruiser'. The armour deck itself was 1.2in thick, with 3.2in slopes, over the machinery, thinning fore and aft. Cofferdams were fitted over the slopes, extending up to the deck above, which was 0.8in thick, and backed by a 1.6in longitudinal splinter bulkhead. The main guns were in armoured turrets. The ship was equipped with relatively low-pressure cylindrical boilers, to aid reliability in her distant-station role. The boiler arrangement was unusual, with four placed ahead of the engines, but the fifth aft of them, producing an odd funnel-spacing.

D'Entrecasteaux entered service in February 1899, and sailed for the Far East on 6 April 1899, arriving at Saigon on 12 May, where she became flagship on 1 June. She remained on the station, apart from a return home to refit, until January 1903, going back once more as flagship in August 1906, while so employed running aground in the Gulf of Tonkin on 9 March 1907, albeit without serious damage; on the other hand, she was present when *Chanzy* ran aground in May and became a total loss (see pp 42–3). The ship returned home again at the end of 1909 and went into reserve. Refitted in in 1911, when her torpedo tubes were removed, she then became flagship of the Mediterranean Training Squadron until November 1913, when relieved by the battleship *Suffren*. *D'Entrecasteaux* remained laid up at Toulon until the outbreak of the First World War, a suggestion that she relieve *Pothuau* as a gunnery training ship not being carried through.

Commerce raiding again

The following year, however, the residual influence of the *Jeune école* was reflected in the ordering of two ships intended for war on commerce. The ships in question, *Châteaurenault (ii)* and *Guichen*, were apparently inspired by the two American commerce-destroyers of the *Columbia* class, and shared their three-shaft machinery layout. As was French practice during the 1890s, competitive designs were invited against the basic specification, to carry two 6.5in and six 5.5in guns, with a protective deck, a large supply of coal and 23kt speed.

D'Entrecasteaux as built. (Author's collection)

Châteaurenault was built to a scheme produced by Lagane at La Seyne, and *Guichen* to one by an unknown engineer at the Ateliers et Chantiers de la Loire at Saint-Nazaire. Although both ships were four-funnelled, they looked very different from one another, *Châteaurenault* having her uptakes conventionally arranged, while *Guichen* had hers separated into two widely-spaced pairs, with the engine-room placed amidships. This feature was to be replicated in many later French big ships down from the *Gueydon* class onwards (see p 68, below). Initial plans had her with the 6.5in guns on the beam, with two of the 5.5in as bow- and sternchasers; however she completed with the 6.5in fore and aft and the 5.5in all on the beam, as in *Châteaurenault*. The latter was given a counter stern of vaguely mercantile shape, the intent being that she might be mistaken at long range for a liner, although no

Perhaps the most extreme example of two ships built to the same specification, but emerging with utterly different appearances, were the two commerce-raiding cruisers laid down in France in 1895. One, *Châteaurenault*, shown here coaling at Toulon during the First World War, was built to vaguely resemble an ocean liner, including a false counter stern. *(NHHC NH 55636)*

The other, *Guichen*, was unmistakably a warship, and introduced the engines-amidships scheme to cruisers, which endured until the end of big cruiser building in France. To speed coaling, *Guichen* joined the fleet fitted with a midships mast carrying a pair of Temperley transporters for trials purposes; these were removed after a few years. *(Author's collection)*

attempt was made to provide such details as promenade decks or less obviously-warship funnels as would have allowed a closer approach to a prospective victim or opponent. Both ships were designed primarily for speed, resulting in a very light armament for their size (as was also the case in the *Columbia*s), while both had problematic trials.

As a result, although *Châteaurenault* began hers in October 1899, modifications and renewed trials (particularly as a result of severe vibration) meant that she did not finally enter service until three years later, although in the end she touched 24.5kt on her final trials, albeit with high coal consumption. *Châteaurenault*'s first deployment was to the Far East, where she was badly damaged by grounding on 7 November 1904, and after her return to France in 1905 underwent repairs before going into reserve at Cherbourg in February 1906. Recommissioned for the Mediterranean at the beginning of 1910, she ran aground on the Moroccan coast while approaching the Straits of Gibraltar on 30 January, and refloated only with the aid of the cruisers *Friant* (1893) and *Du Chayla* (1895); she was then towed by *Victor Hugo* to Toulon for repairs, which lasted until the end of 1911. *Châteaurenault* became flagship of Brest's seagoing training ships in January 1912, but went into reserve in November 1913, returning to service only with the beginning of the First World War.

The trials of *Guichen* lasted from October 1898 to March 1900; given her commerce-raiding role, before entering service she was given an additional mast amidships to carry Temperley transporter fast-coaling gear on an experimental basis; this was later removed, along with the mast. *Guichen* joined the Northern Squadron on commissioning, before leaving for the Far East in January 1905, relieving the damaged *Châteaurenault* in March. The ship returned to France in September 1906, going into reserve until 1910, when she joined the 2nd Squadron in the Mediterranean as repeating-ship. She became a seagoing training ship in 1912, passing into reserve in January 1914, before recommissioning in August for war service.

The Russian Second Generation

Initial plans envisaged the building of a full sister to *Ryurik*, but in 1892 a revised design was ordered, with more extensive armour coverage and additional bunkerage, which then grew further in size as the secondary and tertiary batteries were modified – although sailing rig was now eliminated (albeit leaving three masts).[65] The new ship, to become *Rossiya*, also had a wholly different machinery arrangement, with Belleville boilers (giving a four-funnel profile) and a three-shaft engine set-up, with the small centre engine to be used only for cruising; unfortunately, the drag of the stopped outer propellers was such that the anticipated low-speed efficiencies could not be achieved.

The aim of significantly extending the protected areas was not achieved, the thickness of the belt actually being reduced to 8in – albeit of Harvey armour and thus of similar protective

Rossiya as completed. *(NHHC NH 93615)*

value – although it now ran all the way to the stern. On the other hand, the conning tower was much thicker, there was some protection to the uptakes, and cylinder heads were enclosed in a 5in glacis. Like *Ryurik*, *Rossiya* went to the Far East soon after completion, but in her case returned home after an active role in the Russo-Japanese War (see pp 94–6).

The same was true of a half-sister, *Gromoboi*, ordered under the 1895 programme.[66] Again, the original intent had been to build a full sister of the previous cruiser, but the emerging battlefleet role of the big cruiser (cf. pp 55, 82) made a replication of the relatively weakly protected *Rossiya* unwise. Thus, *Rossiya* was taken now as the basis for a 'squadron' armoured cruiser, with a better armour deck and protection for the guns – a major weakness in *Ryurik* and *Rossiya*. In the resulting trade-offs, the belt was both thinned and shortened, although the former was compensated for by having the now-sloped margins of the armour deck behind it. The glacis over the cylinders was eliminated by having three equal-sized (and so aggregately lower) engines, the overall weight of armour saved being applied to casemating the forward pair of 8in guns and three-quarters of the 6in weapons. The new ship came out 1000 tons larger than *Rossiya*, making her some 500 tons heavier than the contemporary American-built Russian battleship *Retvizan*.

In parallel with the building of *Rossiya* and *Gromoboi*, the Russian navy began work on what the design-documents dubbed 'battleship-cruisers' – fast, seaworthy, well-armed and well-protected vessels that could act as capital ships on distant stations and reinforce the *Ryurik*-type armoured cruisers in their commerce-raiding roles. They were seen as equivalents of, and counters to, the British *Centurion* class (pp 47–8, above). The original intention was that the new ships would

form a Mediterranean squadron, deployable to the Far East in an emergency. However, with the construction of the Japanese battleships *Fuji* and *Yashima* (1896), with the four follow-on battleships and six armoured cruisers of the Japanese '6–6' programme (pp 72–3), the focus of these, and other new construction, shifted to long-term deployment to the Far East.

The design ultimately became the *Peresvet* class,[67] a few hundred tons heavier than *Rossiya*, and 20 per cent bigger than the *Centurion*s. They had a number of design features in common with *Rossiya*, including three shafts and a secondary gun in the stem, but with 10in guns in twin turrets, 6in guns in casemates and a 9in main belt. Only a knot slower than the

A modified *Rossiya* intended for fleet service, *Gromoboi* is shown here in Australian waters in 1901. *(Author's collection)*

cruiser as finally realised, they had, however, with a much lower endurance. The *Peresvet*s also pioneered a much-improved compartmentalised water-discharge system.

As with many Russian warships, a number of changes were made during construction, including replacing the planned mixed 6in/4.7in secondary central battery with uniform casemated 6in, adding a 75mm battery and expanding the original number of 47mm guns. As a result of the increases in weights, while *Peresvet* received two military masts, the second ship, *Oslyabya*, had her mainmast replaced by a pole – but both ships completed so overweight that their entire main belts were

Peresvet in the inner roads at Port Arthur, 31 March 1904, wearing the dark green paintwork adopted during the Russo-Japanese War. (*Author's collection*)

Pobeda at Piraeus on her way out to the Far East at the end of 1902, wearing peacetime white and buff. (*Author's collection*)

submerged at full load. On the other hand, the protection afforded by the armour deck was enhanced by their following *Renown* in adopting slopes at the margins.

A third ship, *Pobeda*, was laid down in 1898, three years after the first pair, in the absence of a new design to occupy the slip left vacant by the launch of *Peresvet* – in spite of the fact that the type had been made obsolescent in its intended role by the Japanese procurement of 1st class battleships, starting with the *Fuji* class, laid down even before the *Peresvet*s had been begun. *Pobeda* (which shared *Oslyabya*'s rig) differed somewhat from the first pair, with a slightly different hull and Krupp (rather than mainly-Harvey) armour, permitting a complete waterline belt, rather than one terminating in transverse bulkheads short of the bow and stern. While the first two ships had been sheathed and coppered, this feature was omitted in *Pobeda*. She possessed the same reduced rig as *Oslyabya*, joining the fleet before the latter, in spite of having been laid down some three years earlier.

Both *Peresvet* and *Pobeda* proceeded to the Far East soon after completion in 1901 and 1902, respectively. *Oslyabya* also left for the Far East once finished in 1903, but ran aground in the Straits of Gibraltar in August, spending until November under repair at La Spezia.

The Ubiquitous *Garibaldis* and their Ramifications

When finances allowed the ordering of the two Italian contract-built cruisers that had been planned alongside the *Pisani*s, they were begun to a modestly enlarged, slightly faster, design. This nevertheless had a much heavier armament, with a heavy mounting – a single 10in or a twin 8in – fitted fore and aft and an extra two 6in. The 4.7in guns of the earlier class were omitted, ten 76mm weapons being fitted in lieu. The first ship, *Giuseppe Garibaldi* (i), was to have two 10in mountings, while the second, *Varese* (i), would have two 8in turrets.

These enhancements over the *Pisani*s were intended to allow the new ships to, if necessary, make up for the shortage of modern battleships in the Italian navy, which the Italian financial crisis was making it difficult to resolve.[68] The *Garibaldis*' big guns were given unusually high angles of elevation for the period, the 10in 35deg and the 8in 25deg resulting in firing ranges in excess of many ships of the era (cf. p 94). To compensate for the added heavy guns, the belt beyond the citadel was thinned by 20 per cent as compared with the *Pisani*s. The citadel extended from the armour deck to the upper deck, with oblique 4.7in bulkheads enclosing the main armament barbettes. Coal bunkers lay behind the belt the full length of the citadel, above the slopes of the armour deck, with splinter decks at upper-deck level within the citadel and at lower-deck level outside it.

The lead ship of the class was begun in July 1893, and launched in May 1895, well ahead of schedule (and even before *Pisani* had taken to the water). However, by that year, relations between the South American neighbours Argentina and Chile had become particularly poisonous over long-term boundary disputes, going back to poor delineations of responsibility during Spanish imperial rule. A naval race had been kindled by the latter's ordering of the battleship *Capitan Prat* in 1887 (for long one of only three 'true' battleships in South America, alongside the Brazilian *Riachuelo* and *Aquidaban*), plus two protected cruisers (*Presidente Errazuriz* and *Presidente Pinto* [1890]).[69] Argentina had then countered with the coast-defence ships *Independencia* and *Libertad* (1890–1) and two protected cruisers (*Veinticinto de Mayo* [1890] and *Nueve de Julio* [1892]). Each country then acquired a further protected cruiser (*Buenos Aires* [1895] and *Blanco Enclada* [1893]), before Chile ordered an armoured cruiser (*Esmeralda* [ii], see below), financed in part by selling a protected cruiser (*Esmeralda* [i – 1883]) to Japan in late 1894. Except for the French-built *Capitan Prat* and *Presidente* class, all these ships were built by Armstrong in the UK.

In reply, an Argentine naval commission was dispatched to Europe, with the potentialities of the *Garibaldi*s leading to negotiations being opened towards obtaining one of them.[70]

The first of her class to complete, Argentina's *Garibaldi* had been launched as the Italian *Giuseppe Garibaldi* in May 1895, but sold two months later; a replacement was laid down immediately, but was herself sold, to Spain as *Cristóbal Colón*. A third *Giuseppe Garibaldi* was sold to Argentina as *Pueyrredón* in 1897, and it was not until 1901 that Italy commissioned a ship of the name. (*Author's collection*)

San Martin on trials; she differed from *Garibaldi* principally in having a main armament of four 8in, rather than two 10in, guns; her rig and arrangement of second battery also displayed differences. (*Author's collection*)

These culminated in an offer from the shipbuilder, Ansaldo, to the Argentine President to sell *Giuseppe Garibaldi* for £750,000, spread over four payments, the first to be paid immediately (14 July 1895), and the last on delivery. This was accepted; the ship retained her name, albeit abbreviated, commemorating her namesake's involvement in South American affairs in the 1840s. Handed over to the Argentine commission at Genoa in October 1896, *Garibaldi* sailed immediately for Buenos Aires, arriving on 10 December and immediately becoming flagship to the 2nd Division for manoeuvres. Permission for the sale was granted by the Italian government on the basis that an eponymous replacement would be delivered against the existing contract completion date, but with watertube, rather than cylindrical, boilers. *Garibaldi* returned to Italy for a refit at Genoa in 1900, modifications including the removal of her torpedo tubes.

In March 1896, Chile ordered a further armoured cruiser (*General O'Higgins*, see below), and the 25th of the following month, Argentina concluded a preliminary agreement to buy *Garibaldi*'s sister *Varese*, just about to be launched for Italy by the Orlando yard at Leghorn. It is unclear whether one transaction was a direct consequence of the other, or just fortuitous synchronicity. The Argentine deal was not, however, finalised until October, as a result of a change of the Italian government in March; in the event, it required the Italian Navy Minister, Benedetto Brin (1833–98), to convince the Foreign Minister to approve the sale, on grounds that to block it would probably turn the Argentines elsewhere for future ship purchases. The sale was, in any case, advantageous financially to the Italian government in view of the ongoing crisis in the naval budget, as it delayed the point at which they would need to pay money to the shipyard until the replacement ship advanced in construction. In addition, until the ship being sold actually left Italian waters, it could be requisitioned in an emergency.

In addition to her 8in main battery, *San Martin*, as the ship was renamed, differed from her sister in having her main-deck guns arranged with the fore and aft mountings sponsored out, giving limited axial fire. In addition, the upper fighting top was lower down the mast in *San Martin*, which also lacked *Garibaldi*'s prominent funnel caps. Handed over in April 1898, *San Martin* reached her new home waters on 13 June, joining *Garibaldi* in the High Seas Squadron; she was fleet flagship until 1911.

Following the sale of the first ships of the class to Argentina, replacements had been laid down for the Italian navy (*Giuseppe Garibaldi* [ii] and *Varese* [ii]), but neither ship was destined to sail under the Italian flag. First, the new *Giuseppe Garibaldi* was purchased by Spain on 14 August 1896, a month before launch, and re-named *Cristóbal Colón*. She had *San Martin*'s sponsons for the end 6in weapons, but otherwise generally followed the design of the original *Garibaldi*, including her two 10in Armstrong-pattern guns. However, the Spanish preferred to use main guns of Hontoria manufacture (presumably 9.4in/35, as mounted in the *Princesa*

The Spanish *Garibaldi*, *Cristóbal Colón*, never received her definitive main guns, being lost with nothing larger than her 6in secondary battery. *(NHHC NH 63229).*

de Asturias class),[71] but these had not been fitted by the time that she was deployed against the Americans in the spring of 1898 (see further p 76, below). There were Spanish plans to acquire a further, new-build, ship named *Pedro de Aragon*, ordered in 1897, but these were abandoned in 1900 and the contract transferred to Argentina, under the name *Rivadavia*, before being cancelled, the name being transferred to a fresh Argentine order (see p 62, below).[72]

Back in South America, in the summer of 1897, Argentina purchased from Italy two more incomplete *Garibaldi*s, a third *Giuseppe Garibaldi* and a second *Varese*, renaming them *Pueyrredón* and *General Belgrano* respectively. The contract for the first-named demanded completion two (!) months after launch, paying a £30,000 premium on the £752,000 asking price; this was not, however, achieved. Attempts had been made by the Chilean minister in Italy to prevent the sale by expressing a interest in buying the ships, but these had not been supported by the Chilean navy. They regarded the *Garibaldi*s as too small for their needs; there were also major financial issues involved, as Chile's economy was weaker than that of Argentina, and funding a response to the Argentine purchases was problematic.

Pueyrredón and *General Belgrano* were both armed with 10in guns and had watertube, rather than cylindrical, boilers, but differed in main-deck battery arrangement (*Pueyrredón* had sponsoned end-guns, like *San Martin*; *Belgrano* did not, like *Garibaldi*), funnels (*Pueyrredón*'s had caps, like *Garibaldi*) and rig (*Belgrano* had no upper fighting top). *Belgrano* was unique amongst the Argentine *Garibaldi*s in lacking 4.7in guns, having four upper-deck 6in mountings instead, giving her a secondary battery of fourteen guns. *Pueyrredón* was accepted in August 1898 and her sister in October, arriving at Mar del

Plata on 1 September and 6 November respectively. The four *Garibaldi*s formed the Argentine navy's 1st High Seas Division, *Garibaldi* herself being refitted in 1899, when her early-model 10in guns were replaced by those of the newer type fitted in *Pueyrredón* and *Belgrano*.

Italy finally received its own *Garibaldi*s just after the turn of the century: like *Belgrano* (the intended *Varese* [ii]), they had an all-6in secondary battery, but had the 3in battery increased to ten guns, and the 47mm reduced to six barrels. In addition, they were all lengthened by 16ft amidships which, and given an extra 500ihp, in a vain attempt to guarantee 20kt. All had watertube boilers, Niclausse in *Giuseppe Garibaldi* (iv) and *Varese* (iii), Belleville in *Francesco Ferruccio*, the latter initially having much taller boiler-room ventilators from her sisters. Each of the trio could be distinguished by differing funnel-caps, while *Varese* also had a much wider fighting top, and *Ferruccio* shallow sponsons for her fore and aft 3in embrasures. *Garibaldi* and *Varese* commissioned in 1901, but *Ferruccio* did not come into service until 1905, although laid down only a year after her sisters. The delay was not only due to the inexperience of her

Francesco Ferrucio as completed; she could be distinguished from her sisters by her funnel casings. *(Author's collection)*

The fourth *Giuseppe Garibaldi*, the first to join the Italian fleet, shown at Genoa. (*Author's collection*)

builders with the design (she was built at Venice Dockyard, the only one of the class not constructed by Ansaldo or Orlando), but also owing to the diversion of her armament to an export order.

Plans existed for the building of four further vessels, to be named *Genova*, *Venezia*, *Pisa* and *Amalfi*, with one to be built at the dockyard of La Spezia and one at Castellamare di Staba.[73] Initially to be simply improved *Garibaldis*, they evolved into a new design, of 8000 tons, with an additional deck forward, twelve 8in in twin turrets, protected by a complete 5.9in belt and 1.6in deck, and with a speed of 22–23kt. However, no orders were placed, the funding being diverted to the first two *Vittorio Emanuele*-class battleships of the 1901–02 programme, which were built at the same two yards. These ships combined twelve 8in guns with two 12in and the then-exceptionally high speed of 21kt, and came close to being more cruisers than battleships, bearing more than a

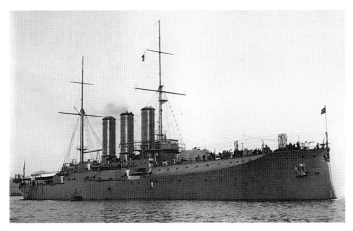

The Italian battleship *Regina Elena* (1904), an example of the blurring between the battleship and cruiser categories during the late nineteenth and early twentieth centuries, with an armament consisting mainly of 8in guns (with only two 12in as armour-piercers) and the high speed of 21kt. She much impressed the German Emperor Wilhelm II, whose desire to fuse the battleship and large cruiser categories was frustrated by the German Fleet Laws' strict division of the two. (*Author's collection*)

passing resemblance to the deferred cruisers, with their raised forecastle and twin 8in turrets on the beam, but a single 12in fore and aft. The actual cruisers would eventually be procured from 1904 onwards, to rather different designs (see pp ***, below).

Chilean reply and Argentine riposte

The aforementioned Chilean armoured cruisers were both purchased from Armstrong's. *Esmeralda*, funded in part from the sale of the 1883 protected cruiser of the name to Japan (as *Izumi*) in November 1894, was first tendered as a slightly enlargement of *Blanco Encalada*, launched for Chile by the same firm the previous year, and armed with two 8in and ten 6in guns.[74] However, by the time an order was placed on 15 May 1895, the ship had grown by a quarter to 6000 tons, while in July Chile requested that she be lengthened, and have belt armour and an extra six 6in added. The shipyard advised against such an enlargement, proposing that *Esmeralda* be built to her May plans, with a new ship to be designed from scratch as an armoured cruiser. Although such a vessel would eventually be built (as *O'Higgins*), the Chileans insisted on going ahead with the 'armoured' *Esmeralda*, which was launched in June 1896, carrying out her gun trials on 16 December, and sailing for South America on 22 March 1897.

Three-quarters of her length was covered by the 7ft-wide belt, the main guns being mounted fore and aft, with the 6in weapons distributed along the beam, with two pairs at shelter-deck level (removed in 1910, when fire-control positions were fitted on the masts). 12pdrs were mounted between each of the four midships pairs of 6in, with two more on the after superstructure.

Work towards the other ship began with a request for tenders in September 1895, for a 7300-ton vessel with a 7in Harvey belt, two turreted 8in (not just shielded, as in *Esmeralda*) and ten 6in, in a mixture of main-deck casemates and upper-deck mountings. Two further 8in were soon added, with options put forward for placing them abreast the forward superstructure in main-deck casemates, in upper-deck casemates, or in upper-deck turrets; displacement jumped by a thousand tons. In the event, as ordered in March 1896 and laid down 4 April, the turret option was taken, with four of

The Chilean *Esmeralda*, an example of the kind of big cruiser offered by Armstrong's at Elswick. (*Author's collection*)

the 6in also so-mounted, the rest being placed in main-deck casemates. Unlike *Esmeralda*, the new ship, *General O'Higgins*, was fitted with watertube boilers, the customer insisting on Bellevilles, giving her a completely different, three-funnelled, profile. Her machinery was very successful, the ship exceeding her original trial speed in service and still being good for 21kt during her last decade of active service. Completed in April 1898, *O'Higgins* arrived in Chile on 5 July 1898, beginning a career that would last six decades.

By May 1898, as *O'Higgins* was completing her final trials in the UK, tensions between Chile and Argentina were such that it was agreed to submit their underlying Andean boundary disputes to the UK for adjudication, while certain other issues were formally resolved, *Belgrano* embarking the Argentine President on 20 January 1899 to meet his Chilean opposite number to sign the peace treaty at Punta Arenas on 15 February. However, the adjudication was not to be completed until 1902, there were continued mutual accusations of violations of the status quo, and agitation for war.

The naval race thus continued, Chile making enquiries in 1901 about acquiring the three American *Indiana*-class battleships,[75] and purchasing from Armstrong's an already-complete protected cruiser (*Chacabuco* [1898]), built on speculation. In reply, Argentina signed as letter of intent with Ansaldo in May 1901 for the building of a pair of 15,000-ton, 12in-armed battleships of the *Regina Margherita* type (1901), and made firm orders with Ansaldo for a further pair of (new-build) *Garibaldi*s on 23 December the same year. Laid down as *Mitra* and *Roca* in March 1902, but launched as *Berndardino Rivadavia* and *Mariano Moreno*, they were very similar to the Italian-completed ships of the class, but reverted to cylindrical boilers (presumably as a result of negative experiences with *Pueyrredón* and *Belgrano*'s Bellevilles), exhausting through half-cased funnels. They also had three-bladed, rather than four-bladed screws, in an attempt to ensure their designed 20kt speed, *Garibaldi* (iv) having only made 19.66kt on trial, in spite of making 5 per cent more than designed power. While originally both were to have the 'Italian' gun arrangement of a single 10in forward and a twin 8in aft, the armament of *Moreno* was later changed to four 8in, presumably to allow her to tactically combine with *San Martín*.[76] Both ships had the fourteen-6in/ten-3in

Argentina's final pair of *Garibaldi*s were actually laid down for them. *Bernardino Rivadavia* is shown here at her launch in October 1902, although in the end she was sold to Japan, becoming their *Kasuga*. (*Author's collection*)

Sold to Japan following the Argentine-Chilean agreement on naval limitations, *Nisshin* (ex-*Mariano Moreno*) and *Kasuga* (ex-*Rivadavia*) are shown here completing at Genoa in 1904. (*Author's collection*)

secondary/tertiary batteries of the Italian *Garibaldi*s, but lacked fighting tops, the guns previously fitted in them being moved to the superstructure.

In reply, Chile authorised in late 1901 a pair of vessels (*Constitucion* and *Libertad*) classified as battleships, but actually *Garibaldi*-killers, and thus to all intents and purposes big cruisers. The ships were designed by former British Chief Constructor Edward Reed (then Chile's naval consultant), the initial sketches showing four 10in and ten/twelve 7.5in guns, later increased to fourteen 7.5in at the customer's request. Drawings were agreed with Armstrong's and Vickers, who would each build one ship, orders being placed on 26 February 1902. As well as more than capable of overwhelming a *Garibaldi* by gunfire – the 7.5in battery was clearly intended to directly complement the 10in in this destruction – they had a 15 per cent thicker belt and were just as fast.

However, this ludicrously expensive set of beggar-my-neighbour programmes was brought to an end by the British, fearing for the wider impacts of any hostilities between the two South American powers. Linked with the UK's final adjudication of the Andean boundary dispute, three 'Pacts of May' were signed in 1902, the third dealing with the naval race, finalised by a naval limitation treaty of 9 January 1903. For the next five years, each country could only buy new ships

O'Higgins, also built for Chile at Elswick, but of a very different design, which would provide the prototype for a later series of ships built for Japan. (*Author's collection*)

Also disposed of under the Argentine-Chilean agreement, the Chilean cruiser-killer *Constitucion* became the British *Swiftsure* (ii); she is shown here outbound to the Mediterranean in April 1909. *(Author's collection)*

if the other had been given eighteen months' notice.

Ships under construction would be sold as soon as possible, while *Garibaldi* and *Pueyrredón*, along with the Chilean *Capitan Prat*, would be paid off, 'moored in a basin or port, having on board only the necessary crew to attend to the preservation of the material which could not be removed', without coal, powder and ammunition, small-calibre guns, torpedo tubes and torpedoes, searchlights, boats, and stores. Accordingly, decommissioned in January 1903, the Argentine pair returned to service in 1908, *Garibaldi* as a training ship for stokers, gunners, deck officers, signallers and navigators, remaining as such for the rest of her seagoing career. *Belgrano* went back to fleet service, having been fitted with wireless in 1907 (upgraded in 1912).

The treaty put *Constitucion, Libertad, Rivadavia* and *Moreno*, all either afloat or about to the launched when the naval treaty was signed, 'at the disposal of King Edward VII, who is to ensure that they could only leave the yards at the joint request of Chile and Argentina, either because their sale has been effected, or in virtue of a subsequent agreement'. Agents were appointed to sell the ships, William R Grace of New York being among the appointees of the Chileans.[77]

They approached the Japanese in October 1902 regarding *Constitucion* and *Libertad*, who were not at that time interested. Even when, in February 1903, the British government informed the Japanese that intelligence indicated Germany and Russia were interested in purchasing the ships,

nothing was done owing to lack of funds. However, by the autumn Russo-Japanese relations were deteriorating, and when another Chilean agent, the British Anthony Gibbs & Co, offered the ships for £1.6 million in October, the Japanese entered into negotiations. Russia had also been the object of an offer by Gibbs & Co, in this case with the asking price of £1.8 million, effectively raising the price for the Japanese, who once again withdrew on 20 November, citing lack of funds.

After this, and concerned to avoid *Constitucion* and *Libertad* falling into Russian hands, the British decided to buy the pair themselves, making their own bid on 27 November, the two ships being formally purchased on 4 December. On the 19th, the Japanese managed set an emergency budget, including funds to obtain *Constitucion* and *Libertad* from the British, but the latter refused to sell-on, citing the terms under which Parliament had acquiesced to the acquisition. The vessels thus joined the British fleet as *Swiftsure* (ii – ex-*Constitucion*) and *Triumph* (ii – ex-*Libertad*) on completion in 1904.

The ships were controversial acquisitions, not easily melding with the 12in-armed 'standard' ships of the battle line, and too slow to tactically combine with the British armoured cruisers. Nevertheless, they both served with the fleet at home and in the Mediterranean until 1913, when *Swiftsure* became East Indies flagship and *Triumph* joined the China Station, mirroring the eastern service of their earlier namesakes, and the concept of deploying such second-class vessels as capital ships for distant stations.

However, the British did offer their good offices in acquiring *Rivadavia* and *Moreno* (also of interest to the Russians) which had been considerably more advanced than the Chilean pair, respectively running contractors' trials during July and September, and October and November, 1903. The propeller changes noted above (p 62) seem to have had a positive effect, as both made their design speeds, with a 7 per cent excess in power; vibration was negligible, even compared to the good results achieved by earlier *Garibaldi*s.

Accordingly, Gibbs & Co, instructed by the British Government, but acting for Japan, purchased *Rivadavia* and *Moreno* for £1.53 million on 30 December 1903 (Russia had failed to make a cash offer). They were formally transferred to Japan on 7 January 1904 as *Kasuga* and *Nisshin*, respectively. Delivery was entrusted to Armstrong's – in any case the ships' armour and armament contractor – to take place within thirty-five days; a Royal Navy escort was planned, but dropped for reasons of neutrality. *Kasuga* and *Nisshin* sailed from Genoa under the Japanese merchant flag on the night of 8/9 January, under British command, but with Italian engineers and an international crew, including increasing numbers of Japanese as their voyage east continued. Russian protests ensued, especially as the ships' captains were Royal Navy reservists, but this was circumvented by their commissions being speedily cancelled.

Also crossing the Mediterranean towards the Suez Canal (the Japanese ships arrived at Port Said on 13 January) were a Russian force comprising *Oslyabya*, resuming her interrupted voyage east, with *Dmitri Donskoi* and the protected cruiser *Aurora* (1900). Given the plummeting diplomatic situation between Russia and Japan, there were concerns regarding 'incidents', with the British 'managing' the two forces to ensure they were kept apart until through the Canal (after which the Japanese were shadowed for a while by *Aurora* which was, however, soon outpaced). In any case, the Japanese avoided the final rupture with Russia until after their departure from Singapore on 5 February: diplomatic relations were severed on the 6th, and Port Arthur attacked on the 8th; *Kasuga* and *Nisshin* arrived at Yokosuka on the 16th (see further p 93).

With the completion of this pair, the *Garibaldi* line came to an end. The design had been in production for a decade at a time when warship design had been undergoing year-on-year significant change, and it is a tribute to its perceived qualities that Argentina wished to perpetuate the design as late as 1901 – notwithstanding the strategic imperative to get early delivery to face Chilean new construction.

Even after the outbreak of war between Russia and Japan, the former continued to investigate the acquisition of South American cruisers as a means of reinforcing the fleet now being sent to relieve the Japanese siege of Port Arthur in the Far East. An unnamed neutral (possibly China) was reported in May 1904 as being interested in Chilean cruisers (one assumes, in particular, *O'Higgins* and *Esmeralda*), while Turkey was another alleged go-between for Russia in negotiations with both Chile and Argentina, reported by British diplomats in May/June. While neither Chile nor Argentina were willing to sell directly to the belligerents, they had no qualms about selling to other nations, and would turn a blind eye to any on-sales. British diplomatic pressure was exerted to prevent such transactions, while Turkey's financial credibility as a 'real' buyer was recognised as marginal at best.

On the other hand, Greece appeared in mid-June as a potential buyer on behalf of Russia, while further rumours suggested Persia might make acquisitions on behalf of Japan. Greece remained in the running in October, with Morocco, Bolivia and Paraguay also be mentioned. An actual Greek deal for the Russians was alleged in the middle of October, but was a false alarm, and discussions continued into December, before fizzling out. This removed the last chance of effective reinforcement of the Russian squadron at that time in transit from the Baltic to the Far East, and which would face annihilation at Tsushima (see pp 97–8, below).

Oslyabya and *Dmitri Donskoi* during their abortive 1904 voyage to the Far East. (*NHHC NH 94416*)

Right: *Shannon* is often regarded as the first British armoured cruiser, although she did not actually receive such a classification until 1887, a decade after she first joined the fleet. She was originally an 'iron armour plated ship', as were the functionally similar, and preceding, *Audacious* and *Swiftsure* classes – although these became in 1887 '2nd class armoured battle ships'. The difference in re-classification seems to have been based in part on *Shannon* carrying some heavy guns on an open deck amidships, and in part on her innovative protective deck, the submerged forward part of which being clearly visible in this longitudinal section, showing the ship with modifications to May 1883.
(© National Maritime Museum, Greenwich, London, M0932)

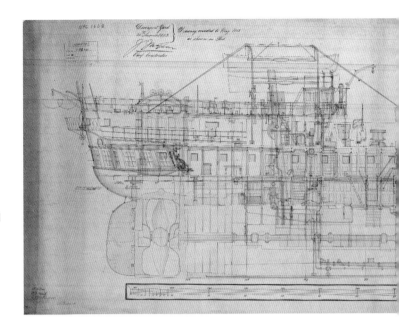

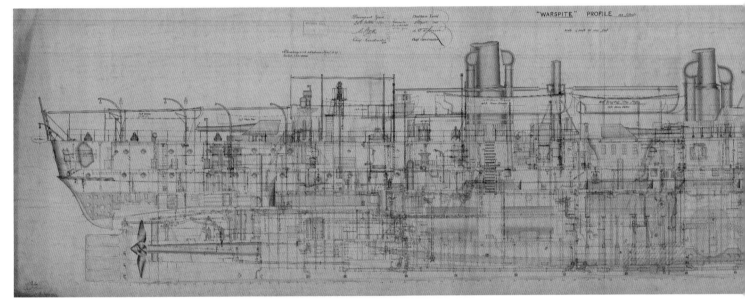

Right: In contrast to earlier British armoured cruisers (and the *Audacious* class), the *Orlando* class, represented here by *Galatea* (as at 27 January 1891, before her funnels were heightened) were intended primarily for fleet, rather than distant, service, although some did indeed serve commissions abroad. Developed from smaller protected cruiser designs they, like the *Imperieuse* class, came out over-weight, making their armour belts all but useless. The *Orlando*s nevertheless formed the basis for the Spanish *María Teresa* class.
(© National Maritime Museum, Greenwich, London, M0934)

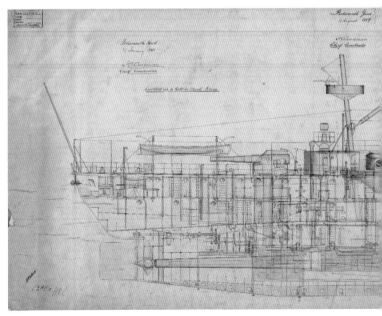

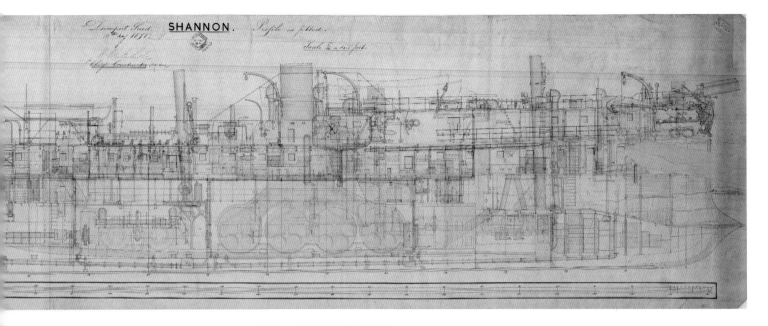

SHANNON. *Profile as fitted.*

Devonport yard
2 Aug 1876.

Scale 1/8 in to one foot.

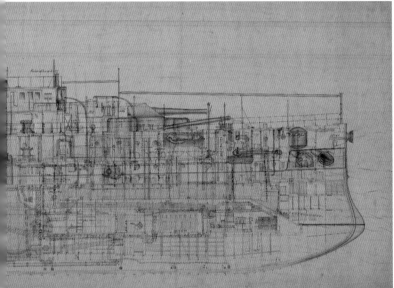

Left: The first British big cruisers to be built of steel, *Warspite* and her sister *Imperieuse* had poor reputations, but were an important move away from the broadside armament-based approach of earlier such vessels, in spite of detail problems (e.g. their abortive sailing rig) and excess weights. Like quite a few similar vessels of their era, they had their engines amidships, between the boiler rooms. *Warspite* is shown as modified down to April 1899, at the beginning of her last commission, as Pacific flagship.
(© National Maritime Museum, Greenwich, London, M0933)

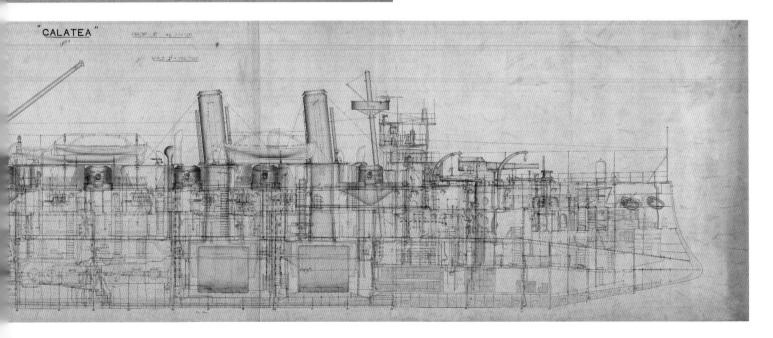

"CALATEA"   PROFILE AS FITTED
1884
SCALE 1/8 in to one foot

Right: A smaller design with the same speed, but omitting 9.2in guns, the *Monmouth* class was produced alongside the *Drake*s. The replacement of eight of the *Monmouth*s' 6in weapons with four of 7.5in calibre, together with a mixed watertube/cylindrical boiler installation, produced the *Devonshire* class, of which *Antrim* is an example. She had sixteen Yarrow boilers in the forward boiler rooms, with six cylindrical units in the aftermost compartment. The drawing shows *Antrim* with modifications to 1920, including a deckhouse directly aft of her foremost 7.5in turret which prevented it from training – of little import given her role at that time as a trials and training vessel. (© National Maritime Museum, Greenwich, London, J9269)

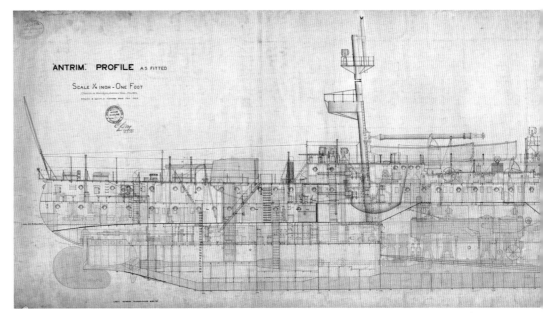

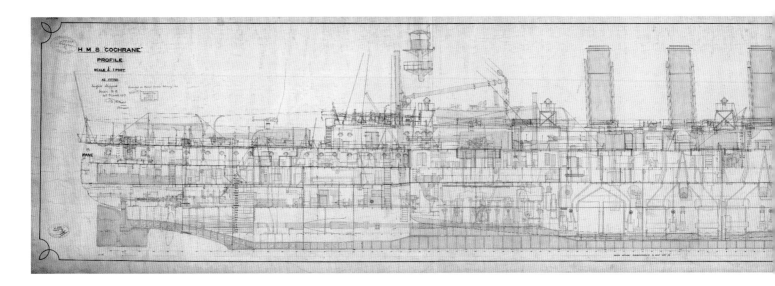

Right: The *Minotaur* class represented the final generation of the 'classic' British big cruiser, with the main 9.2in guns placed for the first time in twin mountings fore and aft, supplemented by single 7.5in turrets on the beam. Compared to their immediate predecessors, funnels and masts reverted to being rigged vertically, to reduce the strain on the mainmast derrick. Completed with short funnels, like the preceding two classes, those of the *Minotaur*s were subsequently raised, as sketched on the forefunnel only in this early drawing. (© National Maritime Museum, Greenwich, London, J9544)

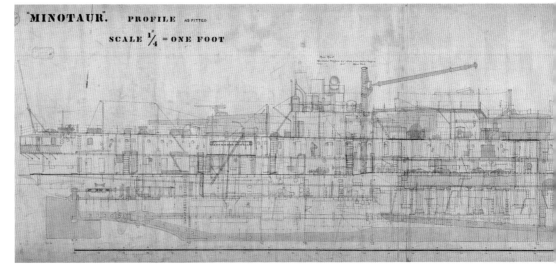

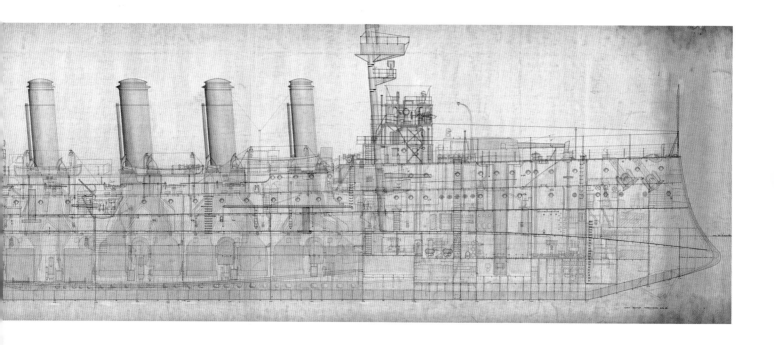

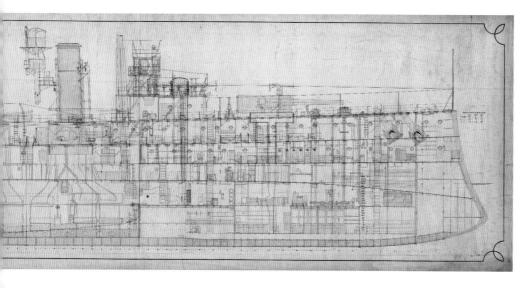

Left: The *Devonshire* class formed the basis for an enlarged design with a main battery of six 9.2in guns. The first pair, the *Duke of Edinburgh* class, carried 6in secondary guns on the main deck, soon realised to be carried too low for normal use. Thus, the final four, the *Warrior* class (represented here by *Cochrane*) replaced these with turreted 7.5in guns on the upper deck. As such, they were regarded as the best of the later British armoured cruisers, although only one was to survive to be scrapped after the First World War. *Cochrane* is shown as in February 1910, before the heightening of her funnels (© National Maritime Museum, Greenwich, London, J9539)

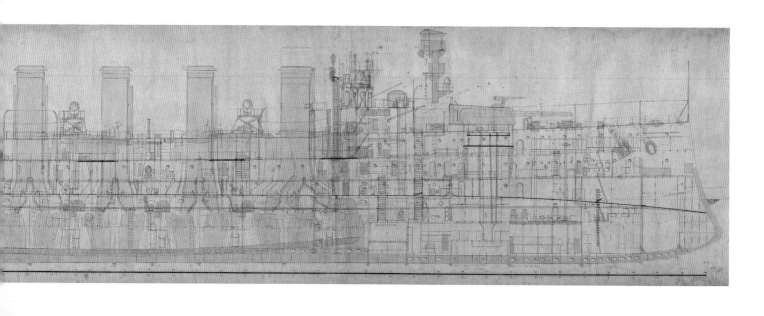

Germanic Expansion

Germany

Prior to the middle of the 1880s, German cruisers had been generally of no more than 3000 tons, and of wooden construction into the 1870s, most vessels being essentially training or overseas-station ships of minimal fighting value. Iron vessels had begun with the *Leipzig* class (1875–6), broadside-armed full-rigged corvettes which, like their wooden predecessors, generally spent much of their operational lives abroad.

The first modern (unrigged) cruisers in the German navy were the two 5000-ton *Irene* class, laid down in 1886, with fourteen 5.9in guns, an armour deck and a speed of 18kts. A third sister was originally envisaged, but was replaced in the programme with a much larger vessel, equally able to serve as a scout for the fleet in home waters and on detached service overseas. As such, *Kaiserin Augusta* (1892) was 1200 tons larger than the *Irene*s, and was designed to have, with a maximum speed of 21kts, a 4.5-knot margin over the *Brandenburg*-class battleships then being designed.

Following from *Kaiserin Augusta*, and following a debate between the Navy Office (one of the tripartite division of naval authority in Germany) favouring a combination of such large cruisers, and small vessels of ~1500 tons, and the High Command, which preferred a uniform force of cruisers of ~3000 tons, five deck-protected ships of something under 6000 tons were laid down during 1895–6, the *Victoria Louise* class, with a main battery of two 8.2in guns.

In addition to these new-construction vessels, between 1891 and 1897 three old (1860s/70s) broadside/central-battery ironclads *König Wilhelm*, *Kaiser* and *Deutschland* were rebuilt, and reclassified as cruisers. They were reboilered, had their superstructures enlarged and military masting added, but retained their old between-decks armaments,[78] albeit with the addition of modern medium and light guns on the upper deck. *König Wilhelm* received eighteen 3.5in, while *Kaiser* and *Deutschland* were more extensively re-armed; the former

Kaiser, as built as a central-battery armoured frigate. *(Author's collection)*

Her sister, *Deutschland*, rebuilt as a cruiser; the alterations to the *Kaiser* class were considerably more extensive than in *König Wilhelm*. *(Author's collection)*

Fürst Bismarck, in many ways the prototype battlecruiser, with the same armament as contemporary German battleships but lighter armour and higher speed. *(Author's collection)*

received a mix of six 4.1in and nine 3.5in guns, while her sister has eight 5.9in and eight 3.5in weapons. As rebuilt, the latter two vessels spent much of their remaining active careers as flagships in the Far East, although *König Wilhelm* remained in home waters.

Such conversions were of course only stop-gaps and, as well as the last two *Victoria Louise*s, 1896 saw the laying-down of

König Wilhelm as rebuilt as a large cruiser; she is shown here after her mizzenmast was removed in 1898 *(NHHC NH 47943)*

the 10,690-tonne *Fürst Bismarck*, the first German armoured cruiser. Nearly double the size of the *Victoria Louise* class, in other navies she could have qualified as a battleship, having exactly the same main battery as the contemporary *Kaiser Friedrich III*-class battleships, and like them had six of her secondary guns in the turrets. The same basic arrangement of armour was, however, generally only two-thirds the thickness of that of the battleships, and through the weight thus saved, coupled with a slightly longer hull (on the same beam) and an extra 500ihp, *Fürst Bismarck* was 1.2kts faster. Suitable as both a a fleet scout or distant-station capital ship, her entire front-line career was spent in the latter role, relieved *Deutschland* as the flagship of the East Asiatic Squadron[79] in 1900, and remaining there until 1909.

Austria-Hungary

As noted above (p 47), the ordering of the fourth 'ram-cruiser' (*D*) was delayed in favour of the construction of the first of a series of new coast-defence ships. A number of options had been investigated in 1891, all displacing 5090 tonnes, but modelled on different prototypes: *Kaiser Franz Joseph I*; the small torpedo-cruiser *Panther*; and HMS *Royal Arthur* (see pp 39–40).[80] The project was revived in 1894, when a 5800-ton vessel was sketched by the naval architect Josef Kellner, armed with two 9.4in (fore and aft), plus eight 5.9in in a main-deck battery, and rigged with a light military foremast and a pole main, with a single funnel. Kellner then followed this with a 6000-tonne ship, with the end pairs of 5.9in guns moved abreast of the 9.4in turrets, and two funnels (June 1895). A competing design was produced by Viktor Lollok (March 1895), of the same size, but with half the secondary battery in main-deck casemates and half in shields on the upper deck.

In the event, the Kellner design was adopted, albeit with watertube boilers (resulting in a three-funnelled silhouette), and laid down in June 1896. Launched as *Kaiser Karl VI* in October 1898 (after a delay caused by a major strike at her shipyard in 1897), the ship had the same new Krupp 9.4in/40 C/94 as the coast-defence ship *Monarch*, a weapon also mounted in the German battleships of the *Kaiser Friedrich III* class and armoured cruiser *Fürst Bismarck*; on the other hand, her 5.9in/40 were of Austro-Hungarian manufacture, by Škoda. A thousand tons larger than *Maria Theresia*, she had a third more power, an extra knot of speed, and much thicker

armour, making her an important addition to the Austro-Hungarian navy's strength when she commissioned in May 1900. She was the last warship to emerge from the Stablimento Tecnico Triestino's San Rocco yard, later construction shifting to the firm's refurbished San Marco facility. Following her trials, concerns were expressed about *Karl VI*'s stability, with the result that during November 1900, the foremast was lightened, the aft bridge and two 47mm/33 guns removed, and some rearrangement of upper coal bunkers undertaken.

Until 1898, the Austro-Hungarians had generally only activated a significant squadron of warships during the summer, which took part in manoeuvres before being laid up for the winter, leaving just one or two unarmoured cruisers active. However, for 1898–9, *Maria Theresia* and the coast-defence ship *Budapest* remained in service over the winter, at least one big ship being active every subsequent winter, *Kaiser Karl VI* serving thus for 1900–1.

Maria Theresia departed the Far East in the summer of 1900, along with *Kaiserin Elisabeth* and the small cruiser *Aspern*, to join the latter's sister *Zenta* (1897) as part of the international fleet operating off the Chinese coast during the Boxer Rebellion. *Maria Theresia* and *Aspern* remained in Far Eastern waters until 1902, being relieved by *Karl VI*, which served there until the autumn of 1903, then reducing to reserve at Pola as tender to the gunnery school.

Planning for *Ram Cruiser E* began alongside work on the *Erzherzog Karl*-class battleships.[81] A July 1899 scheme retained the two single 9.4in guns of earlier cruisers, but with an extra pair of 5.9in weapons, placed on the upper deck. However, the following April it was proposed that the secondary battery might be increased in calibre to 7.6in, although the previous 5.9in battery was for the time being preferred, with two options developed, one with the upper-deck 5.9in just aft of the bridge, the other placing them aft, the two 9.4in guns now being grouped in a twin turret forward.

In the event, when laid down in March 1901, the ship, to be named *Sankt Georg*, followed the latter arrangement for her two 9.4in/40 Škoda guns, but with a single 7.6in/42 mounting aft, four more in the midships battery, and four 5.9in in casemates fore and aft. This heavier secondary battery (also adopted for the *Erzherzog Karl*-class battleships) was intended to allow *Sankt Georg* to counter the three contemporary Italian *Garibaldi* class (p 60), with their 10in + 8in main batteries, and also reflected contemporary international trends. *Sankt Georg* was also another thousand tons larger than *Karl VI*, had an extra 3000ihp, for 2kt extra speed, and a slightly thinner belt (of Krupp, rather than Harvey, plate), but a thicker deck. Her completion, along with that of the *Erzherzog Karl* class, was funded under a special credit of May 1904, which also provided for a large new fleet of large and small torpedo boats.

In the meantime, *Maria Theresia* had been re-rigged with pole masts in 1903, and then had her old 9.4in weapons replaced by modern 7.6in pieces in 1906. She was then rebuilt in 1910, with a rearrangement of armament (including the deletion of the secondary-battery sponsons, and placing all the

Austria-Hungary's second armoured cruiser (nominally a 'torpedo-ram cruiser) *Kaiser Karl VI* as built. (*NHHC NH 87380*)

Sankt Georg at Abbazia (Opatija) on the Dalmatian coast, during 1912. *(NHHC NH 87396)*

5.9in guns in new embrasures on the upper deck) and new fully-cased funnels.

A fourth armoured cruiser was planned in parallel with the *Radetzky*-class battleships (laid down 1907) and what was to become the small cruisers of the *Admiral Spaun* class (laid down from 1908 onwards).[82] The ship was to be of 8000 tons and 23kt speed, with a range of armament options considered. Option A had eight 7.6in/45 in twin turrets fore and aft, and on the beam, amidships; Option B had a single 9.4in/45 fore and aft, with six 7.6in/45 in a main-deck battery; Option C raised the main-battery calibre to 28cm/45, with four 7.6in/45 in the battery; Option D was identical, but with 12in/45 main

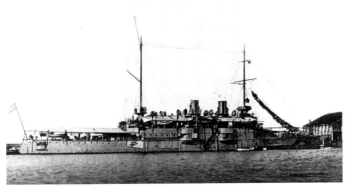

The earlier *Kaiserin und Königin Maria Theresa* around 1908, as rebuilt with pole masts. *(NHHC NH 87353)*

guns; and Option E had ten 7.6in, in twin turrets fore and aft, and six in the battery. In the event, however, no ship was ordered, and no further big cruiser was contemplated by Austria-Hungary until 1915, when a series of fully-fledged battlecruiser designs were begun, ranging from 30,000 to 40,000 tons, and armed with 13.8in, 15in or even 16.5in guns;[83] in addition, in 1918, the 10/12,000t, six 7.6in/45-armed 'Project VII' was also sketched.[84]

A further expansion of the force remaining active over the winter began in 1904, after which three newest battleships were in kept in service year-round, supplemented from 1905–6 by either *Kaiser Karl VI* or *Sankt Georg*, two armoured cruisers being available over the summer from 1906 onwards. Whichever armoured cruiser not active over the winter formed part of a new Reserve Squadron, along with the second-newest three battleships.

During April–June 1907 *Sankt Georg* and the small cruiser *Aspern* (1899) represented Austria-Hungary at the Jamestown Tricentennial Exhibition,[85] participating in the naval review on 10 June, which also included the French armoured cruisers *Kléber* and *Victor Hugo* and the American *Brooklyn*, *Washington* and *Tennessee*. Three years later, during March–September 1910, *Kaiser Karl VI* deployed to South America to participate in the Argentine Centennial celebrations and visit a number of ports in Uruguay and Brazil. That autumn, the newly-rebuilt *Maria Theresia* was sent to Salonika to protect Austro-Hungarian interests and subjects during the First Balkan War (see p 113, below).

4 | THE GOLDEN AGE

The Bertin Era in France

Jeanne d'Arc

A new French Navy Minister, Edouard Lockroy (1838–1913) came into office in November 1895, and replaced the planned second *D'Entrecasteaux* in the 1896 programme with an armoured cruiser of a wholly new design by Emile Bertin, now back from Japan and appointed Principal Director of Naval Construction in 1896. This ship was to be some 40 per cent larger than the planned ship and the two commerce raiders of the previous year. As large as the battleships of the *Charlemagne* class, laid down between 1894 and 1896, the intended purpose of the new ship, *Jeanne d'Arc* (ii), remains somewhat obscure, being described at various points during her construction as both a commerce raider and as a ship for fleet service. At the root of this was the continuing turmoil over French naval policy, with the frequent changes in ministry also making coherent requirement-setting and implementation all but impossible.[86]

Jeanne d'Arc was certainly designed to be fast (23kt), much of her size, like that of the British *Powerful* class, being a result of needing to install machinery nearly three times as powerful as in *Pothuau* and double that in the *Charlemagne*s. However, in spite of exceeding her designed power by more than 15 per cent, *Jeanne d'Arc* made only 21.8kt on trials – over a knot short – in spite of some two years on trial. Her tactical diameter proved to be twice that of comparable vessels, while she also proved to be an uneconomical steamer, and later had her original thirty-six boilers replaced by forty-eight of a different pattern. These were arranged in four boiler rooms in two groups, each exhausting through three funnels, fore and aft of the engine rooms, following the scheme introduced in French practice in *Guichen*, and which would be used in all subsequent French big cruisers; *Jeanne d'Arc* reverted to *Dupuy de Lôme*'s triple shafts, as would all later big cruisers in France.

Forward, protection also followed *Dupuy de Lôme* in extending the entire height of the forecastle, but in contrast only reached up to the main deck aft of the forefunnel. Above main-belt level the side armour was a uniform 3.1in, the belt itself being 5.9in thick (Harvey – the first use of the material in France) amidships, thinning forward and aft. The armour

The French *Jeanne d'Arc* (ii) marked a major increase in dimensions as compared to earlier vessels, much of it owing to a desire for higher speed, and resulting in a relatively light armament for her size. She is shown here early in her career, with various French battleships and a cruiser in the background. *(Author's collection)*

The protected cruiser *Jurien de la Gravière* was envisaged as a reduced *D'Entrecasteaux* for overseas service, but emerged as a prototype for the next generations of French armoured cruisers. *(Author's collection)*

deck was 1.8in thick on the flats, the slopes 2.2in amidships and 1.8in fore and aft. There was also a splinter deck a level above, sandwiching the main belt, with a cofferdam behind the belt and close subdivision within the 'sandwich'. This 'cellular layer' was intended to provide a 'raft' with sufficient volume to preserve floatation, whatever damage was done above it, and would be characteristic of all Bertin-designed or inspired big ships.

Armament comprised a single 7.6in/45 fore and aft, with fourteen 5.5in/45 on the beam, eight in upper-deck casemates and six in shields at forecastle-deck level. All thus had good command, in contrast to the main-deck casemates in contemporary British vessels. Nevertheless, the ship was much criticised for carrying such a light armament for her size, with only two 5.5in more than the 30 per cent smaller *D'Entrecasteaux*: as with the other giant cruisers of the period, armament was a key element traded-off in search of high speed.

After her extended trials, *Jeanne d'Arc* finally joined the fleet in 1903, carrying President Loubet to Algiers in April, before relieving *Bruix* as flagship of Northern Squadron cruisers, including *Guichen* and *Dupuy de Lôme*, on 1 June. In July 1906 she was transferred to the Mediterranean as flagship of the Light Squadron, until relieved by *Jules Ferry* in 1908, when *Jeanne d'Arc* returned to the Northern Squadron, forming the 2nd Division with *Marseillaise* (flag) and *Gueydon* until reduced to reserve the following year. She returned to service in March 1912, when she replaced the former troopship *Duguay-Trouin* (ex-*Tonkin*, 1878) as cadet training ship, in which role she remained until the summer of 1914.

The armoured cruiser programme

A reduced *D'Entrecasteaux* was inserted into the 1897 programme – only to have it rejected by the *Conseil de Traveaux*, who declared the armoured cruiser to be the way ahead. However, with the support of the Chamber of Deputies, the ship was after all built as the 5595-ton protected station cruiser *Jurien de la Gravière* (1899) In overall appearance she looked like a cut-down *Guichen*, but was actually very different in lines, and the ancestor of the next generations of French armoured cruisers. A second ship was projected to be built under contract, but was never ordered.

The desired armoured cruisers appeared in the 1898 programme, an original pair being joined by four more, balanced by the deletion of the battleship originally included. Three (initially four, to be the *Kléber* class) were intended for distant stations (in spite of the *Conseil de Traveaux* objecting that no such dedicated vessels were needed), while the other three (originally two, the *Gueydon* class) would be essentially reduced *Jeanne d'Arcs*, suitable for general duties. Five more of the latter type of ship (which became the *Gloire* class) were added by Lockroy when he returned as Navy Minister in June 1898, three as additions to the 1897–8 programme, the final two under that for 1898–9. Designed again by Bertin, the hull-form of the *Gueydons* would also form the basis of that of the *Patrie* class battleships, approved in 1900.

The new cruisers were seen by Admiral Ernest-François Fournier (1842–1932), the navy's leading theoretician and mentor to Minister Lockroy, as being capable, when combined with torpedo craft, of carrying out all the key tasks of modern naval warfare. Thus, they should be able to successfully engage enemy fleet units, scout, raid commerce, and act as station ships abroad. In Fournier's view, 117 such cruisers and 300 torpedo boats would suffice for all France's needs.

Another view on the role of the big cruiser had been expounded discussed back in 1893, when a paper to the Institute of Naval Architects by Rear-Admiral Samuel Long (1840–93) coined, apparently for the first time, the term 'battle-cruiser' for big vessels with high speed, long endurance and good seakeeping qualities that could act in support of 2nd and 3rd class cruisers patrolling the trade-routes.[87] Such views on the utility of the armoured cruiser would be an important theme over the following two decades.

THE *GUEYDON* CLASS

The first ship of the programme to be laid down was *Gueydon*, which followed *Jeanne d'Arc* in her basic pattern of belt/deck protection, albeit now terminating short of the stern, where a transverse bulkhead closed the belt and decks, and the forward side armour only carried to the upper deck. The main battery remained the same, but *Jeanne d'Arc*'s forecastle-deck 5.5in guns were omitted in favour of four 3.9in mountings at the same level; the forecastle was now extended almost to the stern, raising the aft turret by one deck. In contrast, the 47mm battery was increased by four guns, the latter installed in main-deck embrasures abreast the 6.5in mountings fore and aft; the forward pair will have been particularly difficult to work in a seaway. The remaining guns remained in the superstructure.

The first vessel of the group to complete, *Montcalm*, entered service in March 1902, and proceeded to the Far East in 1903, in the company of *D'Entrecasteaux* and the protected cruisers *Bugeaud* (1893) and *Pascal* (1895), returning in 1906 for repairs to a damaged propeller. After a period in reserve, she returned east in 1910, accompanied by the protected cruiser *Alger* (1889) staying until the following spring,

beginning yet a third tour based on Saigon in January 1913; she was still in the Far East in August 1914.

Gueydon herself spent nearly two years on trials, before commissioning for service in the Far East in September 1903, joining *Montcalm*; the third ship of the class, *Dupetit-Thouars*, arrived on station in 1905. Returning in 1906, *Gueydon* and *Dupetit-Thouars* became members of the Northern Squadron in January 1907. *Gueydon*, with *Jeanne d'Arc* and *Gloire* (p 71, below), moved to the Mediterranean in October 1909. She was employed in various reserve functions from 1910 until 1914, when she became a seagoing training ship. *Dupetit-Thouars* was in reserve from 1911 until the outbreak of the First World War.

THE LAST 'STATION ARMOURED CRUISERS'

Kléber was the second ship of the programme to be laid down, and was some 20 per cent smaller than *Gueydon*, with significantly lighter armament (no 7.6in) and protection (belt 4in maximum, rather than 5.9in, restricted to the waterline and ending at the aft turret). On the other hand, her primary armament of four twin 6.5in/45 mountings introduced a new model gun to service, which that would form the secondary batteries of all later armoured cruisers. The turrets were disposed in the lozenge manner that had been typical of French battleships down to *Bouvet*, laid down in 1893. In appearance, she was much 'lighter' than the *Gueydon*s, with a pole, rather than military, foremast.

Two sisters, *Dupleix* and *Desaix*, were laid down at the beginning of 1899, differing from *Kléber* in having Niclausse, rather than Belleville, boilers. Niclausse units caused problems in many vessels so-fitted (cf. pp 87, 108), the career of *Dupleix* being particularly plagued by problems with hers, reducing to reserve for five years after only a few months' service in 1904, suffering further problems while serving in the Far East during 1910–14, and again while operating off East Africa during the First World War.

Kléber was launched entirely complete (with steam up on some boilers), with a view to her running her first trials within six days, as was long the custom of her builders. Unfortunately, she damaged her bottom during the launch, and it was not until three months later that she was able to leave the yard.

Gloire as completed; she and her sisters differed from the preceding *Gueydon* class principally in the arrangement of their secondary batteries. *(NHHC NH 64264)*

Dupleix, the last French armoured cruiser built specifically for duty on distant stations. *(Author's collection)*

Furthermore, her trials were long and difficult, the ship joining the fleet in July 1904.

Although designed for distant stations, the ships began their careers in home waters, *Desaix* never going abroad in peacetime, while *Kléber* went to the West Indies during 1906–7 and then the Far East during 1911–12, joining *Dupleix*, which was there from 1910 to 1914. From the outset the ships were regarded as weak in comparison with foreign vessels, and combined with questions being raised at the wisdom of building two types of armoured cruisers at the same time, it was decided that future construction would concentrate on the heavier, general-purpose *Gueydon* type.

THE *GLOIRE* CLASS

Although intended to be essentially identical to the *Gueydon*s, in 1898 it was decided to modify the next three ships, *Gloire*, *Condé* and *Sully*, by moving the midships four 6.5in guns up to forecastle-deck turrets, but dropping the aft casemates to the main-deck. Thus, while the command of four weapons was significantly improved, that of the aft two was worsened. The number of 3.9in guns was increased to six, while two more 47mm weapons were also added, eight of them now placed in main-deck embrasures. This low-placement of anti-torpedo-boat battery was common in many ships of the period, being based on the low-lying nature of the target; unfortunately it failed to take into account the reality of fighting guns at that level in any kind of sea. The openings also threatened the safety of the ship, as all-but-impossible to seal and liable to be placed under water in the event of a list caused by damage.[88] Installed power was increased by 900ihp, and displacement by 900 tons. Two more ships of the class, *Marseillaise* and *Amiral Aube*, were subsequently ordered with some minor changes. As with most French cruiser classes, there were differences between vessels concerning the height and shape of the ventilators on the upper deck.

The first of these five ships into service was *Marseillaise*, which joined *Jeanne d'Arc* and *Guichen* in the Northern Squadron in October 1903, being transferred a year later to the Mediterranean, where she joined *Desaix* and *Kléber* in the Light Squadron, as its flagship from October 1905 to July 1907. *Condé* also began her active career in August 1904 in the Northern Squadron, along with *Gloire* and *Amiral Aube*. In September 1905 she went to the Mediterranean, and in April 1906 she accompanied USS *Brooklyn*, carrying the body of John Paul Jones (1747–92), from Paris to Annapolis, MD, for re-interment.

Unlike her full-sisters' initial service in home waters, *Sully* went straight to the Far East to join her half-sisters *Montcalm* and *Gueydon* in 1904, after a year on trials, including a period awaiting repairs to a damaged propeller and rudder. Her service there was short: on 7 February 1905 she ran aground in Along (Ha Long) Bay. Salvage proved impossible and, after guns and equipment had been salvaged, the wreck broke in two during an autumn typhoon. Stricken a month later, the wreck was sold for scrap in 1906.

At around 15.00 on 7 February 1905, *Sully* ran onto rocks in Along Bay while carrying out trials. A 200ft gash was opened in the port side, the ship settling steadily by the head. *Montcalm*, *Gueydon* and smaller vessels brought out salvage equipment, with work continuing into April, with suggestions that the hulk of *Vauban* and the transport *Européen* might be of use in salvage attempts. Ultimately, however, the ship remained stuck, and after guns and equipment had recovered, the wreck was damaged in a typhoon on 30 August, and finally broke in two and sank in 50ft of water following a second typhoon on 28 September. *(Author's collection)*

The Sino-Japanese War

War broke out between China and Japan in July 1894, as the culmination of long-standing disputes over the future of Korea. On 17 September, the Japanese fleet and the Chinese Peiyang fleet, which had just finished escorting a troop convoy, clashed off the mouth of the Yalu River. The Japanese force included *Chiyoda* and seven protected cruisers, plus two older ironclads, while the Chinese one was headed by their two battleships, supported by the two *King Yuen*s, *Ping Yuen* and the three modern protected cruisers, plus smaller vessels. Early on, *Lai Yuen* badly mauled the Japanese gunboat *Akagi* (1888), before herself being set on fire by a single shell from her opponent, and then heavily hit by the Japanese Flying Squadron of fast protected cruisers (*Yoshino* [1892], *Takachiho* [1885], *Akitsushima* [1892] and *Naniwa* [1885]). Although ablaze amidships, and ultimately burnt out in this area, *Lai Yuen*'s machinery remained undamaged, the ship managing to withdraw towards Port Arthur.

Regarding *Lai Yuen* as in a sinking condition, the Flying Squadron switched its attention to her sister *King Yuen*, which had been under fire for over an hour when, with her main magazine apparently flooded, and after an apparent attempt to ram *Yoshino*, she fell over to port at 16.48, heavily on fire; she rolled over and sank soon afterwards, following a large explosion, with only seven survivors. *Ping Yuen* traded salvoes with the Japanese flagship *Matsushima* (1890), receiving a single 12.6in hit, and landing one 10.2in hit in exchange; although this wrecked a torpedo tube, the shell did not explode. *Chih Yuen*, two of the Chinese small cruisers and a sloop were also sunk, and while a number of Japanese ships had suffered significant damage, none was lost.

The Chinese survivors made Port Arthur to begin repairs, but all were withdrawn to Waihaiwei on 20 October, in view of the likelihood of a landward siege from the Japanese army (Port Arthur fell on 20 November). The ships remained largely inactive at Waihaiwei, which itself came under siege in January 1895. Some counter-bombardment was undertaken by *Ting Yuen*, *Tsi Yuen* and *Ping Yuen* (*Chen Yuen* had been damaged by running aground back at Port Arthur, while *Lai Yuen* still required further post-Yalu repairs), but *Ting Yuen* was sunk by Japanese torpedo boats on 2/3 February, and *Lai Yuen* the following night, the latter capsizing in shallow water. Various other ships had also been sunk by the time the port was surrendered on 16 February, only *Ping Yuen*, *Tsi Yuen* and *Chen Yuen* of the bigger ships surviving to be incorporated into the Japanese navy. *Ping Yuen* first became *Pingyuan-go*, was redesignated a first-class gunboat on 21 March 1898, and renamed *Heien* in 1900.

Japan

In 1896, in the wake of the Sino-Japanese War, the doctrine was promulgated that in future the Japanese fleet should be led by six battleships and six protected cruisers (the '6–6 Plan'). However, the ongoing expansion of the Russian Pacific squadron led to concerns that the six battleships would not

Asama as built; she was in essence a development of the Chilean O'Higgins. *(Author's collection)*

Azuma as built, the French interpretation of the Japanese 6–6 programme armoured cruiser specification. *(NHHC NH 58990)*

Iwate, at Plymouth en route from her builders to Japan. *(Author's collection)*

necessarily be sufficient. However, as there was insufficient funding to increase the number of such vessels in the Japanese fleet, the cruisers envisaged under the 6–6 Plan were upgraded to much more powerful armoured cruisers that could form part of the battle line. This added yet another role to the repertoire of the big cruiser, alongside those of commerce raiding/protection, distant station capital ship, and fleet scout that had emerged in various navies over past decades.

Five ships were ordered in 1897 (two under the First Naval Expansion Programme, the rest under the Second), with a

Yakumo completing at Stettin; she would remain in seagoing service for forty-six years. (NHHC NH 58993)

further vessel in 1898.[89] Orders went to three yards, Armstrong's in Great Britain, the Chantiers de la Loire in France, and Vulcan in Germany. The armament and overall capabilities of the new ships were developed in conjunction with Armstrong's, the first pair, *Asama* and *Tokiwa*, being laid down in June 1896 on while negotiations were still underway, and only 'sold' to Japan a year later, by which time they ships had been on the slip for eight and six months, respectively.[90]

Their design was based on the Chilean *O'Higgins*, going through a number of iterations, mainly concerning improving the protection, until finalised in August 1896. Compared with their prototype, they were a thousand tons larger, had cylindrical boilers, had their 8in in twin mountings, and four more 6in, with double-deck casemates for the foremost and rearmost weapons; four of the 6in were in open mountings on the upper deck. Completed in the spring of 1899, both ships would have very long careers, as would be the case with all of the six cruisers of the programme.[91] In her early years, *Asama* would act as Imperial viewing ship during annual naval reviews by the Emperor.

The characteristics of the *Asama* class then formed the basis of the international Japanese specification, although the individual yards had some leeway in the detailed design of the ships. Armstrong's received orders for follow-on vessels in September 1897 and July 1898, *Izumo* and *Iwate* differing from the *Asama*s principally in having watertube boilers (and hence three funnels), slightly different dimensions, one less torpedo tube, and differently arranged armour, now of Krupp type. The belt amidships was now a uniform 7in thickness (rather than tapering to 5in outside the machinery spaces), the armour deck 2.5in (rather than 2in, with a 1in main deck over the machinery), and continued all the way to the stern. The two ships were both completed during the autumn and winter of 1900–01.

The French and German vessels, *Azuma* and *Yakumo*, differed from the British ones principally in having twelve secondary guns, and shared with the second British pair Krupp armour. *Azuma* was also longer than her half-sisters,[92] but a knot slower in service, and with less of the side covered by the

main and upper belts. She could be easily distinguished by the gap between her second and third funnels, caused by a compartment worked-in between the between aft and the forward boiler room. *Yakumo* was actually the second-last to be laid down, but the third to arrive in Japan, on 30 October 1900.

The British Return to Side Armour

While, as noted above (p 38), the British had, during the early 1890s, regarded protective decks as adequate by themselves, developments in armour manufacture were by 1897 making it possible to procure 6in plate as effective as nearly double that thickness only a few years earlier. Thus, 6in of Krupp Cemented armour was as effective as 7.5in of Harvey, which was equivalent of 12in of steel, 13in of compound and 15in of wrought iron armour. This paralleled improvements in shells and guns that made deck-only protection less effective, the two issues combining to mean that the next set of British big cruisers would mark a return to the side armour last seen in the *Orlando*s.

The availability of the new armour also meant a change in the ways in which the British considered that they could use big cruisers, as it was now possible to give a cruiser armour equivalent to that of a battleship, yet keep size and cost down to a reasonable level. Thus, White now argued that it was possible to produce a cruiser that could 'come to *close quarters* with the enemy without running undue risks', operating alongside battleships as their fast wing. Some inspiration came from of the *Garibaldi*s, whose armament and armour had been selected to allow them to make up for Italy's problems with funding battleships. On the other, as well as a fleet role in 'the performance of all duties hitherto devolving on 1st class cruisers attached to [the Channel and Mediterranean] fleets' and having 'the capacity for close action as adjuncts to battleships', the new ships were also to be suitable for detached

Vengeance, one of the British *Canopus*-class battleships, intended for overseas service, but still regarded as a 1st class vessel; their belts were the same thickness as the contemporary *Cressy*-class cruisers. (NHHC NH 52622)

service, 'if required to be used in the protection of shipping, commerce & communications'.

Accordingly, a design was presented to the Board of Admiralty for the 1897–8 Estimates that had the same 6in midships and 2in forward belt armour as the previous year's *Canopus*-class battleships. They also shared the latter's two armoured decks over the citadel, with the curved armour (lower) deck 1.5in thick (in *Canopus* 2in) and the main deck of 1in plate (as in *Canopus*).[93] These equivalences are interesting in that *Canopus* and her five sisters, although classified as 1st class battleships, were actually designed particularly for service in the Far East, as lightweight, faster versions of the *Majestic* class, thus having conceptually much in common with such early 'proto-armoured cruisers' as the *Audacious* class, and also more recent *Centurion*s.

Ships of the new type were ordered under the 1897–8 Estimates, to become the six-ship *Cressy* class. Although superficially similar to the *Diadem*s, they were a thousand tons larger, with 50 per cent more of their displacement dedicated to protection, and greatly enhanced powers of offense provided by two of the new 9.2in/46.7 Mk X gun, placed fore and aft; twelve 6in (also of a new, 45-calibre, Mk VII, type) were installed in the now-usual mix of double and single casemates on the beam.

Machinery was a higher-powered version of that of *Diadem*, producing designed speed of 21kt. This was significantly below the nominal 23kt of *Jeanne d'Arc*, the obvious foreign comparator (her actual maximum of 21.8kt was not yet known), but White argued that the latter was unrealistic as a sustained speed, and that if forced to the degree necessary to get the Frenchman up to 23kt, the *Cressy*s could match it.

Five of the ships commissioned during 1901–2, the name-ship going to the China Station, with the others split between the Mediterranean and Channel Fleets. The exception was *Euryalus*, which, although launched only three months after *Bacchante*, then suffered a series of mishaps[94] and was not finally finished until the beginning of 1904, after which she proceeded to Australia as station flagship.

Following on from the building of the *Cressy*s, a proposal

Cressy, as completed in Victorian livery, which was abandoned by the Royal Navy in 1902, not long after the ship's completion. *(NHHC NH 61848)*

was submitted to the Admiralty by Vickers to bring the *Powerful* and *Diadem* classes up to near-*Cressy* standards, by adding a 4in belt midships, thinning to 2in forward and closed by a 4in bulkhead aft, with the option in the case of the *Diadem*s to replace their forward and aft pairs of 6in guns each with a single 7.5in. This was, however, turned down, there being concerns that the extra weight would bring the main-deck batteries even closer to the waterline, would reduce speed and probably not be cost-effective.

The German Fleet Laws
Driven by the State Secretary at the Navy Office, Admiral Alfred von Tirpitz (1849–1930), the first of a series of laws placing the size of the German Navy on a statutory basis came into effect on 10 April 1898. As far as larger cruisers were concerned, it noted a baseline of ten existing ships (*König Wilhelm*, the *Kaiser*s and *Fürst Bismarck*, plus *Kaiserin Augusta* and the *Victoria Louise*s, which were formally classified together as 'large cruisers'), and set their lifespans as twenty years from date of original authorisation, after which replacements could be procured. It then set the required strength in such ships as six for use as scouting vessels on home service, three on foreign service and three as material reserve.

Thus, under the Law, five new 'large' cruisers were needed – three to replace ships already over-age (the ex-ironclads), plus two additional new-construction vessels. Following German practice (which did not reveal a ship's name until launch), the first three new builds were according given the provisional names *Ersatz-König Wilhelm*, *Ersatz-Kaiser* and *Ersatz-Deutschland*, the other two being *Large Cruiser A* and *Large Cruiser B*.

Large Cruiser A (to be *Prinz Heinrich*) was the first of the additional vessels in this category to be ordered. A desire for economy resulted in a ship 17 per cent smaller than *Fürst Bismarck*, with half the main battery and two less secondary guns; she was also not sheathed and metalled, as intended primarily for home service. As such, *Prinz Heinrich* was comparable to contemporary British *Cressy*, French *Amiral Aube* and Russian *Bayan* (p 79) in armament, capability and fleet role.

Prinz Heinrich marked a significant technical advance over *Fürst Bismarck*, and in many ways represented the prototype for the next generation of not only German armoured cruisers, but capital ships in general, in particular as concerned her protective scheme, which was also adopted by for the *Wittelsbach*-class battleships (1900–01). Taking into account the advent of new armours allowed more strength for a given thickness, the narrow waterline belt in *Fürst Bismarck* was replaced by a 'citadel' arrangement, providing a much greater armoured freeboard amidships.

Her secondary battery was concentrated in this amidships area, in four turrets and six casemates. This not only protected the 5.9in guns in the battery, but also the bases and ammunition-supply to the turreted 5.9in weapons. The new ship's underwater hull-form was also altered, especially aft, with

THE GOLDEN AGE • 75

Prinz Heinrich, the prototype for later German armoured cruisers and protectively also for the following generations of battleships. (*Author's collection*)

the upper-deck arrangement also cleaned up, and military masts replaced by poles.

Prinz Heinrich spent her life in home waters, of which only a few years were in front-line service. She was a gunnery training ship between 1908 and 1912, before paying off in 1912 on relief by the newer *Prinz Adalbert*, remaining out of commission until the outbreak of the First World War.

From the 1900 programme onwards, one large cruiser was authorised each year. The first of these was *Large Cruiser B* (to

be *Prinz Adalbert*), the second the replacement for *König Wilhelm* (to be *Friedrich Carl*), ordered in 1901. In most features they followed *Prinz Heinrich*, with the key exceptions of an enhancement of protection, and the replacement of the single 9.4in main-battery guns with twin 8.2in/40s mountings. However, the *Prinz Adalbert*s looked very different from their prototype, with three funnels, rather than the originally planned two, and military masts.

Although *Friedrich Carl* commissioned within eighteen months of her launch, her elder sister was delayed by a lack of capacity at Kiel Dockyard, taking two-and-a-half years from launch to completion. Both ships spent most of their pre-war service in training and trials roles – indeed, *Prinz Adalbert* did not see any fleet service until August 1914.

A flaw in the 1898 Fleet Law was that once its totals had been reached, and over-age ships replaced, the feast for the shipbuilding industry would be replaced by a famine. A gap in ship-authorisations back in the late 1870s and early 1880s would mean no capital ships being ordered between 1905 and 1912, after which block-obsolescence would produce up to a dozen orders over five years. Such a build-drumbeat was clearly industrially unsustainable, as well as operationally undesirable. Thus, a Second Fleet Law became effective on 14 June 1900, raising, inter alia, the large cruiser establishment to fourteen (eight as scouts at home, three overseas and three in reserve).

Friedrich Carl, which spent much of her career as a torpedo trials ship. (*Author's collection*)

Roon in the Kiel Canal. *(Author's collection)*

The wreck of *Maine* in Havana harbour on 15 February 1898; her loss to an internal explosion was a catalyst for the outbreak of the Spanish-American War. *(NHHC UA 477.26)*

Two further additional constructions were thus needed, *Large Cruisers C* and *D*.

In the meantime, 1902 and 1903 programmes had provided for *Ersatz-Kaiser* (to be *Roon*) and *Ersatz-Deutschland* (*Yorck*). A further modest modification of the *Prinz Heinrich/Prinz Adalbert* design, they were lengthened slightly amidships to accommodate two extra boilers (resulting in four funnels), for an additional 2000ihp and another 0.5kt of speed.

As in the previous class of large cruisers, the Dockyard-built lead ship (*Roon*) languished for over two years fitting-out, while her privately-built and later-started sister, was completed half a year earlier. As completed, neither made their intended 22kts, the length-breadth ratio (dictated by dock-dimensions at Wilhelmshaven) being found inappropriate.

The Spanish-American War

Relations between the USA and Spain had been becoming increasingly tense as the 1890s progressed, particularly over Cuba, the last remaining major Spanish possession in the Americas. An independence movement there culminated in the outbreak of a rebellion in 1895, the Spanish reaction to which appalled US opinion, US commercial interests also being threatened by the conflict. Attempts to reach a settlement effectively ended when *Maine*, which had arrived at Havana on 25 January 1898 to protect US interests, was destroyed by a magazine explosion on 15 February. An official enquiry blamed this on a mine – although later studies indicated a fire in a coal bunker as the most probable cause[95]

– contributing to a sequence of events that culminated in a US ultimatum to Spain demanding Cuban independence; Spain declared war on 23 April.

In the Pacific, the small Spanish naval force in the Philippines was destroyed at the Battle of Manila Bay on 1 May, followed by a blockade of Manila itself. This gave rise to tension, when the commander of the German ships among a group of international vessels (including *Kaiser*, *Immortalité* and *Bruix*) that arrived soon after the battle to protect their national interests objected to the Americans' claim of the right to board foreign warships. Manila fell to US land forces on 13 August, while Guam had been seized by the protected cruiser *Charleston* (i – 1888) on 21 June.

In the Atlantic, a squadron comprising the armoured cruisers *Infanta María Teresa* (flag), *Almirante Quendo*, *Vizcaya* and *Cristóbal Colón* (still awaiting her main guns, leaving her 6in battery as her heaviest weapons), plus the destroyers *Pluton* (1897), *Terror* and *Furor* (1896), was ordered to the east coast of America. Fear that they might bombard US cities led to a division of the American North Atlantic Squadron, *Brooklyn* leading a Flying Squadron, along with the battleships *Texas* and *Massachusetts* (1893). The rump North Atlantic Squadron, led by *New York*, had the monitors *Puritan* (1882) and *Terror* (1883) attached to make up numbers, would, on 27 April, fire the first shots of the war, when *New York*, *Puritan* and the protected cruiser

Cristóbal Colón and *Vizcaya* at the Cape Verde Islands between mid-April 1898, and 29 April, when they sailed for the West Indies. *(NHHC NH 88613)*

Cincinatti (1892) fired on Spanish defences at Matanzas, east of Havana. On 12 May, the squadron, now comprising *New York*, *Terror*, the battleships *Iowa* (1896) and *Indiana* (1893), the monitor *Amphitrite* (1883), the unprotected cruiser *Detroit* (1891), a torpedo boat, a tug and a collier, bombarded San Juan, Puerto Rico.

Having eluded US ships, the Spanish cruiser squadron (less *Terror*, detached to Puerto Rico, where she was damaged in attempting to run the US blockade) arrived at Santiago de Cuba, on 19 May; there they joined the unprotected cruiser *Reina Mercedes* (1887), largely immobilised by boiler defects. An American blockade was, however, imposed from 1 June with the arrival of *New York*, leading a combined force of the North Atlantic Squadron and the Flying Squadron. An attempt was made on 3 June to block the harbour by scuttling the collier *Merrimac* (1894) in the channel, but shore batteries disabled the ship as she approached, the drifting hulk being fired on by *Reina Mercedes*, *Vizcaya* and *Pluton*; *Merrimac* sank clear of the channel. Regular bombardments of Santiago and its environs were carried out by the American force, *Vizcaya*, *Reina Mercedes* and *Furor* all being hit on 6 June. On 1 July, to the southeast of Santiago, at the mouth of the Aguadores River, *New York* led a bombardment that was part of an unsuccessful diversionary attack in support of operations to the east, before returning to the blockade line.

By then, it was clear to the Spanish that their ships could not remain in Santiago, while US land forces were now advancing on the port (albeit decimated by disease). Accordingly, the ships were ordered to break out, their departure being was planned for 09.00 on 3 July, except for *Reina Mercedes*, whose boiler defects could not be repaired.[96] The Spanish ships slipped at 08.45, soon after two ships of the blockading force, *New York*, and the torpedo boat *Ericsson* (1894) had left their positions to convey the admiral to a conference, opening a gap in the western part of the blockade line; the battleship *Massachusetts* and the protected cruisers *Newark* (1888) and *New Orleans* (1896) had also left that morning to coal. Leadership of the American force thus devolved on *Brooklyn*, supported by the battleships *Texas*, *Indiana*,

Oregon (1893) and *Iowa*, and the armed yachts *Vixen* (1896) and *Gloucester* (1891).

The Spanish sortie was spotted from *Brooklyn* at 09.35, the ships clearing the mouth of Santiago Bay around 09.45, led by *María Teresa*, followed by *Vizcaya*, *Colón*, *Oquendo*, *Furor* and *Pluton*. Fire was opened by *Iowa*, the Spanish responding with support from shore batteries; however, the Spanish squadron's speed was hampered by the severe fouling of *Vizcaya*'s hull, as well as poor-quality coal. On the other hand, *Brooklyn*'s engines were still in cruising mode (see p 50–1, above), and there was no time to connect up her second pair (nor was there yet enough steam to feed them), limiting her speed to 17kt; only *Oregon* had full steam up, making her at first the fastest American ship, while *Indiana* had defects that limited her to 9kt.

The Americans also suffered from manoeuvring issues, resulting in *Brooklyn* and *Texas* coming close to collision and masking each other's fire, but soon afterwards *Iowa* hit *María Teresa* with two 12in shells, receiving two 6in hits from *Colón*, one striking near the waterline and reducing the American battleship's speed. This led to *Iowa* shifting her fire to *Oquendo*, at the tail of the Spanish cruiser line. In an attempt to preserve the bulk of his squadron, the Spanish admiral ordered them to head south-west, while *María Teresa* provided cover by engaging *Brooklyn*. Although the latter was hit more than 20 times, she suffered only two casualties; in contrast, *María Teresa* was badly hit, including on the bridge, and suffered severe fires, as a result of which she was run aground on the Cuban coast at 10.20.

Of the rest of the Spanish squadron, *Oquendo* was not only badly mauled by *Iowa*, but also suffered from the premature detonation of a 5.5in shell in the breech, killing the gun's crew. With an uncontrollable fire in the after torpedo room, and having suffered a boiler explosion, she turned out of line and ran for the shore, grounding about 500 yards from the beach around 10.30, some 7nm west of Santiago.

The wreck of *Oquendo*, like her sister-ships run aground in shallow water after heavy damage by gunfire. *(Author's collection)*

New York bombarding Aguadores on 1 July 1898. *(LoC LC-D4-20726)*

Vizcaya exchanged fire with *Brooklyn* for around an hour at close range, disabling a 5in gun aboard the American ship, but was hampered by poor ammunition – some 85 per cent of Spanish shells were subsequently estimated to have been duds. The guns themselves were also defective: as well as the burst breech in *Oquendo*, there were various other failures, including breech closure issues and jammed projectiles. In contrast, the estimated 200 hits *Vizcaya* suffered from *Brooklyn* and *Texas* devastated the Spanish cruiser, culminating in an 8in hit that may have detonated a torpedo warhead. After this, *Vizcaya* struck her colours and turned to beach herself, taking ground at 11.06; her crew were rescued by *Iowa*.

The two Spanish destroyers had been engaged by *Gloucester*, *Iowa* and *Indiana*, later joined by *New York*, which had reversed course as soon as smoke had been spotted at the harbour mouth (and which was, like *Brooklyn*, speed-limited by uncoupled forward engines), *Furor* sinking at 10.50 and *Pluton* being run aground at 10.45 near Cabanas Bay. This just left *Colón*, which continued to draw away, with only *Oregon* able to keep in touch, keeping the cruiser close to shore until a combination of the exhaustion of *Colón's* supply of Welsh coal and switch to poorer fuel and local geography allowed to *Oregon* to close and open fire, finding the range immediately. Unable to escape, *Colón* was run ashore at the mouth of the River Tarquino, with her seacocks open, hauling down her ensign on grounding at 13.20. A prize crew was put aboard from *Oregon*, but flooding from the scuttling was spreading, and when the rising tide put *Colón* back afloat, *New York* attempted to push her back ashore; however, the Spanish cruiser then suddenly capsized to port, leaving the starboard battery above water.

During the last phases of the battle, the Austro-Hungarian *K u K Königin Maria Theresia* approached Santiago, having been diverted from a West Indian cruise by a German request to evacuate neutral citizens from the port prior to an anticipated American bombardment. She narrowly escaped coming under fire from *Indiana*, which mistook her for another Spanish cruiser, but the following day was allowed to enter harbour and pick up Austro-Hungarian and German evacuees and carry them to Jamaica. *Maria Theresia* remained in the West Indies until the end of the year, when she returned to the Adriatic.

After the war, the cruiser wrecks from the battle were surveyed, but only that of *María Teresa* was regarded as worth salvage: the other wrecks remain in situ, albeit now badly denuded.[97] Parties from the repair ship *Vulcan* (1884) succeeded in refloating *María Teresa* in September 1898, the hulk being towed to Guantanamo Bay for preliminary repairs. On 29 October, *María Teresa* was taken in tow by *Vulcan*, bound for Norfolk Navy Yard, VA, for full repairs, but began to take on water during a storm off the Bahamas on 1 November, and was cast adrift, running aground between two reefs off Cat Island; her back subsequently broke, and the ship sank. A number of 5.5in guns from *María Teresa* and her two sisters were taken to the USA, where they were installed as memorials.[98]

A handful of big Spanish ships had been left behind in home waters, principally *Carlos V*, which was still undergoing trials, and the battleship *Pelayo* (1887) which had just completed reconstruction in France; there was also the protected cruiser *Alfonso XIII* (1891), still not fully complete. These were initially formed into three divisions, the 1st led by *Carlos V*, and otherwise made up of four auxiliary cruisers, the 2nd, with *Pelayo*, *Alfonso XIII*, the old ironclad *Vitoria* (1865) and three destroyers, and the 3rd of three auxiliary cruisers. The original plan was for them to make sorties into the Atlantic, with the 1st Division to attack the US coast, while the 2nd made a feint towards the Caribbean, and the 3rd would raid commerce off the Brazilian coast.

This strategy was abandoned, in part in fear of British reaction, in favour of sending *Carlos V*, *Pelayo*, three destroyers, two auxiliary cruisers and six transports (*Alfonso XIII* was judged unseaworthy) to Manila via the Suez Canal, to defeat the US force and land 4000 troops. The squadron left Cadíz on 16 June 1898 and arrived at Port Said on the 26th. They were prevented from coaling there by US intrigue and the Anglo-Egyptian interpretation of neutrality rules, proceeding through the Suez Canal on 5–6 July. By then, the Battle of Santiago had been fought and, given the risk that the victorious US forces would head east and threaten Spain itself (*Iowa*, *Oregon* and *Brooklyn* had actually been nominated for the task), the vessels were ordered home on 7 July, departing Suez on the 11th, and arriving back in Spain on the 23rd. The war was ended by the Protocol of Peace on 12 August, and the Treaty of Paris of 10 December.

Aftermath

After the disaster at Santiago, of her big cruisers, Spain was left with just *Carlos V* and the three interminably-delayed *Princesa de Asturias* class. As noted above, they finally joined the fleet early in the next century, but were soon reduced to two. *Cardenal Cisneros* had spent much of the first half of 1905 on various escort tasks relating to the travels of Spanish and

The capsized wreck of *Cristóbal Colón*. (NHHC NH 72711)

foreign royalty, including attending the fleet reception of the British Duke of Connaught during his visit to Cadíz aboard the armoured cruiser *Essex*, that of the German Emperor Wilhelm II to Mahon with the cruisers *Friedrich Carl* and *Hamburg* (1903), and then accompanying the Spanish royal yacht *Giralda* (1894) on visits that included Cherbourg and Portsmouth. In October, she sailed to participate in exercises off the Galician coast, but on the 28th, while departing Muros for Ferrol to repair boiler defects, she struck an unchartered rock off Meixidos and subsequently foundered.

Her two sisters were active in operations against rebels fighting against the Spanish in Morocco during 1911–12, with *Princesa de Asturias* going to the Dardanelles in May 1913, to relieve the protected cruiser *Reina Regente* (ii - 1906) as the Spanish representative in an international squadron established to protect foreigners during the First Balkan War (see p 113, below).

For the USA, the victory had changed the standing of the navy fundamentally. The next few years would see further expansion of the fleet, including a large new force of big cruisers to build on the perceived success of *New York* and *Brooklyn* (see p 86, below). Of them, *Brooklyn* was transferred to the Asiatic Squadron (Fleet, from 1902) as flagship at the end of 1899, being joined by *New York* the following spring. *New York* remained there until she returned home in 1905 for reconstruction, but *Brooklyn* was back in the North Atlantic Squadron (as flagship) in the spring of 1902, going to the European Squadron during 1903–4, and then to the South Atlantic. On 1 April 1905, a reorganisation left *Brooklyn* as flagship of the 3rd Division, 2nd Squadron, the ship spending time in the Mediterranean in early 1906. Limited service off the east coast of America followed until she paid off for a major refit in 1909.

The two *Columbia*s went back into reserve during 1898–9, recommissioning as receiving ships in 1902. *Columbia* then went to the Atlantic Squadron until 1907, while her sister was on special service during 1905–6; both ships then reduced to reserve until 1915, when *Columbia* became a submarine flagship, and 1917, when *Minneapolis* was recommissioned. By then they had both had their 8in guns replaced by a further 6in weapon, owing to safety issues regarding the original gun (cf. p 87).

Russian Fleet Cruisers

The switch from the commerce-raiding model to that of operating with the fleet begun with *Gromoboi* was completed with the ordering of *Bayan* in 1899.[99] Given the pressures on the Russian shipbuilding industry caused by the extensive 1896–1902 programme, a number of ships were contracted-for overseas, with the battleship *Tsesarevich* and the new cruiser going to the Forges & Chantiers de la Méditerranée at La Seyne. A number of designs were offered by the yard, with Russian clarifications of the requirement producing a vessel rather bigger than the 6700-ton vessel originally envisaged, the final ship being just over a thousand tons larger. Omitted during the redesign was the sheathing-and-coppering employed in the earlier Russian armoured cruisers, a change signalling the end of the idea of such ships as commerce raiders operating far from drydocks.

Bayan carried an 8in mounting fore and aft, with eight 6in in main-deck casemates, plus twenty 75mm weapons. In addition to a main belt running from the stem to the after end of the machinery spaces, she had an upper belt which, with a central battery on the main deck holding 75mm guns, gave her a much greater protected freeboard than *Ryurik* and her successors. Horizontal protection followed French 'cellular'

Bayan (i), as completed in France. (*Author's collection*)

practice in having two decks sandwiching the main belt; there was also armour on the deck above the central battery and the end-casemates. Completing in 1902, *Bayan* carried out a series of Mediterranean visits before sailing for Russian waters, proceeding soon afterwards the Far East.

The Next British Generation

The *Drake* class

The *Cressys*' apparent speed deficit, as compared to *Jeanne d'Arc*, regarded as the exemplar of opposition to be faced by the new generation of British big cruiser, led to demands that the next batch of British ships be designed for 23kt.[100] To make this with a ship armed as *Cressy*, 30,000ihp were required – a 30 per cent increase over the *Cressys*, and the highest power ever to be delivered by reciprocating engines in a British warship. It would in any case require watertube boilers to keep the size-jump to a minimum (there was currently a backlash against watertube units, with the 'battle of the boilers' resulting in some ships reverting to cylindrical boilers for cruising).[101] The ship would also need to be longer, reaching the basic dimensions of the *Powerfuls*, displacement coming within 6 per cent less of than that of the new cruisers' battleship contemporaries, the *London* class (1899).

As for armament, the new ships' role in running-down opponents required heavy axial fire, options put forward being a single 9.2in fore and aft (after renewed proposals for 8in guns had been dropped), a pair of single 6in fore and aft behind an armoured screen, and a twin 6in turret, plus two casemated 6in, fore and aft. The 9.2in-gunned version was adopted, backed-up with sixteen 6in, all in two-storey casemates, and fourteen 12pdrs, eight on the upper deck, six in embrasures at the bow and stern). The resulting *Drake* class had a much-simplified superstructure as compared to earlier vessels, with the boat deck eliminated. Although they retained the basic armour-plan of the *Cressys* (and the *Canopus* class), the thicknesses of the two decks over the citadel were reversed and the forward of the two bulkheads that had closed the citadel in the earlier ships deleted in favour of a thicker forward belt.

Two vessels were ordered under the 1898–9 Estimates, and a further two under that year's Supplementary Estimates (a consequence of the Fashoda crisis between the UK and France[102]). This followed a debate over the appropriate mix between the *Drakes* and a smaller 23kt armoured cruiser that was being worked-up in parallel (and which would become the *Monmouth* class). At one point, it was decided to make all four of the 'Supplementary' ships *Drakes* (making a class of six), but in the event they were split between the two designs. All four *Drakes* (*Drake*, *Leviathan*, *Good Hope* and *King Alfred*) were laid down during 1899, and completed during 1902–3, spending much of their careers as flagships, as befitted their size.

The same programme that produced the *Drakes* also included six 'fast' battleships of the *Duncan* class, capable of 19kt, and with a belt only slightly thicker than that of the *Drakes*. They were intended as 'replies' to the *Peresvets*, believed originally to be 19kt ships (rather than their actual 18kt speed),

Drake, shown at New York in 1909. *(LoC LC-D4-39232)*

Exmouth, one of the *Duncan*-class 'fast battleships' built as a reply to the Russian *Peresvet* class, which made major sacrifices in protection to gain an extra knot of speed. *(Author's collection)*

and as such were another group of vessels that blurred the boundaries between 'battleships' and 'armoured cruisers'. However, they clearly lay on the 'battleship' side of the line, and spent their operational lives firmly in 'line' roles, although their protection was considerably inferior to the *London* class, with a belt 22 per cent thinner, the forward armoured bulkhead omitted, the aft one thinned by 30 per cent, and the deck armour also considerably reduced in thickness.

The *Monmouth* class[103]
In parallel with the design of the *Drakes*, vessels of equal speed but between 7700 and 9750 tons displacement were also investigated. Just as *Drake* had been conceived as a counter to *Jeanne d'Arc*, the smaller vessel was intended to deal with *Chateaurenault* and *Guichen*, as well as with *Jurien de la Gravière*, which was also regarded as having a commerce raiding potential. There were also concerns at 23kt vessels being built for other nations, and an ability to counter the 21kt foreign-station *Kléber*s, whose eight 6.5in guns provided another baseline.

The largest option was taken forward for a ship regarded as primarily for trade protection, to be first built under the 1898–9 Supplementary (see just above) and 1899–1900 Estimates. The main armament of fourteen 6in was largely arranged in a combination of main- and upper-deck casemates, as in earlier British cruisers, but with the chase weapons for the first time in Britain installed in twin turrets. The latter were also unusual in British ships in being electrically, rather than hydraulically, powered. These mountings proved unpopular in

service, in particular owing to their guns being fitted too close together in a common cradle. Indeed, consideration was given in 1911–12 to replacing them with single 7.5in pieces or even single 9.2in mountings; however, nothing was done. The ships were the first British cruisers to omit fighting tops.

Armour was a lighter version of the overall layout used in the *Drake*s, and included a 4in belt, thinning to 2in forward, and closed by a 3in bulkhead aft. Armament employed the now-usual double-storey casemates for the fore and aft broadside 6in guns, with a main-deck single casemate amidships. While most ships had Belleville boilers, two had Niclausse and one Babcock units for comparative purposes; some ships also tried inward-turning screws.

Although (with *Bedford*) of the 1899–1900 programme, the contract-built *Monmouth* was the first ship laid down, well before the dockyard-built 1898–9 *Kent* and *Essex*. The ships thus became the *Monmouth* class, which also comprised the 1900–1 Estimates' *Cornwall* and *Suffolk*. The remaining four 1900–01 ships (*Berwick*, *Cumberland*, *Donegal* and *Lancaster*) had a different mark of 6in twin turret, and were accordingly classified as a separate *Donegal* class, although in all other ways identical to the earlier ships.

The ships were poorly regarded from the outset, being unfavourably compared with contemporary Japanese vessels of similar size, better armament and protection – but significantly lower speed; as usual, speed was expensive. The *Monmouths*' protection had been intended to be proof against 6in shell, but target trials against the old battleship *Belleisle* (1876) in 1900 showed that this was not the case. Accordingly, options for revising the design were considered in March 1902 (by which time the class were either already afloat or close to launch), principally by thickening the belt to 6in, but with more extensive changes (including to the armament) also on the

Essentially a reduced *Drake*, *Monmouth* is shown here before the First World War. *(NHHC NH 60092)*

table. Some of these modifications were taken forward into the follow-on *Devonshire* class (see pp 85–6 below), but nothing was in the event done with the ships already in hand.

Entering service during 1903–4, many of the class began their careers in home waters before moving abroad, although *Lancaster* and *Suffolk* began in the Mediterranean. *Monmouth*, *Kent* and *Bedford* went out to the China Station during 1906–7, where *Bedford* was lost by stranding in 1910.[104] The rest of the class went to the North American & West Indies Station between 1907 and 1913, some operating as training ships there, and some remaining there for the rest of their operational careers.

The Dawn of the Era of the Big Cruiser

This swathe of big cruiser construction during the 1890s produced an unprecedented group of fast and relatively heavily-armed and armoured vessels, which led to a view that such ships were the now the real building-blocks of naval power. However, as already noted, their strategic purpose remained somewhat fluid, with the shift from high-seas commerce raiding/protection seemingly shifting to a battlefleet role not so much by design, but through the fact that new technology permitted such a move – a shift from technology being informed by strategy to strategy being informed by technology.[105] Against this background, the first decade of the new century would see the big cruiser become even bigger and finally transmogrify itself into a wholly new beast: the battlecruiser.

Between 1905 and 1910 no fewer than three big cruisers fell victim to accidental loss in the Far East, beginning with the French *Sully* in 1905, followed by *Chanzy* in 1907 (see pp 42, 71). The final loss was that of *Bedford*, on 21 August 1910, which had been sailing in company with her sisters *Kent* and *Monmouth* and the China Station flagship *Minotaur*, from Wei-Hai-Wei to Nagasaki. Poor visibility had meant that astral navigational fixes had been problematic, and *Bedford* was 24.5 miles north and 8 miles west of her estimated position when she ran onto the Samarang Reef, off Quelpart (Cheju Do, Saishu To) Island. The ship flooded rapidly forward of the engine-room bulkhead, and within the next two days flooding extended throughout the ship. *Bedford* was thus evacuated and work begun with the help of Japanese salvage vessels to take off her guns and other equipment. Work was abandoned on 31 August, and the wreck handed over to Mitsubishi for further salvage on 2 September; it was sold at Hong Kong in October, having previously failed to make its £5000 reserve price at auction. *(Richard Osborne collection)*

Hong Kong in 1910; closest to the shore are: the cruisers USS *Cleveland*, *Chattanooga* or *Denver*; the sloop HMS *Merlin*; an unidentified vessel, with the depot ship *Tamar* behind; and the gunboat USS *Helena*; next out are a *Monmouth* class cruiser (*Monmouth*, *Kent* or *Bedford*), *Hawke*, two more *Monmouth*s (with *St Louis* or *Charleston* directly behind), and *King Alfred*. (NHHC NH 83075)

5 | THE FINAL GENERATION

Ships for the New Century

French politicians and poets

It was not only Germany that passed a law relating to naval strength in 1900. France also did so under a 'Law relative to the Augmentation of the Fleet' which set a target strength of 28 battleships, 24 big cruisers (in 8 divisions of 3), 52 destroyers, 263 torpedo boats and 38 submarines. To move towards this, a seven-year programme was agreed to build, inter alia, six battleships (the *Patrie/Démocratie* class) and five armoured cruisers. The objective was a fleet capable of flexible deployment, combining both fleet and cruiser warfare, against whatever foe might arise, rather than relying on a particular theory of campaign against a particular enemy, as had been implicit in the strategic conflicts within the navy of the preceding decades.

The first four of the five cruisers of the 1900 law were intended to be essentially enlargements of the *Gloire* class, with twin 7.6in and 6.5in turrets replacing the singles mounted in the earlier ships and two more twin 6.5in turrets added – doubling the armament – with displacement raised by 20 per cent and the hull lengthened by 30ft and widened by 7ft. Armour arrangements were slightly modified, with ends of the belt reduced in thickness, but the decks and aft transverse

bulkhead thickened; in addition, Krupp Cemented armour was employed for the first time in French cruisers. Bertin had hoped to enhance protection more extensively than was actually done, but he was constrained by limits placed on displacement increases.

Unlike earlier ships, which generally bore the names of former naval officers, some of which went back to the days of the monarchy, the new series were named for 'Republican' politicians and poets. This reflected the political position of Charles Pelletan (1846–1915), Navy Minister from 1902 to 1905, which also resulted in the naming of the contemporary battleships after 'Republican' concepts and virtues (*Patrie/Démocratie* class), and later after prominent figures of the French Revolution (*Danton* class). The first of the cruisers, *Léon Gambetta* (named for the founder of the Third Republic), came into full commission in July 1905, and relieved *Condé* in the Northern Squadron the following month, becoming flagship of its 1st Division. She moved to the Mediterranean to join her sisters *Jules Ferry* and *Victor Hugo* in April 1911; they had both commissioned for the Mediterranean from the outset, although *Victor Hugo* had gone to New York on 8 May 1907 to participate in the Jamestown celebrations.

The fourth ship of the group, *Jules Michelet*, had her design modified while under construction, and as a result was delayed

Victor Hugo was distinguishable from her sister-ships by the flat top to the ventilator in front of the third funnel and maintopmast is at front of masthead. *(NHHC NH 60092)*

Jules Michelet, shown late in her career, but little changed in appearance from her completion, at Manila in February 1929. *(NHHC NH 65202)*

Ernest Renan. (LoC LC-B2-2462-82)

by two years. In particular, the six rather cramped twin 6.5in turrets were suppressed in favour of eight single mountings,[106] while deck thicknesses were adjusted and power marginally increased, with a view to higher speed, which was not, however, achieved. *Michelet* came into active service at the beginning of 1909, as part of the 1st Light Division in the Mediterranean, but went into reserve in January 1911. She returned to full commission in October, but in January 1912 *Michelet* was reassigned to the Mediterranean Training Division, where she remained until the spring of 1914. She then became flagship of the 1st Light Division, remaining in that role at the outbreak of the First World War.

The fifth vessel authorised under the 1900 law, and actually laid down before *Michelet*, was *Ernest Renan*, built to a 30ft-longer design, with new 50cal 7.6in main guns, but with the same secondary battery and armour as installed in *Michelet*. As in the past, the increased size was primarily an attempt to increase speed, installed power being boosted by 20 per cent, the additional power requiring double the number of boilers and an further pair of funnels, matching *Jeanne d'Arc*'s six. The original intent had been to raise power even further, to 42,000ihp, through the use of small-tube boilers, for up to

25kt; however, it was decided to use Niclausse large-tube units, meaning that the highest speed achieved on trial was 24.24kt – still over a knot faster than *Michelet*. *Renan* joined the fleet in October 1909, briefly joining the 2nd Light Division (recently redesignated from the 1st Light Division), before moving to the newly re-formed 1st Light Division, with which she was serving at the outbreak of war.

The British *Devonshire* class[107]

As in France, the first British vessels of the new century would be updated versions of the last of the old. The 1901–2 Estimates provided for six more ships of the *Monmouth* type, but with single 7.5in mountings in lieu of the twin 6in, and boiler rooms rearranged and expanded to allow a full range of available boiler types to be accommodated. Together with some other modifications to magazine and torpedo arrangements, the new ships were thus to be 10ft longer and 1ft wider. In view of the results of the *Belleisle* experiments, the belt was thickened to 6in. During construction, a further change was made, with single 7.5in guns replacing the forward two-storey 6in casemates.

As completed in 1905, the new *Devonshire* class looked very different from their prototypes, with four funnels, which,

Hampshire, which could be distinguished from her sisters by her narrower funnels. *(NHHC NH 60425)*

along with the masts, were stepped with a significant rake, imposed for aesthetic reasons.[108] This turned out to have an adverse effect on the lifting capacity of the main derrick, stepped from the mainmast, but this would not become wholly apparent for some time, the next two classes also being so-configured. *Hampshire* could be distinguished from her sisters by thinner and taller funnels, while *Argyll* and *Roxburgh* shared raked tops to theirs. The other three, *Devonshire* herself, *Antrim* and *Carnarvon* had flat-topped uptakes. All ships had a mix of watertube and cylindrical boilers (cf. p 80), which proved to be unsatisfactory in service.

Apart for a short stint by *Carnarvon* in the Mediterranean from 1905–7, *Hampshire* on the China Station during 1912–14, and a trip to India by *Argyll* escort King George V during 1911–12, the class spent their peacetime careers in home waters.

The White Swan of Sweden

An 1892 commission had recommended that two types of cruiser were required by the Swedish navy, but owing to a shortage of funds, only five vessels of the smaller type (the 800-ton 'torpedo cruisers' of the *Örnen* class [1896–8]) were ordered at that time. However, in 1901 a new commission reinforced the need for larger vessels for fleet scouting work and capable of engaging enemy small cruisers and destroyers. In peacetime, such ships could also be employed for cadet training purposes. Accordingly, in 1902, funds were made available for building one ship of this type; a request a second vessel in 1903 was turned down.[109]

The ship was to be fitted with a 3.9in belt, and at 4,300 tonnes was long held to be the smallest 'true' armoured cruiser

to be built. Nevertheless, *Fylgia*, as she was named, was of the same displacement as *Oscar II*, the largest of the Swedish navy's coast-defence battleships, and some 70ft longer. Unusually for the period, her main battery, disposed in lozenge fashion, was in twin turrets. The secondary guns were divided between main-deck embrasures and sponsons and the superstructure; in 1916 two 57mm guns were replaced with anti-aircraft weapons of the same calibre, while in 1926–7 the forward 57mm sponsons were removed and plated over.

The American new guard
THE *PENNSYLVANIAS*

New York and *Brooklyn* – and their 8in main batteries – emerged from the Spanish-American War with much credit, and in the wake of the US victory, three 12,000-ton cruisers, 'carrying the heaviest armor and most powerful ordnance for vessels of their class', were requested in November 1898, and approved by Congress on 3 March 1899; three more were authorised on 7 June 1900, with one of each group to be built on the West Coast. Each trio was authorised alongside a batch of the new *Virginia*-class battleships, and as 'first-class' ships were given, like the battleships, state names in accordance with an Act of Congress of 1898,[110] rather than the city-names given to the implicitly second-class *New York* and *Brooklyn* (although the former's name was shared by both city and state, she was named for the city). Initially, the lead cruiser was to be named *Nebraska*, but on 7 March 1901, before laying-down, she swapped her name with that allocated to one of one of the battleships, *Pennsylvania*, to match the state in which she was to be built (by Cramp at Philadelphia).

Initial sketches envisaged four 8in and twelve 6in guns,

Fylgia in the eastern Mediterranean in September 1921. (*LoC LC-M34-90021*)

West Virginia as built. *(LoC LC-D4-21845)*

6in armour and a speed of 22kt; an option of trading the 6in for 5in and an extra knot or two of speed was rejected, the ships actually completing with fourteen 6in. The main guns were mounted in electrically-operated turrets fore and aft; these were of an elliptical, balanced, design, rather than the old circular type used in earlier vessels. The guns themselves were of a new 40cal Mk 5 design, superseding the old 35cal Mk 3. The secondary-battery guns were also of a new type, the 5in/50 Mk 8, ten being placed in a main-deck battery, just over 14ft above the waterline, and which would prove wet (cf. p 132, below); the other four were at upper-deck level, forming double-storey casemates with the endmost main-deck guns. A tertiary, anti-torpedo boat, battery of sixteen 3in/50 was mounted, with eight guns on the main deck fore and aft (the foremost and aftermost pairs in sponsons), with the rest on the upper deck between the 6in guns there.[111] A dozen 3pdrs were divided between the four corners of the boat deck and the tops of the double-storey 6in casemates, with 1pdrs fitted in the fighting tops of the two military masts. A debate was under way on the value of torpedo tubes in big ships at the time the new cruisers were being built; in the event just two tubes being fitted, in a single flat just aft of the forward 8in magazine.

Protection comprised a complete waterline belt (backed by a cellulose cofferdam), 6in thick amidships, reducing to 3.5in fore and aft of the machinery spaces, with 4in transverse bulkheads fore and aft of the main battery. Above the belt, the battery had 5in armour, as did the upper deck 6in casemates. The armour deck was 1.5in on the flat, with the slopes 4in.

The protection incorporated a mixture of nickel steel, Harvey and Krupp armour, with the latter used for all plates over 5in thick. The armour for the whole class was ordered on 28 November 1900 as part of an order to Carnegie and Bethlehem with that also included that intended for the eight *Maine* (1901) and *Virginia*-class battleships and three *St Louis*-class (see below) cruisers. However, by the following year it was clear that existing industrial capacity was insufficient to maintain contracted deliveries, with the problem exacerbated by late delivery of drawings of the plates required to the

steelmakers from the shipyards; there were also issues around quoted prices for armour exceeding authorised average levels. Accordingly, all ships involved suffered delays. From an early stage the *Pennsylvanias*' protection was criticised as inadequate, especially the substructure of the 8in turrets and the amount of the ships' side left unarmoured.

To make the required 22kt speed, 43 per cent more horsepower was required that had been installed in *Brooklyn*. Reflecting a contemporary debate as to the relative benefits of outward- and inward-turning screws (cf. p 81), two vessels (*Pennsylvania* and *Colorado*, both being built by Cramps) were to be fitted with outward-turning shafts, the remaining four ordered with inward-turning ones. As it turned out, only two of these (*West Virginia* and *Maryland*) were actually finished with inward-turning machinery (changed to outward-turning in 1905), the other pair (*California* and *South Dakota*) completing with outward-turning screws.

In contrast to the previous armoured cruisers, steam was supplied by watertube boilers, sixteen Babcock & Wilcox in all but the two Cramp-built ships, which instead had thirty-two Niclausse, a type for which Cramps held the US licence. The Niclausse-boilered ships has a slightly different internal layout, resulting the funnels being slightly closer together, with a noticeably larger gap between them and the bridge, occupied by additional ventilators. Niclausse boilers had caused trouble in other Cramp-built ships (e.g. the battleship *Maine* [ii], and in the Russian protected cruiser *Varyag*, as well as other ships abroad), and *Pennsylvania* and *Colorado* were no exception. Accordingly, in 1911 both went into dock for what was originally to be a complete reboiling with Babcock & Wilcox units, but in the event all that was done was to fit the foremost eight boilers with Babcock & Wilcox drums and tubes, leaving everything else essentially unchanged. All ships underwent main-armament modifications during 1907–10, initially to improve safety, and then to replace the main guns, following an accident in *Colorado* in in June 1907, when an 8in gun had lost its muzzle owing to an inherent weakness in the Mk 5 weapon. Thus, during 1908–10 (starting with *Colorado*), all ships had them replaced by the stronger Mk 6, which was a 45cal piece.

The first ship to commission was *Colorado*, quickly followed by *West Virginia* and *Pennsylvania*. All became the 4th Division of the Atlantic Fleet (with *West Virginia* as flagship), with *Maryland* joining in October. In 1906, a comprehensive reorganisation planned the concentration of all US battleships in the Atlantic Fleet, supported by a division of big cruisers, with another division of the latter forming the Asiatic Fleet. Two of the *St Louis* class and the two *New Orleans*-class ex-Brazilian, British-built protected cruisers (1896–9) would head the Pacific Fleet. Accordingly, in September 1906, *West Virginia*, *Colorado*, *Pennsylvania* and *Maryland* sailed for the Far East, arriving at Cavite in November, with *West Virginia* now becoming Asiatic Fleet flagship. There they replaced the three battleships (*Oregon*, *Wisconsin* [1898, flag] and *Ohio* [1901]) formerly deployed to the station. On 17 April 1907, the Asiatic and Pacific Fleets were merged, the four cruisers now becoming the 1st Division, 1st Squadron of the 'new' Pacific Fleet, with *West Virginia* continuing in the flag role.

During late 1907/early 1908, the four ships operated primarily off the West Coast of the USA, including refits at Mare Island and Bremerton. In August 1908, the division (less *Colorado*, being regunned at Bremerton), joined with the 2nd Division, comprising two of the new *Tennessee* class (*Tennessee* [flag] and *Washington* – see below, pp 89–90), plus the last two *Pennsylvania*s, *California* and *South Dakota*, commissioned respectively in 1907 and 1908. The combined 1st Squadron then cruised to Samoa, returning to the West Coast via Honolulu, where *Colorado* rejoined. They then sailed down the Central and South American coast from December to March 1909, and then deployed to the western Pacific until February 1910.

REFITTING THE OLD GUARD

In parallel with the construction of the new cruisers, work began to rebuild *New York*, in particular replacing all guns and boilers. She was re-armed very much along the lines of the *Pennsylvania*s, with the same main battery and a main-deck secondary/tertiary battery arranged in exactly the same way, albeit with 5in/50s replacing the larger ships' 6in weapons. No upper-deck battery was, however fitted, the old wing 8in locations being used for 3pdr saluting guns. The main-deck changes were achieved by fitting the after two pairs of embrasures (one formerly mounting 6pdrs, the other 4in) with 3in weapons, while the foremost embrasures at the bow were plated over, the next fitted with 3in and a new pair installed slightly further aft, also for 3in guns. The remaining embrasures were dismantled and replaced by completely new ones to hold the 5in mountings.

All boilers were removed and replaced by twelve watertube units. The fore and aft superstructures were also modified, mast platforms drastically lowered and reduced in numbers, and a pair of searchlight gantries installed aft of the third and between the first and second funnels. These were initially kept at their original heights, but all were significantly heightened

Saratoga, formerly *New York*, as reconstructed and following the heightening of her funnels, at Shanghai in 1911. *(NHHC NH 50964)*

Unlike the former *New York*, *Brooklyn* was only modestly upgraded, and appears little changed as shown serving with the Asiatic Fleet on 4 July 1917. *(Author's collection)*

prior to the ship deploying as Asiatic Squadron flagship in 1910. While there, in February 1911, she was renamed *Saratoga* to free her name for the new battleship to be laid down the coming September. The ship remained in the Far East until the beginning of 1916, when she went into reserve at Bremerton, WA.

Brooklyn's 1909 refit was far less extensive than that of *New York*, with few external or machinery changes. However, she received two-stage ammunition hoists to improve survivability, new electrical turret-training gear and updated fire controls. Her flying and after bridges were removed and the remaining torpedo tubes were taken out (the bow tube had been removed in 1899), the 6pdr battery being cut to four guns. On completion, *Brooklyn* remained in reserve at League Island until 1914, when she became a receiving ship at Boston, in reduced commission. She returned to full service in March 1915, undertaking Atlantic neutrality patrols until November, when she transferred to the Asiatic Fleet.

THE *ST LOUIS* CLASS

In 1899, as well as the first three of the *Pennsylvania* class, three 6000-ton vessels, initially envisaged as updates of the protected cruiser *Olympia*, were requested, but not approved until the following year. At first, they were to be 20kt vessels, with two single 8in, ten 6in (or fourteen 5in), and a 3.25–4in deck. However, some embarrassment was felt in that they would be 700 tons smaller than *Varyag* (1899), being built by Cramp's in the USA for Russia, and the trio were re-approved

St Louis as completed. (Author's collection)

at 8000 tons the following year. Displacement had crept up to 8500 tons by July, with an armament of twelve (later fourteen) 6in (no 8in) and 2–5in deck armour. In the end, the deck was thinned and a short 4in waterline belt added – with displacement rising to 9500 tons. This was built as the St Louis class, three ships, St Louis, Charleston (ii) and Milwaukee entering service during 1904–5. They were superficially very similar in appearance to the Pennsylvanias, with two-storey casemates, four funnels and military masts, and shared the sixteen Babcock & Wilcox boilers of that class's later ships.

The three ships spent most of their careers on the West Coast, much of it in reserve or on subsidiary duties, reflecting a general perception of them as under-armed and under-protected for their size. The first to complete was Charleston (ii), in October 1905, which carried out goodwill visits along the South American coast during the summer of 1906, before proceeding to the West Coast, joining the Pacific Fleet in December, with her two sisters forming the 3rd Division of the 2nd Squadron; she served with this until June 1908. After a refit, she spent October 1908 to September 1910 in the Far East, first as flagship of 3rd Squadron, Pacific Fleet, and then as flagship of the Asiatic Fleet, when re-established in 1910.

Returning home later that year, Charleston was decommissioned and spent the next two years laid up. Commissioned into the Pacific Reserve Fleet in September 1912, the ship then served as a receiving ship at Puget Sound as until 1916, except for a voyage to San Francisco in October 1913. She became a submarine tender at Cristobal, the Panama Canal Zone, in May 1916, still being there the following spring.

Commissioned in August 1906, St Louis sailed around Cape Horn on her May–August 1907 voyage from New York to San Diego, before spending the next two years active in the eastern Pacific, before going into reserve in November 1909. Over the next few years, she had a few short periods away from her Puget Sound, before becoming a receiving ship at San

Francisco from April 1914 to February 1916. In July of that year she became a submarine tender and station ship at Pearl Harbor in Hawaii, which remained her duty until April 1917.

Milwaukee commissioned in December 1906 at San Francisco, but reduced to reserve in April 1908, after no more than a year of active service. Apart from a cruise to Hawaii and Honduras that summer, the ship remained in reserve until 1913, out of commission after May 1910. She recommissioned in June 1913, but as part of the Pacific Reserve Fleet, going to sea for only brief periods. In 18 March 1916, she was detached to become tender to Pacific Fleet destroyers and submarines, based at San Diego. As such, Milwaukee participated in exercises, undertook survey work and patrolled off the Mexican coast, before being fitted with additional workshop facilities to enhance her capabilities as a tender. She was lost in January 1917, while attempting to tow one of her charges, the submarine USS H-3, off the beach on which she had grounded. The cruiser herself became lodged on the beach and was abandoned as a total loss.

On 14 December 1916, the submarine H-3 (1913) ran onto the beach off Eureka, CA. Against local mariners' advice, Milwaukee attempted to pull the submarine off on 13 January 1917, but herself grounded on the very same beach. Salvage attempts were of no avail (although the submarine was successfully refloated in April), the hulk breaking its back in a storm in November 1918. Milwaukee was stricken the following year, and although sold for scrap, much of the wreck still exists beneath the sand. (NHHC NH 46151)

THE LAST AMERICAN BIG CRUISERS

Planning in October 1900 for the 1901 programme initially assumed further repeat-Pennsylvanias, but early discussions suggested an enlarged version with additional 8in turrets on the beam on 14,500 tons. A smaller (11,000-ton) vessel was also considered, but the prevailing view was that a bigger ship was needed; concerns also existed over the protection of the Pennsylvanias. The question of increasing main and secondary gun calibres to 10in and 7in (the latter as adopted in the contemporary Connecticut and Mississippi-class battleships)[112] was also considered, a number of alternative schemes being prepared. In the end, an enlarged Pennsylvania, with modified armour and four 10in and sixteen 6in, was adopted, as a 7in secondary battery would have resulted in too many protection trade-offs. Two ships were authorised on 1 July 1902 (along with the first two vessels of the new *Connecticut*-class battleships), and two more (with minor changes in protection, inspired by the Russo-Japanese War) on 27 April 1904 (with the sixth and final *Connecticut*, the protection of which was also amended).

As compared to the much-criticised scheme in the *Pennsylvania*s, barbettes were extended all the way down to the armour deck, while the belt was extended (at its full 5in thickness) up to the main deck between the double 5in transverse bulkheads that were placed fore and aft of the main barbettes. It then continued along the waterline 3in thick to the bow and stern. The armour deck was 1.5in thick on the flats along the whole length, with the slopes 4in amidships and 3in at the ends. In the second pair, barbette armour was thickened, the belt was narrowed somewhat, but the transverse bulkheads thickened to 6in, and the armour deck thickened to 2in amidships, but thinned to 1in at the ends; in addition, the 9in shield placed aft of the conning tower in the first two was omitted, as was the cellulose cofferdam behind the belt.

Washington as completed; she and her sisters could be distinguished from the *Pennsylvania*s in particular by their larger main turrets and their lack of two-storey casemates. *(Author's collection)*

The 10in guns of the new class delivered a broadside nearly half as heavy again as that of the 8in weapons in the *Pennsylvania*s and modernised *New York*, with the secondary battery increased by two barrels as compared to the former. The addition of the extra guns to the main-deck battery changed alignments and avoiding the double-deck casemates used in the *Pennsylvania* and *St Louis* classes. The 3in battery was also increased, to twenty-two weapons, with six incorporated into the main-deck battery amidships, and an extra pair of torpedo tubes, with their calibre increased to 21in, provided forward of the aft magazines. The provision of the latter reduced bunkerage and thus endurance.

Machinery essentially duplicated that of the later *Pennsylvania*s, with Babcock & Wilcox boiler and outward-turning screws, contradicting an original proposal to increase power by 2000ihp to get an extra knot of speed, at the cost of reductions in protection and armament. The two batches of the class could be distinguished by their funnels, the first pair, *Tennessee* and *Washington*, having fully-cased funnels (as found in the *Pennsylvania* class), but the second pair, *North Carolina* and *Montana*, only half-cased funnels, a feature also found in the battleship *New Hampshire*, authorised on the same day as them. A further external means of differentiation was that the later two ships only had single hawse-holes.

Tennessee and *Washington*, began their operational lives with a goodwill voyage to France during June–July 1907, subsequently proceeding together to the Pacific, arriving at San Francisco in February 1908. From June, together with *California* and *South Dakota*, they formed the 2nd Division of the 1st Squadron, with the flag in *Tennessee*, until they moved to the Atlantic in the spring of 1910. There, they joined their

Montana, shown here after the fitting of a cage foremast, and *North Carolina* could be distinguished from their sisters by their half-cased funnels. *(LoC LC-D4-22598)*

Duke of Edinburgh at New York in 1909; the exceptionally low placement of her 6in is readily apparent. *(LoC LC-D4-22628)*

sisters *North Carolina* and *Montana* which, having initially served in the Atlantic Fleet, had spent April–August 1909 in the Mediterranean, providing relief during the Adana massacres that occurred during the abortive counter-coup by the deposed Ottoman Sultan, Abdul Hamid II.

Dukes and *Warriors*[113]

Having built up a force of medium armoured cruisers during under the immediately preceding Estimates, the Royal Navy's next batch of ships reverted to a tonnage akin to that of the *Drakes*. They were, however, an enlargement of the *Devonshire* design, initial options ranging from the replacing the beam 7.5in with four 6in, through twin 7.5in forward and aft, plus four 7.5in and eight 6in in casemates, to a single 9.2in fore and aft, with two twin 9.2in and eight single 6in in upper deck mountings on the beam.

The next step was to place six 9.2in in single mountings, fore, aft and on the beam, with eight 6in in a main deck battery. The latter would be protected by a 1.5in roof, and an upward extension of a 6in main belt. The belt extended the whole length of the waterline (thinned to 4in forward and 3in aft), in contrast to *Cressy* and subsequent ships, which had lacked a belt aft. This basic scheme was then taken forward in April 1902, with a number of potential variations, including the omission of a raised forecastle, to compensate for a twin 9.2in turret forward. Other sketches included a forecastle, and added two extra 6in, or placed the eight 6in in twin mountings on the upper deck. Other areas of variation included the potential boiler-fit, either following the *Devonshires* in a mixed watertube/cylindrical mix, reverting to an all-watertube scheme, or even going to an all-cylindrical outfit, the latter requiring a significantly enlarged ship.

By May 1902, a vessel with single 9.2in arranged fore and aft, with the other four on the upper deck beam, and eight 6in between them (with no decision yet between twin upper-deck and single main-deck mountings), had been agreed upon. The armament decision went in favour of the main-deck battery for the 6in (with an addition gun worked-in in front of the forward beam 9.2in mounting on each side), while an initial plan to move to the new 50-calibre 9.2in Mk XI was dropped to avoid delays. Twenty-two 3pdr Vickers guns were to be installed atop turrets and the superstructure, with three torpedo tubes. It was eventually decided in September that mixed boilers should be fitted. Ideas investigated and dropped included telescopic funnels and armoured redoubts to protect the three 9.2in for and aft, although the former led to abnormally short uptakes in this and the next two classes, which eventually had to be heightened to avoid the smoking-out of the bridge.

Two ships were ordered under the 1902–3 Estimates, *Duke of Edinburgh* and *Black Prince*, with four more under those for 1903–4. However, only three months after *Duke of Edinburgh* had been laid down doubts were being expressed about the placement of the 6in on the main deck, as sea-experience with the newly-completed *Cressy*s and *Drake*s showed that their main-deck guns were unworkable in anything other than a dead calm – and those of the *Duke of Edinburgh*s were even closer to the waterline. Although the earlier idea of moving them to upper-deck twin mountings was raised, the fact that the *Duke of Edinburgh*s' foremost guns were further aft than those of *Drake*, and concerns over topweight, led to no change being made.

In December, it was suggested that the main-deck battery be suppressed in favour of four single 7.5in mountings (of a new 50cal Mk II type), rather than the twin 6in as previously proposed. By then, it was clear that the *Duke of Edinburgh*s would come out light, which would not only allow the change

Cochrane as completed, showing the single 7.5in turrets on the upper deck that replaced the *Dukes*' 6in main-deck batteries. *(NHHC NH 61367)*

Scharnhorst on builders' trials. *(Author's collection)*

of gun, but also allow the battery armour to be retained. Accordingly, and in view of the unanimous view from afloat that main-deck guns would be useless in a moderate seaway, it was decided on 30 March 1904 to change the design of the four follow-on vessels (which now became the *Warrior* class, the other ships being *Achilles*, *Cochrane* and *Natal*). Unfortunately, the original pair was found to be too advanced in construction to make the change affordable; in service *Duke of Edinburgh* and *Black Prince* thus had a poor reputation, and were amongst the first vessels to have main-deck guns taken out during the First World War (see p 126, below).

Apart from the change in secondary battery, there were few other major changes in the *Warriors*, the tertiary armament remaining as 3pdrs, twenty-six Vickers-type being arranged atop turrets and superstructure. All four joined the 5th CS in home waters on commissioning, the first modifications coming in 1910 when the aft searchlight platforms were shifted further astern and the two Hotchkiss guns removed. *Warrior* had her forefunnel raised by 6ft at this time, with all four uptakes heightened across the whole class in 1912.

Germany

As in the UK, the next generation of German vessels marked a major leap in capability. *Large cruiser C* and *Large cruiser D* (to be *Gneisenau* and *Scharnhorst*), funded under the 1904 and 1905 programmes, were again a development of the line begun by *Prinz Heinrich*, but now an additional 2000 tons marked a significant growth in size, fighting power and speed. This was the result of a requirement that they could if necessary substitute for a damaged battleship in the battle line, leading to the main battery being doubled in size by replacing the turreted 5.9in guns of previous classes with casemated 8.2in weapons, the secondary battery being reduced to six guns on the main deck. The tertiary battery was further strengthened, being upgraded to battleship scale with two guns on

each side of both the bow and the stern in main-deck embrasures/sponsons.

It was originally intended to have an additional pair on the bridge, abreast the conning tower, but these were deleted on the basis of experience with so-sited mountings in *Braunschweig*-class battleships. In addition, the belt was thickened by 50 per cent to 5.9in, firing trials on the Meppen range, using a mock-up of *Prinz Heinrich*'s side, having shown that the hitherto-used 3.9in belt was insufficient to defeat medium-calibre shells. Another two boilers were added, boosting horsepower by another 7000ihp, giving *Scharnhorst* and *Gneisenau* an extra knot over the *Roons*.

After initially replacing *Yorck* as flagship of Scouting Ships in the High Seas Fleet, *Scharnhorst* sailed to the Far East on 1 April 1909 to relieve *Fürst Bismarck* as flagship of the East Asiatic Squadron. *Gneisenau* left Germany to join her sister on 8 September 1910, both ships remaining in the east down to the outbreak of the First World War.

Following her return from the Far East in 1909, *Fürst Bismarck* was taken in hand at Kiel in 1910 for reconstruction, but the work seems not to have been pursued with any urgency, and she had not recommissioned by the time the First World War broke out. The modifications were mainly concerned with reducing topweight, masts being reduced to poles, but with the machinery and armament left essentially unchanged. The intent had been that when completed she would relieve the old battleship *Württemberg* (1878) as the torpedo training ship at Flensburg, her torpedo rooms being enlarged accordingly.

Prinz Heinrich was modestly rebuilt along similar lines at Kiel during 1914 – a September 1913 proposal that she be refitted as a training ship having been rejected. Her superstructure bulwarks were cut down and the masts modified, but little else was done.

The Russo-Japanese War

The Russo-Japanese War of 1904–5 – begun by a surprise torpedo-boat attack on the Russian base on 8 February 1904

Nisshin as completed. *(NHHC NH 58999)*

– marked perhaps the high point of the story of the big cruiser, with armoured cruisers on both sides playing prominent roles. To an extent, this was a matter of necessity, following the loss of two of Japan's six 1st-class battleships,[114] and the blockading of the Russian Far East Squadron in Port Arthur from the outset of the conflict.

As already noted, the date of Japan's attack was wholly dependent on the progress east of the newly-acquired *Kasuga* and *Nisshin*: the war could only begin once they were safely on the very last leg of their voyage to Japan. On the Russian side, the eastward-bound *Oslyabya*, *Dmitri Donskoi* and *Aurora* had only reached Djibouti by the outbreak of war; as too small a force to fight their way to Port Arthur, they were ordered to return to Russia.

When attacked by the Japanese, the Russian force at Port Arthur included *Peresvet*, *Pobeda* and *Bayan*, with the 1st-class battleships *Petropavlovsk*, *Sevastopol*, *Poltava* (1894–5), *Retvizan* (1900) and *Tsesarevich* (1901), and the protected cruisers *Pallada*, *Diana* (both 1899), *Askold*, *Novik* (both 1900) and *Boyarin* (1901). *Tsesarevich*, *Retvizan* and *Pallada* were each struck by a torpedo, putting them out of action for some weeks.

The Battle of Chemulpo
For some time, *Chiyoda* had been at Chemulpo (Incheon) in Korea to monitor the Russian protected cruiser *Varyag* and gunboat *Korietz* (1887, with which *Chiyoda* had a accidental exchange of fire early on 8 February – the first shots of the war), which were also based there. Now, *Chiyoda* joined up with the Japanese 4th Division, comprising the protected cruisers *Takachiho*, *Naniwa*, *Niitaka* (1902) and *Akashi* (1897), torpedo boats and troop transports, plus *Asama*, on loan from the 2nd Division, which then landed troops, with no apparent reaction from the Russians. The next day, the Japanese notified all ships present (there were a number of neutral warships in harbour) that unless the Russians sailed by midday, they would be attacked after 16.00. In spite of being urged to surrender, the Russian ships attempted to fight their way out from 11.00; in this they were unsuccessful, retiring, badly battered, back into the harbour at 13.15. *Korietz* was blown up by her crew at 16.00 and *Varyag* scuttled by opening her seacocks (to avoid damage to neutral ships nearby) at 18.10.[115]

Port Arthur
Meanwhile, a Japanese reconnaissance of Port Arthur by the 3rd Division of protected cruisers on the morning of 9 February had made an over-optimistic assessment of the damage caused, leading to the Japanese fleet, comprising the 1st Division of battleships and 2nd Division of 6–6 Plan armoured cruisers (less the detached *Asama*) approaching to follow-up the apparent disarray of their opponents. However, warned by *Boyarin*, on patrol outside, the Russian shore batteries and ships were able to repulse the Japanese, with damage on both sides at the ensuing Battle of Port Arthur; *Bayan* suffered superficial damage from nine hits, with six dead, *Peresvet* from three hits, and *Pobeda* from a small number. War was finally declared the following day (the 10th).

On the 11th, the Russians lost their minelayer *Yenisei* (1899) to one of her own mines, and then the protected cruiser *Boyarin* to two more of the Russian mines. On the 24th, there was an unsuccessful Japanese attempt to plant blockships across the mouth of Port Arthur, while on 8 March a new Russian admiral, the well-respected Stepan Makarov (1849–1904), arrived, and on the morning of the 10th made an unsuccessful attack on the blockading Japanese. Indirect fire from the ships in harbour on the 22nd succeeded in damaging the battleship

Fuji, another attempt at blocking the harbour on the 27th also proving a setback for the Japanese. However, on 13 April, a sortie by *Petropavlovsk* (flag), *Poltava, Sevastopol, Pobeda, Peresvet, Askold, Diana* and *Novik* ended in disaster when *Petropavlovsk* was mined and sunk, with the admiral amongst the dead; *Pobeda* also struck a mine, which flooded a bunker and three compartments. An 11-degree list was corrected to 5 degrees by counter-flooding, repairs being conducted through the use of a caisson down to 9 June. The ships had sailed to support two (lost) destroyers and *Bayan*, which had been trying to succour them. On the other hand, on the 15th, a 10in shell from *Peresvet* succeeded in hitting *Nisshin*, which had been bombarding Port Arthur, by firing from the harbour, over the mountain.

In addition to the ships at Port Arthur, also in the Far East was a cruiser force at Vladivostok, comprising the protected cruiser *Bogatyr* (1901) and the Independent Cruiser Squadron, with the much more powerful *Rossiya, Ryurik* and *Gromoboi*. There were also an auxiliary cruiser, *Lena* (1896), eleven torpedo boats (*201* to *211* [1886–99]) and two icebreakers at the port. The cruisers made six commerce-raiding sorties from Vladivostok during 1904, (9–14 February, 24 February–1 March, 23–27 April, 12–19 June, 28 June–3 July, and 17 July-1 August), sinking fifteen ships, including the transport *Hitachi Maru* (1898) on 15 June, which was carrying over a thousand troops and eighteen 11in howitzers bound for the siege of Port Arthur. The force suffered the loss of the services of *Bogatyr* when she struck a rock in Amur Bay on 15 May, and was so badly damaged that she could not complete repairs with the facilities available at Vladivostok until after the war. As a result of the force's depredations, the Japanese 2nd Division of armoured cruisers was deployed against them, including a long-range bombardment of Vladivostok by *Izumo* (flag), *Iwate, Azuma, Asama* and *Yakumo*, plus the protected cruisers *Yoshino* and *Kasagi* (1898), on 2 March, but with a lack of success that led to significant public disquiet in Japan.

Back at Port Arthur, a final Japanese attempt to block the harbour on 3 May had been a failure, and on 15 May the Japanese battleships *Yashima* and *Hatsuse* (1899) had been sunk by mines. Although this event was successfully kept secret, as noted above it enhanced the importance of the Japanese armoured cruisers, *Kasuga* and *Nisshin* thus now effectively replacing the two lost battleships in the 1st Division. The same day, however, *Kasuga* had further depleted the Japanese fleet, when she ran into the cruiser *Yoshino* in thick fog, which sank with heavy loss of life

Two attempts were made by the Russian fleet to break out from Port Arthur to Vladivostok, the first on 23 June, aborted on meeting the Japanese just before sunset. On 27 July, *Nisshin* and *Kasuga* forced a Russian detachment of one battleship and several cruisers and gunboats to return to port through long-range gunfire after they sortied to provide fire support to the Russian Army. As noted on p 58, the *Garibaldi* class incorporated unusually high angles of elevation for their main guns, and were thus capable to firing at significantly greater ranges than the Japanese fleet's British-built vessels, making them particularly useful for bombardment purposes.

A month later, *Bayan* was mined while returning from a bombardment of Japanese army shore positions on 27 July, and was under repair until September. She was thus excluded from the second break-out attempt on 10 August, by which time the base had come under siege from the Japanese army.

The Battle of the Yellow Sea
Makarov's temporary successor, Wilgelm Vitgeft (1847–1904), led the sortie in *Tsesarevich*, accompanied by *Retvizan, Pobeda, Peresvet* (both without three 6in and two 75mm guns), *Sevastopol, Poltava, Askold, Diana, Novik, Pallada* and fourteen destroyers, making an initial feint to the south-west to conceal his actual plans. The fleets finally met at around 12.25, the Japanese force comprising *Mikasa* (1900, fleet flag), *Asahi* (1899), *Fuji, Shikishima* (1898), *Nisshin* and *Kasuga*, plus eight protected cruisers, eighteen destroyers and thirty torpedo boats. Fire was opened at 13.00, but no hits were scored, but on resuming action around 13.30, hits were scored by both sides, with the lagging *Poltava* suffering badly by 14.45, but saved from worse by *Peresvet* and her division concentrating their gunfire onto *Mikasa* and *Asahi*, causing the Japanese 1st Division to temporarily break off the fight at 15.20. However, the Japanese cruisers of the 3rd Division, led by *Yakumo*, came within range of the Russians around 15.40, *Yakumo* taking a 12in hit, killing twelve and wounding eleven, causing the 3rd Division to withdraw. As nightfall approached, there seemed a chance that the Russians would escape, but by 17.35 both Japanese divisions had caught up with the still-lagging *Poltava* which, nevertheless, scored hits on *Mikasa*, while gun defects on a number of Japanese battleships were reducing their firepower.

By 18.30, although some of the Russian ships were badly damaged, the Japanese were also having problems, with *Mikasa* in poor condition, handing targeting of *Tsesarevich* to *Asahi* which, at 18.40, struck the Russian flagship's conning tower, killing the admiral and jamming her steering, leading the Russian line in a 180-degree turn. *Persevet*, 2nd flag, was unable to take over control owing to damage to her foremast preventing the hoisting of signal flags (she had been hit thirty-nine times – nineteen times by shells of heavy calibre – and was also suffering from flooding above the armour deck, with thirteen dead and seventy-seven wounded). The Russian fleet thus scattered, all but one ship (*Novik*) giving up on the goal of Vladivostok and limping back towards Port Arthur under the cover of darkness. *Pobeda* had taken eleven hits, but without serious damage, with two 6in knocked out, three dead and thirty-eight wounded. Not all made it back to Port Arthur, *Tsesarevich, Askold* and four destroyers being interned in neutral ports through a shortage of fuel. The Vladivostok-bound *Novik* was caught by the Japanese cruisers *Tsushima* (1902) and *Chitose* (1898) on 20 August, run aground and then scuttled, although later salvaged as the Japanese *Suzuya*.

The Russian fleet never emerged again, and as the siege came closer and closer to the naval base, the ships gave up guns to the land defences. *Peresvet* and *Pobeda* had each lost two 6in, two 3in, one or two 47mm and four 37mm guns by 10 August. The ships were now suffering increasing damage from shore artillery, *Peresvet* receiving a 4.7in hit the day before the Yellow Sea action. On the other hand, Russian mines continued to have successes, the old ex-Chinese cruisers *Heien* and *Saien* (ex-*Tsi Yuen*) being lost on 18 September and 30 November. *Heien* was disabled in Piegen Bay, to the west of Port Arthur and foundered in heavy weather later the same day. The much newer protected cruiser *Takasago* was sunk of 13 December while providing gunfire support to the besiegers.

The Battle of Ulsan
As part of the plan for the 10 August breakout, the Vladivostok cruisers were to sail and rendezvous with the Port Arthur squadron in the Sea of Japan. However, as the Port Arthur ships had not been sighted by the following morning, the cruisers were ordered back towards Vladivostok while off Pusan. During the night, the Japanese 2nd Fleet, comprising *Izumo* (flag), *Tokiwa*, *Iwate*, *Azuma* (2nd Division), *Naniwa* and *Takachino* (4th Division) had passed the Russians on a reciprocal course but neither side had spotted the other. However, as the Russian turned north they sighted the Japanese ships, fire being opened by the Japanese at 05.20, beginning the Battle of Ulsan.

Fire was for some reason concentrated on *Ryurik*, the last in the Russian column, which was soon hit and began to fall astern of her squadron-mates. Around 06.00, the latter turned to starboard in the hope that *Ryurik* could re-join, with the Japanese not for initially following, as they were now hampered by engine defects in *Azuma*. However, firing on *Ryurik* recommenced at 06.24, with the ship hit three times aft, flooding the steering compartment and the rudder jamming to port around 06.40. *Rossiya* and *Gromoboi* then attempted to interpose themselves between *Ryurik* and the Japanese, but the latter's damaged steering frustrated this. A series of turns left the two forces on opposite courses, *Iwate* then receiving a hit in a casemate that disabled three 6in and one 12pdr, the fire threatening the ship and leaving thirty-two dead and forty-three wounded.

Further reversals of course followed, at 07.45 on the part of the Russians to shield *Ryurik*. However, at 08.15 *Ryurik* was ordered to make her own way back to Vladivostok, the other two ships then retiring northward. At this point the old *Naniwa* and *Takachiho* caught up, being left to deal with *Ryurik* while the rest of the force chased *Rossiya* and *Gromoboi*. A running battle then ensued for some ninety minutes, the Russians' speed being cut from 18kt to 15kt, although *Azuma's* defects continued to hinder her, her place in the line being taken by *Tokiwa*. However, around 11.15 an erroneous report on ammunition expenditure and concerns at leaving the Tsushima Strait unguarded led to the Japanese cutting short the chase and heading back towards Pusan. In the meantime,

Rossiya in August 1904, after the Battle of Ulsan. *(Author's collection)*

Ryurik, under fire from *Naniwa* and *Takachiho*, had been scuttled.

Aside from the damage to *Iwate*, *Izumo* had received twenty hits, with three dead and sixteen wounded, *Azuma* ten, with eight wounded, and *Tokiwa* three hits but no casualties. On the Russian side, *Rossiya* had 44 dead and 156 wounded, with *Gromoboi* suffering 87 dead and 170 wounded. *Rossiya* had received nineteen hull-hits on the starboard side and nine on the port, losing half her guns. For *Gromoboi* the figures were fifteen and seven, but in neither ship had her belt been penetrated.

Both ships had suffered propellant fires and hits in their funnels, boats and decks, but were repaired within two months in spite of the very basic facilities available at Vladivostok. While under repair, *Rossiya* had her foremost 6in moved from its bow embrasure to the forecastle deck, and six more weapons of the same calibre added on the upper deck, replacing the 75mm mountings previously there.

The Fall of Port Arthur
As a final attempt at saving the situation in the Far East, a 2nd Pacific Squadron (the Port Arthur force now becoming the 1st) had been put together from units of the Baltic Fleet, sailing on 15 October 1904, and comprising seven battleships (five modern, including *Oslyabya*, and two old), *Admiral Nakhimov* and *Dmitri Donskoi*, five protected cruisers, nine destroyers and a range of auxiliary vessels. They were met en route, at Cam Ranh Bay, French Indochina, in February 1905, by the 3rd Pacific Squadron, a further old battleship, three coast-defence ships and *Vladimir Monomakh*, which then joined her half-sister *Donskoi* in the 1st Cruiser Division (*Nakhimov* was grouped with *Oslyabya* and the battleships *Navarin* [1891] and

Vladimir Monomakh in her final form, with only two masts, on her way to the Far East during 1904–5. *(Author's collection)*

Sissoi Veliky [1894] in the 2nd Division). A further force, comprising most of the remainder of the Baltic Fleet, including *Pamiat Azova*, was to have followed later, as part-compensation for Russia's inability to purchase Argentina and Chile's armoured cruisers (p 64, above); however, by the time the ships were ready, it was all too late.

Port Arthur had surrendered on 2 January 1905. On 5 December 1904, the Japanese had captured the key 203 Metre Hill, opening the harbour to direct fire by the army's 11in howitzers. *Poltava* was sunk the same day, *Retvizan* and *Pobeda* (the latter having been hit or near-missed by fifteen 11in shells) following on the 6th, and *Peresvet* (scuttled to prevent capsize, after over twenty hits over two months, and forty-six 11in hits and near-misses on her last day), *Pallada* and *Bayan* on the 9th. The battleship *Sevastopol*, although damaged, was moved out of range, and survived six destroyer attacks during the following three weeks; she was finally scuttled by her crew

Port Arthur after the surrender, with (from the front) the wrecks of *Bayan*, the protected cruiser *Pallada*, *Pobeda* and *Peresvet*. *(Author's collection)*

when Port Arthur surrendered on 2 January 1905. Although the other ships had been further damaged by demolition charges prior to the surrender (*Pobeda* also having her foremast collapse as a result of earlier damage), all the major warships sunk at Port Arthur were salvaged by the Japanese, and taken to Japan for refitting (see further p 98).

With Port Arthur in their hands, the Japanese undertook a programme of incremental refitting over the next few months, the most noticeable alterations being the removal of the lower fighting tops in the major ships. The Russian Vladivostok ships were icebound for the winter, while *Gromoboi* would in any case be unserviceable until February, having run aground on 13 October, not long after completing her repairs from Ulsan. Docking was delayed by the drydock being occupied by *Bogatyr*, still under repair from her own grounding, which then fell off the blocks when being refloated to make way for the bigger ship; it took a week to get her clear.

While under refit, six additional 6in were mounted on *Gromoboi*'s upper deck, protected by light casemates. Her foremost 6in guns were also moved from their casemates to the forecastle and the aftmost 6in moved forward, space being freed-up by removing many lighter guns, the ship keeping only nineteen 75mm and two 37mm guns. In addition, the ship had further rangefinders and new radio equipment installed.

The repaired *Rossiya* and *Gromoboi* made a short raiding cruise into the Sea of Japan from 9–13 May, during which *Rossiya* carried a kite balloon, which was deployed thirteen times over three days before being lost – the first such use of a balloon at sea. No successes were recorded, and, as she approached Vladivostok on 13 May, *Gromoboi* struck a mine. Although able to make port for repairs, she took no further part in the war: on 13 April, *Izumo* and *Kasuga* had been among escorts for a sortie in which the Japanese laid 715 mines off Vladivostok.

The Battle of Tsushima

In spite of the loss of Port Arthur, it was nevertheless decided to send the 2nd and 3rd Pacific Squadrons onwards, with Vladivostok now their destination, if necessary fighting their way through the Japanese blockade. They entered Japanese waters on 26 May, and the following day began the Battle of Tsushima against the Japanese fleet. *Kasuga* and *Nisshin* continued to serve with the four battleships of the 1st Division, the 6–6 armoured cruisers comprising the 2nd Division, with *Chiyoda* in the 6th Division, along with three protected cruisers.

Fire was opened at 14.07, with *Oslyabya* and the flagship *Kniaz Suvorov* (1902) heading the two Russian columns. *Oslyabya* received an early 12in hit close to her port waterline forward, causing significant flooding, and one in a coal bunker on the port side, with consequent leakage into the adjacent boiler room – equipped with a centreline bulkhead and thus encouraging asymmetric flooding. The ship thus took a list to port and settled by the head, her forward turret disabled and the mainmast felled. Counterflooding was attempted, but was not fully successful, additional flooding being caused when holes in the port side above the belt were put under by the increasing list, and then by two further hits forward. Hauling out of line at 14.50, her forward turret was hit by two 12in shells causing major damage to it and the bridge, while failures in the power supply disabled pumps for both flooding and firefighting. With whole ship now ablaze, water began to enter the gunports of the 3in battery around 15.00, damaged shutters preventing them from being closed, the consequent inrush of water causing *Oslyabya* to capsize around 15.10 (385 men were saved by destroyers).

Over the next four hours, all the modern Russian battleships except *Orel* were sunk. The 2nd Division played important roles in the battle, *Asama* being hit aft by a 12in shell at 14.28, temporarily disabling her steering gear. Falling out of line to effect repairs, which were completed within six minutes, while attempting to re-join her division *Asama* received two more 12in hits which caused serious flooding and reduced her speed. Nevertheless, she was able to join the 1st Division at 15.15, but efforts to get back into her proper station were hindered by a 6in hit at the base of her after funnel at 16.10, which reduced boiler draught and so power until repairs could be undertaken. She finally took station aft of *Iwate* at 17.05. At 15.35, the 2nd Division had fired at the disabled *Kniaz Suvorov*, *Azuma* and *Yakumo* firing torpedoes, albeit without effect.

From 17.30 to 18.03, the 2nd Division attempted to chase Russian cruisers, but then turned re-joined the main fleet, spotting Russian vessels that were fired on without any apparent hits from 18.30 to 19.30, once again joining up with the rest of the fleet at 20.08, around nightfall. *Asama*'s flooding was getting worse, which would lead to an hour's stop at 06.30 the next morning for further repairs.

The three remaining ships of the Russian 2nd Division (*Admiral Nakhimov*, plus the battleships *Navarin* and *Sissoi*

Veliky) were still afloat at nightfall. Of them, *Nakhimov* had been hit some thirty times, mainly by the Japanese 2nd Division, with twenty-five killed and fifty-one wounded, and in exchange had hit *Iwate* with three 8in projectiles. Overnight, Japanese destroyers and torpedo boats harried the Russian vessels. All three ships were hit by a torpedo, *Navarin* then being sunk by mines laid in her path. The other two survived until the next morning, when they foundered, *Sissoi* soon after having surrendered to two Japanese armed merchant cruisers (AMCs).[116]

Of the other two Russian armoured cruisers, *Monomakh* had been on the disengaged side of the fleet, guarding the auxiliaries, although she had exchanged fire with the protected cruiser *Izumi*. During this she had lost a 4.7in and suffered an ammunition fire in a 6in shell-hoist, resulting in the flooding of the magazine, with the loss of three men. During the night, she claimed to have sunk a Japanese destroyer at 20.25, but fifteen minutes later was hit by a torpedo from a ship she had mistaken for a Russian destroyer, flooding the starboard forward boiler room and adjacent bunker. By the next morning it was clear that *Monomakh* was in a sinking condition and could not escape; she was thus was abandoned off Tsushima Island and scuttled, sinking at 10.20.

Dmitri Donskoi had also been on auxiliary-ship protection duties, but had escaped significant damage, with just eight wounded. Overnight, she escaped the torpedoes that had claimed the remaining Russian big ships, and was proceeding northward when, the next evening, laden with survivors from *Oslyabya* and the destroyer *Buinyi* (1901), *Donskoi* was spotted by the Japanese 4th Division and badly hit in the ensuing exchange, with some 60 dead and 120 wounded; in return, she scored hits on *Naniwa* and *Otawa*. Although she escaped at nightfall, she was scuttled at 06.45 on the morning of the 29th off Ulleungdo Island, the last ship to be sunk during the battle.

Of the remaining Russian ships, the cruisers *Oleg* (1903), *Aurora* and *Zhemchug* (1903) retreated southwards and found

Nisshin's mutilated forward 8in turret after the Battle of Tsushima: the guns had been hit by two separate 12in shells, over four hours apart. (Author's collection)

internment at Manila, while the 3rd Pacific Squadron, less the coast-defence ship *Admiral Ushakov* (1893), which had become detached during the night, plus *Orel*, the only survivor of the 2nd Pacific Squadron's battleships, surrendered to Japanese warships at 10.30 on the morning of the 28th. *Ushakov*, having initially eluded the Japanese, fell in with *Iwate* and *Yakumo* during the afternoon and, having refused to surrender, was badly mauled by them; abandoned and scuttled, she sank around 18.15. The only ships of the Russian fleet to make it to Vladivostok were the cruiser-yacht *Almaz* (1903) and the destroyers *Groznyi* (1904) and *Braviy* (1901), with *Izumrud* (1903) wrecked within sight of her goal.

Japanese losses were just the torpedo boats *34*, *35* and *69*, although many ships suffered significant damage. Of the 2nd Division, *Asama* was hit eleven times during the battle (with three dead and thirteen wounded), and was the only Japanese ship that was badly-enough damaged to seek immediate repairs back in Japan. *Izumo* had been hit nine times (four dead, twenty-six wounded), *Iwate* sixteen times (sixteen wounded), *Tokiwa* eight times (one dead, fourteen wounded), and *Azuma* and *Yakumo* seven times each (no casualties). In the 1st Division, *Kasuga* had been hit three times and *Nisshin* thirteen, the first hit on the latter, from a 12in shell at 14.40, cutting the forward right 8in gun in half. Another at, 15.00 (when *Nisshin* was in the van of the Japanese fleet) penetrated the belt below the waterline and flooded a coal bunker, although another belt hit above the waterline was resisted by the armour. Yet another 12in hit at 15.30 did no significant damage, but a 9in hit on the forward turret sent splinters into the conning tower, wounding the ship's captain, and a 12in hit at 17.20 severed the left 8in gun of the aft turret. The remaining gun of the forward turret was then blown off by a further 12in hit around 19.00.

The end of the war

On 14 June, *Azuma*, *Yakumo*, *Nisshin* and *Kasuga* were assigned to the 3rd Fleet to support the projected capture of Sakhalin Island in July. Meanwhile, the 2nd Division, now reduced to *Iwate*, *Izumo* and *Tokiwa*, was tasked with defending the Korea Strait, prior to escorting troops to make an amphibious landing in north-eastern Korea, and then covering further landings at Chongjin. The war was, however, ended by the Treaty of Portsmouth on 5 September, *Asama* carrying the Emperor during the victory review in Tokyo Bay on 15 September.

Although all badly damaged by bombardment and attempts at demolition by the Russians at the time of the surrender of Port Arthur, all ships sunk there were successfully raised by the Japanese during the summer and autumn of 1905; they also included the battleships *Retvizan* and *Poltava*, and the cruiser *Pallada*. *Bayan* and *Peresvet* were refloated on 24 and 29 June,[117] respectively, and the more badly-damaged *Pobeda* on 17 October, all being able to proceed to Japan for refit under their own power (as were all other salvaged major vessels). *Bayan*, renamed *Aso*, was little altered, although

Pobeda was extensively refitted following salvage at Port Arthur, recommissioning into the Japanese navy as *Suwo*; external changes included new masts and funnels and the deletion of the 6in bowchaser. (*Author's collection*)

Bayan recommissioned as *Aso*, and spent much time as a cadet training ship; she is shown as such in Australian waters in June 1915. (*State Library of Victoria*)

rearmed with Armstrong-pattern guns and fitted with Mayabara boilers. She commissioned in 1908, and was used during 1909–10 as a cadet training ship in conjunction with another ex-Russian vessel, *Soya*, the former *Varyag*, salvaged at Chemulpo. *Sagami* (ex-*Peresvet*) and *Suwo* (ex-*Pobeda*) recommissioned as 1st class coast-defence ships in April and October 1908, the 6in bow-chaser being suppressed, along with the 47mm and 37mm batteries, their embrasures being plated over. *Suwo* received new pole masts and additional ballast.

Post-war Russia

Of the big cruisers deployed to the Far East, only two survived, *Rossiya* and *Gromoboi*, which returned to the Baltic where they both underwent extensive refits. While at the Baltic Works between 1906 and 1909, *Rossiya* had her

Gromoboi on her way back to the Baltic after the Russo-Japanese War. (NHHC NH 101909)

When refitted in 1904, Pamyat Azova had her rig reduced to two masts, was rearmed and had her funnels heightened; in this form she soon became the training ship Dvina. (Author's collection)

Rossiya after her post-war refit, with her rig reduced, upper-deck 6in fitted with casemates and the 6in bowchaser moved up onto the forecastle. (Author's collection)

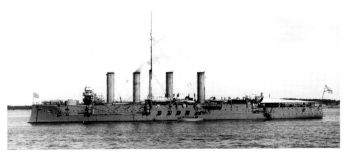

Admiral Makarov as completed with a single mast, which distinguished her from her sisters. (Author's collection)

Gromoboi was also extensively altered; she is seen here in 1911. (Author's collection)

Admiral Makarov following her 1912 re-rigging; behind her is the British battleship Cornwallis (1901). (Author's collection)

cruising engine removed, thus reducing her to two shafts. Her recently-added upper-deck 6in guns were enclosed in casemates and the forward and aft rangefinders and the radio cabin also given protection, while the roof of the conning tower was replaced to make the entry of splinters less likely. New torpedo tubes were fitted, and lighter guns reduced in number, with the rig reduced to two masts, by the removal of the mizzen and resiting the fore and main masts. Gromoboi's 1906–11 refit also reduced the rig and added yet more protection around her guns.

In addition, there still survived in the Baltic Pamiat Azova, whose modernisation had been delayed by the preparation of the 2nd and 3rd Pacific Squadrons. Plans had been prepared for an extensive reconstruction, with new Krupp armour, and the existing guns replaced by fourteen 6in/45, sixteen 47mm and eight 37mm guns. However, in the event the armour

changes were not carried through, alterations begun in 1904 being restricted to twelve new 6in and smaller guns, reboiling with Bellevilles (with heightened funnels), deletion of the mizzenmast, shifting the main further aft and restepping it vertically, the foremast following suit. On completion of her refit, Pamiat Azova returned to her gunnery training role, being formally reclassified as a training ship in October 1907. She was largely disarmed in 1909, when she became a training ship for underwater weapons under the name Dvina.

However, new vessels were already on order, with a repeat Bayan contracted with the original vessel's French builder in the spring of 1905. Although now a relatively old design, the original ship had proved satisfactory in service, and given the pressures of the war a repeat of an existing design was clearly less resource-intensive for Russian design staffs than a new one. The new vessel, Admiral Makarov, benefitted from using

Krupp, rather than Harvey, armour, allowing some thicknesses to be reduced; there were also other detail changes, most noticeably a single-masted rig, although a hope to provide a heavier-calibre tertiary battery was not achievable. Completed in 1908, she spent time in the Mediterranean as well as the Baltic during the years leading up to the First World War.

The contract for *Admiral Makarov* provided for full sets of drawings to be provided for constructing sisters in Russian yards, these being *Bayan* (ii) and *Pallada*, not commissioned until 1911. They were slightly modified as compared with the French-built prototype, having the 75mm guns removed from the main deck embrasures forward to the upper deck amidships where, joined by another pair, they replaced the 47mm guns formerly fitted there; they also completed with two masts. *Admiral Makarov* was re-rigged similarly in 1912 to permit an effective radio installation. Her new masts differed from those of her sisters in having her topmasts carried only half-way down the lower masts, rather than extending almost the whole way to deck level. Both Russian-built ships spent their entire careers in the Baltic, *Pallada* becoming an early war loss, but her sisters playing an important part in the Baltic war at sea (see pp 124, 133–5).

As well as repeating the proven *Bayan* design, an international competition had been launched in July 1904 for a completely fresh design of up to 14,000–15,000 tons, which was won by Vickers. A contract was placed with them for a single ship in June 1905, which became *Ryurik* (ii).[118] A number of sketch-designs were put forward for Russian approval, including one with no fewer than twelve 10in guns; however, the one which was finally selected displaced 13,500 tons and mounted four 10in in twin turrets fore and aft, plus twelve 8in in twin turrets on the beam, backed up by a main-deck battery of twenty 75mm guns.

However, as this sketch was developed into a design for formal approval, it grew by some 1500 tons, while once before the Naval Technical Committee further changes were required, including an increase of the main-deck battery calibre to 4.7in and changes to protection, on the basis of lessons from the war. In compensation, two of the 8in turrets were to be deleted. The ship had a complete waterline belt of Krupp armour, 6in at its thickest, with an upper belt and the battery armour (both 3in) giving complete coverage amidships. Maximising vertical armour was a key lesson that the Russians had taken from the war, contributing to the wholly-armoured sides of the battleships of the *Imperator Pavel I* (1906–7) and *Sevastopol* (1911) class battleships. *Ryurik*'s armour deck was 1in thick (1.5in on slopes), with a 1.5in main deck and 1in upper deck over the battery; a 1.5in torpedo-bulkhead was also fitted.

Gunnery trials in 1907 revealed a need for local strengthening, carried out at Kronstadt after delivery. Although it had been intended to build two sisters in Russia, limited budgets and the fact that the ship's reciprocating machinery and mixed armament were now becoming obsolescent in light of the advent of turbines and the 'all-big-gun' era, none were ordered. *Ryurik* went to the Baltic on completion, although she made a Mediterranean cruise in 1910, and was fleet flagship in 1913.

The Last Classic Armoured Cruisers

Italy

As noted above, p 61, Italian plans included four more armoured cruisers, but it was not until 1904 that the first ship was ordered. This was *San Giorgio*, ordered on 3 August 1904, with a sister, *San Marco*, following on 18 September 1905. Designed by Masdea, they were essentially an enlargement of

Ryurik (ii) after the addition of a full pole foremast. (*NHHC NH 60712*)

San Giorgio, as completed without a foremast. (Author's collection)

San Marco was also completed with a single mast; she could be distinguished from her sister by her fully-cased funnels and higher placement of the aft searchlight platform. (Author's collection)

Amalfi, as completed; she could be distinguished from her sister Pisa by the upper margins of her funnels. (Author's collection)

the 'improved Garibaldis' previously sketched, retaining the raised forecastle but with 10in/45 weapons substituted for the 8in fore and aft, with the beam turrets equipped with a new 7.5in/45 gun, rather than 8in. The engine rooms were, however, as in the Garibaldis, once again placed amidships, with the boiler rooms fore and aft, now exhausting through two sets of twin funnels.[119] San Marco was innovatory in that she was to be the first turbine-powered vessel in the Italian navy; she also differed from her sister in having a simplified superstructure. The ships had a particularly complicated armour scheme, based around a complete waterline belt and an upper belt, with the armour deck complemented by armoured main and upper decks.

Both vessels had their funnels reduced in height after trials,[120] and lacked foremasts as completed, following the pattern of other Italian capital ships of the period (e.g. the second pair of the Regina Elena-class battleships). Light signal foremasts were, however, installed during the First World War, later replaced by heavier examples with a fire-control top.

In the meantime, two ships of very similar characteristics had been laid down by the Orlando and Odero yards to an Orlando design. These looked very different from the San Giorgios, with conventional machinery layout, and owed much to the Regina Elena-class battleships, albeit with a flush deck. Armament was the same as in the San Giorgios (although with different patterns of guns and mountings), but although the main belt was essentially the same, the overall armour scheme was simpler, less extensive and lighter.

While designed in collaboration with the Italian navy, they

had not, however, been formally ordered by it, and it was not until 1907 that the two ships were actually purchased as Amalfi and Pisa. Although stated in contemporary periodicals as having been laid down on speculation, they were much larger than usual 'stock' ships, and it seems more likely that, especially in view of the navy's involvement in their design, that there had been some 'understanding' to smooth state financial programming issues, much as seems to have been the case when the Japanese were procuring the Asamas (see p 73, above). On the other hand, once Amalfi and Pisa had been sold, a further vessel (B, also sometimes referred to as X) was laid down by the Orlando shipyard, which was not then acquired by Italy, and seems then to have been suspended until another buyer came forward.[121] As completed (see p 107, below), this ship would have a 9.2in main battery of Elswick manufacture, rather than the 10in Vickers guns of the Italian pair. It would appear that a further vessel of this modified type was projected, albeit with Vickers guns: this firm manufactured four 9.2in guns intended for a cruiser 'to be built in Italy', but the order for was subsequently cancelled.[122]

The British final generation

Consideration of designs for the armoured cruisers to be ordered under the 1904–5 Estimates had begun in the summer of 1903, well before final decisions had been made on the changes to the Duke of Edinburgh design that would produce the Warriors.[123] Protection would be at least as in the preceding vessels, thicker on the waterline if possible. Eleven armament arrangements were submitted for consideration in December, involving twin and single 9.2in and 7.5in mountings, with one using twin 6in. Some were variants on options considered for the Duke of Edinburghs and by now being considered for the Warriors (six single 9.2in, plus six twin 6in/single 7.5in), while others used new twin 9.2in and 7.5in mountings. All-7.5in sketches ranged up to sixteen (eight twin) or even eighteen (six twin, plus six single) guns, some with a single 9.2in substituted for a twin 7.5in. Those envisaging twin 9.2in turrets backed these up by either six twin or ten single 7.5in mountings.

The 7.5in-only designs were felt to be both crowded and lacking in armour-piercing capability in a fleet-scouting role, with the Director of Naval Ordnance suggesting that 10in guns be substituted for the existing 9.2in to enhance this, pointing to their installation in the American Tennessee class. Cost-pressures were also operating (exacerbated by the purchase of *Triumph* and *Swiftsure*, p 63, above), options for (cheaper) battery-mounting of secondary guns being investigated, resulting in sketches that included ones with both 7.5in and 6in so arranged. However, these were clearly inferior to those with all-turret-mounted guns, and it was decided in February 1904 that any trade-off should be on the basis of total numbers, rather than the cost of individual ships. It was also decided that 7.5in guns should be used, rather than larger numbers of 6in. The final decision was thus between the two options that were built around two twin 9.2in turrets (which gave the same heavy broadside as the six singles of the *Duke of Edinburgh*s), the general preference for single guns over twins leading to the final design having ten such 7.5in mountings, five on each beam.

The twin 9.2in turret, which mounted the new 50cal Mk XI gun, had been designed for the battleships of the *Lord Nelson* class (1906), and was thus somewhat heavier than a dedicated cruiser mounting would have been. The tertiary battery was before completion increased from the *Warriors*' 3pdr weapons to 12pdrs, in view of the increasing size of torpedo craft. Mixed boilering was abandoned for the new ships, an all-watertube fit being applied, giving 4000ihp more than in the *Warriors*.

Protection generally followed that in *Warrior*, but with reductions to make up for the increased length of the new ships. Thus, the upper belt was omitted (but with 7in-armoured ammunition hoists at this level), along with its closing transverse bulkheads, and the main belt thinned by 1in towards the bow. Horizontal protection was concentrated on a single armoured lower deck, with a box citadel around the cylinder heads. Underwater protection was enhanced through the use of unpierced bulkheads in the machinery spaces.

Four ships had originally been planned for 1904–5, *Minotaur* (ii), *Shannon* (ii), *Defence* (ii) and *Orion*, but the aforementioned cost-pressures resulting from the purchase of *Triumph* and *Swiftsure* led to the latter being not proceeded with (likewise a potential third ship of the *Lord Nelson* class of battleships was not built). *Shannon* was constructed with different hull-lines from her sisters to resolve a long-standing dispute over the merits of hollow bow-lines (as generally used), versus full (straight) ones. A comparison of her trial results with those of *Minotaur* showed 0.5kt less (on 1000ihp greater power) in conditions that should theoretically have favoured her hull form. *Defence* also failed to make her designed speed, only *Minotaur* getting to 23kt (she was unique in the class in having Babcock & Wilcox boilers, which exhausted into fatter funnels than the Yarrow units of her two sisters). These and the masts were stepped upright, rather than at the rake fitted in the *Devonshire*s through *Warriors*, operational experience having shown that raked masts suffered over-stressing when derricks stepped from them were used for boat-handling.[124]

Minotaur as completed with short funnels. She and her sisters could be easily distinguished from the immediately-preceding classes by their upright masts and funnels. (*Author's collection*)

Shannon was the first ship to commission, joining the 5th CS of the Home Fleet as flagship, but moving to the 2nd CS on the reorganisation in March 1909, as its flagship from March 1910; on 5 December 1909 she collided with the battleship *Prince George* (1896) at Portsmouth. On relief by *Indomitable* in March 1912, *Shannon* moved to the 3rd CS as its flagship, but resumed the flag of the 2nd CS at the end of 1912, remaining part the squadron for the rest of her active career. In contrast, after beginning her service with the 5th and 1st CS in the Home Fleet, *Minotaur* relieved *King Alfred* as China Station flagship in January 1910, remaining abroad until after the outbreak of the First World War. Pre-1914 modifications were limited to the heightening of funnels by 15ft and the fitting of range-clocks in 1909, and the removal of torpedo nets during 1913–14.

Defence was the last conventional British armoured cruiser to commission, actually being finished after the last of the new *Invincible*-class 12in-gunned cruisers – soon to be reclassified as battlecruisers (see below). As such, after a short period in the 5th and 2nd CS, she joined the 1st CS of the Home Fleet alongside *Minotaur* and the three *Invincibles*, remaining with the latter even after *Minotaur* had left for China in January 1910. *Defence* was detached to escort the royal yacht *Medina* (1911, a P&O liner) to the Delhi *durbar* during 1911–12, being then sent to join *Minotaur* in China.

On 1 January 1913, a reorganisation of the British fleet turned the Mediterranean Fleet into an all-cruiser force, led by four battlecruisers of the 2nd BCS, supported by a reconstituted 1st CS (the 'old' 1st CS transforming into the 1st BCS in home waters). This was led by *Defence*, where she still was in August 1914, leading *Black Prince*, *Duke of Edinburgh* and *Warrior*.

Single-calibre Batteries

In contrast to the mixed batteries of the last generations of these Italian and British vessels, two intended sisters of the French *Ernest Renan*, built under the 1904 and 1905 programmes (the only big ships authorised in France during 1903–5),[125] had their designs re-cast to replace *Renan*'s mix of 7.6in and 6.5in weapons with fourteen 7.6in guns, four in twin turrets fore and aft, six in upper-deck single turrets, and four in casemates; these were backed by eighteen 65mm anti-torpedo-boat weapons. In addition to the armament change, armour thicknesses were adjusted and the upperworks slightly differently arranged compared to *Renan*. The ships also had fully-cased funnels and a new vertical bow, of the same kind adopted for the succeeding *Danton* (and later) classes of battleships. Laid down in 1905–6, *Waldeck-Rousseau* and *Edgar Quinet*, as the new ships were named, were completed in 1911. The last French big ships to be powered solely by reciprocating engines (the *Danton*-class battleships switched to turbines, although the 1912-authorised *Normandie* class battleships adopted a composite turbine/reciprocating installation), the pair joined their half-sister *Renan* in the 1st Light Division of the Mediterranean Squadron.

Germany had never adopted mixed batteries, maintaining a uniform set of 8.2in main guns, backed up by 5.9in secondaries since the *Prinz Adalbert*s. Their final essay into the classic big cruiser genre produced probably the finest example of the breed, although with a reputation besmirched by her demise (pp 125–6, below). To become *Blücher*, the ship was the product of a labyrinthine design process, starting out as a developed, faster, better-protected *Scharnhorst*, and at first retaining her eight 8.2in guns.[126] However, the armament soon grew to twelve 8.2in in six twin turrets, although the associated

Edgar Quinet, as completed. *(Author's collection)*

costs led to the investigation of a reduction to ten or even back to eight guns, but with more secondary guns.

Although sketches were made with a new 9.4in gun, these were judged too big and expensive, and a new cycle of development began in September 1905, which mounted twelve 8.2in on 14,400 tons, significantly larger than previous designs. By the end of the month the essential features of the final vessel had been established, although the ship would not be laid down for another eighteen months – by which time she had been outclassed by new 12in-armed vessels under construction in the UK (see pp 106–7, below). However, as funding had been finalised before the news broke, there was no scope for re-casting the design with bigger guns. The oft-told story that the armament of *Blücher* was the result of planted false documents giving the *Invincible*s a 9.2in armament finds no support in contemporary German design documents, nor in the chronology of the respective ships' design processes.

Blücher commissioned in October 1909, on the completion of her work-up replacing *Yorck* as flagship of the German fleet's Scouting Unit, which now also comprised *Roon* (2nd flag) and *Gneisenau*, plus six light cruisers. However, in September 1911, *Blücher* was relieved by the new 11in-armed *Von der Tann*, and became a gunnery trials ship, although she returned to the fleet for a cruise to Danish waters in 1912, as flagship of the II. SG for that year's manoeuvres, and briefly again during 1913. During the latter stint, she ran aground off the island of Romsø in the Great Belt on 28 May, only being pulled free on 1 June.

During the consequent refit, *Blücher* received a tripod foremast for trials purposes, the first of its kind in German service, allowing for the fitting of a much-enlarged spotting top, with a rangefinder above and a prototype director-type system. The latter was first implemented in the port secondary battery, extended to the starboard battery in 1914, and finally the main battery at the end of the year. Experience in *Blücher* led to a tripod mast being included in the designs of the 1913 and later capital ships. On outbreak of war, along with other ships on secondary duties, *Blücher* re-joined the fleet once again.

Dawn of the Battlecruiser

Genesis

Up to the beginning of the twentieth century, cruiser guns had been generally limited to 10in calibre at the most (the only exception being the 12.6in guns in the Japanese *Matsushima* class of 1889–91, which had been specifically designed to penetrate the belts of Chinese battleship). However, as the new century progressed, this implicit limit was progressively eroded as the logic of longer-range fire and the strategic and tactical evolution of the big cruiser led inexorably towards guns of undoubted battleship size.

One of the first suggestions of such a 'big gun cruiser' was made by the French constructor Bertin to Navy Minister Lockroy in 1899, when he sketched an enlarged (14,500-ton) *Léon Gambetta* with a single 12in fore and aft, backed up by

Blücher, as built. *(Author's collection)*

fourteen 6.5in (six in turrets, the rest in main-deck casemates).[127] This was not carried forward, but during the first year of the the Russo-Japanese War, Japan ordered the first vessel of the genre.

Interestingly, before going down the route of such a vessel, Japan had considered the option of an 'all 6in' design, with twenty guns of that calibre, arranged in eight twin mountings (two each on the centreline of the forecastle and quarterdeck, four at the corners of the citadel) and four single casemates, protected by a 6in main belt.[128] This was clearly not in keeping with the evolving role of the armoured cruiser in the conflict with Russia, leading to a pair of ships being ordered with a main battery of four 12in guns, a significant jump from the 8in guns of the 6–6 series of cruisers.

They were funded under a Temporary Special Budget Law, promulgated a month after the outbreak of the Russo-Japanese War, which included funds for two battleships, four armoured cruisers and forty-seven smaller vessels. *Tsukuba* and *Ikoma*, the first pair of armoured cruisers were authorised on 4 July 1904, but had actually been ordered in anticipation on 23 June.[129] Two more ships of the type were authorised at the end of January 1905, *Kurama* under the Special Budget (along with the first two vessels as part of the 1904 War Naval Supplementary Programme), and *Ibuki* under the pre-war (June 1903) Third Period Naval Extension Programme. The latter had covered three battleships and three armoured cruisers, but only two of the battleships were yet under contract.[130]

The design of the new ships was carried out during the second half of 1904, the first one being laid down in January 1905. Their twin 12in turrets fore and aft gave them a main battery equal to that of contemporary battleships, but combined them with a speed of 20.5kt – 2.5kt greater than the 18kt that was standard for most such vessels. On the other hand, the belt was only 7in thick, rather than the 9in typical of contemporary battleships. *Tsukuba* thus represented a new type of ship that could overwhelm any cruiser, but avoid action with anything capable of matching or over-matching her; a raised forecastle extending well aft guaranteed seaworthiness. The design was also the one of the first big ships for many years to do away with a ram bow, instead sporting an elegant clipper stem; it also incorporated war experience by minimising the amount of superstructure. As the first capital ships to be designed and built in Japan, the construction of the *Tsukuba* class presented major challenges. Nevertheless, *Tsukuba* herself completed two years after laying down, although the other ships took longer.

Tsukuba and *Ikoma* had casemated secondary batteries of twelve 6in/45, backed up by a dozen 4.7in/50s. Eight of the former were in a main-deck battery that proved to be too wet for use; accordingly, the embrasures were plated up around 1913–14, and six guns moved to the upper deck, displacing four of the 4.7in weapons. In *Kurama* and *Ibuki*, the 6in battery was replaced by eight 8in/45 guns, guns mounted in twin turrets at the corners of the citadel. The resulting 10ft additional length amidships and 800 tons displacement

Tsukuba early in her career. (Author's collection)

Kurama. (Author's collection)

required more power, eight further boilers being added, resulting in a third funnel.

Although *Kurama* was laid down in August 1905, not long after the first pair, construction was very slow, with the building of the battleships *Satsuma* and *Settsu* and the rebuilding of captured Russian vessels given higher priority at Yokosuka dockyard. The laying-down of *Ibuki* was delayed by the presence of the battleship *Aki* on the slip intended for her, but once construction of the hull was actually begun in May 1907, progress was rapid, launching occurring only six months later. Soon afterwards, it was decided to fit *Ibuki* with turbines, rather than the reciprocating engines of the other three cruisers, and also with director fire control (both for the first time in Japanese service); however, in spite of the changes needed, she completed in November 1909, now having been given priority over *Aki* which, also adapted for turbine propulsion, did not complete until 1911. *Kurama* was also finally finished that year, differing from her sister and half-sisters in being rigged with tripod masts, to better carry modern fire-control equipment; both these and the funnels were taller than in *Ibuki*. *Tsukuba* had her masts heightened after completion, but those of *Ikoma* and *Ibuki* were not changed.

Of Japan's older armoured cruisers, *Azuma* had her funnels

heightened and fully cased, while *Kasuga* and *Nisshin* also received taller, fully-cased funnels in 1912–14. In their case, this was in conjunction with the replacement of their obsolescent cylindrical boilers by new watertube Kampon units, *Nisshin's* refit being prompted by a boiler explosion in November 1912 that killed twenty. *Tokiwa* had already received new Kampon boilers in 1910, although her sister would not be reboilered until under repair during the First World War.

Fulfilment

In Britain, a move to an all-big-gun armoured cruiser for the 1905–6 programme was clear by the end of 1904 (Admiral Sir John Fisher having become First Sea Lord in October, bringing with him radical ideas for the future). Then, proposals were made that the *Minotaurs* (just about to be laid down) might be modified, to replace their 7.5in beam mountings with three twin 9.2in turrets on each side, with two twins and one single (as in the *Lord Nelson*-class battleships) as an alternative. While nothing was actually done to change the existing ships (presumably because the time taken for such a redesign would have been unacceptable), the concept was taken forward for the next generation of ships. This as at first again based on fourteen/sixteen 9.2in, but then on eight 12in guns, influenced in part by the Japanese move to this calibre for their latest armoured cruisers.

A series of sketches were considered by a Committee on Designs established in December 1904, which should be capable of 25.5kt, be armed with 12in and anti-torpedo boat guns only, and be armoured on the same scale as *Minotaur*. A desire for good ahead fire meant that the first three sketches to be produced had twin 12in turrets set abreast on the forecastle (one also having the same arrangement aft) – an unusual arrangement of turrets last seen in the Russian battleships of the *Ekaterina II* class (1883–9) and the German coast-defence ships of the *Siegfried/Odin* classes (1889–95). Unfortunately, blast effects were prohibitive, as well as producing a poor broadside; accordingly, the next two basic sketches had a lozenge distribution of turrets, the second of which ('E') had the beam turrets placed *en echelon*, to allow limited cross-deck firing in the event that the opposite turret was disabled. A further sketch placed the wing turrets abreast the forward superstructure, with no turret on the forecastle, but it was 'E' that formed the basis for the further work.

In January 1905, in light of the adoption of turbines for the new battleship *Dreadnought*, the idea of replacing the *Minotaur*-type two-shaft reciprocating plant with turbines began to be investigated; a four-shaft turbine arrangement was agreed the following month. Board approval was given in June, although keel-laying of the three ships *Invincible*, *Inflexible* and *Indomitable*, did not take place until the beginning of 1906.

Indomitable as completed. (NHHC NH 60003)

Construction then proceeded rapidly, all three being launched in the spring of 1907 and completed during 1908, preceding the last of the *Minotaur*s, *Defence*, into service. They also beat all but the first of the Japanese big-gun cruisers into service, bitterly disappointing the Japanese navy in having their own revolutionary ships made obsolescent almost immediately.

In spite of the move to 12in guns in *Invincible*, the idea of armoured cruisers with 9.2in was not entirely dead. As a cost-saving measure, a number of 9.2in-armed sketches were considered for the 1908–9 programme.[131] One was essentially reduced a reduced, 9.2in-armed *Invincible*, 1500 tons lighter and 40ft shorter than the prototype, with eight 9.2in/50, sixteen 4in/40 Mk VIII (rather than the heavier 50cal Mk VII), and two torpedo tubes. Protection would have been similar to *Invincible*, but with some reductions in thickness at the margins. Of the other options, one had only three twin turrets, all on the centreline, on 13,000 tons, while another had two twins and two singles.

However, the decision of Germany to include 'big-gun cruisers' in their 1907 later programmes (beginning with *Von der Tann*) led to the next British 'armoured cruiser', *Indefatigable*, being another 12in-gunned vessel. Nevertheless, 9.2in designs continued to be produced down to 1913, when sketches 'E2' and 'E3' represented vessels with eight 9.2in and eight 6in guns, capable of 28kt and protected with 6in belts, on 15,500/17,850 tons.

Although only the British, Germans and Japanese would actually build such big-gun cruisers in the years leading up to the First World War, in the USA the idea of a battleship-armoured version of the *Tennessee*s, with four 12in and twenty-two 3in (no 6in) guns was mooted at a Naval War College conference in 1903. A 1908 conference endorsed the utility of vessels along the lines of *Invincible*, and in November 1909 a set of six 25.5kt designs based on the latest battleships, the *Wyoming* class, were sketched out. These displayed different trade-offs of armament and armour for speed. However, nothing was done until Japanese developments led to further studies that by 1914 had resulted, as in the UK, to the concept of the 'fast battleship' instead.[132]

On 24 November 1911, all British armoured cruisers of the *Invincible* and later classes (by then augmented in service by *Indefatigable*) were redesignated as battlecruisers, formally marking the creation of a new type, and implicitly marking earlier ships as obsolescent. As already noted, in January 1913, the 1st CS became the 1st BCS, marking the tactical separation of the two types of cruiser. Japan also reclassified the *Tsubuka/Kurama*s as battlecruisers as 1912, along with the 14in-gunned *Kongo* class, the first of which had been laid down the previous year. Interestingly, the German navy did not follow suit, continuing to classify its big-gun cruisers (*Von der Tann* commissioned in September 1910, and was followed by one further vessel each year) as 'large cruisers' alongside earlier vessels down to the dissolution of the Imperial Navy in 1919.[133]

Georgios Averof, early in her long career. *(Author's collection)*

The Last of the Line

The suspended third ship of the *Pisa* class (p 101, above) was finally purchased by Greece (in the face of Turkish interest) in October 1909,[134] the one-third downpayment being obtained from a bequest left under the will of the Egypt-based businessman and philanthropist Georgios Averof (1815–99). This had required that one-fifth of his property should be devoted to the construction of a cruiser, to be named after him and capable of acting as a cadet training ship. The remainder of the cost of the ship was covered by the Greek National Fleet Fund.

Apart from the already-noted differences in armament, the now-*Georgios Averof* could be easily distinguished from her Italian sisters by being rigged with two tripod masts. In June 1911, soon after commissioning, the ship visited the UK represent her country at King George V's coronation naval review and to pick up ammunition for her British-made 9.2in and 7.5in guns. Directly following the review, she touched ground while entering Plymouth Sound, and suffered a near-mutiny while drydocked for a month's repairs.

The acquisition of *Averof* was a concern to Turkey, and in December 1909 the German military attaché in Constantinople was informed by the Turkish Grand Vizier (prime minister) that the Ottoman Navy was seeking an armoured cruiser and some destroyers to balance the expanding Greek fleet. The sale of four torpedo boats was rapidly agreed, but the question of a larger ship was more problematic. *Blücher* was initially offered, but discussions included the as-yet-unfinished battlecruisers *Von der Tann*, *Moltke* and *Goeben*. However, in July the offer of a large cruiser was dropped by the German State Secretary, who substituted the option of some or all of the *Brandenburg*-class battleships (1891–2). As a result, *Barbaros Hayreddin* (ex-*Kurfürst Friedrich Wilhelm*) and *Turgut Reis* (ex-*Weißenburg*), were handed over on 1 September 1910. As we will see below, these acquisitions were but initial steps in what would soon turn into armed conflict between Greece and Turkey.

New Big-Cruiser Navies

On 4 May 1910, a Naval Service Act was passed by the Canadian Parliament to provide for a Naval Service of Canada (Royal Canadian Navy from August 1911). To meet the training requirements of the new navy, two cruisers were acquired from the Royal Navy, the 3600-ton *Apollo*-class *Rainbow* was to serve on the Pacific coast, and the much bigger *Niobe* was to be based on the Atlantic. Both vessels were refitted with new heating systems, new galleys and radio. *Niobe* arrived at Halifax, Nova Scotia, on 21 October 1910, being formally transferred on 12 November 1910. While departing for a training cruise, *Niobe* ran aground in fog off Cape Sable, Nova Scotia, on the night of 30/31 July 1911, repairs lasting until January 1912, and leaving the ship with a permanently reduced maximum speed. She was then laid up, only recommissioning at the outbreak of the First World War.

Also in 1910, another nation sought to become a big cruiser owner, when Peru, concerned that Ecuador might be about to buy the Italian protected cruiser *Umbria* (1891), approached France about purchasing an armoured cruiser to over-match her. The initial thought was to offer one of the *Kléber* class, but in the spring of 1911 the French Navy proposed reconditioning for Peru the recently-stricken *Dupuy de Lôme* (p 42, above). Accordingly, a contract was agreed in July 1911, for a price of FF 3 million, plus the cost of reconditioning, estimated at FF 0.7 million. Work proceeded, with the ship ready for trials in January 1912, which were successfully completed in March. The arrival of her new Peruvian crew was delayed, but the ship was formally transferred in September as *Commandante Elias Aguirre*.

However, Peru, with the urgency of the purchase reduced by the fact that in the event *Umbria* had actually been sold to Haiti,[135] were slow in making payments, only the first FF 1 million having been paid by the outbreak of the First World War, when the Peruvian crew were repatriated. Following negotiations, it was agreed in January 1917 that the ship revert to France, the monies paid being offset against the outturn costs of the refit (FF 0.9 million), with any receipts from the sale of the ship over FF 0.4 million paid to Peru. Put up for sale, ex-*Dupuy de Lôme* (her name had now been given to a submarine) was in the interim used as a mooring- and accommodation-hulk at Lorient for American vessels based there. In October 1918, the ship was finally sold – not for scrap, but for yet another career (see p 137 below).

The USA: Modernisation and Beyond

Between 1909 to 1914, all US battleships and post-*Brooklyn* armoured cruisers (excluding the *St Louis* class) had cage masts installed as part of a general fire-control upgrade. While most battleships had both fore and mainmasts replaced, the armoured cruisers only had their foremasts changed (the last refit being that of *Montana* in 1914).[136] The work also included the removal of the ships' 3pdr batteries, flying bridges, aft bridge and wooden charthouses, with the intent that ships should now normally be conned from within the conning tower. The latter intent stemmed from the experience of the Russo-Japanese War, and its high casualty rate among exposed personnel – especially senior officers on the bridge – and was one of the outputs from the key Newport Conference in 1908.[137] All the *Pennsylvania*s except the name-ship had the upper maintop removed as well. *Pennsylvania* and *Colorado* were further modified in 1914, when that the remaining twenty-four Niclausse boilers were replaced with twelve Babcock & Wilcox units, although the eight 'composite' forward boilers were kept.

When the first refits began, the *Pennsylvania*s and the first two *Tennessee*s were still with the Pacific Fleet, but in February 1910 the latter two formed a special service squadron to represent the USA at the centenary of the Argentine Republic, and then headed north to join the Atlantic Fleet, uniting with the other two ships of the class, which had served there since completion in 1908. *Tennessee* and *Montana* were detached as a special service squadron to the Mediterranean from November 1912 to May 1913, to protect US interests during the Balkan Wars (for which, see p 113, below).

In January 1911, *Pennsylvania* was fitted with a temporary

The big American armoured cruisers were fitted with cage foremasts between 1909 and 1914. Here we have *Tennessee* soon after her refit. *LoC LC-D4-22786)*

deck stretching from the mainmast to just beyond the stern, to be used for what proved to be the first successful landing of an aircraft from a ship on the 18th. On the 24th she was the first US vessel to launch a manned kite balloon, although such equipment had previously been used operationally by Russia during 1904–5 (see p 96). However, in July, *Pennsylvania* was reduced to the Pacific Reserve Fleet, owing to personnel shortages that led to most of the American big cruisers spending a period laid up over the next few years.

The Atlantic-based *North Carolina* and *Montana* went into reserve in 1911, the latter vessel then became a torpedo training ship in 1914, with 21in and 18in tubes installed on the upper deck. *Washington* was also withdrawn from service between July 1913 and April 1914 as a receiving ship at Brooklyn. On returning to full commission, she was deployed to the Caribbean, in light of events in Haiti, the Dominican Republic and Mexico, remaining in the area until being taken in hand for refit at the beginning of 1916.

The troubles in Mexico also prompted the return to service of *North Carolina* in August 1914, to relieve the battleship *Mississippi* (1905, now being sold to Greece – cf. p 113) as

aeronautical station ship at Veracruz. However, soon afterwards she proceeded with *Tennessee* (recommissioned after three months as a receiving ship at Brooklyn) and the collier *Jason* (1912), to Europe and the Mediterranean to evacuate Americans and other neutrals following the outbreak of the First World War; they returned in August 1915. *North Carolina* then became station ship at the new Naval Air Center at Pensacola, Florida. As such she was fitted with a primitive catapult, the first to be installed in a warship, from which the first-ever catapult launch of an aircraft was carried out on 5 November 1915.

During her lay-up, *Pennsylvania* was renamed *Pittsburgh* in August 1912, to free her name for a new battleship; down to 1920, all other state-named cruisers would exchange their existing names for major cities – but not the capitals[138] – of their original states. This not only reflected the expansion of US Navy's battleship force, but also the big cruisers' decline from capital status.

In early January 1914, tensions caused by the Mexican revolution led to the recommissioning of *Pittsburgh* for service as Pacific Fleet flagship off the west coast of Mexico, but boiler

Pennsylvania being fitted with a landing deck at Mare Island in January 1911; she had not yet received her cage foremast. *(NHHC NH 70595)*

Memphis (ex-*Tennessee*) was at anchor at Santo Domingo on 29 August 1916 when she was driven ashore by a giant hurricane-generated wave. A total loss, she was stripped of reusable equipment by personnel from the battleship *New Hampshire*, stricken in December 1917 and sold for scrap in 1922, breaking-up continuing until 1938. (*NHHC NH 49912*)

As refitted during 1916–17, the *Pennsylvania* and *Tennessee* classes had new fire-control equipment installed (*Montana* exchanging the lower searchlight on her foremast for a rangefinder), together with two 3in AA guns. In addition, compressed-air aircraft catapults were fitted in *Washington* (March 1916), *North Carolina* (June 1916, replacing her earlier experimental model) and *Huntington* (ex-*West Virginia*, February 1917); *Montana* was fitted for, but not with (May 1916). They were rigged from the mainmast to the stern, in which direction aircraft were launched, aircraft being hoisted inboard by extensions to the boat cranes and stored on the after superstructure, from which rails led to the catapult. While *North Carolina* carried out extensive trials with her installation, including in fleet exercises, the aircraft equipment proved too fragile for operational use, as well as seriously interfering with the aft turret. *Seattle* had hers removed in the summer of 1917 and *Huntington* after her first transatlantic escort voyage in September of that year. *North Carolina* was the last to keep her catapult, which was taken out at the beginning of 1918.

Subsidiary Service

With the advent of Admiral Sir John Fisher as British First Sea Lord in 1904 there was a major upheaval in the Royal Navy. Amongst other things there was a clear-out of the reserves, with the wholesale disposal of many classes of vessels, including the scrapping of *Warspite*, *Northampton* and the whole *Orlando* class between 1905 and 1907. *Nelson* and the *Audacious*/*Swiftsure*s had by then already been hulked, with other aging vessels joining them on subsidiary duties.

Following the disposal of the *Orlando*s, a number of which had been employed on gunnery training duties, various members of the *Edgar* class were appropriated to replace them. Thus *Endymion*, *Theseus* and *Grafton* were refitted for the role in 1905, replacing *Narcissus*, *Immortalité* and *Undaunted*.

defects forced her return to reserve the following month, remaining laid up (including the aforementioned reboiling) until February 1916. She was replaced by *California*, while *West Virginia* and *South Dakota* also recommissioned for Mexican service in April 1914, during the Veracruz crisis, but then returned to reserve; *Colorado* was another ship briefly returned to full commission for Mexican service, during 1914. American interests were also felt to be under threat in the Caribbean, whence *Tennessee* was deployed repeatedly following her return from Europe, culminating in three months of intervention in a revolution in the Dominican Republic. Renamed *Memphis* on 25 May 1916, was driven ashore by a freak wave in August and became a total loss.

Seattle (ex-*Washington*), shown with a catapult and extended cranes in 1917. (*NHHC NH 86410*)

Changes included replacing some of their 6in guns with other marks, and four of the 6pdrs switched for 4.7in. *Theseus* and *Endymion* remained in service as such until 1912, when they were respectively relieved by the battleships *Magnificent* and *Jupiter*. Passing into the 4th Fleet, the cruisers' armaments were reverted to their original fits.

The withdrawal of *Northampton* and other old ships employed for boys' and youths' instruction led to *Gibraltar* and *St George* becoming seagoing boys' training ships, while *Hawke* took a similar role for youths. *Royal Arthur* was at one point considered to become a navigating school ship, but this was not carried forward, the ship replacing *Ariadne* as flagship of the 4th CS.

As previously noted (p 37), three of the *Audacious*es had been converted to unpowered destroyer depot ships during 1902–4. However, the programme for such vessels was terminated in January 1905, and a shift made to self-powered vessels to support such flotilla vessels. To provide the necessary hulls, a number of now-aging cruisers were adapted for the role, *Imperieuse*, renamed *Sapphire II*, replacing *Erebus* (ex-*Invincible*) at Portland in February 1905. She was little altered for the role, with only her 6in guns dismounted to make additional space in the battery. Further cruisers were adapted for the destroyer depot role the following year, including *Blake* and *Blenheim*, as well as the much smaller *Leander* (1882). The former *Imperieuse* would be withdrawn from depot service at the end of 1912 and scrapped, but *Blake* and *Blenheim* served on into the 1920s. *St George* was proposed for conversion for destroyer depot duties in 1907, although her copper sheathing presented a problem in that it could have caused galvanic problems with steel-bottomed vessels alongside. However, in the event she completed her

refit in 1910, relieving *Tyne* (1878) at the Nore. She and the *Blake*s had their armament reduced to four 6in (their sponson mountings).

The former unpowered depot ships were then adapted for harbour training roles. Ex-*Audacious* and ex-*Invincible* became part of the new *Fisgard* establishment at Portsmouth (as *Fisgard* and *Fisgard II*), while ex-*Triumph* became part of the *Tenedos* establishment at Chatham until 1910, when she moved with her role to Devonport, as *Indus IV*.

In 1912 *Powerful* was stripped of her propelling machinery and housed over as a boys' training establishment at Devonport, commissioning as such on 23 September 1913, along with *Powerful II*, the former *Diadem*-class *Andromeda*; these ships were now also beginning to pass from service. *Terrible* was also earmarked for subsidiary duties and was under consideration for conversion to a coal hulk (with a capacity of 12,000 tons), the removal of her guns having been approved on 14 July 1914. Nothing had, however, been done by the outbreak of the First World War, after which she once again saw sea service (see below, pp 120–1).

Diadem herself paid off in 1913, and the following year she was nominated for conversion to replace *Actaeon* (ex-4th rate *Vernon*) as a torpedo school vessel at Portsmouth under the 1914–15 estimates. However, this was also overtaken by the outbreak of war, and *Diadem* continued in service as a stokers' training ship into 1915. Another sister, *Spartiate*, had also reduced to a stoker training role at Portsmouth on paying off in 1913, and remained as such until July 1915. She then transferred to the *Fisgard* training establishment as an accommodation ship, replacing ex-*Audacious* and ex-*Invincible*, which had been withdrawn for use at Scapa Flow in August 1914 (the latter being lost in tow en-route).

The first generations of big iron cruisers began to be disposed of early in the twentieth century. This view of T W Ward's Morecambe scrapyard, taken on 27 October 1905, shows *Northampton* with breaking-up already well underway, and *Raleigh* just arriving. (*Lancashire County Council*)

Powerful as the training hulk *Impregnable I* at Devonport, some time after October 1922. (*Devonport Naval Heritage Centre*)

6 | TRIAL BY COMBAT

The Italo-Turkish war

Italy had coveted Libya since the occupation of Tunisia and Cyprus by France and Britain following the Russo-Turkish War of 1877–8. By 1911 press campaigns in Italy were pushing for an invasion, culminating in an ultimatum to the Ottoman government in September. Although the latter responded by offering to transfer control of Libya to Italy while retaining ultimate suzerainty (akin to the de facto situation with Egypt vis-à-vis the UK), this was rejected and war declared on 29 September. The Italian navy outnumbered its Turkish opposite number both quantitatively and qualitatively, with its Italian armoured cruisers an important component, although *San Giorgio* was under refit following a serious grounding and thus not available at the beginning of the war.

Tripoli was immediately blockaded by *Pisa* and *Amalfi*, together with the battleships *Roma* and *Napoli*. They were then relieved by the battleship *Benedetto Brin* (1901) and the Italian training division, which included three battleships and *Carlo Alberto*, and fired on the coastal defences on 3–4 October, by now joined by *Giuseppe Garibaldi* and *Francesco Ferruccio*; *Varese* led a covering force to seaward. On the morning of the 4th, a naval brigade was landed by *Garibaldi*, reinforced by a force of 1200 men on the 5th, which soon secured the city. However, Ottoman counter-attacks followed, including a reoccupation of the forts that was countered by naval gunfire by ships that included *Carlo Alberto*, which was also involved in repulsing counter-attacks into November. Her sister, *Vettor Pisani*, remained for the time being in Italian waters, as flagship of Luigi Amedeo, Duke of the Abruzzi (1873–1933), the overall war commander.

While landings successfully secured Tobruk, Derna (where the force included *Pisa*, *Amalfi* and *San Marco*) and Khoms (led by *Varese* and *Marco Polo*), there was stronger resistance at Benghazi, with *San Marco* involved in supporting the Italian forces attempting to maintain their positions there. Elsewhere in the Ottoman Empire, the protected cruiser *Piedmont* (1888) led a Red Sea force that defeated a small Ottoman force at the Battle of Kunfuda Bay on 7 January 1912 and blockaded Yemeni ports. In the eastern Mediterranean, *Garibaldi* (flag) and *Ferruccio* arrived off Beirut on 24 February 1912, demanding that the Ottoman governor surrender the two warships present, the armoured corvette *Avnillah* (1869, rebuilt 1907) and the torpedo boat *Angora* (1906). Since no reply was received by the stated deadline, fire was opened at 09.00.

Ottoman fire was ineffective, and by 09.35 *Avnillah* was on fire, struck her flag and was abandoned. *Garibaldi* then closed in and engaged *Angora* at close range, albeit without scoring any hits. The cruiser then fired a torpedo at *Avnillah*, which missed but hit and sank several lighters moored nearby; a second torpedo, however, did hit *Avnillah*, which sank in shallow water. Temporarily withdrawing to the north at 11.00, the Italian cruisers returned at 13.45 to deal with *Angora*, which was finally sunk by *Ferruccio*.

April saw naval operations in a number of areas, supporting ongoing consolidation and occupation efforts on the Libyan coast. While the *Garibaldi*s and *Carlo Alberto* went back to Italy for regunning, significant forces moved to the Aegean to support the Italian occupation of the Dodecanese islands by blockading the Dardanelles and preventing any interference from the Ottoman fleet. On 18 April, *Vettor Pisani* led the two *Pisa*s and the battleships *Vittorio Emmanuele*, *Napoli* and *Roma*, plus torpedo boats, out of Taranto to rendezvous with the three *Garibaldi*s and the battleships *Regina Margherita* (1901), *Brin*, *Ammiraglio di Saint Bon* and *Emmanuele Filiberto* (both 1897) from Tobruk and Augusta.

Around 06.30 the following morning, *Pisa* and *Amalfi* presented themselves off the western entrance to the Dardanelles as bait for the Ottoman fleet, which did not respond. At 09.00 the outer forts opened fire, the Italians responding over a period of two hours, with no damage to the Italian ships, but a number of Ottoman casualties. *Margherita*, *Brin*, *Saint Bon* and *Filiberto* having bombarded the forts at Samos, and severed the Rhodes–Marmarice cable, the main body of the fleet then headed back to Italy, leaving the *Pisa* class and *Margherita*, *Brin*, *Saint Bon* and *Filiberto*, together

The wreck of the Turkish armoured corvette *Avnillah*, sunk at Beirut by *Giuseppe Garibaldi* and *Francesco Ferruccio* in February 1912. (*Author's collection*)

with torpedo boats, to continue operations in the area. Landings, from *Pisa* and *Amalfi*, began on 28 April, with Rhodes occupied on 4–5 May, with the support of *Vittorio Emmanuele*, *Napoli*, *Roma*, *Margherita*, *Brin*, *Saint Bon* and *Filiberto*.

San Giorgio rejoined the fleet in June, but the latter was now largely held in home ports refitting, although the *Regina Elena*-class battleships made an Aegean cruise during July/August, while the Duke of the Abruzzi in *Vettor Pisani*, with two destroyers and five torpedo boats, made a reconnaissance of the Dardanelles in mid-July. In August, *Margherita*, *Brin*, *Saint Bon* and *Filiberto* deployed off the Lebanese and Palestinian coast, extending its scope into the Aegean during September in an attempt to put pressure on the Ottoman delegates at ongoing peace talks. The Treaty of Lausanne (Ouchy) was agreed in October, bringing the war to an end.

The First Balkan War

Just as the Italo-Turkish War had ended, a fresh conflict, the First Balkan War, broke out between the Ottoman Empire and Greece, Bulgaria, Serbia and Montenegro in October 1912. While the war was fought mainly on land, there were two fleet actions between the Greeks and Turks, *Georgios Averof* serving as the Greek fleet flagship. First, at the battle of Elli on 16 November 1912, *Averof* led the three *Spetsai*-class battleships (1889–90) and the new destroyers *Aetos*, *Ierax*, *Panthir* and *Leon* (1911) against a Turkish force comprising the battleships *Barbaros Hayreddin* (flag), *Turgut Reis*, *Mesudiye* (1874) and *Âsâr-ı Tevfik* (1868), the cruiser *Mecidiye* (1903) and the destroyers *Muavenet-i Milliye*, *Yadigâr-ı Millet* (1909), *Taşoz* and *Basra* (1907). *Averof* hit *Barbaros Hayreddin* twice aft, first killing five men, and then jamming the aft turret, killing another thirteen, while splinters damaged the battleship's boilers and started a fire in a bunker; *Turgut Reis* was superficially damaged.

At the battle of Lemnos on 18 January 1913, the same big ships (except for *Âsâr-ı Tevfik*) engaged once again, *Barbaros* being hit on her centre turret by *Averof*, with the loss of its entire crew; altogether, she was hit over twenty times and had thirty-two dead and forty-five wounded. *Turgut Reis* received

The Greek fleet at the battle of Lemnos, with *Averof* leading the three battleships of the *Spetsai* class. (Author's collection)

seventeen hits, with nine dead and forty-nine wounded, while *Mesudiye* received a direct hit on a 5.9in mounting that destroyed it, disabled two adjacent guns and caused sixty-eight casualties. In exchange, *Averof* received just two hits from the Turkish ships. Another encounter in April resulted in no damage on either side, with no further fleet actions before the war was ended by the Treaty of London on 30 May 1913. During the war, various foreign powers deployed vessels to protect their interests in Turkish waters, including in the Dardanelles. These included *Victor Hugo*, *Léon Gambetta*, *Pisa*, *San Marco* and *Hampshire*.

On 30 July 1914, *Averof* was joined in the Greek fleet by the ex-American battleships *Mississippi* and *Idaho* (1905), now re-named *Kilkis* and *Lemnos*, respectively. They represented an interim answer to the Turks' two ex-German battleships, but were just a part of an escalating Aegean naval race which included the building of two, and purchase of one, battleships for Turkey in the UK, and the construction of two Greek ships in France and Germany, none of which were delivered owing to the outbreak of the First World War.[139]

The First World War

By the early summer of 1914, battlecruisers had superseded most of the 'classic' big cruisers in the British and German navies. In the latter, only *Scharnhorst* and *Gneisenau* in the Far East were in first-line service; the *Prinz Adalbert*s and *Blücher* were on trials and training duties, with the rest all in reserve or under refit.

In the Royal Navy, the last-generation vessels were split between the 1st CS (*Defence*, *Black Prince*, *Duke of Edinburgh* and *Warrior*) in the Mediterranean, the 2nd CS (*Shannon*, *Achilles*, *Cochrane* and *Natal*) at home, and the China Station (*Minotaur*, accompanied by *Hampshire*). Of older ships, the 4th CS (*Suffolk*, *Berwick*, *Essex* and *Lancaster*) were active on the North American & West Indies Station, but most of the remainder were at reduced readiness (2nd Fleet – nucleus crews), in reserve (3rd Fleet – care and maintenance) or on training duties. On mobilisation in July, however, the 2nd and 3rd Fleets were brought forward, almost all the big cruisers finding a place on either fleet (3rd CS – *Antrim*, *Argyll*, *Devonshire* and *Roxburgh*) or patrol duties (5th, 6th, 7th and 9th CS). Only a handful, already reduced to harbour service or low-category reserve, remained laid up.

In Germany, big cruisers in reserve or on secondary duties were similarly brought back into front-line service, *Blücher* joining the I. SG, and the remainder being grouped into the IV. SG (redesignated III. SG on 28 August). The exception was *Fürst Bismarck*, which did not finish her reconstruction until mobilisation was complete – and by which time some of the ships brought forward were already being paid off. Thus, as soon as she had completed her post-refit trials, *Fürst Bismarck* was used briefly as mobile target for torpedo trials, and then reduced to a stationary training ship.

On the other hand, the Russian and French navies lacked battlecruisers – or the modern light cruisers that formed an

Russian cruisers alongside around 1914, with *Rossiya* in the foreground, *Bayan* or *Pallada* alongside her, and either *Aurora* or *Diana* beyond; *Ryurik* is to be seen to the right. *(NHHC NH 92426)*

important part of the scouting forces of the British and German navies: France had yet to order any, while the six ships for the Russian Baltic Fleet were all still under construction. Accordingly, the armoured cruisers, together with a range of protected cruisers, formed crucial parts of the French and Russian war fleets, acting not only in pure cruiser roles, but also often in a capital role, given both fleets' small forces of dreadnought battleships – or battleships of any kind on the part of the Russians.

The North Sea and North Atlantic 1914
CRUISER PATROLS
As already noted, only a small number of big cruisers were allocated to fleet roles by the British, the vast majority being allocated to patrol duties. The 7th CS, comprising *Bacchante* (flag), *Euryalus* (flag, Southern Force) *Aboukir*, *Cressy* and *Hogue* was allocated a patrol area in the central North Sea, *Bacchante* and *Euryalus* being present as reserve ships at the Battle of Heligoland Bight on 28 August, when two German light cruisers were sunk.

Concerns were expressed at the utility of the squadron's 'beat', and the vulnerability of the ships being used, whose main virtues were seaworthiness and availability. On 20 September, *Euryalus*, *Aboukir*, *Cressy* and *Hogue* were on patrol, in weather too bad for escorting destroyers, when *Euryalus* was forced to return to port owing to damage to her radio antenna and a shortage of coal. On the morning of the 22nd, the ships were sailing in line ahead, ignoring orders to zig-zag, making them a fine target for the German submarine *U9*, which put a torpedo into *Aboukir* at 06.20, which lost power and took a heavy list: she would capsize twenty-five minutes later. Thinking that she had been mined, the other two cruisers were ordered to close and assist, both stopping to lower boats; *Hogue* was then hit by two torpedoes at 06.55, and sank in ten minutes. *Cressy* now recognised the true

situation, and although she attempted to escape, *U9* managed to hit her as well at 07.20. Initial indications were that she might stay afloat, but the German submarine put a second torpedo into her at 07.55. *Cressy* then capsized, sinking twenty minutes later: 837 men were rescued, but 1459 were lost from the squadron, leading to a withdrawal of ships such as the *Cressy*s from patrol duties. The wrecks, capsized in 90ft of water, were heavily salvaged during the 1950s. The surviving two members of the 7th CS were reallocated to 12th CS, where they joined their sister *Sutlej* (flag) and a number of smaller protected cruisers escorting ships between the UK and Gibraltar.

In the far north, the 10th CS comprised the Northern Patrol, comprising *Crescent* (flag), *Edgar*, *Gibraltar*, *Grafton*, *Hawke*, *Royal Arthur*, *Theseus* and *Endymion*, soon joined by the AMCs *Alsatian* (1913) and *Mantua* (1909).[140] However, on 15 October, while on patrol with the squadron off Aberdeen, *Hawke* was hit by torpedo fired by *U9* and rapidly capsized and sank, with only seventy survivors, giving the submarine a score of four cruisers within a month.

The *Edgar*s were ill-suited to the severe weather encountered on their area of operations, *Crescent* and *Edgar* being so badly damaged on 9 November that they had to be withdrawn. The state of the remaining members of the class was such that the decision was taken to take them out of service as well, the ships being replaced by more AMCs, far better suited to the conditions, no fewer than twenty-three being on station in December.

Some of the *Edgar*s were retained in home waters for guard and subsidiary duties, *Gibraltar* coming back to the Northern Patrol in August 1915 as guard and depot ship at the Patrol's forward base at Swarbacks Minn in the Shetlands. Reduced to 6in guns only, she remained there January 1918, when she was transferred elsewhere, following the withdrawal of the 10th CS from the base. *Crescent* and *Royal Arthur* became guardships before also reducing to depot roles, *Crescent* ultimately being roofed-over at Rosyth. On the other hand, four ships were extensively refitted for further service in the Mediterranean (see below, p 120).

In the south, *Amphitrite*, *Argonaut* and *Europa* were based at Portland along with three smaller cruisers as the 9th CS, while the Bay of Biscay was the responsibility of the French 2nd Light Squadron. It contained three divisions of big cruisers, the 1st comprising *Marseillaise* (squadron flag), *Jeanne d'Arc*, and *Amiral Aube*, the 2nd *Gueydon*, *Gloire* and *Dupetit-Thouars*, and the 3rd *Kléber*, *Desaix*, *Guichen* and *Chateaurenault*, plus four smaller cruisers, two destroyers and eight auxiliary cruisers. The 9th CS later moved to West Africa for southern Atlantic duty, comprising a mix of big cruisers and AMCs. *King Alfred* became flagship in October 1915, remaining with the squadron until 1917; other ships attached during that period including *Essex* and *Swiftsure*.

THE WESTERN ATLANTIC
On the other side of the Atlantic, *Condé* was based in the West Indies, with the British 4th CS, comprising *Suffolk*, *Lancaster*, *Essex*, *Suffolk* and *Berwick*, plus the light cruiser *Bristol* (1910) and the battleship *Glory* (flag) serving on the North American & West Indies Station. At Halifax, *Niobe* was recommissioned and joined *Lancaster* in patrolling the Gulf of Saint Lawrence. *Niobe* then, escorted the transport *Canada* to Bermuda during 11–13 September, but on her return journey developed defects and required a week to repair, meaning that she was unable to escorting the large troop convoy that carried Canadian soldiers to Europe in October. However, she formally became part of the 4th CS on 6 October 1914,

Niobe was reduced to a hulk in 1916, shown here with her original funnels being removed and the first of a new pair being erected. The loss of her funnels has been frequently attributed to the 'Halifax Explosion' of 6 December 1917, when the French merchantman *Mont-Blanc* blew up after a collision, but here their removal is clearly shown as part of her refit. *(Author's collection)*

intercepting German ships along the American coast, chasing the German AMC *Prinz Eitel Friedrich* (1904 – see p 116 below) into internment at Newport News, Virginia, on 11 March. However, she was withdrawn from patrol duties in July 1915 and paid off in September, owing to her poor materiel state. She then became a depot hulk at Halifax, additional deckhouses being fitted, her funnels being taken down and new boilers (with a pair of new uptakes) being fitted in the aft boiler room for ships services.

While the 4th CS dealt with the Atlantic coast of North America, the 5th CS was employed further south, between West Africa and Brazil, comprising *Carnarvon* (flag), *Cornwall*, *Cumberland* and *Monmouth*. However, the ships soon moved to South American waters to counter the German East Asiatic Squadron, now crossing the Pacific (see pp 116–18, below).

WITH THE BATTLEFLEETS
A key objective of the German High Seas Fleet was to reduce the size of the British Grand Fleet to such an extent that it could be met with a greater prospect of success than would otherwise be the case, given the British superiority in numbers at the outbreak of war. Accordingly, alongside wide-ranging minelaying and submarine activity, it was decided to carry out surface operations of sufficient size to tempt out a part – but not all – of the British battlefleet, which would then be surprised and obliterated by the lurking High Seas Fleet. The 'bait' for such operations would be the battlecruisers of the I. SG.

The first such operation began on 2 November 1914, when the I. SG, sailed to bombard the coastal town of Yarmouth, and lay mines between there and Lowestoft. Two squadrons of battleships and supporting vessels sailed some time later to provide the 'ambush' force; the latter included the three III. SG cruisers, *Prinz Heinrich*, *Roon* and *Yorck*. The raid had little effect, but on the fleet's return, *Yorck* strayed into a German defensive minefield at the mouth of the Jade on the morning of 4 November, having missed the swept channel in fog while attempting to reach Wilhelmshaven ahead of the rest of the fleet to rectify defects; she sank with the loss of 336 men.

A further operation of the same type was to be carried out against three further coastal towns, Hartlepool, Scarborough and Whitby, on 16 December, the supporting force including the two surviving ships of the III. SG. The departure of I. and II. SGs was detected by British code-breakers – but not that of the battlefleet. Thus, the response was to dispatch just the 1st BCS (four battlecruisers), the 2nd BS (six battleships) and the 1st LCS (four ships), plus destroyers from the Grand Fleet, together with two light cruisers and forty-two destroyers from Harwich, and the 3rd CS (*Devonshire*, *Antrim*, *Argyll* and *Roxburgh*) from Rosyth.

Blücher was one of the ships bombarding Hartlepool, whose batteries scored four hits on her, one on the forward superstructure disabling two 3.5in guns and killing nine. The second hit was on a starboard 8.2in turret, wrecking its sight and rangefinder, but leaving the mounting still operational. The third shell struck the belt below the turret, while the fourth hit was on the foremast, damaging aerials and other equipment. Their tasks finished, I. and II. SG sailed for their rendezvous point with the battlefleet, beginning the homeward journey around 11.00.

Meanwhile, at 05.15, *Roon* and *Prinz Heinrich*, which were in the van of the High Seas Fleet, ran into two destroyers from the British screen, but no shots were exchanged. At this point, German concerns at exceeding standing orders regarding avoiding action with potentially superior forces meant that it was decided to withdraw the High Seas Fleet – only a few minutes away from encountering just the kind of detached element of the Grand Fleet that the strategy had envisaged as the fleet's victim. This reversal of course placed *Roon* at the tail of the line, and at 05.59 she, and two light cruisers, again encountered British destroyers, which shadowed her until 06.40, at which point the two smaller cruisers were detached to deal with them. However, they were recalled at 07.02, and the German ships continued safely home in the wake of the fleet.

The Pacific 1914–1918

At the outbreak of war, the British ships on the China Station (*Minotaur and Hampshire*, plus the light cruisers *Newcastle* and *Yarmouth* [1909–10]) were reinforced by the battleship *Triumph* recommissioned from reserve at Hong Kong on 6 August, and by the French *Dupleix*. The East Indies Station had *Swiftsure*, the light cruiser *Dartmouth* (1910) and the protected cruiser *Fox* (1893), and the Australian fleet the battlecruiser *Australia* (1911), the light cruisers *Melbourne* and *Sydney* (1912) and the protected cruisers *Encounter* (1902) and *Pioneer* (1899). The latter was joined by the other French armoured cruiser in the region, *Montcalm*.

On the Central Powers side, the news of the assassination of Archduke Franz Ferdinand came while *Scharnhorst* and *Gneisenau* were in the German Caroline Islands, arriving at Ponape on 17 July, where they were still at the beginning of August.[141] The small cruisers of the squadron, which had been in various parts of the Pacific, were recalled, the big cruisers, plus the light cruisers *Nürnberg* (1906) and *Emden* (1908), the liner, *Prinz Eitel Friedrich*, now adapted as an auxiliary cruiser, and colliers concentrating at Pagan in the Marianas on 11 August. A further light cruiser, *Geier* (1894), on passage from Germany at the outbreak of war, was unable to join and was eventually interned at Honolulu on 7 November.

At Tsingtau remained just the light cruiser *Cormoran* (1892), the torpedo boat *S90* (1899) and the gunboats *Iltis*, *Jaguar*, *Tiger* and *Luchs* (1898–9), plus the Austro-Hungarian cruiser *Kaiserin Elisabeth*; the port came soon came under blockade from *Triumph* and the destroyer *Usk* (1903). Japan declared war on Germany on 23 August and on Austria-Hungary on the 25th, the latter's refusal to withdraw *Kaiserin Elisabeth* being a key element of the Japanese ultimatum. On the 27th, *Suwo* led a squadron to join *Triumph*, which had

already captured a German collier, on blockade duty. The blockade squadron, with *Iwate* as flagship, would grow to also contain *Dupleix*, the British light cruiser *Yarmouth* (1911) and further destroyers.

The defenders had some naval successes, in particular when *S90* sank the cruiser-minelayer *Takachiho* on 17 October (although then had to scuttle herself when she ran out of coal), while on 4 September, *Jaguar* destroyed the stranded Japanese destroyer *Shirotaye* (1906), and on 11 November the torpedo boat *33* (1899) was sunk by a mine. However, by then the German position was becoming increasingly untenable, with *Cormoran*, *Iltis* and *Luchs* scuttled on 28 September, *Tiger* on 29 October, *Kaiserin Elisabeth* on 2 November and *Jaguar* on 7 November, the day that the garrison surrendered.

Emden and *Prinz Eitel Friedrich* were detached from the East Asiatic Squadron to act as commerce raiders on 13 August, the remaining ships heading for Enewetak Atoll in the Marshall Islands, arriving and coaling on 20 August. On 8 September *Nürnberg* was sent to Honolulu with dispatches and to gather news, the squadron then sailing to the recently-captured German Samoa in the hope of catching an isolated British warship. However, nothing was found there on the 14th, although better luck was had at the French harbour of Papeete, on Tahiti, on 22 September, where the gunboat *Zélée* (1900) was sunk and the town bombarded by *Scharnhorst* and *Gneisenau*.

On 12 October, the German ships reached Easter Island, where they were joined from American waters by *Dresden* (1907) and *Leipzig* (1905), together three more colliers. A week later, the squadron pushed on to Mas a Fuera, and then towards and down the Chilean coast, seeking the British light cruiser *Glasgow* (1909) which was known to be in the area. *Asama* and *Izumo*, later joined by the battleship *Hizen* (ex-*Retvizan*), had been formed into the American Expeditionary Squadron, and deployed during October into the central Pacific in search of the Germans, seizing the German protectorate of Jaluit Atoll, Marshall Islands, in the process. It was the presence of *Asama* and *Hizen* off Hawaii that forced the internment of *Geier* in November. While also operating against the Germans, *Nisshin* struck an uncharted rock off Sandakan on 12 October and was forced to put into Singapore for repairs. In addition, *Ibuki* went to New Zealand, where she was joined by *Minotaur* to convoy troop transports from there and Australian towards Europe, remaining with their escort while the *Sydney* was detached to destroy *Emden* at the Cocos Islands on 9 November. Other troop convoys from the region included ones from India, *Swiftsure* shepherding ships from Bombay to Aden during September–November, and then being based at Suez in defence of the Suez Canal.

The aforementioned *Glasgow* was part of a force also comprising *Good Hope* (flag) and *Monmouth*, together with the battleship *Canopus* and the AMC *Otranto* (1909); the two armoured cruisers had been detached respectively from the 6th and 5th CS to spearhead a hunting group specifically aimed at the German squadron. There had been plans for them to be joined by the much more modern and powerful *Defence* (detached from the 1st CS, in which she was temporarily replaced as flagship by *Leviathan*) but she was held back in the South Atlantic, and *Canopus*'s speed restricted by defects, so that when the British and German squadrons met off Coronel, Chile, at 16.20 on 1 November, only *Good Hope*, *Monmouth*, *Glasgow* and *Otranto* were in company.

The British big cruisers were outgunned and outranged by their German opposite numbers, exacerbated by half the British 6in guns being in main-deck casemates that were unworkable in the heavy seas then running. While the setting of the sun behind the British ships gave them an initial tactical advantage, the Germans declined action until sunset, after which the British were silhouetted against the horizon, with the German ships lost in the gloom of dusk.

When fire was opened around 19.00, *Good Hope* was engaged by *Scharnhorst*, whose third salvo put the British cruiser's forward 9.2in gun out of action, followed by a series of hits to the forward part of the ship – including the bridge – with more shells amidships setting her on fire; only two 6in shells hit *Scharnhorst* in exchange. *Good Hope*'s aft turret having been hit twice, there was a large explosion at 19.50 between the after funnel and the mainmast, leaving the ship dead in the water, sinking soon afterwards with all hands.

Gneisenau took on *Monmouth*, whose fore turret was demolished and the forecastle set on fire by an early salvo. Hit some thirty to forty times, and having hit her opponent only four times, *Monmouth* attempted to withdraw to the west, but was found around 21.00 by *Nürnberg*, down by the head and with a list to port. She was then sunk with all hands, leaving only *Glasgow*, engaged by *Leipzig* and *Dresden*, but able to escape with five hits. *Scharnhorst* had received two 6in hits and *Gneisenau* four, none of which had done significant damage, but both ships had now expended nearly half their ammunition outfits.

Following the battle, the German squadron proceeded to the Chilean port of Valparaíso; having coaled in relays, owing to neutrality rules, the ships reassembled at St Quentin Bay on the south-east coast of Chile on the 21st. There, they prepared to break through back to Germany across the Atlantic. However, it was agreed to make a raid on the Falkland Islands before pushing on homeward, the squadron sailing on the 6th – a decision that would prove fatal.

In the wake of the battle, additional Japanese ships were deployed westwards, *Ikoma* joining *Kurama* and *Tsukuba* and two destroyers in the 1st Southern Expeditionary Sqn, while the American Expeditionary Sqn was reinforced by two light cruisers. In addition, two battlecruisers (*Invincible* [flag] and

Scharnhorst, with *Gneisenau* beyond at Valparaíso following the battle of Coronel. (*BA 134-C0001*)

Inflexible) were dispatched from the UK to hunt down the German ships, joining *Glasgow* and *Canopus* at the Falklands, along with the newly-refitted *Kent*, and *Carnarvon* and *Cornwall* from West Africa. The force was coaling in harbour as the Germans approached, but a 12in hit on *Gneisenau* from *Canopus* dissuaded the Germans from pressing home what might have been a successful assault on the British force while it was confined in harbour. The German force thus turned away, initially unaware of the presence of the 25kt battlecruisers that could outpace the German ships' best nominal speed of 22kt.

Within three hours, *Invincible* and *Inflexible* had sailed and caught up with the Germans, *Scharnhorst* and *Gneisenau* accepting action with them at 13.20, most of the British smaller cruisers being directed to chase their German opposite numbers. The flagships engaged each other, *Scharnhorst* straddling *Invincible* with her third salvo, but soon afterwards *Scharnhorst* received a number of hits and caught fire, although continuing to score hits on *Invincible*. The British pair then swapped opponents, *Inflexible* causing further damage to *Scharnhorst*, which was now listing and had lost her third funnel. *Gneisenau* had already been badly battered by *Inflexible*, with her secondary battery largely wrecked, the forward boiler room flooded and another leaking badly. Around 16.00, she was briefly hidden by smoke, both battlecruisers thus concentrating on *Scharnhorst*, which capsized to port and sank with all hands at 16.17. Trying to escape, *Gneisenau*, now down to 16kt and under fire from not only the battlecruisers, but also *Carnarvon*, continued to fight, hitting *Invincible* as late as 17.15. However, she hove to at

17.40 and, her seacocks open, sank within twenty minutes, with 190 survivors.

Kent sank *Nürnberg*, while *Glasgow* assisted her in sinking *Leipzig*. Only *Dresden* escaped, to be scuttled at Mas a Tierra, off the Chilean coast, when cornered by the AMC *Orama* (1911), together with *Kent* and *Glasgow* on 14 March 1915. With the departure of the German squadron from the south-western Pacific, *Dupleix* and *Montcalm* returned west, *Dupleix* back to France, and *Montcalm* to join with *Desaix*, originally outbound to for service in the Far East, to provide protection for the Suez Canal. However, until *Dresden* had been dealt with, parts of the Japanese American Expeditionary Squadron remained off the South American coast, while *Nisshin* was stationed at Fiji. While serving with the former, *Asama* ran aground off the Baja California peninsula on 31 January 1915, Mexico. Badly damaged, the ship was not refloated until 21 June, undergoing emergency repairs at San Diego, and finally returning to Yokosuka on 18 December for final repairs; during these, the opportunity was taken to reboiler her with Kampon watertube units. Japanese ships also continued to operate against German merchantmen in Asiatic waters, a squadron being based at Singapore for the purpose.

In January 1917, increasing enemy submarine and raider activity led to a British request that the Japanese provide ships for escort duties in both the Indian Ocean and the Mediterranean. In response to the former, the 1st Special Squadron of light cruisers was formed at Singapore, with two ships detached to the Cape of Good Hope. With the advent of SMS *Wolf* in the theatre in March, the squadron was

Aso at Yokosuka in 1924, while serving as a minelayer. (Author's collection)

reinforced by *Nisshin* (which had served as a destroyer squadron flagship during 1915–17) and *Kasuga* which, with *Izumo*, escorted merchantmen between Fremantle and Colombo during March/April. Some months later, *Kasuga* ran aground at the entrance the Bangka Straits, East Indies, in January 1918, and was not refloated until May. A year earlier, an accident had fatally claimed *Tsukuba*, which had suffered an explosion in her forward magazines while moored in Tokyo Bay, sinking within twenty minutes, with 305 dead. She was later raised and the hulk used temporarily as a target for aviators, before being broken up in 1918. *Tsukuba* was one of two Japanese capital ships lost to internal explosion during the First World War, the battleship *Kawachi* (1910) being sunk in July 1918.

Aso and *Soya* rejoined the Training Squadron on 1 December 1914, but their training cruises were terminated in August 1915. In 1917, *Aso* was converted into a minelayer, to join the also-ex-Russian *Tsuguru* (ex-*Pallada*), refitted in 1915, following the 1914 loss of the Japanese navy's first cruiser-minelayer, *Takachiho*.[142] As modified, *Aso* lost her remaining torpedo tubes and had her 8in guns replaced by two 6in/50 weapons,[143] and could now carry 420 mines, although she would not be formally reclassified until 1 April 1920.

The Mediterranean and Aegean 1914–1915

The main French fleet (*1ʳᵉ Armée Navale*) was concentrated in the Mediterranean, with the four most modern armoured cruisers comprising the 1st Light Division of the 1st Light Squadron (*Jules Michelet* flag), with the next three in the 2nd Light Division (*Léon Gambetta* flag); a number of older cruisers, *D'Entrecasteaux*, *Pothuau* and the three surviving *Amiral Charner* class were in a Special Division with two old battleships, which was employed in escorting colonial troops from Morocco to France during August–November 1914. *Charner* had recommissioned from Special Reserve at the outbreak of war: had peace continued she would probably have been stricken in the near future.

In August 1914, the British force in the Mediterranean was headed by the 2nd BCS (*Inflexible*, *Indefatigable* and *Indomitable*), supported by the 1st CS (*Defence*, *Black Prince*, *Duke of Edinburgh* and *Warrior*), four light cruisers and sixteen destroyers. On the Central Powers side, Austria's fleet was concentrated in the Adriatic, while Germany had the battlecruiser *Goeben* and light cruiser *Breslau* (1911) serving as its Mediterranean Division.

On 3 August, following the outbreak of war between Germany and France, *Goeben* undertook a short secondary-battery bombardment of Philippeville (Skikda, Algeria), while *Breslau* shelled Bone (Annaba). The two ships were then ordered to Constantinople, a destination unsuspected by Anglo-French commanders, who assumed that they would either attempt to break out into the Atlantic, or join the Austro-Hungarian forces in the Adriatic (a large Austro-Hungarian force, including *Sankt Georg*, being mobilised on the 7th to rendezvous with them).

Thus, only the British 1st CS (less *Black Prince*, in the Red Sea) found themselves in a position to intercept when the Germans' direction of travel was realised. They chased until early on the 7th, when the British admiral (Sir Ernest Troubridge [1862–1926]) concluded that *Goeben* represented too superior a force to risk the British ships and withdrew. Thus, having coaled off the Greek island of Donoussa in the Cyclades on 9–10 August, on the afternoon of 10 August *Goeben* and *Breslau* were able to enter the Dardanelles unmolested.

Troubridge's decision was much criticised at the time, the admiral being court-martialled but acquitted. In retrospect, while it was certainly clear that the vessels of the 1st CS were individually inferior to *Goeben* in speed, protection and firepower, the German battlecruiser was being slowed by incompletely-repaired boilers, had guns whose range did not significantly exceed those of the British ships – and would have faced the challenge of dealing with multiple foes simultaneously.

Following the declaration of war by the Ottoman Empire, the defence of British-occupied Egypt and the strategically vital Suez Canal became a priority, with the French *D'Entrecasteaux* was transferred to the Syrian Division in December 1914 to protect the Suez Canal, along with the coast-defence ship *Requin* (1885), the two ships anchoring in Lake Timsah to fire on Ottoman forces threatening the waterway. *D'Entrecasteaux* would remain operational in North African waters, apart from a short break for refitting, until the summer of 1917, primarily in defence of the Canal, but with a spell off Morocco during April–August 1916. *Montcalm* and *Desaix* also joined the protective force from the Indian Ocean, the larger vessel

The French fleet at sea. In the foreground are destroyers of the *Bouclier* class (1909–11), led by *Casque*; behind are (from the far left: a *Courbet*-class battleship; a *Patrie*/*Démocratie*-class battleship; a *Danton*-class battleship; the battleship *Bouvet*; more *Danton*-class battleships. (*Author's collection*)

remaining on station until the end of 1915, and *Desaix* into the spring of 1916.

Other vessels transferred to Egypt to reinforce the Canal's defences were *Bacchante* and *Euryalus*, arriving in late January 1915 to reinforce the defences of the Suez Canal. However, as the Turkish threat had now lessened, they were transferred north to the Dardanelles theatre in March.

On 1 June 1915, a Cruiser Unit was constituted within the French 3rd Mediterranean Squadron, comprising *Dupetit-Thouars*, *Guichen*, *Châteaurenault*, *Desaix*, *Pothuau* and *Admiral Charner*, plus the smaller protected cruiser *Du Chayla* and the coast-defence ship *Requin*, for various duties, including the rescue of Armenians escaping from an Ottoman massacre at Gebel Mousa in Syria in September. The three *Amiral Charner*s assembled as the 3rd Light Division at Alexandria during 1915.

The Dardanelles and Gallipoli campaign

A plan to force the Dardanelles and open up the sea route into the Black Sea was put into effect in February 1915, with bombardments by British and French battleships. However, the loss of three such ships and damage to others from mines on 18 March resulted in a shift of strategy, with landings on the Gallipoli peninsula undertaken in April to begin what would be a long drawn-out, and ultimately unsuccessful, land campaign. Nevertheless, naval bombardments continued to be a key part of operations, *Jeanne d'Arc* and *Latouche-Tréville* being amongst ships carrying out bombardments on 24 April, prior to the latter (together with the coast-defence ship *Henri IV* [1899]) landing two French divisions on the following day.

Submarine torpedoes were now added to the risks posed by minefields, *Triumph* falling victim to *U21* on 25 May 1915, capsizing after fifteen minutes. The battleship *Majestic* (1895)

having been sunk by the same submarine two days later, and *Goliath* (1898) by a Turkish destroyer torpedo on the 15th, it was clear that vessels with better underwater protection were needed for operations off the beaches. To meet this requirement, four of the cruisers withdrawn from the Northern Patrol, *Edgar*, *Endymion*, *Grafton* and *Theseus*, were rebuilt with deep bulges and their 9.2in guns replaced by 6in weapons. Their 9.2in guns (together with weapons taken from sisters reduced to harbour service) were redeployed to arm ten of the new small monitors ordered in early 1915 for shore bombardment purposes.[144] Thus the guns from *Edgar* went to *M19* and *M26*, those of *Theseus* into *M21* and *M27*, those of *Grafton* into *M23* and *M28*, and those of *Gibraltar* into *M20* and *M22*.[145]

The ongoing build-up of land forces in the theatre meant that many ships were pressed into service as troop transports. These included the long-idle *Terrible*, which was one of the ships recommissioned with a special complement for trooping duties on 9 September 1915, the others being the battleships *Magnificent*, *Mars* and *Hannibal* (1894–6), their armaments now reduced to four 6in guns, following the removal of their turrets to provide guns for *Lord Clive*-class monitors. Similarly, although keeping her 9.2in turrets for the time being, *Terrible* recommissioned at Portsmouth, with her her secondary armament reduced to four guns. She sailed for the Mediterranean on the 16th, arriving at Mudros on 2 October, and continuing in a trooping role until the end of November. Suffering from machinery problems, *Terrible* was considered locally for use to reinforce the breakwater at Kephalo Bay, Imbros (as were the three troopship-battleships), but this was rejected by the Admiralty[146] and she was sent home, arriving at Portsmouth on 16 January, to pay off on the 26th.

Nevertheless, the campaign bogged down into an

Endymion, as rebuilt, in 1915, with the scout cruiser *Forward* in the background. (*Author's collection*)

Recommissioned as a troopship in September 1915, with all but four of her 6in guns, and all lighter weapons, removed, *Terrible* sailed for the Mediterranean on the 16th, carrying 34 army officers and 1319 men, arriving at Mudros on 2 October, the troops disembarking from the 5th to 12th. She sailed on the 23rd, arriving at Malta on the 26th, sailing for Marseilles on the 28th, where she arrived on the 31st, proceeding to Toulon on 2 November, in company with the troopship-battleships *Mars*, *Magnificent* and *Hannibal*. Returning to Marseilles on the 10th, *Terrible* embarked 720 troops on the 12th, sailing for Alexandria the next morning, and arriving on the 18th, before pushing on to Port Said, arriving on the 20th. On the 22nd, she sailed for Salonika, arriving on the 26th, spending the night there before proceeding back to Mudros, whence she arrived on the 28th. The old cruiser remained at anchor until the evening of 11 December, when she sailed for home, calling at Malta from 14 December to 6 January 1916 and arriving at Portsmouth on the 16th. It having now been decided that she should be converted into an accommodation hulk along the lines of her sister (p 111) dismantling began soon afterwards; her 9.2in guns were allocated for the re-arming of the monitors *Marshal Ney* and *Marshal Soult* (although only *Ney* was actually so-modified), with her four remaining 6in also going to *Ney*. After a number of duties, carried out while being refitted, *Terrible* joined the *Fisgard* artificers' training establishment at Portsmouth in November 1919, being renamed *Fisgard III* in August 1920. By now she had been roofed over, her aft nineteen boilers having been removed and the remainder, together with the engines, partly dismantled. (*World Ship Society*)

unwinnable stalemate, the decision being taken in December 1915 to evacuate all troops. The last men left on 9 January, with remaining ships redeployed, some, including the *Edgar*s remaining in the Aegean for further action.

The Adriatic 1914–1918[147]
The Austro-Hungarian main fleet was divided into two Battle Squadrons, comprising the twelve battleships, with the three armoured cruisers grouped with the three older small cruisers in the Cruiser Flotilla. Of the latter, *Zenta* became an early casualty, while bombarding the town of Antivari (Bar) in company with the destroyer *Ulan* (1906) on 16 August 1914. The two ships were cut off by a large Franco-British force seeking to provoke a sortie by the main Austro-Hungarian fleet, and grossly outnumbered by the twelve battleships, the armoured cruisers *Victor Hugo*, *Jules Ferry*, plus *Warrior* and *Defence* from the British 1st CS, a protected cruiser and some twenty destroyers, *Zenta* sank with 173 dead, although *Ulan* managed to escape.

Austrian submarines, however, had an early success in damaging the French fleet flagship *Jean Bart* and on 21 December 1914, and on 27 April 1915, *U5* torpedoed and sank *Léon Gambetta* in the Ionian Sea, with the loss of some 700 lives. Larger vessels henceforth kept well away from the Straits of Otranto.

Italy declared war on Austria-Hungary (but not Germany) on 23 May 1915. That very evening, Austro-Hungarian ships put to sea to bombard various Italian coastal targets, *Sankt*

Sankt Georg around 1917. (*NHHC NH 60158*)

Georg firing on Rimini, destroying a freight train and a railway bridge. Of the Italian fleet, the *Pisa* and *San Giorgio* classes were at Taranto, along with the latest battleships, the three *Garibaldi*s at Brindisi with *Vettor Pisani*, and *Carlo Alberto* and *Marco Polo* at Venice. *Marco Polo* had been in the Far East in August 1914, being withdrawn in December, returning to Italy via Red Sea, reaching Naples in March 1915. She became a depot ship, principally for British submarines, at Venice in October, remaining in this role until late 1917.

The *Pisani*s lost their mainmasts early in the war, with searchlights added in the fore fighting top and on a platform aft of the second funnel. *Pisani* herself had her conning tower heightened and fitted with a spotting tower, a feature also added in the *Garibaldi*s, facilitated by the removal of the bridge from atop the conning tower; new bridgework was built up around it. Ventilators were also cut down in height or replaced by windsails. In addition, a searchlight platform had now been installed against the forefunnel in all, with searchlights also added to the mast fighting top. The pair of searchlights on the aft superstructure were later moved to a platform on the second funnel in *Varese* and *Ferruccio*, which additionally had their fore and aft 3in embrasures plated over.

Garibaldi herself had by then been one of two Italian armoured cruisers that fell victim to submarines in July 1915. First, *Amalfi*, which had just been transferred to Venice along with her sister and the *San Giorgio*s, was torpedoed by the nominally-Austro-Hungarian submarine *U26*[148] on 7 July, while 20 miles off Venice; seventy of her complement were lost. The redeployment of the four big cruisers to Venice had been opposed by the Italian CinC, the Duke of the Abruzzi, but implemented by the Chief of Staff, Paolo Thaon di Revel (1859–1948), but on 17 July the Duke ordered the three *Garibaldi*s and *Pisani* to bombard the railway line between Cattaro and Ragusa (now repaired after being severed by a bombardment on 5 June). At 04.00 the next morning, the

Kaiserin und Königin Maria Theresa during 1917–18, disarmed as an accommodation ship for submarine crews at Pola. *(NHHC NH 87360)*

force was some 3 miles off the Dalmatian coast, 17 miles south-east of Dubrovnik, and began shelling the railway.[149] It had been sighted, however, half an hour earlier by the Austro-Hungarian submarine *U4*, which fired two torpedoes at 04.38, one hitting *Garibaldi* (flag) on the starboard side, close to the after boiler rooms. The cruiser sank by the stern within a few minutes of being hit, with the loss of fifty-three men, coming to rest upside down 120m down. As a result, Allied plans for landings on the Adriatic coast were abandoned, and big ships were no longer used for coastal bombardment purposes.

On 29 December, *Kaiser Karl VI* sortied from Cattaro to support the small cruiser *Helgoland* (1912) and three destroyers, retiring from a raid on the Albanian port of Durazzo (Durrës) during which two other destroyers had been mined. *Karl VI* managed to intercept the Anglo-French-Italian force pursuing the Austro-Hungarian vessels, but was too slow to keep up. The armoured cruiser was also active on 8 January 1916 when she, along with the coast-defence ship *Budapest* (1896) and *Kaiser Franz Joseph I*, began three days of bombardments of Montenegrin positions, which contributed directly to the capture of the Montenegrin capital on the 13th.

In April 1916, the three big Italian armoured cruisers were finally withdrawn from Venice, from which they had rarely emerged since the sinking of *Amalfi* the previous summer. They ultimately moved to Brindisi, replacing the *Regina Elena*-class battleships that had previously been based there; they went to Valona, where the cruisers had been briefly based after leaving Venice. The same month *Karl VI* had her original K/94 type 9.4in guns replaced by the K/97 pattern.

Italy finally declared war on Germany on 28 August 1916, leading to a now-overt increase in the German submarine presence in Austro-Hungarian waters. To provide additional accommodation for the German submariners, *Maria Theresia* was paid off at the end of January 1917 to service vessels based at Cattaro; the torpedo cruiser *Panther* was also relegated to a similar role.

Vettor Pisani during the First World War, after the removal of her mainmast. *(Author's collection)*

Older vessels were also passing from combat roles on the other side of the Adriatic, *Marco Polo* being taken in hand in late 1917 to be refitted as a troopship, all guns and the side armour being removed; a few 3in weapons were added. *Carlo Alberto* was similarly modified, after a period as a support ship for motor torpedo boats, also at Venice. Renamed respectively *Cortellazo* and *Zenson*, both ex-cruisers recommissioned in April 1918 and were employed on transport duties until the end of the war and beyond.

Zenson carried troops and equipment to Libya, the Aegean and Albania during the spring of 1919, before being stricken in June 1920. *Cortellazo* remained in service rather longer, and from September 1919 to January 1921, she was active off Fiume following the seizure of the city by the poet and adventurer Gabriele D'Annunzio (1863–1938). She was renamed *Europa* in October 1920, to free her name for an ex-Austro-Hungarian destroyer. The old ship paid off at Pola in January 1921, and was stricken on the 16th, but was simultaneously reinscribed on the navy list under yet another name, *Volta*. Transferred to La Spezia in November 1921, she was definitively stricken in January 1922 and sold for scrap.

Pisani saw little service after the summer of 1915, and from November 1916 to November 1918 served as a headquarters office-ship for the CinC. During the year following the armistice, she was in the Adriatic as flagship of the SNO Albania, but paid off at La Spezia in September 1919, was stricken in January 1920, and sold for scrap soon afterwards.

It was soon found that the single-masted rigs of the later Italian armoured cruisers were inadequate for war service, the surviving *Garibaldi*s, *Pisa* and the two *San Giorgio*s having a signal-yard added high on the forefunnel, with a light mast as well in the newer three vessels. In the latter, this had been replaced by a heavier structure, carrying a top, before, the end of the war. In addition, a number of their 3in guns had been swapped for examples on anti-aircraft mountings.

The two remaining operational Austro-Hungarian armoured cruisers, *Kaiser Karl VI* and *Sankt Georg*, remained part of the Cattaro-based Cruiser Flotilla through 1917, by which time both had received one 2.6in/50, plus one (*Karl VI*) or two (*Sankt Georg*) 8mm machine guns for anti-aircraft use. Although unable to tactically combine with the four fast *Admiral Spaun*-class vessels that also comprised the flotilla (and which shouldered the bulk of the navy's operations in the lower Adriatic), *Sankt Georg* was deployed on 15 May 1917, along with two destroyers, to support the hard-pressed *Novara*, *Helgoland* and *Saida*, under attack from a superior Allied force after a raid on the Otranto Barrage. The sighting of *Sankt Georg*'s smoke led to the latter's withdrawal.

A turning point for the Austro-Hungarian navy came on 1 February 1918, with a mutiny at Cattaro, both *Kaiser Karl VI* and *Sankt Georg* being seized by mutineers. Although both ships surrendered on the 2nd and 3rd respectively, the fallout resulted in major command changes, with many older ships reduced to secondary roles. These included the two armoured cruisers, which were replaced by the three *Erzherzog Karl*-class battleships, and became headquarters ships at Sebenico (*Karl VI* – later disarmed) and Cattaro (*Sankt Georg*) in March.

On 2 October 1918, *Pisa*, *San Giorgio* and *San Marco*, with three British light cruisers, spearheaded an attack on Durazzo, the action ending with the Italian occupation of the port on 16 October. This marked almost the end of the naval war in the Adriatic, the Austro-Hungarians seeking an armistice from the 28th onwards, hostilities ending on 3 November.

The Baltic 1914–1915

In August 1914, the Russian Baltic Fleet was in the first stages of re-equipment. Four modern battleships (the *Sevastopol* class) were completing, but four battlecruisers were still on the stocks, as were five of the six light cruisers on order. Of the latter, two (including the only one actually afloat) were building in a German yard, and thus would soon be seized, and of the rest only one (eventually completed in 1928) would

Gromoboi leading *Admiral Makarov* and the rest of the Russian Cruiser Brigade around 1914. *(NHHC NH 93612)*

ever serve as a cruiser under a Russian flag.[150] Thus, the key ships were the two battleships of the *Imperator Pavel I* class, and the older *Slava* (1903) and the Yellow Sea veteran *Tsesarevich* – and the cruiser force.

At the outbreak of war, the latter was divided into the Cruiser Brigade, comprising *Admiral Makarov, Bayan, Gromoboi* and *Pallada*, supported by the destroyer *Novik* (1911), and the Reserve Brigade, of *Rossiya, Aurora, Bogatyr, Diana* and *Oleg*. A reorganisation in the spring of 1915, after the commissioning of the *Sevastopol* class, created 'manoeuvre groups', three made up of two battleships and one cruiser, one of just two battleships, and the rest of just cruisers. In the initial iteration of this scheme, *Rossiya* was placed in Group 2 with the new battleships *Sevastopol* and *Poltava*, while *Ryurik* and the two surviving *Bayan* class (*Pallada* had by then been lost: see just below) made up Group 5 and *Gromoboi* led *Aurora* and *Diana* in Group 6. However, these were regarded as tactical formations only, the armoured cruisers being grouped administratively into the 1st Cruiser Brigade, the 2nd Cruiser Brigade embracing the protected cruisers.

In practice, it was cruisers that carried out the lion's share of Russian big-ship operations, supplemented by *Slava* and *Tsesarevich*, the more modern battleships being largely restricted to the Gulf of Finland as a 'fleet in being'. In spite of the armoured cruisers' importance, even higher priorities – the need to protect the mouth of the Gulf of Finland – meant that *Rossiya*'s 8in guns were temporarily replaced by 6in weapons during 1914–15 and used to equip shore batteries at Nargan Island and Porkalla Udd.[151]

In view of the nature of Russian heavy forces, and owing to the need to keep 'dreadnought' vessels in the North Sea to oppose the British, the Germans also based their forces in the Baltic around armoured cruisers. Thus, over 3–9 September, *Blücher*, detached from the I. SG, led a sweep into the Baltic, along with four light cruisers, the flagship briefly exchanging fire with *Bayan* and *Pallada* at the entrance to the Gulf of Finland on the 4th. *Pallada* would be torpedoed and sunk the following month by the German submarine *U26* with loss of all hands, following a magazine explosion; her wreck, lying upside down and broken in three pieces in some 120ft of water, was discovered in 2012.

In November 1914, *Ryurik*, until recently Baltic Fleet flagship, was temporarily fitted for minelaying, and laid 120 mines off Danzig on 14 December. On 13 February 1915, while part of the escort of a minelaying sortie off Danzig, she ran aground off the Faro lighthouse, taking on 2400 tons of water, but managed to get off and was able to withdraw safely.

On 17 November, while on a bombardment mission to the Latvian coast, the German now-flagship *Friedrich Carl* struck a mine in a field laid by Russian destroyers west-south-west of Memel on the 5th. Assuming that she had been torpedoed, the ship set a course for shallow water that took her back into the minefield, where she struck a further mine, causing extensive flooding aft and disabling an engine. The rudder jammed soon afterwards, *Friedrich Carl*'s crew being taken off some six hours after the first mine had been struck and shortly before the ship capsized and sank, albeit with only seven fatalities. *Friedrich Carl* was replaced as Baltic flagship by her sister *Prinz Adalbert*, withdrawn from the III. SG in the North Sea.

The mine danger was further emphasised when two light cruisers were damaged in two separate minefields on the night of 24/25 January 1915, while a further submarine threat had arisen in October 1914, with the first deployment of British submarines to the Baltic, which used *Dvina* (ex-*Pamiat Azova*) as their depot ship at Kronstadt. The mine danger led on 24 January to *Prinz Adalbert* taking a course towards Libau that took her through shallow waters in which she ran aground, fortunately being refloated before HMS/M *E9* reached her position.

The heavy naval forces available to the Germans in the Baltic theatre were enhanced in April 1915 when the surviving ships of the III. SG (*Roon* and *Prinz Heinrich*) redeployed there. On 11 May, *E9* sighted *Roon* and several other ships en route to Libau; five torpedoes were fired, but all missed. On 2 July, *Bayan, Admiral Makarov, Bogatyr* and *Oleg* attacked a German minelaying force, resulting in the cruiser-minelayer *Albatross* being forced by heavy damage to seek refuge in neutral Swedish waters. *Roon* and a light cruiser sailed in support, and on arrival *Roon* engaged *Bayan*, the Russians being soon reinforced by *Ryurik* and a destroyer, the German ships being forced to withdraw.

Prinz Heinrich and *Prinz Adalbert* were sent from Danzig to provide further support, but the latter ship was torpedoed below the conning tower by *E9* en route, losing ten men and being flooded by some 2000 tons of water. This increased her draught beyond that which would allow her to re-enter Danzig, but she was able to proceed under her own power to Kiel for repairs, arriving on 4 July.

In the absence of *Prinz Adalbert*, the battleships *Braunschweig* and *Elsaß* joined *Roon* and *Prinz Heinrich* in the III. SG in July, and the following month a major operation was carried out against Russian forces in the Gulf of Riga, when they were joined by battleships and battlecruisers from the High Seas Fleet in an attempt to destroy local Russian forces. Particular objectives were to neutralise *Slava* and mine the entrance to the Moon Sound channel, the northern entrance to the gulf. As part of this, on the 10th, *Roon* and *Prinz Heinrich* shelled Russian positions.

From 9 to 11 September, operating from Libau, the newly-returned *Prinz Adalbert*, with *Roon, Braunschweig* and *Elsaß* (*Prinz Heinrich* was at Kiel for boiler repairs) undertook a sweep towards Gotland, a further operation being carried out by *Prinz Adalbert* and five battleships, plus a light cruiser (*Roon* was also now away for repairs) on 21–23rd. *Prinz Heinrich* returned to Libau on 22 September and covered a minelaying operation on 5–6 October in company with *Prinz Adalbert*. *Roon* returned from her repairs on the 18th, but on 23 October *Prinz Adalbert* was torpedoed by the British submarine *E8* off Libau, the explosion detonating a magazine. She broke in two and sank with the loss of 672 men. The battleship *Braunschweig* was missed by the submarine *E18* the same month.

Ryurik was once again used as a minelayer in November, laying 560 mines off Gotland on the 11th, and 700 more on 6 December. In doing so, she contributed to a decision by the German navy that, in light of the losses and severe damage caused by mines and submarine torpedoes during the latter part of the year, that the continued operation of big ships in the eastern Baltic was too dangerous.[152] *Prinz Heinrich* thus returned to Kiel to be placed at reduced readiness until early 1916, when she paid off for disarmament and relegation to subsidiary duties. *Roon* became the Kiel guardship in February 1916, before reducing to a trials and training ship for the Torpedo Inspectorate in November. During 1917–18 she was the subject of a project to convert her into a seaplane carrier, with a hanger and aircraft handling gear aft (as actually done in the light cruiser *Stuttgart* [1906]), but these plans were dropped in favour of the conversion of the incomplete liner *Ausonia* into a flight-deck aircraft carrier – never carried through owing to the end of the war.[153]

The North Sea 1915

The I. SG's follow-on operation to the Hartlepool, Scarborough and Whitby raid was intended to probe the Dogger Bank and attack the fishing fleet there that was suspected of being a key source of British intelligence on German movements: that German naval codes had been compromised was as yet unsuspected. No High Seas Fleet support was available.

The British were aware of the operation five hours before the German force sailed on 23 January 1915. British and German light cruisers met at 07.05 on the 24th, with the engagement between British battlecruisers and the German force beginning at 08.52. Following an early hit that did little damage, at 10.30 *Blücher* received a hit that penetrated her fore-aft ammunition passage, a number of cartridges catching fire, which spread a forward wing turret. The uptakes from the forward boiler room were also damaged, cutting the ship's speed to 17kt, causing her to fall behind her companions. Soon afterwards a signalling error resulted in the British force turning to attack *Blücher*, rather than chase the rest of the German force, which was able to escape. Overwhelmed, although having scored final hits on the battlecruisers *Tiger*

Prinz Adalbert after being torpedoed on 2 July 1915. (BA 134-B2185)

(1913), *Indomitable* and a destroyer, *Blücher*, hit fifty to a hundred times by heavy shells, finally sank after being hit by two torpedoes fired by the light cruiser *Arethusa* (1913); 260 men survived.

By early 1915, the late-generation British armoured cruisers were all back in home waters, *Defence* (replacing *Leviathan*), *Black Prince*, *Duke of Edinburgh* and *Warrior* constituting the 1st CS of the Grand Fleet, *Shannon*, *Achilles*, *Cochrane* and *Natal* the 2nd. *Minotaur*, after refit, led a reconstituted 7th CS (with *Donegal* and *Hampshire*) from the end of the year until the following May. The 3rd CS (*Antrim*, *Devonshire*, *Argyll* and *Roxburgh*) was formally part of the Grand Fleet, but generally acted on patrol duties, based at Rosyth.

Modifications to these ships down to 1916 focussed on the fitting of one or two anti-aircraft guns, with a reduction in tertiary batteries, and changes to rig and searchlight installations. Ships with main-deck 6in batteries began to have at least some of the guns shifted to open upper-deck locations, with the old casemates plated up. Amongst the first were the *Duke of Edinburgh*s, as still fully-fledged fleet units: in March 1916 it was ordered that the six centremost guns be moved to the upper deck directly above their original locations, and the end guns deleted altogether; the empty main-deck embrasures were all to be closed permanently.

In the *Drake*s, by the end of 1915 deployed on the trade routes, four of the main-deck guns replaced the midships 12pdrs, with two more placed atop the forward casemates, while in the *Monmouth/Donegal*s, now on the Atlantic trade routes and in the Far East, the midships gun was in some ships moved up to the upper deck but the lower guns of the end casemates initially left in place. These were, however, later also were moved to the upper deck, as was also the case in the *Devonshire*s.

Of the latter, *Argyll* had been lost in October, having run onto Bell Rock near Dundee as a result of the local lighthouse not having been lit as requested (lights were not kept lit owing to concerns at aiding enemy vessels); guns and fittings were salvaged. *Roxburgh* had been torpedoed forward by *U39* on 20 June, but had managed to return to Rosyth under her own power; repairs lasted until April 1916.

The next loss of a big British cruiser occurred at the very end of 1915, when a fire broke out aboard *Natal*, lying in the Cromarty Firth at Invergordon. It spread rapidly and the ship capsized after the explosion of her aft 9.2in magazine. This was the second loss of a British big ship to an accidental magazine explosion, the first having been the battleship *Bulwark* in November 1914. Sadly, it would not be the last, with similar losses suffered by the Italian and Japanese navies as well (for the latter, see p 119). Magazine safety issues would also contribute to losses in action (p 127).

The North Sea 1916–18

As already noted, by the beginning of 1916, the surviving British big cruisers were increasingly being concentrated on the trade routes, where their size and seaworthiness made them particularly effective, or on distant stations, where the same qualities were useful – but also where they were unlikely to face modern opposition. A few of the more modern vessels remained with the main battlefleet – ironically in part because their nominal replacements, the battlecruisers, now formed a detached Battlecruiser Fleet based at Rosyth, rather than operating as an integral part of the Grand Fleet itself.

THE BATTLE OF JUTLAND[154]

The next German bombardment sortie, once again with the intent of drawing out a British force that could be overwhelmed by the German battlefleet which would be waiting to the east, was planned to be against Sunderland. Submarines would be deployed off Scapa Flow, the Moray Firth, the Firth of Forth and the Humber, and north of Terschelling, while airships would act as scouts for the I. SG and provide reconnaissance against being surprised by the whole Grand Fleet. On the 30th it was decided to substitute a

On 30 December 1915, a fire broke out aboard *Natal* (shown that year in the left-hand photograph, with reduced or removed topmasts and wearing a false bow-wave and stem-profile), then moored at Invergordon. It spread rapidly and a small explosion took place, followed immediately by a series of further small explosions, and then a final very large one, all within a few seconds. Fire then engulfed the after part of the ship, quickly spreading forward, where attempts to flood the forward magazines were frustrated by thick smoke and a power failure. The ship then took a list to port, capsizing within five minutes, her starboard bilge keel clear of the water; 404 men were lost. The ship's loss was blamed on the ignition of old cordite charges, which started the initial fire, which then spread to first the aft 3pdr magazine, then the small-arms magazine and finally that for the aft 9.2in guns. *(NHHC NH 50154/author's collection)*

Warrior in the North Sea in 1916, showing her final modifications before loss. *(WSS)*

sortie into the Skagerrak for the Sunderland bombardment, British signals intelligence leading to the Grand and Battlecruiser Fleets being deployed on the 30th.

By now, the only armoured cruisers in any of the forces involved were the 1st and 2nd CS of the Grand Fleet, the former 7th CS having been recently dissolved, with *Minotaur* and *Hampshire* joining *Shannon* and *Cochrane* in the 2nd CS, respectively as flagship and as a temporary replacement for *Achilles*, now refitting. The 1st CS was still led by *Defence*, accompanied by *Warrior*, *Black Prince* and *Duke of Edinburgh*. Neither squadron were thus uniform in equipment. Although all but *Hampshire* shared a four x 9.2in main broadside, secondary batteries were in some of 7.5in calibre, in others 6in. *Hampshire* was significantly smaller and more lightly armed than the remainder.

Their participation in what became the Battle of Jutland came as the main body of the Grand Fleet and the German forces came together around 17.50, when *Defence* and *Warrior* exchanged shots with the German II. SG, hitting the light cruiser *Wiesbaden* (1915), immobilised by battlecruiser gunfire shortly before. At 18.13, now joined by their squadron-mates, *Duke of Edinburgh* and *Black Prince* (which also successfully fired on *Wiesbaden*), the 1st CS came under fire from the battleship *König* (1913) and the battlecruiser *Seydlitz* (1912), soon joined by the battlecruiser *Lützow* (1913), and the battleships *Großer Kurfürst, Markgraf, Kronprinz, Kaiser* and *Kaiserin* (1911–14). *Defence* was hit at 18.19, resulting in the explosion of the forward magazines, flash then migrating through the ammunition passages on each beam, venting through each of the 7.5in turrets, before exploding the main magazines at the other end of the ship, the ship sinking within perhaps twelve seconds, with no survivors.

Warrior was also under heavy fire, receiving some fifteen hits from heavy guns and caught fire; she would probably have been sunk then, had the battleship *Warspite* (1913) not suffered a steering failure at 18.19, which caused her to circle

in a way that took her closer to the German fleet, inadvertently (but fortuitously) interposing herself between them and *Warrior*. However, the latter was fatally wounded, in particular by a port waterline hit just forward of the after engine-room bulkhead that seems to have reached the centreline bulkhead before exploding, thus causing flooding in engine rooms. Although the boiler rooms remained dry, leaks caused the gradual flooding of the after magazines, while holes in the side and deck became problematic as the ship later settled and encountered rough weather while in tow by the seaplane carrier *Engadine* (1911), which had succoured the stricken cruiser at 20.40. *Engadine* ultimately took off *Warrior*'s crew when it became clear that the cruiser could not be saved after a tow of 100 miles: she was abandoned with a freeboard of little over

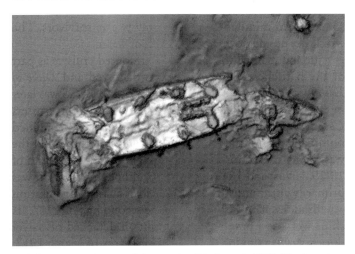

Multibeam sonar image of the wreck of *Defence* in 2015. The bow is to the left, lying on its port side, with the area from the forward 9.2in and the bulkhead between the first and second boiler rooms destroyed by the initial magazine explosion. The flash then passed aft via the 7.5in guns' ammunition passages to the aft magazine, causing a further explosion that severed the stern at the engine-room bulkhead. *(Sea Museum Jutland, courtesy Innes McCartney)*

3ft in worsening weather at 08.25 on 1 June, and subsequently sank.[155]

Of the two remaining ships of the 1st CS, *Duke of Edinburgh* had taken up station to the starboard of the 2nd BS by 18.30, and evaded a torpedo at 18.47, although subsequently reporting a number of phantom submarines. About 19.15 she joined the 2nd CS, which had had an uneventful battle, *Minotaur*, *Cochrane* and *Shannon* not firing their main or secondary guns at all and *Hampshire* only four salvos. The track of *Black Prince* following the sinking of *Defence* and crippling of *Warrior* remains unclear, but by 20.45 she was some 17 miles behind the main body of the British fleet, suggesting that she had suffered some form of machinery damage or defect.

At 23.36, during the confused night phase of the battle, she fell in with the van of the High Seas Fleet, and then engaged and hit the battleship *Rheinland* (1908) twice with 6in shells, albeit for only minor damage. However, less than half an hour later, she encountered *Rheinland*'s squadron-mates, *Nassau* (1908) and *Thüringen* (1909). The latter opened fire at the point-blank range of 1100 yards. Twenty-seven 5.9in and twenty-four 3.5in shells were reported to have hit the cruiser, which was then also fired on by the battleships *Ostfriesland* (1909) *Nassau* and *Friedrich der Große* (1911) between 00.07 and 00.15. *Black Prince* attempted to turn away, apparently having fired a torpedo from her port submerged tube, but the aft 9.2in magazine exploded, blowing the stern off, after which she rolled over to port and sank with all hands.[156]

BEYOND JUTLAND

On 5 June, *Hampshire* was detached to carry the Secretary of State for War, Earl Kitchener, on a mission to Russia, but was mined forward off Orkney at 19.40 in heavy weather, sinking some fifteen minutes later, with only twelve survivors. The wreck lies upside down in over 150ft of water.

Jutland marked the end of the armoured cruisers as part of the battlefleet. The 1st CS was dissolved and *Duke of Edinburgh* consolidated into the 2nd CS; the 1st CS was later re-established in the form of the new large light cruisers *Courageous* and *Glorious* (1916). The 2nd CS remained nominally part of the Grand Fleet through to the end of the war, going to sea during abortive High Seas Fleet sorties of 18/19 August and 18 October 1916, although by 1917 it was primarily an administrative, rather than tactical organisation – without even a flagship during the second half of 1917. Its ships were now employed primarily on detached or patrol duties, *Achilles* sinking the raider *Leopard* on 16 March 1917. On 8 December 1917, the Northern Patrol's AMC-equipped 10th CS was disestablished, and its responsibilities, and a tithe of its ships, devolved on the 2nd CS, which at the point of transfer comprised *Minotaur* and *Shannon* (*Achilles*, *Cochrane* and *Duke of Edinburgh* now on detached service) plus the AMCs *Alsatian*, *Tuetonic* (1889) and *Orvieto* (1909), two armed boarding vessels, and twelve trawlers. The

Shannon in 1918, showing many wartime modifications, but not yet fitted with a tripod foremast. *(WSS)*

Shannon on patrol in heavy weather, now with her tripod mast fitted, and with range-finding baffles on the funnels – which were in fact useless against German stereoscopic equipment. Such conditions experienced in the North Atlantic led to any remaining main-deck guns being removed from big ships employed on convoy duty. *(WSS)*

Achilles in 1918, now typical of the surviving members of the last three classes of classic British armoured cruisers, with a tripod foremast to carry a director and numerous minor modifications. *(WSS)*

The older British vessels were less altered, but most had their main-deck 6in guns removed from their casemates and some or all remounted on the upper deck; hull-mounted 12pdrs were also taken out. *Lancaster* is seen here so-modified. *(WSS)*

Amphitrite following her conversion to a minelayer. *(NHHC NH 63009*

changed nature of the squadron was illustrated by the fact that *Alsatian*, rather than any of the armoured cruisers, was now squadron flagship.

Alterations to the surviving *Duke of Edinburgh*, *Warrior* and *Minotaur* classes from 1916 onwards focussed on the installation of director control for main batteries, with support legs fitted to foremasts during 1917–18 to provide the requisite rigidity, although the actual directors were in some cases only fitted later. There was also a general elaboration of bridgework and a further rearrangement of searchlights. In addition *Duke of Edinburgh* received in 1917 a further of 6in in her forward superstructure.

Regarding older vessels, the rearrangement of secondary batteries continued in ships that remained operational, while others were increasingly relegated to secondary and harbour service. Two of the *Diadem* class, *Ariadne* and *Amphitrite*, were taken in hand in 1916 for conversion to minelayers. The ships recommissioned the following year, armed with four 6in guns and one 4in AA gun, with a capacity of 354–400 mines. *Ariadne* had a short renewed career, being sunk by submarine torpedo four months after recommissioning (having laid 708 mines of the Dover Barrage), with the loss of thirty lives. *Amphitrite*, however, having laid 5053 mines off Dover, went on to play an important role in laying the North Sea Mine Barrage from April 1918, and remained in commission until the middle of 1919. *Euryalus* also began conversion to a minelayer, at Hong Kong in late 1917. However, this work was never finished, and the ship returned incomplete to the UK at the beginning of 1919 to pay off for the final time.

The Mediterranean and Aegean 1916–1918

At the beginning of 1916, the French fleet in the Mediterranean comprised three squadrons of battleships, supported by the 1st and 2nd Light Divisions, comprising respectively *Waldeck-Rousseau* (flag) *Edgar Quinet* and *Ernest Renan*, and *Jules Michelet* (flag), *Victor Hugo* and *Jules Ferry*, the six most modern examples of their type. At Alexandria were the *Amiral Charner*s, forming the 3rd Light Division, with *D'Entrecasteaux* at Port Said; *Pothuau* was flagship of the Syrian Division, leading the battleship *Jauréguberry* and the coast-defence ship *Requin*. However, on 8 February 1916, while off Beirut, en route to Port Said, *Amiral Charner* was hit by a single torpedo fired by *U21*, the vessel that had sunk *Triumph* the previous year. *Charner* sank in two minutes, with only one survivor, not found until five days later.

On 1 May 1916, the 2nd Light Squadron had been disestablished, and most of the second-generation armoured cruisers split between the 4th Light Division (*Gueydon*, *Montcalm* and *Dupetit-Thouars*), which remained based on the Atlantic coast, a re-established 3rd (*Glore*, *Amiral Aube*, *Marseillaise* and *Condé*), which went to the Mediterranean, and the 6th (*Dupleix*, *Kléber* and *Desaix*), which went briefly to the Mediterranean, before moving to Dakar in October. Also in the Atlantic at this time was *Châteaurenault*, which had arrived in February to search for the German raider *Möwe* (1914), and stayed until July, when she proceeded to Bizerte for a refit.

Also during 1916, Russia, wishing to obtain larger ships for service outside the Baltic and Black Seas (the only major warship currently available being the protected cruiser *Askold*, currently in the Mediterreanean), came to agreement with Japan to purchase a number of vessels captured from her during the Russo-Japanese War. These comprised the battleship *Tango*, ex-*Poltava*, which now became *Chesma* (her original name having now been taken by a dreadnought), the protected cruiser *Soya*, which resumed her former name, *Varyag*, and *Sagami*, ex-*Peresvet*, which also took her former name, but was now reclassified as an armoured cruiser. *Chesma* was initially

After nearly a decade's service as the Japanese *Sagami*, *Peresvet* was sold back to her original owners in 1916. She is shown here at Vladivostok before sailing west. *(NHHC NH 94791)*

Nisshin at Port Said in 1918, with the French battleship *Jauréguiberry* (1893) in the background. *(Author's collection)*

intended for the Mediterranean, with the other two for the White Sea, although *Chesma* would also end up there.

Peresvet ran aground near Vladivostok on 23 May 1916, and remained stuck fast until 7 July, meaning that she was left behind when the other two ships sailed on 2 July. Repaired at Maizuru in Japan, she finally sailed on 18 October, but soon after having passed through the Suez Canal and had machinery repairs undertaken at Port Said, she struck two mines (laid by *U73*) a few hours after leaving the latter on 4 January 1917. One caused a magazine explosion that blew off the roof of the forward 10in turret, while the other opened the port side abreast the middle boiler room. A fire broke out on the battery deck, the vessel sinking rapidly by the head, with at least ninety men lost.

In September 1917, *Châteaurenault* and *Guichen* were refitted at Bizerte as fast troop transports, for service between Taranto and Itea in Greece, to support the expanding Salonika front. Both had been employed since January on escort duties from Dakar, alongside the *Kléber*s of the 6th Light Division, *Guichen* after over a year in reserve. *D'Entrecasteaux* was employed at first as an escort and then a transport on the same run. While so-employed in October, *Châteaurenault* rescued survivors from the AMC *Gallia* (1913), torpedoed by *U35* off Sardinia, but on 14 December 1917, while west of Kephalonia,

she was herself hit by a torpedo from *UC38*. The troops onboard were evacuated to the auxiliary cruiser *Rouen* and the escorting destroyers *Mameluck* and *Lansquenet* (1910–11), with the trawler *Balsamine* attempting to take the damaged cruiser in tow. However, some ninety minutes after the first torpedo had struck, *UC38* hit *Châteaurenault* a second time. She sank rapidly, before the submarine was herself sunk by the two French destroyers. The other two cruisers continued as troopships until 1919.

As already noted, in January 1917, the British requested that the Japanese provide destroyers for Mediterranean anti-submarine escort duties. Accordingly, on 13 April 1917 the 2nd Special Squadron arrived at Malta, the protected cruiser *Akashi* leading eight destroyers; in June 1917, *Izumo* arrived at Malta as relief flagship, along with four additional destroyers. *Nisshin* was sent as a further reinforcement in the autumn of 1918, relieving *Izumo* as flagship, and leading the bulk of the Japanese force to Constantinople, arriving on 6 December. *Izumo* and *Nisshin*, plus the destroyers *Hinoki* (1916) and *Yanagi* (1917) then proceeded to the UK, arriving on 5 January 1919, to take over seven surrendered German submarines allocated to Japan. *Nisshin* left with her charges and eight destroyers at the end of March, proceeding via Malta back to Japan, arriving on 18 June, while *Izumo* and

Guichen as fitted as a troop transport, with drawbridges fitted to ease the embarkation and disembarkation of the troops. *(Author's collection)*

Edgar Quinet following the removal of her mainmast to allow the use of a kite balloon. *(Author's collection)*

the rest of the destroyers sailed home via a number of Mediterranean port visits, arriving on 2 July.

During 1917–18 a number of French battleships[157] and armoured cruisers had their mainmasts cut down to allow them to deploy a kite balloon. The latter comprised *Ernest Renan*, *Edgar Quinet* and *Pothuau*, which at the same time lost her foretop and had a second searchlight added to her foremast platform, to which her former bridgetop searchlight had been relocated around the beginning of the war. From the spring of 1918, eight of the French armoured cruisers were moved to the Aegean from the Adriatic, along with the surviving *Danton*-class battleships, to relive the five *Patrie/Démocratie* class battleships previously deployed there.

Atlantic convoys

At the American declaration of war on 6 April 1917, *Pittsburgh* was flagship of the Pacific Fleet, but was soon switched to Atlantic Fleet's Scouting Force, of which *Pueblo* (ex-*Colorado*) was made flagship; the two ships operated in the South Atlantic for the remainder of the year. *Huntington* (ex-*West Virginia*) was undertaking aviation trials in Floridan waters, but in August was assigned to the Cruiser and Transport Force, which would first assemble in August at Brooklyn; this would ultimately comprise a 1st Division of *Seattle*, *North Carolina*, *Montana* and *Huntington*, and a 2nd Division of *San Diego*, *Frederick*, *Pueblo* (from January 1918) and *South Dakota*.

Saratoga (ex-*New York*) was refitted when recommissioned, the after superstructure being cut down, searchlights reduced in number, the bridgework enlarged and a control top installed on the foremast. All 3in guns and the aftermost pair of 5in were removed and a pair of 3in AA guns added. She first served in the Pacific, based on Hawaii, but also moved to the Atlantic Fleet in November 1917 (with the Japanese *Tokiwa* replacing her on station, and *Asama* taking over in August 1918), where she (renamed yet again as *Rochester* on 1 December 1917) undertook convoy escort duties as part of the 4th Division, 2nd Squadron, Cruiser Force. The only big cruisers not to

serve on Atlantic escort duty were *Brooklyn*, which remained in the Far East until 1920, and *Pittsburgh*, which operated principally in the South Atlantic as part of the Scouting Force of the Atlantic Fleet.

The two surviving *St Louis* class were also used as Atlantic escorts. *St Louis* herself had been serving as a submarine tender at Honolulu when the USA declared war, but immediately sailed for the East Coast, completing her crew en route at San Diego, fully commissioning on 20 April 1917. She then proceeded via the Panama Canal, carrying Marines to Cuba before arriving at Philadelphia on 29 May. *St Louis* left with her first convoy on 17 June. *Charleston*, also serving as a submarine tender, in her case in the Canal Zone, had recommissioned on 6 April 1917, beginning with the Patrol Force in the Caribbean, before becoming part of the escort of the first convoy carrying troops of the American Expeditionary Force to France on 14 June; this also included *Seattle* (flag). *Charleston* also carried out escort duties in the Caribbean and to Nova Scotia, before joining the Cruiser and Transport Force at the end of the war to carry occupation troops and to repatriate combat troops. The two *Columbia*-class vessels were also employed on convoy duty, with two of their 4in now taken out. *Columbia* herself covered five convoys between January and November 1918, while *Minneapolis* made four convoy-voyages between February and October.

The American ships served alongside their British counterparts *Duke of Edinburgh* and the surviving *Warrior*s, plus *Drake*, *King Alfred*, *Leviathan*, *Berwick*, *Cornwall* and *Carnarvon*, together with a number of pre-dreadnought battleships from both navies.[158] For example, one twelve-ship 'fast' convoy, which left New York on 13 October 1918, was escorted by *Montana*, *Duke of Edinburgh* and the battleship *Nebraska*. The Brest-based French Atlantic Division (ex-4th Light Division, redesignated in January) and West Indies Divisions, comprising *Gueydon*, *Montcalm*, *Dupetit-Thouars* and *Jeanne d'Arc*, also took part in the operations, as did the Dakar-based 6th Light Division (still comprising the *Kléber* class).

Minneapolis in 1918, camouflaged for convoy duty; the new superstructure aft contained a radio cabin. *(NHHC NH 46198)*

Charleston while on Atlantic escort duty. (Author's collection)

On 3 November 1918, Cochrane sailed from Murmansk, arriving at Scapa Flow on the 10th, after a rough passage that left parts of her forward structure badly strained and buckled. She left on the 12th for the Mersey, coming under command of a river pilot at 07.15 on the 14th, the ship running aground at 07.57. Tugs arrived ninety minutes later, which attempted to tow the cruiser off on the rising tide through the late afternoon and evening. As the ship was clearly stuck fast, work was begun discharging ammunition into lighters that night, but soon after 04.00 the next morning, Cochrane began to take water forward and in 'A' boiler room. At 06.00, tugs once again attempted to tow her off, aided by the ship's own engines running full astern, but again without success, and the discharge of ammunition was resumed at 09.00. That afternoon, 500 ratings were sent ashore, and that evening further attempts were made to tow the ship off, again without success, ammunition discharge continuing. A floating crane arrived at 09.00 on the 16th, with more lightening work proceeding; 170 more ratings were discharged on the afternoon of the 17th, but by the 20th it was clear that refloating was not practicable. The ship soon afterwards broke her back and sank. Her remains, a danger to navigation, were rapidly broken up over the next six months. A court martial on 19 February 1919 found against Cochrane's Navigating Officer. (Author's collection)

Although the size and seaworthiness of all these ships apparently made them ideal for Atlantic conditions, the duty reinforced the already-noted decision to delete main-deck guns from British ships, the Americans also being forced to land their similarly-sited weapons, with permanent plating-over installed in a number of ships. *Frederick*, for example, had her main-deck 3in removed while in the South Atlantic in 1917, then the forward six 6in in January 1918, and the remaining four in March. No attempt was made, as had been the case in British ships, to reinstall any of these guns on the upper deck (partly owing the re-allocation of some of the weapons to defensively-armed merchant ships),[159] reducing these huge vessels' secondary batteries to only four guns. Only *Pittsburgh*, serving in the South Atlantic, kept some main-deck guns, losing only four. Experience also showed that the drastically-reduced bridgework mandated by the Newport Conference (p 108) was wholly inadequate for conning ships in operational circumstances, and thus significant new structures were added at the same time.[160]

In addition to the ships operating across the North Atlantic and on patrol duties northern waters, the 9th CS continued to provide a long-range force based in West Africa for more southerly operations. In September 1917, it comprised *Bacchante* (flag) and *King Alfred*, plus the battleships *Africa* and *Britannia* and four AMCs. By June 1918, only *Bacchante* and the two battleships were left, with *Africa* withdrawn in October and *Britannia* sunk in November; at the end of the war, just *Bacchante* remained, supported by a pair of whalers.

As already noted, organisationally *Minotaur* and *Shannon* remained formally in the Grand Fleet's 2nd CS throughout, reverting to being an armoured-cruisers-only formation in March 1918. *Cochrane* had rejoined early in 1918, as had *Achilles*, although she would be under refit from February to November 1918. *Cochrane* went to the White Sea in March 1918, during the first phase of the Allied intervention in the Russian Civil War (see further below, p 135), returning to the UK in November, only to run aground in the Mersey on the 14th, becoming a total loss. The majority of British big cruisers on convoys were, however, now part of the North American & West Indies station; the French merged their Atlantic Division into the West Indies Division in September 1917.

Four big cruisers were lost to enemy action while on Atlantic convoy duty, in three cases while close to home shores. First, on 26 June 1917 *Kléber* struck a mine on the approach to Brest at 06.00. The forward boiler room flooded rapidly and power was lost. The anti-submarine gunboat *Inconstant* (1916) attempted to take the cruiser in tow, but by 06.45 the situation had deteriorated, with the collapse of a boiler room bulkhead; she sank with the loss of thirty-eight men. Next, *Drake* was torpedoed by *U79* in the North Channel in October 1917, having just arrived with a convoy; she capsized some five hours later. *San Diego* (ex-*California*) struck a mine (laid by the German submarine *U156*) in July 1918 off Long Island,

On 2 October 1917, having just arrived the North Channel with a convoy from North America, *Drake* was struck at 09.15 on the starboard side abreast the second funnel by a torpedo fired by *U79*, killing eighteen men. While limping, with ineffective steering, towards Church Bay on Rathlin Island at 10.37 she collided with the merchant ship *Mendip Range*, which was so damaged that she had to be beached. The cruiser anchored at 11.46, to await the arrival of salvage vessels, but her list gradually increased as flooding spread, it being decided to evacuate the ship to the destroyer *Martin* (1910), as seen her; this was completed at 14.05. *Drake* capsized thirty minutes later, coming to rest on her side in 15–20m of water, with much of her port bilge above water. The wreck was sold for £5,350 on 4 March 1918, some salvage work being carried out during the 1920s. Ammunition was removed from the hull by naval divers during the 1970s, after which the wreck was blown up with depth charges. Much remains on the bottom, however. *(Tommy Cecil collection)*

Another vessel lost on escort duty was *San Diego* (ex-*California*, shown here under her original name at Mare Island on 10 September 1915). She struck a mine (laid by the German submarine *U156*) in on 19 July 1918 off Long Island, while en-route from Portsmouth, NH, to New York to pick up a convoy. The explosion took place abreast the port engine room, flooding both this and the adjacent boiler room, giving a 9-degree list that soon led to flooding through the port 6in gunports. The ship was abandoned ten minutes after hitting the mine and capsized and sank twenty minutes later. As the water was fairly shallow (110ft), the wreck was sold for scrap in the 1950s, but little was done and it remains upturned on the seabed. *(Author's collection)*

capsized and sinking soon afterwards. Finally, *Dupetit-Thouars* was sunk by *U62* 400nm west of Brest on 7 August 1918: she had been stationed at the head of a convoy at 20.51, when hit by two torpedoes on the starboard side. She sank in fifty minutes, albeit with no loss of life, the crew being taken off by American destroyers.

After the war, the American big cruisers, together with the battleships also on escort duty, were employed to carry troops back to the United States. In doing so, they in part utilised space freed-up on the battery deck by the removal of some or all of their secondary batteries.

The Baltic and Russia 1916–1919

During 1915–16, the armament of the earlier armoured cruisers was upgraded, *Rossiya* having the 8in guns removed in 1914–15 replaced, and two more added on the quarterdeck, with the intention of fitting a further pair on the forecastle; to accommodate these extra guns, the ship's forecastle was removed to maintain stability, although it remains unclear whether the two extra guns were ever actually installed.[161] Her 6in battery was as a result reduced to fourteen guns, the guns on the starboard side being replaced with new ones, but only the most worn on the port.

In *Gromoboi*, the pairs of 6in under the forecastle and quarterdeck were taken out (along with all 75mm and 47mm weapons), and single 8in placed fore and aft at forecastle-deck level. In the surviving two *Bayan*s, all 75mm weapons were taken out and midships bulwarks cut down, with the intent

Pueblo (ex-*Colorado*) arriving at New York from France on 22 February 1919. The form of her now greatly-expanded bridgework reflects a common scheme for US warships by the end of the war; note also the absence of main-deck guns. *(NHHC NH 55270)*

The removal of *Rossiya's* forecastle in preparation for the fitting of two additional 8in guns forward. *(Author's collection)*

Rossiya with her forecastle removed, but no 8in guns yet fitted. *(Author's collection)*

It was planned to upgun the *Bayan* class as well during the war: this is *Admiral Makarov* in 1917 with an extra 8in gun worked-in amidships. *(Author's collection)*

Ryurik in 1917 at Reval, following completion of repairs to mine damage and the conversion of the foremast to a tripod. *(Author's collection)*

(apparently implemented only in *Makarov*) that a single 8in be installed on the centreline directly in front of the mainmast, and four 6in fitted in lieu of the shielded 75mm guns.

Ryurik continued to be active, and in June 1916 undertook a number of anti-shipping raids, but with only one German vessel sunk. On 7 November, *Ryurik* struck a mine off Hogland in the Gulf of Finland, with severe damage to her bow. She did not return to service until April 1917, now with her foremast converted to a tripod. By then, brigade allocations had changed, with the 1st Cruiser Brigade containing *Ryurik* and the *Bayan*s, plus *Bogatyr* and *Oleg*, the 2nd *Rossiya*, *Gromoboi*, *Aurora* and *Diana*.

The effectiveness of the Russian fleet was greatly degraded by the revolutionary events of 1917. Nevertheless, when the Germans launched Operation 'Albion' in October, aiming to seize the West Estonian Archipelago that closed off the Gulf of Riga from the Baltic,[162] units of the Baltic Fleet put up a spirited resistance, in spite of the size and nature of the German naval force deployed. This included ten modern battleships, a battlecruiser, eleven light cruisers, a minelayer, forty-three destroyers and thirteen submarines, plus minesweepers and other supporting vessels. In opposition, the Russian Navy could only deploy the battleships *Slava* and *Grazhdanin* (ex-*Tsesarevich*), the cruisers *Bayan*, *Admiral Makarov* and *Diana*, thre gunboats *Khrabryi* (1895), *Groziashchiy* (1890) and *Khivinetz* (1905), and three divisions of destroyers, torpedo boats and other subsidiary vessels.

German bombardments began on 11 October, *Admiral Makarov*, *Groziashchii* and six destroyers engaging German torpedo boats that afternoon. On the 13th, further actions took place between Russian destroyers, later joined by *Khivinetz*, and German light vessels. *Grazhdanin* and *Admiral Makarov* joined the fray late the following afternoon, but the range was too great and fire ceased at nightfall. On the 17th, *Grazhdanin*, *Slava*, *Bayan* and supporting destroyers launched an attack on German minesweepers, with the German battleships *König* and *Kronprinz* soon being deployed to support the latter. The German battleships concentrated on their Russian opposite numbers, *Bayan* was for the time being ignored.

Grazhdanin received only minor damage, but *Slava* was badly mauled, before *Bayan* was belatedly taken under fire by *König*, and at 10.36 was hit by a shell that penetrated both the upper and the battery decks and exploded deep inside the ship, where it caused a fire that was only put out the next day. The German battleships ceased fire at 10.40, the Russians having begun to withdraw towards the Moon Sound dredged channel ten minutes earlier. Unfortunately, *Slava* now drew too much water to pass, and had to be scuttled. The other ships, however, successfully retreated into the Gulf of Finland and back to Kronstadt, the Germans being in full control by the 20th.

Following the Bolshevik seizure of power in November, an armistice was agreed between Russia and the Central Powers on 15 December. The consequent Treaty of Brest-Litovsk confirmed the already incipient independence of Finland,

Many old and incomplete Russian big ships were sold to German shipbreakers by the new Soviet government. *Gromoboi* was one of these, but she ran aground adjacent to the breakwater at Liepaja while in tow to Germany, and was subsequently broken up *in situ*. (Author's collection)

Brooklyn and *Suffolk* at Vladivostok on 10 March 1918; they had respectively arrived on 1 March and 24 January. The large vessels out in the harbour are the Japanese battleships *Iwami* (1902, left, ex-Russian *Orel*, captured at Tsushima) and *Asahi* (1899). (NHHC NH 69711)

meaning that the principal fleet anchorage at Helsingfors (Helsinki) had to be evacuated to Kronstadt in March 1918 in the so-called 'Ice Voyage'. Following this, the majority of the bigger ships were placed in reserve, most never to return to service. These included the armoured cruisers, some of which gave up guns for use on land, and of which all but *Ryurik* were sold for scrap in Germany in 1922, *Gromoboi* being wrecked en-route. *Ryurik* was, although listed for long-term retention on 21 May 1921, in very poor condition, with

key systems to be removed for preservation, and it was decided in November 1923 to scrap the by-now-disarmed hulk. The 8in turrets were subsequently emplaced for coast defence.

The collapse of the Russian war effort was of great concern to her erstwhile allies, including the potential fate of stockpiles of equipment at Murmansk and Vladivostok. Accordingly, ships, in particular big cruisers, were deployed to both ports during 1917–18 to look after Allied interests. An American contribution was from *Brooklyn*, which made a first visit to Vladivostok on 25 November 1917, returning in March 1918. The flagship of the British China Station, *Suffolk* arrived on 14 January, donating 6in and 12pdr guns for railway and later river use, being joined by *Kent* in January 1919, which also landed guns for use inland.

Cochrane's detachment to the White Sea has already been noted, where a British force had been landed at Murmansk from the battleship *Glory* to on 6 March 1918. *Gueydon* and *Amiral Aube* arrived there in August 1918, being relieved by *Montcalm* in December 1918, the latter nominally part of a new Baltic Squadron, remaining there until May 1919. *Gueydon* went to the Baltic in November 1919, relieving *Marseillaise*, which had been there since December 1918.

The British were also in the Baltic, providing direct naval support to White, Finnish and Balt forces fighting the Bolsheviks from November 1918 to February 1920. During the summer of 1919 a number of raids were made on Kronstadt,[163] with *Pamiat Azova* (which had resumed her old name in 1917) regarded as a key target, owing to her submarine depot role. As such she was the objective of an air-strike from the carrier *Vindictive* on 30 July, although not hit on this occasion. Then, on 17 August 1919, a raid by coastal motor boats was carried out, *CMB79* (herself sunk soon afterwards) sinking *Pamiat Azova*, and *CMB4* the protected cruiser *Oleg*; the battleship *Andrei Pervosvannyi* was also damaged.[164] Work to salvage and scrap the former armoured cruiser's wreck began in late 1923, one of the salvage vessels sinking herself in September 1924 after striking one *Pamiat Azova's* submerged davits.

The wreck of *Pamiat Azova* (ex-*Dvina*, ex-*Pamiat Azova*) at Kronstadt after being torpedoed by *CMB79* on 17 August 1919. The ships in the background are the protected cruisers *Diana* (rear) and *Aurora*. (Author's collection)

7 | THE LONG DYING

The Post-War World

At the end of the First World War, of the surviving Central Powers' big cruisers, the one German vessel left (*Roon*) was disarmed and on harbour service, and thus not affected by the 1919 Treaty of Versailles. The only restriction was that she could not be sold abroad when disposed-of for scrap.

On the other hand, all Austro-Hungarian warships had fallen under Allied control in November 1918, being concentrated in a number of locations, *Maria Theresia* at Pola, *Karl VI* at Sebenico and *Sankt Georg* at Cattaro. Under the Treaty of Saint-Germain-en-Laye of September 1919, the three cruisers all fell to the British share of the ex-Austro-Hungarian navy, although at one point *Sankt Georg* was slated for handover to Italy as a 'propaganda' ship – a sub-division of prizes given to each of the principal Allied powers without reference to war losses, and primarily intended for target service.[165] There was no question of bringing the ships to the UK, all (together with the other ships surrendered to the UK[166]) being sold to Italian companies 'as lies' in Adriatic ports, although some were subsequently re-sold after a number of vessels had not reached the required level of dismantlement by the contractual date.

The remaining operational British ships were removed from active service soon after the Armistice (the 2nd CS was disestablished at the end of 1918), as there were ample modern ships to fulfil most cruiser needs of the post-war navy, with even the earlier battlecruisers already being paid off into reserve. On the other hand, most of the new ships were 'fleet' cruisers intended for North Sea service, meaning that the older *Weymouth*, *Chatham* and *Birmingham* classes needed to be used for overseas roles, while immediate post-war plans envisaged the use of AMCs for high seas patrol and convoy duty in the event of war, at least until such time as new larger cruisers were completed.[167]

The only vessels left at sea for a while were *Cumberland*, which was used as a cadet training ship until April 1920, *Roxburgh*, which was a wireless training ship during 1919, and *Antrim* which acted as an Asdic trials ship from March 1920 to 1922. *Achilles* replaced *Diadem* as a stokers' training ship in June 1919, and *Shannon* was an accommodation ship for the *Actaeon* torpedo school at Sheerness from 1919 to 1922, but the rest lay essentially idle until sold for scrap. On the other hand, some of the long-hulked vessels lasted considerably longer, the former *Powerful*, *Terrible*, *Spartiate* surviving until 1929–32, and *Andromeda*, now transferred to the *Defiance* establishment, beyond the Second World War.

However, the lack of modern cruisers that had left most old big cruisers in front-line service in other navies continued to be a factor after the war as well, and although some of the oldest vessels were indeed removed from service and sold, others would continue to remain listed, and in quite a number of cases in front-line service into the 1920s, occasionally even beyond.

Most pre-war British warships went to the breakers in the early years of peace, in particular such obsolete vessels as the big armoured and protected cruisers. *Leviathan* is shown arriving at Blyth to be broken up in the spring of 1920, still bearing her late-war camouflage. *(WSS, David K Brown Collection)*

A small number of British vessels survived for a while on harbour service. The *Fisgard* training establishment at Portsmouth, seen here in 1920, incorporated two, *Fisgard I* (ex-*Spartiate*, nearest the camera) and *Fisgard III* (ex-*Terrible*, the housed-over vessel beyond) as accommodation hulks. The vessel to the right is *Fisgard II*, the former central-battery ironclad *Hercules*. *(Author's collection)*

Swords to Ploughshares?

While the all-but universal fate of surplus hulls was the scrapyard, the shortage of mercantile tonnage immediately after the war led to a number of warships being converted for peaceful purposes. This was not only true for smaller vessels, but also a handful of armoured warships, whose heavy construction and layouts entirely antithetical to the needs of a merchantman would normally have made such a conversion wholly uneconomic. During the war, Italy had modified the old battleship *Italia* (1880) as a grain carrier, while the British protected cruiser *Charybdis* (1893) had become a cargo carrier between Bermuda and New York, with many of her boilers taken out and their space used for cargo.[168] Then, in October 1918, the ex-*Dupuy de Lôme* was sold to a Belgian company, delivered in December and then rebuilt at Bordeaux as a cargo vessel.[169]

The conversion followed the basic pattern found in most such reconstructions, with all armament and as much armour as possible removed, propulsion machinery cut down to a minimum, and vacant machinery and magazine spaces converted to cargo holds. In the ex-*Dupuy de Lôme*'s case, all superstructure was removed, apart from the after deckhouse (to act as passenger accommodation), as was all side armour. The forward two boiler rooms and engine rooms were stripped out and their dividing bulkheads removed, leaving just the aft (centre shaft) engine and aft boiler room, with six boilers (for 1700–2000ihp and 10–10.5kt). A forecastle was built over the existing extended prow, including crew accommodation (more being provided on the main deck aft), and four cargo-holds were created. One comprised the former forward magazines, one the two vacated boiler rooms, one the vacated engine rooms and one the aft magazines, all serviced by nine derricks. Bridgework and officers' accommodation was installed over the fore-end of the remaining boiler room.

Renamed *Peruvier*, her first commercial voyage began at Cardiff on 20 January 1920, en route to Rio de Janeiro with a

In light of the post-war shortage of merchant ships, attempts were made to adapt a handful of cruisers as such. The former *Dupuy de Lôme* was rebuilt as *Peruvier*, but her career was unsuccessful and short. (The Engineer *129 [1920], p 270*)

Although some French vessels were retained, the surviving *Amiral Charner*s were soon disposed of, *Latouche-Treville* being shown here in 1922 while being used as a hulk for the salvage of the battleship *Liberté*, sunk by internal explosion in 1911. (*Author's collection*)

cargo of coal. However, the ship broke down in mid-Atlantic and had to be towed to Las Palmas, whence she was then towed to Pernambuco in Brazil, arriving on 1 June – where one of her coal-filled holds was found to be on fire. The fire was only extinguished nineteen days later, by which time the mainmast – directly aft of the hold in question (the former forward engine rooms) – had collapsed and the machinery made unusable. Towed to her home port of Antwerp during October/November, she remained laid up there until sold for scrap in 1923.

The conversion had been closely watched as a potential prototype for further similar reconstructions, *Latouche-Tréville* being mooted as the next subject, but in the event she was used as hulk during the salvage of the battleship *Liberté* (1905), sunk by a magazine explosion in 1911, before being broken up. *Jules Michelet* was proposed as a 15kt-liner, but again nothing was done.[170] The British *Europa* was sold to become an emigrant carrier in September 1920, but sank in a storm off Corsica four months later, without having begun her refit.

Sailing On

As noted above, in contrast to the Royal Navy, which had built a wide range of cruising vessels during the war, including the 9750-ton *Cavendish* class that had been designed for overseas service, the other victorious nations did not have the option of removing all their aging big cruisers from service, no matter how obsolete they manifestly now were. Although she now had the ten *Omaha* class under construction, until the first one commissioned in 1923 the USA had only three vaguely modern light cruisers (the *Chester* class of 1907). Italy was similarly afflicted, with only three modern scout-cruisers (*Quarto* and the *Nino Bixio* class [1911–12]), and the fairly new but archaic-in-design *Libia* (begun for Turkey) and *Basilicata* class (all 1914). However, France was in an even worse position, having been unable to proceed with her first modern light cruisers of the *Lamotte-Piquet* class owing to the exigencies of the war.[171] All three nations thus needed to retain at least some of their armoured and protected cruisers in commission to maintain any kind of cruiser force until new ships could come into service, whether through fresh construction or, in the case of France and Italy, the acquisition of surrendered German and Austro-Hungarian tonnage as well.[172]

Japan was much better situated, with a large programme of light cruisers of the *Tenryu*, *Kuma* and follow-on classes well underway. However, she opted to keep the old big cruisers long-term for secondary duties, in particular as cadet training vessels, a role in which they had begun to be employed even before the war (cf. pp 99, 213). Even before peace had been declared, *Tokiwa* had begun to be so-employed by the Etajima Naval Academy in April 1917, joined by her sister in 1918. Such duty had also been long a function of the South American big cruisers, their seaworthiness, roominess and impressive appearance well fitting them for the role. Indeed, it would be in this role that the very last example of the kind would still be at sea beyond 1950.

The old *Chiyoda* was also retained, being converted into a submarine depot ship during 1919–20; as such, she was largely disarmed and the mainmast was struck. She served as such until December 1924 when she became a training ship at the Naval College. Hulked in February 1927, she was expended as a target that August during an Imperial review, although her bridge survived at the Naval Academy as a reviewing stand until the end of the Second World War.

France

In France, the surviving pair of *Amiral Charner*s had already been laid up by the Armistice and were subsequently disposed of, while the surviving *Kléber*s only lasted a short while before being condemned, as was also the case with *Guichen*. *D'Entrecasteaux* was condemned after spending 1919–21 as a training vessel at Brest, but was then lent to the Belgian navy as a stationary training ship and depot ship for their ex-German torpedo boats from May 1923. Her screws were removed along with all armament, while two of her old boilers were replaced by hardly-used Bellevilles from the coast-defence ship *Furieux* (1883).

A potential issue was that Article XVIII of the Washington Naval Treaty, agreed on 6 February 1922 between the British Empire, France, Italy, and Japan, forbade the 'gift, sale or any mode of transfer of any vessel of war in such a manner that such vessel may become a vessel of war in the Navy of any foreign Power'. However, the work already undertaken on *D'Entrecasteaux* was accepted by the signatories as meaning that she was 'disarmed and . . . immobile and therefore had been deprived of its character as a combat ship'; she accordingly took up duty with the Belgians. This was terminated in 1926, when the Belgian navy was abolished, its combat ships being disposed of or converted to civilian roles. *D'Entrecasteaux* herself was towed to Cherbourg, with a view to sale for scrap.

However, back on 18 June 1923, Poland had had begun negotiations with France to acquire *Desaix* for conversion to a similar role.[173] The French Navy had initially recommended permanently lending the vessel to the Poles, subject to the payment of the costs of conversion and towage, along the same lines as Belgium was receiving *D'Entrecasteaux*. However, in March 1924 the French Foreign Minister agreed to gift the vessel to Poland, although by early 1925 the Naval Ministry

D'Entrecasteaux had a long career as a disarmed stationary training ship, first at Brest, and then at Bruges on loan to the fledgling Belgian navy, in which role she is seen here. On the winding-up of that navy in 1926, she passed to the Polish navy, surviving to be captured by the Germans in 1939. (*Author's collection*)

was taking the view that the Poles should now pay for the hull as well as its conversion. Concerns then arose that such a move might alienate Poland, and have a negative impact on attempts to sell new ships to the country.[174] In June, it was concluded that gifting the ship would require parliamentary approval – something that could be problematic – and that other options needed to be considered. An agreement was finally reached on 14 July 1926, under which Poland would pay FF 1.2 million for the hull, plus 2.42 million for the refit and the tow to Gdynia, funds to come from a long-term loan granted to Poland by France; alterations were to be undertaken at Toulon.

However, there were concerns in the UK and US over whether the sale might contravene Article XVIII of the Washington Treaty, which had already prevented a number of potential sales by the UK – although as *Desaix* was to become an immobile hulk, it was not clear that she would still be a 'vessel of war' (a term not actually defined in the Treaty). Matters dragged on until the end of the year, when the availability of *D'Entrecasteaux* produced a way out of the difficulty, as not only a vessel already adapted as a stationary training vessel, but had already been accepted as being no longer a 'vessel of war' when transferred to Belgium.

Poland accordingly requested *D'Entrecasteaux* in lieu of *Desaix*, the ship being commissioned into the Polish Navy as *Król Władysław IV* on 30 July 1927, and then towed via the Kiel Canal to Gdynia, arriving on 11 August; in September she was renamed *Baltyk*, undergoing refit at Danzig and at Gdynia until June 1928. Further work begun later in the year removed the funnel caps and made various internal changes.

Suggestions that the ship be used as a floating anti-aircraft battery were not carried through, and she continued in her training role until September 1939. *Baltyk* was slightly damaged by a bomb hit aft on 1 September, abandoned on the 11th and captured by the Germans on the 19th. She was then used as an accommodation hulk, and scrapped sometime during 1940–2.

Other vessels remained active with the French navy for some time. *Jeanne d'Arc* resumed her pre-war cadet training role, making nine voyages between December 1919 and 1928; she was little altered, except for the removal of her casemated 5.5in guns and the plating-over of their embrasures. The original intent had been that *Jeanne d'Arc* should be directly replaced by a homonymous new ship, but the order for the

Jeanne d'Arc remained seagoing in her pre-war role as a cadet training ship for a few years, but ultimately found her stripped at Landévennec awaiting a tow to the scrapyard. (*Author's collection*)

Other vessels were consigned to the 'graveyard' of Landévennec, near Brest. Here may be seen *Guichen* and *Dupleix*, together with the battleships *Justice* and *Flandre*; the latter had been launched in 1914, but never completed owing to the war. (*Author's collection*)

latter was delayed and *Edgar Quinet* converted as a stop-gap to serve for three years, the old ship going into reserve under the name *Jeanne d'Arc II*, being stricken in 1933 and sold for scrap the following year.

For the new role, *Edgar Quinet* was extensively refitted, with her first and sixth funnels removed, the boiler spaces being been taken over for training purposes; she had also had the four casemated 7.6in guns removed and various modifications to the superstructure. However, having successfully carried out her first cruise, which took the ship as far as California during 1928–9, *Edgar Quinet*'s career came to a sudden halt at the very beginning of 1930, when she was wrecked off the Algerian coast.[175] The three heavy cruisers of the 1st Light Division, *Duquesne*, *Tourville* and *Suffren* (1925–7), took on the cadet

Edgar Quinet was rebuilt as an interim replacement for *Jeanne d'Arc*, with a new bridge and two less funnels, re-entering service in 1928. (*Author's collection*)

Unfortunately *Edgar Quinet*'s new career lasted little over a year. Having left Brest in October 1929, on 4 January 1930, while steaming at 12kt and acting as a torpedo target for the destroyer *Enseigne Roux* (1915) she struck an uncharted rock in some 90ft of water just under a mile off Cape Blanc, Algeria. Lodged on the rock, with a 50ft gash in the starboard side of the hull and the forward boiler rooms flooded, stopping violently, *Quinet*'s crew were taken off, save a hundred to undertake salvage operations. Although some lighter guns were taken off, bad weather led to the ship breaking in half aft of the second funnel the following evening, the rear half sinking immediately, although the forepart remained afloat for four days. (*L'Illustration, 18 June 1930*)

training role for the 1930 cruise, before the new *Jeanne d'Arc* commissioned in October 1931.

Of the remaining French vessels, *Montcalm* was in the Far East from January 1921 to August 1922, relieved by the light cruiser *Colmar* (ex-German *Kolberg*). *Victor Hugo* and *Jules Michelet* also deployed to the Far East down to the summer of 1923, *Hugo* going into reserve on her return (to be stricken in 1928). However, *Michelet* returned from July 1925 to May 1929 to replace *Colmar*, being herself was relieved in turn by *Waldeck-Rousseau* in June 1929.*Michelet* then became an artificers' training ship, in place of the battleship *Saint-Louis*, before being stricken in 1936. Henceforth used as a target ship for aircraft and submarines, she was finally sunk by the submarine *Thétis* a year later.

Marseillaise, *Gloire* and *Condé* all served in the Atlantic Squadron from 1920 to 1922, after which they paid off. *Gloire* was disposed of shortly afterwards, but *Condé* was kept as a stationary training ship for marines at Lorient throughout the 1930s; *Marseillaise* was attached to the gunnery school at Toulon until stricken in 1929. Her sale for breaking-up was delayed (along with that of *Saint Louis*) until 1933 owing to poor scrap prices.

Ernest Renan was also part of the gunnery school during 1927–8; she became a target in 1931, until stricken in 1936 and

Surviving armoured cruisers continued their historic service on distant stations, *Jules Michelet* and *Pittsburgh* (ex-*Pennsylvania*) being seen here at Shanghai in 1927; on the far right is the Italian light cruiser *Libia* (1914). (*NHHC NH 60439*)

By the beginning of the 1930s, most French armoured cruisers had passed from seagoing service. *Condé* became a harbour training ship at Lorient, and is seen here with large destroyers of the *Vauban* or *Aigle* classes (1930–4) during the early 1930s. (*Author's collection*)

Gueydon was rebuilt during 1925–6 as a gunnery training and trials vessel, replacing the old *Pothuau*. She is seen here as first converted, with new guns and greatly enlarged bridge. *(Author's collection)*

broken up the following year. *Montcalm*, stricken in 1926, was a training hulk at Brest from 1931, renamed *Tremintin* in 1934 to free her name for a new ship; she then joined *Armorique* (the former troopship *Mytho*, 1879) as part of the seamen's training establishment at Brest. *Pothuau* resumed her pre-war seagoing gunnery training and trials role, with a modified armament, her main guns being replaced by prototype anti-aircraft mountings, until relieved by *Gueydon* in June 1926; the older ship was stricken the following year and sold for scrap in 1929.

In her new role, *Gueydon* was entirely rearmed with modern 5.5in/40, of the type M1923 type carried by the new *Guépard*-class large destroyers (1928–30) on the forecastle and in the main deck casemates, while 75mm AA guns were installed abreast the aft funnel, on the former aft 6.5in barbette and on the upper deck aft of that. Lighter guns were also installed for trials and training purposes. The bridgework was modified and extended, with a number of rangefinders fitted to the upper bridge for training purposes, and struts added to the foremast to steady the director in the foretop. *Gueydon* received the first operational remote power control (RPC) system in the French navy in 1928, and was also later fitted with a modern main-battery director in an enlarged lower top (the old foretop being stripped and its additional supports removed), and a pair of searchlights added abreast the midships ventilator-tower. The ship remained in her role until 1933, when relieved by the cruiser-minelayer *Pluton*, equipment transferred to the new ship including the main-battery director, the four 75mm AA guns, and two 13.2mm weapons.

The central and eastern Mediterranean

In Italy, *Varese* was the Naval Academy training ship from 1920 to 1922, when she was relieved by her sister *Francesco Ferruccio*, which was so-employed from 1923 until 1929, joined by *Pisa* in 1925. The pair were replaced by the new purpose-built *Cristoforo Colombo* and *Amerigo Vespucci* and (completed in 1928 and 1931, respectively), *Ferruccio* being stricken in 1930, but survived to be used for bombing trials in 1937, along with the old destroyer *Fuciliere* (1909).

The three surviving big Italian cruisers, including *Pisa*, had been refitted soon after the war, most noticeably having heavier foremasts installed, to carry fire-control equipment; they were reclassified as '2nd class ships of battle' in 1921. In *Pisa*, her 3in guns were removed from the superstructure and remounted on the turret tops, the ship being used for various training roles from 1921, when she was further reclassified as

Having spent a number of years as a cadet training ship, *Francesco Ferruccio* was withdrawn in 1929 and stricken. However, her hulk was retained, and used in bombing trials during 1937. *(LoC LOT 5213)*

Pisa was also used in a cadet training role, her appearance considerably altered by the addition of a heavy foremast towards the end of the war. (*Author's collection*)

Pisa's Greek half-sister *Averof* was rebuilt in France in mid-1920s, receiving a new foremast and fire-control equipment; she is seen here at Malta during the 1930s. (*Author's collection*)

a coast-defence ship. She became a second Naval Academy training ship in 1925, with the 3in guns removed from atop the 7.5in turrets. Like a number of other Italian cruisers, she carried the navy's then-standard Macchi M.7 flying boat, handled by booms stepped from the second funnel. *Pisa* carried out annual training cruises between 1925 and 1930, mainly within the Mediterranean, but in some cases extending to the UK or even the Baltic (1929). After returning from her last cruise on 14 October 1930, she was placed on harbour service at La Spezia, until stricken in 1937.

San Giorgio had finished the First World War as flagship of the Eastern Squadron, and was relieved in this role by the ex-Austro-Hungarian scout cruiser *Brindisi* (ex-*Helgoland*) on 16 July 1921 at Istanbul. After that, she served in the Far East and China, during July–September 1924 carrying Crown Prince Umberto to Argentina, Chile, Uruguay and Brazil, accompanied by her sister, *San Marco*. During 1925–6, *San Giorgio* served with Red Sea and Indian Ocean Naval Division,

The *San Giorgio*s had also received foremasts, and served extensively until after the war. This is the name ship. (*Author's collection*)

San Marco continued to be distinguishable from her sister by her funnels and searchlight arrangements. (*Author's collection*)

supporting operations in Italian Somaliland, while *San Marco* became a Pola-based training ship until the end of the decade, as did *San Giorgio* from September 1928.

Averof had been the Greek flagship at Constantinople at the end of the First World War, and took part in the Graeco-Turkish war of 1919–22, carrying Greek refugees from Turkey at the end of the conflict. She underwent a major refit at La Seyne in France during 1925–7, receiving a new foremast and fire–control system. She also had most of her tertiary battery removed, along with her torpedo tubes, and new anti-aircraft guns installed. Her boilers were refurbished, but remained coal-fired.

The United States

Most of remaining American big cruisers saw further seagoing service during the period directly after the war. *Columbia* was flagship of Squadron 2, Destroyer Force, Atlantic Fleet, during the first half of 1919, and remained operational until June 1921, with *Minneapolis* serving as Pacific Squadron flagship from February 1919 to March 1921. Both then paid off and were scrapped soon afterwards.

Rochester became flagship of Atlantic destroyers in May 1919, while *Brooklyn* operated as Pacific destroyer flagship from her return from the Far East until January 1921. She was then sold for scrap at the end of the year. *Brooklyn* was then relieved by *Charleston*, which served until June 1923.

A 1919 plan envisaged keeping four of the *Pennsylvania*s and *Tennessee*s in full commission, with the other four in reduced commission (65 per cent crew). Suggestions were also made at this time that the *Pennsylvania*s be modernised, by converting them to oil firing, replacing their armoured turrets with lighter mountings, fitting new secondary (6in or 5in) guns at upper-deck level, installing two 12in mortars for anti-submarine or shore bombardment purposes, removing the battery armour and re-rigging with tripod or pole masts. After the Washington Treaty banned new-build cruisers over 10,000 tons, serious consideration was given to modernising both classes. A 1922–3 study envisaged that new oil-fired boilers and the bow modified along the lines of the *Lexington*-class battlecruisers might push speed up to 25kt – perhaps as high as 27kt – with triple 8in turrets as envisaged for the new 'Washington' cruisers also considered for installation. Although nothing was done then, the issue re-emerged in 1928, investigations including machinery of the type being built for the carrier *Ranger*, increased main-battery elevation, a new fire-control system (with a tripod foremast), six secondary guns moved to upper-deck level, and a catapult on the quarterdeck. However, studies showed the ships, even in modernised form, to compare unfavourably with the new cruiser *Pensacola*, while modernising the old ships would undermine the case for continuing the planned series of new 8in cruisers. Accordingly, nothing again was done and the ships remained in most cases largely unaltered.

As noted above, main-deck batteries had been removed while the ships had been operating on Atlantic escort duty but, by December 1919, the Bureau of Ordnance was pressing hard for the 6in guns' restoration, given the large loss of nominal capability caused by their removal. However, this was not carried through: although all the surviving *Pennsylvania*s and *Tennessee*s continued to be listed with their full designed batteries, only four guns were noted as actually aboard (except in *Pittsburgh*, which still kept ten in place), with the remainder listed as held in reserve.

Pittsburgh went to the Mediterranean as flagship of the CinC US Naval Forces Adriatic & US High Commissioner to Turkey in June 1919, and then became flagship of US Naval Forces Europe in April 1920, which also included *St Louis*. *Pittsburgh* returned to the USA to decommission in October 1921; *St Louis* followed a month later, to decommission for the last time in March 1922. *Huntington* became flagship of

the 1st Squadron, Cruiser Force, at the end of her repatriation service in 1919, but decommissioned for the last time on 1 September 1920. *Frederick* was used as a seagoing naval reserve and Naval Academy training ship during the second half of 1920, before going to the West Coast as flagship of the fleet train, until decommissioned in February 1922. *Seattle* spent a few months from the end of 1919 to early 1920 as flagship of the Pacific Fleet Cruiser Force, before going into reduced commission.

Both *Montana* and *North Carolina* went straight into reduced commission on the West Coast after completing repatriation duty, being decommissioned for the final time in February and September 1921 respectively. As such, they never saw sea service under the new names, *Missoula* and *Charlotte*, bestowed in June 1920. *Pueblo* likewise went into reduced commission from repatriation duty, and was decommissioned in September 1919. However, she was recommissioned for stationary duty as receiving ship at Brooklyn Navy Yard in April 1921, remaining as such until decommissioned for the final time in September 1927.

South Dakota was withdrawn early from repatriation duty, and sent east as the Asiatic Squadron flagship in September 1919, replacing *Brooklyn*. Renamed *Huron* in June 1920, she operated in Philippine waters during the winter months and out of Shanghai and Chefoo (Yantai) during the summer until the end of 1926 when, her boilers deteriorating, she was relieved by *Pittsburgh*. *Huron* arrived at Puget Sound in March 1927, paying off into reserve three months later. During her last years on station, she had been without searchlights on the front of her foremast. *Pittsburgh* had recommissioned in October 1922 to resume the flag of US Naval Forces Europe, which she flew until relieved by the new light cruiser *Memphis* (ii – 1924) in the summer of 1926.

Seattle returned to full commission in March 1923 as US Fleet flagship, with a new bridge, long-base rangefinders on her turrets (as being fitted in battleships), a rangefinder on a foremast platform (as previously fitted in *Montana*) and various detail alterations to fit her for her new role. She then served primarily in the Pacific, until relieved by the newly-reconstructed battleship *Texas* (1912) in June 1927. For much of that time her maximum speed was restricted to 15kt, owing

Frederick and the battleship *Rhode Island* (1904), laid up at Mare Island in 1922; the battleship would soon be sold, but the cruiser survived until the end of the decade. (*Author's collection*)

Huron (ex-*South Dakota*) in the Yangtze during 1922–4; the ship to the left is the French ex-German cruiser *Colmar*. (*NHHC NH 68989*)

Seattle at Melbourne in 1925, with CinC US Fleet embarked and a collier alongside. (*Author's collection*)

Pittsburgh around 1931, at the end of her career in, Far East. By then she had lost her forward boilers and funnels, together with some of her main-deck 6in guns. (*NHHC NH 94170*)

to the poor state of her boilers. *Seattle* then relieved *Pueblo* as a receiving ship, remaining as such for nearly twenty years.

After her return to the USA in July 1926, and before proceeding east to relieve *Huron*, *Pittsburgh* had been extensively refitted, including receiving an enclosed bridge, a new fire-control system, having her unoccupied gun-deck ports plated in to provide additional accommodation, and the

having her eight 'composite' boilers, now useless, removed along with the forward funnel. She then served as Asiatic Fleet flagship until February 1931, when she was relieved by the new heavy cruiser *Augusta* (1930) and returned to the USA via the Mediterranean. Decommissioned in July, she was used for weapons-effect bombing trials in Chesapeake Bay in October, before being broken up.[176]

However, she was not the last American big cruiser to be in full commission. That honour fell to oldest of them all, *Rochester*, which continued to serve on the East Coast and in the Caribbean into the 1930s. Refitted in 1927, when her forward boilers and funnel were removed, she was redeployed to Asiatic waters in June 1932, where she decommissioned at Cavite on 29 April 1933.

Spain

Princesa de Asturias, *Cataluña* and *Carlos V* were all still in service at the beginning of the 1920s. *Carlos V* had been employed as a training ship since 1916, and in 1923 became a stationary school for seamen, torpedomen and electricians at Ferrol. Stricken in December 1931, she remained at Ferrol as a hulk until broken up at Bilbao in 1933.

Princesa de Asturias was active during the Rif revolt in Morocco during 1921–4, and while bombarding M'Ter in April 1924 was hit by a rebel shell, the dead including two officers. She was paid off in December 1927, *Cataluña*, having spent her last years as a midshipmen's training ship, following her in November 1928. Stricken in 1930, they were both subsequently sold at Bilbao and broken up from 1932–3.

The old *New York*, by now further renamed as *Rochester*, was still operational when pictured here on 14 April 1923, and would continue in active service for another decade, by which time she was the last, as well as the first, American armoured cruiser. (*NHHC 80-G-464248*)

Rochester following her final refit, during which her forward boilers and funnel were removed. *(NHHC NH 58663)*

South America

In Argentina, all four ships were assigned to the Instruction and Training Division in 1923 and reclassified as coast-defence ships in 1932. *Garibaldi* had continued in the training role that she had fulfilled since 1908, joining the Artillery School in 1917, and was host ship for the visit of the Italian *San Giorgio* and *San Marco*, carrying Crown Prince Umberto and an Italian Naval Division in 1924. Formally reclassified as a training ship on 31 August 1930, she spent 1932 and 1933 laid up and stricken in March 1934. Sold for scrap in November 1935, and subsequently re-sold, she was sailed to Rio Santiago by a Swedish crew and broken up during 1936–7.

Pueyrredón had been used as a cadet training ship during 1918–19, while the regular schoolship *Presidente Sarmiento* (1897) was under refit. *San Martin* having also acted as a cadet training ship in 1920, she transported an army squadron to Peru in May 1921, to celebrate the country's centenary; that November she represented Argentina at celebrations in Brazil.

During 1922–3 *Pueyrredón* had her boilers converted to oil firing, *San Martin* being similarly modified at Puerto Belgrano in 1926. *General Belgrano* was under refit at Puerto Belgrano from 21 October 1926 to July 1927, and the following month she carried crews for the new destroyers

Cervantes and *Juan de Garay* (1925) to Spain, and then in October went to Brazil for the unveiling of a statue of her namesake army officer. *Belgrano* then proceeded to Genoa for a similar ceremony in October 1927, and after a visit to Spain, returned to Genoa in November for an extensive refit by Orlando, involving the replacement of her boilers, the fitting of a tripod mast, control top and director, and rangefinders atop the 10in shields. The main-deck battery was also removed (along with its armour), with eight 4.7in being fitted on the upper deck, and on the shelter deck abreast the bridge. On 25 October 1929 she departed for home, arriving at Buenos Aires on 24 November. *Pueyrredón* was similarly modified at Puerto Belgrano from 1924 to 1926, the main difference being that her upper/shelter-deck battery was of 6in calibre; she completed in 1934.

San Martin was disarmed in preparation for a similar refit in May 1926, but this was cancelled and the ship hulked at Rio Santiago in 1927; stricken in 1935, she was finally scrapped in 1947. In spite of her recent reconstruction, *Belgrano* became a submarine depot ship at Mar del Plata in 1933, not going to sea after 1934. She served in her new role until 1947, being stricken in May. However, her hulk was not towed away from Rio Santiago for scrap until 1953, running aground outside

Garibaldi in the 1920s, with the protected cruiser *Buenos Aires* moored ahead of her. *(Author's collection)*

General Belgrano on 6 October 1927 at Genoa. *(Author's collection)*

General Belgrano on 15 May 1929, with her reconstruction at Leghorn nearly complete. (Author's collection)

O'Higgins around 1930, showing her enlarged fore and aft bridgework and modified rig. (Author's collection)

Buenos Aires on 31 March, before being refloated three days later and placed in her final berth. On the other hand, Pueyrredón would remain at sea for another two decades.

Of the two Chilean armoured cruisers, Esmeralda was stricken in 1929, and sold for scrap the following year. In 1919 O'Higgins was fitted to carry a floatplane, handled by a crane; on 24 August 1920 an aircraft crashed into the cruiser, killing the pilot. Now serving mainly as a training ship, O'Higgins was refitted twice: in 1919–20, when fire-control equipment was fitted in both lower tops and the searchlights removed from the upper tops; and in 1928–9, when the upper tops were removed altogether and two searchlights fitted in the aft lower top, the fore bridge enlarged, and the aft bridge removed. She was seized by her crew on 1 September 1931 during the major mutiny that swept the fleet, and was reduced to an accommodation ship two years later.

Japan

Three vessels completed as armoured cruisers fell victim to the Washington Treaty. While no numerical limitation was placed on cruisers by this agreement, it *was* on capital ships, and thus embraced the 12in-gunned ships that had been reclassified

from armoured cruisers to battlecruisers in 1912; accordingly Ikoma, Ibuki and Kurama were all stricken in September 1923 and broken up.[177] The turrets of Ibuki and Ikoma were refitted for shore use, although the aft mounting of the latter was retained as a reserve asset, rather than emplaced on the Japanese coast with the others.

However, the older vessels (reclassified as coast-defence ships in 1921) were not affected, and most would remain in for service for a considerable time. Initially, all the 6–6 Plan armoured cruisers were employed as cadet training vessels, but in contrast to the British- and German-built vessels, which continued in ocean-going service for another two decades, Azuma was reduced to harbour training duties at Maizuru in 1921, and formally hulked in 1941. The two Japanese Garibaldis were never employed in the cadet training role, both serving in home waters until 1927, when Kasuga became a navigation and engineering training ship, with an enlarged bridge for instructional purposes and her main-deck guns taken out; Nisshin became a stationary depot and training ship at Yokosuka. The two ships' 8in guns (removed in 1942 and the 1930s, respectively) were amongst many of the same vintage redeployed for coast-defence purposes in the south Pacific during the Second World War, including at Truk Lagoon.[178]

Tokiwa made her last training cruise in May 1920, and then refitted as a minelayer, replacing Tsuguru and joining Aso in the role, although it was envisaged that the latter would not be retained long-term. Work was completed in 1924, Tokiwa losing her aft 8in turret and main deck 6in, to carry 500 mines. While undertaking training in this role, at 09.39 on 1 August 1927, in Saeki Bay, Kyushu, a mine exploded while being disarmed, triggering the explosion of a number of others and causing substantial damage to the ship's stern; thirty-five men were killed and sixty-five wounded. Repairs were undertaken in September.

The remaining four 6–6 ships continued their cadet training voyages through the 1920s, Asama and Iwate making six each, and Yakumo and Izumo five each, variously within the Pacific region, to American waters, the Mediterranean and Europe.[179] All, except Asama, which had already received new boilers in 1917, were reboilered during the 1920s–1930s, installed power being halved, but perfectly adequate for their training roles. Main-deck secondary guns were progressively reduced in number, with the shielded upper-deck weapons also taken out during the 1930s, leaving just the four upper-deck

Yakumo at Cristobal in the Canal Zone on 6 August 1936, while serving as a cadet training ship. (NHHC NH 111701)

Azuma serving as a cadet training ship during 1919–20; her funnels had been changed before 1914. *(Author's collection)*

Tokiwa, now a minelayer, at Shanghai in 1932. *(NHHC NH 51896)*

casemates. By the 1920s, *Izumo* could be distinguished from *Iwate* by the former having enclosed platforms added to both masts in the locations formerly occupied by the fighting tops removed during the Russo-Japanese War.

The London Treaty and Beyond

The London Naval Treaty of 1930 marked end of the remaining American big cruisers, as it placed on the UK, USA and Japan total tonnage limits on the number of cruisers to be in service on 31 December 1936. Every ton of ship represented by the *Pennsylvania*s and *Tennessee*s (and other reserve vessels) was thus now needed for modern vessels, although they had already begun to be stricken even before the Treaty had been signed. On the other hand, Japan was explicitly permitted under Article 12 of the Treaty to retain *Asama*, *Yakumo*, *Izumo*, *Iwate* and *Kasuga* until replaced by three *Kuma*-class light cruisers (1919–20) that were to be converted to training ships when themselves replaced by new tonnage. The ex-cruisers *Aso* and *Tokiwa* could also be kept as minelayers until replaced by new ships: *Okinoshima* and *Tsuguru* (ii) had originally been planned for the 1927 Supplementary Programme, but delayed. In the event, *Aso* was stricken on 1 April 1931 and sunk as a target in August 1932, but *Okinoshima* was not completed until October 1936. *Tsuguru* (ii) was not laid down until 1939, completing in 1941. *Tokiwa* continued in service into the Second World War.

Vessels hulked prior to 1 April 1930 could also be retained in a non-seagoing condition by all signatories. The futures of *Seattle*, *Nisshin*, ex-*Andromeda*, ex-*Terrible* and ex-*Spartiate*

were thus unaffected – although the last two would soon be scrapped with the closure of the *Fisgard* establishment in 1932.

With the squeeze on tonnage, the remaining US big cruisers were sold for scrap during 1930–1, except for the apparently-immortal *Rochester* which, as already noted, was simply laid up, and not actually stricken until 1938. Towed to Subic Bay, she was moored off the Olongapo, where she served as an auxiliary power plant and machine shop for the Naval Station. Two of the other vessels would, however, have an afterlife when, cut down to the waterline, the hulks of

Rochester paid off for the last time in 1933, and was hulked in Philippine waters in 1938. She is seen here at Olongapo on 27 October 1941, two months before she was scuttled in the adjacent Subic Bay in the face of the Japanese invasion. *(NHHC 80-G-178319)*

Charleston (foreground) and *Huron* being broken up at Seattle by the Lake Union Dry Dock and Machine Works; their lower hulls were resold and became floating breakwaters in the Powell River, British Columbia. Arriving there in October 1930 and August 1931 respectively, they remained in use until, in February 1961, *Huron* sank in 78ft of water in a storm. *Charleston* was assessed as vulnerable to a similar fate, and was thus redeployed to Kelsey Bay on Vancouver Island as a grounded breakwater, where she remains today. *(Powell River Museum PH004414)*

Charleston and *Huron* became as floating breakwaters during 1930–1, acting as such for three decades.[180]

France and Italy were not, however, bound by any cruiser limits, although Anglo-French-Italian negotiations did attempt to come to an agreement on the matter during 1930–1. The surviving armoured cruisers were factored into the Bases of Agreement that it was hoped would result in a Franco-Italian treaty, with two Italian ships scrapped for each of two new battleships to be allowed under the agreement.[181] While both nations' vessels were to be usable as sacrificial tonnage to allow other overage cruisers and destroyers to be retained, the proposals failed to address whether the French armoured cruisers could be directly replaced by new vessels. The negotiations ultimately collapsed, however, leaving the old ships without any legal constraints on their future.

However, their front-line deployment ended in May 1932, when *Waldeck Rousseau* returned to France from the Far East and was laid up at Landévennec; she was stricken in June 1936, but not immediately sold. The former gunnery training ship *Gueydon* was stricken in 1935, when she became a training hulk at Brest, joining *Tremintin* and *Armorique* in a constellation of training vessels for seamen and petty officers. *Ernest Renan* lingered as a target until sold for scrap in 1937.

On the other hand, in Italy, *San Giorgio* was retained in a seagoing training role throughout the 1930s, while *San Marco* was refitted during 1931–5 for service as a radio-controlled target, akin to the converted battleships operated by the British, US and Japanese navies. The conversion involved disarmament and the dismantling of much of her superstructure, plus the provision of new boilers, giving her a maximum speed of 18kt; her control vessel was the torpedo boat (ex-destroyer) *Audace* (1916). *San Giorgio* was sent to Spanish waters protect Italian interests at the beginning of the Spanish Civil War in 1936, but the following year she was taken in hand for reconstruction at La Spezia, with six boilers and two funnels removed, the remaining boilers converted to oil firing, her torpedo tubes removed and a new anti-aircraft suite fitted, comprising four twin 100mm mountings and a mix of 37mm and 20mm weapons. As such, she was to be employed as a cadet training ship.

The Swedish *Fylgia* also continued in her cadet training role until laid up following the return from a European voyage – her 31st training cruise – in July 1933, owing to her poor materiel condition, and pending reconstruction. This was finally carried out during 1939–40, with new boilers, funnels reduced to two, the bow rebuilt, a new bridge, the main guns' range increased, fire-control equipment installed, and new anti-aircraft guns and torpedo tubes fitted.

In Greece, *Averof* was now the navy's sole big ship, the battleships *Kilkis* and *Lemnos* having been paid off in 1932. On 1 March 1935, *Averof* found herself on the side of the military faction attempting a coup against the current Second Hellenic Republic, resulting in the government's hurried recommissioning *Kilkis* to oppose her. However, the coup collapsed after less than a week; in 1937, *Averof* represented Greece at King George VI's coronation review at Spithead.

The last operational French armoured cruiser, *Waldeck-Rousseau*, paid off in 1932; she is shown here disarmed and laid up at Landévennec after 1936. In the background are sloops of the *Marne* (left) and *Amiens* classes. (*Author's collection*)

Having completed her service as a gunnery training ship, *Gueydon* was hulked and in 1935 joined the 'Armorique Group' of training hulks in the Rade-Abri at Brest, serving as training ships. The others were *Armorique* herself, the former troop/hospital ship *Mytho* (1879), which had become a training hulk in 1910, renamed *Bretagne*, and then *Armorique* in 1912, and *Gueydon*'s sister, *Tremintin* (ex-*Montcalm* – with her aft pair of funnels removed). (*Author's collection*).

Ernest Renan about to be towed away from Toulon to the breakers' yard in 1937. (*Wilfried Langry collection*)

San Marco converted to a radio-controlled target ship.
(Author's collection)

The rebuilt San Giorgio about to leave for Tobruk in 1940.
(Author's collection)

Fylgia in 1941–2, following her reconstruction. (Author's collection)

Rochester and Izumo at Shanghai during 1932–3. (NHHC NH 76480)

After 1935, only Pueyrredón remained seagoing in Argentina. In 1941, she was once again used for cadet training voyages, the purpose-built new training cruiser La Argentina (1937, replacement for Presidente Sarmiento) having been assigned to active service in view of the Second World War. In Chile, General O'Higgins continued in her role as an accommodation ship, serving as such for a total of twenty-four years, being finally disposed of for scrap in 1958.

Having secured the survival of her ships, Japan continued the employment of Asama, Iwate and Yakumo in the cadet training role, Iwate being reboiled in 1931. Her light armament was also modified and an enclosed platform added on the foremast, but not the mainmast. Asama continued in

service until soon after her return from the 1935 cruise when, on 13/14 October 1935, she ran onto rocks near Hiroshima Shiraishi lighthouse, while returning to Kure after an air-defence exercise. She was eventually refloated with the aid of a floating crane, but was not felt worthy of full repairs. Stricken in 1937, she was, however, soon restored to the list as a training hulk for midshipmen. Iwate and Yakumo then maintained the programme of cadet training voyages until December 1939, when the Training Squadron was deactivated, pending its re-establishment with new purpose-built training cruisers Katori and Kashima (1939).[182]

On the other hand, Izumo returned to first-line service in 1932 as flagship of the China Area Fleet, based at Shanghai for a decade, with the exception of April–July 1934, when she was reboiled and had her anti-aircraft armament enhanced at Sasebo. While serving in China, she was the target for a number of air raids by the Chinese Air Force during August 1937, and for a torpedo attack by the Chinese torpedo boat 102 (which was sunk) two days later. Tokiwa was also active in Chinese waters during 1932–3, following the so-called 'Shanghai Incident' that provided the excuse for Japan's formal intervention in China, before returning to reserve. In 1937 she was reboiled with eight Kampon units, giving her 8000ihp, for 16kt, plus some light AA guns.

Nisshin, now a hulk, was stricken 1 April 1935. Renamed Hai-Kan No. 6, she was sunk as a target at the Kamegakubi Naval Proving Ground off Kure in 1936. Subsequently refloated, on 18 January 1942 the hulk was towed out by the battleship Mutsu (1920) to be sunk once again, off Kurahashi, Hiroshima, as a target for the 18.1in guns of the new battleship Yamato (1940) Her capsized hulk was later broken up.

The Second World War

In 1939, apart from Pueyrredón, six ships remained seagoing. Three were also Italian-built, the Greek Averof and the Italian San Giorgio and San Marco, plus the Japanese Izumo, Iwate and Yakumo. Various other vessels still remained afloat as hulks.

Of the latter, *Seattle* still lay at New York, as receiving ship for the 3rd Naval District, managing personnel for a wide range of purposes. Over in the Philippines, *Rochester* was still extant, but on 14 December 1941, with Japanese forces approaching, she was towed out into Subic Bay and scuttled, settling on her starboard side in 100ft of water. The wreck was damaged, especially on the starboard side of the bow, by the USN Harbor Clearance Unit-1 during 10–22 July 1967, but much of the ship still remains intact.

In French waters, as well as the vessels being formally employed in stationary roles, *Waldeck-Rousseau* was still laid up at Landévennec in September 1939. During May–June 1940 she was towed around from Landévennec and anchored around half a mile south-west of the southern breakwater of the Rade Abri at Brest. She had been for some time taking on water and, after the German occupation of the port at the end of June prevented access to the ship to run pumps, she foundered there on 8 August.[183] The wreck was dismantled between 1941 and 1944, although some remains are still in situ.

Of the vessels on harbour service, at Lorient, *Condé*'s hulk was first used by the Germans as a accommodation ship for submarine crews, but in 1942 was towed to Verdon and sunk in shallow water near Royan an aircraft bombing target; the remains were broken up from 1951. At Brest, *Tremintin*, abandoned and unmaintained, foundered at her berth some time before February 1942.[184]

Gueydon was partly dismantled and, with the hulls of the old avisos *Oise* and *Aisne* (1917) moored either side of her stern to increase length, used as the basis for a dummy of the

Waldeck-Rousseau moored off Brest on 18 June 1940, with the battleship *Richelieu* sailing for Dakar in the background. Recently towed back from Landévennec, the old cruiser foundered in this location in August. (*Author's collection*)

Condé being expended as a German bombing target in 1942. (*Author's collection*)

With the French surrender, the *Armorique* Group at Brest landed its trainees, and the ships anchored close to breakwater in the south-west corner of the Rade-Abri; here, they lie there derelict in 1941, with the first works for the German submarine bunker visible at the top of the image. *Tremintin* foundered *in situ* later that year; *Armorique*, sold to the Germans, was towed away in February 1942 to Landévennec to become a floating workshop; she was scuttled there in 1944. (*Wilfried Langry collection*)

Gueydon was removed from the group and in late 1941, transformed, together with the old avisos *Oise* and *Aisne*, into a decoy for the German cruiser *Prinz Eugen*. (*Author's collection*)

German heavy cruiser *Prinz Eugen*, 'construction' being ordered in August 1941, and completed on 8 December. The 'dummy' was recognised as unlikely to fool aerial reconnaissance, but possibly viable as a decoy during an air-raid. No attempt was made link the dummy's placement with that of the real German cruiser, and it was dismantled after a short period. *Gueydon* was bombed and sunk in August 1944 in a daylight raid by the RAF, prompted by intelligence received from the French Resistance that her hulk was being prepared for use as a blockship, along with that of the unfinished battleship *Clemenceau*, which lay close to the capsized wreck of *Tremintin*. The latter was later cut into five sections, the last being removed in 1952.

Action in the Mediterranean

In contrast to these ships whose seagoing lives had been long over by 1939, a number were not only still operational in the Mediterranean, but would play important roles in the conflict. In particular, *San Giorgio* was sent to Tobruk in Italian North Africa in early May 1940 to reinforce its defences as a floating battery, with an additional twin 3.9in mounting added on the forecastle, together with further light guns. Following Italy's declaration of war, Tobruk was attacked by British naval and air forces on 12 June, *San Giorgio* receiving a single bomb hit that caused a fire. On 19 June, HMS/M *Parthian* (1929) fired two torpedoes, but both detonated prematurely. Further light guns were added following these attacks. *San Giorgio* fired on attacking Australian troops on 21 January 1941, and was scuttled the following morning as Anglo-Australian forces entered Tobruk. From March 1944 to 1945, the hulk was commissioned by the British Royal Navy as a repair platform. The forward two-thirds of the wreck of *San Giorgio* was partly raised for scrap in 1952 (with the twin 3.9in mounting on the forecastle left in place, presumably for symbolic reasons), but sank in tow to Italy. *San Marco* spent the war at La Spezia, where she was captured by the Germans on 9 September 1943. She was found sunk there in shallow water in 1945 and later broken up.

Italy attacked Greece on 28 October 1940, *Averof* being a target of an air raid on Salamis on 1 November; she was undamaged, although the disarmed battleship *Lemnos* was hit once. Following Germany's intervention and the Greek collapse in April 1941, an order to scuttle was ignored, and

San Giorgio was scuttled at Tobruk in January 1941 as British troops occupied the port, where she had served as a floating anti-aircraft battery since the previous summer. (*Author's collection*)

The hulk of *San Marco* at the end of the Second World War; captured by the Germans in 1943, she had been scuttled at La Spezia in 1945. (*Author's collection*)

Averof in standard British-pattern camouflage in 1942, with a 3in AA gun added on the forward 9.2in turret. (*Author's collection*)

Averof sailed, via Crete, towards Egypt, as part of a force of three destroyers and five submarines, arriving at Alexandria on 23 April 1941. In August 1941 she sailed for the Indian Ocean, arriving at Bombay on 10 September; from then until the end of 1942 the ship carried out convoy escort and patrol duties from there. Low morale owing to relative inactivity led to a number of disciplinary incidents, the ship spending 1943–4 moored at Port Said. *Averof* returned to Greece on 17 October 1944, once again fleet flagship and she carrying the Greek government-in-exile back to Athens.

The Pacific War

In the Far East, *Izumo* sank the British gunboat *Peterel* (1927) on 8 December 1941 at Shanghai, but was damaged by a mine on the 31st, when at Lingayen, in the Philippines. After emergency repairs, she left under the tow of the salvage vessel *Yusho Maru* on 4 February 1942; she was then repaired at Hong Kong. While under repair she, along with *Iwate* and *Yakumo* were re-classified back to 1st class cruisers, but in 1943 *Izumo* was withdrawn from her role as China flagship, and was re-rated as a training ship, joining the other two ships on instructional duties in home waters, which would continue until the very end of the war.

Tokiwa, on the other hand, was in front-line service throughout the war, as part of *Sentai* 19, the Fourth Fleet's minelaying squadron. As such, she formed part of the Gilbert Islands Invasion Force along with *Okinoshima* and *Tsuguru* – all acting as troop transports – in December 1941. Supported by auxiliary minelayers, the trio took part in the invasion of Rabul in January 1942, but on 1 February 1942, aircraft from the carrier USS *Enterprise* damaged *Tokiwa* at Kwajalein, which had to return to Sasebo for repairs, following preliminary repairs at Truk. In August, *Tokiwa* carried troops to react to an American landing on Makin Island, Gilberts.

In 1943, *Tokiwa*'s remaining 8in mounting was removed (leaving just four 6in – the main-deck weapons had now been removed – and the 3in AA), and new light AA guns added; in May the ship was reassigned to the 52nd Base Force, Ominato Naval District. In January 1944 she moved to the 18th Escort Squadron, Seventh Fleet, as flagship, leading a force that laid 1650 mines off Okinawa on 19/20 June. Aided by the auxiliary minelayer *Koei Maru*, *Tokiwa* laid 1000 mines south of Yaku Shima on 27 February 1945, but herself struck a mine off

Asama at Matsure Shima in October 1945, where she had been moored as a stationary training/accommodation ship since 1942. She had not been to sea since being badly damaged by grounding (for the second time in her career) in 1935. *(NHHC NH 86279).*

Her sister *Tokiwa*, on the other hand, was still operational as a minelayer when mined in June 1945, and forced to beach in August. *(Author's collection)*

Izumo survived in service until sunk by bombs at Kure in July 1945. *(NHHC 80-G-351724)*

Iwate suffered the same fate, although remaining upright; both ships are both shown in October, with all guns removed from the wrecks. *(NHHC 80-G-351365)*

Hesaki, Kyushu on 14 April 1945. Although repaired, on 3 June she struck an air-laid mine off Bakuchizaki, and on 9 August was bombed by aircraft from US Task Force 38 at Ominato, receiving a direct hit amidships and four near-misses, necessitating her being run ashore to avoid sinking.

The other three seagoing cruisers had their 8in mountings replaced by twin 5in anti-aircraft guns and had a number of 25mm mountings added during March–April 1944 (*Izumo*) and 1945 (*Iwate* and *Yakumo*), reflecting the air threat now facing ships even in Japanese home waters. Having hitherto escaped American raids, *Izumo* and *Iwate* fell victim to bombing on 27 July 1945. *Kasuga*, hulked in 1942, had sunk ten days earlier, coming to rest in shallow water with a 60-degree list.[184]

However, although the hulk of *Azuma* had been badly damaged at Yokosuka, *Asama* (from 1944 an accommodation ship) and the still-seaworthy *Yakumo* survived the aerial onslaught, the latter's career continuing even after the Japanese surrender. She was assigned to the Allied Repatriation Service as a special cargo ship. She began her first voyage in this role on 7 December 1945, and between then and June 1946 she carried 9010 Japanese personnel from Taiwan and China back to Japan. *Yakumo* was finally delivered for breaking up in July 1946, a process that was declared complete on 1 April 1947. The remaining Japanese ships were, where necessary, refloated during 1945–6, and all also broken up.

Ironically, as these veterans of the classic age of the big cruisers were coming to the ends of their lives, the breed was undergoing its final revival, in the form of the American *Alaska* class. Although often dubbed 'battlecruisers', they were actually classified as 'large cruisers' (CB), and were enlargements of the post-Washington Treaty 10,000-ton/8in-gun cruiser type. First mooted as 'killers' of such vessels as the German *Deutschland*-class 'pocket battleships', the result was a 12in-armed 30,000-ton upsizing of the contemporary *Baltimore*-class 8in heavy cruisers, with six authorised in 1940, three laid down during 1941–3, and two (*Alaska* and *Guam*) completed in 1944. Their initiation prompted Japan to project similar vessels, the 31,500-ton B-65 type, two of which were ordered, but never laid down.

The idea of the big-gun cruiser (as against the transformed battlecruiser as it had emerged by 1914) had also been revived in the Soviet Union, where the 40,000-ton Project 69 large cruiser had emerged, initially armed, like the American and Japanese designs, with nine 12in, later swapped for six 15in. Two were laid down as the *Kronshdadt* class in 1939, but neither was to be completed.[186] However, Josef Stalin's love for the concept of the big cruiser led after the Second World War to the 35,500-ton, nine 12in-armed, Project 82, laid down as the three-ship *Stalingrad* class in 1951–2, but abandoned at the death of Stalin in March 1953.[187] A 26,330-ton, 8.7in armed vessel, the Project 66,[188] was also approved in December 1951, to be laid down from 1952 onwards, but also fell victim to the post-Stalin review of Soviet naval requirements – the last big gun-armed cruiser to be seriously considered in the world.

Alone of the Japanese '6–6' cruisers, *Yakumo* was still seaworthy at the end of the war. She is shown here at the top-right of the photograph at Kure around October 1945, moored with a range of surrendered vessels; they include the destroyers *Hanatsuki*, *Natsutsuki*, *Harutsuki*, *Yoisuki*, *Kiri* (all 1944) and *Yukaze* (1921), the submarines *I-47* (1943), *I-36* (1941), *I-402* (1944), *Ha-203*, *Ha-204* (1945), *I-203* (1944), *Ha-106*, *I-58* (1944) and *I-53* (1943), and the transport *T-22* (1945). *(NHHC 94884)*

The large cruiser *Guam* (CB-2, 1943) in the Delaware River around January 1945, in many ways a lineal descendant of the big cruisers of the late nineteenth century. *(NHHC NH 92283)*

The End

The arrival of peace spelled the end for *Seattle*, decommissioned for the last time on 28 June 1946. She was then towed to Philadelphia, where she was sold for scrap.

Other ships' careers continued, however. *Averof* served as headquarters ship for the Greek navy between 1947–9, but was not was decommissioned until 1952, when she was laid up at Salamis. *Fylgia* had spent the war both on neutrality duties and acting in her old cadet training role, albeit restricted to Swedish coastal waters. She made her last overseas cruise in 1948, and was stricken in January 1953. She was then stripped and used as a target at Kalixlinjen in northern Sweden. In spite of damage from gunfire and missiles, the old ship remained afloat, and was sold for scrap in 1957.

The last big cruiser at sea was *Pueyrredón*, the Argentine vessel continuing in her cadet training role through to 1952, having made eight overseas cruises since 1941. Her last one lasted from March to November 1952, after which, owing to the condition of her boilers, she was laid up at Puerto Belgrano

Pueyrredón at Genoa on 19 September 1951, during her penultimate cruise as a cadet training ship. The last operational armoured cruiser, and now in her sixth decade of service, she is little altered from her 1933 post-reconstruction form, with just some modest additions to her bridgework and the removal of searchlights from the platforms on the tripod-mast legs. *(Author's collection)*

Seattle at Pier 92, North River, New York City, as a receiving ship during the 1940s; to the right is the accommodation ship, ex-submarine tender, *Camden* (IX-42, ex-AS-6, 1900). *(NHHC NH 89402)*

The last remaining British big cruiser was the former *Andromeda*, which survived as the lead ship of the *Defiance* establishment at Devonport into the 1950s, narrowly avoiding being replaced by the heavy cruiser *Frobisher* in 1946. Here she is shown during the 1930s with *Defiance II* (ex-*Inconstant*) in front of her, behind which can be seen *Defiance III* (ex-*Vulcan*). *(Author's collection)*

Averof was the last surviving big ship of the Greek navy, the two ex-American battleships having been bombed and sunk in April 1941. Here she is shown alongside the mole in Salamis harbour in the early 1950s, with the wreck of *Kilkis* (ex-*Mississippi*, 1905) under salvage. *(Author's collection)*

Defiance, ex-*Andromeda*, is broken up at Bruges in late 1956. *(Richard Osborne collection)*

in 1953. Paid off on 2 August 1954 and stricken on 4 January 1955, she was sold to the Boston Metal Company of Baltimore, but the re-sold and finally towed away from Rio Santiago for Italy for scrapping.[189] The previous year, HMS *Defiance* (I), once *Andromeda*, had also been sold for scrap, arriving at Burgt, in Belgium, on 14 August 1956, six months after *Defiance II* – once HMS *Inconstant* and the ancestress of all big metal cruisers. The breed was almost extinct.

Yet, while never to sail again, the Greek navy seemed never to be able to bring themselves to dispose of their old flagship, which remained moored at Salamis until 1956, when she was towed to Poros, where she remained until 1983, still on the navy list as 'gate guard' of the petty officers' school. During this period many fittings were pilfered, as the ship's state deteriorated. Early in 1973, under the military regime of 'the Colonels', funds were allocated to mark the sixtieth anniversary of the battle of Lemnos, including moving the ship to Piraeus as a museum; however, the regime fell the following summer and nothing was done. Nevertheless, in the early 1980s, a decision was made to take forward the idea of turning the old cruiser into a museum, and in 1984 *Averof* was removed from Poros to Salamis for dry-docking and repainting. In January 1985 it was agreed that she should be refitted in Niarchos Yard, Skaramangas, but the yard closed in May of that year. The refit was therefore moved to the Elefsis Shipyard; completed in October 1985, the ship was towed to her new berth in Phaleron Bay, Athens, where she remains, the last of the line, and thus a memorial to the ingenuity and resources that were invested in such ships before the battlecruiser superseded them as perhaps the most glamorous of all fighting ships.

Averof is towed from her long lay-up at Poros to Salamis in 1984 to begin her restoration. *(Author's collection)*

8 | RETROSPECT

Looking back over the half-century that separates the building of *Belliqueuse* from the battle of Jutland, which marked the end of the 'classic' big cruiser as a truly first-class warship, one is particularly struck by the variety of approaches taken by designers, and also the ever-changing roles envisaged for the ships in question, even when few (if any) changes in physical capability were involved. Of course, any review of naval history in the steam age makes it obvious that warships are rarely called upon to do what they were designed to do. Even where the requirement and design are clear and unambiguous, the moment a ship enters service she is likely to become simply another hull to be deployed as and where needed to meet the fleet's broad needs, and will rarely be in a position to fulfil the niche role so often envisaged at the requirement or design stage. This is thrown particularly into relief where a ship has been specifically designed to 'counter' a particular foreign rival, seemingly oblivious to the fact that the likelihood of both of them ever finding themselves in the same piece of sea in wartime was remote. The case of the *Powerful*s versus the original *Ryurik* is perhaps the most glaring, producing a pair of ships that, although a great technical achievement, could be seen ultimately as a misuse of resources that could have been used for a larger number of smaller, and more flexibly-deployable, vessels.

On the other hand, the original French conception of *Belliqueuse* and the follow-on *Alma* class as capital ships for distant stations was sound, at least as long as their potential opponents were wooden (or at least unprotected) vessels, which would be unable to face them with any chance of success, or likely to be able to successfully run away from them (*Rodney*, the last British wooden battleship on the China Station, was, like *Belliqueuse*, an 11.5kt vessel). However, later generations of French vessels represented only a modest improvement over the prototype ships, in spite of being already outclassed by the much bigger, more heavily armed and faster *Audacious* class that had come into service in parallel with the *Alma*s. Nevertheless, the French ships were still far superior to the Chinese fleet, the only significant non-European force in the Far East, as evidenced by the outcome of the battle of Foochow.

But the ordering of the *Ting Yuen*-class battleships and new cruisers by China at the beginning of the 1880s marked the end of the French ships' even potential dominance, particularly as until the last pair they continued to be wooden-hulled. Curiously, the concept of a modernised 'station' type endured into the 1890s, with the construction of *D'Entrecasteaux* and the *Kléber* class, none of which could be seen as having any

capability against the full-sized battleships of the emerging regional (and soon to be world) power of Japan.

The other early pioneer of the big cruiser, Russia, had a rather different conception of her first generations of ships. Also designed for Far Eastern service, and implicitly a capital role in Russia's embryonic forces in the region, their endurance and intended (although not realised) speeds fitted

The chasm between the old and new in the history of the big cruiser is well illustrated here by the recently-commissioned *Indomitable* in the foreground, and the *Monmouth/Donegal*-class vessel in the background, a mere half-decade older, but technologically and conceptually of a different era. The vessel to the left is the protected cruiser *Furious* (1896). *(NHHC NH 60004)*

them for the commerce raiding role that had been an important part of Russian maritime strategy since the 1850s, with the *General-Admiral* class the direct successors of the previous *General-Admiral* and her smaller half-sisters. This conceptual line would continue down to the 1890s, *Rossiya* being the last vessel laid down as such, although her half-sister *Gromoboi* would emerge with a very different strategic role. The commerce-raiding concept would also give rise to the hybrid battleship-cruisers of the *Peresvet* class, with much of their capability built around support for the true commerce-raiding big cruisers.

The odd man out in the nineteenth-century Russian big cruiser fleet was *Admiral Nakhimov*, which as an 'oceangoing armourclad' was in many ways akin to the French idea of a distant-station light battleship. Indeed, her construction as essentially a copy of the British *Imperieuse* sheds an interesting light on the byzantine lines of evolution of men-of-war during the later nineteenth century. The British vessel was a comprehensive update of the Royal Navy's perceived need for an overseas capital ship, borrowing ideas from contemporary French first class ships to supersede the antiquated layout of the preceding *Nelson* class, an update of *Shannon* – intended as a counter to the *General-Admirals* which, as already noted, were a very different kind of ship. The non-linearity of development is further underlined when the direct successors of the *Imperieuse* class, like their direct predecessors clearly 'cruisers' (and classified as such in the 1887 formal split of armoured ships into 'battle ships' and 'cruisers'), turned out to be the small battleships of the *Centurion* class, although all-but-indistinguishable in role and capability from the *Imperieuses*. To complete the circle, the *Centurions* then became an inspiration for the Russian *Peresvets* (one of which was later reclassified as a cruiser)!

In contrast to the broadly task-based approach taken by the French and the Russians, British building policy was frequently reactive, most glaringly in the already-mentioned case of the *Powerfuls* as counters to *Ryurik* (i), but also in the building of the *Audaciouses* and *Shannon* in the wake of *Belliqueuse* and her successors. Indeed, this reactivity continued into the twentieth century, with the speed (and consequent size) of the *Drakes* being determined by what was understood to be that of *Jeanne d'Arc* (which she never actually made). On the other hand, the *Cressy* class represented a genuine new start in producing a big cruiser designed to be capable of operating with the battlefleet (albeit picking up a thread already running in Italy: see below), although France and Russia were also reorienting their big cruisers towards a 'squadron' role from their previous anti-commerce conception.

In the French case, this reorientation emerged from a decade or more of flux, during which various strategic conceptions for the navy had struggled for supremacy amid the upheavals of the ascendancy of the *Jeune école*. As well as the building of dedicated commerce-raiders, this had led, as noted above, to the perpetuation of the dedicated 'station' big cruiser, arguably by the 1890s an obsolete concept. On the

other hand, as the decade progressed, a 'standard' general-purpose big armoured cruiser emerged, that provided the French navy with a useful fleet of broadly uniform vessels that would serve it well into the 1920s. The down side of this programme was that by concentrating on 'high-end' big cruisers to meet the overall cruiser requirement it meant that the French navy was left bereft of the kind of smaller vessels pioneered by the Germans and evolved by the British which would prove ideal for many roles during the First World War and beyond.

The USA had begun its building of big cruisers very much with an eye to commerce-raiding, *New York* being seen as both a commerce raider and an anti-commerce raider (as well as implicitly a general-purpose 'oceangoing armourclad' akin to *Admiral Nakhimov*), while the *Columbia* class were (probably over-)specialised commerce-destroyers modelled on French prototypes. However, when the time came to build the *Pennsylvania* class, under the influence of the performance of *New York* and *Brooklyn* during the Spanish-American War, the international shift towards the use of such ships as a fast wing of the battlefleet had come to the fore in the USA as well. But in practice a major use of the *Pennsylvania* and *Tennessee* classes was as the capital ships of the Asiatic and Pacific fleets, replacing the battleships that had formerly been deployed to these waters. Like France, the USA essentially standardised on the big cruiser, rather than building smaller cruisers on the Anglo-German model, which would lead to careers for these vessels extending well beyond their obsolescence.

Germany took a more explicit approach to the use of her big cruisers for both fleet and overseas roles, going back to the prototype *Kaiserin Augusta*, with an innovative gap-filling to meet the latter requirement by rebuilding the old *Kaiser*-class ironclads pending the completion of *Fürst Bismarck*. The latter represented a particularly interesting approach to the big cruiser, in being as large as, and having a main battery identical to, contemporary battleships, sacrificing secondary guns and protection for speed, thus anticipating in some ways the mature battlecruiser. The use of battleship-sized guns (albeit in the context of the German practice of employing relatively light main guns for her battleships) was, however, soon dropped in the smaller ships that followed *Bismarck*, which nevertheless grew within six years from the four-gun, 9000-ton *Prinz Adalbert* to the twelve-gun 15,800-ton *Blücher*. The latter represented what could have been a been a new standard, had the big-gunned battlecruiser supervened.

Alongside strategic determinations to reorient big cruisers, at least in part, to the needs of the battlefleet lay decisions in the same direction driven by financial realities. This was true not only of South American navies, for which true battleships were all-but-unaffordable, and where big cruisers could both fulfil a capital role and be usable as true cruisers in the fastness of their Pacific and Atlantic seaboards. It was also an approach taken by cash-strapped major navies. Thus, in Italy the distinctly under-armed *Vettor Pisani* design was re-worked as the *Giuseppe Garibaldi* class to squeeze in single 10in or/and twin 8in mountings to allow them to substitute for the battleships that were currently unaffordable in the wake of financial crisis.

Similarly, budget restrictions were key a factor in the specification laid down for the Japanese 6–6 programme cruisers, and their subsequent employment as a key part of the battlefleet, as well as in more typically 'cruiser' roles. This was exacerbated by the loss of two battleships early in the Russo-Japanese War, which not only increased the value of the existing big cruisers, but also made the acquisition of the two ex-Argentine *Garibaldi*s even more crucial to the war effort, both vessels substituting directly for the lost battleships in the Japanese order of battle.

It was this Japanese employment of their big cruisers that led to the step that marked the end of the type in its classic form – the upgrade of the main battery to 'full' battleship size.

While many earlier ships had shared main-gun calibres with battleships, the latter had generally been second-class vessels, on occasion essentially themselves better seen as big cruisers (e.g the *Centurion*s and *Peresvet*s), or fitted with relatively light guns as a matter of policy (e.g. the German *Kaiser Friedrich III* and *Wittelsbach* class contemporaries of *Fürst Bismarck* and *Prinz Heinrich*). However, with the *Tsukuba* class, the Japanese fitted the same kind of 12in weapons as being fitted in the latest first-class ships around the world.

The genie now being out of the bottle, there could no longer be any question of the new generation of single-calibre British armoured cruisers adopting the heavy 9.2in batteries that formed part of the original options analysis, leading instead to the eight 12in fitted in the *Invincible*s. Having reached parity with battleships, this had to be maintained, with the result that in British service 13.5in-gunned 'cruisers' were

The last of her kind, *Averof* lies peacefully at Palaio Faliro, near Athens, as a museum ship in 2016. *(Author's photograph)*

being laid down within four years, of a size that not simply matched their battleship contemporaries, as had been the case with a number of earlier big cruisers, but now exceeded it by nearly 20 per cent. That a wholly-new kind of warship was now in existence was recognised by the reclassification of the *Invincible*s and their successors as 'battlecruisers'; Japan soon followed suit.

Such vessels both pushed 'classic' big cruisers towards obsolescence, as ships that could both out-gun and out-run them: ships under construction were completed, but no further examples were begun. Yet the new battlecruisers were fiendishly expensive ships that only a handful of powers could afford, meaning that at least the most recent of the 'classics' were still likely to maintain their position in a number of theatres and strategic contexts, and if operating together would have a fighting chance against a single battlecruiser (*pace* Troubridge!).

The loss of the three armoured cruisers at Jutland has often been held up as a condemnation of the type, but *Defence*, *Black Prince* and *Warrior* were still powerful units, with a 2kt speed advantage over the main battle-line, and thus still of tactical value to the Grand Fleet. The circumstances of *Defence*'s destruction were such that a battlecruiser (or even a battleship) would probably have suffered similarly: numerous hits followed by a magazine explosion caused by the same poor safety procedures that lay behind the loss of *Invincible*, *Indefatigable* and *Queen Mary* (which, apart from the last, were hardly better protected than *Defence* and her compatriots). As for the other two, *Black Prince* was faced with an impossible tactical position, resulting in a similar outcome to *Defence*, which no ship would have been likely to escape. *Warrior*, on the other hand, stood up to the hail of fire quite well, and with more luck might have made it home.

On the other hand, as the *Renown* and *Courageous* classes came into service, there was no longer a need for the surviving armoured cruisers as fleet units, yet their size and seaworthiness gave them, and older British vessels, an important role in conjunction with American and French opposite numbers in shepherding important convoys across the Atlantic. Indeed, it was their qualities as ships, rather than as fighting units, that kept many big cruisers in service after the war – coupled with an almost complete, or even complete, lack of any other kind of cruising vessels in some navies. It was only with the completion of their first 10,000-ton 'Washington' cruisers that such navies as those of the USA and France could dispose of their last front-line examples.

The same 'ship' qualities contributed to many being employed as cadet training ships for the long oceanic voyages that played an important role in the education of new naval officers. Roomy, relatively economical and impressive in appearance, a number thus remained at sea into their fourth decades, or even beyond, *Pueyrredón* clocking up fifty-four years in seagoing service before being finally withdrawn though sheer old age. Others lingered on harbour service duties, their spaciousness proving appealing for such roles, with some ships' 'afterlives' far exceeding their service at sea, *Andromeda*'s ratio being 13:43 years.

Many of the ships covered in this book have received a decidedly negative press over the years – both from modern historians and from contemporary commentators. Yet when looked at in their own terms, as solutions to what at least *seemed* to be the requirement at the time of ordering, most appear as creditable attempts at harnessing rapidly-changing technologies to the (not-infrequently incoherent) demands of naval and political hierarchies. Brave attempts were often made by their designers to square circles in trying to reconcile the usually-contradictory demands for speed, firepower and protection, with the ships themselves ultimately faced with situations for which they had not been designed, or ships of generations far removed from their own.

They were also often impressive-looking ships, well able to 'show the flag', an important quality for vessels which by design or circumstance would spend important parts of their careers in distant waters. It is thus to be celebrated that the very last of the breed to be launched survives to this day as a monument to some of the most complex and innovative warships of their age.

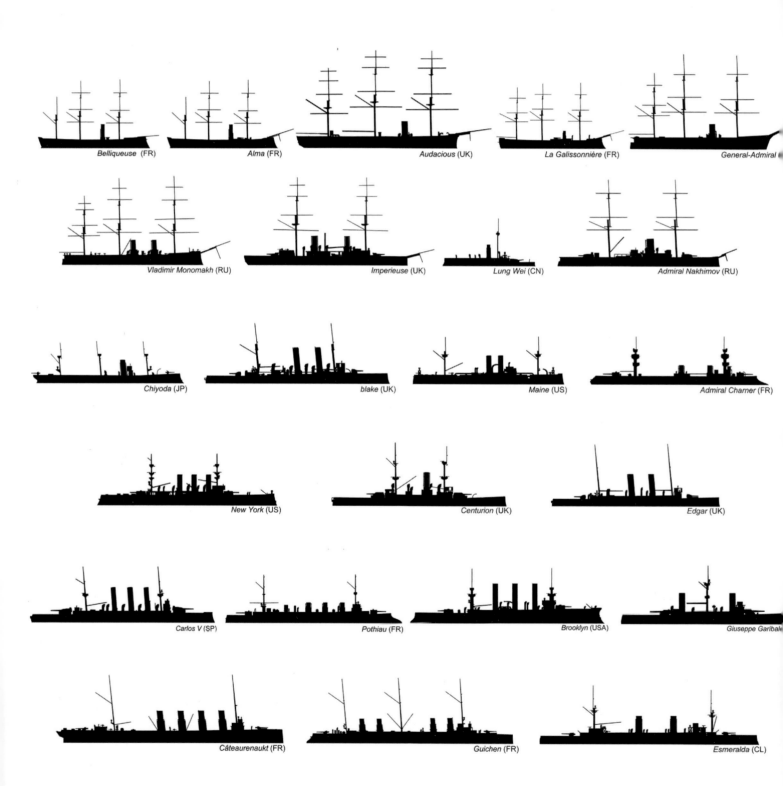

Belliqueuse (FR)

Alma (FR)

Audacious (UK)

La Galissonnière (FR)

General-Admiral

Vladimir Monomakh (RU)

Imperieuse (UK)

Lung Wei (CN)

Admiral Nakhimov (RU)

Chiyoda (JP)

blake (UK)

Maine (US)

Admiral Charner (FR)

New York (US)

Centurion (UK)

Edgar (UK)

Carlos V (SP)

Pothiau (FR)

Brooklyn (USA)

Giuseppe Garibal

Câteaurenaukt (FR)

Guichen (FR)

Esmeralda (CL)

AND CAREER DATA

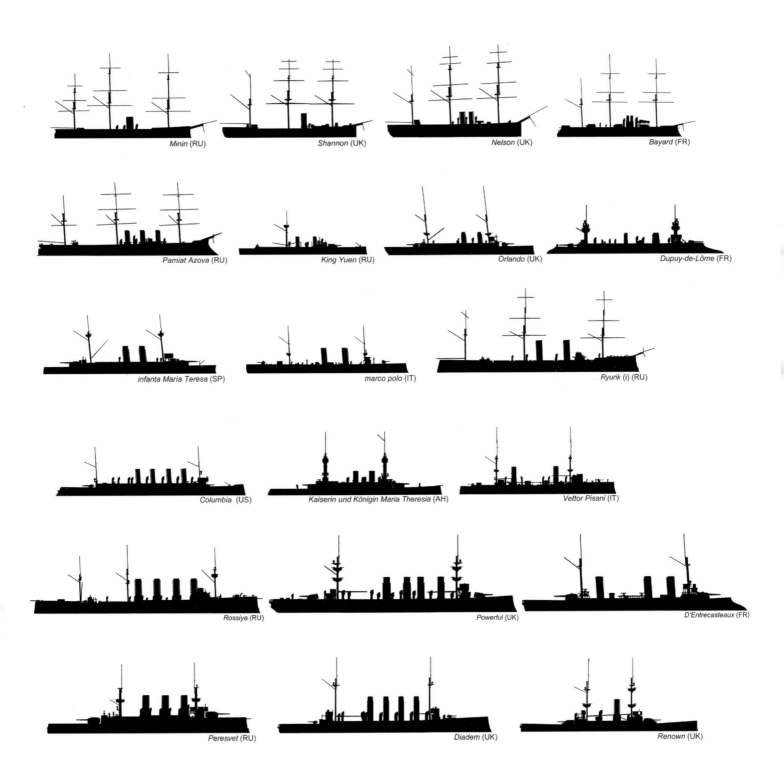

Minin (RU)

Shannon (UK)

Nelson (UK)

Bayard (FR)

Pamiat Azova (RU)

King Yuen (RU)

Orlando (UK)

Dupuy-de-Lôme (FR)

infanta María Teresa (SP)

marco polo (IT)

Ryurik (i) (RU)

Columbia (US)

Kaiserin und Königin Maria Theresia (AH)

Vettor Pisani (IT)

Rossiya (RU)

Powerful (UK)

D'Entrecasteaux (FR)

Peresvet (RU)

Diadem (UK)

Renown (UK)

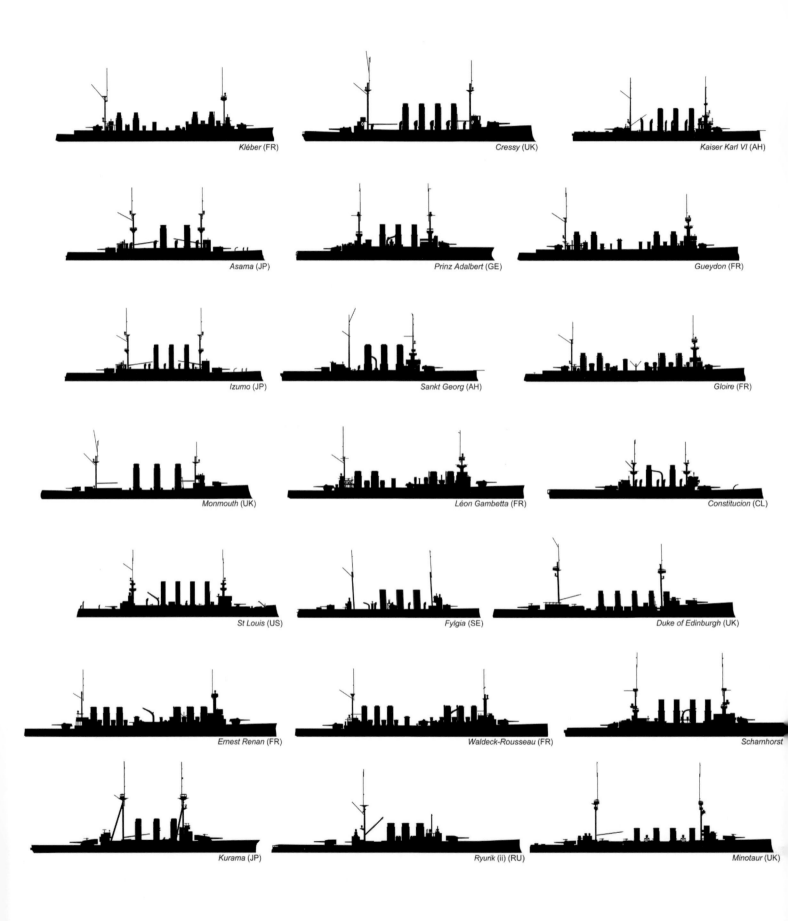

Kléber (FR)

Cressy (UK)

Kaiser Karl VI (AH)

Asama (JP)

Prinz Adalbert (GE)

Gueydon (FR)

Izumo (JP)

Sankt Georg (AH)

Gloire (FR)

Monmouth (UK)

Léon Gambetta (FR)

Constitucion (CL)

St Louis (US)

Fylgia (SE)

Duke of Edinburgh (UK)

Ernest Renan (FR)

Waldeck-Rousseau (FR)

Scharnhorst

Kurama (JP)

Ryurik (ii) (RU)

Minotaur (UK)

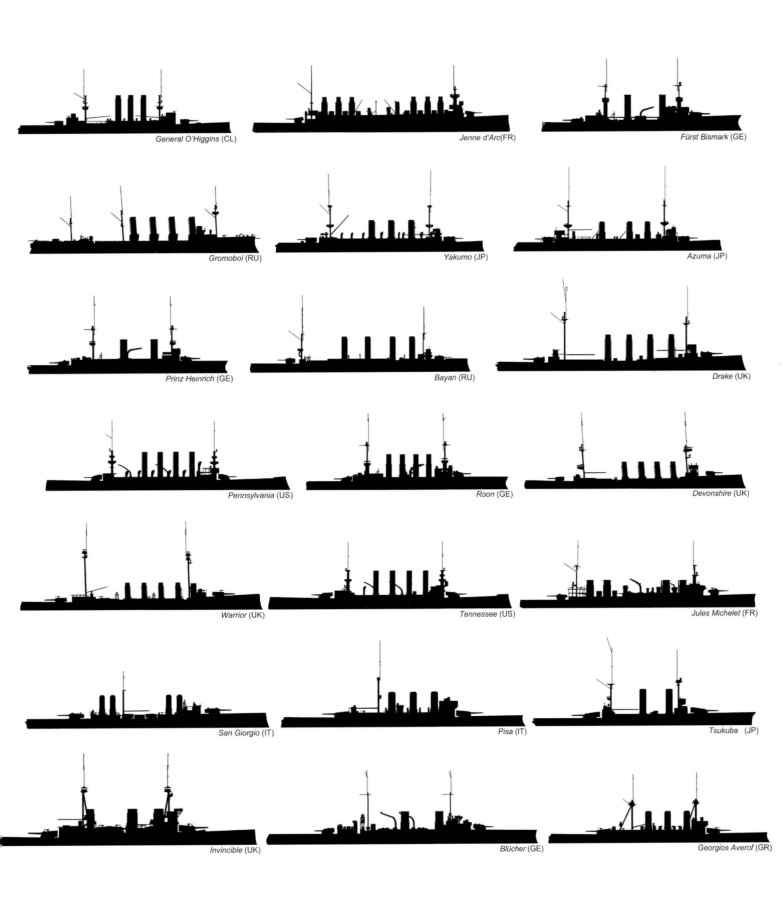

General O'Higgins (CL)

Jenne d'Arc (FR)

Fürst Bismark (GE)

Gromoboi (RU)

Yakumo (JP)

Azuma (JP)

Prinz Heinrich (GE)

Bayan (RU)

Drake (UK)

Pennsylvania (US)

Roon (GE)

Devonshire (UK)

Warrior (UK)

Tennessee (US)

Jules Michelet (FR)

San Giorgio (IT)

Pisa (IT)

Tsukuba (JP)

Invincible (UK)

Blücher (GE)

Georgios Averof (GR)

9 | ARGENTINA

	1865	1870	1875	1880	1885	1890	1895	1900	1905	1910	1915	1920	1925	1930	1935	1940	1945	1950	1955
Garibaldi				ex-Italian *Giuseppe Garibaldi* (i)															
San Martin					ex-Italian *Varese* (i)														
General Belgrano					ex-Italian *Varese* (ii)														
Pueyrredón			ex-Italian *Giuseppe Garibaldi* (iii)																
Bernardo Rivadavia								Japan = *Kasuga*											
Mariano Moreno								Japan = *Nisshin*											

Giuseppe Garibaldi class

Armoured cruisers; 1915: armoured ships;
1922: armoured cruisers; 1927 coast-defence ships

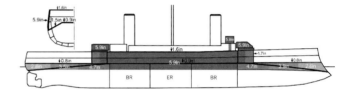

Displacement: 6732 (*Garibaldi*), 6773 (*San Martin*), 7069 (*Belgrano*), 6773 (*Pueyrredón*) tons.

Dimensions: 328.1 (pp) 363.7 (oa) (*Rivadavia* & *Moreno*: 344 [pp] 366.7 [oa]) x 59.75 x 23.3 feet.
100 (pp) 107.8 (oa) (*Rivadavia* & *Moreno*: 104.9 [pp] 111.8 [oa]) x 18.2 x 7.1 metres.

Machinery: Eight cylindrical (*Belgrano* & *Pueyrredón* sixteen Belleville; *Pueyrredón* and *Belgrano* 1930–4, eight Yarrow) boilers; two shafts; reciprocating (VTE), IHP 13,000 = 20kt; coal 400/1000 tons (*Pueyrredón*), 1150 tons (*Belgrano*) or 1137 tons; range 6000nm (*Belgrano* 4800nm) @ 10kt.

Armament:

		10in/40	8in/45	6in/40	4.7in/40	4.7in/45	3in	47mm	37mm	1pdr AA	18in torpedo tubes
Garibaldi	as built	2	–	10	6	–	–	10	–	10	4
	1900	2	–	10	6	–	2	6	–	–	–
	1930	2	–	10	6	–	–	4	–	–	–
San Martin	as built	–	4	10	6	–	–	10	–	10	4
	1924	–	4	10	6	–	2	6	–	–	–
Pueyrredón	as built	2	–	10	6	–	–	10	–	12	4
	1924	2	–	10	6	–	2	4	–	–	–
	1934	2	–	8	–	–	–	4	1	–	–
Belgrano	as built	2	–	14	–	–	2	10	–	12	4
	1924	2	–	14	–	–	4	4	–	–	–
	1930	2	–	–	–	8	–	4	2	–	–
Rivadavia	as built	1	2	14	–	–	10	–	–	–	4
Mariano Moreno	as built	–	4	14	–	–	10	–	–	–	4

Protection: Belt 2.8–3.5–4.7–5.9–4.7–3.5–2.8in; battery 5.9in; turrets 5.9in; armour deck 0.9/1.5in; conning tower 5.9in.

Complement: 500.

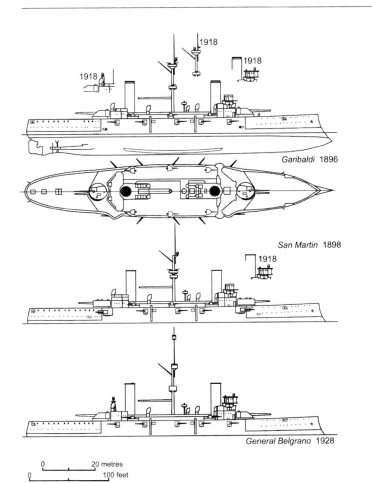

Garibaldi 1896

San Martin 1898

General Belgrano 1928

0   20 metres
0   100 feet

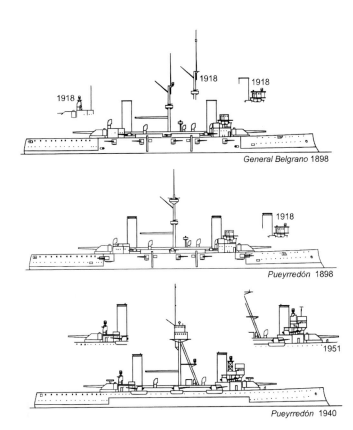

General Belgrano 1898

Pueyrredón 1898

Pueyrredón 1940

1951

Name	Builder	Laid down	Launched	Purchased	Completed	Fate
Garibaldi (ex-IT Giuseppe Garibaldi [i])	Ansaldo (Genoa-Sestri Ponente)	[25 Jul 93]	[27 May 95]	14 Jul 95	14 Oct 96	Stricken 20 Mar 34; sold Julián Nery Huerta 5 Nov 35; resold Empresea Trasatlàntica S.A. Argentina Comercial y Maritima; resold and BU Sweden 1936–7.
San Martin (ex-IT Varese [i])	Orlando (Leghorn)	[1895]	[25 May 96]	26 Oct 96	25 Apr 98	Stricken 18 Dec 35; BU Buenos Aires 1947.
General Belgrano (ex-IT Varese [ii])	Orlando (Leghorn)	[Jun 96]	[25 Jul 97]	1897	8 Oct 98	Submarine depot ship 1933; stricken 8 May 1947; arrived Buenos Aires 3 Apr 53 to BU.
Pueyrredón (ex-IT Giuseppe Garibaldi [iii])	Ansaldo (Genoa-Sestri Ponente)	[Aug 96]	[25 Sep 97]	1897	4 Aug 98	Stricken 4 Jan 55; sold Boston Metals (Baltimore); re-sold Ardemsa & arrived Savona-Vado Ligure Jul 57 to BU.
Rivadavia (i) (ex-SP Pedro de Aragon)	Ansaldo (Genoa-Sestri Ponente)	–	–	1900	–	Cancelled 1902.
Bernardino Rivadavia (ii) (ex-Mitra) = JP Kasuga (1904)	Ansaldo (Genoa-Sestri Ponente)	10 Mar 02	22 Oct 02	–	[Jan 04]	Sold to Japan 7 Jan 04.
Mariano Moreno (ex-Roca) = JP Nisshin (1904)	Ansaldo (Genoa-Sestri Ponente)	29 Mar 02	9 Feb 03	–	[Jan 04]	Sold to Japan 7 Jan 04.

Garibaldi

2nd Division (flag) 1897; Armoured Cruiser Division 1898; 1st Division 1901; disarmed reserve 1903–7; 1st Division 1908; seagoing training ship 1912–31 Aug 31.

San Martin

Training Division Apr 07–1908; 1st Division 1908–10; Training Division 1914; cadet training ship 1920–1; Training Division 1924–20 May 26.

General Belgrano

1st Division 1902; reserve May 03–23 Dec 06; 2nd Division 1909; 1st Division 1910; training division 1911; 2nd Division 1917–22; training division 1923–12 Oct 26; Europe and reconstruction 1927–9; gunnery training ship 1930–1; training ship 1932–3; submarine depot ship Mar del Plata 31 Aug 33–1946.

Pueyrredón

Bahia Blanca Division 1901; 1st Division 1902; disarmed reserve 1903–6; 1st Division 1907; 2nd Division 1909; refit 1911–12; reserve and gunnery training ship 1913–14; 1st Division 1914; cadet training ship 1918–21; refit 1922–3, 1924–6; training ship 1930–53.

10 | AUSTRIA-HUNGARY

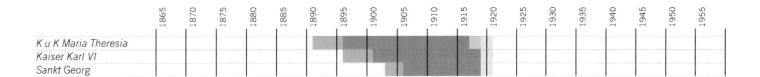

	1865	1870	1875	1880	1885	1890	1895	1900	1905	1910	1915	1920	1925	1930	1935	1940	1945	1950	1955
K u K Maria Theresia																			
Kaiser Karl VI																			
Sankt Georg																			

Kaiserin und Königin Maria Theresia
ARMOURED CRUISER

Displacement:	5247 tons.
Dimensions:	349.7 (pp) 366.5 (wl) 373(oa) x 53.4 x 22.4 feet. 106.6 (pp) 111.7 (wl) 113.67 (oa) x 16.26 x 6.13 metres.
Machinery:	Six cylindrical boilers; two shafts; reciprocating (HTE), IHP 9000 = 19kt; coal 746 tons; range 3500nm @ 10kt.
Armament:	Two 9.4in/35 (1906: two 7.6in/42), eight 5.9in/35, twelve 47mm/44, six (1904: four) 37mm/33 guns, two 8mm MG; four 17.7in torpedo tubes. Four (1910: two) 37mm MG added 1904; two 47mm/33 added 1910.
Protection:	Belt 3.9in; barbettes 5.9in; casemates 3.1in; armour deck 1.5–2.2in; conning tower 2in.
Complement:	32+443.

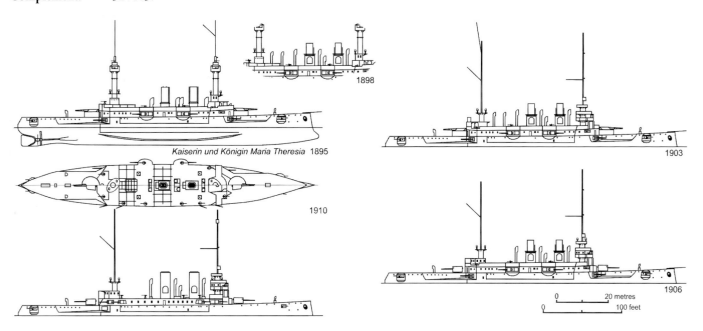

Kaiserin und Königin Maria Theresia 1895

1898

1903

1910

1906

0   20 metres
0   100 feet

Name	Builder	Laid down	Launched	Completed	Fate
Kaiserin und Königin Maria Theresia	Stablimento Tecnico Triestino (San Rocco)	6 Oct 91	29 Apr 93	24 Mar 95	To UK Jan 1920; sold Fiat Motor Co (Turin) 27 Aug 20; re-sold Vaccaro & Co; BU Portoferraio (Elba).

Cruiser Squadron (flag) Apr–Sep 95; Exercise Squadron Apr–Aug 96; Aegean May 96–Sep 97; reserve Sep 97–May 98; West Indies May–Oct 98; Active Squadron (flag) Jan–Feb 99; reserve Mar 99–May 00; Active Squadron (I. Cruiser Division) May–Jun 00; Far East Jun 00–Dec 02; reserve Dec 02–Oct 04; Active Squadron Oct–Nov 04; under repair after grounding Nov 04–Jul 05; Active Squadron Jul–Dec 05; refit and reserve 1906–8; reconstructed 1909–10; Summer Squadron (Cruiser Division [flag] Jun–Sep 10; reserve Squadron Sep 10–Feb 11; Levant Feb 11–Dec 12; Feb–May 13; Adriatic 1914–Feb 17; accommodation ship Pola Feb 17–Nov 18; hulked 3 Feb 19.

Kaiser Karl VI
ARMOURED CRUISER

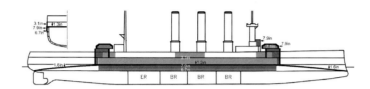

Displacement:	6265 tons.
Dimensions:	367.5 (pp) 386.8 (wl) 393.6 (oa) x 56.6 x 20.5 feet. 112 (pp) 117.9 (wl) 119.96 (oa) x 17.25 x x 6.26 metres.
Machinery:	Sixteen Belleville boilers; two shafts; reciprocating (VTE), IHP 12,000 = 20kt; coal 500/818 tons.
Armament:	Two 9.4in/40, eight 5.9in/40, sixteen (1906: fourteen) 47mm/44, two 47mm/33 guns, two 8mm MG (1906: two 37mm; removed 1917); two 17.7in torpedo tubes. One 2.6in/50 AA and one 8mm AA added 1917; disarmed 1918.
Protection:	Belt 7.9in; battery 3.1in; turrets 7.9–7.1–2in; barbettes 7.9in; armour deck 1.6–1.3–1.6/2.4in; conning tower 7.9in.
Complement:	550.

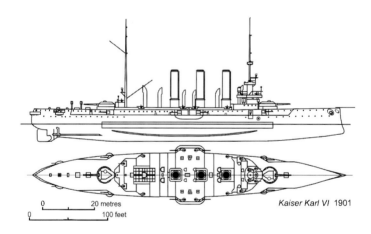

Kaiser Karl VI 1901

Name	Builder	Laid down	Launched	Completed	Fate
Kaiser Karl VI (San Rocco)	Stablimento Tecnico Triestino (San Rocco)	1 Jun 96	4 Oct 98	23 May 00	To UK Jan 1920; sold Vaccaro & Co 21 Aug 20; BU Naples to 1922.

Adriatic 1900–Sep 02; Far East Sep 02–Sep 03; reserve squadron & tender to gunnery school Oct 02–Jun 06; Summer Squadron Jun–Sep 06; reserve squadron Sep 06–Jun 07; Summer Squadron Jun–Sep 07; reserve squadron Sep 07–Jun 08; Summer Squadron 15 Jun–15 Sep 08; reserve squadron Sep–Dec 08; Leader, Torpedo Flotilla Jan–Mar 09; Aegean Apr–Jun 09; Home Jun 09–Feb 10; South America Mar–Aug 10; Leader, Torpedo Flotilla, and Home 1911; refit & reserve Sep 11–Mar 13; Adriatic 13 Mar 13–Jun 14; Mediterranean Jun–Aug 14; Adriatic Aug 14–Mar 18; paid off Sebenico 19 Mar 18; Pola Feb 19.

Sankt Georg
ARMOURED CRUISER

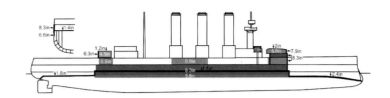

Displacement:	7300 (normal) 8070 (full load) tons.
Dimensions:	383.8 (pp) 404.2 (wl) 407.8 (oa) x 65.4 x 22.4 feet. 117 (pp) 123.2 (wl) x 124.3 (oa) x 19 x 6.8 metres.
Machinery:	Twelve Yarrow boilers; two shafts; reciprocating (VTE), IHP 12,300/15,000FD = 21/22kt; coal 600/1000 tons; range 4500nm @ 10kt.
Armament:	Two 9.4in/40 (1 x 2), five 7.6in/42, four 5.9in/40, nine 66mm, six (1914: ten) 47mm/44, two (removed 1914) 47mm/33, four (removed 1914) 37mm/33 guns; two 17.7in torpedo tubes. One 2.6in/50 AA and one 8mm AA added 1917; disarmed 1918.
Protection:	Belt 0–8.3–0in; battery 5.9in; barbette 8.3in; fore turret 7.9–5.9in; aft turret 6.3–4.5in; armour deck 1.8–1.4–2.4in; conning tower 7.9in.
Complement:	628.

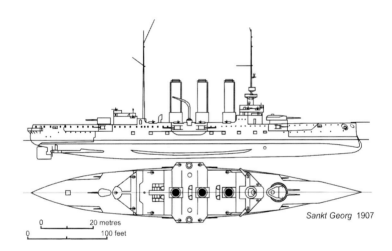

Sankt Georg 1907

Name	Builder	Laid down	Launched	Completed	Fate
Sankt Georg	Pola DYd	11 Mar 03	8 Dec 03	21 Jul 05	To UK 1920; sold Count Taverna & Alessandro Piaggio 12 Aug 20; re-sold Vaccaro & Co; BU Taranto.

Summer Squadron Sep–Nov 05; Aegean Nov–Dec 05; Levant Mar–May 06; Summer Squadron (Cruiser Division flag) Jun–Sep 06; Heavy Division Sep–Dec 06; Atlantic/North America/Mediterranean Mar–Jul 07; Summer Squadron (Cruiser/III. Division flag) Jun–Sep 07; Aegean Dec 07; Summer Squadron (Cruiser/III. Division flag) Jun–Sep 08; reserve squadron Dec 08–May 11; Summer Squadron (Cruiser/III. Division flag) Jun–Aug 11; Cruiser Flotilla (flag) Dec 11–May 12; Summer Squadron (Cruiser/III. Division flag) May–Aug 12; Cruiser Division flag 1913–14; Adriatic 1914–Apr 18; paid off 7 Apr 18; HQ ship Tivat Apr–Nov 18.

11 | CHILE

	1865	1870	1875	1880	1885	1890	1895	1900	1905	1910	1915	1920	1925	1930	1935	1940	1945	1950	1955

Esmeralda
General O'Higgins
Constitucion UK = *Swiftsure* (ii)
Libertad UK = *Triumph* (ii)

Esmeralda

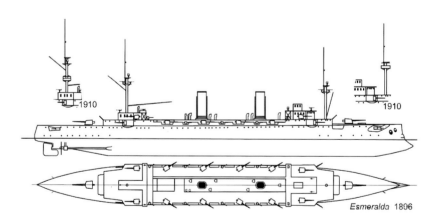

Displacement:	7032 tons.
Dimensions:	436 (pp) 468.25 (oa) x 52.4 x 20.5 feet. 132.9 (pp) 142.7 (oa) x 15.9 x 6.2 metres.
Machinery:	Six cylindrical boilers; two shafts; reciprocating (VTE), IHP 16,000 = 22.25kt; coal 550/1374 tons; range 7680nm @ 10kt.
Armament:	Two 8in/40, sixteen 6in/40, eight 12pdr, ten 6pdr guns; three 18in torpedo tubes.
Protection:	Belt 0–6–0in; armour deck 1.5/2in; shields 4.5in; conning tower 8in (Harvey).
Complement:	513.

Esmeralda 1806

0   20 metres
0   100 feet

Name	Builder	Laid down	Launched	Completed	Fate
Esmeralda (ii)	Armstrong (Elswick)	4 Jul 95	14 Apr 96	Dec 96	Stricken 1929; BU 1930.

General O'Higgins

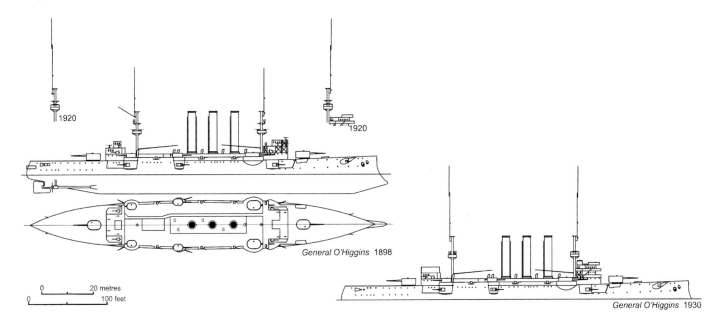

Displacement:	8476 tons.
Dimensions:	412 (pp) 446 (oa) x 62 x 22 feet. 125.6 (pp) 135.94 (oa) x 18.9 x 6.7 metres.
Machinery:	Thirty Belleville boilers; two shafts; reciprocating (VTE), IHP 16,000 = 21kt; coal 550/1253 tons.
Armament:	Four 8in/45, ten 6in/40, four 4.7in/45 (removed 1920), eight (1920: ten; 1929: twelve) 12pdr, ten 6pdr (removed 1929) guns; three 18in torpedo tubes.
Protection:	Belt 0–5–7–5–0in; armour deck 1.5/3in; main turrets 5–7in; secondary turrets & casemates 5–6in; conning tower 9in (Harvey-Nickel).
Complement:	489.

General O'Higgins 1898

General O'Higgins 1930

Name	Builder	Laid down	Launched	Completed	Fate
General O'Higgins	Armstrong (Elswick)	19 Mar 96	17 May 97	2 Apr 98	Accommodation ship 1933; BU 1958.

Constitucion class

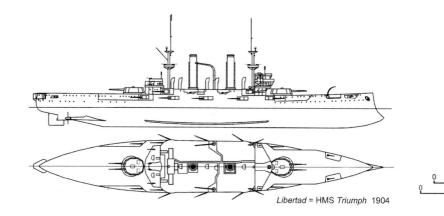

Displacement:	11,740 (*Constitucion*)/11,985 (*Libertad*) tons.	
Dimensions:	436 (pp) 462.5 (wl) 475.2 (oa) x 71.2 x 26.6 feet. 132.9 (pp) 139.6 (wl) 146.2 (oa) x 21.6 x 7.7 metres.	
Machinery:	Twelve Yarrow boilers; two shafts; reciprocating VTE) IHP 12,500 = 19kt; coal 800/2048 tons; range 6210nm @ 10kt.	
Armament:	Four 10in/45 (2 x 2), fourteen 7.5in/50, fourteen 14pdr, two 12pdr/8cwt, four 6pdr, four 3pdr guns; two 18in torpedo tubes.	
Protection:	Belt 0–3–6–7–6–3–2in; battery 7in; barbettes 10in; turrets 9–8in; armour deck 3–1.5–3in; conning tower 11in.	
Complement:	800.	

Libertad = HMS Triumph 1904

Name	Builder	Laid down	Launched	Completed	Fate
Constitucion = UK *Swiftsure* (ii – Dec 03)	Armstrong-Whitworth (Elswick)	13 Mar 02	12 Jan 03	[Jun 04]	Sold UK 3 Dec 03.
Libertad = UK *Triumph* (ii – Dec 03)	Vickers (Barrow)	13 Mar 02	15 Jan 03	[Jun 04]	Sold UK 3 Dec 03.

12 | CHINA

	1865	1870	1875	1880	1885	1890	1895	1900	1905	1910	1915	1920	1925	1930	1935	1940	1945	1950	1955

Lung Wei = Ping Yuen   Japan = *Haien*
King Yuen   ✚
Lai Yuen   ✚

Lung Wei

Displacement:	2067 tons.
Dimensions:	196.8 (pp) 215 (oa) x 40 x 13.7 feet. 60 (pp) 65.5 (oa) x 12.2 x 4.2 metres.
Machinery:	Four locomotive boilers; two shafts; reciprocating (VTE), IHP 2500 = 10.2kt; coal 300 tons.
Armament:	One 10.2in/25, two 5.9in, eight 3pdr guns; four 18in torpedo tubes.
Protection:	Belt 5–8–5in; barbette 5in; shield 1in; armour deck 2in; conning tower 5in.
Complement:	204.

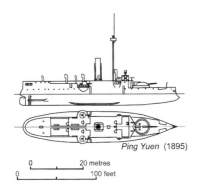

Ping Yuen (1895)

```
0            20 metres
0            100 feet
```

Name	Builder	Laid down	Launched	Completed	Fate
Lung Wei = *Ping Yuen* (16 May 90) = JP *Ping Yuen-go* (Feb 95)	Foochow DYd	Late 1886	Mid 1889	End 1889	Captured Japan, Weihaiwei 16 Feb 95.

King Yuen class

Displacement:	2900 tons.
Dimensions:	270.3 (oa) x 39.3 x 16.7 feet. 82.4 (oa) x 12 x 5.1 metres.
Machinery:	Four cylindrical boilers; two shafts; reciprocating (HTE), IHP 3400/5000 = 15.5kt; coal 320 tons.
Armament:	Two 8.2in/22 (1 x 2), two 5.9in guns; four 18in torpedo tubes.
Protection:	Belt 9.5in; armour deck 1.5/3in; barbette 8in; conning tower 6in.
Complement:	202–270.

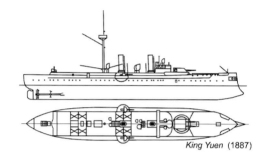

King Yuen (1887)

Name	Builder	Laid down	Launched	Completed	Fate
King Yuen	Vulcan (Stettin)	Late 1885	3 Jan 87	Jul 87	Gunfire battle of the Yalu 17 Sep 94.
Lai Yuen	Vulcan (Stettin)	Late 1885	25 Mar 87	Jul 87	Torpedoed by Japanese torpedo boat *Kotaka*, Weihaiwei, 5 Feb 95.

13 | FRANCE

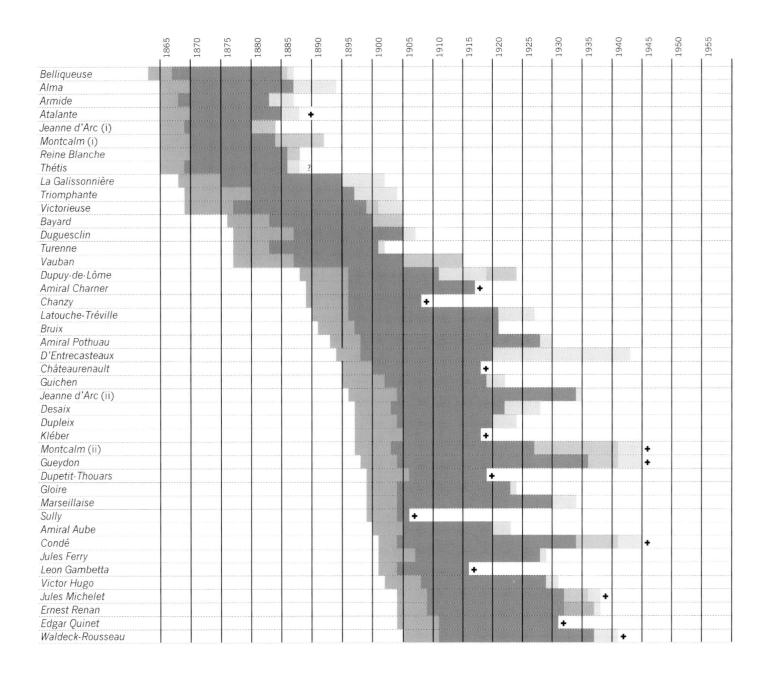

Belliqueuse
ARMOURED CORVETTE

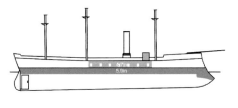

Displacement:	3717 tons.
Dimensions:	223.1 (wl) 229.7 (oa) x 46 x 23 feet. 68 (wl) 70 (oa) x 14 x 7 metres.
Machinery:	Four oval boilers; one shaft; reciprocating (HRCR), IHP 1,200 = 11kt; coal 250 tons; range 1410nm @ 10kt.
Armament:	Four 7.6in, six (1876: four) 6.5in guns; five 5.4in added 1876.
Protection:	Belt 5.9in; battery 4.7in (wrought iron).
Complement:	300.

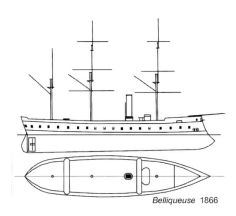

Belliqueuse 1866

Name	Builder	Laid down	Launched	Completed	Fate
Belliqueuse	Toulon DY	Sep 63	6 Sep 65	30 Oct 66	Condemned 3 May 86; expended as target Toulon.

Pacific 22 Dec 66–26 May 69; Levant Nov 69–Jul 70; Pacific Aug 70–5 Jun 71; China & Japan Oct 72–May 74; Evolutionary Squadron Jun 77–Dec 77; reserve 1877–83; decommissioned Nov 84.

Alma class
ARMOURED CORVETTES

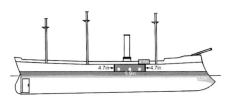

Displacement:	3513–3828 tons.
Dimensions:	226 (wl) 236.9 (oa) x 45 x 21 feet. 69 (wl) 72.2 (oa) x 14 x 6.5 metres.
Machinery:	Four oval boilers; one shaft; reciprocating (HRCR), IHP 1600–1800 = 11.7–12kt.
Armament:	Six 7.6in guns.
Protection:	Belt 5.9in; battery 5.9in; barbettes 3.9in.
Complement:	316.

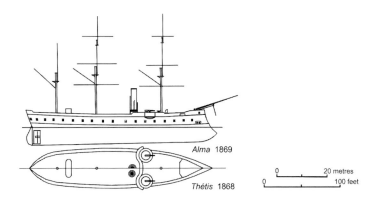

Alma 1869

Thétis 1868

Name	Builder	Laid down	Launched	Completed	Fate
Alma	Lorient DY	1 Oct 65	26 Nov 67	24 Aug 69	Condemned 12 Mar 86; sold May 93 & BU.
Armide	Rochefort DY	1865	12 Apr 67	5 Oct 67	Condemned 25 Oct 82; expended as target Mar 86.
Atalante	Cherbourg DY	Jun 65	9 Apr 68	1 Apr 69	Condemned 1887; foundered Saigon.
Jeanne d'Arc (i)	Cherbourg DY	1865	28 Sep 67	9 Mar 68	Condemned 28 Aug 83.
Montcalm (i)	Rochefort DY	26 Oct 65	16 Oct 68	16 Jun 69	Condemned 2 Apr 91.
Reine Blanche	Lorient DY	1865	10 Mar 68	15 Apr 69	Condemned 12 Nov 86.
Thétis	Toulon DY	20 Jul 65	22 Aug 67	1 May 68	Hulked Nouméa, New Caledonia after 1885.

Alma
China & Japan Jun 70–Jan 73; Evolutionary Squadron Oct 73; Cherbourg reserve 1876–81; Levant Mar 81; Cherbourg reserve Jan 83; decommissioned 1884.

Armide
Brest reserve Oct 67–Jul 70; Baltic Jul–Nov 70; Levant Aug 74; Brest reserve Dec 75–1877; China Jan 78–Mar 80; decommissioned Toulon Mar 80.

Atalante
Brest reserve Jul 69–Feb 70; Evolutionary Squadron Feb 70; Heligoland Aug 70; Pacific Aug 72–Feb 74; Lorient reserve Feb 74–Dec 75; China Jan 76–May 78; Lorient reserve May 78–1882; Far East Jul 82–1885; decommissioned Saigon 1885.

Jeanne d'Arc
Brest reserve 1869–Apr 70; Northern Squadron Apr 70; Brest reserve 1 Jan 76–1879; Levant Apr 79.

Montcalm
Brest, Cherbourg & Mediterranean Jun 69–May 70; Cherbourg reserve 1871–3; China & Japan Jan 74–May 76; Cherbourg reserve 1878–80; Pacific 1882–4; Cherbourg reserve 1884–91.

Reine Blanche
Lorient reserve Sep 70–1871; 2nd Division, Evolutionary Squadron Jul 71; reserve Feb–Apr 76; Toulon reserve Jan 78–1879; Levant Apr 79; Pacific Jan 84–May 86.

Thétis
Brest reserve 1869–70; Northern Squadron Jun 70; Evolutionary Squadron 1871; Levant May 72; Evolutionary Squadron Apr 77; Pacific 1885.

La Galissonnière
ARMOURED CORVETTE; 1885: ARMOURED CRUISER

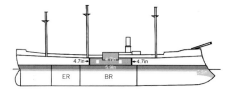

Displacement:	4645 tons.
Dimensions:	251.6 (wl) 261.8 (oa) x 48.8 x 23 feet. 76.7 (wl) 79.8 (oa) x 14.9 x 7 metres.
Machinery:	Four oval boilers; two shafts; reciprocating (VC), IHP 2370 = 13kt; coal 500 tons; range 3240nm @ 10kt.
Armament:	Six 9.4in/19, six 4.7in/25 (1880: 3.9in) guns.
Protection:	Belt 5.9in; battery 4.7in; barbettes 4.7in.
Complement:	352.

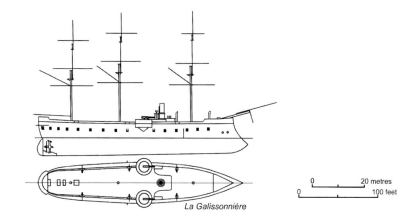

La Galissonnière

Name	Builder	Laid down	Launched	Completed	Fate
La Galissonnière	Brest DY	22 Jun 68	7 May 72	20 Apr 74	Stricken 24 Dec 94; target 1896; sold at Cherbourg before 1902.

Pacific Oct 74–Mar 77; West Indies Oct 78–May 80; Cherbourg reserve May 80–May 81; Levant Nov 83; Far East Mar 84–Feb 86; Cherbourg reserve 1888; decommissioned 1893.

Victorieuse class
ARMOURED CORVETTES; 1885: ARMOURED CRUISERS

Displacement:	4434 (*Victorieuse*)/4585 (*Triomphante*) tons.
Dimensions:	261.8 (*Victorieuse*)/252.1 (*Triomphante*) (oa) x 48.8 x 20.7 feet. 79.80/76.85 (oa) x 14.9 x 6.3 metres.
Machinery:	Four oval boilers; one shaft; reciprocating (VC), IHP 2360 = 12.5kt; coal 330 tons; range 2740nm @ 10kt.
Armament:	Six 9.4in/19, one 7.6in/20, eight 5.4in/21 guns; *Triomphante* 1880s: four 14in torpedo tubes.
Protection:	Belt 5.9in; battery 4.7in; barbettes 4.7in.
Complement:	382.

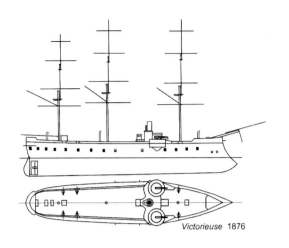

Victorieuse 1876

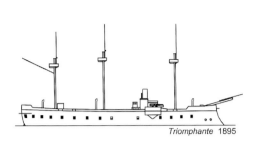

Triomphante 1895

Name	Builder	Laid down	Launched	Completed	Fate
Victorieuse = *Semiramis* 1900	Toulon DY	5 Aug 69	18 Nov 75	1 Nov 76	Condemned 8 Mar 00; BU 1904.
Triomphante	Rochefort DY	5 Aug 69	28 Mar 77	6 May 79	Stricken 18 Jul 96; sold Chinese interests, Saigon, 1903.

Victorieuse
Toulon reserve Nov 76; Pacific Aug 78–May 81; China Dec 81–Apr 84; Levant Dec 84; Cherbourg reserve 1888–91; Northern Squadron Feb 92; condemned May 97, but reversed; destroyer tender Bizerte 1898; parent ship at Landevennec 1900.

Triomphante
Pacific Oct 80; Levant Feb 83; Far East from Aug 83; reserve 5 Feb 94.

Bayard class
ARMOURED CORVETTES; 1885: ARMOURED CRUISERS

Displacement: 5891 (*Bayard*)/6263 (*Turenne*)/6094 (*Duguesclin*)/6024 (*Vauban*) tons.

Dimensions: 267.7 (wl) 276.6 (oa) x 57.3 x 25.6 feet.
81.6m (wl) 84.3m (oa) x 17.5 x 7.8 metres.

Machinery: Six cylindrical boilers; two shafts; reciprocating (VC), IHP 4500 = 14.5kt; coal 400–450 tons; range 3600nm @ 10kt.

Armament: Four 9.4in/18, two 7.6in/20 (first two)/one 6.5in (last two), six 5.4in/21 guns; two 14in torpedo tubes (last three only).

Protection: Belt 6.3–9.8–7.9in; barbettes 7.9in; armour deck 1.2in (wrought iron; barbettes compound in last two).

Complement: 451.

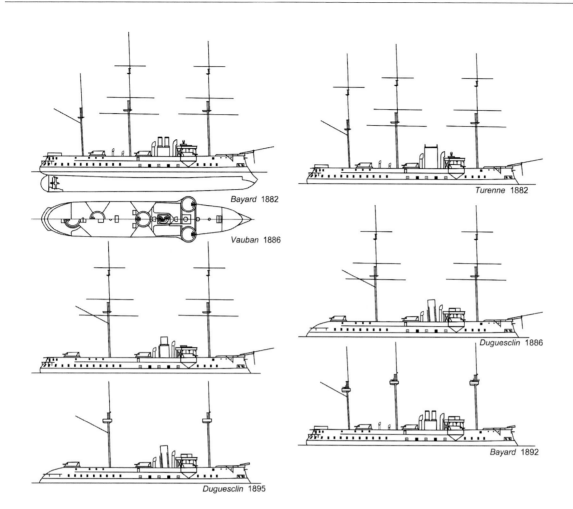

Bayard 1882

Turenne 1882

Vauban 1886

Duguesclin 1886

Bayard 1892

Duguesclin 1895

Name	Builder	Laid down	Launched	Completed	Fate
Bayard (ex-Condé)	Brest DY	19 Sep 76	Mar 80	22 Nov 82	Condemned 26 Apr 99; hulked Along 1899; BU Saigon 1904.
Turenne	Lorient DY	1 Mar 77	Oct 79	4 Feb 82	Stricken 11 Sep 00; sold at Cherbourg 1901 to BU.
Duguesclin	Rochefort DY	Mar 77	7 Apr 83	1 Jan 86	Stricken 10 Oct 04; sold at Toulon 1906 to BU.
Vauban	Cherbourg DY	1 Aug 77	3 Jul 82	9 Mar 86	Stricken 1904; sold at Saigon 1914 to BU.

Bayard
Far East 1883–5; Toulon reserve Aug 88; Far East 1894–9.

Turenne
Far East 1885–Mar 1890; Cherbourg reserve Mar 90.

Duguesclin
Reserve Jul 87.

Vauban
Levant 8 Jun 87; Mediterranean Jan 88; Far East from Apr 92; hulked 1904; torpedo boat depot ship Along Bay 1906–10; submarine depot ship Saigon/Rach Dua 1911–13.

Dupuy de Lôme
1ST CLASS ARMOURED CRUISER

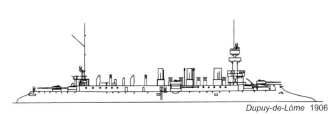

Displacement:	6676 (as *Peruvier*: 8100) tons.
Dimensions:	364.2 (pp) 374 (oa) x 51.5 x 23 feet. 111 (pp) 114 (oa) x 15.7 x 7 metres.
Machinery:	Thirteen cylindrical (1905: twenty Guyot-du-Temple) boilers; three shafts; reciprocating (HTE+VTE), IHP 13,000 = 19.7kt; coal 1080 tons; range 7000nm @ 10kt; as *Peruvier*: six Guyot-du-Temple boilers; 1 shaft; reciprocating (VTE), IHP 2000 = 10.5kt.
Armament:	Two 7.6in/45, six 6.5in/45, four 65mm/50, eight 47mm/40, eight 37mm/20 guns; four 17.7in torpedo tubes.
Protection:	Belt 3.9in; armour deck 1.2in; turrets 3.9in; 3.9in; conning tower 4.9in.
Complement:	526.

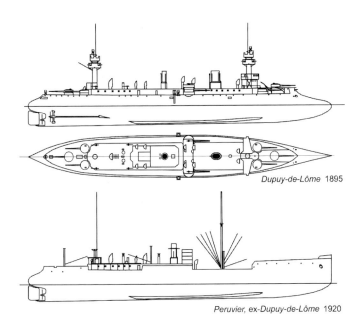

Dupuy-de-Lôme 1895

Dupuy-de-Lôme 1906

Peruvier, ex-Dupuy-de-Lôme 1920

```
0                    20 metres
0                              100 feet
```

Name	Builder	Laid down	Launched	Completed	Fate
Dupuy de Lôme = *Commandante Aguirre* 1912 = ex–*Dupuy de Lôme* 1917 = *Peruvier* 1919	Brest DY	4 Jul 88	27 Oct 90	15 May 95	Condemned 20 Mar 10; stricken 20 Feb 11; to Peru 12 Sep 12; retroceded 17 Jan 17; sold Soc. Commeriale & Industriel de Paris Oct 18; resold Consortium du Nord; resold Lloyd Royal Belge and mercantile; sold Dutch sbkr; arrived Flushing 4 Mar 23 to BU.

Northern Squadron 1895–1902; reconstructed Brest 1902–6; Brest reserve Oct 06–Sep 08; Morocco Dec 08–Sep 09; Lorient reserve Sep 09–Mar 10.

Amiral Charner class

2ND CLASS ARMOURED CRUISERS; 1891:
1ST CLASS ARMOURED CRUISERS

Displacement:	4700 tons.
Dimensions:	363.5 (pp) 374 (wl) x 47.3 x 20.3 feet. 106.1 (pp) 110.2 (wl) x 14.04 x 6 metres.
Machinery:	Sixteen Belleville boilers; two shafts; reciprocating (HTE; *Bruix*: VTE), IHP 8000 (*Bruix*: 8900) = 18.5kt; coal 406/535 tons; range 4000nm @ 10kt, 950nm @ 18kt.
Armament:	Two 7.6in/45, six 5.5in/45, six 65mm, four 47mm, six 37mm guns; four 17.7in torpedo tubes (removed 1906–7).
Protection:	Belt 3.6in; armour deck 1.6/2in; turrets 3.6in; conning tower 3.6in.
Complement:	16+378.

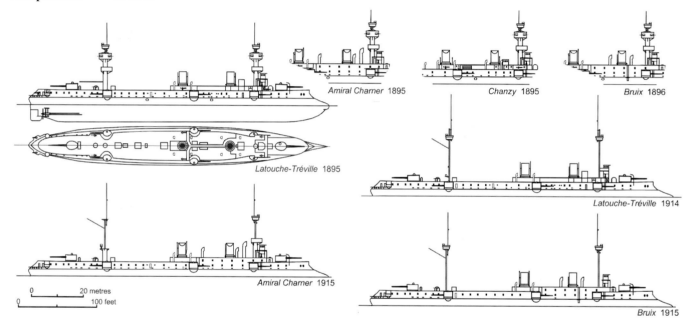

Amiral Charner 1895

Chanzy 1895

Bruix 1896

Latouche-Tréville 1895

Latouche-Tréville 1914

Amiral Charner 1915

Bruix 1915

Name	Builder	Laid down	Launched	Completed	Fate
Amiral Charner (ex-*Charner*)	Rochefort DY	15 Jun 89	18 Mar 93	19 Aug 95	Torpedoed *U21* W of Beirut 18 Feb 16.
Bruix	Rochefort DY	9 Nov 91	2 Aug 94	1 Dec 96	Sold 9 Jun 20.
Chanzy	Societe de la Gironde (Bordeaux)	18 Dec 89	24 Jun 94	1 May 95	Wrecked Balard Island (Chusan archipelago) 20 May 07; blown up 12 Jun 07.
Latouche-Treville	Forges et Chantiers de la Mediterranée (Granville-Le Havre)	25 Apr 90	5 Nov 92	6 May 95	Condemned 21 Jun 21; salvage hulk 1922; BU 1926.

Amiral Charner

Training Division 1895; Mediterranean 1896–1901; Far East 1901–2; Mediterranean 1911–Jul 12; Bizerte reserve 1912–Aug 14; Mediterranean Aug 14 to loss.

Bruix

Far East 1906–9; Atlantic 1914–15; Red Sea 1915; Aegean 1916–17; Salonika reserve 1918.

Chanzy
Mediterranean 1895; Levant 1897; Mediterranean 1898; Toulon reserve 3 May 04; Far East Sep 06 to loss.

Latouche-Treville
Training Division 1895; Levant 1897; Toulon reserve May 97; Mediterranean Oct 97–1899; tender to gunnery school Feb 07; Toulon reserve 1912; Mediterranean Dec 12–1918.

Pothuau
1ST CLASS ARMOURED CRUISER

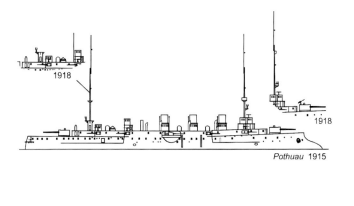

Displacement:	5365 tons.
Dimensions:	370.75 (wl) x 50 x 22.5 feet. 113 (wl) x 15 x 6.5 metres.
Machinery:	Eighteen Belleville boilers; two shafts; reciprocating (HTE), IHP 10,400 = 19kt; coal 538/630 tons; range 4500nm @ 10kt.
Armament:	Two 7.6in/40, ten 5.5in/45, twelve 47mm, eight 37mm guns; four 17.7in torpedo tubes. 1919: ten 5.5in/45, four 75mm AA guns.
Protection:	Belt 1.2–2.4–1.4in; armour deck 1.4–3.3in; turrets 7.1in; casemates 2.2in; conning tower 9.4in.
Complement:	626.

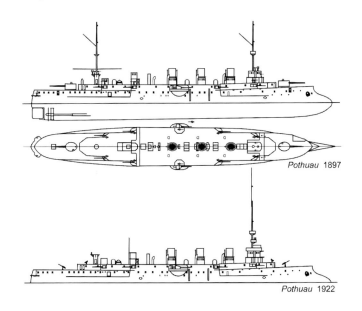

Pothuau 1897

Pothuau 1915

Pothuau 1922

1918

1918

Name	Builder	Laid down	Launched	Completed	Fate
Pothuau	Forges et Chantiers de La Méditerranée (Granville)	25 May 93	19 Sep 95	8 Jun 97	Stricken 3 Nov 27; sold Societé due Matérial Naval du Midi 25 Sep 29 to BU.

Northern Squadron Jul 97; Mediterranean Sep 98–mid 05; gunnery training & trials ship Aug 06–Jul 14; Cameroon Oct 14–Jun 15; Red Sea/Indian Ocean Jan 16–1917; Far East May–Sep 17; Mediterranean Nov 17–1918; gunnery training & trials ship 1919–Jun 26.

D'Entrecasteaux
1ST CLASS ARMOURED CRUISER

Displacement:	8114 tons.
Dimensions:	383.8 (pp) 393.5 (wl) x 58.5 x 26 feet. 117 (pp) 120 (oa) x 17.9 x 7.5 metres.
Machinery:	Five cylindrical boilers; two shafts; reciprocating (VTE), IHP 13,500 = 19.5kt; coal 650/1000 tons; range 5000/2700nm @ 10/19kt.
Armament:	Two 9.4in/40, twelve 5.5in/30, twelve 47mm, six 37mm guns; six 18in torpedo tubes (removed 1911).
Protection:	Armour deck 0.8/2–1.2/3.2–0.8/2in; longitudinal bulkhead 1.6in; main turrets 9in; secondary shields 2.8in; casemates 2in; conning tower 9.8in.
Complement:	521.

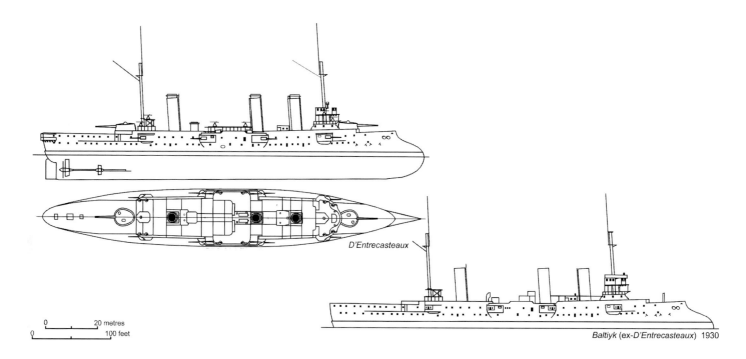

D'Entrecasteaux

Baltiyk (ex-D'Entrecasteaux) 1930

Name	Builder	Laid down	Launched	Completed	Fate
D'Entrecasteaux = Polish *Król Władysław IV* (30 Jul 27) – *Bałtyk* (Sep 27)	Forges et Chantiers de la Méditerranée (La Seyne)	Jun 94	12 Jun 96	15 Feb 99	Stricken 27 Oct 22; Belgian 25 May 23; Polish 30 July 27; German 19 Sep 39; BU Gdynia 1940–2.

Far East 1898–1900, 1901–3; Indian Ocean 1905–6; Far East 1906–9; Toulon reserve Jan 10–Jan 12; Mediterranean Training Squadron Jan 12–Nov 13; Toulon reserve Dec 13–Aug 14; Mediterranean Aug 14–1919; Brest reserve 2 Jul 19; condemned 1 Jun 21; depot/training ship under Belgian and Polish flags.

Châteaurenault

2ND CLASS CRUISER

Displacement:	8200 tons.
Dimensions:	443 (wl) 457 (oa) x 56 x 22.5 feet. 135 (wl) 140 (oa) x 18 x 7.5 metres.
Machinery:	Twenty-eight Normand-Sigaudy boilers; three shafts; reciprocating (VTE), IHP 24,000 = 23kt; coal 1460/2100 tons; range 7500nm @ 10kt.
Armament:	Two 6.5in/40, six 5.5in/45, twelve 47mm, three 37mm guns.
Protection:	Armour deck 2.4/3.9in; casemates 2.4in; shields 2.1in.
Complement:	18+569.

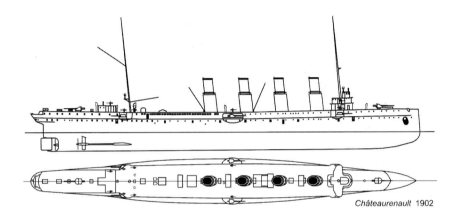

Châteaurenault 1902

Name	Builder	Laid down	Launched	Completed	Fate
Châteaurenault	Forges et Chantiers de la Méditerranée (La Seyne)	1895	12 May 98	10 Oct 02	Torpedoed German *UC38* off Cephalonia 14 Dec 17.

Far East Oct 02–1905; Cherbourg reserve Feb 06–Jan 10; Mediterranean Jan 10; seagoing training ship Jan 12–Nov 13; reserve Nov 13–Aug 14; Atlantic Aug 14–Apr 15; Mediterranean May 15–Feb 16; Atlantic Feb–Jun 16; troop transport Sep 16 to loss.

Guichen
1ST CLASS CRUISER

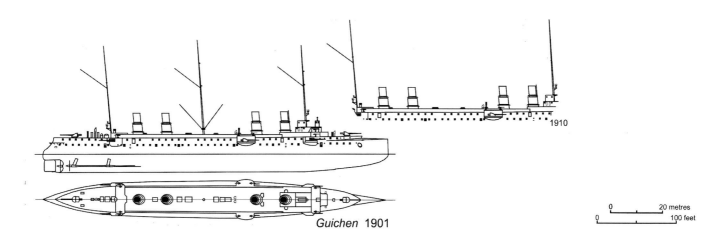

Displacement:	8300 tons.
Dimensions:	436 (pp) x 55 x 27 feet. 133 (pp) x 16.7 x 7.4 metres.
Machinery:	Thirty-six Lagrafel d'Allest boilers; three shafts; reciprocating (VTE), IHP 24,000 = 23kt; coal 1460/2000 tons; range 7500nm @ 10kt.
Armament:	Two 6.5in/40, six 5.5in/45, twelve 47mm guns; two 17.7in torpedo tubes.
Protection:	Armour deck 2.4/3.9in; casemates 2.4in; shields 2.1in; conning tower 6.3in.
Complement:	625.

Guichen 1901

Name	Builder	Laid down	Launched	Completed	Fate
Guichen	Ateliers et Chantiers de la Loire (Saint-Nazaire)	Oct 95	17 May 98	May 00	Stricken 29 Nov 21; condemned 1922 & sold at Brest.

Northern Squadron Mar 00–Jan 05; Far East Jan 05–Sep 06; Brest reserve 1906–10; Mediterranean 1910; seagoing training ship Apr 11–Jan 14; Brest reserve Jan–Aug 14; Atlantic Aug 14–May 15; Mediterranean Jun 15–Jan 17; East Africa Jan–Jul 17; troop transport Aug 17–Jul 19; reserve Jul 19.

Jeanne d'Arc
1ST CLASS ARMOURED CRUISER

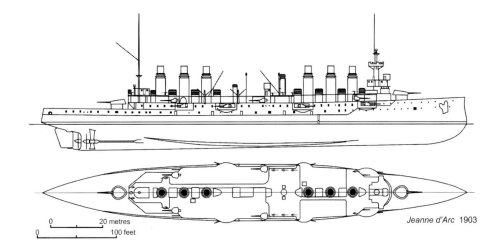

Displacement: 11,270 tons.

Dimensions: 477 (pp) x 63.7 x 26.7 feet.
145 (pp) x 19.4 x 8.1 metres.

Machinery: Thirty-six Guyot du Temple (1912: forty-eight Normand-Sigaudy) boilers; three shafts; reciprocating (VTE), IHP 20,500 = 23kt; coal 1400/2100 tons; range 13,500nm @ 10kt.

Armament: Two 7.6in/40, fourteen (1919: six) 5.5in/45, sixteen 47mm guns; two 17.7in torpedo tubes. Two 75mm AA added c. 1918.

Protection: Belt 3–5.9–3.9in; armour deck 1.8/2.2in; turrets 7.9in; barbettes 6.6in; casemates 5in; conning tower 5.9in.

Complement: 626.

Jeanne d'Arc 1903

Name	Builder	Laid down	Launched	Completed	Fate
Jeanne d'Arc (ii) = *Jeanne d'Arc II* (1929)	Toulon DY	24 Oct 96	8 Sep 99	19 May 03	Stricken 15 Feb 33; condemned 21 Mar 33; sold Bon Sacré (La Seyne) 9 Jul 34; BU Chantiers de démolition de La Seyne Aug 34

Northern Squadron Jun 03–Jul 06; Mediterranean (Light Squadron) Jul 06–1908; Northern Squadron (2nd Cruiser Division) 1908–9; reserve 1909–12; cadet training ship Mar 12–Jul 14; Northern Squadron (1st Cruiser Division/2nd Light Division) Aug 14–Apr 15; 3rd Squadron (Dardanelles) Apr 15–Jan 17; 4th Light Division Jan 17–1919; cadet training ship Dec 19–1928.

Gueydon class

1ST CLASS ARMOURED CRUISERS

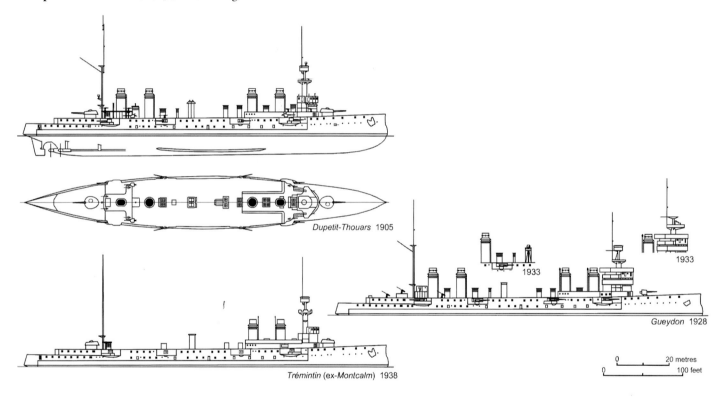

Displacement:	9517 tons.
Dimensions:	452.8 (wl) 460 (oa) x 63.6 x 24.5 feet. 138 (wl) 140.2 (oa) x 19.4 x 7.45m.
Machinery:	Twenty-eight Niclausse (*Gueydon*), Belleville (*Dupetit-Thouars*) or twenty Normand (*Montcalm*) boilers; three shafts; reciprocating (VTE), IHP 20,000 = 21kt; coal 1000/1600 tons; range 10,000nm @ 10kt.
Armament:	Two 7.6in/40, eight 5.5in/45, four 3.9in, sixteen 47mm M1885 guns; two 17.7in torpedo tubes. Two 75mm AA added c. 1918. *Gueydon* 1927: nine 5.5in/45, four 75mm AA, twelve 40mm, four 37mm guns.
Protection:	Belt 0–3.1–5.9–3.5in; armour deck 2/2.2in; turrets 6.9in; casemates 4.7in; conning tower 6.3in.
Complement:	26+565 (35+629 as flag).

Dupetit-Thouars 1905

Trémintin (ex-Montcalm) 1938

1933

1933

Gueydon 1928

0   20 metres

0   100 feet

Name	Builder	Laid down	Launched	Completed	Fate
Gueydon	Lorient DY	13 Aug 97	20 Sep 99	1 Sep 03	Stricken 24 Jul 35 & hulked; bombed RAF aircraft Brest-Laninon 27 Aug 44; salved 1 Apr 48 and BU.
Montcalm (ii) = *Tremintin* (1 Oct 34)	Forges et Chantiers de la Méditerranée (La Seyne)	27 Sep 98	27 Mar 00	20 Mar 02	Stricken 28 Oct 26 & hulked; foundered Brest 1941; BU to 1952.
Dupetit-Thouars	Toulon DY	17 Apr 99	5 Jul 01	28 Aug 05	Torpedoed German *U62* 400nm west of Brest 7 Aug 18.

Gueydon

Far East 1903–6; Northern Squadron Jan 07–Oct 09; Mediterranean 5 Oct 09–1910; reserve 1910; Light Squadron Reserve Division, Brest Oct 12–Jan 14; Oceanic Training Division 1914; 2nd Division, 2nd Light Squadron Aug 14–Apr 16, 4th Division 1 May 16–Jun 17; Brest reserve 15 Jun 17–Aug 18; Arctic 11 Aug 18–Nov 19; Baltic Nov 19–Mar 20; Atlantic Division 15 Mar 20–Nov 21; Flying

Squadron Nov 21–1 May 22; refit as gunnery training ship 1923–6; gunnery training ship 1926–33; training hulk for topmen 24 Jul 35; dummy *Prinz Eugen* 1941–2.

Montcalm
Far East 7 Feb 03–1906; Brest reserve 27 Dec 06–1909; Far East Jan 10–21 Apr 11; Brest reserve 25 Jun 11–Oct 12; Far East Jan 13–1915; Suez Canal Mar 15–Jan 16; Atlantic (4th Division) May 16–27 Apr 17; West Indies Squadron Jul–27 Nov 18; Baltic Dec 18–May 19; Atlantic Division May 19–1920; Far East 11 Mar 21–27 Jun 22; Brest reserve 16 Aug 22; annex to apprentice's school 1931; accommodation ship for petty officers' training establishment 25 Sep 34.

Dupetit-Thouars
Far East 1905–6; Northern Squadron 1 Jan 07–Oct 09; Mediterranean Oct 09–Jan 11; reserve 1911–14; 2nd Division, Light Squadron Aug 14–Apr 16, 4th Division 1 May 16–Jan 17; West Indies Division Jan 17–Aug 17; reserve Aug 17–Feb 18; West Indies Division Feb 18 to loss.

Kléber class
ARMOURED CRUISERS

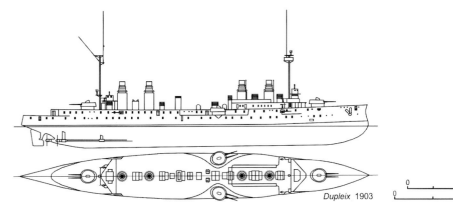

Dupleix 1903

Displacement:	7580 tons.
Dimensions:	426.8 (pp) x 433.3 (oa) x 58.3 x 24.3 feet. 130 (pp) 132.1 (oa) x 17.9 x 7.4 metres.
Machinery:	Twenty-four Niclausse or twenty Belleville (*Kléber*) boilers; three shafts; reciprocating (VTE), IHP 17,000 = 21kt; coal 880/1200 tons; range 6400nm @ 10kt.
Armament:	Eight 6.4in/45 (4 x 2), four 3.9in, ten 47mm, four 37mm guns; two 17.5in torpedo tubes. Two 75mm AA guns added c. 1918
Protection:	Belt 0–3.9–3.5in; armour deck 1.6–2.6in; turrets 3.9in; conning tower 5.9in.
Complement:	19+551 (24+584 as flag).

Name	Builder	Laid down	Launched	Completed	Fate
Kléber	Chantiers de la Geronde (Bordeaux)	Apr 98	20 Sep 02	4 Jul 04	Mined (*UC61*) off Molène 27 Jun 17.
Dupleix	Rochefort DY	18 Jan 99	28 Apr 00	15 Sep 04	Stricken 27 Sep 19; BU Brest(?) 1923.
Desaix	Penhoët (St Nazaire)	18 Jan 99	21 Mar 01	5 Apr 04	Condemned 30 Jun 21; sold to BU 1927.

Kléber
Mediterranean (Light Division) Jul 04–Nov 06; West Indies Nov 06–Oct 07; Moroccan Division Feb 08–Feb 09; Brest/Cherbourg reserve 1909–Mar 11; Far East May 11–Feb 13; Brest reserve Mar 13–Jul 14; 3rd Division, 2nd Light Squadron 1 Aug 14–Apr 15; Dardanelles Apr–Dec 15; 2nd Cruiser Division Jan–May 16; 6th Cruiser Division (Dakar) Jul 16 to loss.

Dupleix
Atlantic Division Sep 04; Brest reserve 1905–10; Far East 1 Nov 10–Dec 14; Dardanelles Division 1915–Jan 16; 6th Light Division (Dakar) Oct 16–Apr 19; Brest reserve Apr 1919; decommissioned 1 May 1919; parent ship Landévennec reserve 1920–2.

Desaix
Mediterranean (Light Division) Apr 04–Oct 05; Atlantic Division Oct 05–Nov 06; Mediterranean (Light Division) Oct 06–Jan 08; Northern Squadron (3rd Division) Jan–Sep 08; Cherbourg reserve 1908–Apr 13; Brest reserve Apr 13–Jul 14; 3rd Division, 2nd Light Squadron Aug–Dec 14; Dardanelles Division Jan 15; Indian Ocean/Suez 1915; Syrian Squadron 1915–May 16; 6th Cruiser Division (Dakar) May 16–Jul 18; West Indies Division Jul 18–1919; Far East 1919–Mar 21; decommissioned Mar 21.

Gloire class
1ST CLASS ARMOURED CRUISERS

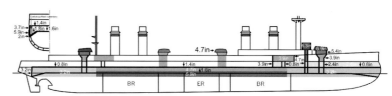

Displacement:	10,236 tons.
Dimensions:	452.8 (wl) 458.7 (oa) x 66.3 x 25.6 feet. 130 (wl) 140 (oa) x 20.3 x 7.7 metres.
Machinery:	Twenty-eight Belleville (*Amiral Aube* and *Marseillaise*) or Niclausse boilers; three shafts; reciprocating (VTE), IHP 20,500 = 21.4kt; coal 970/1590 tons; range 12,000nm @ 10kt.
Armament:	Two 7.6in/45, eight 6.5in/45, six 3.9in, eighteen 47mm guns; two 17.7in torpedo tubes. Two 75mm AA added c. 1918.
Protection:	Belt 0–3.1–5.9–3.5in; armour deck 1.6/1.8in; main turrets 6.9in; secondary turrets 4.7in; casemates 3.9in; barbettes 3.9in; conning tower 7.9in.
Complement:	612.

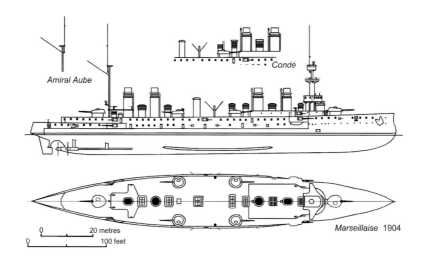

Name	Builder	Laid down	Launched	Completed	Fate
Amiral Aube	Penhoët (St Nazaire)	9 Aug 99	9 May 02	1 Apr 04	Condemned 7 Jul 22; sold to BU 1922.
Sully	Forges et Chantiers de la Méditerranée (La Seyne)	24 May 99	4 Jun 01	26 Jan 04	Stranded Along Bay 7 Feb 05; foundered 28 Sep 05; stricken 31 Oct 05; wreck sold at Tonkin 1906.
Gloire *Marseillaise* = *Marseillaise II* (Dec 33)	Lorient DY Brest DY	5 Sep 99 Jan 00	27 Jun 00 14 Jul 00	28 Apr 04 Oct 03	Condemned 7 Jul 22; BU 1923 Stricken 1929; condemned 13 Feb 32; BU Brégaillon (Toulon) Dec 33.
Condé	Lorient DY	20 Mar 01	12 Mar 02	12 Aug 04	Stricken 15 Feb 33 & hulked; beached Pointe de Suzac as aircraft target 1942; bombed Allied aircraft 1944; BU 1952.

Amiral Aube
Northern Squadron Apr 04–Apr 10; Mediterranean Apr 10–Apr 12; reserve Group Apr–Dec 12; Brest reserve Jan–Dec 13; Atlantic (1st Division, 2nd Light Squadron) Jan 14–May 16; Mediterranean (3rd Light Division) May–Dec 16; Atlantic Jan 17–May 18; West Indies Division May–Aug 18; Arctic Aug 18–1919; Atlantic Division 1919–20; decommissioned Mar 20.

Sully
Far East 29 Jan 04 to loss.

Gloire
Northern Squadron (1st/2nd Cruiser Division) Apr 04–Oct 09; 2nd/3rd Light Division, 2nd Mediterranean Squadron Oct 09–1914; reserve 1914; Oceanic Training Division 1914; Atlantic (2nd Division, Light Squadron) Aug 14–Apr 16; Mediterranean (3rd Light Division) 1 May 16–Jan 17; Atlantic Division Jan–May 17; West Indies Division 18 May 17–1918; Atlantic Naval Division 1918–Sep 20; Mediterranean (1st Light Division) 1920–2.

Marsellaise
Northern Squadron (1st Cruiser Division) Oct 03–Oct 04; Mediterranean (Light Squadron) Oct 04–1907; reserve Jul 07–Jan 08; Northern Squadron (2nd Cruiser Division) Jan 08–Oct 09; Mediterranean (2nd/3rd Light Division, 2nd Squadron) Oct 09–Dec 12; Atlantic (1st Division, 2nd Light Squadron) Jan 13–Apr 16; Mediterranean (3rd Light Division) 1 May 16–Jan 17; Atlantic Division Jan–Aug 17; West Indies Division Aug 17–Dec 1918; Baltic 18 Dec 18–Mar 20; Atlantic Naval Division Mar–Sep 20; reserve 1921; Mediterranean Training Division 1925–9.

Condé
Northern Squadron (1st Cruiser Division) Oct 04–Sep 05; Mediterranean (Light Squadron) Sep 05–1909; Mediterranean (2nd/3rd Light Division, 2nd Squadron) Oct 09–1911; West Indies 1911; Mediterranean (3rd Light Division, 2nd Squadron) Apr–Dec 12; Atlantic (1st Division, 2nd Light Squadron) Jan–Aug 13; West Indies Division 1 Aug 13–Jul 16; 3rd Light Division 1916–Jan 17; reserve Jan–Aug 17; 3rd Light Division 11 Aug 17–Mar 20; Brest reserve Mar 20–1928; marines' training ship Lorient 1928–33; training hulk Lorient 1933; German submarine depot ship 1940.

Léon Gambetta class

1ST CLASS ARMOURED CRUISERS

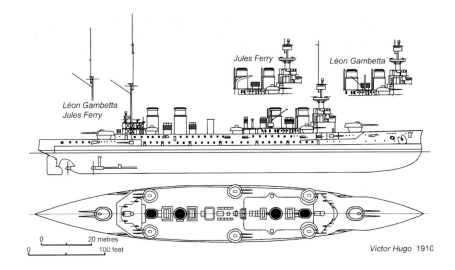

Displacement:	12,550 tons.
Dimensions:	476 (wl) 486.6 (oa) x 70.25 x 26.5 feet. 148 (pp) x 21.4 x 8.2 metres.
Machinery:	Twenty-eight Niclausse (*Léon Gambetta*), Belleville (*Victor Hugo*) or twenty-four Guyot du Temple (*Jules Ferry*) boilers; three shafts; reciprocating (VTE), IHP 27,500 = 22kt; coal 1320/2100 tons; range 12,000nm @ 10kt.
Armament:	Four 7.6in/45 (2 x 2), sixteen 6.5in/45 (6 x 2 + 4 x 1), two 65mm, twenty-two 47mm guns; four (later two) 17.7in torpedo tubes. Two 75mm AA added c. 1918.
Protection:	Belt 0–3.5–5.9–3.5in; armour deck 1.6/2.6in; main turrets 7.9in; secondary turrets & casemates 5.4in; barbettes 7.9in; conning tower 7.9in.
Complement:	26+708 (30+749 as flag).

Name	Builder	Laid down	Launched	Completed	Fate
Léon Gambetta	Brest DY	Jan 01	26 Oct 02	21 Jul 05	Torpedoed Austrian *U5* Adriatic 24 Apr 15.
Jules Ferry	Cherbourg DY	Oct 01	23 Aug 03	1 Jun 07	Stricken 19 Jan 27; sold to BU 1928.
Victor Hugo	Lorient DY	3 Jul 02	30 Mar 04	16 Apr 07	Condemned 20 Jan 28; sold to BU 26 Nov 30.

Léon Gambetta
Northern Squadron Aug 05–Aug 09; Mediterranean (1st Light Division, 1st Squadron) Oct 09–Apr 11; Mediterranean (2nd Division, 1st Light Squadron) 4 Apr 11–Oct 13; Mediterranean (2nd Light Division) Oct 13 to loss.

Jules Ferry
Mediterranean (Light Squadron) Jun 07–Oct 09; Mediterranean (1st Light Division, 1st Squadron) Oct 09–Apr 11; Mediterranean (2nd Division, 1st Light Squadron) 4 Apr 11–Oct 13; Mediterranean (2nd Light Division) Oct 13–12 Aug 17; 1st Light Division Aug 17–Jul 18; Bizerte reserve Jul 18–Oct 23; Far East Nov 23–Sep 25; Toulon reserve Oct 25–1926.

Victor Hugo
Mediterranean (Light Squadron) Jun 07–Oct 09; Mediterranean (1st Light Division, 1st Squadron) Oct 09–Apr 11; Mediterranean (2nd Division, 1st Light Squadron) Apr 11–Oct 13; Mediterranean (2nd Light Division) Oct 13–Aug 17; 1st Light Division Aug 17–1918; reserve 1918–1922; Far East Oct 22–Jul 23; Toulon reserve 11 Aug 23.

Jules Michelet
1ST CLASS ARMOURED CRUISER

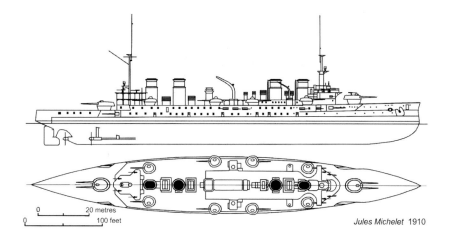

Displacement:	12,600 tons.
Dimensions:	485 (wl) 493 (oa) x 70 x 27 feet. 148 (wl) 150.25 (oa) x 21.4 x 8.2 metres.
Machinery:	Twenty-eight Guyot du Temple boilers; three shafts; reciprocating (VTE), IHP 29,000 = 23kt; coal 1400/2300 tons; range 12,000nm @ 10kt.
Armament:	Four 7.6in/45 (2 x 2), twelve 6.5in/45 (4 x 2 + 4 x 1), twenty-two 47mm M1902 guns; four 17.7in torpedo tubes. Two 75mm AA added c. 1918. 1923: two aircraft.
Protection:	Belt 0–3.5–5.9–3.5in; armour deck 1.8/2.6in; main turrets 7.9in; secondary turrets 6.5in; casemates 4.5in; barbettes 7.2in; conning tower 7.9in.
Complement:	770.

Jules Michelet 1910

Name	Builder	Laid down	Launched	Completed	Fate
Jules Michelet	Lorient DY	Jun 04	31 Aug 05	Jan 09	Stricken 3 May 36; gunfire heavy cruiser *Tourville* and torpedoed submarine *Thétis* off Toulon 8 May 37.

Mediterranean (1st/2nd Light Division) Jan 09–Dec 11; Mediterranean Training Division Jan 12–Apr 14; 1st Light Division 1914–15; 2nd Light Division 1915–Mar 20; Toulon reserve Jul 20–1921; Atlantic Flying Squadron Nov 21; Far East Oct 22–Jul 23; Far East Jul 25–May 29; decommissioned 1929; condemned 1931 and artificers' training ship Toulon.

Ernest Renan

1ST CLASS ARMOURED CRUISER

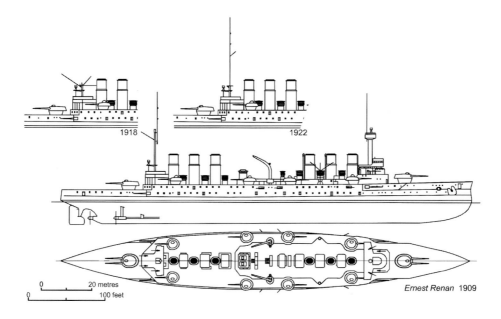

Displacement:	13,644 tons.
Dimensions:	515 (wl) x 70.3 x 27 feet. 157 (wl) x 21.36 x 8.2 metres.
Machinery:	Forty Niclausse boilers; three shafts; reciprocating (VTE), IHP 37,000 = 23kt; coal 1350/2300 tons; range 10,000nm @ 10kt.
Armament:	Four 6.7in/50 (2 x 2), twelve 6.5in/45 (4 x 2 + 4 x 1), sixteen 65mm, eight 47mm guns; two 17.7in torpedo tubes.
Protection:	Belt 0–3.3–5.9–4in; armour deck 1.8/2.6in; main turrets 7.9in; secondary turrets & casemates 5.2in; conning tower 7.9in.
Complement:	750.

Ernest Renan 1909

Name	Builder	Laid down	Launched	Completed	Fate
Ernest Renan	Penhoët (St Nazaire)	Oct 03	9 Mar 06	1 Feb 09	Stricken 3 May 36; BU 1937.

2nd Light Division Oct 09–Jan 10; 1st Light Division Jan 10–1919; Light Division, E. Mediterranean Squadron 1919–Jul 21; Levant Division Jul 21–1924; reduced commission Toulon Jun 24; gunnery training ship 1927–31; target 1931.

Waldeck-Rousseau class

1ST CLASS ARMOURED CRUISERS

Displacement:	14,000 tons.
Dimensions:	515 (wl) 527.5 (oa) x 70.5 x 27 feet. 157 (wl) 159 (oa) x 21.36 x 8.4 metres.
Machinery:	Forty Niclausse boilers; three shafts; reciprocating (VTE), IHP 37,000 = 23kt; coal 1242/2300 tons; range 10,000nm @ 10kt.

Armament:	Fourteen 7.6in/50 (2 x 2 + 10 x 1), eighteen 65mm (later also two 75mm AA, four 47mm) guns; two 17.7in torpedo tubes. *Waldeck Rousseau* late 1920s: fourteen 7.6in/50, eight 75mm, two 75mm AA guns; two 17.7in torpedo tubes. *Edgar Quinet* 1929: ten 7.6in/50 (2 x 2 + 6 x 1), four 75mm, two 75mm AA guns; two 17.7in torpedo tubes.
Protection:	Belt 0–3.3–5.9–2.8in; armour deck 2.5/2.6in; turrets 7.9in; casemates 7.6in; conning tower 7.9in.
Complement:	23+818 (34+890 as flag).

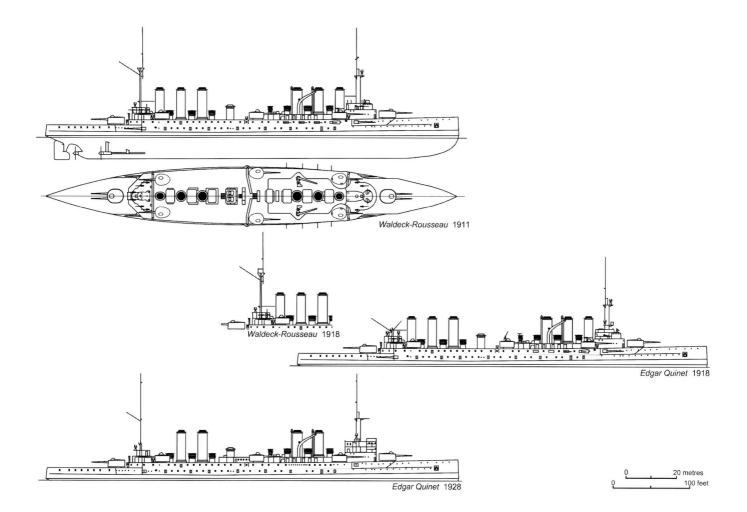

Waldeck-Rousseau 1911

Waldeck-Rousseau 1918

Edgar Quinet 1918

Edgar Quinet 1928

Name	Builder	Laid down	Launched	Completed	Fate
Waldeck-Rousseau	Lorient DY	31 Jul 05	4 Mar 08	15 Aug 11	Stricken 14 Jun 36; foundered Brest 9 Aug 40; BU 1941–4.
Edgar Quinet	Brest DY	Aug 04	21 Sep 07	15 Dec 10	Wrecked off Cape Blanc 4 Jan 30.

Waldeck-Rousseau
1st Light Division Aug 11–1919; 2nd Division Mar 1919–21; Light Division, E. Mediterranean Squadron/Levant Division Aug 21–Sep 23; Toulon reserve 1924–Apr 29; Far East Jun 29–May 32; Brest reserve 1932–6.

Edgar Quinet
1st Light Division Apr 11–1919; Bizerte reserve 1 Jul 19–Jun 20; Light Division, E. Mediterranean Squadron/Levant Division Jul 21–Sep 23; Mediterranean Squadron 1 Oct 23–1924; reduced commission Toulon Jun 24–Jan 27; cadet training ship 12 Oct 1928 to loss.

14 | GERMANY

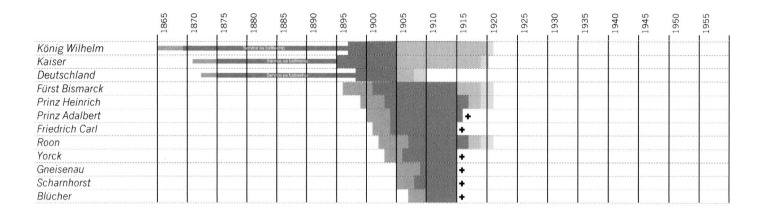

König Wilhelm

II. CLASS ARMOURED SHIP
(EX-ARMOURED FRIGATE EX-ARMOURED SHIP);
25 JAN 97: I. CLASS CRUISER; 1899: LARGE CRUISER

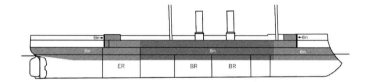

Displacement:	9600 tons.
Dimensions:	356.3 (wl) 368.1 (oa) x 60 x 28 feet. 108.6 (wl), 112.2 (oa) x 18.3 x 8.6 metres.
Machinery:	Eight rectangular boilers; one shaft; reciprocating (HSE), IHP 8000 = 14kt; coal 1013 tons; range 2240nm @ 10kt.
Armament:	Twenty-two 9.4in/20, one 5.9in/30, eighteen 3.5in/30 guns, six 37mm MG; five 13.8in torpedo tubes.
Protection:	Main belt 6–8–6in; battery 8in; fore and aft casemates 6in; conning tower 1.2–4in (wrought iron).
Complement:	38+1102.

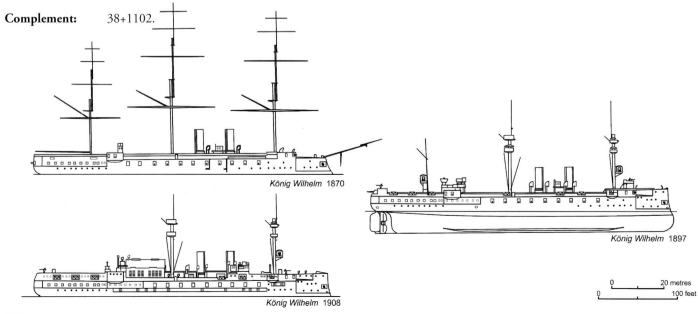

König Wilhelm 1870

König Wilhelm 1897

König Wilhelm 1908

0 ___ 20 metres
0 ___ 100 feet

Name	Builder	Laid down	Launched	Commissioned	Recommissioned as cruiser	Fate
König Wilhelm (ex-*Wilhelm I*, ex-*Fatikh* [i])	Thames Iron Works (Blackwall)	1865	25 Apr 68	20 Feb 69	16 Apr 96	Stricken 4 Jan 21; BU F Oltmann, Rönnebeck, 1921.

Active service 16 Apr 96–30 Sep 97; harbour service 3 Apr 04; accommodation and training hulk Kiel Oct 07–Oct 09; Flensburg-Mürwick Oct 09–Nov 19 (paid off at Kiel).

Kaiser (i) class

II. CLASS ARMOURED SHIPS (EX-ARMOURED FRIGATES,
EX-ARMOURED SHIPS); 1897: I. CLASS CRUISERS; 1899: LARGE CRUISERS

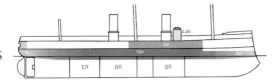

Displacement:	7770 tons.
Dimensions:	290.4 (wl) 293.1 (oa) x 62.7 x 23.5 feet. 88.5 (wl) 89.34 (oa) x 19.1 x 7.15 metres.
Machinery:	Eight rectangular boilers; one shaft; reciprocating (HSE), IHP 5700 = 14kt; coal 680/880 tons; range 2470/3300nm @ 10kt.
Armament:	*Kaiser*: eight 10.2in/20, one 5.9in/30, six 4.1in/35, nine 3.5in/30 guns, twelve 37mm MG; five 13.8in torpedo tubes. *Deutschland*: eight 10.2in/20, eight 5.9in/35, eight 3.5in/30, twelve 37mm MG; five 13.8in torpedo tubes.
Protection:	Main belt 5–10–5in; armour deck 1.5–2in; battery 7–8–7in; conning tower 2.2in (steel).
Complement:	36+620 (47+677 as flag).

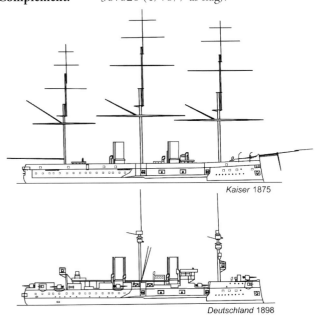

Kaiser 1875

Deutschland 1898

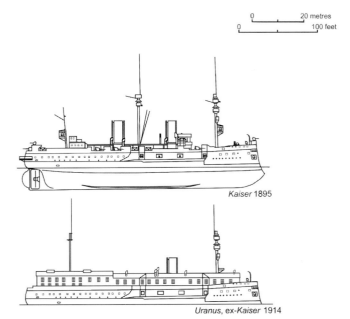

0 ——— 20 metres
0 ——— 100 feet

Kaiser 1895

Uranus, ex-Kaiser 1914

Name	Builder	Laid down	Launched	Commissioned	Recommissioned as cruiser	Fate
Kaiser (i) = *Uranus* (12 Oct 05)	Samuda (Poplar)	1871	15 Sep 71	13 Feb 75	27 Apr 95	Stricken 21 May 06 & hulked; BU Securitas Werke, Harburg 1920
Deutschland (i) = *Jupiter* (22 Nov 04)	Samuda (Poplar) Samuda	1872	12 Sep 74	20 Jul 75	2 Dec 97	Stricken 21 Jun 06; target ship 1907; sold Neugebauer & Co. (Lemwerder) 1908; BU Hamburg-Moorburg 1909.

Kaiser

Far East Cruiser Squadron Apr 95–Oct 99; harbour service 3 May 04; accommodation hulk for torpedo school Flensburg-Mürwick 1906–Nov 18.

Deutschland

Far East Cruiser Squadron Dec 97–Mar 00; harbour service 3 May 04.

Fürst Bismarck

I. CLASS CRUISER; 1899: LARGE CRUISER

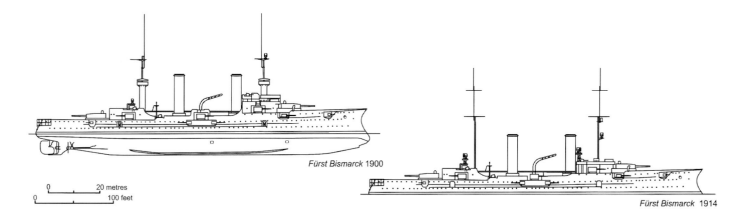

Displacement:	10,690t (design), 11,461t (full load).
Dimensions:	412.4 (wl), 416.7 (oa) x 67 x 27.5 feet. 125.7 (wl), 127.0 (oa) x 20.4 x 8.5 metres.
Machinery:	Four Schulz-Thornycroft and eight cylindrical boilers; three shafts; reciprocating (VTE), IHP 13,500 = 18.7kt; coal 900/1400 tons; oil 120 tons during 1908–9; range 4560nm @ 10kt.
Armament:	Four 9.4in/40 (2 x 2), twelve 5.9in/40, ten 3.5in/30 guns; six 17.7in torpedo tubes. Disarmed Sep 16.
Protection:	Main belt 3.9–7.9–3.9in; armour deck 1.2–2in; barbettes 7.9in; turrets 1.6–7.9in; secondary turrets 2.8–3.9in; casemates 3.9in; fore conning tower 7.9in; aft conning tower 3.9in.
Complement:	36+585 (50+647 as flag).

Fürst Bismarck 1900

0   20 metres
0   100 feet

Fürst Bismarck 1914

Name	Builder	Laid down	Launched	Completed	Fate
Fürst Bismarck	Kiel DYd	1 Apr 96	25 Sep 97	1 Apr 00	Stricken 17 Jun 19; sold Schleswig-Holstein Wirtschaftgemeinschaft 1919; re-sold Brand & Sohn, Audorf; BU Audorf-Rendsburg 1919–20.

Far East Cruiser Squadron 30 Jun 00–26 Jun 09; rebuilt Kiel DYd. 1910–29 Nov 14; Torpedo Research Command as target ship Feb 15–Mar 15; I. Marine Inspectorate as engineering training ship Mar 15–31 Dec 18; office-ship for Baltic Parent Ship Unit Jan 19–27 May 19.

Prinz Heinrich
LARGE CRUISER

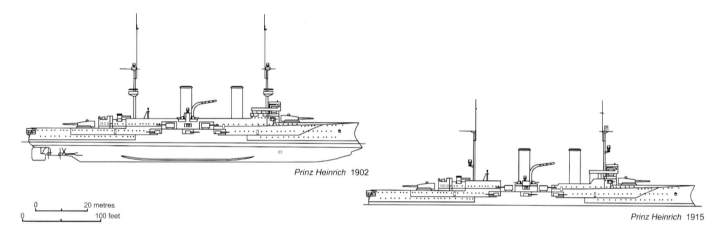

Displacement:	8930 tons.
Dimensions:	409.6 (wl) 415 (oa) x 64.4 x 26.3 feet. 124.9 (wl) 126.5 (oa) x 19.6 x 8 metres.
Machinery:	Fourteen Dürr boilers; three shafts; reciprocating (VTE), IHP 13,500 = 20kt; coal 900/1590 tons; oil 175 tons during 1908–9; range 4580nm @ 10kt.
Armament:	Two 9.4in/40, ten 5.9in/40, ten 3.5in/30 guns; four 17.7in torpedo tubes. Disarmed 1916.
Protection:	Main belt 3.1–3.9–3.1in; armour deck 1.4–1.6/2in; barbettes 3.9in; turrets 1.6–5.9in; secondary turrets 2.8–3.9in; battery 3.9in; fore conning tower 5.9mm; aft conning tower 0.5in.
Complement:	35+532 (44+676 as flag).

Prinz Heinrich 1902

```
0        20 metres
0              100 feet
```

Prinz Heinrich 1915

Name	Builder	Laid down	Launched	Completed	Fate
Prinz Heinrich	Kiel DYd.	01 Dec 98	23 Mar 00	11 Mar 02	Stricken 25 Jan 20; BU Brandt & Sohn, Audorf-Rendsburg 1920.

Scouting Unit Jul 02–Apr 06; Ship Artillery Inspectorate as gunnery training ship May 08–Oct 12; rebuilt Kiel 1914; III. SG Apr 14–Nov 15; Readiness Division, Kiel Nov 15–Mar 16; tender, accommodation and office ship for High Command Baltic Forces 1916–18; tender for submarine-cruisers 1918.

Prinz Adalbert class
LARGE CRUISERS

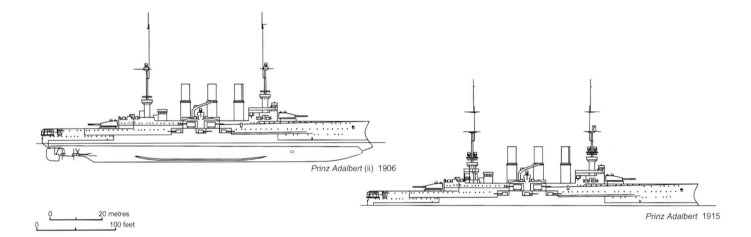

Displacement:	9050 tons.
Dimensions:	409.8 (wl) 415 (oa) x 64.3 x 25.6 feet.
	124.9 (wl) 126.5 (oa) x 19.6 x 7.80 metres.
Machinery:	Fourteen Dürr boilers; three shafts; reciprocating (VTE), IHP 16,200 (*Prinz Adalbert*)/17,000 (*Friedrich Carl*) = 20/20.5kt; coal 750/1630 tons; oil 200 tons during 1908–9; range 5000nm @ 12kt.
Armament:	Four 8.2in/40 (2 x 2), ten 5.9in/40, twelve 3.5in/35 guns; four 17.7in torpedo tubes.
Protection:	Main belt 0–3.1–3.9–3.1in; armour deck 3.1–1.6–3.1/3.1–2–3.1in; barbettes 3.9in; turrets 3.1–5.9in; secondary turrets 2.6–3.9in; battery 3.9in; fore conning tower 5.9in; aft conning tower 0.8in.
Complement:	35+551 (44+595 as flag).

Prinz Adalbert (ii) 1906

Prinz Adalbert 1915

0   20 metres
0   100 feet

Name	Builder	Laid down	Launched	Completed	Fate
Prinz Adalbert (iii)	Kiel DYd.	5 Jun 00	22 Jun 01	12 Jan 04	Torpedoed HMS/M *E8* W of Libau 23 Oct 15.
Friedrich Carl (ii)	Blohm & Voss (Hamburg)	18 Aug 01 .	21 Jun 02	12 Dec 03	Mined SW of Memel 17 Nov 14

Prinz Adalbert
Gunnery trials ship May 04–Sep 11; gunnery training ship Nov 12–Aug 14; IV./III. SG Aug 14 to loss.

Friedrich Carl
Scouting Unit Mar 04–Mar 08; torpedo trials ship Mar 09–Aug 14; III. SG Aug 14 to loss.

Roon class

LARGE CRUISERS

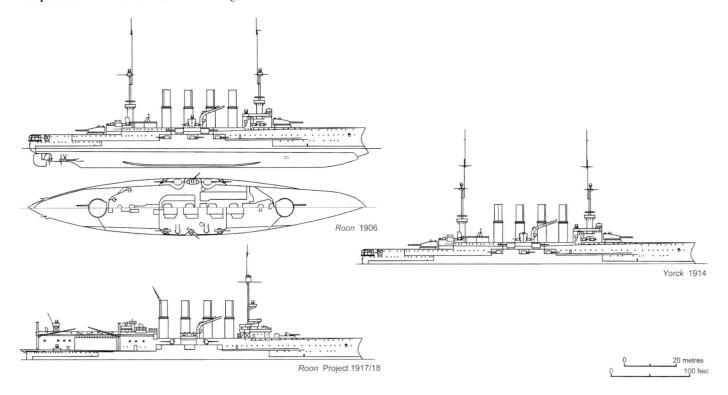

Displacement:	9585 tons.
Dimensions:	417.7 (wl) 422.6 (oa) x 66.3 x 25.5 feet. 127.3 (wl) 127.8 (oa) x 20.2 x 7.76 metres.
Machinery:	Sixteen Dürr boilers; three shafts; reciprocating (VTE), IHP 19,000 = 21kt; coal 750/1570 tons; oil 207 tons during 1908/9; range 4200nm @ 12kt.
Armament:	Four 8.2in/40 (2 x 2), ten 5.9in/40, fourteen 3.5in/35 guns; four 17.7in torpedo tubes. Disarmed 1916.
Protection:	Main belt 0–3.1–3.9–3.1in; armour deck 1.6–2.4/1.6–2in; barbettes 3.9in; turrets 3.1–5.9in; secondary turrets 2.8–3.9in; battery 3.9in; fore conning tower 5.9in; aft conning tower 3.1in.
Complement:	35+598 (48+660 as flag).

Roon 1906

Yorck 1914

Roon Project 1917/18

0   20 metres
0   100 feet

Name	Builder	Laid down	Launched	Completed	Fate
Roon	Kiel DYd.	1 Aug 02	27 Jun 03	5 Apr 06	Stricken 25 Nov 20; BU Kiel-Nordmole 1921.
Yorck	Blohm & Voss (Hamburg)	25 Apr 03	14 May 04	21 Nov 05	Mined Jade Estuary 4 Nov 14.

Roon
Scouting Unit Jul 06–Sep 11; IV. SG Aug 14; III. SG Aug 14–Feb 16; guard and accommodation ship Kiel to Oct 16; Torpedo Inspectorate as trials and training ship Nov 16–Dec 18, Kiel.

Yorck
Scouting Unit Mar 06–May 13; IV. SG Aug 14; III. SG Aug 14 to loss.

Scharnhorst class
LARGE CRUISERS

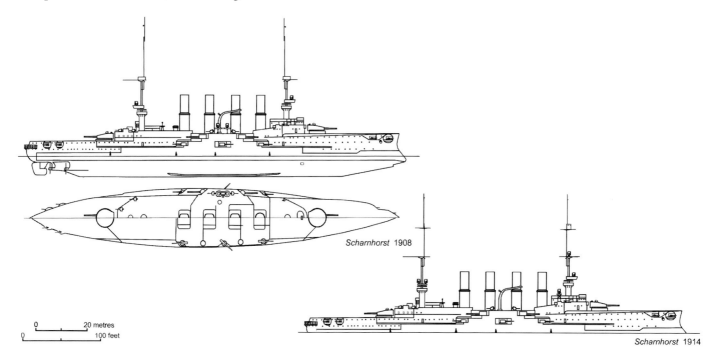

Displacement:	11,435 tons.	

Dimensions: 471.8 (wl) 474.4 (oa) x 70.9 x 27.5 feet.
143.8 (wl) 144.6 (oa) x 21.6 x 8.4 metres.

Machinery: Eighteen Navy boilers; three shafts; reciprocating (VTE), IHP 26,000 = 22.5kt; coal 800/2000 tons; range 5120nm @ 12kt.

Armament: Eight 8.2in/40 (2 x 2, 4 x 1), six 5.9in/40, eighteen 3.5in/35 guns; four 17.7in torpedo tubes.

Protection: Main belt 0–3.1–5.9–3.1mm; armour deck 2.4–1.4/1.6–2.2in; barbettes 5.4in; turrets 1.2–6.7in; secondary turrets 2.8–3.9in; battery 5.9in; fore conning tower 7.9in; aft conning tower 2in.

Complement: 38+726 (52+784 as flag).

Scharnhorst 1908

Scharnhorst 1914

Name	Builder	Laid down	Launched	Completed	Fate
Scharnhorst	Blohm & Voss (Hamburg)	3 Jan 05	23 Mar 06	24 Oct 07	Gunfire UK *Invincible* and *Inflexible* off Falklands 8 Dec 14.
Gneisenau (ii)	AG Weser (Bremen)	28 Dec 04	14 Jun 06	6 Mar 08	Gunfire UK *Invincible* and *Inflexible* off Falklands 8 Dec 14.

Scharnhorst
Scouting Unit (flag) 1 May 08–30 Mar 09; East Asiatic Squadron (flag) 1 Apr 09 to loss.

Gneisenau
Scouting Unit 12 Jul 08–9 Nov 10; East Asiatic Squadron 11 Nov 10 to loss.

Blücher

LARGE CRUISER

Displacement:	15,600 tons.
Dimensions:	528.5 (wl) 530.8 (oa) x 80 x 29 feet. 161.1 (wl) 161.8 (oa) x 24.5 x 8.84 metres.
Machinery:	Eighteen Navy boilers; three shafts; reciprocating (VTE), IHP 32,000 = 24.5kt; coal 900/2510 tons; range 6600nm @ 12kt.
Armament:	Twelve 8.2in/45 (6 x 2), eight 5.9in/45, sixteen 3.5in/45 guns; four 17.7in torpedo tubes.
Protection:	Main belt 0–3.1–7–3.1in; armour deck 2–2.8mm; torpedo bulkhead 1.4in; turrets 3.1/7in; battery 5.4in; fore conning tower 10in; aft conning tower 5.4in.
Complement:	41+812 (55+874 as flag).

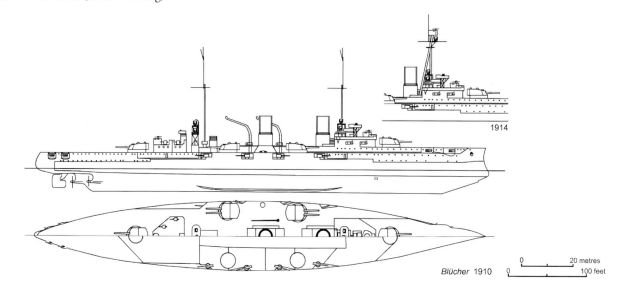

Blücher 1910

Name	Builder	Laid down	Launched	Completed	Fate
Blücher (ii)	Kiel DYd	21 Feb 07	11 Apr 08	01 Oct 09	Gunfire and torpedoes UK battlecruisers, light cruisers and destroyers, Battle of Dogger Bank, 24 Jan 15.

Scouting Unit (flag) Apr 10–Sep 11; gunnery training/trials ship Sep 11– Aug 14 (flag II. SG for manoeuvres Sep 12); I. SG Aug 14 to loss.

15 | GREECE

	1865	1870	1875	1880	1885	1890	1895	1900	1905	1910	1915	1920	1925	1930	1935	1940	1945	1950	1955
Georgios Averof																			

Georgios Averof
ARMOURED CRUISER

Displacement:	9832 tons.
Dimensions:	426 (pp) 461 (oa) x 69 x 24.3 feet. 130 (pp) 140.5 (oa) x 21.1 x 7.4 metres.
Machinery:	Twenty-two Belleville boilers; two shafts; reciprocating (VTE), IHP 19,000 = 22.5kt; coal 600/1560 tons; range 7125nm/2489 @ 10/17kt.
Armament:	Four 9.2in/45 (2 x 2), eight 7.5in/45 (4 x 2), sixteen (1927: eight) 3in/40, four 3pdr (1927: replaced by four 3in AA and six 37mm AA) guns; three 18in torpedo tubes (removed 1927).
Protection:	Belt 3.5–8–3.5in; main turrets 6.5in; main barbettes 8in; secondary turrets 7.1in; main barbettes 8in; armour deck 1.6in; conning tower 7.1in.
Complement:	550.

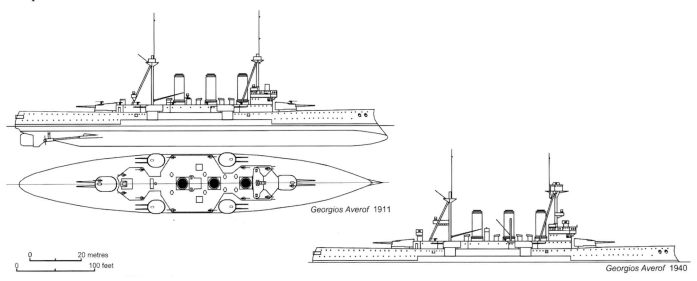

Georgios Averof 1911

Georgios Averof 1940

Name	Builder	Laid down	Launched	Completed	Fate
Georgios Averof	Orlando (Leghorn)	1907	12 Mar 10	16 May 11	Museum Athens 1985.

Egypt 23 Apr 41; Indian Ocean Aug 41–1942; Egypt 1942–4; Fleet HQ Oct 44–1952; laid up Poros 1957–83.

16 | ITALY

	1865	1870	1875	1880	1885	1890	1895	1900	1905	1910	1915	1920	1925	1930	1935	1940	1945	1950	1955
Marco Polo																			
Carlo Alberto																			
Vettor Pisani																			
Giuseppe Garibaldi (i)							Argentina = Garibaldi												
Giuseppe Garibaldi (ii)							Spain = Cristóbal Colón												
Varese (i)							Argentina = San Martin												
Giuseppe Garibaldi (iii)							Argentina = Pueyrredón												
Varese (ii)							Argentina = General Belgrano												
Giuseppe Garibaldi (iv)											✚								
Varese (iii)																			
Francisco Ferruccio																			
Amalfi											✚								
Pisa																			
San Giorgio																✚			
San Marco																	✚		

Marco Polo

3RD CLASS SHIP OF BATTLE; 1918: 1ST CLASS AUXILIARY

Displacement:	4510 tons.
Dimensions:	327 (pp) 347 (oa) x 48.2 x 21.5 feet. 99.7 (pp) 106 (oa) x 14.7 x 6 metres.
Machinery:	Four cylindrical boilers; two shafts; reciprocating (VTE), IHP 10,000 = 17kt; coal 620 tons; range 5800nm @ 10kt.
Armament:	Six 6in/40, ten (1910: four) 4.7in/40, two (1910: one), 75mm, (1910: six) nine 57mm, (1910: two) four 37mm guns; five (1910: four) 17.7in torpedo tubes. 1917: two 3in.
Protection:	Belt 0–3.9–0in (removed 1917); armour deck 0.9–2–0.9in; shields 2.2in; conning tower 2.2in.
Complement:	22+372.

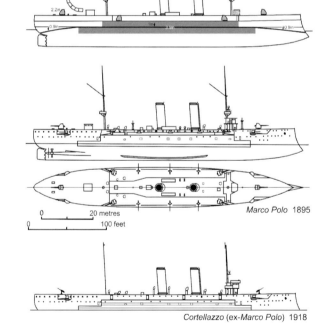

Marco Polo 1895

Cortellazzo (ex-Marco Polo) 1918

Name	Builder	Laid down	Launched	Completed	Fate
Marco Polo = *Cortelazzo* (4 Apr 18) = *Europa* (1 Oct 20) = *Volta* (16 Jan 21)	Castellamare di Stabia DYd7	Jan 90	27 Oct 92	21 Jul 94	Stricken 5 Jan 22 and BU.

Flying Division 1896–7; Far East Feb 98–Aug 99, Oct 01–Feb 03, Mar 04–Jan 07; Mediterranean/Adriatic 1907–13; Far East Mar 13–Dec 14; submarine depot ship Oct 15–May 17; refitted as troopship, Venice, 1917–18; troopship from Apr 18; paid off 5 Jan 21.

Vettor Pisani class
2ND CLASS SHIPS OF BATTLE; 1918:
1ST CLASS AUXILIARY SHIP (*ZENSON* [EX-*CARLO ALBERTO*])

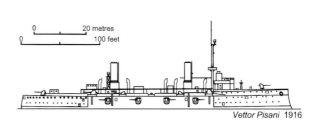

Displacement:	6720 tons (*Pisani*), 6,832 tons (*Alberto*).
Dimensions:	324.8 (pp) 346.8 (oa) x 59 x 23 feet. 99 (pp) 105.7 (oa) x 18 x 7 metres.
Machinery:	Eight cylindrical boilers; twos shaft; reciprocating (VTE), IHP 13,000 = 19kt; coal 600/1000t, oil 120t; range 6000nm @ 10kt.
Armament:	Twelve 6in/40, six 4.7in/40, two 75mm, ten 57mm, ten 37mm guns; four 17.7in torpedo tubes. *Carlo Alberto* disarmed 1917.
Protection:	Belt 4.3–5.9–4.3in; battery 5.9in; shields 2in; armour deck 1.5in; conning tower 5.9in.
Complement:	28+476 (*Pisani*), 27+403 (*Alberto*).

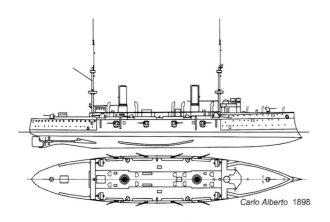

Carlo Alberto 1898

Vettor Pisani 1916

Name	Builder	Laid down	Launched	Completed	Fate
Vettor Pisani	Castellamare di Stabia DYd	7 Dec 92	18 Aug 95	1 Apr 98	Stricken 2 Jan 20; sold 13 Mar 20 to BU.
Carlo Alberto = *Zenson* (4 Apr 18)	La Spezia DYd	Jan 93	23 Sep 96	1 May 98	Stricken 12 Jun 20 & BU.

Vettor Pisani
Far East, 1900–1, Apr 03–Jun 04; Mediterranean/Adriatic 1905–16; headquarters ship 1 Nov 16–27 Nov 18; Adriatic Nov 18–Aug 19; paid off 11 Sep 19.

Carlo Alberto
South America Jun 98–Feb 99; Far East 1899–Jan 00; royal yacht Jun–Sep 02; North America Oct 02; Venezuela Dec 02–Feb 03; Mediterranean 1903–06; gunnery/torpedo training ship 1907–10; Mediterranean/Adriatic 1911–17; MTB support ship 1 Oct 16–1917; refitted as troopship Venice & Taranto 1917–18; troopship 1918–20; paid off Apr 20.

Giuseppe Garibaldi class

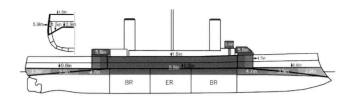

Displacement: 6730–6790 (*Garibaldi* [i], [ii] & [iii], *Varese* [i] & [ii]), 7280 (last three) tons.

Dimensions: 328.1 (pp) 363.7 (oa) (last three: 344 [pp] 366.7 [oa]) x 59.75 x 23.3 feet.
100 (pp) 107.8 (oa) (last three: 104.9 [pp] 111.8 [oa]) x 18.2 x 7.1 metres.

Machinery: Eight cylindrical (*Garibaldi* [ii], [iv], *Ferrucio,* twenty-four Niclausse; *Giuseppe Garibaldi* [iii] sixteen Belleville; *Varese* [iii], twenty-four Belleville) boilers; two shafts; reciprocating (VTE), IHP 13,500 = 20kt; coal 400/1000–1150 tons (first five), 650/1200 tons (last three); range 4400–6000nm @ 10kt

Armament: Two (last three: one) 10in/45, four (*Varese* [i] only, last three: two 8in/45 (2/1 x 2), ten (last four: fourteen) 6in/45, six 4.7in/44 (first three only), ten (last three: six) 47mm guns.

Protection: Belt 2.8–3.5–4.7–5.9–4.7–3.5–2.8in; battery 5.9in; turrets 5.9in; armour deck 0.9/1.5in; conning tower 5.9in.

Complement: 25+530 (last three).

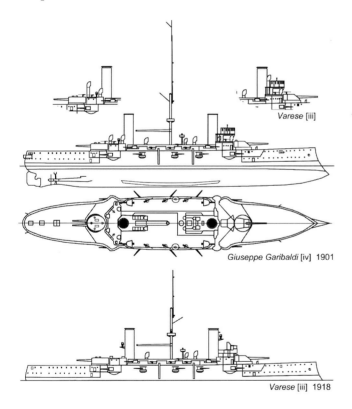

Varese [iii]

Giuseppe Garibaldi [iv] 1901

Varese [iii] 1918

0   20 metres
0   100 feet

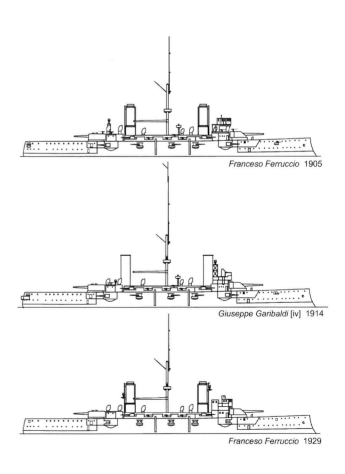

Franceso Ferruccio 1905

Giuseppe Garibaldi [iv] 1914

Franceso Ferruccio 1929

Name	Builder	Laid down	Launched	Completed	Fate
Giuseppe Garibaldi (i) = Argentine Garibaldi (Jul 95)	Ansaldo (Genoa-Sestri Ponente)	25 July 93	27 May 95	–	Sold Argentina 14 Jul 95.
Varese (i) = Argentine San Martin (Oct 96)	Orlando (Leghorn)	1895	25 May 96	–	Sold Argentina 26 Oct 96
Giuseppe Garibaldi (ii) = Spanish Cristóbal Colón (Aug 96)	Ansaldo (Genoa-Sestri Ponente)	1895	[16 Sep 96]	–	Sold to Spain 14 Aug 96.
Giuseppe Garibaldi (iii) = Argentine Pueyrredón (1897)	Ansaldo (Genoa-Sestri Ponente)	Aug 96	25 Sep 97	–	Sold Argentina 1897.
Varese (ii) = Argentine General Belgrano (1897)	Orlando (Leghorn)	Jun 96	25 Jul 97	–	Sold to Argentina 1897.
Giuseppe Garibaldi (iv)	Ansaldo (Genoa-Sestri Ponente)	21 Sep 98	26 Jun 99	1 Jan 01	Torpedoed Austrian submarine U4 off Cavtat 18 Jul 15.
Varese (iii)	Orlando (Leghorn)	15 Sep 98	6 Aug 99	5 Apr 01	Stricken 4 Jan 23
Francesco Ferruccio	Venice DYd	18 Sep 99	23 Apr 02	1 Sep 05	Stricken 1 Apr 30; expended at La Spezia as target August/September 1936. Giuseppe Garibaldi (iv) Mediterranean/Adriatic 1902 to loss.

Varese (iii)
Mediterranean/Adriatic 1902–18; cadet training ship 1920–2.

Francesco Ferruccio
Mediterranean/Adriatic 1905–18; Libya 1919–23; cadet training ship 4 Jan 23.

Projected ships
1st class ships of battle

Displacement: 8000 tons

Dimensions: 400 x 63 x 22 feet.
122 x 16 x 6.7 metres.

Machinery: . . . boilers; two shafts; reciprocating (VTE), IHP 15–19,000 = 22/23kt; coal 600/2100 tons; range 15,000nm @ 10kt.

Armament: Twelve 8in/45 (6 x 2), twelve 3in/40, twelve 47mm guns; four 17.7in torpedo tubes.

Protection: Belt 5.9in; turrets 5.9in; armour deck 1.6in; conning tower 5.9in.

Complement: . . .

Name	Builder	Laid down	Launched	Completed	Fate
Genova	First two to be built at	–	–	–	Cancelled 1901.
Venezia	La Spezia & Castellmare DYds	–	–	–	Cancelled 1901.
Pisa (i)	DYds	–	–	–	Cancelled 1901.
Amalfi (i)		–	–	–	Cancelled 1901.

Pisa class

1ST CLASS SHIPS OF BATTLE; 1 JUL 21:
COAST-DEFENCE SHIP (2ND CLASS SHIP OF BATTLE)

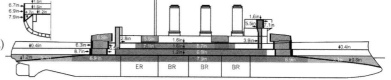

Displacement:	9676 tons.
Dimensions:	426 (pp) 460 (oa) x 68.9 x 23 feet. 130 (pp) 140.5 (oa) x 21 x 7 metres.
Machinery:	Twenty-two Belleville boilers; two shafts; reciprocating (VTE), IHP 20,000 = 23kt; coal 670/1560 tons; range 2500/1400nm @ 12/21kt.
Armament:	Four 10in/45 (2 x 2), eight 7.5in/45 (4 x 2), sixteen (1918: fourteen) 3in/45, eight 47mm/50 (replaced by six 3in/45 AA 1918) guns; three 17.7in torpedo tubes.
Protection:	Belt 3.1–6.9–7.9–9.9–3.1in; main turrets 6.3in; secondary turrets 5.5in armour deck 2in; conning tower 7in.
Complement:	32+655.

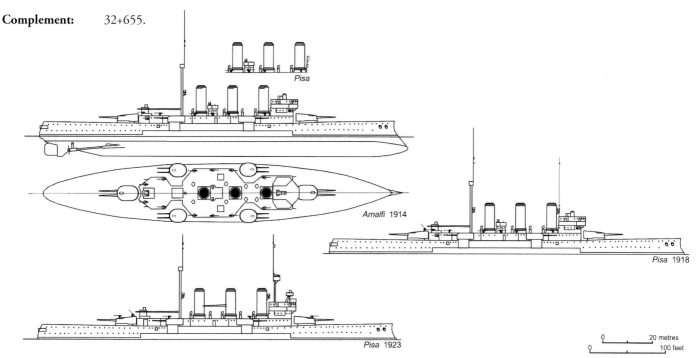

Name	Builder	Laid down	Launched	Completed	Fate
Pisa (ii)	Orlando (Leghorn)	20 Feb 05	15 Sep 07	1 Sep 09	Stricken 28 Apr 37 & BU.
Amalfi (ii)	Odero (Sestri Ponente)	24 Jul 05	5 May 08	1 Sep 09	Torpedoed Austrian *U26* N Adriatic 7 Jul 15.

Pisa
Training ship 1921–30.

San Giorgio class

1ST CLASS SHIPS OF BATTLE; 1 JUL 21:
2ND CLASS SHIPS OF BATTLE; *SAN GIORGIO* 1938:
COAST-DEFENCE SHIP; *SAN MARCO*, 1931: TARGET SHIP

Displacement:	0,167 (*San Giorgio*)/10,720 (*San Marco*) tons; *San Giorgio* 1938: 9470 tons; *San Marco* 1935: 8600 tons.
Dimensions:	430 (pp) 451.5 (wl) 462.3 (oa) x 68.9 x 24 (*San Marco* 25.6) feet. 131 (pp) 137.6 (wl) 140.9 (oa) x 21 x 7.3 (7.8) metres.

Machinery: *San Giorgio*: fourteen (1938: eight) Blechynden boilers; two shafts; reciprocating (VTE), IHP 18,000 = 22.5/16kt; coal 700/1500 tons (1938: oil 1,300 tons); range 3100/6270nm @ 12/10kt (4237/2368nm @ 12/17kt).
San Marco: fourteen Babcock & Wilcox (1935: four Thornycroft) boilers; four shafts; Parsons turbines, SHP 20,000 (13,000) = 23/18kt; coal 700/1400 tons; range 3100/4800nm @ 12/10kt.

Armament: Four 10in/45 (2 x 2), eight 7.5in/45 (4 x 2), eighteen (1918: ten) 3in/40, two 47mm/50 (six 3in/40 AA added 1918) guns; three 17.7in torpedo tubes. *San Giorgio* 1938: four 10in/45 (2 x 2), eight 7.5in/45 (4 x 2), eight (1940: ten) 3.9in/47 AA (4 x 2), four (1940: ten) 13.2mm AA (six 37mm/54 AA, twelve 20mm/65 AA added 1940) guns. *San Marco* 1935: disarmed.

Protection: Belt 2.4–3.5–7.1–7.9–7.1–3.5–2.4in; armour deck 1.2/1.8in; barbettes 6.3–7.1in; turrets 7.9in (main) 7.1in (secondary); CTs 10in.

Complement: 699 (*San Giorgio*), 703 (*San Marco*).

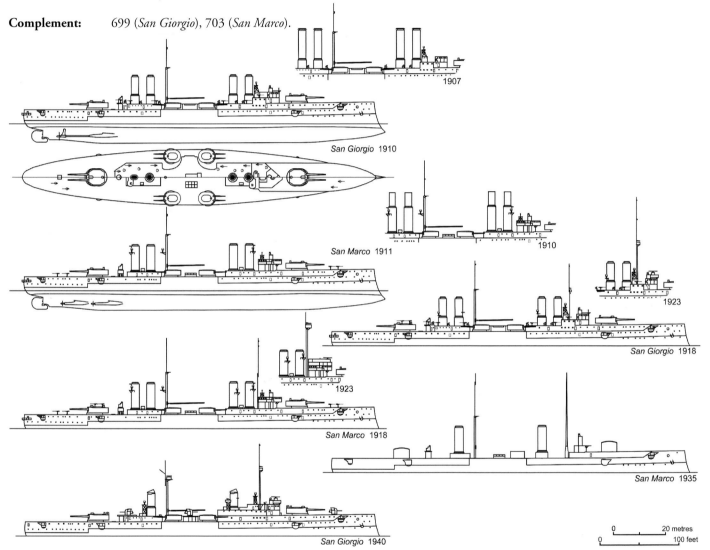

1907

San Giorgio 1910

San Marco 1911

1910

1923

San Giorgio 1918

1923

San Marco 1918

San Marco 1935

San Giorgio 1940

0   20 metres
0   100 feet

Name	Builder	Laid down	Launched	Completed	Fate
San Giorgio		4 Jul 05	27 Jul 08	1 Jul 10	Scuttled Tobruk 22 Jan 41; salved 1952; foundered E of Malta 1952.
San Marco		2 Jan 07	20 Dec 08	7 Feb 11	Target ship 1935; scuttled La Spexia 1945; BU (stricken 27 Feb 47).

San Giorgio
Special Naval Division Jun 24; Red Sea Naval Division Nov 25–Apr 26; seagoing training ship Sep 28–Dec 36; Training Ships Group Jun 38–1939; Tobruk May 40 to loss.

San Marco
Special Naval Division Jun 24; seagoing training ship 1924–Sep 29.

17 | JAPAN

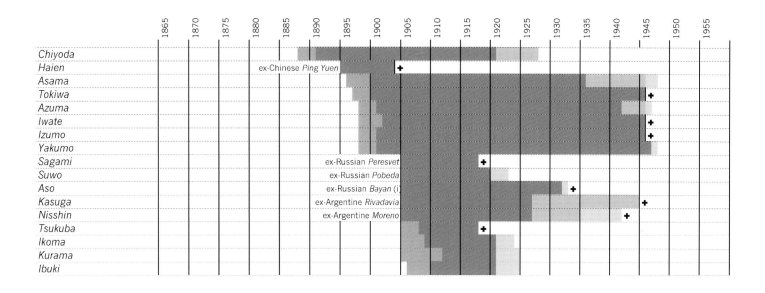

	1865	1870	1875	1880	1885	1890	1895	1900	1905	1910	1915	1920	1925	1930	1935	1940	1945	1950	1955
Chiyoda																			
Haien							ex-Chinese *Ping Yuen*		✚										
Asama																	✚		
Tokiwa																	✚		
Azuma																			
Iwate																	✚		
Izumo																	✚		
Yakumo																			
Sagami							ex-Russian *Peresvet*			✚									
Suwo							ex-Russian *Pobeda*												
Aso							ex-Russian *Bayan* (i)								✚				
Kasuga							ex-Argentine *Rivadavia*										✚		
Nisshin							ex-Argentine *Moreno*									✚			
Tsukuba										✚									
Ikoma																			
Kurama																			
Ibuki																			

Chiyoda

FIRST CLASS VESSEL; 21 MAR 98: 3RD CLASS CRUISER;
28 AUG 12: 2ND CLASS COAST-DEFENCE SHIP; MAR 1920:
SUBMARINE DEPOT SHIP; 1921: SUBMARINE TENDER;
1922: SUBMARINE DEPOT SHIP; 1 DEC 24: TRAINING VESSEL

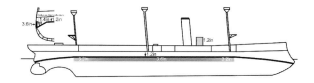

Displacement:	2439 tons.
Dimensions:	310 (wl) 302 (pp) x 42 x 14 feet. 94.5 (wl) 92 (pp) x 13 x 4.3 metres.
Machinery:	Six locomotive (1898: Belleville) boilers; two shafts; reciprocating (VTE), IHP 5600 = 19kt; coal 330/427 tons; range 8000nm @ 10kt.
Armament:	Ten 4.7in/40, fourteen (later six) 47mm guns, three 25mm Gatling (later eleven 37mm) MG; three 14.2in torpedo tubes.
Protection:	Belt 0–3.2–3.6–3.2–0in; armour deck 1.2/1.4in; conning tower 1.2in.
Complement:	350.

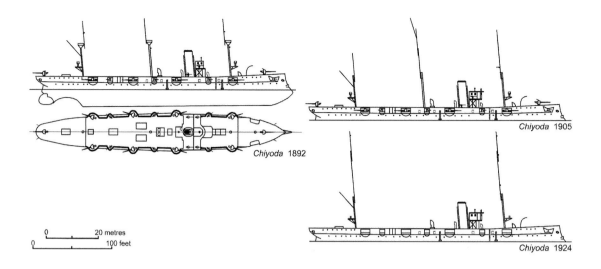

Chiyoda 1892

Chiyoda 1905

Chiyoda 1924

0   20 metres
0   100 feet

Name	Builder	Laid down	Launched	Completed	Fate
Chiyoda	J & G Thompson (Clydebank)	4 Dec 88	3 Jun 90	1 Jan 91	Hulked 1927; expended as target, gunfire cruiser *Furutaka*, Bungo Strait 5 Aug 27.

Ping Yuen-go

21 MAR 98: 1ST CLASS GUNBOAT

See Chinese *Lung Wei*, except:

Armament: One 10.2in, two 6in, eight 3pdr guns; four 18in torpedo tubes.

Name	Acquired	Commissioned	Fate
Ping Yuen-go (ex- *Ping Yuen*)	Feb 95	16 Mar 95	Mined Piegen Bay 18 Sep 04.= *Heien* (1900)

Asama class

1ST CLASS CRUISER; 1921: 1ST CLASS COAST-DEFENCE S
TOKIWA 1922: MINELAYER; *ASAMA* 1930: COAST-DEFENCE
SHIP; *TOKIWA* 1931: COAST-DEFENCE SHIP; *ASAMA* 1942:
TRAINING SHIP

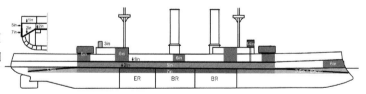

Displacement: 9670 tons.

Dimensions: 408 (pp) 442 (oa) x 67 x 24.4 feet.
124.36 (pp) x 134.72 (oa) x 20.5 x 7.42 metres.

Machinery: Twelve cylindrical (*Tokiwa* 1910: sixteen Belleville; *Asama* 1917: sixteen Miraybara; *Tokiwa* 1938: eight Kampon) boilers; two shafts; reciprocating (VTE), IHP 13,000 (*Tokiwa* 1938: 8000) = 20kt (1938: 16kt); coal 600/1200 tons; range 10,000nm @ 10kt.

Armament: Four 8in/45 (2 x 2), fourteen 6in/40, twelve 12pdr, eight 47mm guns; five 18in torpedo tubes.
Tokiwa 1924: two 8in/45 (1 x 2), eight 6in/40, two 12pdr, one 3in/40 AA guns; 200–300 mines.
Tokiwa 1943: four 6in/40, one 3in AA, two 40mm AA, thirty/thirty-five 25mm AA (10 x 2 + 10/15 x 1) guns; 200–300 mines.

Protection: Belt 0–3.5–5–7–5–3.5in; armour deck 2in; casemates 6in; turrets 6in; conning tower 14in (Harvey-Nickel).

Complement: 661.

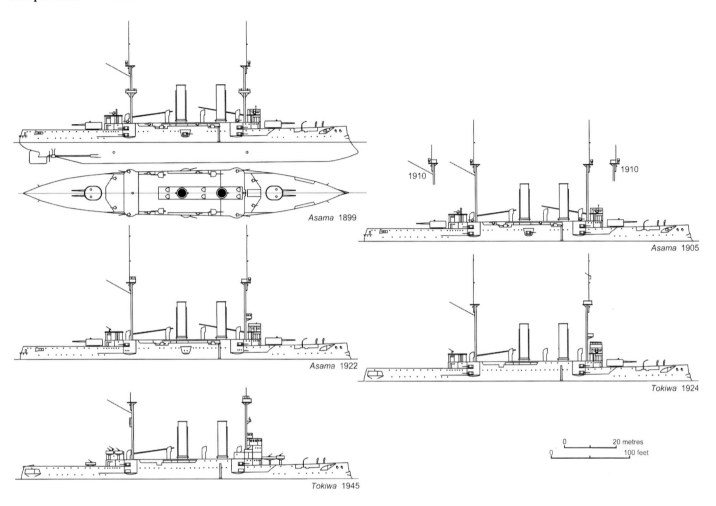

Asama 1899

Asama 1905

Asama 1922

Tokiwa 1924

Asama 1945

Name	Builder	Laid down	Launched	Completed	Fate
Asama	Armstrong (Elswick)	20 Oct 96	22 Mar 98	18 Mar 99	Hulked 1935; stricken 30 Nov 45; BU Hitachi (Innoshima) 15 Aug 46–25 Mar 47.
Tokiwa	Armstrong (Elswick)	6 Jan 97	6 Jul 98	18 May 99	Bombed off Ominato 9 Aug 45 and beached; stricken 30 Nov 45; salved 5 Apr 47; BU Hakodate Oct 47.

Asama
Europe Aug 02–May 03; cadet training cruise (with *Kasagi*) 16 Oct 10–6 Mar 11, (with *Azuma*) 20 Apr–11 Aug 14; E. Pacific Oct 14–Dec 15; cadet training cruise (with *Iwate*) 2 Mar–6 Jul 18, 21 Aug 20–2 Apr 21, (with *Iwate* & *Izumo*) 26 Jun 22–8 Feb 23, (with *Iwate* & *Yakumo*) 7 Nov 23–5 Apr 24, (with *Izumo* & *Yakumo*) 10 Nov 24–4 Apr 25, 30 Jun 26–17 Jan 27, (with *Iwate*) 30 Jun–26 Dec 1927, 1 Jul–27 Dec 29, 1 Mar–14 Jul 32, 15 Feb–26 Jul 34, (with *Yakumo*) 20 Feb–22 Jul 35; hulked as midshipmen's training ship Kure 5 Jul 38; gunnery training/accomodation hulk Matsure Shima 2 Aug 42.

Tokiwa
Second Fleet, 4th Squadron 17 Aug–31 Oct 14; First Fleet 9 Nov 14; cadet training cruise (with *Yakumo*) 5 Apr–17 Aug 17, (with *Azuma*) 1 Mar–26 Jul 19, 24 Nov 19–20 May 20; rebuilt as minelayer, Sasebo 30 Sep 22–Mar 24; reserve 1927; North China Jan 32–17 May 33; reserve 1933–9; Fourth Fleet, 18th Squadron, 15 Nov 39; 19th Mine Division 15 Nov 40; 52nd Base Force, Ominato Naval District 1 May 43; Seventh Fleet, 18th Escort Squadron, 20 Jan 44; Seventh Fleet 5 Apr 45; General Escort Command 10 Apr 45.

Izumo class

1ST CLASS CRUISER; 1921: 1ST CLASS COAST-DEFENCE SHIP;
1931: COAST-DEFENCE SHIP; 1942: 1ST CLASS CRUISER; 1943:
TRAINING SHIP

Displacement:	9600 tons.
Dimensions:	400 (pp) 434 (oa) x 68.5 x 23.75 feet.
	121.9 (pp) 132.2 (oa) x 20.9 x 7.24 metres.
Machinery:	Twenty-four Belleville (*Iwate* 1931: six Yarrow; *Izumo* 1934: six Kampon) boilers; two shafts; reciprocating (VTE), IHP 14,500 (1931/34: 7000) = 20.75kt (1931/34: 16kt); coal 600/1551 tons; 5500nm @ 10kt (*Iwate* 1931/*Izumo* 1934: coal 1412/1405 tons+ oil 324/324 tons).
Armament:	Four 8in/45 (2 x 2), fourteen 6in/40, twelve 12pdr, eight 2½pdr guns; four 18in torpedo tubes.
	1924: four 8in/45 (2 x 2), fourteen 6in/40, eight 3in/40, one 3in AA guns.
	1930s: four 8in/45 (2 x 2), eight (later four) 6in/40, four 3in/40, one 3in AA guns.
	Izumo Apr 44: four 6in/40, four 5in AA (2 x 2), one 3in AA, fourteen 25mm AA (2 x 3, 2 x 2, 4 x 1), two 13mm AA guns.
	Iwate Apr 45: four 6in/40, four 5in AA (2 x 2), three 3in AA, nine 25mm AA (1 x 3, 2 x 2, 2 x 1), two 13mm AA guns.
Protection:	Belt 3.5–7–3.5in; armour deck 2.5in; barbettes, turrets & casemates 6in; conning tower 14in (Krupp).
Complement:	682.

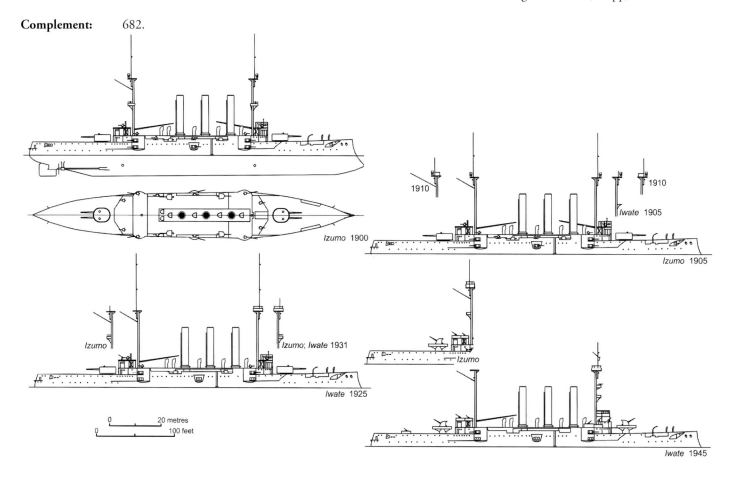

Name	Builder	Laid down	Launched	Completed	Fate
Izumo	Armstrong (Elswick)	14 May 98	19 Sep 99	25 Sep 00	Bombed near Kure 24 Jul 45; salved and BU 1947.
Iwate	Armstrong (Elswick)	11 Nov 98	29 Mar 00	18 Mar 01	Bombed near Kure 24 Jul 45; salved and BU 1946.

Izumo

N. America 20 Sep–Dec 07; Mediterranean Jun 17–May 19; Training Squadron flag Aug 21; cadet training cruise (with *Yakumo*) 20 Aug 21–4 Apr 22, (with *Iwate* & *Asama*) 26 Jun 22–17 Feb 23; (with *Asama* & *Yakumo*) 10 Nov 24–4 Apr 25, (with *Yakumo*) 30 Jun 26–17 Jan 27, 23 Apr–3 Oct 28, 5 Mar–15 Aug 31; Third Fleet, China Area Fleet (flag) 2 Feb 32–1943; Kure Training Squadron 20 Feb 44.

Iwate

Mediterranean and Indian Ocean 25 Jan 15–1916; cadet training cruise (with *Azuma*) 20 Apr–22 Aug 1916, (with *Asama*) 2 Mar–6 Jul 18, 21 Aug 20–2 Apr 21, (with *Izumo* & *Asama*) 26 Jun 22–8 Feb 23, (with *Asama* & *Yakumo*) 7 Nov 23–5 Apr 24, (alone) 10 Nov 25–6 Apr 26, (with *Asama*) 30 Jun–26 Dec 27, 1 Jul–27 Dec 29, 1 Mar–14 Jul 32, (with *Yakumo*) 6 Mar–26 Jul 33, (with *Asama*) 15 Feb–26 Jul 34, (with *Yakumo*) 9 Jun 36–20 Nov 36, 7 Jun–19 Oct 37, 6 Apr–29 Jun 38, 16 Nov 38–30 Jan 39, 4 Oct–20 Nov 39; Third Support Fleet, 12th Squadron 1 Feb 40.

Yakumo

1ST CLASS CRUISER; 1921: 1ST CLASS COAST-DEFENCE SHIP;
1930: COAST-DEFENCE SHIP; 1942: 1ST CLASS CRUISER

Displacement:	9850 tons.
Dimensions:	415.4 (pp) 434 (oa) x 64.3 x 23.7 feet. 124.6 (pp) 132.3 (oa) x 19.6 x 7.2 metres.
Machinery:	Twenty-four Belleville (1927: six Yarrow) boilers; two shafts; reciprocating (VTE), IHP 15,500 (1927: 7000) = 20.5kt (1927: 16kt); coal 550/1300 tons; range 7000nm @ 10kt.
Armament:	Four 8in/45 (2 x 2), twelve 6in/40, twelve 12pdr/40, eight 47mm guns; five 18in torpedo tubes. 1924: four 8in/45 (2 x 2), twelve 6in/40, eight 12pdr/40, one 3in AA guns; two 18in torpedo tubes. 1933: four 8in/45 (2 x 2), eight 6in/40, four 12pdr/40, one 3in AA guns. Feb 1945: four 6in/40, four 5in (2 x 2) AA, one 3in AA, twelve 25mm (2 x 3, 2 x 2, 2 x 1) AA guns.
Protection:	Main belt 88–178–88mm; armour deck 63mm; barbettes 6in; turrets 6in; secondary turrets 70–150mm; casemates 6in; conning tower 254mm.
Complement:	648.

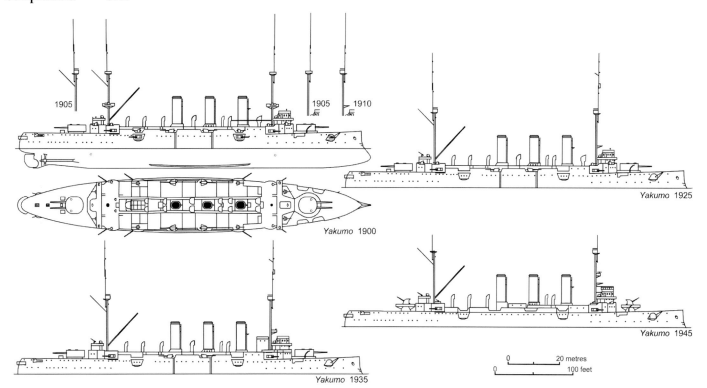

Yakumo 1900

Yakumo 1925

Yakumo 1935

Yakumo 1945

Name	Builder	Laid down	Launched	Completed	Fate
Yakumo	AG Vulcan (Stettin)	1 Sep 98	8 Jul 99	20 Jun 00	Arrived Maizuru 20 Jul 46 for BU by Hitachi Shipbuilding & Engineering to 1 Apr 47.

Cadet training cruise (with *Tokiwa*) 5 Apr–17 Aug 17, (with *Izumo*) 20 Aug 21–4 Apr 22, (with *Asama* & *Iwate*) 27 Nov 23–5 Apr 24, (with *Asama* & *Izumo*) 10 Nov 24–4 Apr 25, 30 Jun 26–17 Jan 27, (with *Izumo*) 23 Apr 28–3 Oct 28, 18 Nov 30–30 Dec 30, 5 Mar 31–16 Aug 31, (with *Iwate*) 6 Mar–26 Jul 33, (with *Asama*) 20 Feb–22 Jul 35, (with *Iwate*) 9 Jun 36–20 Nov 1936, 7 Jun–Oct 37, 6 Apr–Jun 38, 16 Nov 38–30 Jan 39, 4 Oct–20 Nov 39; First Fleet, 5 Sep 43; Kure stricken 1 Oct 45; Allied Repatriation Service 1 Dec 45–19 Jun 46; to Home Ministry 15 Jul 46.

Azuma

1ST CLASS CRUISER; 1921: 1ST CLASS COAST-DEFENCE SHIP

Displacement:	9278 (normal) 9953 (full load) tons.
Dimensions:	431.6 (pp) 452.4 (oa) x 58 x 23.6 feet. 131.56 (pp) 137.9 (oa) x 17.7 x 7.2 metres.
Machinery:	Twenty-four Belleville boilers; two shafts; reciprocating (VTE), IHP 17,000 = 20kt; coal 550/1200 tons; range 7000nm @ 10kt.
Armament:	Four 8in/40 (2 x 2), twelve (1930: eight) 6in/40, twelve (1924: eight; 1930: four) 12pdr/40, twelve (1924: removed) 47mm guns; five (1930: two) 18in torpedo tubes. One 3in AA gun added by 1924.
Protection:	Main belt 3.5–7–3.5in; barbettes, turrets & casemates 6in; armour deck 2.5in; conning tower 14in.
Complement:	670–726.

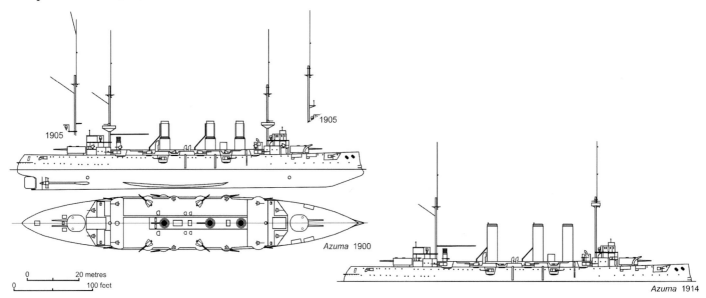

Name	Builder	Laid down	Launched	Completed	Fate
Azuma	Chantiers de la Loire (St Nazaire)	1 Feb 98	24 Jun 99	28 Jul 00	Stricken 1941 & hulked; BU 1946.

Cadet training cruises (with *Soya*) 5 Dec 12–21 Apr 13, (with *Asama*) 20 Apr–11 Aug 14, (with *Iwate*) 20 Apr–22 Aug 16, (with *Tokiwa*) 1 Mar–26 Jul 19, 28 Nov 19–20 May 20; TS Maizuru Naval Corps 7 Sep 21; harbour TS Engineering School, Maizuru, 1 Oct 27.

Garibaldi class

1ST CLASS CRUISER; 1921: 1ST CLASS COAST-DEFENCE
SHIP; 1942: TRAINING SHIP

Displacement:	7500 tons.
Dimensions:	344 (pp) 366 (wl) x 61.3 x 24 feet. 104.9 (pp) 111.7 (wl) x 18.7 x 7.3 metres.
Machinery:	Eight cylindrical (1914: twelve Kampon) boilers; two shafts; reciprocating (VTE), IHP 14,800 = 20kt; coal 500/1190 tons; range 5500nm @ 10kt.
Armament:	One 10in/45 (*Kasuga* only), two (*Nisshin*: four) 8in/45 (1/2 x 2), fourteen (*Kasuga* 1927: four) 6in/45, ten (1924: eight; *Kasuga* 1927: four) 3in/40, six (*Nisshin*: four, removed 1914) 47mm guns; four 18in torpedo tubes. One 3in/40 AA gun added c.1918.
Protection:	Belt 2.8–3.5–4.7–5.9–4.7–3.5–2.8in; battery 5.9in; turrets 5.9in; armour deck 0.9/1.5in; conning tower 5.9in.
Complement:	560.

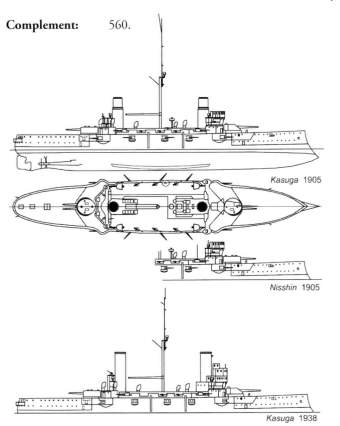

Kasuga 1905

Nisshin 1905

Kasuga 1938

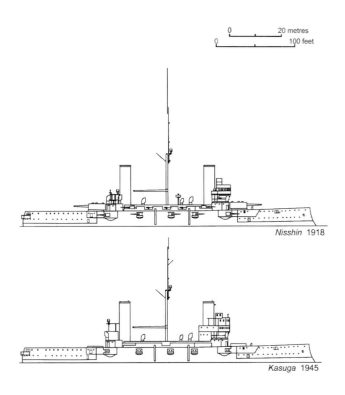

Nisshin 1918

Kasuga 1945

Name	Laid down	Launched	Completed	Fate
Kasuga (ex-*Bernardino Rivadavia*) 1948.	[10 Mar 02]	[22 Oct 02]	7 Jan 04	Hulked 1942; bombed Yokosuka 18 Jul 45; BU Uraga
Nisshin (ex-*Mariano Moreno*) = *Hai-kan No 6* (1935).	[29 Mar 02]	[9 Feb 03]	7 Jan 04	Hulked 1927; stricken 1 Apr 35; expended as target off Kure 1936; salved; expended as target off Kurahashi, Hiroshima, 18 Jan 42; BU.

Kasuga
Seamanship training ship 1927; hulked as accommodation ship Yokosuka Jul 42.

Nisshin
Pacific patrols 1914–15; Destroyer Squadron 1 (flag) 13 Dec 15–13 May 16, 12 Sep–1 Dec 16; Destroyer Squadron 2 (flag) 28 Mar–13 Apr 17; Indian Ocean 1917; Mediterranean 1918–19; hulked Yokosuka 1927.

Ex-Russian *Peresvet* class

As p. 231, except as follows:

Machinery: Thirty Mayabara boilers; three shafts; reciprocating (VTE), IHP 14,500 = 18kt; coal 1,060/2060 tons; range 6200nm @ 10kt.

Armament: Four 10in/45, ten 6in/45, eighteen (*Sagami*)/sixteen (*Suwo*) 3in/40 guns; two 18in torpedo tubes.

Name	Captured	Commissioned	Fate
Sagami (ex-*Peresvet*)	5 Jan 05	Apr 08	Sold Russia 1916 (p 231)
Suwo (ex-*Pobeda*)	5 Jan 05	Oct 08	Stricken 1 Apr 22; capsized while de-armouring Kure 13 Jul 22; BU Mitsugo Shima (Kure) to 25 Sep 22; completed BU after 1945.

Ex-Russian *Bayan* class

1ST CLASS CRUISER; 1 APR 20: MINELAYER

As pp 231–4, except as follows:

Displacement: 7726 tons.

Machinery: Twenty-four Miyabara boilers.

Armament: Two (1913: two 6in/50) 8in/45, eight 6in/40, sixteen 12pdr guns; two 15in torpedo tubes (removed 1913). 1917: 420 mines added.

Complement: 570.

Name	Captured	Commissioned	Fate
Aso (ex-*Bayan* [i]) = *Hai Kan No. 4* (1 Apr 31)	5 Jan 05	1908	Stricken 1 Apr 31; sunk as target gunfire *Myoko* and *Nachi* and submarine torpedoes 8 Aug 32.

Aso
Cadet training cruises (with *Soya*) 14 Mar–7 Aug 09, 25 Nov 11–12 Mar 12, 20 Apr–23 Aug 15; converted to minelayer 1917.

Tsukuba class

1ST CLASS CRUISERS; 1912: BATTLECRUISERS;
1921: 1ST CLASS CRUISER

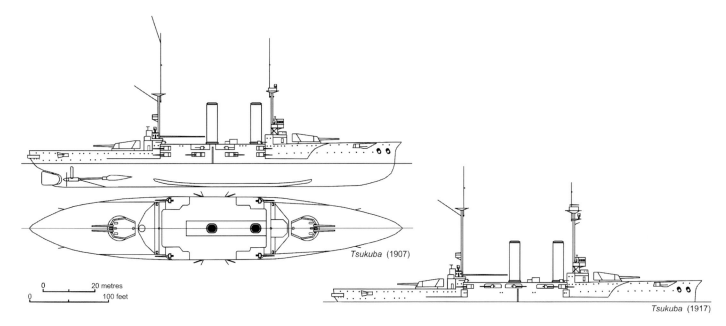

Displacement:	13,750 tons
Dimensions:	440 (pp) 450 (wl) 475 (oa) x 75 x 26 feet. 134.11 (pp) 137.16 (wl) 144.78 (oa) x 22.9 x 7.9 metres.
Machinery:	Twenty Miyabara boilers; two shafts; reciprocating (VTE), IHP 20,500 = 20.5kt; coal 1,600 tons (*Ikoma*: 1,911 tons + 160 tons oil).
Armament:	Four 12in/45 (2 x 2), twelve (1914: ten) 6in/45, twelve (1914: eight) 4.7/40, four 3in/40, guns; three 18in (*Ikoma*: two 21in, one 18in) torpedo tubes. By 1918: two 3in/28 AA guns added.
Protection:	Belt 4–7–4in; turrets 9.6–9–6in; barbettes 7in; battery 5in; armour deck 1.5/2in; conning tower 8in.
Complement:	820.

Tsukuba (1907)

Tsukuba (1917)

Name	Builder	Laid down	Launched	Completed	Fate
Tsukuba	Kure DY	14 Jan 05	26 Dec 05	14 Jan 07	Internal explosion Yokusuka 14 Jan 17; salved 1917 and target; stricken 1 Sep 17; BU 1918.
Ikoma	Kure DY	15 Mar 05	9 Apr 06	24 Mar 08	Stricken 20 Sep 23; sold Mitsubishi & BU Nagasaki to 13 Nov 24.

Kurama class

1ST CLASS CRUISERS; 1912: BATTLECRUISERS;
1921: 1ST CLASS CRUISERS

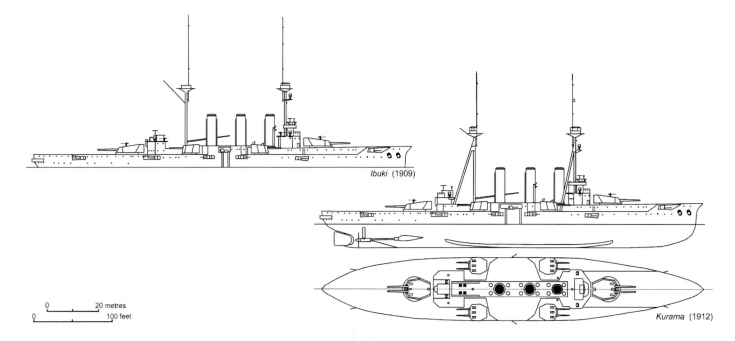

Displacement:	14,635 tons.
Dimensions:	450 (pp) 475.45 (wl) 485 (oa) x 75.5 x 26.1 feet. 137.16 (pp) 144.3 (wl) 485 (oa) 23 x7.97 metres.
Machinery:	Twenty-eight Miyabara boilers; two shafts; reciprocating (VTE - *Kurama*) or Curtis turbines (*Ibuki*), IHP 22,500 = 21.25kt/SHP 24,000 = 22.5kt; coal 600/1868 tons + oil 288 tons or coal 600/2000 tons + oil 218 tons.
Armament:	Four 12in/45 (2 x 2), eight 8in/45 (4 x 2), fourteen 4.7in/40, four 3in/40, three 47mm guns; three 18in torpedo tubes. Four 3in/28 AA added by 1918.
Protection:	Belt 4–7–4in; main turrets 9.6–9–6in; barbettes 7in; secondary turrets 6in; battery 5in; armour deck 2in; conning tower 8in.
Complement:	845.

Ibuki (1909)

Kurama (1912)

0   20 metres
0   100 feet

Name	Builder	Laid down	Launched	Completed	Fate
Kurama	Yokosuka DY	23 Aug 05	21 Oct 07	28 Feb 11	Stricken 20 Sep 23; sold Seiko Zosen & BU Kobe 24-25
Ibuki	Kure DY	22 May 07	21 Nov 07	1 Nov 09	Stricken 20 Sep 23; sold Kawasaki & BU Kobe to 9 Dec 24.

18 | RUSSIA

	1865	1870	1875	1880	1885	1890	1895	1900	1905	1910	1915	1920	1925	1930	1935	1940	1945	1950	1955
Kniaz Pozharskiy																			
Minin											✚								
General Admiral																			
Gerzog Edinburgskiy																			
Vladimir Monomakh									✚										
Dmitri Donskoi									✚										
Admiral Nakhimov									✚										
Pamiat Azova												✚							
Ryurik (i)									✚										
Rossiya																			
Oslyabya									✚										
Peresvet									Japan = *Sagami*										
Gromoboi																			
Pobieda									Japan = *Suwo*										
Bayan (i)									Japan = *Aso*										
Admiral Makarov																			
Bayan (ii)																			
Pallada											✚								
Ryurik (ii)																			

Kniaz Pozharskiy

SEMI-ARMOURED BATTERY FRIGATE; 1ST CLASS CRUISER
13 FEB 92; 24 MAR 06: TRAINING SHIP

Displacement: 4730 tons.

Dimensions: 267.7 (wl) 279.5 (oa) x 49 x 20.8 feet.
82.2(wl) 85.2 (oa) x 14.9 x 6.3 metres.

Machinery: Six (1877: eight) cylindrical boilers; one shaft; reciprocating (HDA), IHP 2835 = 11kt; coal 365 rons; range 1200nm @ 10kt.

Armament: Eight 8in/22, two 6in/22 guns; eight 87mm added 1877.
1892: eight 8in/35, two 6in/23, eight 87mm, four 47mm, six 37mm guns; two torpedo tubes. 1890s: two 8in, two 6in, four 87mm guns.
1906: one 6in, four 87mm, two 47mm, six 37mm guns.

Protection: Belt 4.5in; battery 4.5in; conning tower 2in (added 1871).

Complement: 24+471.

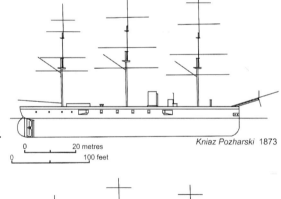

Kniaz Pozharski 1873

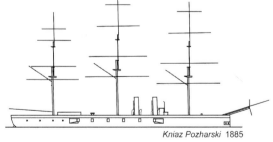

Kniaz Pozharski 1885

Name	Builder	Laid down	Launched	Completed	Fate
Kniaz Pozharskiy = *Blokshiv No 1* 1909	Mitchell (Galernyi Island, St Petersburg)	30 Nov 64	12 Sep 67	1869	Stricken 14 Apr 11; BU

Pacific 1873–5; Mediterranean May 78; Pacific Apr 80–1881; training ship 24 Mar 06; hulked 27 Oct 09.

General-Admiral class

ARMOURED CORVETTES; 27 MAR 75: ARMOURED FRIGATES;
13 FEB 92: 1ST CLASS CRUISERS; 24 MAR 06: TRAINING SHIPS;
25 OCT 09: MINELAYERS; 13 JUN 20: TRAINING SHIP
(*GENERAL-ADMIRAL*)

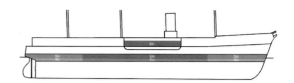

Displacement:	4600 tons.
Dimensions:	281.3 (pp) 282.2 (wl) 285.5 (oa) x 47.9 x 23 feet. 85.75 (pp) 86 (wl) 87 (oa) x 14.6 x 7 metres.
Machinery:	Five (*Gerzog Edinburgskiy* four; *General Admiral* 1886: three; 1892: five; 1911: eight) cylindrical (*General Admiral* 1913: six Belleville) boilers; one shaft; reciprocating (VC), IHP 5300 = 14kt; coal 1000 tons; range 5900nm @ 10kt.
Armament:	*General-Admiral*: six 8in/30, two 6in/28, six 87mm, two 47mm guns; one torpedo tube. 1885: six 8in/30, one 6in/28, six 87mm, eight 37mm guns; two torpedo tubes. 1900s: one or four 6in/45, six 47mm, eight 37mm guns. 1911: four 75mm/50 guns; 658–800 mines. *Gerzog Edinburgskiy*: four 8in/30, five 6in/28, six 9pdr guns; three torpedo tubes. 1880s: ten 6in guns. c.1890: six 6in/45, six 75mm, eight 47mm, two 37mm guns. 1911: four 75mm/50 guns; 700 mines.
Protection:	Belt 5–6–5in; battery 6in.
Complement:	482.

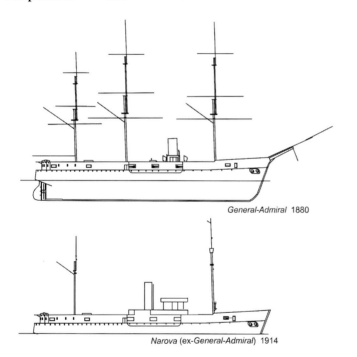

General-Admiral 1880

Narova (ex-General-Admiral) 1914

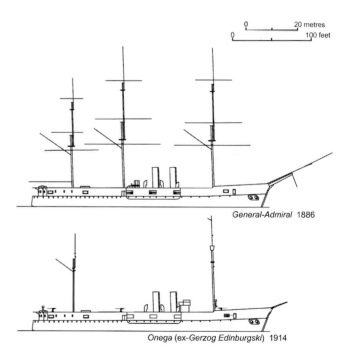

General-Admiral 1886

Onega (ex-Gerzog Edinburgski) 1914

Name	Builder	Laid down	Launched	Completed	Fate
General-Admiral (ii) = *Narova* (25 Oct 09) = *25 Oktiabrya* (5 Sep 24)	Society of Metal & Mining Works (St Petersburg)	27 Nov 70	8 Oct 73	20 Sep 75	Stricken 13 Jun 37; discarded 28 Jul 44; foundered Leningrad; salved and BU 1953.
Gerzog Edinburgskiy (ex-*Alekandr Nevskiy* [ii]) = *Onega* (25 Oct 09) = *Blokshiv No 9* (14 Oct 15) = *Barrikada* (28 Nov 18) = *Blokshiv No 5* (1 Jan 22)	Baltic Works (St Petersburg)	27 Sep 70	10 Sep 75	1877	BU after May 45

General-Admiral
Far East 1882–3; Baltic 1884; Mediterranean 1884–5; training ship 1886–1908 minelayer 1909; in German-Finnish hands at Helsinki Apr–May 18; returned 14 May 18; reserve May 22–Mar 24; workshop hulk Jun 37.

Gerzog Edinburgskiy
Far East 1881–4; seagoing training ship 1890s–1908; minelayer 1909; hulked 14 Oct 15; floating office, Mines & Torpedoes Authority Jul 39.

Minin
SEMI-ARMOURED FRIGATE; 13 FEB 92: 1ST CLASS CRUISER;
24 MAR 06: TRAINING SHIP; 25 OCT 09: MINELAYER

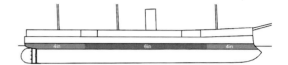

Displacement:	5725 tons.
Dimensions:	295 (wl) 302 (oa) x 49 x 23.6 feet. 89.9 (wl) 92 (oa) x 14.9 x 7.2 metres.
Machinery:	As turret ship: eight/nine boilers; one shaft; reciprocating (HDA), IHP 4000 = 14kt; coal 300T+; range 3000nm @ 10kt. As completed: twelve cylindrical (1887: . . . Belleville; 1911: six Belleville) boilers; 1 shaft; reciprocating (VC), IHP 6000 (1911: 4000) = 10.3kt (1911: 12.2kt); coal 850/1200 tons; range 5300nm @ 10kt.
Armament:	As turret ship: four 11in/20 (2 x 2), two 6in guns. As completed: four 8in/30, twelve 6in/28 guns (three 14in torpedo tubes added 1887). 1901: four 8in/30, six 6in/45 QF, six 75mm, eight 47mm, four 37mm. c.1905: ten 6in/45, six 75mm, eight 47mm, four 37mm. 1909: four 47mm guns; 1000 mines.
Protection:	Belt 4–6–4in (iron).
Complement:	46+505 (1879); 24+295 (1906); 14+299 (1914).

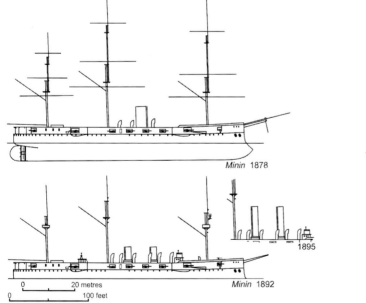

Minin 1878

Minin 1892

1895

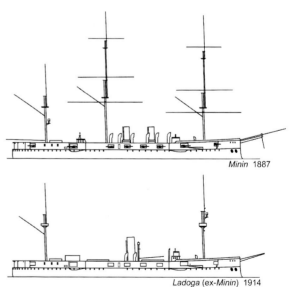

Minin 1887

Ladoga (ex-*Minin*) 1914

Name	Builder	Laid down	Launched	Completed	Fate
Minin	Baltic Works (St Petersburg)	24 Nov 66	3 Nov 69	1878	Mined off Ere, Gulf of Finland, 15 Aug 15 (laid by *UC4*); stricken 28 Mar 17; wreck sold Edward Campbell 30 Apr 19.

Mediterranean and Far East Nov 1878–Sep 81; Mediterranean and Pacific Sep 83–Nov 85; cadet and boys' training ship 1889–91; gunnery training ship 1891–1908; minelayer 1909.

Vladimir Monomakh class

SEMI-ARMOURED FRIGATES; 13 FEB 92: 1ST CLASS CRUISERS

Displacement:	5754 (*Monomakh*)/5900 (*Donskoi*) tons.
Dimensions:	*Monomakh*: 295 (wl) 307.75 (oa) x 51 x 25 feet.
	90.2 (wl) 93.8 (oa) x 15.8 x 7.6 metres.
	Donskoi: 296.7 (wl) 306.5 (oa) x 52 x 25 feet.
	90.4 (wl) 93.4 (oa) x 15.8 x 7.6m
Machinery:	Six (*Donskoi* eight, 1895: twelve; *Monomakh* 1897: eight/twelve) cylindrical boilers; two (*Donskoi*: one) shaft; reciprocating (VC; *Donskoi* 1895, *Monomakh* 1897: VTE), IHP 7000 = 16kt; coal 900/1200 tons; range 6200/8500nm @ 10kt.
Armament:	*Monomakh*: four 8in/22, twelve 6in/28, four 3.4in/24, two 2.5in/19, four 47mm, eight 37mm guns; three torpedo tubes. 1897: five 6in/45, six 4.7in, sixteen 47mm, four 37mm guns, two 37mm MG; three 14in torpedo tubes. *Donskoi*: two 8in/30, fourteen 6in/28, six 87mm guns, four torpedo tubes. 1895: six 6in/45, ten 4.7in, six 47mm, twenty-two 37mm guns; five 14in torpedo tubes. 1903: six 6in/45, four 4.7in, six 75mm, six 47mm, ten 37mm guns; five torpedo tubes. 1904: six 6in/45, ten 75mm, six 47mm, twelve 37mm guns; four torpedo tubes.
Protection:	Belt 4.5–6–4.5in; deck 0.5in.
Complement:	14+478 (*Monomakh*); 24+527 (*Donskoi*).

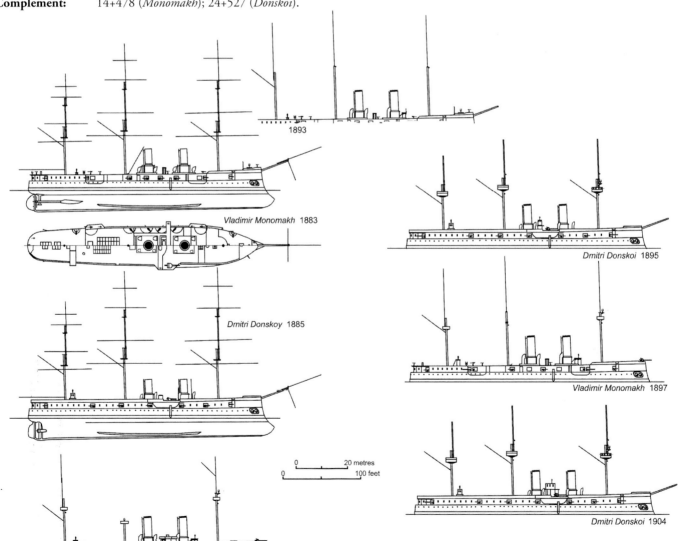

Vladimir Monomakh 1883

Dmitri Donskoy 1885

Vladimir Monomakh 1904

1893

Dmitri Donskoi 1895

Vladimir Monomakh 1897

Dmitri Donskoi 1904

0   20 metres

0   100 feet

Name	Builder	Laid down	Launched	Completed	Fate
Vladimir Monomakh	Baltic Works (St Petersburg)	24 Feb 81	22 Oct 82	13 Jul 83	Torpedoed Japanese TB off Tsushima 27 May 05 and foundered next day.
Dmitri Donskoi	New Admiralty (St Petersburg)	24 Feb 81	30 Aug 83	Feb 85	Scuttled off Tsushima 29 May 05 (NS) after gunfire Japanese cruisers.

Vladimir Monomakh

Mediterranean & Pacific Oct 84–May 87; Nov 89–Aug 92; Oct 93–Oct 02; 3rd Pacific Squadron Feb 05 to loss.

Dmitri Donskoi

Mediterranean & Pacific Aug 85–May 89; Oct 91–Mar 93; Columbian Exposition, New York, Apr 93; Mediterranean & Pacific Nov 95–1902; Mediterranean Oct 03–Mar 04; 2nd Pacific Squadron Oct 04 to loss.

Admiral Nakhimov

1ST CLASS ARMOURED CRUISER; 13 FEB 92: 1ST CLASS CRUISER

Displacement: 8260 tons.

Dimensions: 330.9 (pp) 333 (wl) 339 (oa) x 61 x 26.3 feet.
97.8 (pp) 101.5 (wl) 103.3 (oa) x 18.6 x 8.0 metres.

Machinery: Twelve cylindrical boilers; two shafts; reciprocating (VC; 1899: VTE), IHP 8000 = 16.1kt; coal 1100/1200 tons; range 4000nm @ 10kt.

Armament: Eight 8in/30 (4 x 2), ten 6in/28, twelve 47mm, six 37mm guns; three 15in torpedo tubes.
1900: eight 8in/30 (4 x 2), ten 4.7in/45, fourteen 47mm, two 37mm guns.
1904: eight 8in/30 (4 x 2), ten 4.7in/45, six 87mm, four 37mm guns.

Protection: Belt 10in; barbettes 7–8in; turrets 2–2.5in (1900: 6in); armour deck 3–2–3in; conning tower 6in.

Complement: 23+549; 1904: 28+696.

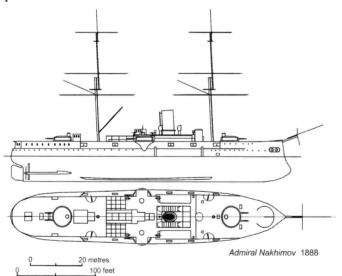

Admiral Nakhimov 1888

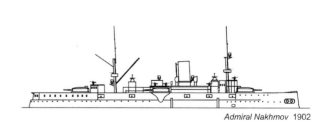

Admiral Nakhmov 1902

Name	Builder	Laid down	Launched	Completed	Fate
Admiral Nakhimov	Baltic Works (St Petersburg)	Jul 84	2 Nov 85	15 Dec 87	Torpedoed Japanese TB Tsushima 27 May 05 and foundered next day.

Baltic 1888; Far East 1889–91, 1894–8, 1900–2; 2nd Pacific Sqn 15 Oct 04 to loss.

Pamiat Azova

SEMI-ARMOURED FRIGATE; 13 FEB 92: 1ST CLASS CRUISER;
10 OCT 07: TRAINING SHIP

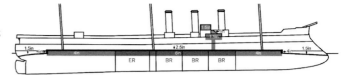

Displacement:	6734 tons.
Dimensions:	377.7 (pp) 385 (oa) x 51.2 x 24 feet. 115.2 (pp) 117.3 (oa) x 15.6 x 7.2 metres.
Machinery:	Six cylindrical (1904: eighteen Belleville) boilers; two shafts; reciprocating (VTE), IHP 8500 = 17kt; coal 967/1200 tons; range 6100nm @ 10kt.
Armament:	Two 8in/35, thirteen 6in/35, seven 47mm, eight 37mm guns; three 18in torpedo tubes; 1904: twelve 6in/45; 1909: four 47mm guns; two 18in torpedo tubes.
Protection:	Belt 0–4–6–4–0in; barbettes 1.5in; armour deck 1.5–2.5in; conning tower 1.5in.
Complement:	23+546.

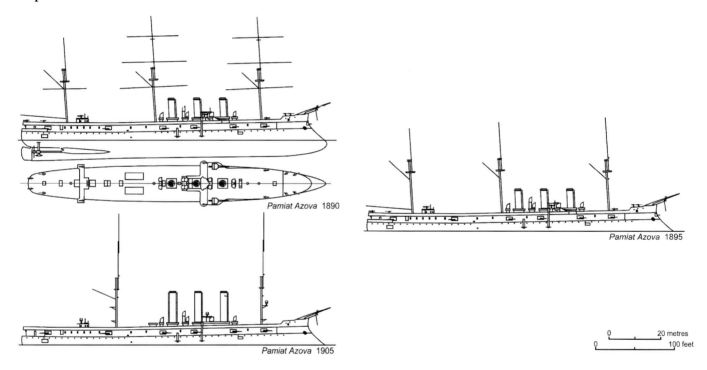

Pamiat Azova 1890

Pamiat Azova 1895

Pamiat Azova 1905

Name	Builder	Laid down	Launched	Completed	Fate
Pamiat Azova = *Dvina* (25 Feb 09) = *Pamiat Azova* (13 Apr 17)	Baltic Works (St Petersburg)	4 Mar 86	20 May 88	1890	Torpedoed British *CMB79* Kronstadt 18 Aug19; salved Dec 23 and BU.

Far East 1890–2; Mediterranean 1893–4; Far East 1894–9; gunnery training ship 1900–7; training ship 1907; torpedo/mining training ship 1909; submarine depot ship 1915–17.

Ryurik (i)

1ST CLASS CRUISER

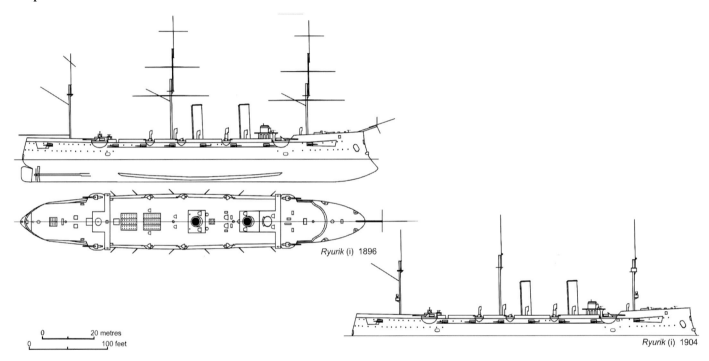

Displacement:	11,690 tons.
Dimensions:	412 (pp) 426.9 (wl) 435 (oa) x 67 x 26 feet. 129.8 (pp) 130.1 (wl) 132.6 (oa) x 20.4 x 9.1 metres.
Machinery:	Eight cylindrical boilers; two shafts; reciprocating (VTE), IHP 13,500 = 18kt; coal 1933 tons; range 6700nm @ 10kt.
Armament:	Four 8in/35, sixteen 6in/45, six 4.7in/45, six 47mm/43, ten 37mm/23 guns; six 15in torpedo tubes.
Protection:	Belt 0–8–10–8–0in; armour deck 2in; conning tower 6in (steel).
Complement:	27+692.

Ryurik (i) 1896

Ryurik (i) 1904

0   20 metres
0   100 feet

Name	Builder	Laid down	Launched	Completed	Fate
Ryurik (i)	Baltic Works (St Petersburg)	19 May 90 (OS)	22 Oct 92 (OS)	16 Oct 95 (OS)	Scuttled after gunfire battle of Ulsan 14 Aug 04.

Far East 1896 to loss.

Rossiya
1ST CLASS CRUISER; 10 OCT 07: ARMOURED CRUISER

Displacement:	12,195 (1909: 13,060) tons.
Dimensions:	461.3 (pp) 473.1 (wl) 485 (oa) x 68.6 x 26.2 (1909: 28.3) feet. 140.6 (pp) 141.4 (wl) 146.3 x 20.7 x 7.9 (1909: 8.63) metres.
Machinery:	Thirty-two Belleville boilers; two + one shafts; reciprocating (VTE), IHP 14,500 + 2500 cruising (removed 1909) = 19kt; coal 2530/2700 tons; range 7740nm/5700nm @ 10kt/12kt.
Armament:	Four (1915: nil; 1916: six) 8in/45, sixteen (1904: twenty-two; 1915: twenty-six; 1916: fourteen; removed 1919) 6in/45, twelve (removed 1909) 75mm/50, twenty (1916: two) 47mm/43, eighteen (removed 1909) 37mm/23 guns; five 15in torpedo tubes.
Protection:	Belt 5–6–8–6–0in; armour deck 2–3–2.5in; lower casemates 5in; upper casemates 4in; conning tower 12in (Harvey).
Complement:	28+811.

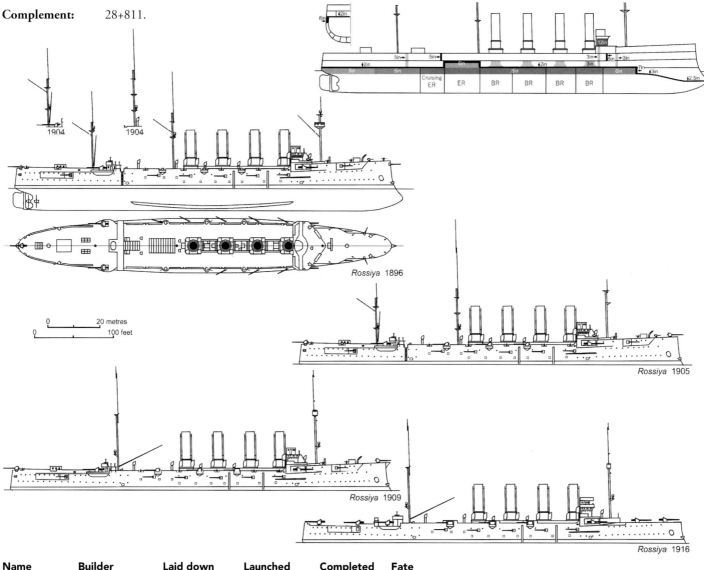

Rossiya 1896

Rossiya 1905

Rossiya 1909

Rossiya 1916

Name	Builder	Laid down	Launched	Completed	Fate
Rossiya	Baltic Works	20 May 95	30 Apr 96 (OS)	13 Sep 97 (OS)	Sold Derumetall 1 Jul 22; resold Rudmetalltorgu 3 Oct 22; stranded on Develsy Bank (Talinn) late 22; salved and BU Kiel.

Far East Oct 97–Mar 06; Baltic 1909–18 (Atlantic training cruises 1912–13, Mediterranean 1914); Kronstadt reserve 1918.

Peresvet class

SQUADRON ARMOURCLADS; 1916: ARMOURED CRUISER
(*PERESVET*)

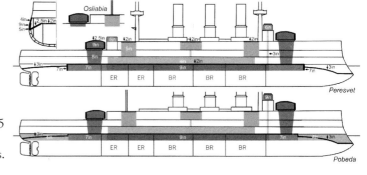

Displacement:	13,810 (*Peresvet*)/14,408 tons(*Oslyabya*)/13,320 (*Pobeda*) tons.
Dimensions:	401.25 (pp) 426.5 (wl) 434.4 (oa) x 71.5 x 26.25 feet. 122.3 (pp) 130 (wl) 132.4 (oa) x 21.8 x 8 metres.
Machinery:	Thirty Belleville boilers; three shafts; reciprocating (VTE), IHP 14,500 = 18kt; coal 1060 (*Pobeda*: 1142)/2,060 tons; range 6200nm @ 10kt.
Armament:	Four 10in/45, eleven 6in/45, twenty 3in/40, twenty 47mm/43, eight 37mm/23 guns; five 18in torpedo tubes.
Protection:	Belt 0–4–7–9–7–4in (*Pobeda*: 4–7–9–7–4in); turrets 9in; barbettes 8in; casemates 5in; armour deck 3–2/2.5–3in; conning tower 6in (Harvey, except *Pobeda* Krupp).
Complement:	27+744.

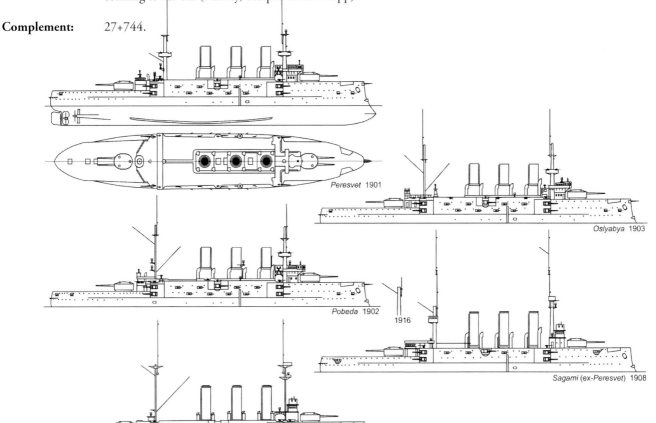

Peresvet 1901

Oslyabya 1903

Pobeda 1902

1916

Sagami (ex-*Peresvet*) 1908

Suwo (ex-*Pobeda*) 1908

Name	Builder	Laid down	Launched	Completed	Fate
Peresvet = *Sagami* (1905) = *Peresvet* (5 Apr 16)	Baltic Works (St Petersburg)	21 Nov 95	19 May 98	Aug 01	Gunfire Japanese army & scuttled Port Arthur 7 Dec 04; salved 29 Jun 05 & Japanese; sold Russia 1916; mined off Port Said (laid by *U73*) 4 Jan 17.
Oslyabya	New Admiralty (St Petersburg)	21 Nov 95	8 Nov 98	Aug 01	Gunfire Japanese fleet off Tsushima 27 May 05.
Pobeda = *Suwo* (1905)	Baltic Works (St Petersburg)	21 Feb 99	10 May 00	Oct 02	Gunfire Japanese army & scuttled Port Arthur 7 Dec 04; salved 29 Jun 05 & Japanese.

Peresvet

Far East Oct 01 to first loss; on passage for Northern Fleet 1916 to loss

Oslyabya

Mediterranean on passage to Far East Aug 03–1904; 2nd Pacific Squadron 15 Oct 04 to loss.

Pobeda

Far East Oct 02 to loss.

Gromoboi

1ST CLASS CRUISER; 10 OCT 07: ARMOURED CRUISER

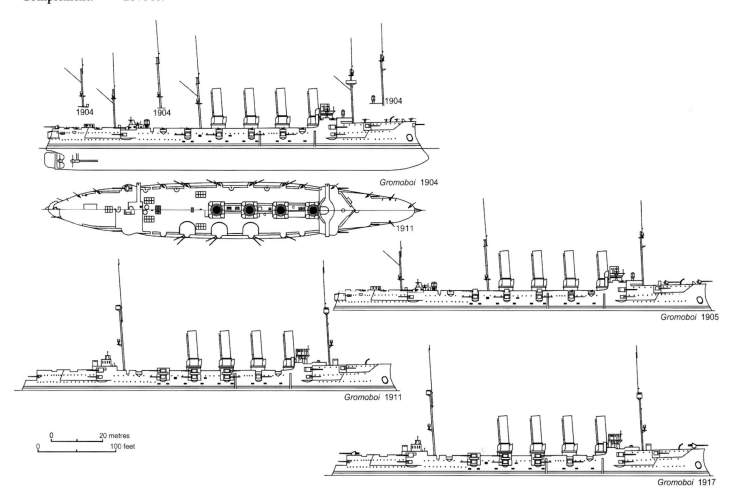

Displacement:	12,455 tons.
Dimensions:	461.3 (pp) 472.5 (wl) 481 (wl) x 68.5 x 27.7 feet.
	140.6 (pp) 144 (wl) 146.6 x 20.9 x 8.4 metres.
Machinery:	Thirty-two Bellevilles boilers; three shafts; reciprocating (VTE), IHP 14,500 = 19kt; coal 800/2500 tons; range 8100nm @ 10kt.
Armament:	Four (1916: six) 8in/45, sixteen (1911: twenty-two; 1916: twenty; removed 1919) 6in/45, twenty-four (1904: nineteen; 1911: four; removed 1916) 75mm/50, twelve (1911: four; removed 1916) 47mm/43, eighteen (1911: two) 37mm/23 guns; four (1911: two) 15in (1911: two 18in) torpedo tubes. Two 2.5in, two 47mm AA guns added 1916–17.
Protection:	Belt 6in; casemates 4.76in; armour deck 1.5/2.5–2.5/3in; conning tower 12in (Harvey).
Complement:	28+846.

Gromoboi 1904

1911

Gromoboi 1905

Gromoboi 1911

0   20 metres
0   100 feet

Gromoboi 1917

Name	Builder	Laid down	Launched	Completed	Fate
Gromoboi	Baltic Works (St Petersburg)	14 Jul 97 (OS)	26 Apr 98 (OS)	Oct 00	Sold Derumetall 1 Jul 22; resold Rudmetalltorgu 12 Oct 22; stranded in tow Liepaja 30 Oct 22; BU in situ.

Far East 1901–7; Baltic 1911–18; Kronstadt reserve May 18.

Bayan class

1ST CLASS CRUISERS; 10 OCT 07: ARMOURED
CRUISERS

Displacement: 7802 (last three: 7750) tons.

Dimensions: 443 (wl) 449.6 (oa) x 57.5 x 22 feet
135 (wl) x 137 (oa) x 17.5 x 6.3 metres.

Machinery: Twenty-six Belleville boilers; two shafts;
reciprocating (VTE), IHP 16,500 = 21kt;
coal 750/1100 tons; range 3900nm @ 10kt.

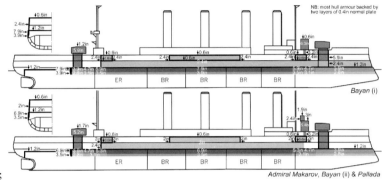

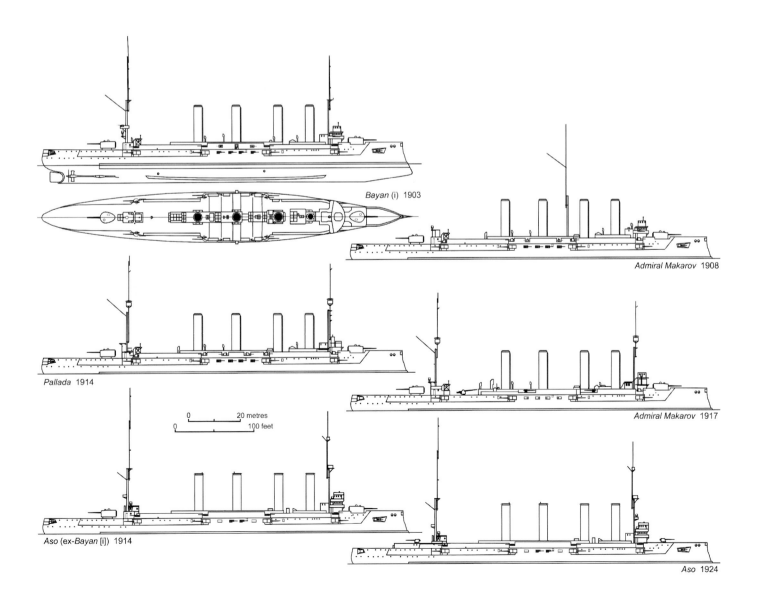

Bayan (i) 1903

Admiral Makarov 1908

Pallada 1914

Admiral Makarov 1917

Aso (ex-*Bayan* [i]) 1914

Aso 1924

Armament:	Two (1916: three) 8in/45, eight (1916: twelve; removed from *Bayan* [ii] 1919) 6in/40, twenty (1916: four) 75mm/50, eight (last three: four) 47mm/43, two 37mm/23 (*Bayan* [i] only) guns; two 18in (*Bayan* [i]: 15in) torpedo tubes.
Protection:	*Bayan* [i]: belt 3.9–7.9–3.9in; turrets 5.9in; casemates 2.3in; barbettes 6.7in; armour deck 1.2in, conning tower 6.3in (Harvey – on two layers of 0.4in hull plating).
	Last three: belt 3.5–6.9–3.5in; turrets 5.3in; casemates 2.3in; barbettes 6.7in; armour deck 1.2in, conning tower 5.4in (Krupp – on two layers of 0.4in hull plating).
Complement:	20+589.

Name	Builder	Laid down	Launched	Completed	Fate
Bayan (i)	Forges & Chantiers de la Méditerranée (La Seyne)	End 1898	2 Jun 00	14 Jan 03	Gunfire Japanese army Port Arthur 26 Nov 04 (OS); salved 24 Jun 05 and Japanese (see p 220).
Admiral Makarov	Forges & Chantiers de la Méditerranée (La Seyne)	4 Apr 05	8 May 06	26 May 08	Sold Derumetall 15 Aug 22 and BU Germany; stricken 21 Nov 25.
Bayan (ii)	New Admiralty (St Petersburg)	28 Apr 05	15 Aug 08	14 Jul 11	Sold Derumetall 1 Jul 22 and BU Germany
Pallada (ii)	New Admiralty (St Petersburg)	30 May 05	10 Nov 07	15 Feb 11	Torpedoed *U26* Gulf of Finland 11 Oct 14 (NS).

Bayan (i)
Baltic 1903; Far East Aug 03 to loss.

Admiral Makarov
Baltic 1908; Mediterranean 1908–9; Baltic 1909–10; Mediterranean 1910; Baltic 1911–18; Petrograd reserve 7 Sep 18; HQ ship Petrograd Jul 21.

Bayan (ii)
Baltic 1911–18; Petrograd reserve May 18.

Pallada
Baltic to loss.

Ryurik (ii)
ARMOURED CRUISER

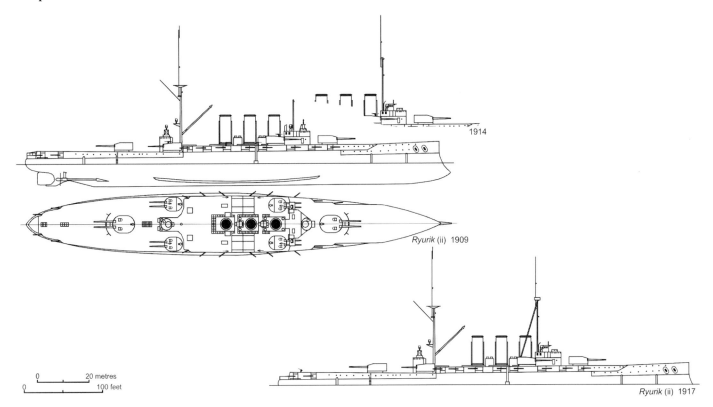

Displacement:	15,130 tons.
Dimensions:	490 (pp) 517 (wl) 529 (oa) x 75 x 26 feet.
	149.4 (pp) 157.6 161.2 (oa) x 22.9 x 7.9 metres.
Machinery:	Twenty-eight Belleville boilers; 2 shafts; reciprocating (VTE), IHP 19,700 = 21kt; coal 1200/2000T; range 6100nm @ 10kt.
Armament:	Four 10in/50 (2 x 2), eight 8in/50 (4 x 2), twenty 4.7in/50, four 47mm/43 guns; two 18in torpedo tubes.
Protection:	Belt 3–6–4–3in; turrets (main) 8in; (secondary) 7in; casemates 3in; armour deck 1/1.5in; conning tower 8in.
Complement:	26+910.

Ryurik (ii) 1909

Ryurik (ii) 1917

Name	Builder	Laid down	Launched	Completed	Fate
Ryurik (ii)	Vickers (Barrow)	9 Aug 05 (OS)	4 Nov 06 (OS)	Aug 08 (OS)	Stripped Kronstadt 1921–2 and Petrograd 1923; stricken 1 Nov 23; BU Leningrad 1924–5.

Baltic 1909–10; Mediterranean Jul 10; Baltic 1910–1918; Kronstadt reserve Oct 18.

19 | SPAIN

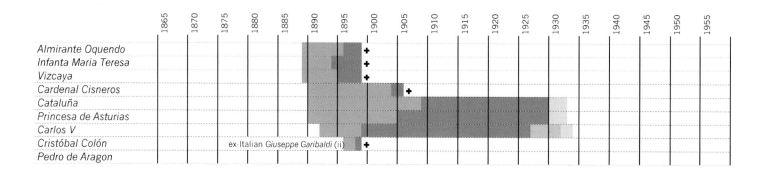

	1865	1870	1875	1880	1885	1890	1895	1900	1905	1910	1915	1920	1925	1930	1935	1940	1945	1950	1955
Almirante Oquendo								+											
Infanta Maria Teresa								+											
Vizcaya								+											
Cardenal Cisneros									+										
Cataluña																			
Princesa de Asturias																			
Carlos V																			
Cristóbal Colón						ex-Italian *Giuseppe Garibaldi* (ii)		+											
Pedro de Aragon																			

Infanta María Teresa class
1ST CLASS PROTECTED CRUISERS; 1898:
2ND CLASS ARMOURED SHIPS

Displacement:	6890 tons.
Dimensions:	340 (pp) x 65 x 21.5 feet. 103.6 (pp) x 19.8 x 6.6 metres.
Machinery:	Six cylindrical boilers; two shafts; reciprocating (VTE), IHP 9000/13,000FD = 18/20kt; coal 1200 tons; range 9700nm @ 10kt.
Armament:	Two 11in/35, ten 5.5in/35, eight 57mm, eight 37mm guns; eight (*Maria Teresa*)/six 14in torpedo tubes.
Protection:	Belt 11.8in; barbettes 10.5in; armour deck 2in (2in/3in fore and aft); conning tower 11.8in.
Complement:	500.

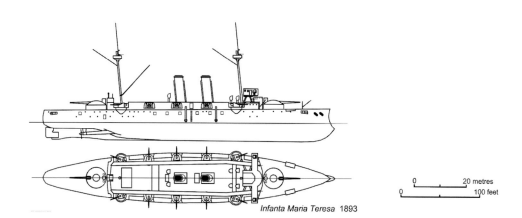

Infanta Maria Teresa 1893

0   20 metres
0   100 feet

Name	Builder	Laid down	Launched	Completed	Fate
Infanta María Teresa	Sociedad Astilleros del Nervión (Sestao)	24 Jul 89	30 Aug 90	28 Aug 93	Stranded after gunfire USS *Iowa* and *Brooklyn*, Santiago de Cuba, 3 Jul 98; salved 23 Sep 98 and US; stranded off Cat Island (Bahamas) in tow Guantanamo–Norfolk VA 3 Nov 98.
Vizcaya	Sociedad Astilleros del Nervión (Sestao)	7 Oct 89	8 Jul 91	2 Aug 94	Stranded after gunfire USS *Texas* and *Brooklyn*, Santiago de Cuba, 3 Jul 98.
Almirante Oquendo	Sociedad Astilleros del Nervión (Sestao)	16 Nov 89	3 Oct 91	21 Aug 95	Stranded after gunfire USS *Iowa*, Santiago de Cuba, 3 Jul 98.
Princesa de Asturias	Sociedad Española de Construcció Naval (La Carraca)	23 Sep 89			Completed as *Princesa de Asturias* class.
Cardenal Cisneros	Sociedad Española de Construcción Naval (Ferrol)	1 Sep 90			Completed as *Princesa de Asturias* class.
Cataluña	Sociedad Española de Construcción Naval (Cartagena)	Jan 90			Completed as *Princesa de Asturias* class.

Princesa de Asturias class
1ST CLASS PROTECTED CRUISERS

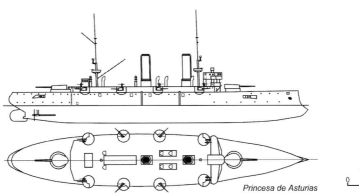

Displacement: 7500 tons.

Dimensions: 347.7 (pp) 358.6 (oa) x 60.7 x 23.5 feet.
106 (pp) 109.3 (oa) x 18.5 x 7.2 metres.

Machinery: Six cylindrical boilers; two shafts; reciprocating (VTE), IHP 10,500/15,000FD = 18/20kt; coal 750/2000 tons; range 6500nm @ 10kt.

Armament: Two 9.4in/42.5, eight 5.5in/40, eight 57mm, eight/ten 37mm guns; two (*Cisneros* five) 14in torpedo tubes (removed 1910).

Protection: Belt 8–11.8–8–6in; barbettes 8in; casemates 2.75in; armour deck 2in; conning tower 8in.

Complement: 546.

Princesa de Asturias

Name	Builder	Laid down	Launched	Completed	Fate
Princesa de Asturias	Sociedad Española de Construcción Naval (La Carraca)	23 Sep 89	17 Oct 96	10 Jun 03	Stricken 1930; sold at Bilbao & BU 1932–3.
Cardenal Cisneros	Sociedad Española de Construcción Naval (Ferrol)	1 Sep 90	19 Mar 97	30 Mar 03	Wrecked Ria de Muros 28 Oct 05.
Cataluña	Sociedad Española de Construcción Naval (Cartagena)	Jan 90	24 Sep 00	7 Apr 08	Stricken 1930; sold at Bilbao & BU 1932–3.

Princesa de Asturias
Paid off 28 Dec 1927.

Cataluña
Cadet training ship 1920s; paid off Nov 28.

Carlos V
1ST CLASS CRUISER

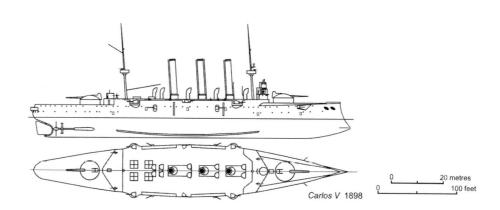

Displacement: 9090 tonnes.

Dimensions: 380 (oa) x 67 x 25 feet.
115.8 (oa) x 20.4 x 7.6 metres.

Machinery: Twelve cylindrical boilers; two shafts; reciprocating (VTE), IHP 18,500FD = 20kt; coal 1200/1800 tons; range 9600nm @ 10kt.

Armament: Two 11in/35, eight 5.5in/35, four 3.9in/35 (later 4.1in), two 70mm, eight 57mm guns; six (later two) 14in torpedo tubes.

Protection: Armour deck 2.5/6.5in; battery 2in; barbettes 9.75in; shields 3.9in; conning tower 11.8in.

Complement: 590.

Carlos V 1898

| | 0 | | 20 metres |
| 0 | | 100 feet |

Name	Builder	Laid down	Launched	Completed	Fate
Carlos V (ex-*Emperador Carlos V*)	Vega-Murguia (Cadíz)	4 Mar 92	13 Mar 95	2 Jun 98	Stricken 5 Dec 31; BU Bilbao 1933.

Training ship 1916; training hulk, Ferrol, 1923.

Giuseppe Garibaldi class

1ST CLASS CRUISER

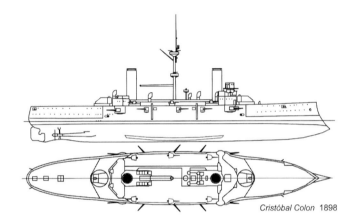

Displacement:	6840 tons.
Dimensions:	328.1 (pp) 363.7 (oa) x 59.75 x 23.3 feet. 100 (pp) 107.8 (oa) x 18.2 x 7.1 metres.
Machinery:	Twenty-four Niclausse boilers; two shafts; reciprocating (VTE), IHP 15,000 = 20kt; coal 400/1000 tons; range 8300nm @ 10kt.
Armament:	Two 9.4in/40 (not fitted), ten 6in/40, six 4.7in, eighteen 57mm guns; four 18in torpedo tubes.
Protection:	Belt 2.8–3.5–4.7–5.9–4.7–3.5–2.8in; battery 5.9in; turrets 5.9in; armour deck 0.9/1.5in; conning tower 5.9in.
Complement:	500.

Cristóbal Colon 1898

Name	Builder	Laid down	Launched	Completed	Fate
Cristóbal Colón (ex-Italian *Giuseppe Garibaldi* [ii])	Ansaldo (Genoa-Sestri Ponente)	1895	16 Sep 96	16 May 97	Grounded and scuttled Rio Tarquino, Cuba, 3 Jul 98.
Pedro de Aragon = Argentine *Rivadavia* (i) 1900	Ansaldo (Genoa-Sestri Ponente)	–	–	–	To Argentina 1900.

20 | SWEDEN

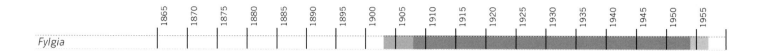

	1865	1870	1875	1880	1885	1890	1895	1900	1905	1910	1915	1920	1925	1930	1935	1940	1945	1950	1955
Fylgia																			

Fylgia
ARMOURED CRUISER

Displacement:	4800 tons.
Dimensions:	377.6 (wl) 383.8 (oa) x 48.5 x 20.6 feet.
	115.1 (wl) 117 (oa) x 14.8 x 6.3 metres.
Machinery:	Twelve Yarrow (1941: four Penhoët) boilers; two shafts; reciprocating (VTE), IHP 12,000 = 21.5kt; coal 900 tons; range 5770nm @ 10kt.
Armament:	Eight 6in/50 (4 x 2), fourteen (1913: twelve; 1918: ten) 57mm/48, two 37mm/39 guns; two 17.3in torpedo tubes. Two 57mm AA added 1918.
	1941: eight 6in/50 (4 x 2), four 57 mm AA, two 40mm AA, one 25mm AA, one 20mm AA gun; two 21in torpedo tubes.
Protection:	Belt 3.9in, turrets 2–4.9in, armour deck 0.9/1.4in; conning tower 3.9in.
Complement:	322.

Name	Builder	Laid down	Launched	Completed	Fate
Fylgia	Bergsunds Mekaniska Verkstad (Finnboda)	Oct 02	20 Dec 05	21 Jun 07	Stricken 30 Jan 53; target; sold 1957 & BU Copenhagen.

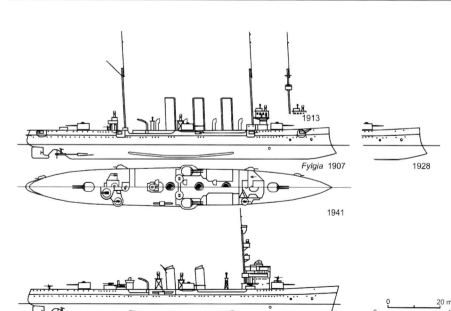

Fylgia 1907

1913

1928

1941

Cadet training cruises Jul–Sep 07; Nov 07–Apr 08; Nov 08–Apr 09; Jun 09–Aug 09; May 10–Jul 10; May 11–Jun 11; May 12–Aug 12; 1912–13; Nov 13–May 1914; Nov 11–Apr 20; 1920–1; Oct 21–Apr 22; Nov 22–Apr 23; 1923; 1923–4; Apr 24; Nov 24–Apr 25; 1925; Oct 25–Mar 26; Nov 26–Apr 27; Nov 27–Mar 28; May 28–Jul 28; Nov 28–Mar 29; Nov 30–Mar 31; May 31–Jul 31; Nov 31–Mar 32; May 32–Jul 32; Nov 32–Mar 33; May–Jul 33; reserve 1933–9; cadet training cruises 1945–6; Jan 46–Mar 46; Apr–Jun 46; Nov 47–Mar 48; Apr–Jun 48.

21 | UNITED KINGDOM

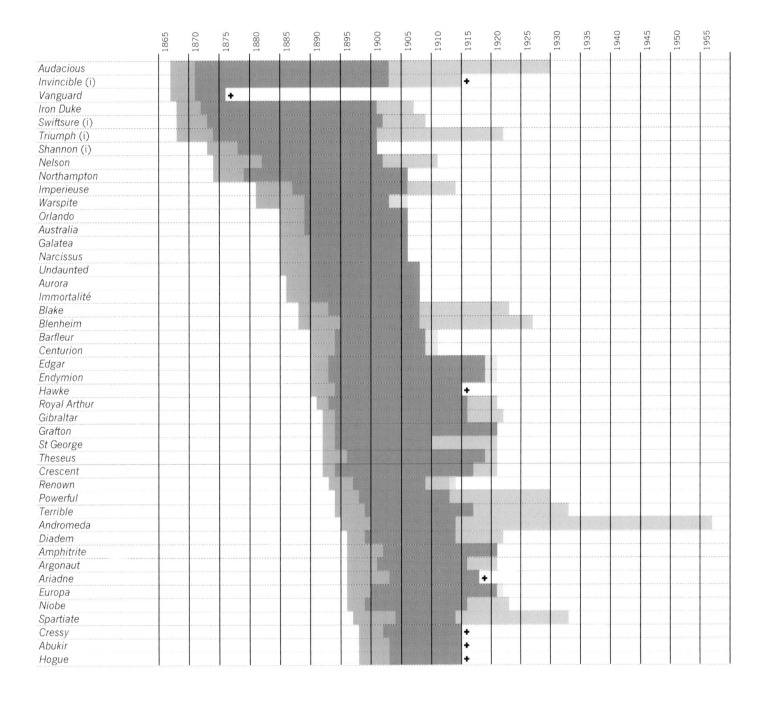

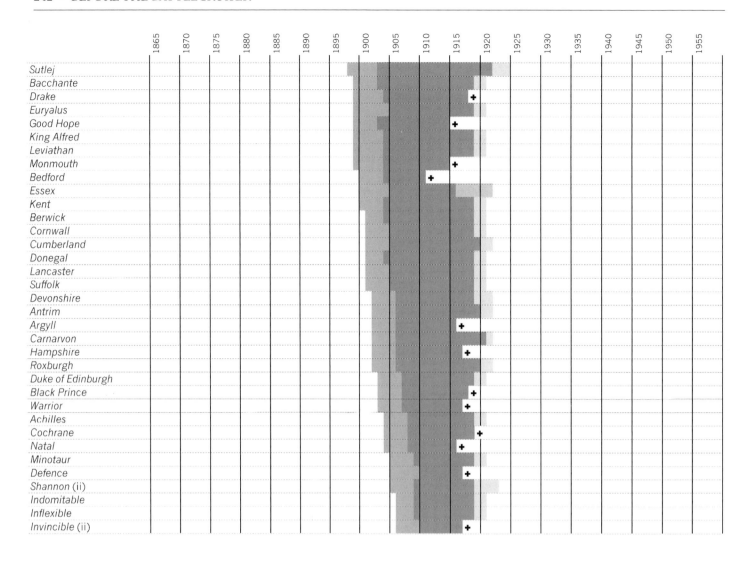

Audacious & Swiftsure classes

IRON ARMOUR-PLATED SHIPS;
1887: 2ND CLASS ARMOURED BATTLE SHIPS;
1892: 3RD CLASS ARMOURED BATTLE SHIPS

Displacement:	6010 (*Swiftsure*: 6910; *Triumph* 6640) tons.
Dimensions:	280 (pp) x 54 (*Swiftsure* & *Triumph*: 55) x 23.2 (26.1) feet. 85.3 (pp) x 16.5 (16.8) x 7.1 (7.8) metres.
Machinery:	Six rectangular boilers; two (*Swiftsure* & *Triumph*: one) shafts; reciprocating (HRCR), IHP 4830 (4900) = 13kt (12.6kt); coal 460 tons; range 1260nm @ 10kt.
Armament:	Ten 9in/14 12-ton MLR, four 6.3in/15.5 64pdr MLR, six 20pdr (*Triumph* 1882: four 5in/25; *Swiftsure* 1882: eight 4in/25; others 1885: six/eight 4in/27) guns; four 14in torpedo tubes from 1875.
Protection:	Belt 6–8in; battery 4–6in.
Complement:	450.

Audacious 1870

Triumph 1873

Iron Duke 1880

Audacious 1890

Erebus ex-Invincible 1904

Iron Duke 1905

0   20 metres
0   100 feet

Name	Builder	Laid down	Launched	Completed	Fate
Audacious = *Ariadne* (21 Mar 04) = *Fisgard* (31 Mar 04) = *Imperieuse* (14 Oct 14)	Napier (Govan)	26 Jun 67	27 Feb 69	10 Sep 70	Hulked 1902; sold TW Ward 15 Mar 27 & BU Inverkeithing.
Invincible (i) = *Erebus* (21 Mar 04) = *Fisgard II* (12 Oct 05)	Napier (Govan)	28 Jun 67	29 May 69	1 Oct 70	Hulked 1904; foundered off Portland 17 Sep 14.
Iron Duke	Pembroke DYd	23 Aug 68	1 Mar 70	21 Jan 71	Hulked 1900; sold Galbraith 15 Jun 06 & BU Glasgow.
Vanguard	Laird (Birkenhead)	21 Oct 67	3 Jul 70	28 Sep 70	Collision *Iron Duke* off Dublin 1 Sep 75.
Swiftsure (i) = *Orontes* (21 Mar 04)	Palmer (Jarrow)	31 Aug 68	15 Jun 70	27 Jun 72	Hulked 1901; sold Castle 14 Jul 08 & BU.

Triumph (i) = *Tenedos* (21 Mar 04) = *Indus IV* (1910) = *Algiers* (Jan 15)	Palmer (Jarrow)	31 Aug 68	27 Sep 70	8 Apr 73	Hulked 1904; sold B Fryer (Sunderland) 11 Nov 21; re-sold Petersen Ralbeck 25 Jul 22 & BU.

Audacious
Kingstown guardship Oct 70; Humber guardship Nov 71–1874; China (flag) Sep 74–1878; Hull guardship Feb 79–1881; China (flag) Sep 82–1889; Hull guardship Apr 90–1894; Chatham reserve 1894–1900; destroyer depot hulk Felixtowe Sep 03–14 Mar 05; artificers' training hulk Portsmouth 1 Jan 06–Sep 14; receiving hulk Scapa Oct 14–Mar 20; store hulk Rosyth 1920–1927.

Invincible
Hull guardship Oct 70–1871; Mediterranean Aug 72–1876; Mediterranean/Channel Mar 78–1880; Mediterranean 1880–5; Southampton guardship Nov 86–1893; Portsmouth reserve 1893–1900; destroyer depot hulk Portsmouth 30 May 04–21 Mar 05; artificers' training hulk Portsmouth 1 Jan 06–Sep 14.

Iron Duke
Plymouth guardship Jan–Sep 71; China (flag) Aug 71–1874; Hull guardship Jul–Sep 75; Kingstown guardship Sep 75–Jul 77; China (flag) Jul 78–1883; Particular Service Squadron Apr–Aug 85; Channel Sep 85–1890; Queensferry guardship May 90–1893; Portsmouth reserve 1893–1902; coal hulk Portsmouth 1902–5; Kyles of Bute 1905–6.

Vanguard
Kingstown guardship Jul 71 to loss.

Swiftsure
Devonport reserve 1871–2; Mediterranean May 72–Oct 78; Pacific (flag) Mar 82–Dec 85; Apr 88–Oct 90; Devonport reserve 1890–1; Devonport guardship Aug 91–1893; Portsmouth reserve 1893–1901; office & workshop hulk Portsmouth 1901–8.

Triumph
Channel Mar 73–Sep 77; Pacific (flag) May 78–Oct 82; Jan 85–Dec 88; Devonport reserve 1889–90; Queenstown (flag) Feb 90–Sep 92; Devonport reserve 1892–Jul 00; destroyer depot hulk Chatham 1904–20 Feb 05; artificers' training hulk Chatham 1 Jan 06–1910; mechanicians' training hulk Devonport 1910–Oct 14; store hulk Invergordon Oct 14–Jan 21.

Shannon (i)
IRON ARMOUR-PLATED SHIP; 1887: 1ST CLASS ARMOURED CRUISER,

Displacement:	5095 tons.
Dimensions:	260 (pp) x 54 x 22.5 feet. 79.2 (pp) x 16.5 x 6.9 metres.
Machinery:	Eight cylindrical boilers; one shaft; reciprocating (HCRCR), IHP 3500 = 13kt; coal 280 tons; range 2260nm @ 10kt.
Armament:	Two 10in/14.5 18-ton MLR, seven 9in/14 12-ton MLR, six 20pdr guns. 1881: six 4in/27 guns and two 14in torpedo tubes added.
Protection:	Belt 6–9–0in; battery 9in; armour deck 1.5in.
Complement:	452.

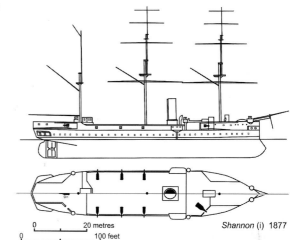

Shannon (i) 1877

Name	Builder	Laid down	Launched	Completed	Fate
Shannon	Pembroke DYd	29 Sep 73	11 Nov 75	17 Sep 77	Sold King 15 Dec 99 & BU Garston.

Particular service 17 Jul 77; Channel Mar 78; China Apr–Jul 78; Channel Dec 78; Mediterranean 1879; Pacific Jul 79–Jul 81; tender to *Warrior* May 83; Greenock coastguard Jun 83; Bantry guardship Aug 83; Particular Service Squadron Jun–Jul 85; Fleet reserve May 93; Dockyard reserve Jan 98.

Nelson class
IRON ARMOUR-PLATED SHIP;
1887: 1ST CLASS ARMOURED CRUISERS

Displacement: 7473 (*Nelson*)/7630 (*Northampton*) tons.

Dimensions: 280 (pp) x 60 x 25.8 feet.
85.5 (pp) x 18.3 x 7.8 metres.

Machinery: Ten oval boilers; two shafts; reciprocating (IC), IHP 6600 (*Nelson*)/6000 (*Northampton*) = 14/13.1kt; coal 1150 tons; range 5000nm @ 10kt.

Armament: Four 10in/14.5 18-ton MLR, eight 9in/14 12-ton MLR, six (removed in 1886 [*Northampton*]/1891 [*Nelson*]) 20pdr guns; four 4.7in (*Nelson* only), six 6pdr, eight/fourteen 3pdr guns. Two 14in torpedo tubes added 1886–91.

Complement: 560.

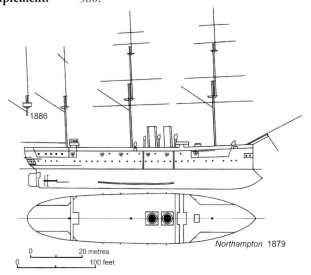

Northampton 1879

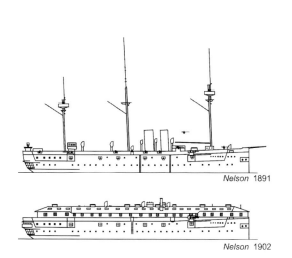

Nelson 1891

Nelson 1902

Name	Builder	Laid down	Launched	Completed	Fate
Nelson	Elder (Hull)	2 Nov 74	4 Nov 76	26 Jul 81	Hulked 1901; sold 12 Jul 10; BU Netherlands.
Northampton	Napier (Glasgow)	26 Oct 74	18 Nov 76	7 Dec 78	Sold T W Ward 5 Apr 05; arrived Morecambe 30 Sep 05 to BU.

Nelson
Australia (flag) Jul 81–1888; Portsmouth guardship Oct 91; Fleet reserve Nov 94; Dockyard reserve Apr 01; hulked as stokers' training ship Dec 01.

Northampton
North America & West Indies Sep 79–Apr 86; 3rd reserve Chatham Nov 86; Sheerness flagship Mar 89; 'A' reserve Sheerness Aug 93; Fleet reserve Feb 94; seagoing training & recruiting ship for boys Jun 94–Nov 04; Fleet reserve Nov 04–Apr 05.

Imperieuse class

STEEL ARMOUR-PLATED BARBETTE SHIP;
1887: 1ST CLASS, ARMOURED CRUISERS

Displacement: 8500 tons.

Dimensions: 315 (pp) 62 x 27.2 feet
96 (pp) x 18.9 x 8.3 metres.

Machinery: Twelve cylindrical/oval boilers; two shafts; reciprocating (IC), IHP 8000/10,000FD = 16/16.7kt; coal 1130 tons; range 5,500nm @ 10kt.

Armament: Four 9.2in/32, six (1892: ten) 6in/25, four 6pdr guns; six 14in torpedo tubes.

Protection: Belt 10in; barbettes 8in; armour deck 4in; conning tower 9in.

Complement: 555.

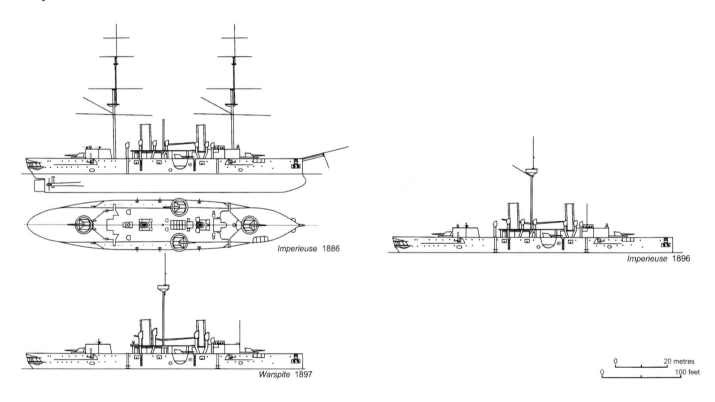

Imperieuse 1886

Imperieuse 1896

Warspite 1897

Name	Builder	Laid down	Launched	Completed	Fate
Imperieuse = *Saphire II* (Feb 05) = *Imperieuse* (Jun 05)	Portsmouth DYd	10 Aug 81	18 Dec 83	Sep 86	Sold T W Ward 24 Sep 13; arrived Morecambe 29 Oct 13 to BU. BU.
Warspite	Chatham DYd	25 Oct 81	29 Jan 84	Jun 88	Sold T W Ward 4 Apr 05; BU Preston.

Imperieuse
China (flag) Mar 89–1894; Pacific (flag) Mar 96–1899; destroyer depot ship Portland Feb 05–Dec 12.

Warspite
Pacific (flag) Feb 90–1893; Queenstown guardship Aug 93–Dec 96; Pacific (flag) Mar 99–1902; Chatham reserve Jul 02.

Orlando class
1ST CLASS ARMOURED CRUISERS

Displacement: 5600 tons (load).

Dimensions: 300 (pp) x 56 x 26 feet.
91.4 (pp) x 17.1 x 7.9 metres.

Machinery: Four cylindrical boilers; two shafts; reciprocating (HTE), IHP 5500/8500FD = 17/18kt; coal 900 tons; range 8000m @ 10kt.

Armament: Two 9.2in/32, ten 6in/25, three 9pdr, ten 3pdr guns; six 14in torpedo tubes (removed 1897–1900).

Protection: Belt 10in; armour deck 2/3in; conning tower 12in.

Complement: 484.

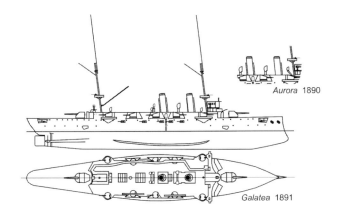

Galatea 1891 / *Aurora* 1890

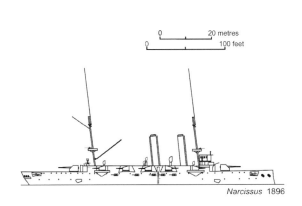

Narcissus 1896

Name	Builder	Laid down	Launched	Completed	Fate
Orlando	Palmers (Jarrow)	23 Apr 85	3 Aug 86	Jun 88	Sold T W Ward 11 Jul 05; arrived Morecambe 17 Jan 06 to BU.
Australia	Fairfield (Govan)	21 Apr 85	25 Nov 86	Oct 88	Sold J J King 4 Apr 05; BU Troon.
Galatea	Napier (Glasgow)	21 Apr 85	10 Mar 87	Mar 89	Sold J J King g 4 Apr 05; BU Troon.
Narcissus	Earle (Hull)	27 Apr 85	15 Dec 86	Jul 89	Sold 11 Sep 06; BU Briton Ferry.
Undaunted	Palmer (Jarrow)	23 Apr 85	25 Nov 86	18 Sep 90	Sold Harris (Bristol) 9 Apr 07; BU Falmouth.
Aurora	Pembroke DYd	1 Feb 86	28 Oct 87	1 Jul 90	Sold Payton 2 Oct 07; BU Milford Haven.
Immortalité	Chatham DYd	18 Jan 86	7 Jun 87	1 Jul 90	Sold Shipbreaking Co 1 Jan 07; BU Blackwall

Orlando
Australia (flag) 1888–98; Portsmouth 1898–9; China 1899–1902; Portsmouth 1903–5.

Australia
Chatham 1888–9; Mediterranean 1889–93; Coast Guard, Southampton, 1893–1903; Chatham 1904.

Galatea
Portsmouth 1889–90; Channel 1890–2; Portsmouth 1892–3; Coast Guard, Queensferry 1893–5; Coast Guard, Hull, 1895–1903; Chatham 1904.

Narcissus
Chatham 1889–92; Channel 1892–4; Portsmouth 1895; China 1895–9; Portsmouth 1899–1901; gunnery training ship Portsmouth 1901–5.

Undaunted
Devonport 1889–90; Mediterranean 1890–3; China 1893–1900; gunnery training ship Devonport 1901–4.

Aurora
Devonport 1889–90; Channel 1890–2; Devonport 1892–3; Coast Guard, Bantry Bay, 1893–5; Devonport 1895–9; China 1900–2; refit 1902–3; Devonport 1904; Holy Loch 1905.

Immortalité
Channel 1890–4; Chatham 1894–5; China 1895–9; Sheerness 1899–1901; gunnery training ship, Sheerness, 1901–5; Holy Loch 1905–7.

Blake class

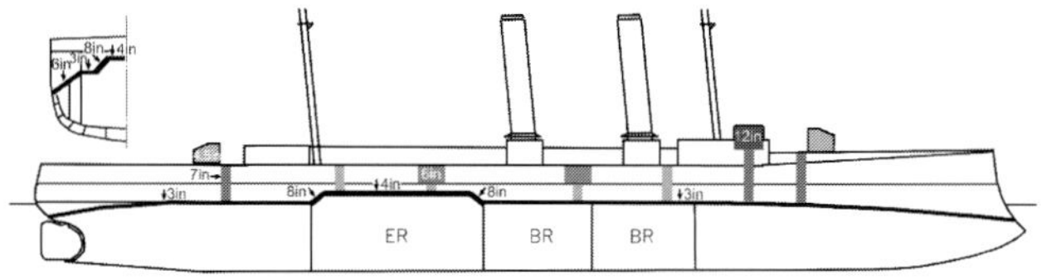

1st class cruisers; 1905: 1st class protected cruisers.

Displacement: 9000 tons.

Dimensions: 375 (pp) 387 (wl) 399 (oa) x 65 x 24 feet.
114.3 (pp) 118 (wl) 121.8 (oa) x 19.8 x 7.3 metres.

Machinery: Six cylindrical boilers; two shafts; reciprocating (VTE – two/shaft), IHP 13,000/20,000FD = 20/22kt; coal 1500/1800 tons; range 15,000nm @ 10kt.

Armament: Two 9.2in/30, ten 6in/26, eighteen 3pdr guns; four 14in torpedo tubes.
Blake 1907: four 6in/40, four 4in/50, four 12pdr guns.
Blenheim 1905: four 6in/40, four 12pdr guns; 1919: three 4in/45, one 12pdr guns.

Protection: Armour deck 3/6in; glacis over cylinders 4/8in; casemates 6in; main shields 4.5in; conning tower 12in.

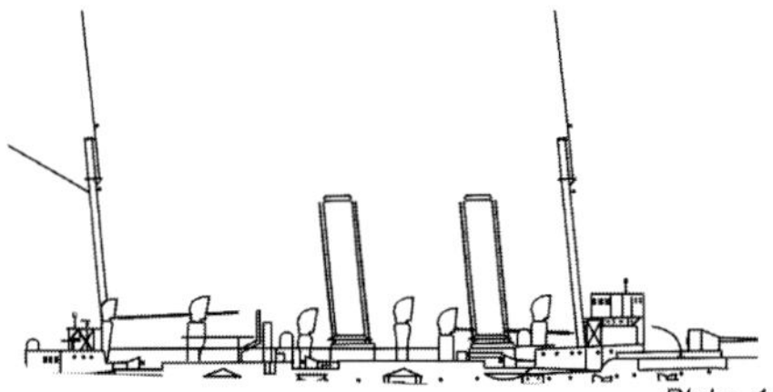

Blake 1894

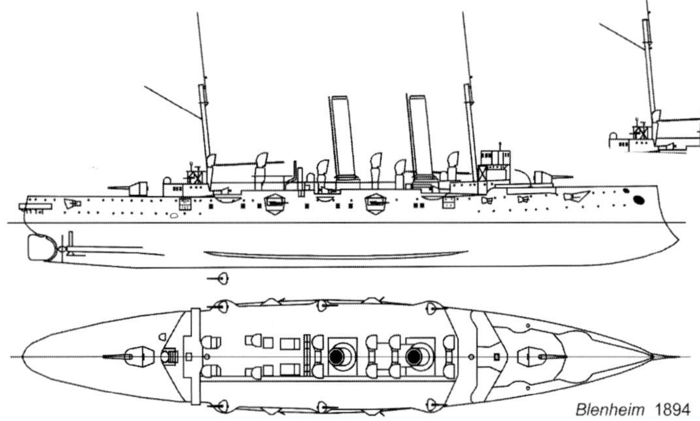

Blenheim 1894

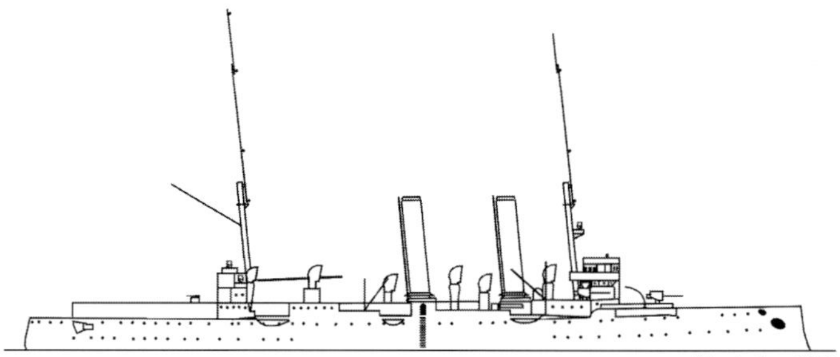

Blenheim 1919

Name	Builder	Laid down	Launched	Completed	Fate
Blake	Chatham DY	Jul 88	23 Nov 89	1892	Sold Edgar G Rees Ltd 9 Jun 22; BU Llanelli from Aug 22.
Blenheim	Thames Iron Works (Poplar)	Oct 88	5 Jul 90	26 May 94	Sold T W Ward 13 Jul 26 & BU Pembroke Dock.

Blake
North America & West Indies 1892–5; Channel 1895–8; Devonport reserve 1897–1907; destroyer depot ship 1907: Nore 1908–9; Home 1909–14; Grand Fleet (2nd, then 11th, DF) 1914–19.

Blenheim
Chatham reserve 1891–4; Channel 1894–8; Chatham reserve 1898; China Jun 98; Chatham reserve 1898–1901; China 1901–4; destroyer depot ship 1905: Home 1906–13; Mediterranean 1912–20; minesweeper depot ship Harwich/Sheerness 1921–5.

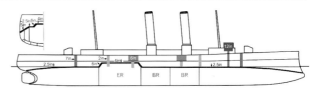

Edgar class

1ST CLASS CRUISERS; 1905: 1ST CLASS PROTECTED
CRUISERS; 1913: CRUISERS.

Displacement: 7350 tons (load); *Gibraltar, St George, Crescent & Royal Arthur* 7700 tons.

Dimensions: 360 (pp) 387.5 (oa) x 60 (*Edgar, Endymion, Grafton & Theseus* 1915: 90) x 24 feet.
109.7 (pp) 118.1 (oa) x 18.3 (27.5) x 7.2 metres.

Machinery: Four cylindrical boilers; two shafts; reciprocating (VTE), IHP 7700/12,000FD = 18/19.5kt; coal 850/1250 tons.

Armament: Two (*Crescent & Royal Arthur* one; removed 1915) 9.2in/30, ten (*Crescent & Royal Arthur* twelve; *Edgar, Endymion, Grafton & Theseus* 1915: twelve) 6in/40, twelve 6pdr (eight 6pdr, four 4.7in in *Endymion, Theseus & Grafton* 1905–12), five 3pdr guns; four 18in torpedo tubes. *Royal Arthur* 1915: disarmed. *St George* 1910: four 6in/40, eight 12pdr; 1919: two 6in, two 12pdr AA, two 3pdr AA guns. *Crescent* Feb 15: four 6in/40 guns.

Protection: Armour deck 2.5/5in; glacis over cylinders 4/6in; casemates 6in; conning tower 12in.

Complement: 544.

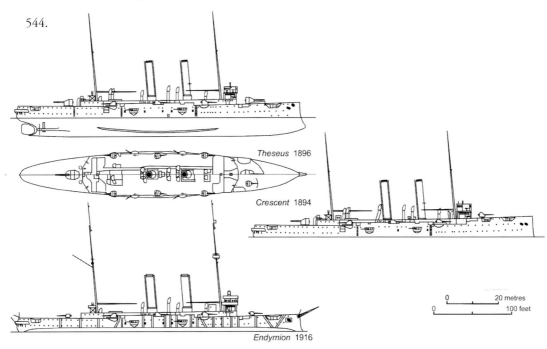

Theseus 1896

Crescent 1894

Endymion 1916

Name	Builder	Laid down	Launched	Completed	Fate
Edgar	Devonport DYd	3 Jun 89	24 Nov 90	2 Mar 93	Sold T W Ward 9 May 21; arrived Morecambe 3 Apr 23 to BU.
Endymion	Earle (Hull)	21 Nov 89	22 Jul 91	26 May 94	Sold E Evans 16 Mar 20 & BU Cardiff.
Gibraltar	Beardmore (Dalmuir)	2 Dec 89	27 Apr 92	1 Nov 94	Sold J Cashmore Sep 23 & BU Newport.
Grafton	Thames Iron Works (Blackwall)	1 Jan 90	30 Jan 92	18 Oct 94	Sold S Castle 1 Jul 20 & BU Plymouth.
Hawke	Chatham DYd	17 Jun 89	11 Mar 91	16 May 93	Torpedoed *U9* North Sea 15 Oct 14.
St George	Earle (Hull)	23 Apr 90	23 Jun 92	25 Oct 94	Sold S Castle 1 Jul 20 & BU Plymouth.
Theseus	Thames Iron Works (Blackwall)	16 Jul 90	8 Sep 92	14 Jan 96	Sold Stanlee 1921; resold Slough Trading Co 8 Nov 21 & BU Germany.
Crescent	Portsmouth DYd	13 Oct 90	20 Mar 92	22 Feb 94	Sold Cohen 22 Sep 21; BU Germany.
Royal Arthur (ex-*Centaur*)	Portsmouth DYd	20 Jan 90	26 Feb 91	2 Mar 93	Sold Cohen 22 Sep 21; BU Germany.

Edgar
Mediterranean 1893–4; China 1894–7; transport 1898–1900; Devonport 1901–2; Holyhead guardship 1903–4; Chatham 1905; North America & West Indies (Boys' TS) 1905–6; nucleus crew, Nore 1907; trooping 1907–8; 4th Div Portsmouth 1909–11; 3rd Fleet 1912; Training Sqn Queenstown 1913–14; 10th CS 1914; Dardanelles 1915–16; Aegean 1917; Gibraltar 1918; Queenstown, paid off 1919.

Endymion
Channel 1894–5; Particular Service 1896–7; Chatham 1899–1902; Channel 1904; gunnery TS Sheerness 1905–12; 3rd Fleet Portsmouth 1912–13; Training Sqn Queenstown (flag) 1913–14; 10th CS 1914; Dardanelles 1915–16; Mediterranean 1916–18; Aegean 1918; Nore, paid off 1919.

Gibraltar
Particular service 1894–5; Flying Sqn 1896; Mediterranean 1896–9; Portsmouth 1899–1901; Cape (flag) 1901–4; North America & West Indies 1904–6; nucleus crew & 4th Div Devonport 1906–13; Anti-submarine School Portland 1914; 10th CS 1914; depot ship Swarbacks Minn Oct 15–Jan 18; Longhope Feb 18–Dec 18; destroyer depot ship Portland Mar 19–1923; paid off 24 Apr 23.

Grafton
Particular Service 1894–5; China (flag) 1895–9; Chatham 1899–1901; Pacific 1902–4; gunnery TS Portsmouth 1905–13; Training Sqn Queenstown 1913–14; 10th CS 1914; Dardanelles 1915–16; Mediterranean 1916–17; Red Sea 1917–18; Aegean 1918; depot ship Black Sea 1919; Nore, paid off 1919–20.

Hawke
Mediterranean 1893–9; Chatham 1899–1902; Special service 1902; Home 1903–4; 4th CS North America & West Indies 1904–6; Torpedo school Sheerness 1906–7; nucleus crew Nore 1907; 3rd Fleet Portsmouth/Nore 1908–13; Training Sqn Queenstown 1913–14; 10th CS 1914 to loss.

St George
Cape & West Africa (flag) 1894–8; Portsmouth 1898–9; Cruiser Sqn 1899–1902; Chatham 1902–4; South Atlantic 1904; North America & West Indies (Boys' TS) 1905–6; nucleus crew Devonport 1906–9; destroyer depot ship 1910; 3rd DF Nore Feb 10–1912; 9th DF Firth of Forth 1913–14; 7th DF Humber 1914–15; Mediterranean 1915–17; submarine depot ship 1917; Aegean 1918–19.

Theseus
Flying Sqn 1896; Mediterranean 1896–8 (Cape 1897); Mediterranean 1899–1902; Chatham 1902–5; gunnery TS Devonport 1905–11; 3rd Fleet Devonport 1912; Training Sqn Queenstown 1913–14; 10th CS 1914; Dardanelles 1915–16; Mediterranean 1916–18; trawler depot ship Aegean 1918; Black Sea 1918–19; Devonport, paid off 1919.

Crescent
Special service (China/Australia) 1894–5; North America & West Indies (flag) 1895–7; Portsmouth 1897–9; North America & West Indies (flag) 1899–1902; Portsmouth 1902–3; Cape (flag) 1904–7; 3rd Fleet Portsmouth 1907–13; Training Sqn Queenstown 1913–14; 10th CS 1914 (flag); guardship, Hoy 1915; Portsmouth 1915–17; submarine depot ship Scapa Flow 1917–18; Firth of Forth 1919.

Royal Arthur
Pacific (flag) 1893–6; Portsmouth 1896–7; particular service 1897; Australia (flag) 1897–1904; North America & West Indies (flag) 1905–6; nucleus crew/4th Div Portsmouth 1906–13; Training Sqn Queenstown 1913–14; 10th CS 1914; guardship Scapa Flow 1915; submarine depot ship 12th S/MF 1918; 1st S/MF Rosyth 1919–20; paid off 1920.

Old battleships reclassified as 1st class armoured cruisers in May 1892

Name	Displacement	Launched	Fate
Warrior = *Vernon III* (1 Apr 04) = *Warrior* (1 Oct 23) = *C77* (27 Aug 42) =*Warrior* (1860) (1974)	9137 tons	29 Dec 60	Paid off Jun 83; destroyer depot hulk 16 Jul 02–31 Mar 04; workshop/power plant 1 Apr 04–Oct 23; oil pipeline jetty Milford Haven Mar 29–1978; museum ship 1979.
Black Prince = *Emerald* (Mar 04) = *Impregnable III* (Jul 10) = *Black Prince* (12 Oct 22)	9137 tons	27 Feb 61	Training hulk 1896; sold 21 Feb 23 & BU.
Hector	7000 tons	26 Sep 62	Paid off 1886; sold 11 Jul 05 & BU.
Achilles = *Hibernia* (1902) = *Egmont* (Mar 04) = *Egremont* (19 Jun 16) = *Pembroke* (6 Jun 19)	9820 tons	23 Dec 63	Paid off 1885; depot ship 1901; sold Granton Shipbreaking Co. 26 Jan 23 & BU.
Minotaur = *Boscowen* (Mar 04) = *Ganges* (21 Jul 06) = *Ganges II* (25 Apr 08)	10,627 tons	12 Dec 63	Training ship 1895; sold 30 Jan 22.
Agincourt = *Boscowen III* (Jun 04) = *Ganges II* (21 Jun 06) = *C108* (Sep 08)	10,627 tons	27 Mar 65	Training ship 1895; coal hulk 1910; sold & arrived Greys to BU 21 Oct 60.
Northumberland = *Acheron* (Mar 04) = *C8* (1909) = *C68* (1926) = *Stedmound* (1927)	10,584 tons	14 Apr 66	Training ship 1898; coal hulk 1909; sold T.W. Ward 26 Apr 27; re-sold Steamship Owners Co-operative Ltd as coal hulk; sold at Dakar 1935.

Centurion class
1ST CLASS ARMOURED BATTLE SHIPS; 1905: BATTLE SHIPS

Displacement:	10,634 (load), 11,120 (deep) tons.
Dimensions:	360 (pp) x 390.8 (oa) x 70 x 25.6/26.7 feet. 109.7 (pp) 119.1 (oa) x 21.3 x 7.8/8.1 metres.
Machinery:	Eight cylindrical boilers; two shafts; reciprocating (VTE), IHP 9000/13,000FD = 17/18.5kt; coal 750/1440 tons; range 5230nm @ 10kt.
Armament:	Four 10in/32 (2 x 2), ten 4.7in/40 (1904: 6in/45), eight 6pdr, twelve 3pdr guns; seven (1904: three) 18in torpedo tubes.
Protection:	Main belt 0–9–10–12–10–9–0in; upper belt 0–4–0in; barbettes 9in; main shields 6in; casemates 4in (1904: 5in); armour deck 2.5–2–2.5in; conning tower 12in (fore), 3in (aft) (compound).
Complement:	600.

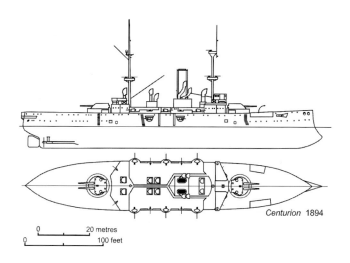

Centurion 1894

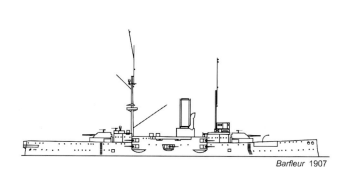

Barfleur 1907

Name	Builder	Laid down	Launched	Completed	Fate
Centurion	Portsmouth DYd	30 Mar 90	3 Aug 92	14 Feb 94	Sold T W Ward 12 Jul 10; arrived Morecambe 4 Sep 10 to BU.
Barfleur	Chatham DYd	12 Oct 90	10 Aug 92	22 Jun 94	Sold C Ewen (Glasgow) Jul 10; resold Hughes Bolckow; arrived Dunston Aug 10 to BU.

Centurion
China (flag) Feb 94–Sep 01; China Nov 03–Aug 05; Portsmouth Division, Home Fleet Sep 05–Mar 09; paid off Portsmouth 1 Apr 09.

Barfleur
Mediterranean Feb 95; China Sep 98–Dec 01 (2nd flag to Sep 00); Fleet reserve Jan 02; commissioned reserve Jan 05; Portsmouth reserve (flag) May 05; nucleus crew Mar 07; 4th Division, Home Fleet, Apr 09; paid off Portsmouth Jun 09.

Powerful class

1ST CLASS CRUISERS; 1905: 1ST CLASS
PROTECTED CRUISERS;
1913: CRUISER (TERRIBLE)

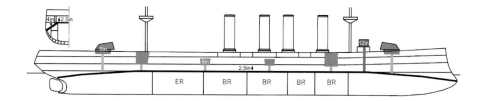

Displacement: 14,200 tons.

Dimensions: 500 (pp) 521 (wl) 538 (oa) x 71 x 27 feet.
152.4 (pp) 158 (wl) 164 (oa) x 21.6 x 8.2 metres.

Machinery: Forty-eight Belleville boilers; two shafts; reciprocating (VTE), IHP 18,000/25,000FD = 20/22kt; coal 1500/3000 tons+ oil 100 tons.

Armament: Two 9.2in/40, twelve (Powerful 1903: sixteen) 6in/40, sixteen 12pdr/12cwt, two 12pdr/8cwt, twelve 3pdr guns; four 18in torpedo tubes.

Protection: Casemates, barbettes & turrets 6in; armour deck 2.5/4in; conning tower 12in.

Complement: 894.

Name	Builder	Laid down	Launched	Completed	Fate
Powerful = Impregnable (1 Dec 19)	Naval Construction & Armaments (Barrow)	1894	24 Jul 95	8 Jun 97	Hulked 1913; sold Hughes Bolckow 19 Aug 29; 29; arrived Blyth Sep 29 to BU.
Terrible = Fisgard III (Aug 20)	J & G Thomson (Clydebank)	1894	27 May 95	24 Mar 98	Hulked 1916; sold J Cashmore 25 Jul 32; arrived Newport Sep 32 & BU to 8 Jun 34.

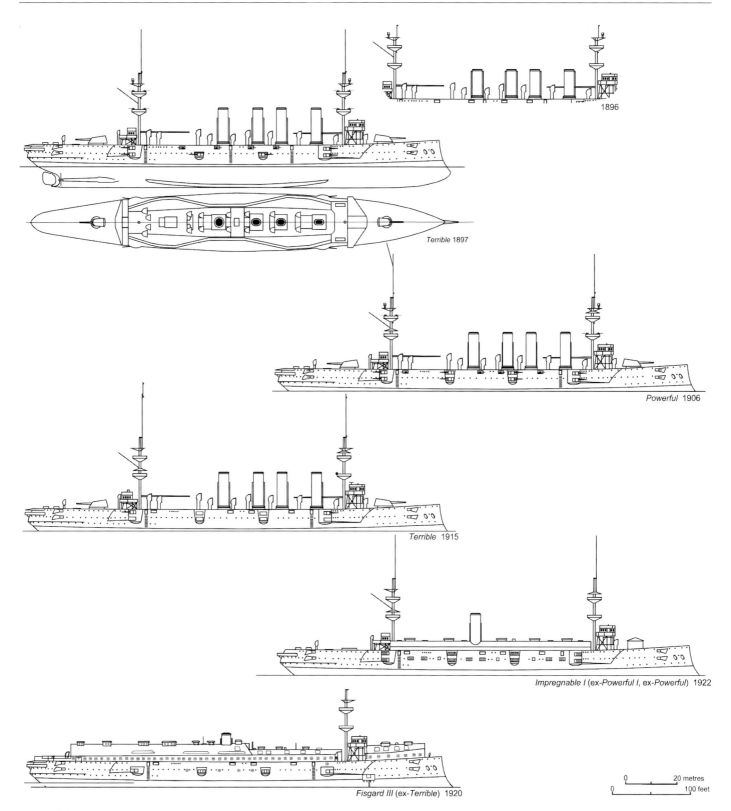

Terrible 1897

Powerful 1906

Terrible 1915

Impregnable I (ex-Powerful I, ex-Powerful) 1922

Fisgard III (ex-Terrible) 1920

1896

0   20 metres
0   100 feet

Powerful
China 1898–9; Cape Oct 99– Mar 00; Portsmouth reserve 1903–6; Australia (flag) Oct 07–Jan 12; 3rd Fleet (attached 7th CS) Mar–Aug 1912; boys' TS Devonport Sep 13–1 Jan 29.

Terrible
Special service 1898–9; Cape Oct 99–Mar 00; China Apr 00–Oct 02; special service 21 Jun–22 Dec 04; Portsmouth commissioned reserve/special service 3 Jan 05–1906; Portsmouth nucleus crew/4th Div 1906–4 May 08; Portsmouth nucleus crew/4th Div 1 Apr 09–Dec 13; Pembroke reserve Dec 13–Jul 14; trooping to Dardanelles 9 Sep 15–26 Jan 16; accommodation ship Portsmouth Mar 16–1 Sep 19 (commissioned from 29 Jan 18); accommodation ship for *Fisgard* establishment Nov 19–1 Jan 32.

Renown
BATTLE SHIP, 1ST CLASS, ARMOURED; 1905: BATTLE SHIP

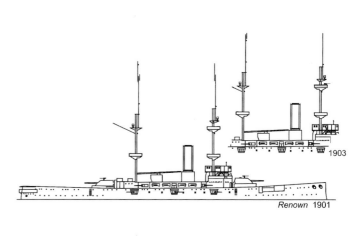

Displacement:	11,690 tons.
Dimensions:	380 (pp) 412.2 (oa) x 72.3 x 25.4 feet. 115.8 (pp) x 125.6 (oa) x 22 x 7.7 metres.
Machinery:	Eight cylindrical boilers; two shafts; reciprocating (VTE), IHP 10,000/12,000FD = 17/18kt; coal 800/1890 tons; range 6400nm @ 10kt.
Armament:	Four 10in/32 (2 x 2), ten (1902: four; 1905: nil) 6in/40, twelve 12pdr/12cwt, two 12pdr/8cwt, eight 3pdr guns; five 18in torpedo tubes.
Protection:	Main belt 0–6–8–6–0in; upper belt 0–6–0in; barbettes 10in; main shields 6–1in; casemates (upper) 4in (lower) 6in; armour deck 3–2–3in; conning tower (fwd) 12in (aft) 3in (Harvey).
Complement:	650.

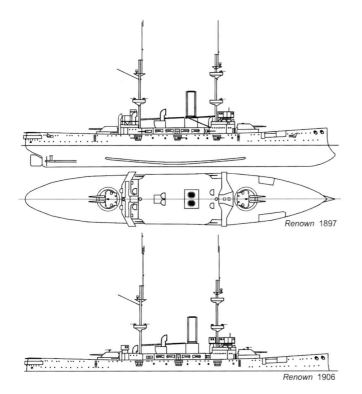

Renown 1897

Renown 1906

1903

Renown 1901

Name	Builder	Laid down	Launched	Completed	Fate
Renown	Pembroke DYd	1 Feb 93	8 May 95	8 Jun 97	Sold Hughes Bolckow 2 Apr 14; arrived Blyth to BU Apr 14.

North America & West Indies (flag) Aug 97–Apr 99; Mediterranean Jul 99–Oct 02 (flag to May 02); royal yacht Nov 02–Mar 03; Mediterranean Apr 03–May 04; Devonport reserve May 04–Apr 05; royal yacht Oct 05–May 06; Portsmouth reserve May 06–May 07; Home Fleet as subsidiary yacht May 07–Mar 09; 4th Division, Home Fleet, Apr–Sep 09; stokers' training ship Portsmouth Oct 09–Jan 13.

Diadem class

1ST CLASS CRUISERS; 1905: 1ST CLASS
PROTECTED CRUISERS; 1913: CRUISERS

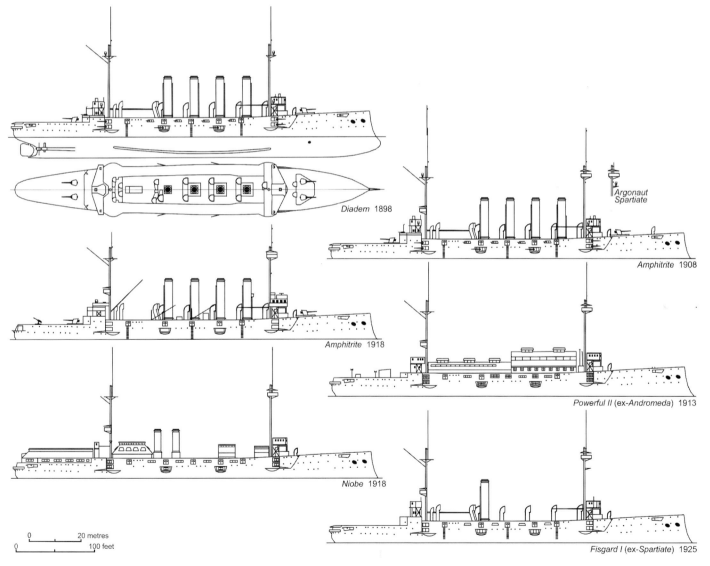

Displacement:	11,000 tons.
Dimensions:	435 (pp) 456 (wl) 462.5 (oa) x 69 x 25.5 feet. 132.6 (pp) 139 (wl) 141 (oa) x 21 x 7.8 metres.
Machinery:	Thirty Belleville boilers; two shafts; reciprocating (VTE), IHP 16,500 (last four: 18,000) = 20.25kt (20.75kt); coal 1000/1900 tons.
Armament:	Sixteen (*Ariadne* & *Amphitrite* 1917: four) 6in/40, twelve 12pdr/12cwt, two 12pdr/8cwt, twelve 3pdr guns; two 18in torpedo tubes. *Ariadne* & *Amphitrite* 1917: one 4in AA gun, 400 mines.
Protection:	Casemates & shields 4.5in; armour deck 2.5/4in; conning tower 12in.
Complement:	677.

Diadem 1898

Argonaut
Spartiate

Amphitrite 1908

Amphitrite 1918

Powerful II (ex-*Andromeda*) 1913

Niobe 1918

Fisgard I (ex-*Spartiate*) 1925

0   20 metres
0   100 feet

Name	Builder	Laid down	Launched	Completed	Fate
Diadem	Fairfield (Govan)	23 Jan 96	21 Oct 96	19 Jul 97	Sold T W Ward 5 Sep 21; arrived Morecambe 1 Oct 21 to BU.

Andromeda = *Powerful II* (1913) *Impregnable II* (Nov 19) = *Defiance* (20 Jan 31)	Pembroke DYd	2 Dec 95	30 Apr 97	5 Sep 99	Hulked 1913; sold 14 Aug 56 & BU Bruges.
Europa	J & G Thomson (Clydebank)	10 Oct 96	20 Mar 97	23 Nov 99	Sold Giulio Fradeletto, for Societa Anonyma di Construczione ed Imprese, Genoa 19 Aug 20 (to be mercantile); foundered off Corsica Jan 21; raised & BU.
Niobe	Vickers (Barrow)	16 Dec 95	20 Feb 97	6 Dec 98	To Canada 6 Sep 10; sold 1922 & BU Philadelphia.
Amphitrite	Vickers (Barrow)	8 Dec 96	5 Jan 98	17 Sep 01	Minelayer 1917; Sold T W Ward 4 Dec 20 & BU Milford Haven.
Argonaut Haven Sep	Fairfield (Govan)	23 Nov 96	24 Jan 98	19 Apr 00	Sold T W Ward 18 May 20; arrived Milford 20 to BU.
Ariadne	Thomson (Clydebank)	29 Oct 96	22 Apr 98	5 Jun 02	Minelayer 1917; torpedoed *UC65* off Beachy Head 26 Jul 17.
Spartiate = *Fisgard I* (1915)	Pembroke DYd	10 May 97	27 Oct 98	17 Mar 03	Sold T W Ward 25 Jul 32; arrived Pembroke Dock Aug 32 & BU to 8 Jun 34. Aug 32 & BU to 8 Jun 34.

Diadem
Channel 1898–1902; particular service/Chatham reserve 1904–5; China 1905–7; Portsmouth nucleus crew 1907–9; 4th Division 1909–13 (attached 7th CS, 3rd Fleet, 1912); stokers' TS Portsmouth 1914–18 (closed Oct 15–Jan 18); accommodation ship 1 Jan 18–Oct 20.

Andromeda
Mediterranean 1899–1902; China 1904–6; Chatham nucleus crew 1906; Devonport nucleus crew & 4th Division 1907–11; attached 9th CS, 3rd Fleet, 1912; boys' TS Devonport 1913–29; torpedo school 20 Jan 31.

Europa
Trooping to Australia 1899–1900; Portsmouth reserve 1900–4; Devonport commissioned reserve/4th Division 1904–11 (special service 1908); attached 9th CS, 3rd Fleet, 1912–14; 9th CS 1914–15; Mudros (flag) Jul 15–Oct 19; Smyrna 29 Oct 19–Mar 20; Malta (paid off) Mar 20 to sale.

Niobe
Channel 1898–1902 (detached to Cape 1899–1900, and escort to HMY *Ophir* to India 1901); Devonport nucleus crew & 4th Division 1905–10; sold to Canada 1910; Atlantic 10 Oct 10–1912; 4th CS North America & West Indies Oct 14–Jul 15; depot ship Halifax NS 6 Sep 15–31 May 20; paid off.

Amphitrite
Special service 1901–2; China 1902–5; Chatham, nucleus crew 1905–7; Devonport 1908–9 (trooping 1908); stokers' TS Devonport 1910–14 (attached 9th CS, 3rd Fleet, 1912–14); 9th CS 1914–15; accommodation ship Portsmouth 22 Jun 15–18 Jun 16; converted to minelayer Devonport 1916–9 Aug 17; Nore Command Aug 17–Jun 19; Portsmouth reserve 1919–20.

Argonaut
China 1900–4; Chatham commissioned reserve 1904–5; nucleus crew 1909–11; Portsmouth 4th Div 1909–11; attached 7th CS 3rd Fleet 1912–14 (TS special entry cadets 10 Oct 13; 9th CS 1914–15; hospital ship Portsmouth 1915–17; accommodation ship for stokers 1 Jan 18–Mar 20.

Ariadne
North America & West Indies (flag) 1902–5; Portsmouth commissioned reserve/nucleus crew 1905–9; 4th Div 1909–11; attached 7th CS 3rd Fleet 1912–13; stokers' TS Portsmouth Oct 13–1915; accommodation ship Devonport for *Impregnable* 7 Jul 15 & overflow ship *Vivid* 9 Sep 15; converted to minelayer Devonport 1916–20 Mar 17; Nore Command 1917.

Spartiate
Portsmouth reserve 1903–4; Chatham reserve 1904–5; Portsmouth nucleus crew 1906–9 (trooping 1907); 4th Div 1909–11; attached 7th CS 3rd Fleet 1912–13; stokers' TS Portsmouth 1913–15; accommodation ship for *Fisgard* establishment 17 Jul 15–14 Jan 32 (paid off).

Cressy class
1ST CLASS ARMOURED CRUISERS; 1905:
ARMOURED CRUISERS; 1913: CRUISERS

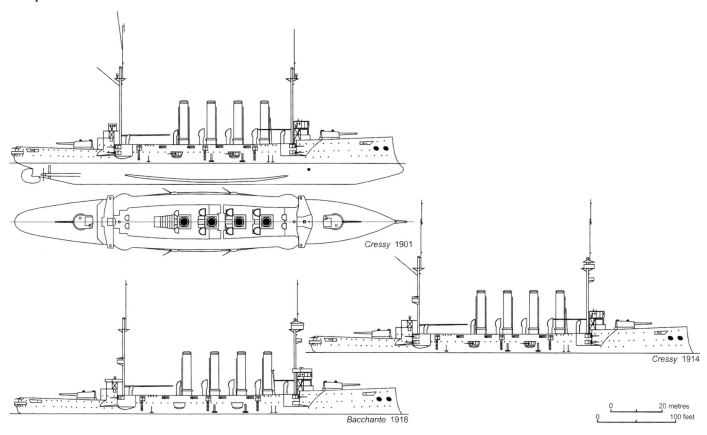

Displacement:	12,000 tons.
Dimensions:	440 (pp) 460 (wl) 472 (oa) x 69.5 x 26 feet. 134.1 (pp) 140.2 (wl) 143.9 (oa) x 21.2 x 7.9 metres.
Machinery:	Thirty Belleville boilers; two shafts; reciprocating (VTE), IHP 21,000 = 21kt; coal 800/1600 tons.
Armament:	Two 9.2in/46.7, twelve (*Bacchante, Sutlej* & *Euryalus* 1916: four) 6in/45, twelve 12pdr/12cwt, two 12pdr/8cwt, three 3pdr guns; two 18in torpedo tubes.
Protection:	Belt 0–6–2in; turrets & barbettes 6in; casemates 5in; armour deck 3–2.5–1.5in; main deck 0–0.5–0in; conning tower 12in.
Complement:	760.

Cressy 1901

Cressy 1914

Bacchante 1918

Name	Builder	Laid down	Launched	Completed	Fate
Hogue	Vickers (Barrow)	14 Jul 98	13 Aug 00	19 Nov 02	Torpedoed *U9* North Sea 22 Sep 14.
Sutlej	John Brown (Clydebank)	15 Aug 98	18 Nov 99	6 May 02	Sold T W Ward 9 May 21; arrived Belfast Mar 24 for lightening & Preston 15 Aug 24 to BU to 30 Jun 25.
Cressy	Fairfield (Govan)	12 Oct 98	4 Dec 99	28 May 01	Torpedoed *U9* North Sea 22 Sep 14.
Aboukir	Fairfield (Govan)	9 Nov 98	16 May 00	3 Apr 02	Torpedoed *U9* North Sea 22 Sep 14.
Bacchante	John Brown (Clydebank)	15 Feb 99	21 Feb 01	25 Nov 02	Sold S Castle 11 Nov 20; transferred to Plymouth & Devonport Shipbreaking Co 18 Sep 24; BU to 1928.
Euryalus	Vickers (Barrow)	18 Jul 99	20 May 01	5 Jan 04	Sold S Castle 29 Aug 21; arrived Deutsche Werke Kiel to BU by A Kubatz 10 Oct 22.

Hogue
Channel 1902–4; China 1904–6; boys' TS, attached 4th CS North America & West Indies 1906–8 (*vice St George*); Devonport nucleus crew 1908–9; Nore 3rd Fleet 1909–11, 1913–14; 7th CS to loss.

Sutlej
Channel 1902–4; China 1904–6; boys' TS, attached 4th CS North America & West Indies 1906–9; Devonport 3rd Fleet 1909–14 (flag 1909–12, attached 6th CS 1912–13, 7th CS 1913, 6th CS 1913–14); 9th CS 1914; 11th CS 1914–15; stokers' TS Devonport 7 Jul–6 Aug 15; 9th CS 1916–17; paid off Devonport 4 May 17; Rosyth overflow ship May 17–1918.

Cressy
China 1901–4; Portsmouth nucleus crew 1904–7; boys' TS, attached 4th CS North America & West Indies 1907–9; Nore 3rd Fleet 1909–14 (attached 6th CS 1912); 7th CS to loss.

Aboukir
Mediterranean 1902–5; Nore nucleus crew 1906, Devonport 1906–7; 3rd CS 1907–9; 6th CS 1909–12; 3rd Fleet 1912–14 (attached 4th CS 1912, 6th CS 1913, 7th CS 1914); 7th CS to loss.

Bacchante
Mediterranean (cruiser flag) 1902–4; Portsmouth nucleus crew 1905–6; 3rd CS 1906–8; 6th CS 1909–12; Nore 3rd Fleet 1912–14 (attached 6th CS 1912); 7th CS (flag) 1914; 12th CS 1914–15; Mediterranean 1915–16; 9th CS (flag) 1917–Apr 19 (at Nore from 31 Dec 18); paid off 30 Apr 19.

Euryalus
Australia (flag) 1904–5; Portsmouth nucleus crew 1905–6; boys' TS, attached 4th CS North America & West Indies 1906–9; Portsmouth 3rd Fleet 1909–10, Devonport 1911–13, Nore 1913–14; 7th CS 1914; 12th CS 1914–15; Mediterranean 1915–16; depot ship Port Said Oct 15–Jan 16; East Indies (flag) 1916–17; under refit as minelayer Hong Kong from Nov 17 (paid off 20 Dec 17; work abandoned Aug 18); to Nore Apr 19.

Drake class
1ST CLASS ARMOURED CRUISERS; 1905: ARMOURED CRUISERS; 1913: CRUISERS

Displacement:	14,150 tons.
Dimensions:	500 (pp) 521 (wl) 533.5 (oa) x 71.3 x 26 feet. 152.4 (pp) 158.8 (wl) 162.6 (oa) x 21.7 x 7.9 metres.
Machinery:	Forty-three Belleville boilers; two shafts; reciprocating (VTE), IHP 30,000 = 23kt; coal 1250/2500 tons
Armament:	Two 9.2in/46.7, sixteen (1916: fourteen) 6in/45, fourteen 12pdr, three 3pdr guns; two 18in torpedo tubes.
Protection:	Belt 0–6–5–2in; turrets & barbettes 6in; casemates 5in; armour deck 3–2.5–1–1.5in; main deck 0–1.5–0in; conning tower 12in.
Complement:	900.

Name	Builder	Laid down	Launched	Completed	Fate
Drake	Pembroke DYd	24 Apr 99	5 Mar 01	13 Jan 03	Torpedoed *U79* North Channel 2 Oct 17.
Good Hope (ex-*Africa*)	Fairfield (Govan)	11 Sep 99	21 Feb 01	8 Nov 02	Gunfire SMS *Scharnhorst* off Coronel 1 Nov 14.
King Alfred	Vickers (Barrow)	11 Aug 99	28 Oct 01	22 Dec 03	Sold R S Heard (ex-Montague Yates) 10 Feb 20; BU Netherlands.
Leviathan	John Brown (Clydebank)	30 Nov 99	3 Jul 01	16 Jun 03	Sold Hughes Bolckow 3 Mar 20 & BU Blyth.

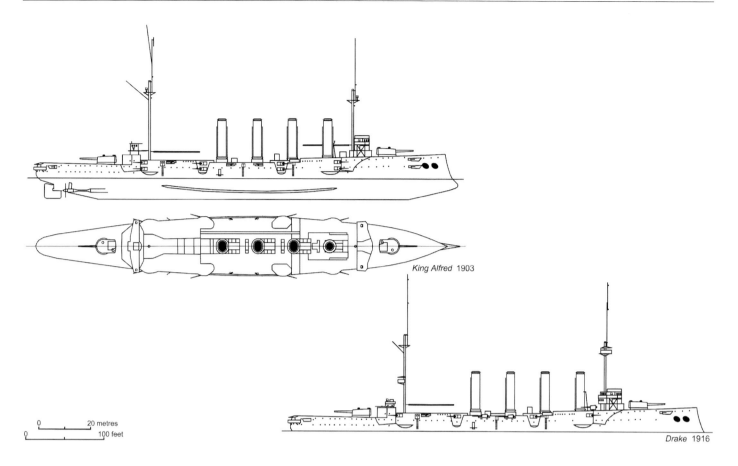

King Alfred 1903

0   20 metres

0   100 feet

Drake 1916

Drake
Channel 1903–4; 2nd Atlantic (flag) 1905–8; 1st CS (Channel) (flag) 1908–10; 5th CS (Atlantic) 1910–11; Australia (flag) 1911–13; 2nd Fleet (attached 6th CS) 1913–14; 6th CS Grand Fleet 1914–15; North America & West Indies 1916 to loss.

Good Hope
Channel 1903–4; 1st CS (Channel) (flag) 1905–7; 2nd CS (Atlantic) (flag) 1907–9; 5th CS (Atlantic) 1911; Mediterranean 1912; 2nd Fleet (attached 6th CS) 1913–14; 6th CS (Grand Fleet) 1914; South America (flag) 1914 to loss.

King Alfred
Particular service 1902; nucleus crew Chatham 1905; China (flag) 1906–10; 3rd Div Devonport 1911; 2nd Fleet (attached 5th, then 6th CS) 1912–14; 6th CS (Grand Fleet) 1914; 9th CS (Atlantic) 1915–17; North America & West Indies 1917–19.

Leviathan
Channel 1903–4; 3rd CS (Mediterranean) 1905–6; 5th CS Home 1908–9; 4th CS North America & West Indies 1909–12; Training Sqn (flag) 1912; 2nd Fleet (attached 6th CS) 1913–14; 6th CS (Grand Fleet) 1914–15; North America & West Indies (flag) 1915–19; paid off 27 Feb 19.

Monmouth/Donegal class

1ST CLASS ARMOURED CRUISERS; 1905:
ARMOURED CRUISERS; 1913: CRUISERS

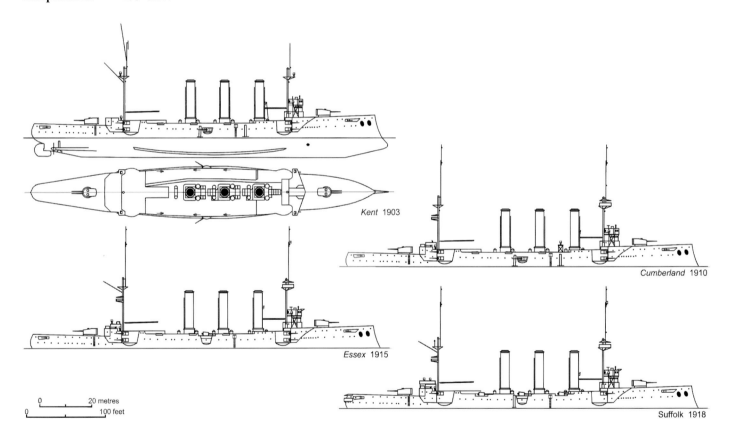

Displacement:	9800 tons.
Dimensions:	440 (pp) 455 (wl) 467.5 (oa) x 68 x 25 feet. 134.1 (pp) 138.7 (wl) 142.5 (oa) x 20.7 x 7.6 metres.
Machinery:	Thirty-one Belleville (*Berwick* & *Suffolk*: Niclausse; *Cornwall*: Babcock) boilers; two shafts; reciprocating (VTE), IHP 9800 = 23kt; coal 800/1600 tons.
Armament:	Fourteen 6in/45 (2 x 2, 10 x 1), eight 12pdr, three 3pdr guns; two 18in torpedo tubes.
Protection:	Belt 0–4–2in; turrets, barbettes & casemates 4in; armour deck 2–0.75–1.5in; main deck 0–1.5–0in; conning tower 10in.
Complement:	675–720.

Kent 1903

Cumberland 1910

Essex 1915

Suffolk 1918

| 0 | 20 metres |
| 0 | 100 feet |

Name	Builder	Laid down	Launched	Completed	Fate
Monmouth	London & Glasgow (Govan)	29 Aug 99	13 Nov 01	2 Dec 03	Gunfire SMS *Gneisenau* & *Nürnberg* off Coronel 1 Nov 14
Bedford	Fairfield (Govan)	19 Feb 00	31 Aug 01	11 Nov 03	Stranded Quelpart (Cheju Do, Saishu To) Island 21 Aug 10; wreck sold Oct 10.
Essex	Pembroke DYd	1 Jan 00	29 Aug 01	22 Mar 04	Sold Slough Trading Co 8 Nov 21; arrived Rustringen 11 Apr 22 to BU by A Kubtz.
Kent	Portsmouth DYd	12 Feb 00	6 Mar 01	1 Oct 03	Sold Tuckcheong 3 Jun 20 & BU Hong Kong.
Cornwall	Pembroke DYd	11 Mar 01	29 Oct 02	1 Dec 04	Sold T W Ward 7 Jun 20 & BU Briton Ferry.

Suffolk	Portsmouth DYd	25 Mar 01	15 Jan 03	21 May 04	Sold S Castle 29 Aug 22; arrived Wilhelmshaven to BU by A Kubatz 6 Sep 22.
Donegal	Fairfield (Govan)	14 Feb 01	4 Sep 02	5 Nov 03	Sold S Castle 13 Jan 21 (registered as merchantship); transferred to Plymouth & Devonport Shipbreaking Co 18 Sep 24; resold Granton Shipbreaking Co. 1927; arrived Granton to BU Jul 27.
Berwick	Beardmore (Dalmuir)	19 Apr 01	20 Sep 02	9 Dec 03	Sold S Castle 28 Aug 22; arrived Ronnebeck to BU by A Kubatz 3 Sep 22.
Cumberland	London & Glasgow (Govan)	19 Feb 01	16 Dec 02	1 Dec 04	Sold T W Ward 9 May 21; arrived Briton Ferry Apr 23 to BU.
Lancaster	Armstrong (Elswick)	4 Mar 01	22 Mar 02	5 Apr 04	Sold T W Ward 3 Mar 20; stripped Birkenhead & BU Preston.

Monmouth
1st CS (Channel) 1903–6; China 1906–13; 3rd Fleet 1913–14; 5th CS (Atlantic) 1914; South America 1914 to loss.

Bedford
Channel 1903–6; nucleus crew Nore 1906–7; China 1907 to loss.

Essex
2nd CS (Atlantic) 1904–6; nucleus crew Devonport 1906; Home 1907–9; 4th CS North America & West Indies 1909–12; Training Sqn 1912; 4th CS North America & West Indies 1914–16; destroyer depot ship Devonport 1916–19; paid off 1919.

Kent
1st CS (Channel) 1903–5; China 1906–13; South America 1914–15; Pacific 1915–16; Cape 1916–18; China 1918; Vladivostok Jan–Jun 19; paid off Hong Kong 7 Aug 19.

Cornwall
2nd CS (Atlantic) 1904–6; cadet TS North America & West Indies 1908–14; 5th CS (Atlantic) 1914; South America 1914–15; East Africa 1915; Dardanelles 1915; China 1915–17; North America & West Indies 1917–19; cadet TS 1919; paid off 1919.

Suffolk
3rd CS (Mediterranean) 1904–9; 6th CS (Mediterranean) 1909–12; 4th CS North America & West Indies 1913–16; China (flag) 1917–18; Vladivostok 1918–19; paid off Devonport late 1919.

Donegal
Channel 1903–5; nucleus crew Devonport, and Home Fleet 1907–9; 4th CS North America & West Indies 1909–12; Training Sqn 1912; 3rd Fleet (attached 5th CS) 1913–14; 5th CS (Atlantic) 1914; 6th CS Grand Fleet 1915; 7th CS Grand Fleet Nov 15–1916; 2nd CS Grand Fleet Mar–Sep 16; 9th CS (Atlantic) Sep 16–17; 4th CS North America & West Indies 1917–18; paid off Devonport Jun 18; Devonport Care & Maintenance 10 Feb 20.

Berwick
1st CS (Channel) 1903–4; 2nd CS (Atlantic) 1904–7; Portsmouth Div, Home Fleet, 1908; 4th CS North America & West Indies 1909–19 (Training Sqn 1912); 8th LCS North America & West Indies 1919; paid off 1919.

Cumberland
2nd CS (Atlantic) 1904–6; nucleus crew Devonport 1907; North America & West Indies as cadet TS 1907–14; 5th CS (Atlantic) 1914–15; 6th CS Grand Fleet 1915; North America & West Indies 1915–19; cadet TS 1919–20; paid off Queenstown 15 Apr 20.

Lancaster
3rd CS (Mediterranean) 1904–9; 6th CS (Mediterranean) 1909–12; 5th CS, 2nd Fleet 1912–13; 4th CS North America & West Indies 1913–15; Pacific 1916–19; paid off Sheerness 21 Jun 19.

Devonshire class
ARMOURED CRUISERS; 1913: CRUISERS

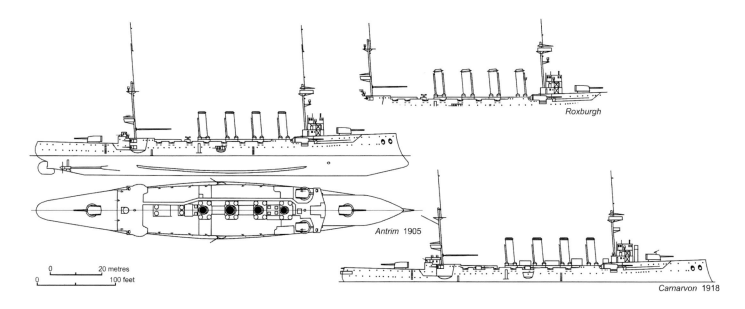

Displacement:	10,700 tons.
Dimensions:	450 (pp) 465 (wl) 473.5 (oa) x 68.6 x 25 feet. 137.2 (pp) 141.7 (wl) 144.3 (oa) x 20.9 x 7.6 metres.
Machinery:	Fifteen Niclausse (*Devonshire*), seventeen Yarrow (*Antrim* & *Hampshire*), sixteen Babcock (*Argyll*) or seventeen Dürr (*Roxburgh*) + six cylindrical boilers; two shafts; reciprocating (VTE), IHP 21,000 = 23kt; coal 800/1800 tons.
Armament:	Four 7.5in/45, six 6in/45, two 12pdr, twenty (1916: ten) 3pdr guns; two 18in torpedo tubes.
Protection:	Belt 0–4–2in; turrets, barbettes & casemates 4in; armour deck 2–0.75–1.5in; main deck 0–1.5–0in; conning tower 10in.
Complement:	655–700.

Roxburgh

Antrim 1905

Carnarvon 1918

0 20 metres
0 100 feet

Name	Builder	Laid down	Launched	Completed	Fate
Devonshire	Chatham DYd	25 Mar 02	30 Apr 04	24 Mar 05	Sold T W Ward 9 May 21; arrived Preston Nov 23 for stripping; BU Barrow.
Antrim	John Brown (Clydebank)	27 Aug 02	8 Oct 03	23 Jun 05	Sold Hughes Bolckow 16 Dec 22; arrived Dunston Mar 23 to BU.
Argyll	Scott's (Greenock)	1 Sep 02	3 Mar 04	Dec 15	Stranded on Bell Rock 28 Oct 15.
Carnarvon	Beardmore (Dalmuir)	1 Oct 02	7 Oct 03	29 May 05	Sold Slough Trading Co 8 Nov 21; left Chatham 28 Mar 22 to BU in Germany.
Hampshire	Armstrong (Elswick)	1 Sep 02	24 Sep 03	15 Jul 05	Mined off Orkneys 5 Jun 16.
Roxburgh	London & Glasgow (Govan)	13 Jun 02	19 Jan 04	5 Sep 05	Sold Slough Trading Co 8 Nov 21; arrived Deutsche Werke, Rustringen, 18 Apr 22 to BU.

Devonshire
1st CS (Channel) 1905–6, (Atlantic) 1906–7; 2nd CS (Atlantic) 1907–9; 3rd Fleet Devonport 1909–11; 3rd CS 2nd Fleet 1913–14; 3rd CS Grand Fleet 1914–16; 7th CS Grand Fleet 1916; North America & West Indies 1916–19; paid off Devonport 31 Mar 20.

Antrim

1st CS (Channel) 1905–6, (Atlantic) 1906–7; 2nd CS (Atlantic) 1907–9; 3rd Fleet Nore 1909–11; 5th CS 2nd Fleet 1912; 3rd CS 2nd Fleet 1913–14; 3rd CS Grand Fleet (flag) 1914–16; Archangel Jun 16; North America & West Indies 1916–18; Nore reserve Sep 18; ASDIC trials ship Mar 20–1921; cadet TS 1922; paid off Portsmouth 1922.

Argyll

1st CS (Atlantic) 1906–7, (Channel) 1907–9; 5th CS (Atlantic) 1909–12; 3rd CS 2nd Fleet 1913–14; 3rd CS Grand Fleet 1914 to loss.

Carnarvon

3rd CS (Mediterranean) 1905–7; 2nd CS (Atlantic) 1907–9; 3rd Fleet Devonport 1909–11; 5th CS 2nd Fleet 1912–14; 5th CS (Atlantic) (flag) 1914; South Atlantic 1914–15; North America & West Indies 1915–18; cadet TS Apr 19–1921.

Hampshire

1st CS (Channel) 1905–6, (Atlantic 1906–7), (Channel) 1907–8; 3rd Fleet Portsmouth 1909–11; 6th CS (Mediterranean) 1911–12; China 1912–14; 6th CS Grand Fleet Dec 14; 7th CS Grand Fleet Jan 15 to loss.

Roxburgh

1st CS (Channel) 1905–6, (Atlantic) 1906–7, (Channel) 1907–9; 3rd Fleet Portsmouth 1909–11; 5th CS 2nd Fleet 1912; 3rd CS 2nd Fleet 1913–14, Grand Fleet 1914–16; North America & West Indies 1916–19; wireless TS 1919–20 paid off Jan 20.

Chilean *Constitucion* class

As p 172.

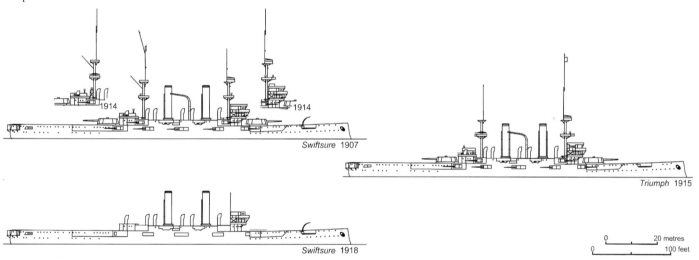

Swiftsure 1907

Triumph 1915

Swiftsure 1918

0   20 metres
0   100 feet

Name	Former namer	Purchased	Completed	Fate
Swiftsure (ii)	*Constitucion*	27 Nov 03	21 Jun 04	Sold Stanlee 18 Jun 20 & BU Dover.
Triumph (ii)	*Libertad*	27 Nov 03	21 Jun 04	Torpedoed German *U21* off Gaba Tepe (Dardanelles) 25 May 15.

Swiftsure

Home/Channel Jun 04–Oct 08; reserve Oct 08–Apr 09; Mediterranean Apr 09–May 12; 3rd Fleet May 12–Mar 13; East Indies Mar 13–Feb 15; Dardanelles Feb 15–Feb 16; 9th CS Feb 16–Mar 17; reserve Apr 17–late 1918; target end 1918.

Triumph

Home/Channel Jun 04–Apr 09; Mediterranean Apr 09–May 12; 3rd Fleet May 12–Aug 13; China Aug 13–Jan 15; Dardanelles Feb 15 to loss.

Duke of Edinburgh class
ARMOURED CRUISERS; 1913: CRUISERS

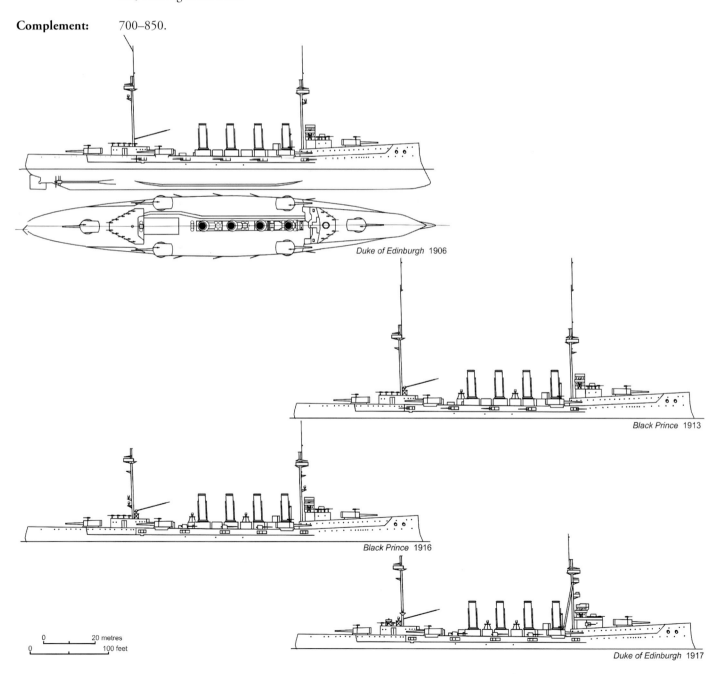

Displacement:	13,550 tons.
Dimensions:	480.27 (pp) 505.3 (oa) x 73.5 x 27 feet.
	146.4 (pp) 154.0 (oa) 22.4 x 8.2 metres.
Machinery:	Twenty Babcock & Wilcox + six cylindrical boilers; two shafts; reciprocating (VTE), IHP 23,500 = 23.3kt; coal 1000/2050 tons + oil 600 tons.
Armament:	Six 9.2in/45, ten (1916: six; 1917: eight) 6in/45, twenty-two 3pdr guns; two 18in torpedo tubes. AA added 1915–16.
Protection:	Belt 4–6–3in; turrets 7.5–4.5in; barbettes 6in; armour deck 1.5–0.75in; main deck 1–0.125–1in; upper deck 0–1–0in; conning tower 10in.
Complement:	700–850.

Duke of Edinburgh 1906

Black Prince 1913

Black Prince 1916

0   20 metres
0   100 feet

Duke of Edinburgh 1917

Name	Builder	Laid down	Launched	Completed	Fate
Duke of Edinburgh	Pembroke DYd	11 Feb 03	14 Jun 04	20 Jan 06	Sold Hughes Bolckow 12 Apr 20 & BU Blyth.
Black Prince	Thames Iron Works (Blackwall)	3 Jun 03	8 Nov 04	17 Mar 06	Gunfire German battleships North Sea 1 Jun 16.

Duke of Edinburgh
2nd CS (Atlantic) 1906–8; 1st CS (Channel) 1908–9; 5th CS (Atlantic) 1909–13; 1st CS (Mediterranean) 1913–14; 1st CS Grand Fleet 1914–16; 2nd CS Grand Fleet Jun 16–1917; North America & West Indies 1918; paid off Portsmouth 3 Aug 18.

Black Prince
2nd CS (Atlantic) 1906–8; 1st CS (Channel) 1908–9; 5th CS (Atlantic) 1909–12; 1st CS (Mediterranean) 1912–14; 1st CS (Grand Fleet) 1914 to loss.

Warrior class
ARMOURED CRUISERS; 1913: CRUISERS

Displacement: 13,550 tons.

Dimensions: 480.27 (pp) 505.3 (oa) x 73.5 x 27 feet
146.4 (pp) 154.0 (oa) 22.4 x 8.2 metres.

Machinery: Nineteen Yarrow + six cylindrical boilers; two shafts; reciprocating (VTE), IHP 23,650 = 23.3kt; coal 1000/2050 tons + oil 600 tons.

Armament: Six 9.2in/45, four 7.5in/50, twenty-six (1910: 1915–16: twenty-four; 1917: twenty) 3pdr guns; three 18in torpedo tubes. One 6pdr (1916: 3in) and two 3pdr AA added 1915–16.

rotection: Belt 4–6–3in; turrets 7.5–4.5in; barbettes 6in; armour deck 1.5–0.75in; main deck 1–0.125–1in; upper deck 0–1–0in; conning tower 10in.

Complement: 712.

Name	Builder	Laid down	Launched	Completed	Fate
Warrior (ii)	Pembroke DYd	5 Nov 03	25 Nov 05	12 Dec 06	Foundered North Sea 1 Jun 16 after gunfire German battleships 31 May 16.
Natal	Vickers (Barrow)	6 Jan 04	30 Sep 05	5 Mar 07	Internal explosion Invergordon 30 Dec 15; wreck sold Stanlee 16 Jun 20; resold Eagle Towing & Barging Co (Southampton) 1924; resold Upnor Shipbreaking Jul 25; resold Middlesbrough Salvage Co 22 Feb 30; resold South Stockton Shipbreaking 23 Feb 37.
Achilles (ii)	Armstrong (Elswick)	22 Feb 04	17 Jun 05	22 Apr 07	Sold T W Ward 9 May 21; arrived Briton Ferry Aug 23 & BU to Oct 25.
Cochrane	Fairfield (Govan)	24 Mar 04	20 May 05	18 Feb 07	Stranded Mersey 14 Nov 18, abandoned 20 Nov 18, BU 1919.

Warrior
5th CS (Atlantic) 1907–09; 2nd CS (Atlantic) 1909–13; 1st CS (Mediterranean) 1913–14; 2nd CS (Grand Fleet) Dec 14 to loss.

Natal
5th CS (Atlantic) 1907–09; 2nd CS (Atlantic /Grand Fleet) 1909 to loss.

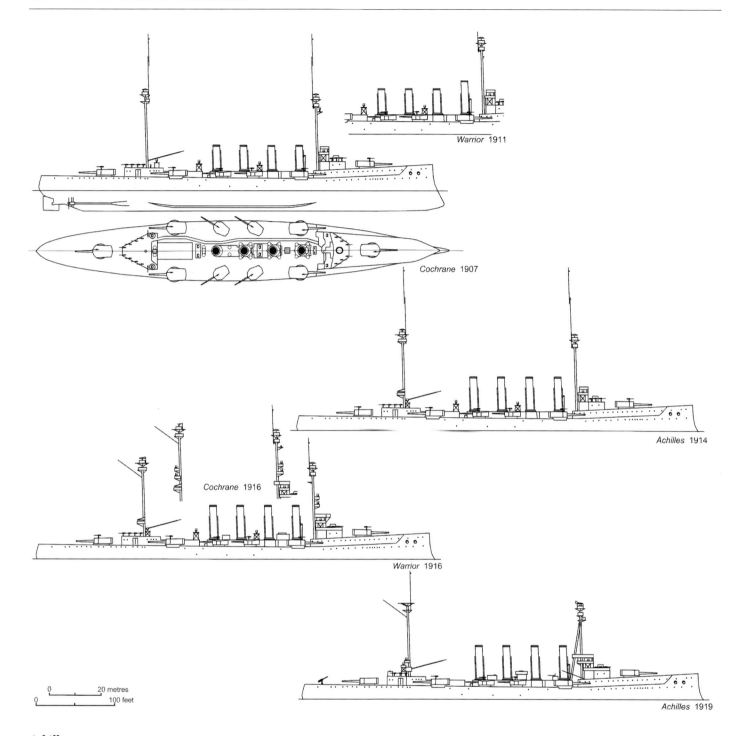

Warrior 1911

Cochrane 1907

Achilles 1914

Cochrane 1916

Warrior 1916

Achilles 1919

0   20 metres
0   100 feet

Achilles
5th CS (Atlantic) 1907–09; 2nd CS (Atlantic/Grand Fleet) 1909–18; Chatham reserve as TS Nov 18–1919; parent ship Reserve Fleet Portsmouth 1 Feb 19–Jun 19; stokers' TS Jun 19–1920.

Cochrane
5th CS (Atlantic) 1907–09; 2nd CS (Atlantic/Grand Fleet) 1909–17; N America & West Indies Nov 17–early 18; 2nd CS (detached to N Russia May–Nov 18) 1918 to loss.

Minotaur class
ARMOURED CRUISERS; 1913: CRUISERS

Displacement:	14,600 tons.
Dimensions:	490 (pp) 519 (oa) x 74.5 (*Shannon* 75.5) x 26.5 feet. 149.4 (pp) 158.2 (oa) x 22.7 (23.0) x 8.1 metres.
Machinery:	Twenty-four Yarrow (*Minotaur* Babcock & Wilcox) boilers; two shaft; reciprocating (VTE), IHP 27,000 = 23kt; coal 1000 (*Shannon* 950)/2010 tons + oil 830 tons; range 8150nm @ 10kt, 2920nm @ 20.6kt.
Armament:	Four 9.2in/50 (2 x 2), ten 7.5in/50, sixteen 12pdr; five 18in torpedo tubes. One 12pdr, one 3pdr AA added 1915/16.
Protection:	Belt 3–6–4–3in; main turrets 8–7in; secondary turrets 8–4.5in; barbettes 7in; armour deck 2–1.5/2.5–2in; conning tower 10in.
Complement:	779.

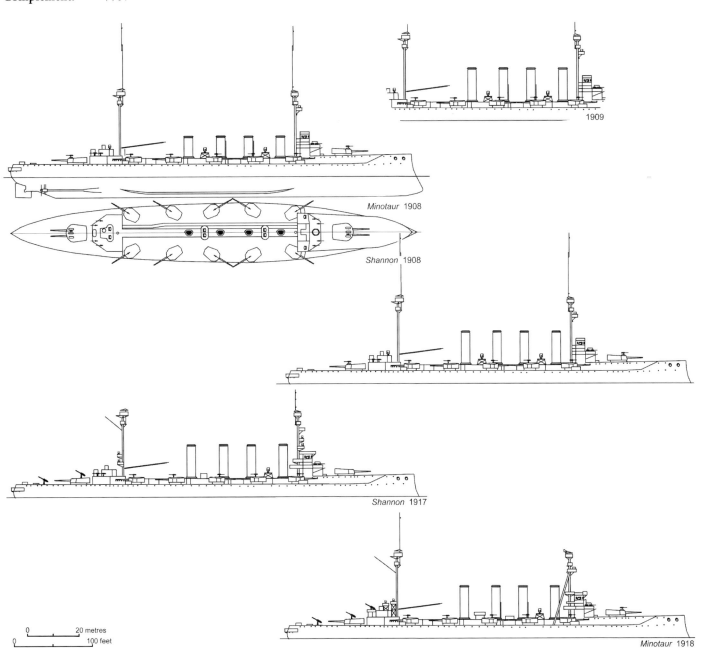

Minotaur 1908

Shannon 1908

1909

Shannon 1917

Minotaur 1918

0   20 metres
0   100 feet

Name	Builder	Laid down	Launched	Completed	Fate
Minotaur (ii)	Devonport DYd	2 Jan 05	6 Jun 06	1 Apr 08	Sold T W Ward 12 Apr 20 & BU Milford Haven.
Shannon (ii)	Chatham DYd	2 Jan 05	20 Sep 06	10 Mar 08	Sold P & W Maclellan Ltd 12 Dec 22; arrived Bo'ness Jan 23 to BU.
Defence (ii)	Pembroke DYd	2 Feb 05	27 Apr 07	9 Feb 09	Gunfire German battleships North Sea 31 May 16.
Orion	–	–	–	–	Cancelled.

Minotaur

5th CS (Atlantic) Apr 08–Mar 09; 1st CS (Atlantic) 23 Mar 09–Jan 10; China (flag) Jan 10–Dec 14; 7th CS (Grand Fleet) Jan 15–May 16; 2nd CS (Grand Fleet) 30 May 16–5 Feb 19 (paid off); disposal list May 19; sale list Mar 20.

Shannon

5th CS (Atlantic) 19 Mar 08–Mar 09; 2nd CS (Atlantic) 23 Mar 09–12 Mar 12; 3rd CS (Atlantic) Mar–Dec 12; 2nd CS (Atlantic/Grand Fleet) Jan 13–2 May 19; accommodation ship for *Acaeton* establishment Sheerness 1919–22.

Defence

5th CS (Atlantic) Feb 09–Mar 09; 2nd CS (Atlantic) 23 Mar 09–Jun 09; 1st CS (Mediterranean) 1912; China 1912; 1st CS (Atlantic/Grand Fleet) Dec 12 to loss.

Invincible class

ARMOURED CRUISERS;
1913: BATTLE CRUISERS

Displacement:	17,250 tons.
Dimensions:	530 (pp) 560 (wl) 567 (oa) x 78.5 x 26.7 feet. 161.5 (pp) 170.7 (wl) 172.8 (oa) x 23.9 x 8.1 metres.
Machinery:	Thirty-one Yarrow (*Indomitable*: Babcock & Wilcox) boilers; four shafts; Parsons turbines, SHP 41,000 = 25kt; coal 1000/3084 tons + oil 725 tons; range 6210nm @ 10kt, 3050nm @ 22.3kt.
Armament:	Eight 12in/45 (4 x 2), sixteen (1917: twelve) 4in/40 (1917: 4in/45 [*Inflexible*] or 4in/50 [*Indomitable*]) guns; five 18in torpedo tubes. One (1916: two, 1917: one) 3in AA added 1915, one 4in/50 AA added 1917.
Protection:	Belt 0–6–4in; turrets 7–3in; barbettes 7in; armour deck 2.5–1.5/2–1.5in; conning tower 10in.
Complement:	780.

Name	Builder	Laid down	Launched	Completed	Fate
Invincible (ii)	Armstrong (Elwick)	2 Apr 06	13 Apr 07	20 Mar 09	Gunfire SMS *Lützow*, Jutland, 31 May 16.
Inflexible	John Brown (Clydebank)	5 Feb 06	16 Jun 07	20 Oct 08	Sold Stanlee (Dover) 1 Dec 21; arrived Dover Apr 22; resold Apr 22 and BU Germany.
Indomitable	Fairfield (Govan)	1 Mar 06	16 Mar 07	25 Jun 08	Sold Stanlee (Dover) 1 Dec 21; arrived Dover 31 Aug 22 to BU.

Invincible

1st CS 20 Mar 09–31 Dec 12; 1st BCS 1 Jan–Aug 13; Mediterranean (2nd BCS) Aug 13–Mar 14; 2nd BCS 19 Aug–Sep 14; 1st BCS Sep–Oct 14; 2nd BCS Oct–5 Nov 14; South Atlantic Nov 14–Jan 15; 3rd BCS Mar 15 to loss.

Inflexible

1st CS Mar 09–Nov 12; Mediterranean (flag) 5 Nov 12–18 Aug 14; 2nd BCS Aug–5 Nov 14; South Atlantic Nov–Dec 14; Mediterranean Jan–Jun 15; 3rd BCS 19 Jun 15–4 Jun 16; 2nd BCS 5 Jun 16–Mar 19; Nore reserve Mar 19–31 Mar 20 (paid off).

Indomitable
1st CS Mar 09–25 Nov 11; 2nd CS 21 Feb–10 Dec 12; 1st CS Dec 12; 1st BCS 1 Jan–26 Aug 13; Mediterranean (2nd BCS) 27 Aug 13–
Nov 14; 2nd BCS Jan–Feb 15; 3rd BCS Feb 15–4 Jun 16; 2nd BCS 5 Jun 16–Feb 19; Nore reserve Mar 19–31 Mar 20 (paid off).

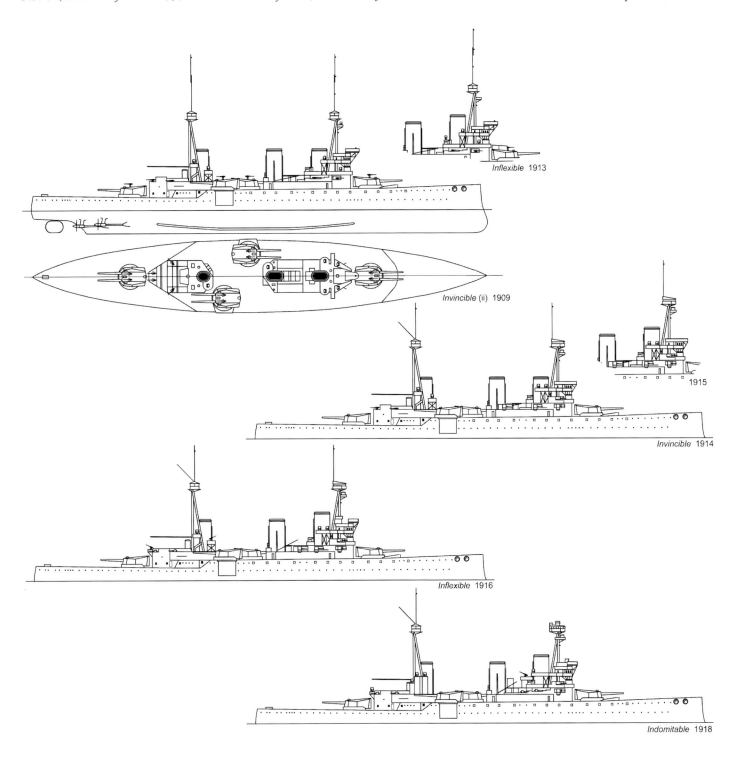

Inflexible 1913

Invincible (ii) 1909

1915

Invincible 1914

Inflexible 1916

Indomitable 1918

	1865	1870	1875	1880	1885	1890	1895	1900	1905	1910	1915	1920	1925	1930	1935	1940	1945	1950	1955
Maine							+												
New York																+			
Columbia																			
Minneapolis																			
Brooklyn																			
Pennsylvania										= Pittsburgh									
West Virginia										= Huntington									
California										= San Diego +									
Charleston																			
Colorado											= Pueblo								
Maryland											= Frederick								
St Louis																			
Milwaukee										+									
South Dakota											= Huron								
Tennessee										+ = Memphis									
Washington										= Seattle									
Montana											= Charlotte								
North Carolina											= Missoula								

Maine

ARMORED CRUISER; 1894; 2ND CLASS BATTLESHIP

Displacement:	6682 tons.
Dimensions:	318 (wl) 324.3 (oa) x 57 x 21.5 feet. 96.9 (wl) 98.8 (oa) x 17.4 x 6.6 metres.
Machinery:	Eight cylindrical boilers; two shafts; reciprocating (VTE), IHP 9000 = 17kt; coal 896 tons; range 3000nm @ 10kt.
Armament:	Four 10in/30 (2 x 2), six 6in/30, seven 6pdr guns; four 18in torpedo tubes.
Protection:	Belt 12in; barbettes 10–11in; turrets 8in; armour deck 2/3in; conning tower 10in.
Complement:	31+343.

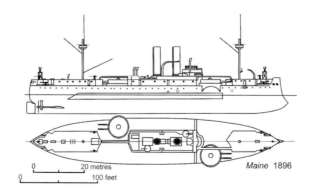

Maine 1896

0   20 metres

0   100 feet

Name	Builder	Laid down	Launched	Completed	Fate
Maine	Brooklyn NY	17 Oct 88	18 Nov 90	17 Sep 95	Internal explosion Havana, Cuba, 15 Feb 98; salved 13 Mar 12; scuttled off Havana 16 Mar 12.North Atlantic Squadron to loss.

New York
ARMORED CRUISER

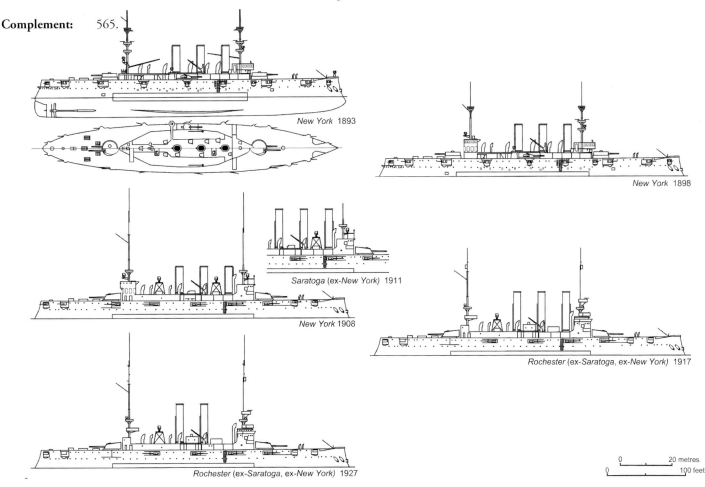

Displacement: 8150 tons.

Dimensions: 380.5 (wl) 384 (oa) 64.8 x 26.7 feet.
116 (wl) 117 (oa) x 19.8 x 8.1 metres.

Machinery: Eight cylindrical (1908: twelve [1927: four] Babcock & Wilcox) boilers; two shafts; reciprocating (VTE – two per shaft), IHP 16,000 (1927: 7,700) = 21kt; coal 750/1150 tons; endurance 4200nm @ 10kt.

Armament: Six 8in/35 (2 x 2, 2 x 1), twelve 4in/40, eight 6pdr guns; three 14in torpedo tubes.
1908: four 8in/45 (2 x 2), ten 5in/50, eight 3in/50, four 3pdr guns.
1917: four 8in/45 (2 x 2), eight 5in/50, two 3in AA guns.

Protection: Belt 4in; armour deck 6in; turrets 5.5in; conning tower 7in.

Complement: 565.

New York 1893

New York 1898

Saratoga (ex-New York) 1911

New York 1908

Rochester (ex-Saratoga, ex-New York) 1917

Rochester (ex-Saratoga, ex-New York) 1927

Hull No[1]	Name	Builder	Laid down	Launched	Completed	Fate
ACR-2 CA-2	*New York* = *Saratoga* (16 Feb 11) = *Rochester* (1 Dec 17)	William Cramp & Son (Philadelphia)	19 Sep 90	2 Dec 91	1 Aug 93	Stricken 28 Oct 38; scuttled Subic Bay, Philippines, 24 Dec 41.

South Atlantic 1893–4; North Atlantic 1894; Europe 1895; Atlantic Fleet 1896–1901; Asiatic Squadron 1901–3; Pacific Squadron 1903–31 Mar 05; reconstructed 1907–8; Armored Cruiser Squadron, Atlantic Fleet 15 May–31 Dec 09; Asiatic Fleet 1 Apr 10–Jan 16; decommissioned 6 Feb 16; Pacific reserve Feb 16–23 Apr 17; Pacific Patrol Force 7 Jun–Nov 17; Atlantic Nov 17–1922; Caribbean & Central America 1923–25 Feb 32; Asiatic Fleet 27 Apr 32–Apr 33; decommissioned 29 Apr 33; hulked Olongapo.

Columbia class
CRUISERS

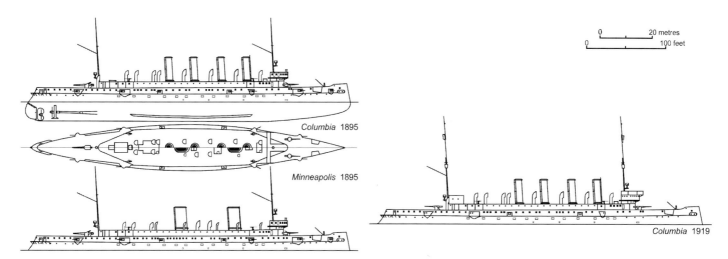

Displacement:	7350 tons.
Dimensions:	411.6 (pp) 413.2 (oa) x 58.3 x 22.6 feet. 125.4 (pp) 125.9 (oa) x 17.7 x 6.9 metres.
Machinery:	Eight cylindrical boilers; three shafts; reciprocating (VTE), IHP 21,500 = 22.5kt; coal 800/1576 tons.
Armament:	One 8in/40 (removed by 1914), two (three by 1914) 6in/40, eight (1917: six; 1918: four) 4in/40, twelve (two by 1914) 6pdr, four 1pdr guns; four 14in (*Columbia*) or 18in (*Minneapolis*) torpedo tubes. Two 3in AA added 1918.
Protection:	Armour deck 2.5/4in, shields and sponsons 4in; conning tower 5in.
Complement:	30+447.

Columbia 1895

Minneapolis 1895

Columbia 1919

Hull No	Name	Builder	Laid down	Launched	Completed	Fate
C-12 CA-16	*Columbia* = *Old Columbia* (17 Nov 21)	W Cramp & Sons (Philadelphia)	30 Dec 90	26 Jul 92	23 Apr 94	Sold 26 Jan 22 & BU.
C-13 CA-17	*Minneapolis*	W Cramp & Sons (Philadelphia)	16 Dec 91	12 Aug 93	13 Dec 94	Sold 5 Aug 21 & BU.

Columbia
Atlantic Sqn Apr 94–May 97; decommissioned 13 May 97; Philadelphia reserve May 97–Mar 98; Atlantic/West Indies 15 Mar 98–Mar 99; decommissioned 31 Mar 99; Philadelphia reserve Mar 99–Aug 02; receiving ship New York 31 Aug 02–Nov 03; Atlantic Training Squadron 9 Nov 03–May 07; decommissioned 3 May 07; Philadelphia reserve May 07–Jun 15; Submarine Flotilla 22 Jun 15–19 Apr 17; Sqn 5, Patrol Force 21 Apr–Jul 17; Cruiser Force Jul 17–Jan 19; Sqn 2, Destroyer Force 7 Jan–29 May 19; decommissioned 29 Jun 21.

Minneapolis
Atlantic Sqn Dec 94–Nov 95; European Sqn 27 Nov 95–6 Jul 97; Philadelphia reserve 7 Jul 97–Mar 98; Atlantic/West Indies 15 Mar–Aug 98; decommissioned 18 Aug 98; Philadelphia reserve Aug 98–Apr 02; receiving ship 23 Apr 02–Jun 02; Philadelphia reserve 2 Jun 03; special service 5 Oct 03–Nov 06; decommissioned 17 Nov 16; Philadelphia reserve Nov 06–Jul 17; Atlantic 2 Jul 17–Feb 18; Cruiser Force 24 Feb–19 Oct 18; Pacific Station 7 Feb 19–Mar 21; decommissioned 15 Mar 21.

Brooklyn
ARMORED CRUISER

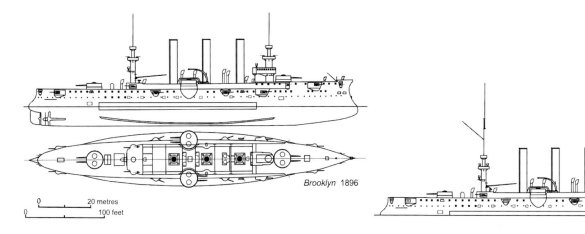

Displacement:	9215 tons.
Dimensions:	400.5 (wl) 402.6 (oa) x 64.7 x 28 feet. 122.1 (wl) 122.7 (oa) x 19.7 x 8.5 metres.
Machinery:	Seven cylindrical boilers; two shafts; reciprocating (VTE – two/shaft), IHP 16,000 = 20kt; coal 900/1461 tons; range 5290nm @ 10kt.
Armament:	Eight 8in/35 (4 x 2), twelve (1918: eight) 5in/40, twelve (1909: four) 6pdr, four 1pdr guns (two 3in AA added 1918); five (1899: four) 18in torpedo tubes (removed 1909).
Protection:	Belt 3in; barbettes 8–4in; turrets 5.5in; armour deck 2.5–3–2.5/3in; secondary sponsons 4in; conning tower 7.5in (belt, turrets and barbettes Harvey).
Complement:	41+440.

Brooklyn 1896

Brooklyn 1919

Hull No	Name	Builder	Laid down	Launched	Completed	Fate
CA-3 ACR-3	*Brooklyn*	W Cramp & Sons (Philadelphia)	2 Aug 93	2 Oct 95	1 Dec 96	Stricken and sold 20 Dec 21; BU.

North Atlantic Squadron 1897–9; Asiatic Squadron/Fleet 16 Oct 99–1 Mar 02; North Atlantic Squadron May–Jun 02; 2nd Squadron, Atlantic Fleet 30 Jun–7 Oct 02; European Squadron 7 Jun 03–Feb 04; South Atlantic Squadron 1904–5; 3rd Division, 2nd Squadron, Atlantic Fleet 1 Apr 05–May 06; decommissioned 8 May 06; special service, Havana, 30 Jun–Aug 06; Jamestown Exposition 12 Apr–4 Dec 07; decommissioned 2 Aug 08; reserve 1909–14; receiving ship, Boston 1914–Mar 15; Atlantic Mar 15–Nov 15; Asiatic Fleet Nov 15–Jan 20; Pacific Fleet Jan 20–15 Jan 21; decommissioned 9 Mar 21.

Pennsylvania class
ARMORED CRUISERS

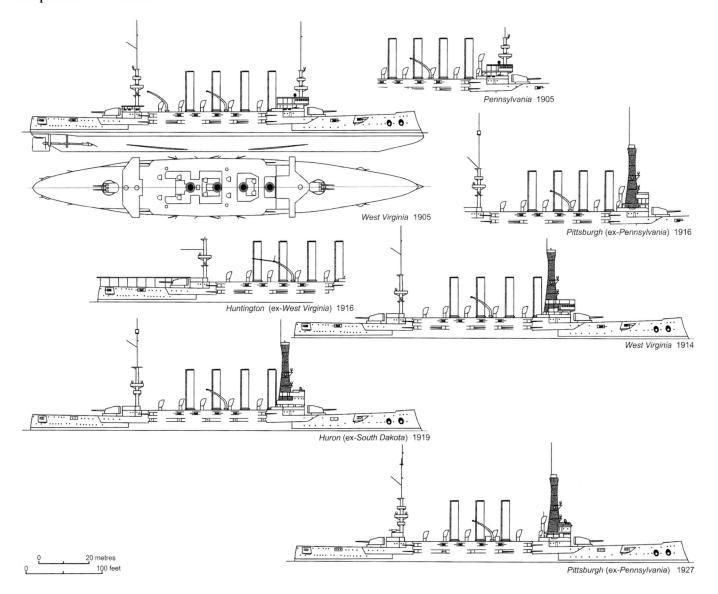

Displacement:	13,680 tons.

Dimensions: 502 (wl) 504 (oa) x 67.6 x 54.2 feet.
153 (wl) 153.6 (oa) x 21.2 x 7.3 metres.

Machinery: Sixteen Babcock & Wilcox (*Pennsylvania* & *Colorado* thirty-two Niclausse, 1911 twenty-four Niclausse & eight Niclausse/ Babcock & Wilcox composite, 1914 twelve Babcock & Wilcox & eight Niclausse/Babcock & Wilcox composite [latter removed in *Pittsburgh* 1926]) boilers; two shafts; reciprocating (VTE), IHP 23,000 = 22kt; coal 900/2025 tons; range 5900nm @ 10kt.

Armament: Four 8in/40 (1908/10: 8in/45 – 2 x 2), fourteen (1918: four, except *Pittsburgh* ten) 6in/50, sixteen 3in/50, two 6pdr (removed 1918), twelve (1910: removed) 3pdr, eight 1pdr (removed 1911) guns; two 18in torpedo tubes.

Protection: Belt 3.5–6–3.5in; battery 5in; barbettes 6in; turrets 1.5–6.5in; armour deck 1.5/4in; fwd conning tower 9in; aft conning tower 5in.

Complement: 41+791.

Pennsylvania 1905

West Virginia 1905

Pittsburgh (ex-Pennsylvania) 1916

Huntington (ex-West Virginia) 1916

West Virginia 1914

Huron (ex-South Dakota) 1919

0   20 metres
0   100 feet

Pittsburgh (ex-Pennsylvania) 1927

Hull No	Name	Builder	Laid down	Launched	Completed	Fate
ACR-4 CA-4	*Pennsylvania* (ex-*Nebraska*) = *Pittsburgh* (27 Aug 12)	W Cramp & Sons (Philadelphia)	7 Aug 01	22 Aug 03	9 Mar 05	Stricken 26 Oct 31; sold Union Shipbuildig (Baltimore) 21 Dec 31 and BU Baltimore.
ACR-5 CA-5	*West Virginia* = *Huntington* (11 Nov 16)	Newport News Sbdg & DD Co (Newport News)	16 Sep 01	18 Apr 03	23 Feb 05	Stricken 12 Mar 30; sold 30 Aug 30 and BU.
ACR-6	*California* = *San Diego* (1 Sep 14)	Union Iron Works (San Francisco)	7 May 02	28 Apr 04	1 Aug 07	Mined (laid by *U156*) off Fire Island, NY, 19 9 Jul 18; wreck sold Maxter Metals Co (New York) 1950s.
ACR-7 CA-7	*Colorado* = *Pueblo* (9 Nov 16)	W Cramp & Sons (Philadelphia)	25 Apr 01	25 Apr 03	19 Jan 05	Stricken 21 Feb 30; sold 2 Oct 30 and BU.
ACR-8 CA-8	*Maryland* = *Frederick* (9 Nov 16)	Newport News Sbdg & DD Co (Newport News)	29 Oct 01	12 Sep 03	18 Apr 05	Stricken 13 Nov 29; sold 11 Feb 30 and BU.
ACR-9 CA-8	*South Dakota* = *Huron* (7 Jun 20)	Union Iron Works (San Francisco) (San Francisco)	30 Sep 02	21 Jul 04	27 Jan 08	Stricken 15 Nov 29; sold Abe Goldberg (Seattle) 11 Feb 30 and BU Lake Union Dry Dock and Machine Works (Seattle); lower hull re-sold Powell River Co., BC; arrived as breakwater Aug 31; foundered Feb 61.

Pennsylvania
Atlantic Fleet 1905–6; Asiatic Fleet 1906–7; Pacific Fleet 1907–4 Jan 11; aviation trials Jan 11–Jun 11; decommissioned 1 Jul 11; reserve Jul 11–Feb 16 (commissioned 30 May 13); Pacific Fleet Jul 16–1917; Atlantic Fleet 1917–1919; Mediterranean Jun 19–Apr 20; Europe Apr 20–Oct 21; decommissioned 15 Oct 21; reserve Oct 21–Oct 22; Europe 2 Oct 22–26; Asiatic Fleet (flag) Dec 26–Jul 31; decommissioned 10 Jul 31; target Chesapeake Bay 5 Oct 31.

West Virginia
Atlantic Fleet 1905–6; Asiatic Fleet 1906–7; Pacific Fleet 1907–12; Pacific Reserve Fleet 1912–20 Sep 16 (Mexico Apr–Jul 14); Pacific Fleet Sep 16–11 May 17; catapult trials Pensacola, FL, Jun–Jul 17; Cruiser and Transport Force 1917–Dec 18; Transport Service Dec 18–8 Jul 19; 1st Cruiser Squadron, Cruiser Force Jul 19–Aug 20; decommissioned 1 Sep 20; reserve Sep 20–Mar 30.

California
Pacific Fleet 1907–17; decommissioned 12 Feb 17; reserve Feb–7 Apr 17; Cruiser and Transport Force 1917 to loss.

Colorado
Atlantic Fleet 1905–6; Asiatic Fleet 1906–7; Pacific Fleet 1907–11; Asiatic Fleet 1911–12; decommissioned 17 May 13; reserve May 13–9 Feb 15; Pacific Fleet 1915–16; Cruiser and Transport Force 1917–Dec 18; Transport Service 1919; decommissioned 22 Sep 19; reserve Sep 19–2 Apr 21; receiving ship 1921–Sep 27; decommissioned 28 Sep 27.

Maryland
Atlantic Fleet 1905–6; Asiatic Fleet 1906–7; Pacific Fleet 1907–17; Cruiser and Transport Force 1917–Dec 18; Transport Service 1919; Pacific Fleet 1920–22; decommissioned 14 Feb 22; reserve Feb 22–1929.

South Dakota
Pacific Fleet 1908–17; Cruiser and Transport Force 1917–Dec 18; Transport Service 1919; Asiatic Fleet 1919–26; decommissioned 17 Jun 27; reserve Jun 27–1929.

St Louis **class**

CRUISERS

Displacement:	9700 tons.
Dimensions:	424 (wl) 426.5 (oa) x 66 x 24.1 feet. 129.2 (wl) 130 (oa) x 20 x 7.35 metres.
Machinery:	Sixteen Babcock & Wilcox boilers; two shafts; reciprocating (VTE), IHP 21,000 = 22kt; coal 650/1776 tons.
Armament:	Fourteen (1918: twelve) 6in/50, eighteen (1918: four) 3in/50, twelve (1911: two/four) 3pdr guns; two 3in AA added 1918.
Protection:	Belt 4in; armour deck 2/3in; shields 4in; conning tower 5in.
Complement:	670.

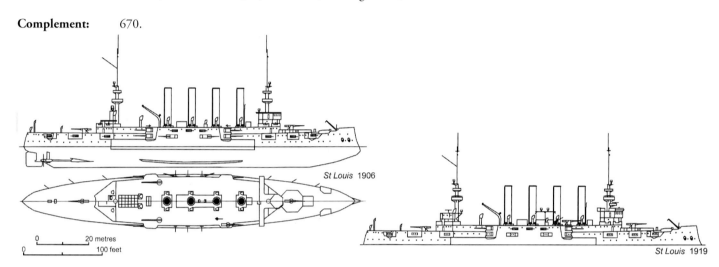

St Louis 1906

St Louis 1919

Hull No	Name	Builder	Laid down	Launched	Completed	Fate
C-20 CA-18	*St Louis*	Neafie & Levy Co., (Philadelphia, PA)	21 Jul 02	6 May 05	18 Aug 06	Stricken 10 Mar 30; sold 13 Aug 30 to BU.
C-21	*Milwaukee*	Union Iron Works (San Francisco, CA)	30 Jul 02	10 Sep 04	10 Dec 06	Stranded Samoa Beach, off Eureka, CA 13 Jan 1917; stricken 23 Jun 1919; wreck sold 5 Aug 19.
C-22 CA-19	*Charleston* (ii)	Newport News Shipbuilding & Dry Dock Co., (Newport News, VA)	30 Jan 02	23 Jan 04	17 Oct 05	Stricken 11 Feb 1930; sold Abe Goldberg (Seattle) 11 Feb 30; re-sold General Salvage Co. (Seattle) 6 Mar 30 and BU Lake Union Dry Dock and Machine Works (Seattle); lower hull re-sold Powell River Co. (BC) as breakwater; beached Kelsey Bay 1961.

St Louis

Pacific 31 Aug 07–May 10; decommissioned 3 May 10; Pacific reserve 7 Oct 11–Jul 12; Oregon Naval Militia 14 Jul 12–26 Apr 13; Pacific reserve Apr 13–24 Apr 14; receiving ship, San Francisco 27 Apr 14–Feb 16; Pacific Reserve Fleet 17 Feb 16–10 Jul 16; Pacific, Submarine Division 3/Station Ship, Pearl Harbor 29 Jul 16–6 Apr 17; Atlantic May 17–Jul 19; Europe Sep 20–11 Nov 21; decommissioned 3 Mar 22.

Milwaukee

Pacific 1907–8; Pacific reserve 1908–May 10; decommissioned 3 May 10; Pacific reserve 17 Jun 13–Mar 16; destroyer/submarine tender, San Diego 18 Mar 16 to loss (decommissioned 6 Mar 17).

Charleston

Pacific 1906–Jun 08; Far East (flag) Oct 08–Oct 10; decommissioned 8 Oct 10; Pacific reserve Fleet 14 Sep 12–1916; submarine tender, Cristobal, Canal Zone, 7 May 16–Apr 17; Patrol Force (Caribbean) 6 Apr 17; Atlantic 1917–19; Pacific 1919–20; flag Pacific destroyers 1920–4 Jun 23; decommissioned 4 Dec 23.

Tennessee class
ARMORED CRUISERS

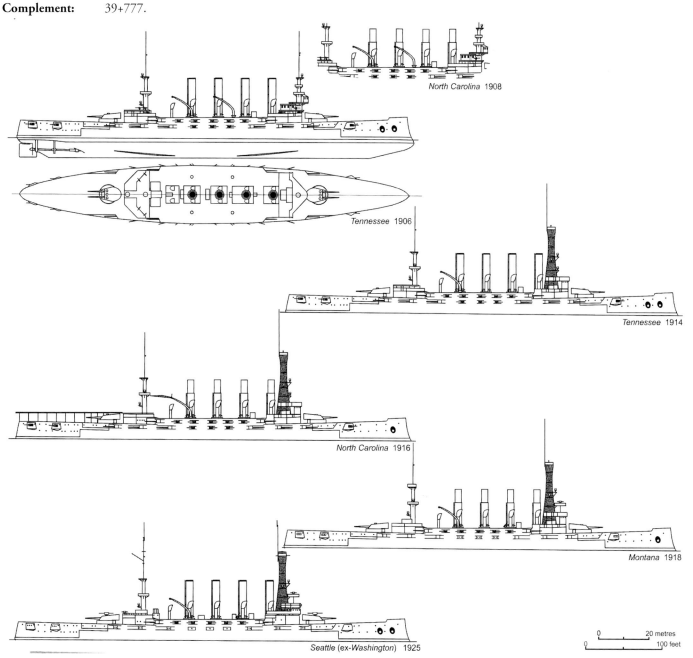

Displacement:	14,500 tons.
Dimensions:	502 (pp) 504.4 (oa) x 72.9 x 25 feet.
	153 (pp) 153.75 (oa) x 22.2 x 7.6 metres.
Machinery:	Sixteen Babcock & Wilcox boilers; two shafts; reciprocating (VTE), IHP 23,000 = 22kt; coal 900/2020 tons (2nd pair 900/2200 tons); range 4710nm @ 10kt.
Armament:	Four 10in/40 (2 x 2), sixteen (1918: four) 6in/50, twenty-two (1918: ten [*North Carolina*, twelve]) 3in/50, twelve 3pdr (removed 1912–14), two 1pdr (two 3in AA added 1918 [not *North Carolina*] guns; four 21in torpedo tubes.
Protection:	Belt 3–5–3in; barbettes: 7–4in (2nd pair 8–4in); turrets: 9–5in; armour deck 1.5/3–4–3in (2nd pair 1–2–1/3–4–3in); fwd conning tower 9in; aft conning tower 5in (Krupp/Harvey).
Complement:	39+777.

North Carolina 1908

Tennessee 1906

Tennessee 1914

North Carolina 1916

Montana 1918

Seattle (ex-Washington) 1925

0   20 metres
0   100 feet

Hull No	Name	Builder	Laid down	Launched	Completed	Fate
ACR-10	*Tennessee* = *Memphis* (25 May 16)	William Cramp & Sons (Philadelphia)	20 Jun 03	3 Dec 04	17 Jul 06	Wrecked Santo Domingo 29 Aug 16; stricken 17 Dec 17; sold A H Radetsky Iron & Metal Co. (Denver, CO) 17 Jan 1922; BU in situ to 1938.
ACR-11 CA-11 IX-39 (17 Feb 41)	*Washington* = *Seattle* (9 Nov 16)	New York Shipbuilding (Camden, NJ)	23 Sep 03	18 Mar 05	7 Aug 06	Stricken 19 Jul 1946; sold Hugo Neu (New York) 3 Dec 46 to BU.
ACR-12 CA-12	*North Carolina* = *Charlotte* (7 Jun 20)	Newport News Shipbuilding & Dry Dock Co. (Newport News, VA)	1 Mar 05	6 Oct 06	7 May 08	Stricken 15 Jul 30; sold 29 Sep 30 to BU.
ACR-13 CA-13	*Montana* = *Missoula* (7 Jun 20)	Newport News Shipbuilding & Dry Dock Co. (Newport News, VA)	29 Apr 05	15 Dec 06	21 Jul 08	Stricken 15 Jul 30; sold John Irwon, Jr, 29 Sep 30 to BU.

Tennessee
Atlantic 1906–7; Pacific Fleet 1908–10; Atlantic Fleet 1910–13; reserve 1913–14; Atlantic Fleet Aug 14 to loss (decommissioned 29 Aug 17).

Washington
Atlantic 1906–7; Pacific Fleet 1908–10; Atlantic Fleet 1911–Jul 12; reserve Jul 12–Apr 14; Atlantic Fleet 23 Apr 14–3 Jun 17; Cruiser and Transport Force 1917–Dec 18; Transport Service Dec 18–Sep 19; Pacific Fleet Nov 19–1920; reserve 1920–23; flagship, US Fleet 1 Mar 23–Jun 27; receiving ship, Brooklyn, 1927–28 Jun 46 ('Unclassified' from 1 Jul 31); decommissioned 28 Jun 46.

North Carolina
Atlantic Fleet 1908–9; Mediterranean Apr–Aug 09; Atlantic Fleet Aug 09–1911; reserve 1911–Aug 14; station ship, Pensacola 7 Aug 14–Jun 17; Cruiser and Transport Force 1 Jul 17–Dec 18; Transport Service Dec 18–Jul 19; Pacific Fleet Jul 19–Feb 21; decommissioned 18 Feb 21; reserve Feb 21–Jul 30.

Montana
Atlantic Fleet 1908–9; Mediterranean Apr–Aug 09; Atlantic Fleet Aug 09–1911; reserve 26 Jul 11–29 Dec 13; torpedo training ship Jan 14–17 Jul 17; Cruiser and Transport Force 1917–Dec 18; Transport Service Dec 18–Jul 19; Pacific Fleet Aug 19–1 Feb 21; decommissioned 2 Feb 21; reserve Feb 21–Jul 30.

APPENDIX 1

Principal guns mounted in big cruisers[2]

Calibre[3]		Other designation	Length (cal)[4]	Mark/ model[5]	Country of origin	Maker/ Designer	Muzzle velocity (ft/sec)	Class/Ships[6]	User(s)
in	mm								
12	305	30cm	45	Type 41	JP	Armstrong	2800	Tsukuba class Kurama class	JP
12	305	–	45	X	UK	Vickers	2746	Invincible class	UK
11	280	–	35	Model 1883	SP	Hontoria	2034	Infanta María Teresa class Carlos V	SP
10	254	–	45	–	RU	Obukhov	2270	Peresvet class	RU
10	254	–	45	Mk VII Mk A	UK	Vickers	2656	Libertad = Triumph (ii)	CL UK
10	254	–	45	Mk VI Pattern S	UK	Elswick/Armstrong	2656	Constitucion = Swiftsure (ii)	CL UK
10	254	–	32	Mk IV	UK	Woolwich	2040	Renown	UK
10	254	–	32	Mk III	UK	Woolwich	2040	Centurion class	UK
10	254	–	14.5	MLR Mk II	UK	Woolwich	1365	Shannon Nelson class	UK
10	254	–	40	Pattern P1	UK	Elswick/ Armstrong	2460	Garibaldi General Belgrano Pueyrredón	AR
10	254	–	40	Pattern P A 1899	UK/IT	Elswick/Armstrong	2460	Giuseppe Garibaldi class	IT
10	254	25cm	40	Pattern R	UK	Elswick/ Armstrong	2400	Kasuga	JP
10	254	–	45	Pattern W A 1907	UK/IT	Elswick/ Armstrong	2850	San Giorgio class	IT
10	254	–	50	Mk C	UK	Vickers	2950	Ryurik (ii)	RU
10	254	–	40	Mk D V 1906	UK/IT	Vickers	2840	Pisa class	IT
10	254	–	40	Mk III	US	BuOrd	2700	Tennessee class	US
9.4	238	24cm	40	K.01	AH	Škoda	2380	Sankt Georg	AH
9.4	238	24cm	40	K.97	AH	Krupp/Škoda	2300	Kaiser Karl VI R	AH
9.4	238	24cm	40	K.97	AH	Krupp	2265	Kaiser Karl VI	AH
9.4	238	24cm	40	M1893	FR	Ruelle	2625	D'Entrecasteaux	FR
9.4	238	24cm	40	C/97	GE	Krupp	2740	Fürst Bismarck Prinz Heinrich	GE
9.4	238	24cm	35	C/88	GE	Krupp	2265	K u K Maria Theresia	AH
9.4	240	24cm	42.5	Model 1896	SP	Guillén	2122	Princesa de Asturias class	SP
9.4	240	24cm	19	M1870	FR	Ruelle	4592	La Galissonnière Victorieuse class Bayard class	FR
9.2	234	–	45	Mk XIV	UK	Vickers	2748	For cancelled sister . to Averof	–
9.2	234	-	45	Pattern H	UK	Elswick/ Armstrong	2770	Giorgios Averof	GR
9.2	234	–	50	Mk XI	UK	Vickers	2940	Minotaur class	UK
9.2	234	–	46.7	Mk X	UK	Woolwich	2778	Cressy class Drake class Duke of Edinburgh class Warrior class	UK

9.2	234	–	40	Mk VIII	UK	Woolwich	2329	*Powerful* class	UK
9.2	234	–	32	Mk VI	UK	Woolwich	2119	*Blake* class *Edgar* class	UK
9.2	234	–	32	Mk V/VI	UK	Woolwich	2119	*Warspite* *Aurora* *Galatea* *Narcissus*	UK
9.2	234	–	32	Mk V	UK	Woolwich	2119	*Australia* *Orlando* *Undaunted*	UK
9.2	234	–	32	Mk III	UK	Woolwich	2119	*Imperieuse*	UK
9	229	12-ton MLR	14	Mk I–VI	UK	Woolwich	1420	*Audacious/ Swiftsure* (i) class *Shannon* *Nelson* class	UK
8.2	209	21cm	45	C/09	GE	Krupp	2953	*Blücher*	GE
8.2	209	21cm	40	C/04	GE	Krupp	2559	*Prinz Adalbert* class *Roon* class *Scharnhorst* class	
8	203	–	45	Pattern S A 1897	IT	Armstrong	2526	*Giuseppe Garibaldi* class *San Martin*	IT AR
8	203	–	40	Pattern P	UK	Elswick/Armstrong	2370	*Esmeralda* (ii)	CL
8	203	–	50	Mk B	UK/RU	Vickers/Obukov	2600	*Ryurik* (ii) *Rossiya* R	RU
8	203	–	45	–	RU	Obukhov	2800	*Ryurik* (i) *Rossiya* *Gromoboi* *Bayan* class	
8	203	–	45	Pattern U Type 41	UK/JP	Elswick/ Armstrong	2495	*Asama* class *Izumo* class *Yakumo* *Azuma* *Kasuga* class	JP
8	203	–	45	Pattern T	UK	Elswick/Armstrong	2575	*O'Higgins*	CL
8	203	–	45	Pattern S	UK	Elswick/Armstrong	2650	*Esmeralda* (ii)	CL
8	203	–	29.6	Mk IV	UK	Woolwich	2145	*Triumph* (i) and R *Swiftsure* (i) (planned only)	UK
8	203	–	25.6	Mk III	UK	Woolwich	1987	*Triumph* (i) R (planned only)	UK
8	203	–	45	Mk VI	US	BuOrd	2750	*Pennsylvania* class R *New York* R	US
8	203	–	40	Mk V	US	BuOrd	2500	*Pennsylvania* class *New York* R	US
8	203	–	35	Mk III	US	BuOrd	2080	*New York* *Columbia* class	US
7.6	194	19cm	42	G	AH	Škoda	2700	*Sankt Georg* *K u K Maria Theresia* R	
7.6	194	19cm	50	M1902	FR	Ruelle	3117	*Jules Michelet* *Ernest Renan* *Waldeck-Rousseau* class	FR
7.6	194	19cm	45	M1893–6	FR	Ruelle	2800	*Jeanne d'Arc* *Gueydon* class *Gloire* class *Léon Gambetta* class	FR
7.6	194	19cm	45	M1893	FR	Ruelle	2600	*Pothuau*	FR
7.6	194	19cm	40	M1887	FR	Ruelle	2600	*Amiral Charner*	

in	mm	cm	cal	Model/Mark	Country	Maker	Weight	Ship class	Country
7.6	194	19cm	20	M1870	FR	Ruelle	2477	Dupuy de Lôme	FR
								Belliqueuse R	
								Alma class R	
								La Galissonnière	
								Victorieuse class	
								Bayard class	FR
7.6	194	19cm	–	M1866	FR	Ruelle	–	Alma class	FR
7.6	194	19cm	–	M1864	FR	Ruelle	–	Belliqueuse	FR
								Alma class	
7.5	190	–	45	Mk D V 1908	UK	Vickers	2850	San Marco	IT
7.5	190	–	45	Pattern C A 1908	UK/IT	Armstrong	2850	San Giorgio	IT
7.5	190	–	45	V 1906	UK/IT	Vickers	2850	Pisa class	IT
7.5	190	–	45	Pattern B	UK	Elswick/ Armstrong	2850	Georgios Averof	GR
7.5	190	–	50	Mk III Pattern A	UK	Elswick/ Armstrong	2781	Constitucion = Swiftsure (ii)	CL UK
7.5	190	–	50	Mk IV Mk B	UK	Vickers	2781	Libertad = Triumph (ii)	CL UK
7.5	190	–	45	Mk II	UK	Vickers	2827	Warrior class	UK
								Minotaur class	
7.5	190	–	45	Mk I	UK	Vickers	2765	Devonshire class	UK
6.5	165	16cm	45	M1893–6M	FR	Ruelle	2950	Jules Michelet	FR
								Ernest Renan	
6.5	165	16cm	45	M1893–6	FR	Ruelle	2950	Gueydon class	FR
								Kléber class	
								Gloire class	
6.5	165	16cm	45	M1893	FR	Ruelle	2600	Guichen	FR
								Chateâurenault	
6.5	165	16cm	45	M1887	FR	Ruelle	2600	Dupuy de Lôme	FR
6.5	165	16cm	–	M1864	FR	Ruelle	–	Belliqueuse	FR
								Alma class	
6.3	160	64pdr MLR	16	Mk I–III	UK	Woolwich	1252	Audacious	UK
6	152	–	40	A 1899	IT	Armstrong	1755	Vettor Pisani class	IT
								Giuseppe Garibaldi class	AR SP
6	152	–	40	A 1891	IT	Armstrong	2297	Marco Polo	IT
6	152	–	45	Pattern GG Type 41	UK/JP	Elswick/ Armstrong	2706	Tsukuba class	JP
6	152	–	45	M1891	RU	Canet/ Obukhov	2600	Ryurik (i) Rossiya Gromoboi Bayan class	RU
6	152	15cm	44	M/98	SE	Bofors	2460	Fylgia	SE
6	152	–	40	Pattern Z3/Z4	UK	Elswick/ Armstrong	2500	O'Higgins Esmeralda (ii) [?]	CL
6	152	–	40	Pattern Z Type 41	UK/JP	Elswick/ Armstrong	2500	Asama class Izumo class Yakumo Azuma Kasuga class	JP
6	152	–	50	BL Mk XI	UK	Elswick/ Armstrong	2921	Duke of Edinburgh class	UK
6	152	–	45	BL Mk VII/VIII	UK	Vickers	2536	Cressy class Drake class Monomouth/ Donegal class Devonshire class Centurion class R	UK

6	152	–	26	BL Mk III/IV/VI	UK	Woolwich	1960	Imperieuse class	UK
								Orlando class	
								Blake class	
6	152	–	40	QF Mk I/II	UK	Elswick/ Armstrong Woolwich	2230	Renown	UK
								Edgar class	
								Powerful class	
								Diadem class	
6	152	–	44	Mk IX	US	Bethlehem	2250	Columbia class R	US
6	152	–	50	Mk VI/VIII	US	BuOrd	2800	Pennsylvania class	US
								Tennessee class	
								St Louis class	
6	152	–	30	Mk III	US	BuOrd	1950	Maine	US
								Columbia class	
5.9	149	15cm	40	K.96	GE/AH	Škoda/ Krupp	2265	Kaiser Karl VI	AH
								Sankt Georg	
5.9	149	15cm	35	K.86	GE/AH	Krupp	2130	K u K Maria Theresia	AH
5.9	149	15cm	45	C/09	GE	Krupp	2739	Blücher	GE
5.9	149	15cm	40	C/97	GE	Krupp	2625	Prinz Adalbert class	GE
								Roon class	
								Scharnhorst class	
5.5	138.6	14cm	30	M1893 (court)	FR	Ruelle	2000	D'Entrcasteaux	FR
5.5	138.6	14cm	45	M1893	FR	Ruelle	2500	Jeanne d'Arc	FR
								Guichen	
								Chateâurenault	
5.5	138.6	14cm	45	M1891	FR	Ruelle	2500	Amiral Charner class (some?)	FR
								Pothuau	
5.5	138.6	14cm	45	M1887	FR	Ruelle	2500	Amiral Charner class	FR
5.5	140	14cm	35	Model 1883	SP	Hontoria	1960	Infanta María Teresa class	SP
								Princesa de Asturias class	
								Carlos V	
5	127	–	25	BL Mk I–V	UK	Woolwich	1750	Triumph (i) R	UK
5	127	–	50	Mk VI	US	BuOrd	3000	New York R	US
5	127	–	40	Mk III	US	BuOrd	2300	Brooklyn	US
4.7	120	–	40	A 1891	IT	Armstrong	2116	Vettor Pisani class	IT
4.7	120	–	50	Mk A	UK/RU	Vickers/Obukhov	2600	Ryurik (ii)	RU
4.7	120	–	40	Pattern BB					
				Type 41	JP	Armstrong/Kure	2150	Kurama class	JP
								Tuskuba class	
4.7	120	–	40	QF Mk I–IV	UK	Elswick	2125	Centurion class	UK
4	102	–	25	BL Mk I	UK	–	–	Swiftsure (i) R	UK
4	102	–	27	BL Mk II–VII	UK	–	1900	Audacious class R	UK
4	102	–	40	QF Mk I/III	UK	Woolwich	2370	Invincible class	UK
4	102	–	50	BL Mk VII	UK	–	2864	Indomitable R	UK
4	102	–	45	BL Mk IX	UK	–	2642	Inflexible R	UK
4	102	–	30	Mk I	US	BuOrd	2000	New York	US
3.9	100	10cm	45	M1891, 1893	FR	Ruelle	2000	Gueydon class Gloire class	
								Kléber class	
3.5	88	8.8cm	35	C/01	GE	Krupp	2132	Blücher	GE
								Prinz Adalbert class	
								Roon class	
								Scharnhorst class	
3	76	14pdr	50	V 1908	IT	Vickers	3051	Pisa class	IT
3 AR	76	12pdr	40	A 1897	IT	Armstrong	2297	Giuseppe Garibaldi class	IT

3	76	8cm 12pdr	40	Type 41	JP	Armstrong/Kure	2230	*Asama* class *Izumo* class *Yakumo* *Azuma* *Kasuga* class *Tsukuba* class *Kurama* class	JP
3	76	14pdr	50	QF Mk I	UK	Elswick/ Armstrong	2548	*Constitucion* = *Swiftsure* (ii) *Georgios Averof*	CL UK GR
3	76	14pdr	50	QF Mk II	UK	Vickers	2548	*Libertad* = *Triumph* (ii)	CL UK
3	76	12pdr 18cwt	50	QF Mk I	UK	Elswick/ Armstrong	2660	*Minotaur* class	UK
3	76	12pdr 12cwt	50	QF Mk I–III	UK	–	2359	*Cressy* class *Drake* class *Monmouth/ Donegal* class	UK
3	76	–	50	Mk III	US	BuOrd	2700	*Pennsylvania* class *Tennessee* class *St Louis* class	US
2.9	75	–	50	M1891	RU	Canet/Obukhov	2828	*Ryurik* (i) *Rossiya* *Gromoboi* *Bayan* class	RU
2.6	66	7cm	45	–	AH	Škoda	2380	*Sankt Georg*	AH
2.25	57	–	55	M/92	SE	Bofors	2810	*Fylgia*	SE
2.25	57	6pdr	50	Mk II	US	BuOrd	2249	*Pennsylvania* class *Tennessee* class	US
1.85	47	4.7cm	44	–	AH	Škoda	2330	*Kaiser Karl VI*	AH
1.85	47	4.7cm	33	–	AH	Škoda/ Hotchkiss	1840	*K u K Maria Theresia*	AH
1.85	47	3pdr	50	M1885	FR	–	2264	*Jules Michelet* *Ernest Renan* *Waldeck-Rousseau* class	
1.85	47	3pdr	40	M1885	FR	Hotchkiss	2132	*Gueydon* class *Amiral Charner* class *Dupuy de Lôme* *Kléber* class *Gloire* class *Guichen* *Chateâurenault*	FR
1.85	47	–	40	V 1908	IT	Vickers	2329	*Pisa* class	IT
1.85	47	3pdr	50	Mk I	UK	Vickers	2587	*Warrior* class *Duke of Edinburgh* class *Devonshire* class	UK
1.85	47	3pdr	50	Mk XIV	US	Driggs-Seabury	2026	*St Louis* class	US

APPENDIX 2

Metric–Imperial–Metric ready-reckoner

mm	in	in	mm
5	0.2	0.25	6
205	8.1	10.25	260
10	0.4	0.50	13
210	8.3	10.50	267
15	0.6	0.75	19
215	8.5	10.75	273
20	0.8	1.00	25
220	8.7	11.00	279
25	1.0	1.25	32
225	8.9	11.25	286
30	1.2	1.50	38
230	9.1	11.50	292
35	1.4	1.75	44
235	9.3	11.75	298
40	1.6	2.00	51
240	9.4	12.00	305
45	1.8	2.25	57
245	9.6	12.25	311
50	2.0	2.50	64
250	9.8	12.50	318
55	2.2	2.75	70
255	10.0	12.75	324
60	2.4	3.00	76
260	10.2	13.00	330
65	2.6	3.25	83
265	10.4	13.25	337
70	2.8	3.50	89
270	10.6	13.50	343
75	3.0	3.75	95
275	10.8	13.75	349
80	3.1	4.00	102
280	11.0	14.00	356
85	3.3	4.25	108
285	11.2	14.25	362
90	3.5	4.50	114
290	11.4	14.50	368
95	3.7	4.75	121
295	11.6	14.75	375
100	3.9	5.00	127
300	11.8	15.00	381
105	4.1	5.25	133
305	12.0	15.25	387
110	4.3	5.50	140
310	12.2	15.50	394
115	4.5	5.75	146
315	12.4	15.75	400
120	4.7	6.00	152
320	12.6	16.00	406
125	4.9	6.25	159
325	12.8	16.25	413
130	5.1	6.50	165
330	13.0	16.50	419
135	5.3	6.75	171
335	13.2	16.75	425
140	5.5	7.00	178
340	13.4	17.00	432
145	5.7	7.25	184
345	13.6	17.25	438
150	5.9	7.50	191
350	13.8	17.50	445
155	6.1	7.75	197
355	14.0	17.75	451
160	6.3	8.00	203
360	14.2	18.00	457
165	6.5	8.25	210
365	14.4	18.25	464
170	6.7	8.50	216
370	14.6	18.50	470
175	6.9	8.75	222
375	14.8	18.75	476
180	7.1	9.00	229
380	15.0	19.00	483
185	7.3	9.25	235
385	15.2	19.25	489
190	7.5	9.50	241
390	15.4	19.50	495
195	7.7	9.75	248
395	15.6	19.75	502
200	7.9	10.00	254
400	15.7	20.00	508

NOTES

Part 1

[1] Which are in any case problematic, with entries often repeated year after year, without any attempt at updating or correcting glaring errors. A most curious example of the latter concerns differences between members of the *Amiral Charner* class (pp 42–3), which *Jane's* consistently states are restricted to 'constantly changing' matters of rig, whereas the two pairs of vessels making up the class had gross differences in their forward upperworks, with individual ships all having easily-spottable differences in ventilator and steampipe layout.

[2] Such as Parkes's *British Battleships* and the Ian Allan volumes of the 1960–80s, and in some cases the *Conway's All the World's Fighting Ships* series.

[3] Such as *Warship* and *Warship International*.

[4] R Perkins, *British Warship Recognition: The Perkins Identification Albums*, II, III (Barnsley: Seaforth, 2016, 2017).

[5] I W Toll, *Six Frigates: The Epic History of the Founding of the US Navy* (New York: W. W. Norton, 2006), pp 49–53.

[6] F Dittmar and D Hepper, 'British Ship of the Line Conversions', *Warship International* XXXIII/3 (1996), pp 307–9.

[7] Cf. A Lambert, *Battleships in Transition: the creation of the steam battlefleet 1815–1860* (London: Conway Maritime Press, 1984), p 114.

[8] There were also plans in 1860 to razee the surviving American ships-of-the-line into steam frigates of 50 (*Pennsylvania*, 120) or 40 (*Ohio, Delaware, North Carolina, Alabama, Vermont, New York* and *Virginia*, 90) guns, or a 35-gun steam sloop (*Columbus*, 74). This was abandoned in view of the Civil War priority for shallow-draught warships, as well as the scuttling of *Pennsylvania, Delaware, New York* and *Columbus* at Norfolk in April 1861 (R B Koehler, 'British Ship of the Line Conversions', *Warship International* XXXIV/3 (1997), pp 319–20).

[9] B Drashpil, 'Re: Question by A. Mach', *Warship International* XX/3 (1983), pp 226–8.

[10] Although (e.g.) the German navy retained 'frigate' and 'corvette' as base-classification for their fleet until the 1880s.

[11] For the naval aspects of which see C Jones, 'The Limits of Naval Power', *Warship* XXXIV (2012), pp 162–8.

[12] See N J M Campbell, 'British Naval Guns 1880–1945, No 8', *Warship* VII (1983), pp 40–2.

[13] It was for this reason that even the extensive rebuilds undertaken of *Hercules* and *Sultan* during the 1890s left their muzzle-loaded main batteries intact.

[14] S McLaughlin, 'Russia's Coles "Monitors": *Smerch, Rusalka* and *Charodeika*', *Warship* XXXV (2013), p 155.

[15] See C C Wright, 'Cruisers of the Imperial Russian Navy, Part 1', *Warship International* IX/1 (1972), pp 38–42; R M Melnikov, 'Fregat "Kniaz' Pozharskii"', *Sudostroenie* 1979/2, pp 63–4. It should be noted that these and other published sources frequently disagree with each other on many details of *Pozharskí's* technical details; Melnikov has generally been followed here.

[16] See C C Wright, 'Cruisers of the Imperial Russian Navy, Part 1', *Warship International* IX/1 (1972), pp 43–53; R M Melnikov, 'Polubronenosnyi fregat "General-Admiral"', *Sudostroenie* 1979/4, pp 64–7. As with *Pozharski*, much of the published data on these ships is contradictory.

[17] Respectively stricken in 1869 (scrapped the following year), and wrecked off Jutland in September 1868.

[18] *General-Admiral* got one of her boilers in 1887 and *Minin* another engine in 1909–11; two of her engines were also initially proposed for the new battleship *Imperator Nikolai I* in 1884, and also for *Dvenadstat Apostilov* in 1886, before being rejected in favour of new engines.

[19] For *Minin*, see C C Wright, 'Cruisers of the Imperial Russian Navy, Part 2', *Warship International* XII/3 (1975), pp 205–23.

[20] See A Dodson, *The Kaiser's Battlefleet: German capital ships 1871–1918* (Barnsley: Seaforth, 2016), p 20.

[21] During this service, the navy of the Australian state of Victoria contained the wooden steam frigate *Nelson* (1814 – razeed from a ship of the line in 1878), leading to frequent confusion in modern works.

[22] For this, and subsequent French naval policy down to 1904, see T Ropp, *The Development of a Modern Navy: French Naval Policy 1871–1904* (Annapolis, MD: Naval Institute Press, 1987).

[23] See C C Wright, 'Cruisers of the Imperial Russian Navy, part 4', *Warship International* XIV/1 (1977), pp 62, 65–8.

[24] For a history of the Chinese Navy in the late nineteenth and early twentieth centuries, see R N J Wright, *The Chinese Steam Navy, 1862–1945* (London: Chatham Publishing, 2000).

[25] A Mach, 'The Chinese Battleships', *Warship* VIII (1984), pp 9–18; R N J Wright, 'The Peiyang and Nanyang Cruisers of the 1880s', *Warship* XX (1996), pp 95–110; Dodson, *Kaiser's Battlefleet*, pp 27–30, 237.

[26] D Kisieliow, 'Krążownik pancernopokładowy „Jiyuan"', *Okręty Wojenne* 113 (2012), pp 15–29.

[27] Two further cruisers (*Nan Rui* and *Nan Chen*) built in Germany had, however, been allowed to leave, as all guns were to be installed by Armstrong in Great Britain, and were permitted to proceed to China by the British authorities.

[28] C C Wright, 'Cruisers of the Imperial Russian Navy, Part 3', *Warship International* XIII/2 (1976), pp 123–47.

[29] Sources differ over whether *Monomakh* and *Donskoi* were re-engined with VTE at the same time as their reboilering; it is possible that their old compound machinery was converted to triple-expansion.

[30] See C C Wright, *Warship International* XIV/1, pp 53–77; R M Melnikov, 'Bronenosnyi kreiser "Admiral Nakhimov"', *Sudostroenie* 1979/9, pp 66–9.

[31] C C Wright, *Warship International* XIV/1 (1977), pp 53–77; V Ia Krestianinov, *Kreisera Rossiiskogo imperatorskogo flota. 1856–1917 gody* (St Petersburg: Galeia Print, 2009), pp 113–18.

[32] R N J Wright, 'The Peiyang and Nanyang Cruisers of the 1880s', *Warship* XX (1996), pp 102–10.

[33] K Milanovich, *Chiyoda* (II): First "Armoured Cruiser" of The Imperial Japanese Navy', *Warship* XXVIII (2006), pp 126–36.

[34] P Brook, 'Two Unfortunate Warships: *Unebi* and *Reina Regente*', *Mariner's Mirror* 87/1 (2001), pp 53–62; K Milanovich, 'Two Ill-Fated French-Built Japanese Warships', *Warship* XXXII (2010), pp 170–6; the year of her last

[35] sighting has often been given in error as 1887: for definitive correction see *Warship* XXXIII (2011), p 180.

[35] R Parkinson, *The Late Victorian Navy: The Pre-Dreadnought Era and the Origins of the First World War* (Woodbridge: The Boydell Press, 2008), pp 84–6.

[36] D Topliss and C Ware, 'First Class Cruisers, Part One', *Warship* XXIII (2000–2001), pp 9–11.

[37] This debacle led to the adoption of the 'Board Margin' of weight in the specification of future ships.

[38] Other cruisers of the period were similarly modified for the same reasons.

[39] The exceptions were *Alexandra*, *Temeraire* and *Superb*, which were 1st class; of early turret ships, *Monarch* was in the 2nd class and *Devastation* and *Neptune* in the 1st.

[40] For a convenient list of classifications as at 1 December 1894 (including the British view of foreign fleets), see Parkinson, *Late Victorian Navy*, pp 248–56.

[41] *Hector*'s sister *Valiant* and the two *Defence*s had ceased to be regarded as even potentially effective units by 1887, when they had become simply 'ships, armour plated' on the non-effective list.

[42] A Dodson, 'The Incredible Hulks: The *Fisgard* Training Establishment and its Ships', *Warship* XXXVII (2015), pp 29–37.

[43] C C Wright, 'Impressive ships – The story of Her Majesty's cruisers *Blake* and *Blenheim*', *Warship International* VII/1 (1970), pp 40–51; Topliss and Ware, 'First Class Cruisers, Part One', *Warship* XXIII, pp 9–15.

[44] Topliss and Ware, 'First Class Cruisers, Part One', *Warship* XXIII, pp 9–11.

[45] Parkinson, *Late Victorian Navy*, pp 81–117.

[46] It was not until 1914 that France considered small cruisers of the type long built by the British and German navies – by which time it was too late (see p ***, below).

[47] L Feron, 'The Armoured Cruisers of the *Amiral Charner* class', *Warship* XXXVI (2014), pp 8–28.

[48] W A Becker and C C Wright, 'The French Armored Cruiser *Pothuau*', *Warship International* LI/2 (2014), pp 136–45.

[49] V L Sanahuja Albíñana, 'Los cruceros acorazados de la clase Princesa de Asturias', *Vida Maritima*, 1 Septiembre 2011 <http://vidamaritima.com/2011/09/los-cruceros-acorazados-de-la-clase-princesa-de-asturias/>

[50] Finally commissioned in May 1900, she was stricken soon afterwards and discarded in 1907.

[51] It should be noted that the pre-1920 Italian classification system did not distinguish between 'line' and 'cruising' armoured vessels – all were 'Nave di Battaglia' – 'ships of battle', divided into 1st, 2nd and 3rd classes. Most battleships fell into the 1st class, while the vessels discussed just below fell into the 2nd (the *Pisani* class and their lineal successors) or 3rd (*Marco Polo*).

[52] See Ropp, *Development of a Modern Navy*, pp 198–201.

[53] See E F Sieche, 'Austria-Hungary's *Monarch* class coast defense ships', *Warship International* XXXVI/3 (1999), pp 220–60.

[54] L Sondhaus, *The Naval policy of Austria-Hungary, 1867–1918: navalism, industrial development and the politics of dualism* (West Lafayette, IN: Purdue University Press, 1994), pp 102–3.

[55] For a detailed account of *Maria Theresia* and her origins, see E F Sieche, *Kreuzer und Kreuzerprojekte der k.u.k. Kriegsmarine* (Hamburg: Mittler, 2002), pp 58–71.

[56] Of the type employed in the ex-Chilean *Triumph*: see p 279, below.

[57] F J Allen, 'Steel at Sea – the First Steps: USS *Atlanta* and USS *Boston* of 1883', *Warship* XII (1988), pp 238–49.

[58] J C Reilly and R L Scheina, *American Battleships 1886–1923: pre-dreadnought design and construction* (Annapolis MD: Naval Institute Press, 1980), pp 18–33; W C Emerson, 'The Second Class Battleship USS *Maine*', *Warship* XVI (1992), pp 31–46

[59] W C Emerson, 'The Armoured Cruiser USS *Brooklyn*', *Warship* XV (1991), pp 19–33.

[60] The Italian *Italia*-class battleships (1880–3) had employed a similar conception, with two engines on each shaft, only one cylinder of each of which was used for cruising.

[61] For a detailed account of the ship's development and career, see S McLaughlin, 'From *Riurik* to *Riurik*: Russia's Armoured Cruisers', *Warship* XXII (1999–2000), pp 44–51, 74–7.

[62] Cf German debates over the size of the main guns to be fitted in their *Kaiser Friedrich III*-class battleships, with the decision taken to use 9.4in weapons as having a rate of fire sufficient for them to *supplement* the 5.9in battery (see Dodson, *Kaiser's Battlefleet*, p 45).

[63] R Burt, 'The *Powerful* class cruisers of the Royal Navy, Part I', *Warship* XII (1988), pp 197–207; Topliss and Ware, 'First Class Cruisers, Part One', *Warship* XXIII, pp 15–17.

[64] K McBride, 'The *Diadem* class cruisers of 1893', *Warship* XI (1987), pp 210–16; Topliss and Ware, 'First Class Cruisers, Part Two', *Warship* XXIV (2001–2002), pp 9–11.

[65] See McLaughlin, 'From *Riurik* to *Riurik*', *Warship* XXII, pp 47–54, 74, 77.

[66] McLaughlin, "From *Riurik* to *Riurik*', *Warship* XXII, pp 55–60, 74, 77–8.

[67] E C Fisher, 'Battleships of the Imperial Russian Navy Part 3', *Warship International* VI/1 (1969), pp 26–32; McLaughlin, 'From iunk to *Warship* XXII, p 54; id, *Russian and Soviet Battleships* (Annapolis: Naval Institute Press, 2003), pp 107–15.

[68] The *Re Umberto* class, begun back in 1884–5, were only just commissioning when *Garibaldi* was laid down, and apart from the pair of 2nd class, 10in-gunned, low-freeboard, *Ammiraglio di Saint Bon* class, laid down at the same time as *Garibaldi*, no new battleships would be begun until the two *Regina Margheritas*, laid down in 1898–9.

[69] On the Chilean-Argentine naval race, see R L Scheina, *Latin America: A Naval History, 1810–1987* (Annapolis, MD: Naval Institute Press, 1987), pp 46–52; J A Grant, *Rulers, Guns, and Money: the Global Arms Trade in the Age of Imperialism* (Cambridge, MA: Harvard University Press, 2007), pp 122–32.

[70] For the Argentinian *Garibaldi*s, see G von Rauch, 'Cruisers for Argentina', *Warship International* XV/4 (1978), pp 297–317; on the class as a whole, see N Soliani, 'The Armoured Cruisers "Kasuga" and "Nisshin" of the Imperial Japanese Navy', *Transactions of the Institution of Naval Architects* XLVII/1 (1905), pp 43–62.

[71] There remains some doubt as to whether she was delivered with main guns, which were then removed and returned to the manufacturer in Italy, or was never fitted with them at all.

[72] E Bagnasco and A Rastelli, *Le costruzioni navali italiane per l'estero: centotrenta anni di prestigiosa presenza nel mondo* (Rome: Rivista marittima, 1991).

[73] G Ransome and P F Silverstone, 'Cancelled GARIBALDI class Italian Cruisers', *Warship International* VII/2 (1970), pp 193–4; Brook, 'The Cancelled AMALFI Class Armored Cruisers', *Warship International* IX/I (1972), 88.

[74] On the development of both *Esmeralda* and *O'Higgins*, see P Brook, *Warships for Export: Armstrong's Warships 1867–1927* (Gravesend: World Ship Society, 1999), pp 101–7.

[75] Reilly and Scheina, *American Battleships 1886–1923*, p 210 n 5.

[76] Writing of *Rivadavia* when she was the Japanese *Kasuga*, *Jane's Fighting*

Ships 1914, p 231, states that she 'formerly carried 2–10 inch, but was altered'; however, it is clear that her armament remained unchanged throughout her career.

77 For the sale of the Chilean and Argentine ships, see P Towle, 'Battleship Sales During the Russo-Japanese War', *Warship International* XXIII/4 (1986), pp 402–9, F Kolonits, 'A present by the Meiji Tenno for the delivery of KASUGA and NISSHIN', *Academic & Applied Research in Military Science* 6/4 (2007), pp 761–3, and C Inaba, 'Military co-operation under the Anglo-Japanese Alliance: Assistance in purchasing battleships', in P P O'Brien (ed.), *The Anglo-Japanese Alliance, 1902–1922* (London and New York: RoutledgeCurzon, 2004), pp 67–9.

78 Essentially for practical reasons, as modern longer-barrelled guns could not easily be fought from the confines of a battery.

79 Raised to squadron status in 1897, and since 1896 always led by a big cruiser (for its early history, see P Caresse, 'The Odyssey of Von Spee and the East Asiatic Squadron, 1914', *Warship* XXX (2008), p 67)

80 Sieche, *Kreuzer und Kreuzerprojekte*, pp 72–90.

81 Sieche, *Kreuzer und Kreuzerprojekte*, pp 89–102.

82 Sieche, *Kreuzer und Kreuzerprojekte*, p 103.

83 Sieche, *Kreuzer und Kreuzerprojekte*, pp 175–84.

84 Sieche, *Kreuzer und Kreuzerprojekte*, pp 173–4.

85 Sieche, 'Austria-Hungary's Last Naval Visit to the USA', *Warship International* XXVII/2 (1990), pp 142–64.

86 Cf. Ropp, *Development of a Modern Navy*, pp 283–93.

87 See Parkinson, *Late Victorian Navy*, pp 216–17

88 As would be demonstrated in particular by Russian experience in the Russo-Japanese War.

89 For this programme, see Milanovich, 'Armoured Cruisers of the Imperial Japanese Navy', *Warship* XXXVI (2014), pp 70–92.

90 For these two ships, see Brook, *Warships for Export*, pp 107–11.

91 For a detailed tabulation of the careers of all but *Azuma*,
see www.combinedfleet.com/asama_t.htm,
www.combinedfleet.com/tokiwa_t.htm,
see www.combinedfleet.com/Izumo_t.htm,
www.combinedfleet.com/Iwate_t.htm,
and www.combinedfleet.com/Yakumo_t.htm.

92 Which for a time restricted her to one dry dock in Japan, at the Uraga Dock Co.

93 Topliss and Ware, 'First Class Cruisers, Part Two', *Warship* XXIV, pp 11–13.

94 Three weeks after launch (on 10 June 1901), while berthed on the south side of Ramsden Dock at Barrow, she was damaged by a fire there, which spread to her wooden deck. Towed to Cammell Laird at Birkenhead for docking and repairs, the ship there slipped off the blocks and was badly damaged. Further damaged in collision with the auxiliary vessel *Traveller* on 27 June 1903 at Devonport, *Euryalus* was finally completed in January 1904, nearly two years late.

95 For a summary of the debate, see L Fisher, *Destruction of the* Maine *(1898)* (Washington, DC: Library of Congress, 2009) <http://loc.gov/law/help/usconlaw/pdf/Maine.1898.pdf>.

96 She would be scuttled as a blockship the following day.

97 *Reina Mercedes* was salvaged from the harbour and towed to the USA, to be repaired and spend half a century on harbour service until sold for scrapping in 1957.

98 For a summary of locations, see P A Marshall, '1898 Spanish Cruiser Guns', *Warship International* LII/1 (2015), p 81.

99 See McLaughlin, 'From *Riurik* to *Riurik*', *Warship* XXII, pp 60–8, 75, 78.

100 Topliss and Ware, 'First Class Cruisers, Part Two', *Warship* XXIV, pp 13–16.

101 See S Hill, 'The Battle of Boilers', *The Engineer* 198 (1954), pp 83–6,

199.

102 A territorial dispute over an area in Sudan at a juncture between British and French zones of interest.

103 K McBride, 'The First County Class Cruisers of the Royal Navy Part I: The *Monmouths*', *Warship* XII (1988), pp 93–100; Topliss and Ware, 'First Class Cruisers, Part Two', *Warship* XXIV, pp 16–18.

104 K McBride, 'The Wreck of HMS *Bedford*', *Warship* XII (1988), pp 214–17.

105 Parkinson, *Late Victorian Navy*, pp 225, 237, 245.

106 Originally to have been of a new M1902 type, but in the event the M1893–96 was fitted as in the *Gambetta*s. This was also the case in the contemporary *Ernest Renan* (just below) and *République*-class battleships.

107 K McBride, 'The First County Class Cruisers of the Royal Navy Part II: The *Devonshires*', *Warship* XII (1988), pp 147–51.

108 Prompted by a note from 'WHM', dated 26 June 1901.

109 C Borgenstam, P Insulander and B Åhlund, *Kryssare: med svenska flottans kryssare under 75 år* (Västra Frölunda: CB Marinlitteratur, 1993), pp 33–60.

110 On the legal basis for US warship names, see Reilly and Scheina, *American Battleships 1886–1923*, pp 12–15.

111 A further pair of 3in were originally planned for just in front of the main-deck 6in battery but, although officially listed down to 1917, appear never to have been installed; a pair of 6pdrs are, however, visible in photographs but never listed!

112 Reflecting a current trend for heavier secondary batteries, also seen in Germany (6.7in guns in *Braunschweig* and *Deutschland*-class battleships, and in Austria-Hungary in the *Erzherzog Karl*-class battleships and the armoured cruiser *Sankt Georg* – for which see p 68. France had been using guns of this size since the early 1890s – see p 41).

113 J Roberts, 'HMS Cochrane', *Warship* III (1979), pp 34–7; K McBride, 'The Dukes and the Warriors', *Warship International* XXVII/4 (1990), pp 362–94.

114 She also had the old, ex-Chinese, *Chin Yen*.

115 *Varyag* was later salvaged and became the Japanese *Soya*; she was to be sold back to Russia in 1916 (cf. p 98).

116 Although there is no contemporary evidence for such a thing, it has been later claimed that *Nakhimov* went down carrying a large cargo of bullion (N Pickford, *Lost Treasure Ships of the Twentieth Century* [London: Pavilion Books, 1999], pp 34–41).

117 Some sources give 3 July as the date of *Peresvet*'s raising.

118 McLaughlin, 'From *Riurik* to *Riurik*', *Warship* XXII, pp 69–76, 78–9.

119 Masdea would also use the same layout in *Dante Alighieri*, the first Italian dreadnought, laid down in 1909.

120 Similar reductions in funnel height after trials also occurred in the contemporary battleships *Napoli* and *Roma* (1905, 1907).

121 Published accounts of the history of this vessel are contradictory, some alleging that the third ship had been ordered, and then cancelled by, Italy, but there seems no evidence for this.

122 Subsequently taken into British shore service as the Mk XIV.

123 R A Burt, '*Minotaur*: Before the Battlecruiser', *Warship* XI (1987), pp 83–95.

124 Ships' Cover 131A, p 253.

125 Cf. p 84 on the policies practiced by the French Navy Minister during this period; the battleships laid down under the 1900 and 1902–3 programmes (the *Patrie/Démocratie* classes were also significantly delayed (J Jordan and P Caresse, *French Battleships of the First World War* [Barnsley: Seaforth, 2017], p 88).

126 On the development of the design, see A. Grießmer, *Große Kreuzer der Kaiserlichen Marine 1906–1918: Konstruktionen und Entwürfe in Zeichen des*

Tirpiz-Panes (Bonn: Bernard & Graefe Verlag), pp 19–39.

[127] H Le Masson, *Propos maritimes* (Paris: Editions maritimes et d'outre mer, 1970), p 211; C C Wright, 'Question 46/88', *Warship International* XXV/4 (1988), p 421.

[128] J Hansen, 'IJN Battleship and Battle Cruiser Project Numbers', *Warship International* LIII/2 (2016), p 111 n 16;, LIV/2 (2017), p 121.

[129] J Itani, H Lengerer and T Rehm-Takahara, 'Japan's Proto-Battlecruisers: The Tsukuba and Kurama Classes', *Warship* XVI (1992), pp 47–79.

[130] The *Katori* class, laid down in the UK in 1904. The third battleship would ultimately become *Fuso*, not laid down until 1912, and the two other armoured cruisers the battlecruisers *Haruna* and *Kirishima* (also 1912). The fourth armoured cruiser of the 1904 War Programme would become the battlecruiser *Hiei* (1911).

[131] N Friedman, *British Cruisers of the Victorian Era* (Barnsley: Seaforth Publishing, 2012), p 329 n.33; D K Brown, *The Grand Fleet: warship design and development 1906–1922* (London: Chatham Publishing, 1999), pp 60–1.

[132] N Friedman, *U.S. Cruisers: an illustrated design history* (London: Arms and Armour Press, 1985), pp 56, 61–5.

[133] The 'battlecruiser' classification was formally adopted by Germany only in the late 1930s, for the abortive *O* class.

[134] J Carr, *R.H.N.S. Averof: Thunder in the Aegean* (Barnsley: Pen & Sword Maritime, 2014), p 23, states that Brazil had previously made payments towards the ship. However, this is not corroborated by any contemporary sources, while a purchase of such a 'pre-dreadnought' ship would not be consistent with Brazil's ongoing acquisition of dreadnought battleships from the UK at this time, the first two, *Minas Geraes* and *São Paulo* (1908–9), having been laid down in 1907 and completed in 1910.

[135] Where she began an inglorious career; renamed *Antoine Simon*, she soon went aground, after salvage and provisional repairs being renamed *Ferrier*. In 1912 she went to Charleston, USA, for further repairs and re-arming, where her crew mutinied. Back in Haiti she then lay idle, being renamed *Hayti* in 1921, but sold for scrap shortly afterwards (http://warshipsresearch.blogspot.co.uk/2011/09/dreadnought-of-haiti-according-to-dutch.html).

[136] Contrary to what is stated in a number of publications, *Maryland* was not excluded from this change. This idea seems to derive from a mislabelling of a photograph of *Charleston* (see our p 132) as of *Frederick* (ex-*Maryland*), and widely published without verification.

[137] N Friedman, *U.S. Battleships: an illustrated design history* (Annapolis MD: Naval Institute Press, 1985), pp 80–3.

[138] Presumably because the most of capitals of the states whose names were to be reallocated were already borne by ships on the navy list, and that a further level of renaming was regarded as undesirable; the same renaming practice was applied to half of the monitors of the *Arkansas* class (*Florida* and *Wyoming* were actually renamed for their states' capitals, respectively *Talahassee* and *Cheyanne*).

[139] Of the Turkish ships, *Reshadieh* and *Sultan Osman I* (ex-Brazilian *Rio de Janeiro*) were taken over by the UK, and *Fatikh* broken up on the slip. The French-built *Vasilefs Konstantinos* was never started, while *Salamis* (to be renamed *Vasilefs Georgios*) never left her German builders and was eventually broken up incomplete in 1932 (Dodson, *Kaiser's Battlefleet*, pp 96, 153–4).

[140] For a history of the Northern Patrol, see R Osborne, H Spong and T Grover, *Armed Merchant Cruisers 1878–1945* (Windsor, World Ship Society, 2007), pp 50–83.

[141] On the following, see Caresse, 'The Odyssey of Von Spee and the East Asiatic Squadron, 1914', *Warship* XXX, pp 71–84.

[142] On the Japanese navy's minelayers, see H Lengerer, 'Imperial Japanese Navy Minelayers *Itsukushima*, *Okinoshima*, and *Tsugaru*', *Warship* XXX

[143] Many sources state that the 8in guns were replaced in 1913, but photographs explicitly dated to June 1915 exist showing the 8in mountings still in place (e.g. that on our p 98).

[144] I Buxton, *Big Gun Monitors: design, construction and operations 1914-1945* (Barnsley: Seaforth, 2008), pp 114–18.

[145] Four more small monitors were armed using spare 9.2in Mk X on Mk V mountings intended for some of the *Cressy* and *Drake*-class vessels, freed-up by the loss of *Abukir*, *Cressy* and *Good Hope* during 1914 (see pp 114, 117).

[146] Instead, *Oruba*, a merchantman converted to a dummy of the battleship *Orion*, and a collier were so-employed, the latter being refloated and replaced by a second dummy battleship, *Michigan* ('*Collingwood*').

[147] See E Cernuschi and V P O'Hara, 'The Naval War in the Adriatic', *Warship* XXXVII (2015), pp 161–73, XXXVIII (2016), pp 62–75.

[148] Actually the German *UB14*, and still with her German crew (although the latter as yet legally neutral in the Italo–Austro-Hungarian conflict).

[149] Z Freivogel, 'The Loss of the *Giuseppe Garibaldi*', *Warship* XXXIV (2012), pp 40–51.

[150] Two more were completed as oil tankers in 1926, while the sixth languished incomplete until broken up in the in the 1950s(!).

[151] Personal communication from Sergei Vinogradov, via Stephen McLaughlin, based on Russian archives RGAVMF, F. 479, Op 3, D. 227, LA 111–21.

[152] The light cruisers *Danzig* and *Lübeck*, plus two minesweepers, were all damaged in minefields laid by *Ryurik*.

[153] See P Schenk, 'German Aircraft Carrier Developments', *Warship International* XLV/2 (2008), pp 129–32.

[154] Of the myriad works on the battle, N J M Campbell, *Jutland: an analysis of the fighting* (London: Conway Maritime Press, 1986) is the most technically detailed, including full analysis of the damage suffered by individual ships, with the damage suffered by sunken ships, based on direct examination of their wrecks, covered in I McCartney, *Jutland 1916: the archaeology of a naval battlefield* (London: Conway, 2016)

[155] R D Layman, 'Engadine at Jutland', *Warship* XIV (1990), pp 97–9.

[156] On the basis of the examination of the wreck (McCartney, *Jutland 1916*, pp 166–76).

[157] *Bretagne, Democratie, Vergniaud, Condorcet* and *Voltaire*.

[158] On the American side, *Louisiana, Georgia, Nebraska, Rhode Island, Virginia, New Hampshire* and *South Carolina* were all employed.

[159] Cf. Friedman, *U.S. Battleships*, pp 175.

[160] See Friedman, *U.S. Battleships*, pp 174–5.

[161] Cf. I I Chernikov, 'Perevooruzhenie kreiserov v 1906-1916 gg', *Sudostroenie* 1983/3, pp 60–3.

[162] For a detailed treatment of this campaign see M B Barrett, *Operation Albion: The German Conquest of the Baltic Islands* (Bloomington, IN: Indiana University Press, 2008), with the naval side covered particularly in pp 199–220.

[163] M Head, 'The Baltic Campaign, 1918–1920, Part II', *Warship International* XLVI/3 (2009), pp 227–33.

[164] But not *Petropavelovsk*, as has been frequently claimed (see McLaughlin, *Russian and Soviet Battleships*, p 322.

[165] See, conveniently, Dodson, *Kaiser's Battlefleet*, p 144 n 4.

[166] Including the battleships *Budapest, Monarch, Hapsburg, Árpád, Babenburg* and *Ferdinand Max*, seven small cruisers and twenty-five torpedo boats.

[167] Of the 9750-ton war-programmed *Cavendish* class, only *Hawkins* had commissioned as a cruiser by 1919, *Vindictive* (ex-*Cavendish*) having completed as an aircraft carrier and not recommissioned as a cruiser until 1925. Of the others, *Raleigh* was finished in 1921, but lost the following

year, with *Frobisher* completed in 1924 and *Effingham* in 1925. The first wholly post-war cruiser was the 10,000-ton *Berwick*, completed in February 1928.

[168] 'Naval Notes', *The Engineer* 129 (1920), p 47.

[169] *The Engineer* 129 (1920), pp 270–1; E Fisher, G Ransome, I Sturton, J Wilterding and C Wright, 'Last Years of the French Armored Cruiser DUPUY DE LOME', *Warship International* VI/4 (1969), pp 344–5.

[170] 'Naval Notes', *The Engineer* 129 (1920), p 47.

[171] H Le Masson, 'The Complex Development of the French Light Cruiser 1910–1926', *Warship International* XXII/4 (1985), pp 374–83.

[172] For the latter, see Aidan Dodson, 'After the Kaiser: The Imperial German Navy's Light Cruisers after 1918', *Warship* XXXIX (2017).

[173] D J Stoker, 2003, *Britain, France, and the Naval Arms Trade in the Baltic, 1919-1939: Grand Strategy and Failure* (London/Portland OR: Frank Cass, 2003), p 89.

[174] The destroyers of the *Wicher* class (1928–9) and submarines of the *Wilk* class (1929–31) would eventually be ordered from French yards.

[175] For her wreck, see http://www.archeosousmarine.net/quinet.html.

[176] It had been originally hoped to use the battleship *Florida*, due for disposal under the 1930 London Naval Treaty, but this proved too expensive; the hulk of the former battleship *North Dakota* (originally slated to be converted to a radio-controlled target ship, but never rebuilt, used briefly as a static target in 1924, but then laid up and stripped of her engines in 1927, to be reused in rebuilding *Nevada*) was then considered, but rejected owing to 'nil' watertight integrity. *Pittsburgh* was accordingly used (R S S Hownam-Meek, K D McBride and C C Wright, 'Target Ships', *Warship International* XXXIX/1 [2002], p 26).

[177] The surviving British 'first generation' battlecruisers, also built prior to the adoption of that classification, had already been stricken prior to the treaty.

[178] The latter also received 8in from *Iwami* (ex-*Orel*) and later from *Iwate*. A number of 6in from *Kasuga/Nisshin* also made their way to Truk (*Field survey of Japanese defenses on Truk*, part 1 [CINCPAC-CINCPOA Bulletin No. 3-46, 15 March 1946]).

[179] For full details, see E Lacroix and L Wells III, *Japanese Cruisers of the Pacific War* (Annapolis, MD: Naval Institute Press, 1997), p 657.

[180] See J A Campbell, *Hulks: The Breakwater Ships of Powell River* (Powell River: Works Publishing, 2003), pp 9–15.

[181] Actually, by then only three were left on the naval list, given that *Francesco Ferrucio* had been stricken in April 1930, but not yet disposed of.

[182] Their first and only cruise was terminated prematurely that autumn; the next year, cadets were distributed among the ships of a 'Special Squadron', comprising a battleship and three cruisers, while subsequently cadets were spread among a wide range of fleet units.

[183] Statements in many sources that she was scuttled are incorrect.

[184] Frequent statements in print that she was used as a German submarine depot ship and sunk by RAF bombing in August 1944 are disproved by photographs showing her foundering spontaneously at some point before *Armorique* was removed to Landévennec on 10 February 1942 (see http://forum.netmarine.net/viewtopic.php?f=20&t=3996).

[185] For the state of Japanese ships at the end of the Second World War see S Fukui, *Japanese Naval Vessels at the End of World War II* (London: Greenhill Books, 1992).

[186] V Iu Usov and E Mawdsley, 'The *Kronshtadt* Class Battle Cruisers', *Warship International* XXVIII/4 (1991), pp 380–6; S McLaughlin, 'Project 69: The *Kronshtadt* Class Battlecruisers', *Warship* XXVI (2004), pp 99–117.

[187] S McLaughlin, 'Project 82: the *Stalingrad* class', *Warship* XXVIII (2006), pp 102–23. Project 82 had actually started life in 1941 as a modified *Admiral Hipper*-class 8in cruiser (of which one [*Lützow*] had been sold to the USSR by Germany in 1939); this had grown by 1944 into a 26,000-ton vessel with 8.7in guns, and by 1947 to the guns to 12in calibre, with an extra 10,000 tons displacement.

[188] McLaughlin, 'Admiral Kuznetzov's Cruiser Killer: The Project 66 Design', *Warship International* XLV/3 (2008), pp 221–8.

[189] There has been considerable confusion over the ship's final scrapping, a number of sources placing it in Japan; for confirmation of its location in Italy (see M. Brescia, 'Re: "Cruisers for Argentina"', *Warship International* XVI/3 [1979], p 199).

Part II

[1] US ships began to be given hull-classifications in the 1890s, which were written out in full (e.g. 'Cruiser No. 1' or 'Armored Cruiser No. 1'), although informally abbreviated at the time, and used in modern sources ('C-1', 'ACR-1'). A revised unified system was instituted on 17 July 1920, with two-letter core codes for each ship type: 'CA' was adopted for older, slower, cruisers, including the armoured cruisers, using their original 'ACR' sequence-numbers: this resulted in gaps in the series where 'ACR' ships had been lost prior to July 1920; the remaining larger protected cruisers then followed as CA-14 upwards, the two *Columbia*s and surviving *St Louis* class becoming CA-16, 17, 18 and 19; CA-14 and 15 were *Chicago* and *Olympia* (reclassified again as CL-14 and 15 on 8 August 1921). *Baltimore* and *San Francisco*, converted to minelayers, became CM-1 and 2. The 'CA' classification was redefined as cruisers with guns over 6.2in calibre in 1931, in the wake of the London Naval Treaty, by which time only *Rochester* and *Seattle* still survived from the earlier vessels.

[2] Data is in the main derived from Friedman, *Naval Weapons of World War One: Guns, Torpedoes, Mines and ASW Weapons of All Nations* (Barnsley: Seaforth Publishing, 2011); Campbell, 'British Naval Guns 1880–1945, No 5–7', *Warship* VI (1982), pp 43–5, 214–17, 282–4, '... No 9–11', *Warship* VII (1983), pp 119–43, 170–2, 240–3; '... No 15', *Warship* IX (1985), pp 48–53; '... No 17–18', *Warship* X (1986), pp 53–5, 117–20.

[3] Bores are rounded to the nearest millimetre or tenth of an inch (where precise bore diameters are available).

[4] While most navies expressed length in terms of the part of the barrel with rifling, Germany, Austria-Hungary and Russia used the whole barrel length for official designations.

[5] The first designation is that allocated by the primary user or manufacturer, with other users' designations following. The Italian navy changed its system from 1 June 1910; before this date, guns were designated by their calibre in millimetres, followed by a single-letter manufacturer code (e.g., '254 V' was a 254mm [10in] gun made by Vickers). Subsequently, the calibre, length and year of construction/design were added (e.g. '254/45 V 1906'). The later version (omitting the calibre/length) is given in the table. Japan used Imperial measurements for its guns (mostly of British origin) until 25 December 1905, when official designations changed to the calibre, rounded to the nearest centimetre, plus a type number based on the regnal year of the current emperor when a weapon was introduced – except that all guns extant in December 1905 were classified as 'Type 41'. Germany also used a rounded centimetre figure for its guns, as did France at various points in time, in particular from November 1908 for guns over 100mm bore.

[6] R = as rearmed.

MAPS

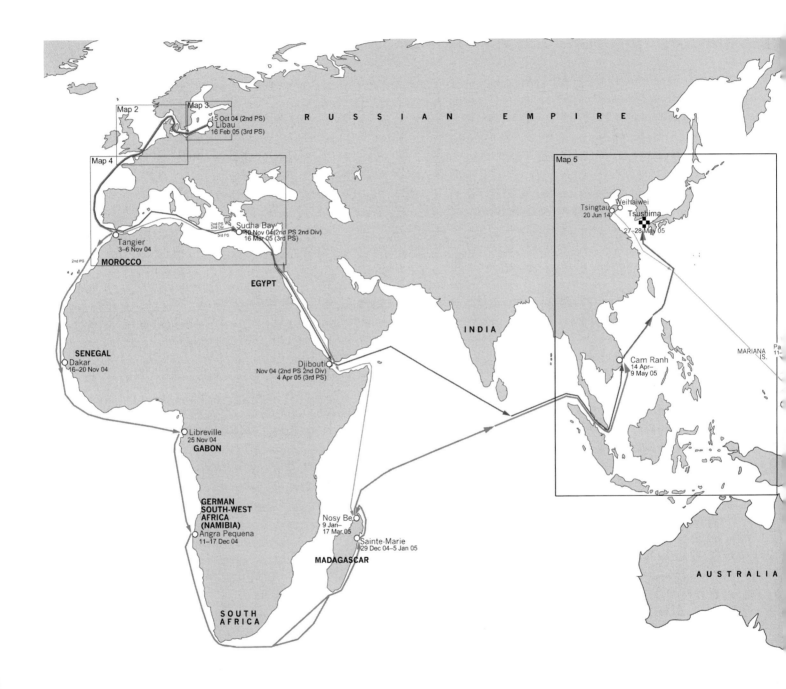

Map 1

The world, showing locations of actions involving big cruisers or their losses, and simplifed tracks of the Russian fleet in 1905 and the German East Asiatic Squadron in 1914. *(Author's graphics)*

Key: ✠ Large-scale action
⸸ Sinking site
——— Track of Russian 2nd Pacific Squadron
------- Track of Russian 2nd Pacific Squadron (2nd Division)
——— Track of Russian 3rd Pacific Squadron
——— Track of German East Asiatic Squadron

Esquimalt
Bremerton
Milwaukee†
13 Jan 17
Eureka
Mare Island
San Francisco

C A N A D A

U N I T E D   S T A T E S

Boston
New York
Philadelphia†*San Diego*
19 Jul 18
Norfolk

Pensacola

MEXICO

Map 1a

HAWAII

am

BAJA CALIFORNIA

Veracruz

Puerto
Rico

Eniwetok
19–22 Aug 14

IS. Ponape
17 Jul–6 Aug 14

Kiribati
7 Sep 14

MARQUESAS IS.
26 Sep–3 Oct 14

SAMOA
14 Sep 14

Papeete
22 Sep 14
TAHITI

VENEZUELA

COLUMBIA

ECUADOR

B R A Z I L

BOLIVIA

PARAGUAY

Easter Is.
12–18 Oct 14

Mas a Fuera
26–28 Oct 14
6–18 Nov 14

Valparaíso
3 Nov 14

URAGUAY

Buenos Aires

Coronel*Good Hope*†
1 Nov 14 *Monmouth*

CHILE

ARGENTINA

NEW ZEALAND

St Quentin Bay
21–28 Nov 14

Falklands *Scharnhorst*†
8 Dec 14 *Gneisenau*

Punta
Arenas

Picton Is.
3–6 Dec 14

Map 1a inset

0   300nm
0   400km

BAHAMAS †*Infanta María Teresa*
2 Nov 98

†*Maine*
15 Feb 98
Havana

CUBA

Infanta María Teresa
Almirante Oquendo† Santiago
Vizcaya   de Cuba
Cristóbal Colón 3 Jul 98

Santo
Domingo

Memphis†
29 Aug 16

Map 1a JAMAICA

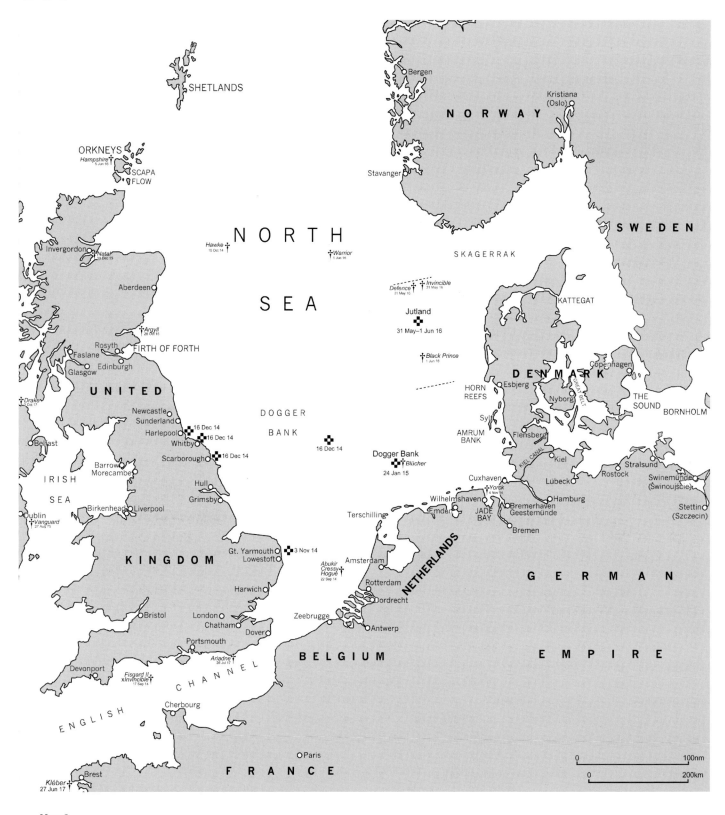

Map 2

Map 3

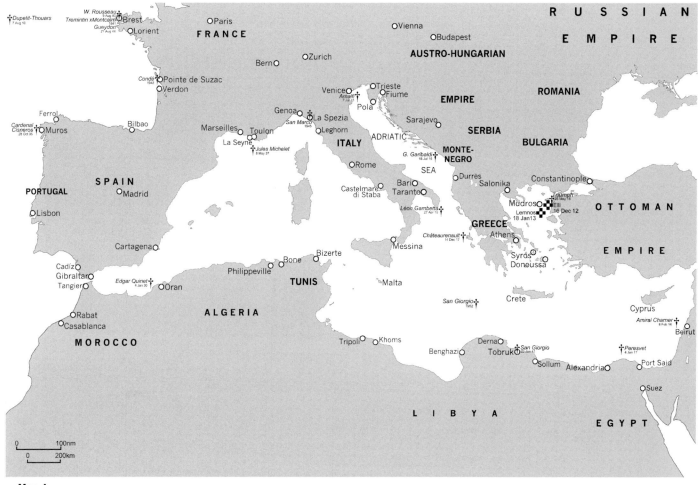

Map 4

Toulon was the principal French Mediterranean dockyard, with the major private shipyard of Forges & Chantiers de la Méditerranée at La Seyne directly to its west, the latter building ships particularly for foreign customers, including two armoured cruisers for Russia. The Toulon roadstead is shown here during the First World War with *Châteaurenault* and *Guichen* in company with the battleship *France*. *(NHHC NH 55992)*

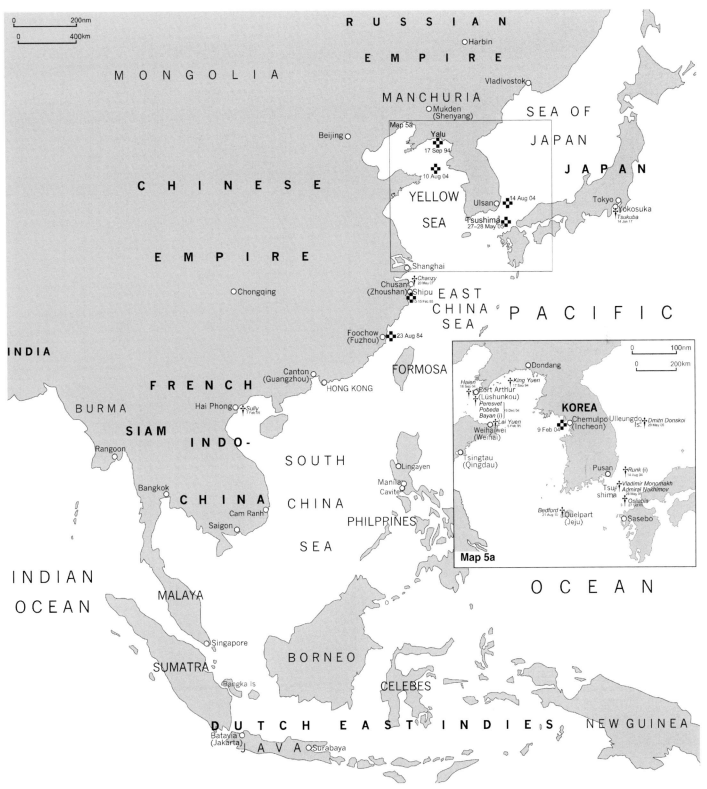

Map 5

BIBLIOGRAPHY

Allen, F J, 'Steel at Sea – the First Steps: USS *Atlanta* and USS *Boston* of 1883', *Warship* XII (1988), pp 238–49.

Anon, 'Cressy, Aboukir and Hogue Uncovered: Underwater research at the wrecks of the ill-fated cruisers', *Warship* XXVI (2004), p 166.

Arnold-Baker, R and G P Cremos, *Averof: The ship that changed the course of history* (Athens: Akritas Publications, 1990).

Bagnasco, E and A Rastelli, *Le costruzioni navali italiane per l'estero: centotrenta anni di prestigiosa presenza nel mondo* (Rome: Rivista marittima, 1991).

Barrett, M B, *Operation Albion: The German Conquest of the Baltic Islands* (Bloomington, IN: Indiana University Press, 2008).

Becker, W A and C C Wright, 'The French Armored Cruiser *Pothuau*', *Warship International* LI/2 (2014), pp 136–45.

Borgenstam, C, P Insulander and B Åhlund, *Kryssare: med svenska flottans kryssare under 75 år* (Västra Frölunda: CB Marinlitteratur, 1993).

Brescia, M, 'Re: "Cruisers for Argentina"', *Warship International* XVI/3 (1979), p 199.

Brook, P, 'The Cancelled AMALFI Class Armored Cruisers', *Warship International* IX/1 (1972), p 88.

_____, *Warships for Export: Armstrong's Warships 1867--1927* (Gravesend: World Ship Society, 1999).

_____, 'The Battle of the Yalu, 17 September 1894', *Warship* XXII (1999–2000), pp 31–43

_____, 'Armoured Cruiser versus Armoured Cruiser: Ulsan, 14 August 1904', *Warship* XXIII (2000–2001), pp 34–47.

_____, 'Two Unfortunate Warships: *Unebi* and *Reina Regente*', *Mariner's Mirror* 87/1 (2001), pp 53–62.

_____, 'Spain's Farewell to greatness: The Battle of Santiago, 3 July 1898', *Warship* XXIV (2001–2002), pp 33–51.

Brown, D K, 'The Russo-Japanese War: Technical Lessons as Perceived by the Royal Navy', *Warship* XX (1996), pp 66–77.

_____, *The Grand Fleet: warship design and development 1906–1922* (London: Chatham Publishing, 1999).

Burt, R A, *British Battleships 1889–1904*, new revised edition (Barnsley: Seaforth, 2013).

_____, '*Minotaur*: Before the Battlecruiser', *Warship* XI (1987), pp 83–95.

_____, 'The *Powerful* class cruisers of the Royal Navy, Part I', *Warship* XII (1988), pp 197–207.

Burzaco, R, *Acorazados y Cruceros de la Armada Argentina* (Buenos Aires: Eugenio B. Ediciones, 1997).

Buxton, I, *Big Gun Monitors: design, construction and operations 1914-1945* (Barnsley: Seaforth, 2008).

Campbell, J A, *Hulks: The Breakwater Ships of Powell River* (Powell River: Works Publishing, 2003).

Campbell, N J M, 'British Naval Guns 1880–1945, No 5', *Warship* VI (1982), pp 43–5.

_____, 'British Naval Guns 1880–1945, No 6', *Warship* VI (1982), pp 214–17.

_____, 'British Naval Guns 1880–1945, No 7', *Warship* VI (1982), pp 282–4.

_____, 'British Naval Guns 1880–1945, No 9', *Warship* VII (1983), pp 119–43.

_____, 'British Naval Guns 1880–1945, No 10', *Warship* VII (1983), pp 170–2.

_____, 'British Naval Guns 1880–1945, No 11', *Warship* VII (1983), pp 240–3.

_____, 'British Naval Guns 1880–1945, No 15', *Warship* IX (1985), pp 48–53.

_____, 'British Naval Guns 1880–1945, No 17', *Warship* X (1986), pp 53–5.

_____, 'British Naval Guns 1880–1945, No 18', *Warship* X (1986), pp 117–20.

_____, *Jutland: an analysis of the fighting* (London: Conway Maritime Press, 1986).

Caresse, P, 'The Odyssey of Von Spee and the East Asiatic Squadron, 1914', *Warship* XXX (2008), pp 67–84.

Carr, J, *R.H.N.S. Averof: Thunder in the Aegean* (Barnsley: Pen & Sword Maritime, 2014).

Cernuschi, E, and V P O'Hara, 'The Naval War in the Adriatic', *Warship* XXXVII (2015), pp 161–73, XXXVIII (2016), pp 62–75.

Chernikov, I I, 'Perevooruzhenie kreiserov v 1906-1916 gg', *Sudostroenie* 1983/3, pp 60–3.

Dittmar, F, and D Hepper, 'British Ship of the Line Conversions', *Warship International* XXXIII/3 (1996), pp 307–9.

Dodson, A, 'The Incredible Hulks: The *Fisgard* Training Establishment and its Ships', *Warship* XXXVII (2015), pp 29–37.

_____, *The Kaiser's Battlefleet: German capital ships 1871–1918* (Barnsley: Seaforth Publishing, 2016).

_____, 'After the Kaiser: The Imperial German Navy's Light Cruisers after 1918', *Warship* XXXIX (2017), pp 140–60.

Dittmar, F and D Hepper, 'British Ship of the Line Conversions', *Warship International* XXXIII/3 (1996), pp 307–9.

Drashpil, B, 'Re: Question by A. Mach', *Warship International* XX/3 (1983), pp 226–8.

Eger, C L, 'Hudson-Fulton Naval Celebration'. *Warship International* 49 (2012), pp 123–51.

Eberspaecher, C, 'Arming the Beiyang Navy. Sino-German Naval Cooperation 1879–1895', *International Journal of Naval History* 8/1 (2009), pp 1–10.

Emerson, W C, 'The Armoured Cruiser USS *Brooklyn*', *Warship* XV (1991), pp 19–33.

————, 'The Second Class Battleship USS *Maine*', *Warship* XVI (1992), pp 31–46.

Fernández Núñez, P, J M Mosquera Gomez, J M Rudíño Carlés, *Buques de la Armada Española Historiales* (Gijón: Instituto de Historia y Cultura Naval – Fundación Alvargonzález).

Feron, L, 'Cent ans: croiseurs', *100 ans Marine français: Croiseurs; Gardes-côtes* (Nantes: Marines Éditions, 2002), pp 5–69.

————, 'The Cruiser *Dupuy-de-Lôme*', *Warship* XXXIII (2011), pp 32–47.

————, 'The Cruiser Dupuy-de-Lôme', *Warship* XXXIV (2012), p 182.

————, 'The Armoured Cruisers of the *Amiral Charner* class', *Warship* XXXVI (2014), pp 8–28.

Fisher, E C, 'The *Rurik* – Progenitor of the armored cruisers', *Warship International* IV/4 (1967), pp 263–7.

————, 'Battleships of the Imperial Russian Navy Part 3', *Warship International* VI/1 (1969), pp 26–32;

Fisher, E, G Ransome, I Sturton, J Wilterding and C Wright, 'Last Years of the French Armored Cruiser DUPUY DE LOME', *Warship International* VI/4 (1969), pp 344–5.

Fisher, L, *Destruction of the* Maine *(1898)* (Washington, DC: Library of Congress, 2009) <http://loc.gov/law/help/usconlaw/pdf/Maine.1898.pdf>.

Fotakis, E, *Greek Naval Strategy and Policy 1910–1919* (London: Routledge, 2005).

————, 'Greek Naval Policy and Strategy, 1923-1932', *Nausivios Chora: a Journal in Naval Sciences and Technology* (2010), pp 365–93. <http://nausivios.snd.edu.gr/nausivios/ed2010.php>

Freivogel, Z, 'The Loss of the *Giuseppe Garibaldi*', *Warship* XXXIV (2012), pp 40–51.

Friedman, N, *U.S. Battleships: an illustrated design history* (Annapolis MD: Naval Institute Press, 1985), pp 80–3.

————, *U.S. Cruisers: an illustrated design history* (London: Arms and Armour Press, 1985).

————, *Naval Weapons of World War One: Guns, Torpedoes, Mines and ASW Weapons of All Nations*

(Barnsley: Seaforth Publishing, 2011).

————, *British Cruisers of the Victorian Era* (Barnsley: Seaforth Publishing, 2012).

Fukui, S, *Japanese Naval Vessels at the End of World War II* (London: Greenhill Books, 1992).

Gille, E, *Cent ans de cuirasses français* (Nantes: Marines Edition, 1999).

Giorgerini, G and A Nani, *Gli Incrociatori Italiani 1861–1967* (Rome: Ufficio Storico della Marina Militare, 1967).

Grant, J A, *Rulers, Guns, and Money: the Global Arms Trade in the Age of Imperialism* (Cambridge, MA: Harvard University Press, 2007).

Grießmer, A, *Große Kreuzer der Kaiserlichen Marine 1906–1918: Konstruktionen und Entwürfe in Zeichen des Tirpiz-Panes* (Bonn: Bernard & Graefe Verlag, 1996).

Gröner, E, *German Warships 1815-1945*, I: *Major Surface Vessels*, revised and expanded by D Jung and M Maass (London: Conway Maritime Press, 1990).

Hansen, J, 'IJN Battleship and Battle Cruiser Project Numbers', *Warship International* LIII/2 (2016), pp 102–12, LIV/2 (2017), pp 121–3.

Head, M, 'The Baltic Campaign, 1918–1920, Part II', *Warship International* XLVI/3 (2009), pp 217–39.

Hill, S, 'The Battle of Boilers', *The Engineer* 198 (1954), pp 83–6, 199.

Hownam-Meek, R S S, K D McBride and C C Wright, 'Target Ships', *Warship International* XXXIX/1 (2002), pp 24–36.

Inaba, C, 'Military co-operation under the Anglo-Japanese Alliance: Assistance in purchasing battleships', in P P O'Brien (ed), *The Anglo-Japanese Alliance, 1902–1922* (London and New York: RoutledgeCurzon, 2004), pp 67–9.

Itani, J, H Lengerer and T Rehm-Takahara, '*Samkeikan*: Japan's Coast Defence Ships of the *Matsushima* Class', *Warship* XIV (1990), pp 34–55.

————, 'Japan's Proto-Battlecruisers: The Tsukuba and Kurama Classes', *Warship* XVI (1992), pp 47–79.

Johnson, H and J P Roche, 'French Amiral Charner Class Armored Cruiser Differences'. *Warship International* 43/3 (2006), pp 243–5.

Jones, C, 'The Limits of Naval Power', *Warship* XXXIV (2012), pp 162–8.

Jordan, J, and P Caresse, *French Battleships of the First World War* (Barnsley: Seaforth, 2017).

Jordan, J, and J Moulin, *French Cruisers 1922–1956* (Barnsley: Seaforth Publishing, 2013).

Kisieliow, D, 'Krownik pancernopokładowy „Jiyuan". *Okrty Wojenne* 113 (2012), pp 15–29.

Koehler, R B, 'British Ship of the Line Conversions', *Warship International* XXXIV/3 (1997), pp 319–20.

Kolonits, F, 'A present by the Meiji Tenno for the delivery of KASUGA and NISSHIN', *Academic & Applied Research in Military Science* 6/4 (2007), pp 757–69.

Koop, G, and K-P Schmolke, *Die grossen Kreuzer: Kaiserin Augusta bis Blücher* (Bonn: Bernard und Graefe, 2002).

Krestianinov, V Ia, *Kreisera Rossiiskogo imperatorskogo flota. 1856–1917 gody* (St Petersburg: Galeia Print, 2009).

Lacroix, E, and L Wells III, *Japanese Cruisers of the Pacific War* (Annapolis, MD: Naval Institute Press, 1997).

Lambert, A, *Battleships in Transition: the creation of the steam battlefleet 1815–1860* (London: Conway Maritime Press, 1984).

Lambi, I N, *The Navy and German Power Politics, 1862–1914* (Boston: Allen & Unwin, 1984).

Layman, R D, 'Engadine at Jutland', *Warship* XIV (1990), pp 93–101.

Le Masson, H, *Propos maritimes* (Paris: Editions maritimes et d'outre mer, 1970).

_____, 'The Complex Development of the French Light Cruiser 1910–1926', *Warship International* XXII/4 (1985), pp 374–83.

Lengerer, H, 'Imperial Japanese Navy Minelayers *Itsukushima*, *Okinoshima*, and *Tsugaru*', *Warship* XXX (2008), pp 52–66.

Lindgren, S M, 'The genesis of a cruiser navy: British first-class cruiser development 1884-1909' (PhD thesis, University of Salford, 2013).

Maber, J M, 'The Iron Screw Frigate *Greenock*', *Warship* VI (1982), pp 218–21, 247–9.

Mach, A, 'The Chinese Battleships', *Warship* VIII (1984), pp 9–18.

Marshall, P A, '1898 Spanish Cruiser Guns', *Warship International* LII/1 (2015), pp 81–2.

McBride, K, '*Minotaur*: Before the Battlecruiser', *Warship* XI (1987), pp 83–93.

_____, 'The *Diadem* Class Cruisers of 1893', *Warship* XI (1987), pp 210–16.

_____, 'The First County Class Cruisers of the Royal Navy: Part I The *Monmouths*' *Warship* XII (1988), pp 83–90.

_____, 'The First County Class Cruisers of the Royal Navy: Part II The *Devonshires*', *Warship* XII (1988), pp 147–51.

_____, 'The Wreck of HMS *Bedford*', *Warship* XII (1988), pp 136–41.

_____, 'The Dukes and the Warriors', *Warship International* XXVII/4 (1990), pp 362–94.

_____, 'The Cruiser Family *Talbot*', *Warship* XXXIV (2012), pp 136–41.

McCartney, I, *Jutland 1916: the archaeology of a naval battlefield* (London: Conway, 2016).

McLaughlin, S, 'From *Riurik* to *Riurik*: Russia's Armoured Cruisers', *Warship* XXII (1999–2000), pp 44–51, 74–7.

_____, *Russian & Soviet Battleships* (Annapolis: Naval Institute Press, 2003).

_____, 'Project 69: The *Kronshtadt* Class Battlecruisers', *Warship* XXVI (2004), pp 99–117.

_____, 'Project 82: the *Stalingrad* class', *Warship* XXVIII (2006), pp 102–23.

_____, 'Admiral Kuznetzov's Cruiser Killer: The Project 66 Design', *Warship International* XLV/3 (2008), pp 221–8.

_____, 'Russia's Coles "Monitors": *Smerch*, *Rusalka* and *Charodeika*', *Warship* XXXV (2013), pp 149–63.

Melnikov, R M, 'Fregat "Kniaz' Pozharskii"', *Sudostroenie* 1979/2, pp 63–4.

_____, 'Polubronenosnyi fregat "General-Admiral"', *Sudostroenie* 1979/4, pp 64–7.

_____, 'Bronenosnyi kreiser "Admiral Nakhimov"', *Sudostroenie* 1979/9, pp 66–9.

Milanovich, K, '*Chiyoda* (II): First "Armoured Cruiser" of The Imperial Japanese Navy', *Warship* XXVIII (2006), pp 126–36.

_____, 'Two Ill-Fated French-Built Japanese Warships', *Warship* XXXIII (2010), pp 170–6.

_____, 'Armoured Cruisers of the Imperial Japanese Navy', *Warship* XXXVI (2014), pp 70–92.

Murfin, D, *Directory of British Cruiser Designs 1860–1960* (Haverfordwest: Croft Books, 2011).

Muscant, I, *U.S. Armored Cruisers: a Design and Operational History* (Annapolis, MD: Naval Institute Press, 1985).

Oliver, D H, *German Naval Strategy 1856–1888: Forerunners of Tirpitz* (London: Frank Cass, 2004).

Osborne, R, H Spong and T Grover, *Armed Merchant Cruisers 1878–1945* (Windsor, World Ship Society, 2007).

Parkinson, R, *The Late Victorian Navy: The Pre-Dreadnought Era and the Origins of the First World War* (Woodbridge: The Boydell Press, 2008).

Parkes, O, *British Battleships: "Warrior" 1860 to "Vanguard" 1950; a history of design construction and armament* (London: Seeley Service, 1957).

Perkins, R, *British Warship Recognition: The Perkins Identification Albums* (Barnsley: Seaforth, 2016ff).

Pickford, N., *Lost Treasure Ships of the Twentieth Century* (London: Pavilion Books, 1999).

Ransome, G and P F Silverstone, 'Cancelled GARIBALDI class Italian Cruisers', *Warship International* VII/2 (1970), pp 193–4.

Reilly, J C, and R L Scheina, *American Battleships 1886–1923: pre-dreadnought design and construction* (Annapolis MD: Naval Institute Press, 1980).

Roberts, J, 'HMS *Cochrane*', *Warship* III (1979), pp 34–7.

Roche, J-M, *Dictionnaire des bâtiments de la flotte de guerre français de Colbert à nos jours*, 2vv (self-published, 2013).

Rodger, N A M, 'British Belted Cruisers', *The Mariner's Mirror*, 64/1 (1978), pp 23–36.

Rodríguez, H, and P E Arguindeguy, *Buques de la Armada*

Argentina 1852–1899: sus commandos y operaciones (Buenos Aries: Instituto Nacional Browniano, 1999).

Ropp, T, *The Development of a Modern Navy: French Naval Policy 1871–1904* (Annapolis, MD: Naval Institute Press, 1987).

Rohwer, J, and M S Monakov, *Stalin's Ocean-Going Fleet: Soviet Naval Strategy and Shipbuilding Programmes 1935-1953* (London/Portland OR: Frank Cass, 2001).

Sanahuja Albíñana, V L, 'Los cruceros acorazados de la clase Princesa de Asturias', *Vida Maritima*, 1 Septiembre 2011 <http://vidamaritima.com/2011/09/los-cruceros-acorazados-de-la-clase-princesa-de-asturias/>

Scheina, R L, *Latin America: A Naval History, 1810–1987* (Annapolis, MD: Naval Institute Press, 1987).

Schenk, P, 'German Aircraft Carrier Developments', *Warship International* XLV/2 (2008), pp 128–60.

Sieche, E F, 'Austria-Hungary's Last Naval Visit to the USA', *Warship International* XXVII/2 (1990), pp 142–64.

_____, 'Austria-Hungary's *Monarch* class coast defense ships', *Warship International* XXXVI/3 (1999), pp 220–60.

_____, *Kreuzer und Kreuzerprojekte der k.u.k. Kriegsmarine* (Hamburg: Mittler, 2002), pp 58–71.

Soliani, N, 'The Armoured Cruisers "Kasuga" and "Nisshin" of the Imperial Japanese Navy', *Transactions of the Institution of Naval Architects* XLVII/1 (1905), pp 43–62.

Sondhaus, L, *The Naval policy of Austria-Hungary, 1867–1918: navalism, industrial development and the politics of dualism* (West Lafayette, IN: Purdue University Press, 1994).

_____, *Preparing for Weltpolitik: German Sea Power Before the Tirpitz Era* (Annapolis: Naval Institute Press, 1997).

Staff, G, *Battle on the Seven Seas: German Cruiser Battles 1914–1918* (Barnsley: Pen and Sword Maritime, 2011).

Stoker, D J, *Britain, France, and the Naval Arms Trade in the Baltic, 1919-1939: Grand Strategy and Failure* (London/Portland OR: Frank Cass, 2003)

Tarrant, V E, *Jutland: the German perspective* (London: Arms and Armour Press, 1995).

Toll, I W, *Six Frigates: The Epic History of the Founding of the US Navy* (New York: W. W. Norton, 2006).

Topliss, D, and C Ware, 'First Class Cruisers, Part One', *Warship* XXIII (2000–2001), pp 9–17.

_____, 'First Class Cruisers, Part Two', *Warship* XXIV (2001–2002), pp 9–18.

Towle, P, 'Battleship Sales During the Russo-Japanese War', *Warship International* XXIII/4 (1986), pp 402–9.

Usov, V Iu, and E Mawdsley, 'The *Kronshtadt* Class Battle Cruisers', *Warship International* XXVIII/4 (1991), pp 380–6.

von Rauch, G, 'Cruisers for Argentina', *Warship International* XV/4 (1978), pp 297–317.

Ware, C, 'First Class Cruisers: Part Three', *Warship* XXX (2008), pp 136–45.

Wright, C C, 'Impressive ships – The story of Her Majesty's cruisers *Blake* and *Blenheim*', *Warship International* VII/1 (1970), pp 40–51.

_____, 'Cruisers of the Imperial Russian Navy, Part 1', *Warship International* IX/1 (1972), pp 28–53.

_____, 'Cruisers of the Imperial Russian Navy, Part 2: the *Minin*', *Warship International* XII/3 (1975), pp 205–23.

_____, 'Cruisers of the Imperial Russian Navy, Part 3', *Warship International* XIII/2 (1976), pp 123–47.

_____, 'Cruisers of the Imperial Russian Navy, Part 4', *Warship International* XIV/1 (1977), pp 62, 65–8.

_____, 'Question 46/88', Warship International XXV/4 (1988), p 421.

Wright, R N J, 'The Peiyang and Nanyang Cruisers of the 1880s', *Warship* XX (1996), pp 95–110.

_____, *The Chinese Steam Navy, 1862–1945* (London: Chatham Publishing, 2000).

INDEX